"HONORARY PROTESTANTS"

The Jewish School Question in Montreal, 1867–1997

PATRONS OF THE SOCIETY

Blake, Cassels & Graydon LLP

Chernos Flaherty Svonkin LLP

Gowlings

McCarthy Tétrault LLP

Osler, Hoskin & Harcourt LLP

Paliare Roland Rosenberg Rothstein LLP

Torys LLP

WeirFoulds LLP

The Osgoode Society is supported by a grant from The Law Foundation of Ontario.

The Society also thanks The Law Society of Upper Canada for its continuing support.

"HONORARY PROTESTANTS"

The Jewish School Question in Montreal, 1867–1997

DAVID FRASER

Published for The Osgoode Society for Canadian Legal History by
University of Toronto Press
Toronto Buffalo London

www.utppublishing.com
www.osgoodesociety.ca

ISBN 978-1-4426-3048-2

Library and Archives Canada Cataloguing in Publication

Fraser, David, 1953–, author
"Honorary Protestants" : the Jewish school question in Montreal, 1867–1997 / David Fraser.

(Osgoode Society for Canadian Legal History)
Includes bibliographical references and index.
ISBN 978-1-4426-3048-2 (bound)

1. Jews – Education – Law and legislation – Québec (Province) – Montréal – History – 19th century. 2. Jews – Education – Law and legislation – Québec (Province) – Montréal – History – 20th century. 3. Jews – Legal status, laws, etc. – Québec (Province) – Montréal – History – 19th century. 4. Jews – Legal status, laws, etc. – Québec (Province) – Montréal – History – 20th century. 5. Educational law and legislation – Québec (Province) – Montréal – History – 19th century. 6. Educational law and legislation – Québec (Province) – Montréal – History – 20th century. 7. Education and state – Québec (Province) – Montréal – History – 19th century. 8. Education and state – Québec (Province) – Montréal – History – 20th century. I. Title. II. Series: Osgoode Society for Canadian Legal History (Series)

KEQ923.F73 2015 344.714′270791 C2015-904100-7

University of Toronto Press acknowledges the financial assistance to its publishing program of the Canada Council for the Arts and the Ontario Arts Council, an agency of the Government of Ontario.

Contents

Foreword

THE OSGOODE SOCIETY FOR CANADIAN LEGAL HISTORY

When the British North America Act was passed in 1867, section 93 guaranteed existing religious minority educational rights. Catholics and Protestants in Quebec, and elsewhere, have since then enjoyed the right to denominational schools, but those rights do not extend to any other group. This deeply researched and comprehensive study by David Fraser of the challenges, legal and otherwise, encountered by Jewish parents in educating their children in Montreal in the shadow of section 93 will undoubtedly become the standard work on the subject. Faced with alternating periods of hostility and tolerance, the Jewish community of Montreal carved out an educational *modus vivendi* based on complex and continuing negotiations with the Protestant and Catholic school boards, the provincial government, and individual municipalities. Divisions within the Jewish community itself, with different groups alternating between cooperation and militancy, only added to this complexity. In the face of the Constitution's exclusionary language, all parties engaged in modes of informal normative ordering that were at times unconstitutional, but unavoidable if Jewish children were to have access to public schools. Bargaining in the shadow of the law, the parties made their own constitution long before a constitutional amendment of 1997 finally put an end to the Jewish School Question.

The purpose of the Osgoode Society for Canadian Legal History is to encourage research and writing in the history of Canadian law. The Society, which was incorporated in 1979 and is registered as a charity, was founded at the initiative of the Honourable R. Roy McMurtry and officials of the Law Society of Upper Canada. The Society seeks to stimulate the study of legal history in Canada by supporting researchers, collecting oral histories, and publishing volumes that contribute to legal-historical scholarship in Canada. This year's books bring the total published to 100 since 1981, in all fields of legal history – the courts, the judiciary, and the legal profession, as well as on the history of crime and punishment, women and law, law and economy, the legal treatment of ethnic minorities, and famous cases and significant trials in all areas of the law. Reaching such a milestone is a wonderful tribute to the leadership and inspiration of our founder and, until recently, President. Roy McMurtry stepped down as President in June 2015. We will be forever in his debt.

Current directors of the Osgoode Society for Canadian Legal History are Robert Armstrong, Susan Binnie, David Chernos, J. Douglas Ewart, Philip Girard, Mahmud Jamal, William Kaplan, C. Ian Kyer, Virginia MacLean, Patricia McMahon, Roy McMurtry, Madeleine Meilleur, Janet Minor, Dana Peebles, Paul Perell, Jim Phillips, Paul Reinhardt, William Ross, Linda Rothstein, Paul Schabas, Robert Sharpe, Jon Silver, Alex Smith, Lorne Sossin, Mary Stokes, and Michael Tulloch.

The annual report and information about membership may be obtained by writing to the Osgoode Society for Canadian Legal History, Osgoode Hall, 130 Queen Street West, Toronto, Ontario, M5H 2N6. Telephone: 416-947-3321. E-mail: mmacfarl@lsuc.on.ca. Website: www.osgoodesociety.ca.

Robert J. Sharpe
President

Jim Phillips
Editor-in-Chief

Acknowledgments

While the usual declaration of sole responsibility applies, many groups and individuals still need to be mentioned. This book could not have been written without the support of the British Academy's invaluable and sometimes endangered small grants program. Funding from the BA permitted me to undertake the travel and to spend the time necessary to complete the bulk of the archival research on which this project is based.

The Library and Archives Canada in Ottawa, the Jewish Public Library in Montreal, the Centre de Référence de l'Amérique Française in Quebec City, and the Archives Nationales du Québec in Montréal all gave me access to their holdings. The British Library, especially Jonathan Sims in the Social Sciences Division, provided important materials. The staff of the Archives Nationales du Québec in Ste Foy offered a warm welcome and assistance beyond what could normally be expected. Mr Joseph Muyal, executive director of the Spanish and Jewish congregation of Montreal, Shearith Israel, kindly granted me access to historical documents. Shannon Hodge of the Jewish Public Library also provided invaluable assistance. The Sir Wilfrid Laurier School Board and the staff of the McGill University Archives assured access to important documents on the extraordinary history of the Ste Sophie "Protestant" School Board. The McLennan-Redpath, Education, and Nahum Gelber Law Libraries at McGill University, and the libraries of Concordia University also provided help.

Thanks are also due to Vaughan Black, Didi Herman, and above all Kathryn McMahon for patiently reading through parts of the book and offering invaluable feedback. Philip Girard of Osgoode Law School and Jim Phillips of the University of Toronto saw the project through the review stages with aplomb, and they, along with the anonymous readers from the Osgoode Society, deserve special gratitude for comments and critiques. Ian MacKenzie provided copy-editing talents *extraordinaire,* and Len Husband and Wayne Herrington of the University of Toronto Press saw the book into the world. To all, my thanks.

Above all, the Archives of the Canadian Jewish Congress and the staff in Montreal provided a research home away from home. Janice Rosen and Hélène Lavallée went above and beyond the call of duty in assisting my work and they deserve a special expression of gratitude. Without the rich documentary record maintained at the CJC and the extraordinary kindness of Janice and Hélène, this project would have been impossible.

"HONORARY PROTESTANTS"

The Jewish School Question in Montreal, 1867–1997

1

Introduction: Constituting Law, Constituting Justice in the Jewish School Question

The Jewish School Question in Two Stories

This book traces the evolution of the so-called Jewish School Question in Montreal by underscoring the normative debates and political battles that informed the struggle by Montreal's Jewish communities to obtain the "right" to educate their children in the public schools as part of their collective understandings of what it meant to be Jewish and British subjects, and later Canadian citizens. The battles waged by the Jewish communities to obtain formal and legal equality in the field of education took place in a constitutional framework in which school rights were legally guaranteed only to Quebec's Protestant and Roman Catholic communities. The book takes part of its title, "Honorary Protestants," from the characterization employed by Roderick MacLeod and Mary Anne Poutanen, historians of Quebec Protestant education, to describe the place of Jewish children in a world of education formally divided between Roman Catholic and Protestant common schools.[1] Yet, as the history set out in what follows will demonstrate, even this idea that Jews were treated as "Protestants for school purposes" in Montreal is incomplete and often inaccurate. The historical, legal, and political record shows that Jews were never really or fully "honorary Protestants." Instead they sat as a category apart, neither Protestant nor Roman Catholic, yet otherwise fully equal British subjects and Canadian citizens. The compromises and refusals, which make up the history of the Jewish School Question in Montreal, took place in a limited and limiting legal constitutional framework that was, more often than not, ignored by the parties involved. Both Protestant and Roman Catholic populations, their elected politicians, and the school officials in each system insisted upon the constitutional guarantees of the Protestant or Roman Catholic nature of Montreal's school systems and stood on their legal rights when faced with challenges emanating from Jewish communities in the city. Yet for almost a hundred years, Jewish children attended the public schools, mostly in the Protestant system, under a provincial legal order that was constitutionally suspect.

Throughout, the book attempts to demonstrate the ways in which the complex and multifaceted political, social, cultural, and religious conflicts that grew up around the presence of increasing numbers of Jewish school children in the public, common, but always denominational schools of Montreal were dealt with by all parties involved. The Jewish communities of Montreal engaged with the dominant Roman Catholic and Protestant educational authorities, as well as with municipal and provincial government officials, and with broader public opinion, in a variety of forums. The book seeks to place these interactions in the context of the legal, constitutional framework governing the structures of education in the city of Montreal (and beyond). But it also attempts to underscore the ways in which the parties sidelined or simply ignored formal legal norms, institutions, and discourses as they sought to embody and concretize their often-conflicting ideas of justice and identity in the context of the Jewish School Question. An important focus of what follows is on the ways in which all the parties engaged in constituting their collective identities in situations in which formal legal normativity might have served as a barrier to collective fulfilment and citizenship. Two brief stories set the context for the discussion that follows. The first is a fictionalized telling from a noted Canadian novelist, the second a brief summary of one of the two legal cases that will frame significant aspects of the remaining narrative.

Mordecai Richler, in his account of the lives of the students in Room 41, voiced by the inimitable Duddy Kravitz, offers this example of life in the Protestant Fletcher's Field High School for its overwhelmingly Jewish pupils.

> Mr Feeney was something else again. He would seize on each new boy and ask him, "Do you know what the Jewish national anthem is?"
>
> "No, Sir."

So Mr Feeney would go to the board and write, "To the Bank, To the Bank."
"Do you know how the Jews make an 'S'?"
"No, Sir."
Mr Feeney would go to the board, make an "S," and draw two strokes through it. Actually he meant his jokes in a friendly spirit and the sour reactions he usually got puzzled him.[2]

Fletcher's Field High School of fiction was Baron Byng High School of the historical Jewish School Question. In addition to Richler, its alumni include a Nobel laureate, Rudolph Marcus, a justice of the Supreme Court of Canada, Morris Fish, the captain of the Starship *Enterprise*, William Shatner, as well as two of Canada's greatest poets, A.M. Klein and Irving Layton.

Richler's stories of Duddy and his classmates occur in the period immediately following the Second World War, while much of the early focus of this book precedes this by some twenty to fifty years. Yet the basic demographic fact of Richler's fictionalized accounts of his Montreal school days had remained relatively unchanged. The students of Fletcher's Field/Baron Byng were predominately Jewish. And the constitutional, legal framework that informed and shaped the experience of these Jewish students had also remained unchanged. While the body of students was Jewish, the school itself, its teachers, its curriculum, and its governing body were Protestant. This conflict between demography and formal legality underpins the discussions that follow and is the source of the clash that informed the second story of the Jewish School Question, the case of *Pinsler ès qual. v The Protestant Board of School Commissioners*.[3]

The year 1901 started out as a very good one for young Jacob Pinsler. He had just completed the sixth and final year of his primary schooling at Dufferin School in Montreal, an institution like Baron Byng, with a largely Jewish student body and a formal Protestant governing structure. He wished to continue his education at the high school level. While most parents could, with judicious saving, afford the fees attached to the primary education of their children, progress to secondary school carried with it a financial burden few could manage. This was especially true for the immigrant Jews who were coming to Montreal in ever increasing numbers as the nineteenth century approached the twentieth. Jacob's father, Paul, was identified as a "Russian" hat-maker in the 1891 census.[4] More accurately perhaps, given the ever-shifting character of Eastern European nation states and Canadian bureaucrats' shaky understandings of world geography, he was described as "Romanian" in the 1901 census. He was by then employed as an upholsterer (*bourreur*).[5] The family lived in rented accommodation in the St Laurent Ward, one of the predominantly Jewish sections of the city. Given the difficult economic circumstances of his family and of his time, in order to pursue his studies beyond primary school, Jacob had to obtain a scholarship. In the annual competition held across all the schools of the Protestant School Commission, he passed with flying colours, scoring 83 per cent and taking the Frothingham Medal. As a result, he "won" the Commissioners' Scholarship, which provided free tuition for his entire secondary schooling.

Before he could begin the next stage of his education, however, the Protestant School Board of Montreal informed Jacob Pinsler that he was, as a Canadian-born Jew, not eligible for the scholarship. His father, as his legal guardian, brought a lawsuit against the Board of School Commissioners seeking a writ of mandamus to compel the School Board to re-establish the scholarship in his son's name. In a judgment detailing the history of Quebec school law and the position of Montreal's Jewish community, Justice Davidson came to the conclusion that the Protestant School Board was entirely within its rights to withdraw Jacob's scholarship. The judge held that Jews were allowed to attend the Protestant schools in Montreal only by the Christian grace and goodwill of the Protestant Board of School Commissioners and not as of right. The legal framework of primary education established only Protestant and Roman Catholic schools in the city. As far as Jewish students were concerned, it was therefore within the sole discretion of the Protestant commissioners as to whom to allow to attend their schools. Likewise, any grant or refusal of a scholarship to a Jewish student was within the unfettered discretion of the commission. Because he was a Jew, Jacob Pinsler had no legal right to schooling or to financial aid. His educational future was dependent on the presence or absence of Christian charity from the Protestant school authorities, the same authorities who had refused to give a scholarship to the Jew, Jacob Pinsler.

These brief narrative introductions to the Jewish School Question in Montreal also share two elements, sometimes contradictory and sometimes complementary, that will resurface as core aspects of the debates and controversies discussed throughout. On the one hand, the story of Duddy Kravitz and Mr Feeney offers a clear example of the anti-Semitism that was an almost daily reality for Jewish students and parents. This blatant anti-Semitism manifests itself throughout the entire history of the Jewish School Question. At the same time, there is a complementary and perhaps mirror-image idea that also emerges, particularly in the *Pinsler* example. A key element of the history of the events that would always be known by all parties as the Jewish School Question is that of the complex relationships between Jews and Protestants in Montreal education. Protestants were always aware not just of their minority status in Roman Catholic Quebec, but more particularly of the need to ensure their survival as a minority. This was an acute part of the discourses of Protestant identity that emerged throughout the Jewish School Question and that are narrated in what follows. For Montreal's Protestants, the legal guarantees enshrined in the provisions of section 93 were existential. The Protestant school system ensured the survival of the Protestant communities and their culture. It is possible to grasp, in part at least, many of the debates and conflicts throughout the Jewish School Question as emanating from the collective desire of Protestants to ensure their future within Montreal. Thus, the incidents and debates that constitute the Jewish School Question in its various iterations must be understood both as manifestations of an almost inherent anti-Semitism that forms part of certain versions of Protestant theology, and of an assertion by Protestants of their right to exist and to constitute themselves as a community in Roman Catholic Quebec. These existential collective assertions of rights, especially, but not only, when constitutional legal norms form part of these claims, operate as positive ideals of community identity. They also, and at the same time, function as negative, violent, exclusions of the Other. In this case, the identity of Protestant Montrealers and Protestant schools was for many in those communities almost necessarily predicated on the exclusion of Jewish students. Protestant anti-Semitism operated hand-in-hand with some ideas of Protestant identity.

This book tells the stories of the Jewish communities of Montreal and their relationship with an educational system that, while public in the North American sense, was also always, and at the same time, parochial, or more precisely, denominational in that same sense. In the city of Montreal, until very recently, there were two public school systems, one run by the Roman Catholic Commission and the other by the Protestant Board of School Commissioners. There were no neutral, non-denominational, state-supported schools, which would become the norm in the United States and in most other Canadian provinces. Tens of thousands of Jewish immigrants, like Mordecai Richler's grandparents and Jacob Pinsler's father and mother, arrived in the port city of Montreal at the end of the nineteenth and in the early years of the twentieth century. As they settled into life in their adopted Canadian homeland, they sought to educate their children in order to allow them to make a better life by becoming "Canadian." They wanted their children to gain a formal education and, more broadly and informally, entry into their new country's mores and social practices through public schooling. For many but not all Montreal Jews, the idea of citizenship and belonging was central to the promise of education for their children. But the only public schools to which they could send those children were denominational, Roman Catholic or Protestant. This, broadly, is the Jewish School Question in Montreal, which is the subject of the chapters that follow. How did the Jews of Montreal, among the largest Jewish communities in Canada, carve out for themselves and for their children a place in a public school system, which in its very structures and legal framework seemed to countenance only the Protestant and Roman Catholic populations of the city? How did they struggle within a constitutional structure that merely allowed them to attend school, not as of right but as a matter of Christian charity? How much of this Christian charity was really on offer to these European and later North African Jewish immigrants? These are the questions within the Jewish School Question that this book seeks to illuminate though a study of the history of the Jewish presence in the public schools of Montreal. In the chapters that follow, the historical and social narratives will demonstrate how and why these issues manifested themselves in a constitutional and political context in which the Jewish population sought to obtain practical educational equality for their children. While Jews sought equality and justice in educational matters, schooling and especially school finance were sites of ongoing conflict between the numerically dominant Roman Catholic population and the economically powerful Protestant communities of the city of Montreal.

The Jewish School Question was never, nor could it ever be, a question only for Jews. The dynamic interactions between and among these communities and their political representatives, all within a limited and limiting formal constitutional framework, again inform what follows. There has been, since the days of Legal Realism at least, an extensive literature on the ways in which social order and dynamic relationships are maintained without reference to the rigid formalities of legal discourse.[6] But the struggles for Jewish educational equality in Montreal were not engaged with issues of land use, studied by Ellickson, nor were they conflicts between commercial rivals highlighted by Lisa Bernstein's work on the diamond trade.[7] They were foundational, constitutional, and constitutive struggles on issues of identity, equality, and belonging, and concomitant exclusion. But they did not result in or ever really involve serious claims for a radical restructuring of the constitutional order.[8] To some extent, the struggles surrounding Jewish claims for educational equality in Montreal were similar, but not identical to, the dynamics of a narrative, legal and extra-legal, construction of religious communities described in the works of Robert Cover. Cover argued in some depth not just about the inherently violent character of law and adjudication, with its enormous hermeneutic powers of inclusion and exclusion, but more significantly perhaps about the complex and myriad ways in which formal constitutional legality is supplemented, challenged, questioned, and sometimes replaced by sets of political and social practices that define and constitute in the broadest sense not just the limits of minority communities in their relationship with the dominant legal and constitutional social discourses and rules, but also the relationships between and among minority and majority groups.[9] Some of these insights are reflected in the discussions that follow in different instances of law creation, jurisgenesis, by collective action and interaction. In the constitutional liminal zones highlighted in the historical narratives of the Jewish School Question, the contingent social practices of constructing group and individual identities as Jews, Protestants, and Roman Catholics were always highlighted, but in very specific debates about what it meant to be equal British subjects, and then Canadians.

While American socio-legal work on law outside law is useful in framing a broad idea, the legal history of the Jewish School Question in Montreal demonstrates how the communities at the heart of the issues, in the particular context of a Canadian legal framework fundamentally different from one wrapped in the First Amendment and the founding mythologies of religious freedom in the United States, set about constructing and constituting their visions of life in Canada. The Jewish School Question was, throughout its various incarnations, always about the tensions surrounding Canadian identity as understood by Jews, Protestants, and Roman Catholics – Yiddish, English, and French-speaking citizens – democrats, oligarchs, and emerging ultramontane elements who would challenge the earlier modus vivendi between the church and Liberals.[10] How these various elements that made up Montreal from the 1880s to the 1990s managed their interactions in the educational domain without being self-destructive is at the core of the stories that follow.

Constituting Canada, Constituting Jews: The Montreal School Question and Narratives of Legality

The provinces, and not the federal government, obtained, in section 93 of Canada's originating constitution, the British North America Act 1867 (BNA Act),[11] exclusive jurisdiction over education. But section 93 (2) imposed an important limitation on provincial power. It stated, "All the Powers, Privileges, and Duties at the Union by Law conferred and imposed in Upper Canada on the Separate Schools and School Trustees of the Queen's Roman Catholic Subjects shall be and the same are hereby extended to the Dissentient Schools of the Queen's Protestant and Roman Catholic Subjects in Quebec."

In essence the Canadian Constitution in section 93 instituted a school system in the Province of Quebec, which mirrored in reverse the set-up in the neighbouring province of Ontario. There, the minority Roman Catholic population had their rights to separate schools entrenched in the Constitution. In Quebec, the mostly anglophone Protestant population obtained a constitutional guarantee for their own school system. Meanwhile, the schools of the majority francophone inhabitants were left in the hands of the Roman Catholic Church. The legal consequences of this constitutional and constitutive arrangement frame the core of this book. The politics within and often outside that technical constitutional form, make up the substantive heart of many of the stories that unfold herein. While it is not the intention here to write a book on the history of section 93 or of educational rights under the Canadian Constitution, it is nonetheless important to put some meat on the bones of the constitutional skeleton that was so important to the evolution of the Jewish School Question in Montreal.

The central purpose of section 93 was to protect the established school rights of the religious minorities, Roman Catholic in Ontario (Canada West) and Protestant in Quebec (Canada East) at the time of Confederation.[12] The situation in each jurisdiction was socially and politically complex. Following the conquest of Quebec, the British government had guaranteed religious freedom to its Roman Catholic inhabitants, while at the same time ensuring the "Encouragement of the Protestant Religion."[13] Prior to Confederation, then, both local governments and the Colonial Office in London had to seek a careful balance between and among the competing denominational constituencies in Britain's colonies of Upper and Lower Canada.[14] In Quebec, government attempts to institute a more advanced, colony-wide system of education ultimately failed when they met with both local opposition in communities and more significantly with objections from the hierarchy of the Roman Catholic Church.[15] This meant not just dealing with the broad conflict between Protestant and Roman Catholic majorities and minorities, but also with issues arising within the Protestant populations insofar as the institutionalized dominance of Anglicanism was concerned.[16] Throughout this period, the politics and social framework within the non–Roman Catholic population of Lower Canada gave rise to attempts to avoid sectarianism, or the dominance of one branch of Protestantism, in schools, while at the same time ensuring their primarily Christian (Protestant) character.[17] In Upper Canada, similar struggles against Anglican hegemony also took place.[18] In addition, the influx of American Loyalist settlers into what would become Ontario led to attempts to introduce schools along the model of publicly funded common schools that was beginning to emerge in the United States.[19] At the same time, the Roman Catholic minority in Upper Canada sought to protect their parochial schools. In the end, in Ontario, a system of public schools was created, within which the Roman Catholic schools were subsumed, but with a legally protected existence.[20] The ultimate consequence of the battles over religion, language, and educational rights would mean that in the country of Canada, education would be a local, provincial matter and not one falling within the ambit of national or federal power.[21]

When representatives of the four colonies, Nova Scotia, New Brunswick, Quebec (Canada East), and Ontario (Canada West), met to hash out the terms of Confederation, conflicts between Roman Catholics and Protestants were at the forefront of debates and negotiations, not just in terms of educational rights, but as to whether Confederation should proceed at all.[22] When most of the issues had been settled to the satisfaction of representatives of the four colonies, the school rights issue flared near the end of negotiations. While some might believe that the separate school issue has been the domain of Canada's Roman Catholic populations, in fact the most important debates on the issue were invoked by the representative of Quebec's Protestants, Sir Alexander Galt.[23] The Protestant minority of Quebec not only wanted their school rights protected; they wanted them "confirmed by statute before they passed under the control of the provincial legislature in which French-speaking Roman Catholics would possess an overwhelming majority."[24] In turn, and as a response to Galt's insistence on the protection of Canada East's Protestants, Canada West's Roman Catholic representatives demanded reciprocal guarantees for their schools, although again within the slightly different institutional context in which Roman Catholic schools existed under the broad framework of the public school system.[25]

Now the Roman Catholics of the two Maritime colonies, Nova Scotia and New Brunswick, entered the debate. While the compromise that would eventually become section 93 of the BNA Act was being worked out, Maritime bishops pointed out that the rights of their parishioners were being dangerously ignored. "In Nova Scotia and New Brunswick, education was not exclusively provided by the churches as in Canada East, nor organized by the state, with Roman Catholic separate schools as an integral part of the provincial system, as in Canada West. Most of the privileges that the Maritime – and particularly the Nova Scotian – Roman Catholics possessed in respect to education were extra-legal and acquired simply by usage and custom."[26]

In the end, it proved impossible to construct a compromise or a constitutionally enshrined system of education for Roman Catholics in New Brunswick and Nova Scotia that mirrored those of either Canada East or Canada West. Existing structures and practices simply had the force of inertia and the urgency of a confederative arrangement in their favour. The right to appeal to the federal government against provincial attempts to adversely affect minority religious rights in the education field was extended to the two Maritime provinces under section 93 (3), but that right protected only legally established school systems. In the dynamics of post-Confederation Canadian federalism, the idea of federal interference in education in the provinces was anathema to many. The right to appeal existed in the text of the Constitution but never really in the practice of Canadian federalism.

The constitutional textual framework, which would inform the evolution of the Jewish School Question in Montreal, was now formally in place. Roman Catholic and Protestant minorities in Ontario and Quebec enjoyed a basic right to their own school systems as part of the key political and legal arrangements, which had led to the creation of the new country, Canada. But complex and often messy political and social arrangements do not always fit comfortably or completely within the simple wording of the constitutional text. The taxonomical structures that were adopted by the framers of these constitutional documents cannot truly be said to have completely contained or constricted these social and political complexities. For example, the evolving debates within the province of Quebec over national identity and minority rights would (and still do) take place predominantly in terms of linguistic issues between the francophone majority, the historically anglophone minority, and as time passed, the difficult place of newer so-called allophone immigrant populations. But while these issues have played themselves out in the educational context, section 93 did not guarantee language rights at all. It protected the rights of Protestants and Roman Catholics, religion not language. While at the time of Confederation, the English language and the Protestant religion and conversely the French-speaking population and Roman Catholicism may have been seen as broadly synonymous, this has never really been the case in fact. There are and have been francophone Protestants in Quebec, just as there have been English-speaking Catholics, particularly with the arrival of Irish immigrants, in that province.[27] While English and French may have been easy and commonly invoked shorthand for Protestant and Catholic, the sociology of Quebec has never been so straightforward.[28]

Nor was the situation in Ontario at the time of Confederation or thereafter as simple as French/Roman Catholic, English/Protestant. While it was true that for many francophone Ontarians, the Roman Catholic Church was an essential bulwark in protecting their language and culture, other more complex social and political situations muddied the constitutional and political waters.[29] Francophone dominance over Roman Catholic education in Ontario met with opposition not only from English-speaking Protestants, but more significantly from English-speaking, largely Irish heritage, Roman Catholics. Irish Roman Catholics in Ontario wanted a Roman Catholic education for their children, but one provided in the English language.[30] These disputes over the extent and nature of Roman Catholic school rights in Ontario were played out to some extent before the courts in two cases, *Trustees of the Roman Catholic Separate Schools of Ottawa v Mackell* and *Roman Catholic School Trustees for Tiny v The King*.[31] *Mackell* dealt with the question of language versus religion, while *Tiny* was concerned with broader issues of the regulation of school curriculums, matriculation standards, and the division of school tax monies, by the provincial education authorities, in other words with the place of the Roman Catholic schools of Ontario within a public school system.

In *Mackell*, the issue was ultimately a simple one. Did the phrase "nothing in any such Law affect any Right or Privilege with respect to Denominational Schools which any Class or Persons" in section 93 (1) include the right to an education in French? The Privy Council confirmed the fears that had been expressed by the Roman Catholic hierarchy of the Maritimes in the pre-Confederation debates. Following its earlier decision in *City of Winnipeg v Barrett*,[32] the Privy Council held that section 93 protected only legal rights and privileges and not "any practice, instruction or privilege of a voluntary character which at the date of the passing of the Act might be in operation."[33] The Privy Council found that the education provisions of the BNA Act referred only to religion and not to language, and that there was nothing in statute or regulation in force at the time of Confederation that would enshrine linguistic education rights. The "class of persons" in section 93 referred to Roman Catholics as a whole and "that class cannot be subdivided into other classes by considerations of the language of the people by whom that faith is held."[34]

In *Tiny*, Viscount Haldane recognized the social and political importance of the case, referring to it as "among the most important that have come before them from Canada in recent years."[35] At the same time, however, he also underlined that "so far as concerns the question brought before the Judicial Committee of the Privy Council, it will be found to be a question of pure law, turning on the interpretation and application of words in that Act."[36] The Privy Council, as it had in other cases dealing with educational rights under the BNA Act, recognized that the legal question of the meaning of section 93 could be answered only by a historical inquiry into the state of education and of rights, if any, in relation to separate schools, as they existed at the time of Confederation, since it was those rights that were enshrined in the constitutional text at that time.[37] Thus, every judicial inquiry into section 93 would be largely historical, with the courts seeking to determine the legal situation that obtained in 1867, with as much exactitude as possible. In *Tiny*, the Privy Council confirmed that the arrangement in Ontario at the time of Confederation was that while Roman Catholic schools were constitutionally protected, they had existed within the overarching framework of the public school system and were therefore subject to the general regulatory measures put into place under and within that system. While regulation did not carry with it the power to abolish the Roman Catholic school system in Ontario,[38] the existence of which was protected and guaranteed under section 93, it did allow the secular, governmental school authorities to exercise broad powers over Roman Catholic schools in curricular and other matters.[39]

This historically informed and strictly limited legal reading of the constitutional text as judicial interpretive approaches in education cases had already been seen in controversies dealing with the vexed and politically sensitive Manitoba School Question that had arisen following Manitoba's entry into Confederation.[40] They had also manifested themselves in New Brunswick, the other province in which there was a large Roman Catholic citizenry that was mostly, but not uniquely, francophone. In *Maher v The Town Council of Portland*,[41] the Privy Council considered the constitutional validity of a decision to withdraw taxpayer funding from parish schools in which "the special doctrines of the Roman Catholic religion were taught."[42] Again, the court engaged in a careful historical analysis of the legislative record involving schooling in the province, relying heavily on the decision of Chief Justice Ritchie of the New Brunswick Supreme Court.[43] While he was sympathetic to the claims of Roman Catholics, the chief justice was clear that the question of common schooling was one that the Constitution left to the political wisdom of the provincial legislature, and the courts could not be influenced by the practical hardships that might befall Roman Catholic ratepayers compelled to support a school system to which they had confessional objections.[44] The Privy Council determined that, for the purposes of the case, the New Brunswick legislature had established a non-sectarian, common school system in the province at the time of Confederation, with the legal aim of "guarding the law and in preserving the schools from any denominational or sectarian tendency."[45] Under the operative legislative scheme establishing a public school system, the fact, for example, that a local population may have been unanimously Protestant or Roman Catholic, and therefore that the schools may have come to take on "a denominational character or denominational hue" was simply a matter of social and demographic chance. It did not create any "legal right to that denomination, which was the right alone which was intended to be protected by the Federation Act of the Dominion of Canada."[46]

In these cases, the Privy Council enunciated the understanding it had of the limited and limiting denominational character of educational rights embodied in the Canadian Constitution. It highlighted the historical nature of any judicial inquiry into the precise meaning of section 93. It also underlined the position that the only rights and privileges that were protected by the constitutional provisions were legal rights and not those enshrined by lesser practices, customs, or demographic happenstance. Indeed, the history of Canadian constitutional federalism would be troubled and defined by the issue of religion and schooling throughout the twentieth century. As late as 1949, with Newfoundland's entry as the tenth Canadian province, negotiations hinged on enshrining protections for the province's Roman Catholic population.[47]

Each of these elements within the judicial approach to the educational rights under section 93 would come to play a vital role in the evolution of the Jewish School Question in Montreal.

Constituting Education: Law and the Narratives of Confessional Identity

The history of the educational system in the province of Quebec and particularly in the city of Montreal is long and complex.[48] The key constitutional issue under section 93 was, of course, the state of legal rights to education in denominational terms in 1867. Yet both prior arrangements and the post-Confederation developments would come in their own ways to influence the fate of the Jewish School Question throughout its long history. The situation in 1867 was the result of a long history after the English conquest. Likewise, the institutional structures and the legal framework after 1867 were those actually in place when the problems of educating Jews within a common school system divided along (Christian) denominational lines arose in the 1880s. The constitutionality of those post-1867 laws and administrative arrangements, as well as the room for manoeuvre left within these legal normative frameworks for political and social practices and compromises at the margins and in the shadow of legality, would be central to the practical solutions of the Jewish School Question. The narratives of education, national identity, sectarian divides, and the place, if any, open within these narratives of constituting embedded and nascent identities in Montreal would not always or necessarily take place within, or in obedience to, strict legal norms, but those norms would have an inevitable influence in shaping the available narrative spaces.

Immediately following the conquest of Quebec, the educational system remained largely unchanged. Francophone Roman Catholic elementary education was in the hands of the local priests throughout the province. Likewise, higher levels of education were in the hands of the church. For the newly arrived anglophone Protestant population, education was largely private or run by some church-related bodies. But the new English-speaking settlers soon demanded a general non-denominational public system of schooling, a demand that met with some sympathy from the English governing authorities.[49] Unfortunately it also met with firm opposition from clerical authorities in the Roman

Catholic Church who saw proposals for such a system as the first step in the diminution of their authority. In addition, calls for public schooling were seen as attempts to assimilate the majority population into an anglophone world. Despite pleas and arguments from the Protestant minority concerning the common nature of the schools, which would produce peace and harmony between the two communities, and from liberal members of the French-Canadian elite who sought both to promote these harmonious feelings and to undermine what they saw as the negative influence of conservative, narrowly nationalist clergy, these arguments ultimately failed.[50] The 1840s saw the establishment of nominally common schools. These legislative and governance changes occurred in the context of the Union between Canada East (Quebec) and Canada West (Ontario) and concomitant political discourses about representative government following the rebellions of 1837–8. Changes in the legal architecture of education fit into these evolving state structures and in emerging ideologies and debates about "the novel belief that governments ought to take over the instruction and socialization of children."[51] The changes in school governance reflected these broader political and cultural shifts more clearly in Canada West, where the idea of public schools became entrenched.[52] The same period also witnessed the formal establishment of both the right to dissent and form schools for religious minorities and the reinforcement of the role of the church in Roman Catholic schooling, both in Ontario and in Quebec.[53] In Quebec, the political dynamic supported the church's position. Local school authorities, under the influence of the church, eventually refused to cooperate with any modernization attempts.[54] The legislative discourse of the time attached the label common to Quebec schools, but the normative provisions of the laws and the organizational structures of education became grounded in the religious divide that would inform the debates leading to Confederation and become constitutionalized in section 93. For the historian of Quebec education Roger Magnuson, this led to a period characterized by the "triumph of denominationalism."[55]

In 1841, a School Act was passed following debate about the issue of public education and the role, if any, of denominationalism.[56] Another Act to improve elementary education in Lower Canada was passed by the legislature in 1846.[57] Again while ostensibly aimed at the establishment of common schools, the statute in fact began the separation of public education in Quebec along religious lines. Section 26 of the statute granted to the religious minority in a given school district the right to establish their own dissentient schools. Religious minorities were granted the right to create their own schools, to govern them, and to do so to the exclusion of the majority population, and to raise funds for those schools. In practice this meant the separation of the Protestant minority from the Roman Catholic majority throughout most of the province, and, in some areas predominantly settled by anglophone Protestants, the converse isolation of Roman Catholic schools. Significantly for subsequent developments, school administration was given to local municipalities, and the right to elect school commissioners, or trustees for dissentient schools, was granted to local taxpayers. From the earliest period of common schooling in Quebec, there was a distinct and strong element of local and democratic, or at least electoral, control over the running of the school systems of both the majority and the minority populations. Somewhat ironically perhaps, rural Protestant minorities enjoyed significant autonomy in school matters, but at the same time, they continued to perceive themselves as being more broadly under attack by the local majority, Roman Catholic population.[58] The existential threat posed by this minority status meant that for many Protestants in Quebec, schools became the institution that, along with their churches, they controlled, and gave concrete meaning to being Protestant in a predominantly Roman Catholic province.[59]

The 1846 statute also created a separate and distinct method of administration for common schools in the two large cities of the province, Quebec and Montreal. There school commissioners were not elected but nominated by the local government. Under the 1846 law, twelve commissioners were to be named, six each for the Roman Catholic community and the Protestant population.[60] Two separate and equal school commissions were thereby created, and each technically was in charge of common schools. Each system was broadly held to the general rules and practices of province-wide school regulation established by the statute.[61] This early legislation introduced a system of funding for the schools in Montreal that would change subsequently, but at the time provided for the payment to each commission of funds for education from the municipal treasury in proportion to the population represented by each.[62]

An amending Act in 1849 expanded and specified the rights of dissentient school trustees to finance their schools.[63] Another statute passed two years later clarified and solidified the rights of the Protestant and Roman Catholic commissioners in Quebec and Montreal to claim their due from the city treasury.[64] Again these statutes did not operate any fundamental changes to the arrangements and principles governing the issue of common and dissentient schools in the province. They did, however, further concretize several vital aspects of the constitutional and dominant cultural narratives around the Jewish School Question. First, it was established that Protestant and Roman Catholic communities had rights to operate and control their own schools to the exclusion of the other religious group. Protestants controlled Protestant common and dissentient schools and Roman Catholics likewise controlled their majority, common schools and their minority dissentient establishments. Second, as a consequence, throughout the province, it was now evident that while schools were common or dissentient according to the circumstances, all common schools were in reality controlled by one or the other of the two dominant denominational groups in the province. Third, the principle of local control over schools, by way of election by taxpayers was confirmed throughout the province. Montreal and Quebec were exceptions to most of these rules. The dominant principle of denominationalism in schools was confirmed and concretized in the cities, but there neither system was the creature of a majority or a dissentient minority population. Each system operated common schools, and the management of the Roman Catholic and Protestant school systems, like common schools throughout the province, was in the hands of school commissioners and not trustees. Finally, the system of governance was different in Montreal (and Quebec), where these school commissioners were appointed and not elected.

Another vital statutory change occurred in 1856 when the legislature again situated the rights of majority and dissentient populations at the centre of the constitutive arrangements for the governance of education.[65] Section 1 of the Act provided both for further taxation powers for dissentient school trustees and for the payment of additional sums from the municipal treasuries of Quebec and Montreal to the two school commissions in those cities. But the most significant change to the legal and administrative horizons of education law in Quebec came at the level of provincial governance. The 1856 statute created the Council of Public Instruction, a provincial body appointed by the governor, to comprise eleven to fifteen individuals, working in collaboration with the provincial superintendent of public instruction. The council was charged with making regulations for schools, including the choice of texts and other curricular matters, and to take charge of the provincial examination process.[66] The Council of Public Instruction would come to play a key role not just in the creation and implementation of school policy and practice throughout the province, but in the various iterations of what would become the Jewish School Question, where its input would often be vital.[67]

Minor amendments were made again in 1859, this time giving a more solid statutory and regulatory basis to the conduct of provincial examinations. Section 4 confirmed the separation of examination boards into Roman Catholic and Protestant panels.[68] More significantly, perhaps, the consolidation of 1861, the last statutory norms prior to the all-important date of 1867, continued and reinforced the denominational divide in public education.[69] That consolidation confirmed and entrenched the positions of the Council of Public Instruction (sections 18 and following) and the superintendent of public instruction (sections 23 and following). The key provision, which would echo throughout the Jewish School Question and the tortured history of the place of Jews in the system of common schools in Quebec, was section 27 of the 1861 consolidation. Once and for all, it provided the basic principle for education under section 93 of the BNA Act for the cities of Montreal and Quebec, and the rest of the province: "There shall be in each of the Cities of Quebec and Montreal, and in each Municipality, Town or Village in Lower Canada, one or more Common Schools for the elementary instruction of youth, to be managed by School Commissioners, – or in the event of dissentient schools being established therein, then by Trustees of such schools, – in the manner hereinafter provided."

The legal die was cast. Majority and minority schools were now firmly established and entrenched in the statutory regime governing education in Quebec. Throughout the province, the majority schools would be common schools, and in Montreal and Quebec, both Roman Catholic and Protestant schools were common schools. The right to dissent and to establish dissentient schools was reserved for religious minorities, which interestingly and importantly were not further described in these statutory provisions, as they would later be, in terms of Protestant or Roman Catholic. The electoral systems for commissioners and trustees were again set out in some detail.[70] Intriguingly, the consolidated statute also contained one of the few instances in which provincial legislation countenanced and recognized the potential complexities involved in a system in which Protestants were treated as a single entity. While section 103 (2) provided for a single Board of Examiners divided into Roman Catholic and Protestant sections, section 103 (1), which dealt with the nomination of members of the board, did so not in terms of choosing members who were Roman Catholic or

Protestant, but provided instead that "there shall be, in each of the Cities of Quebec and Montreal, a Board of Examiners, composed of fourteen persons, chosen, in as fair and equitable manner as possible, from among the different religious denominations."

While it is obvious from the subsection that followed, and from historical practice, that there would be an equal division between Roman Catholics and Protestants, it is also clear from the use of the word "among" in the context of "different religious denominations," rather than "between," that the composition of the Protestant board was intended to be, as was the Protestant population, more heterogeneous and representative in as fair a manner as possible of the various branches of Protestantism. At the same time, of course, it was patently obvious that, despite the presence of several hundred Jews in the province at the time, there was no institutional place open to them. Religious denominations for school purposes, within the provincial statutory scheme governing education, meant only Roman Catholic and Protestant.

Finally the 1861 consolidation dealt with the special circumstances that obtained in Montreal and Quebec.[71] Section 130 clearly confirmed that of the twelve appointed, not elected, school commissioners, six would be Roman Catholic and six Protestant, and that they would "form two separate and distinct Corporations." They were again to be financed from the city treasury (section 131). At the moment of Confederation, then, there was in the Province of Quebec a system of common and dissentient schools in which the rights of religious minorities, Roman Catholic and Protestant, were enshrined in statute, and where, while the general provincial statutory regime applied, in Montreal special provisions in relation to Protestant and Roman Catholic schools, as common schools, were in effect.

While most of these arrangements would not change over the years following Confederation, in part because of the looming shadow of section 93, some important modifications to the governance of Quebec schools did take place in subsequent years. Most importantly, these were the actual operating political, cultural, and legal arrangements and accommodations that were in effect both within and outside the bounds of strict legality and operated to influence and to be influenced by the Jewish School Question. Thus, in 1869, statutory change was made to the broad structures of provincial school governance.[72] A ministry was created, placing primary political and legal responsibility for education ultimately in the hands of an elected member of the government. More importantly in the long run, the Council of Public Instruction was fundamentally altered. The council would henceforth consist of twenty-one members, fourteen Roman Catholics and seven Protestants. The council was then subdivided into two committees along denominational lines, with each committee given exclusive jurisdiction over matters affecting each of them (sections 1, 2). The minister or the superintendent was to be an ex officio member of each committee but would have voting rights only in the committee of his or her religious faith (section 2). At the provincial level, educational governance was now more clearly divided than ever on denominational lines, as the two committees were given exclusive jurisdiction over matters relating to their own school systems.

The 1869 law also operated a key change in school finances in Montreal, a change that would also have profound affects on subsequent manifestations of the Jewish School Question. The former system of allocating funds from the general revenue of the city in a proportion related to denominational populations was replaced by a new mode for financing schools within Montreal that imposed a specific real estate–based school tax.[73] Section 26 specified, "The said 'city school tax' shall be payable by the proprietors of real estate to the exclusion of the tenant, and the tenant shall not be bound to reimburse the same to the proprietor, except in the case of special agreement to that effect."

Protestant and Roman Catholic tax assessors were to be appointed to regularly compile information about all real estate holdings in the city. The annual tax statement would be divided into panels: Panel 1 would be constituted by Roman Catholic–owned real estate, while Protestant-owned real estate would be placed in Panel 2. Panel 3 would comprise corporate property and property owned by "persons not belonging to the roman catholic or protestant faith, or whose religious faith shall not have been ascertained" (e.g., Jews), jointly owned property belonging to owners of more than one religious denomination, and undeclared (in denominational terms) property (which would become known as the neutral panel). Finally, Panel 4 would be made up of property exempted from taxation (mostly educational and religious property) (section 29). In addition to the new taxation system, the 1869 Act also permitted schools in Montreal to demand payment of monthly fees for enrolled students.

The final relevant statutory change to the system of public schooling in Quebec at the time of the first crisis in the Jewish School Question occurred in 1875.[74] The Ministry of Public Instruction was abolished, largely at the urging of the Roman Catholic Church, which sought to entrench its control over education and to formally reduce the power of politicians over schooling. The powers of the provincial superintendent of education were confirmed and expanded.[75] For most of the period relevant to the Jewish School Question, then, public education was not a matter for an elected minister with direct political and legislative responsibility, and a departmental bureaucracy, of which the minister was in charge, that ran the education portfolio. Instead, at the insistence of the rising ultramontane elements in the Roman Catholic Church, education was taken out of the hands of elected politicians and placed firmly under the control of those most directly concerned. Hand-in-hand with the abolition of the ministry came the further recomposition of the Council of Public Instruction, most importantly of its Roman Catholic Committee. All Roman Catholic bishops whose diocese was situated partly or wholly in the province became ex officio members of the committee. Moreover, they were given the right, unlike other members, to appoint representatives in cases where they could not be personally present at meetings of the council or the Roman Catholic Committee.[76] Thus, the ever-present position of the Roman Catholic episcopate came to dominate the majority of common schools in the province. As Audet and Gauthier point out, this statutory regime created in 1875 would embody the essential characteristics and governance structures of the denominational and common school system in Quebec until the 1960s. It consolidated the power of the Roman Catholic hierarchy over the majority of educational institutions in the province and completed the separation of the two denominational systems, both in law and subsequently in practice.[77] After this final reorganization of the Council of Public Instruction (later changed to the Council of Public Education in its English version) in 1875, the two denominational committees operated in virtual isolation from one another, meeting jointly only thirteen times between 1876 and 1908. From 1908 to 1960, they held no joint sessions at all.[78]

By 1875, then, the educational system in the province of Quebec, and more particularly in Montreal, had been legally and politically constituted along denominational lines. For many, this was the great achievement of Quebec in the field of education. Religious minorities had been protected at Confederation, and subsequent governance arrangements instituted by the province had put flesh on the bare bones of section 93 in Quebec's public education system. In doing so, the province had given a political and social structure to the wishes and desires of the two founding nations at the time of Confederation. The education system as it existed in its final form after the 1875 changes embodied more broadly the ideal of a bi-national Canada. For almost a century this Canadian version of separate but equal would inform broad and basic ideas and ideals of national identity (not just in Quebec). The denominational common school system of Quebec became a predominant signifier of the politics of Canadian and Canadien identity.

"Our dual school system is an achievement of the Province of Quebec, and I regret to have to point out that our English-speaking historians do not appear to have seized its significance and its fundamental contribution to the cause of unity and amity between the races, first and foremost in our own Province, and also throughout our country by illustrating the possibilities of constructive co-operation when the rights of majority and minority are fully respected."[79]

These institutional arrangements for the governance of identity and difference, at least in terms of Roman Catholics and Protestants, in the educational system came at a time of important changes and developments in Quebec society. In both Protestant and Roman Catholic schools, ideas of national identity and the importance of education itself were of growing significance, albeit in different ways. In the Protestant system in particular, but in French-Canadian Roman Catholic society as well, the question of gender would arise in important contexts.[80] The role of schoolteacher became more and more one for women, while the leadership position of headmaster or school principal continued to be held by men.[81] Much of the post-1875 period was also characterized by an increasing urbanization of Quebec society. This would have a direct impact on the school systems of Montreal as immigrants arrived not just from overseas, but also from rural Quebec, in ever-increasing numbers. The Roman Catholic and Protestant School Commissions would be faced with these and many other issues as the dual education structures of Montreal were established and grew. While the debates around the Jewish School Question are to be understood largely in denominational terms – Jewish, Roman Catholic, and Protestant – each of these denominations must also be understood in the complex terms of internal organizational dynamics of gender and class in a new set of economic and social circumstances.[82] In addition, the sociological history of education in Montreal and the Jewish School Question must also be placed and grasped in terms of alliances between some of these groups and others, alliances that would emerge from complex economic and social circumstances, which would always render the Jewish School Question more complex than simple general denominational taxonomies might indicate.

Dual Denominationalism in Montreal's Schools: Educating and Creating Roman Catholics and Protestants

The economic and social evolution of the province, and of the city of Montreal in particular, witnessed an increasing French-Canadian working-class presence, as well as a growing bourgeois francophone elite. Almost exclusively, the children of the French-speaking majority were educated in church-run schools. While provision for working-class education was poor, the bourgeoisie could send their children to the *collèges classiques*, where they would be trained for entry into the medical and legal professions, or the priesthood.[83] To a large extent, the Roman Catholic educational system at this stage reproduced the class and economic structure of the French-Canadian population. However, the rise of an educated elite, whose professional lives brought them into contact with anglophones and with different world views and broader social and political experiences, also led to the creation of a minority among French Canadians who came to adopt a more commercial, and therefore a more liberal, individualized political and social philosophy. This *rouge* mentality would allow for the development of a different set of ideas about identity, in which Canada would for some come to embody ideas of freedom and emancipation outside a traditional Roman Catholic Canadien ideal. The *rouge* faction would be in almost constant conflict with the church for years to come.[84] More liberal elements of French-Canadian society would also be more broadly opposed to more compliant, accommodationist government and party officials within the Liberal Party itself. On occasion this disharmony would manifest itself in the educational domain, but conservative church views, with the support of successive Liberal governments, would always dominate all parts of the Jewish School Question.[85]

While the Protestant mercantile elite of Montreal had long educated their children in a system of private establishments, and many would continue to do so, the school structure began to change as the numbers of Protestants in the city increased dramatically.[86] The Protestant School Board began to take on an increasingly prominent role in the lives of the city's Protestant population as the number of students and the number of schools in the public education system grew.[87] A review of tax monies made available to the Protestant schools of Montreal reveals not just the ways in which the changing legal framework for school finance affected the income of the commission, but also makes evident the increasing need created by the growing school population. From 1868 to 1870, payments to the Protestant board increased from

$1031 to $8,900, $19,400, and $18,300. With the implementation in 1870 of the direct school tax system in the city, based on real estate evaluations and in the creation of the separate panels, the revenue from public monies was increased to $26,000. The Protestant citizens of Montreal were apparently more than happy to support the needs of the expanding common school system. "In the year 1873, in answer to an application from the City Council, supported by a petition of citizens, the School Tax was doubled, and the income of the Board became more nearly adequate to the work devolving to it."[88]

This increase gave the Protestant school system of Montreal an annual tax income of $75,000, which was supplemented by an annual grant from general provincial revenues of around $4,000, and a further $23,000 obtained from compulsory school fees.[89] From these revenues, the Protestant board supported a high school for boys,[90] a high school for girls, a senior school, and the elementary school system of Protestant education. From the modest beginnings of two elementary schools in 1850, with a student body of 244, by 1878, the Protestant Commission had nine elementary schools teaching 3,125 pupils.

While the Roman Catholic population of Montreal also increased rapidly in this period after Confederation and before the turn of the twentieth century, the education system of the majority population was somewhat slower to adapt to the changing demographic circumstances. Broadly speaking, the dominant sociological and ideological position of Quebec Roman Catholics valued an idealized vision of Canadiens as a predominantly rural people, close to the land, more concerned with spiritual than material values, and deeply embedded in a collective identity that eschewed individualism. This meant that the majority of French-speaking Quebeckers were ill equipped, educationally and ideologically, to prosper from the economic growth spurts that characterized this period of North American history. One important consequence was that the minority Protestant group had much more wealth, in terms of the real estate base on which school taxes were grounded, than the impoverished Roman Catholic residents of Montreal, who filled mostly unskilled places in the economy. Education depended, not just as an administrative matter, on the power of the church; in the Roman Catholic primary school system, it also relied on the wealth and charity of the church to support its own schools.[91] The increase in Montreal's population of more than 3 per cent per year imposed a constant economic burden that fell heavily on the Roman Catholic school system.[92] The Roman Catholic elementary system in

1886 was made up of twelve schools for boys, eight schools for girls, and ten mixed schools, run by principals, Christian Brothers, nuns, and "other lady teachers."[93]

This necessarily brief historical overview of the evolution of the school system in Montreal in its legal, administrative, and practical aspects is necessary for several reasons. It situates the context of the synagogue schools of the two principal Jewish congregations in Montreal, around which the first crisis over the education of Jewish students in Montreal emerged in the 1880s. The synagogue schools of the 1870s and 1880s came into being and existed at the same time as the bi-denominational common school structure of schools in the city was beginning to take on a more solid form. As with other aspects of the context in which Jews in Montreal had to construct narratives and political practices to ensure the concretization of their legal rights to equality and their social right to community, in the school environment, they would have to engage concretely and ideologically with the Roman Catholic and Protestant school systems. That engagement would, of course, always occur in the shadow of the formal legal structure embodied constitutionally in section 93 and legally in the bi-confessional statutory framework established by provincial legislation. As well, it would have to occur in the context of the dominant Roman Catholic ideological construction of the vision of Canada and Canadian identity grounded in a bi-nationalist frame from which, by definition, Jews were excluded.

Of course, the *rouge* ideal of a new Canadian citizenship beyond French- or English-Canadian identities would have a significant influence on debates about nationalism and belonging throughout the period.[94] At the same time, Jewish Montrealers would invoke the ideals of citizenship and equality they enjoyed as British citizens.[95] But whatever room for manoeuvre might have been left in provincial politics for the embodiment of *rouge* ideals in the Liberal party, that ideological space was essentially closed in the world of education.[96] Any manifestation of liberal or *rouge* ideals would confront and be stymied by the bi-confessional, bi-national constitutional structures of the provincial education system. Likewise, broad claims to citizenship equality and British principles of justice and fair play would simply become irrelevant within an educational structure enshrined in section 93 and concretized by the omnipresence and power of the most conservative elements of the Roman Catholic hierarchy at the provincial level and in the Montreal school system. Liberal views had almost no place in Roman Catholic school governance in Montreal or in Quebec.[97]

Setting out the overview legislative and social history of common schools in Quebec and Montreal is also useful for another aspect of the political and rhetorical narrations of the constitutional issues of the Jewish School Question. The rivalries between the Protestant and Roman Catholic communities in relation to education would play an important part in the different historical manifestations of the Jewish School Question. But there was not always conflict between the two. The tax increase in Montreal in 1873 had come about following an approach from the Roman Catholic board to their Protestant counterparts to join together in seeking more money for education.[98] At this time, Roman Catholic officials sought to broaden the financial base of school funding and to relieve the church itself of an increasingly onerous burden. But a few years later in 1880–1, the Roman Catholic Commission attempted to force changes to the way the system operated in relation to the corporate bodies that paid into the neutral panel. The two commissions had previously agreed that the revenues would be divided according to the express wish or intention of the different bodies corporate. Because of the nature of capitalist life in Montreal, English-speaking Protestants controlled the vast majority of the largest and most wealthy corporate institutions, which had the consequence that most of that part of neutral panel taxes came to the Protestant board. The Roman Catholic Commission now claimed that the agreement reached with the Protestant board in the 1870s was in fact illegal. They sought legislative approval for the idea that neutral panel taxes be distributed on a pro rated basis, depending on the number of students in each common school system. The consequence of such a division of neutral panel revenues would have been the radical reversal of the distribution in neutral taxes in favour of the numerically superior, but economically poorer, Roman Catholic system.[99]

It is also important to bear in mind the legal context of the governance arrangements in public, common education in Quebec, because neither the Roman Catholic nor the Protestant governing bodies operated as hegemonic monoliths with never-changing practices and policies. Protestant representatives differed on a number of issues and at several levels. Members of the Protestant Committee of the Council of Public Instruction would not always see eye-to-eye among themselves. They represented different Protestant denominations, as well as rural and urban school systems, each of which had different demographic needs and different financial arrangements. Likewise, members of the Protestant School Board in the city of Montreal, who also represented different churches within the broad Protestant framework, often differed fundamentally on a variety of issues. Relations between the Montreal board and the provincial committee were also sometimes strained, as were those between rural boards and trustees and the central authorities. In Montreal, as local, formerly independent boards from outlying areas were absorbed as the result of urban expansion and amalgamation, the loss of local autonomy could and did result in acrimony.[100]

Likewise, the Roman Catholic Commission in Montreal experienced tension as various governments attempted to consolidate school administration on the island of Montreal as population movements made new demands on public education and other parts of the broader infrastructure.[101] Tensions arose around the democratic deficit in Montreal, where, unlike the rest of the province, members of the school commissions were appointed and not elected.[102] As the representation on the Roman Catholic Commission came to include more liberal members of the francophone elite of Montreal, dangerously secular ideas occasionally competed with clerical dominance of the governing structures. For most of the relevant period, however, until the Quiet Revolution (*la Révolution tranquille*) of the 1960s and perhaps even beyond, more traditionalist church views still continued to dominate and to hold sway over Roman Catholic school governance in Montreal.[103]

As a consequence, all narrative constructions of identity and attempts to arrive at transgressive moments in the constitution of Jewish identities in the context of the School Question always occurred in a further complex set of often cacophonous attempts to articulate competing and sometimes multiple Protestant and Roman Catholic identities and to constitute rival polities in the school context. The Jewish School Question was never and could not have been solely Jewish, nor solely a School Question, in the constitutional, legal, political, economic, and social contexts of Montreal at the relevant historical junctures.

Schools and Citizenship: The Dream behind the Jewish School Question

The text of section 93 and the set of judicial interpretations arising out of the pronouncements form the technical legal framework within which the Jewish School Question in Montreal must be legally understood. The interpretation of various statutory schemes and provisions must, despite the importance of history and social and political context, be constructed according to the canons of legal interpretation. Nonetheless broader social attitudes and positions always informed the political circumstances in which the debates took place. The most obvious point of conflict and controversy within the history of the Jewish School Question, and one that might still strike present-day readers as containing a chord of dissonance, can be found in the conceptions of education and the role of schools in the construction of citizenship and national identity.

Many of the issues that arose and the debates that took place in Montreal, beginning in the 1880s, had a distinctively modern flavour, where claims to equality, rights of citizenship and democratic participation, and respect for minority religious practices and cultures, among others, were in turn asserted, accepted, or rebuffed, both in law and in broader political and social contexts. Nonetheless it is still important to situate the discussions and controversies in their own temporal frame. While the same terminology about identity, equality, and citizenship may have been present from the late nineteenth into the early years of the twentieth century in Montreal, that terminology was being invoked in Victorian and Edwardian – not postmodern, multicultural – circumstances. The claims of equality and assertions about the centrality of education to the formation of citizens have not changed, but the circumstances in which they were and are invoked and articulated have.

For example, in their editors' introduction to a collection of studies of current culturally diverse and complex societies, Will Kymlicka and Wayne Norman write, "The last ten years have witnessed a remarkable upsurge of interest in two topics amongst political philosophers: the rights and status of ethnocultural minorities in multi-ethnic societies (the 'minority rights–multiculturalism' debate) and the virtues, practices and responsibilities of democratic citizenship (the 'citizenship–civic virtue' debate)."[104]

These debates, both in theory and practice, circulate around broad concerns, informed by evolving demographic and political realities, and are situated, as Kymlicka and Norman point out, within contexts in which multiculturalism and citizenship in an increasingly multi-polar world become central foci for debates about identity and belonging.[105] Whether one wishes to engage with these debates in terms of multiculturalism, or cosmopolitan identity and citizenship, or any of their multiple variants, there can be little doubt that underlying the various signifiers are central political and legal concerns.[106] One of the most important consequences of the cultural and political phenomena that give rise to the often vigorous and not always helpful debates that surround important questions of identity in cosmopolitan and/or multicultural circumstances is the apparent contingent, and consequent vulnerability, of legal understandings of citizenship. As Michel Rosenfeld puts it, "The constitutional subject and its identity may be more fragile than would initially appear. Their trajectory and future potential confront manifold obstacles and complexities and require painstaking and belabored deployment on many distinct fronts."[107]

Many of these debates, concerns, and anxieties can be found in a nascent form in the struggles of Montreal Jewry for educational rights for their children. Equality rights were invoked; pleas for comparable treatment of all citizens could be heard in the courts and before the legislative tribune; arguments for the respect and recognition of immigrant, minority groups and their practices were often at the heart of assertions coming from various parts of the Jewish communities within Montreal. All participants in the politics of the Jewish School Question in Montreal would witness a set of constitutional and constitutive discourses that were often, as Tully puts it, "overlapping, interacting and negotiated in use because these are the ways they are handled in practice, thereby constituting the aspectival and diverse identity of the constitutional associations they describe."[108] But the private and political practices that would define the negotiated understandings in this context would always be informed by overarching and competing constructions of national identity, by religious normativity, and by formal legal text, all of which left little room for "diverse identity" in the educational domain. All these pleas for equality and democratically informed constitutive dialogue and negotiation took place at a specific time and place and within an established constitutional framework, each element of which informed and constrained the debate and its consequences.

A brief comparison with another culturally powerful narrative of Jewish immigrants to North America might situate more precisely some of the key elements of the contexts informing the Jewish School Question in Montreal.[109] A dominant and important story of immigration in United States history is the role played by public schools in the acculturation of new arrivals to that country.[110] Even if we must recognize both that the ways in which these processes of Americanization worked were different for different groups and that other education models, such as parochial Roman Catholic schools for Italian or Irish immigrants, were also in place in many cities, the reality and mythology of public schooling, immigration, and assimilation are strong in American history.[111]

Dominant and culturally resonant accounts of Jewish immigrants to the United States situate the influx of newly arrived migrants within the overarching narrative of the American melting pot, the historically powerful counter-narrative to later ideas of multiculturalism and cosmopolitan citizenship. A key component of this idealization of the process through which Jews became Americans is the role played by the public school system in the United States generally and the culturally dominant locus, New York City, more specifically.

This story in its broad outlines is one of an immigrant community that achieved some sort of acculturalization, identity, and acceptance as American through the processes of formal and informal education in the public school system. Language and cultural values were passed on to Jewish children as they attended school, studied civics, and interacted daily with Americans.[112] As the public schools became central to the creation of an American identity among the Jewish immigrant population, they also became a desirable professional destination for increasingly well-educated members of the Jewish communities. When Fiorella La Guardia did away with the old patronage systems that had kept Jews from employment as teachers, a whole new class of schoolteachers, whose professional and personal identities were informed by their intimate relationship with the public school system as an American locus, emerged. "The new mayor changed the system completely, championed competitive exams, and required candidates to posses a high school education even to sit for the entrance test. Jews, with their diplomas in hand, were first in line for these jobs, at the expense of the more poorly educated Irish."[113]

Of course, the real-life version of the story is somewhat more complex. The influx of Jewish public school teachers and the lost jobs of now unqualified Irish Americans fostered anti-Semitism. Many well-educated Jews turned to school teaching because university quota systems kept them from pursuing careers in medicine or law.[114] At the same time, Jewish students met with anti-Semitism in the school system, ranging from abuse and taunts to physical attacks. They also had to deal with the attitudes, biases, and stereotypes of the dominant social groups – attitudes not dissimilar to those encountered in fact and fiction by Mordecai Richler and Duddy Kravitz. These biases informed attempts by their teachers and school administrators to put them, as new immigrants, into vocational training streams rather than academic paths within the school system. Throughout much of their time in public schools, Jewish children struggled to assimilate within a system that sought to marginalize and exclude them. This, of course, does not mean that there is no truth to the myth of public schools, Jews, and the American melting pot. It simply means that, like all immigrants to America, or any other country for that matter, creating new identities, becoming citizens in the broad sense, and finding equality through schooling are all matters of political and social struggle, rather than the natural consequences of an ineffable truth embodied in the experience of going to public school.[115] Additionally, as the Jewish School Question in Montreal demonstrates, the constitutive processes of citizenship, whether through education or more broadly, always created a space in which the immigrant population played an active role. While they constituted themselves as citizens and dealt with the quotidian realities of anti-Semitism, Jewish immigrants also created complex understandings of the other participants in the political and social hermeneutic.[116]

There is, despite the necessary nuanced and contextual analyses that are always part of such inquiry, no doubt that the public school system was a locus for the construction of American identity among Jewish and other immigrant groups. Nevertheless, the idea of the public school, which was so central to the mythological and practical processes of Americanization, was not itself a transcendental truth. It grew out of particular social and economic necessities, within which the roles and functions of both education and the state were being rethought and continually contested.[117] It is not the intention here to trace the detailed history of public education at the primary and secondary levels in the United States. However, it is necessary, not just in terms of the American experience itself, but more concretely for understanding the Jewish School Question in Montreal in some comparative historical, political, and legal context, to briefly outline the controversies surrounding the denominational versus secular issue in public education taking place in the United States, as thousands upon thousands of Italian, Irish, German, Jewish, and other immigrants came to the promised land.

Many elements, shifting over time, informed the atmosphere that had shaped important debates over the establishment of a public primary and secondary school system in the United States. With their origins in the New England states, common schools began, to summarize a complex history perhaps beyond recognition, as schools that were meant to be non-denominational or non-sectarian, but at the same time Christian.[118] Non-sectarianism originally and for a long period simply meant that no particular version of Protestantism would be invoked within what would eventually be a common public school system. In other words, an overarching Protestant character informed the school, but no sect could have its teachings form part of the general curriculum. Layered within these understandings of non-sectarianism within the school system was a not so subtle and often blatant, sometimes violent, anti-Catholicism (and later anti-Semitism).[119] Proponents and activists for the common school system originally understood the provision of Christian education as non-sectarian, just as they also understood the provision of study informed by the Bible as universal. For them there was no contradiction between an education system infused with Protestantism and a belief that the schools were non-sectarian. They preached universal values – values that were American and Protestant, true – and if Roman Catholics rejected this model, then that could only be because they were anti-American.

While what emerged from heated and hotly contested political debate in a number of states would eventually come to resemble the truly secular public school that is the ideal and ideological embodiment of the American model today, the issue of what place, if any, religion should play in schools has not disappeared from American political and legal debate, but this is not the focus here.[120] Suffice it to say, again by way of gross generalization, these debates now occur in a context in which the contours of both public schools and religion have been, however contingently, constructed through First Amendment jurisprudence. Issues of the right to dissent, released time for religious study, separate schools and compulsory education statutes, prayer in public schools, whatever one might think of particular decisions on specific questions or cases, have been dealt with within a broad liberal constitutional and political understanding of the public school as a secular place, where all students are, or are about to become, Americans, and where issues of establishment and free exercise are dealt with in a specific, if contested, constitutional tradition.[121]

The basic constitutional structure of Canada is fundamentally different from that of the United States in that the right to religious schooling was specifically enshrined in the provisions of section 93. There was in fact and in law no wall of separation between church and state insofar as the school systems of some provinces were concerned, always depending on the state of legal rights on 1 July 1867, or when the various provinces joined Confederation thereafter. But this enshrined constitutional status did not prevent the question of denominational schools from arising before the courts, particularly in those provinces where no legally protected religious rights to schooling had been in effect at the time of union. The New Brunswick experience is again illuminating. The school system in that province was, at the time of Confederation, one of common, non-denominational schools. While in practice, as in the province of Quebec outside of Montreal and Quebec City, schools might come to be dominated by a single, perhaps unanimous, local population in terms of the community's religious adherence, this again did not mean that the denomination acquired any legal rights over education, nor did it therefore mean that the school was anything other than common or non-denominational. But the question about the nature and character of the content of education, who could be employed as teachers in non-denominational schools, what to do about absences of pupils for religious motives, all these issues that arose in the United States, and that would arise in the clearly denominational context of Montreal's school system, also came before the courts in the province of New Brunswick with its non-denominational system of education.

Again, the Privy Council had clearly confirmed that the school system established in New Brunswick at the time of Confederation was a non-denominational one where common schools were found. In the Bathurst School Case, the courts in that province had to determine with more precision what was meant by such a system when faced with the customs and practices arising from a set of local circumstances in which Roman Catholics and Protestants sought to establish a modus vivendi.[122] In this case, the legality both of a school board employing female members of a Roman Catholic religious order, who wore their religious garb in the classroom, as teachers, and of the holding of catechism classes in the school after hours, was challenged. It was claimed by those opposed to such practices that their continuation transformed the schools from common schools into denominational schools in which the Roman Catholic appearance and adherence of the teachers, and the use of school facilities, albeit out of hours, for Roman Catholic doctrinal education gave an overwhelmingly and inescapable denominational character to the schools.

The Court found support in foundational notions of the common school system in which the school trustees had statutory control over all teachers within a legislative framework that enshrined the non-denominational character of the school system. It held that since the members of the order, when they were fulfilling their roles as schoolteachers, fell not under the direct control of the church, but of the local school Trustees, they were in the same situation as any other provincial teacher in any common school.[123] Likewise, events before and after regular school hours were not part of the education system set out in the provincial statute governing common schools and therefore could have no bearing on the appropriate characterization of the schools in a particular district.

Once the general principle had been established, the question of school holidays arose. For three holy days of obligation, the teachers and their students were released from school attendance. As a result of these missed school days, the local trustees simply substituted three Saturdays, which were not normal teaching days, into the school calendar. School Regulation 20 allowed for such substitutions in cases of illness or unavoidable absence of teachers or in "other extraordinary circumstances," such as time lost due to inclement winter weather. Justice Barker accepted the argument that because the vast majority of students were Roman Catholics and would adhere to the teachings of their faith and absent themselves from school in any event, common sense, and an interpretation of regulation 20, would allow for the creation of substitute Saturdays by the local school trustees. For the majority of students, the decision of the trustees may have been understood as one made to allow them to meet their religious obligations. But, the Court was quick to point out, the decision neither impeded the efficiency of the common school program, nor did it alter the fundamental character of the school system itself. In other words, this accommodation of the religious practices of the student did not turn the common school into a Roman Catholic school. The substitution of the Saturdays in order to permit the students to make up for work missed on the three days of holy obligation was simply "a matter of administration," like the use to which school buildings might be put outside teaching hours. Such decisions relating to administrative matters remained in the hands of the trustees in running the school system according to the specificities and demands of the local environment.[124] The strictures of section 93 and the limits imposed by a careful study of the legal history of education in New Brunswick revealed the limits of what Paul Bowlby has called the "Victorian social imaginary" of a bi-confessional Canada.[125] At the same time, the local political practices of communal self-constitution, aided by a degree of judicial sensitivity, allowed for the creation of a common school system in which the two denominations, Protestant and Roman Catholic, maintained some form of self-governance. "The result was the creation of a unified public education system with a religiously dual practice."[126]

This brief digression into the history of denominational and non-denominational schooling in the United States and in other parts of Canada highlights many of the issues that would arise subsequently in Montreal throughout the episodes and disputes that fall under the broad rubric of the Jewish School Question. The duality recognized in the New Brunswick situation again offered limited equality only to the two founding Christian denominations. The question of a broader understanding that would include religious Others would form the core of the Jewish School Question in Montreal. What is the place of minorities in a common school system that is at once public and denominational? What precisely is meant by denominational? What is the nature of a Protestant school? Who is a Protestant? Does the presence of an increasing number of Jewish students or the absence of these same Jewish students on high holy days transform a Protestant school into something else? Each of these questions, in its own way, would play an important role in the Jewish School Question in Montreal. Courts, legislatures, school commissioners, and the broader communities would all have to answer them in ways that were consistent both with the law as it stood in 1867, and with claims about equality and national identity, or identities, that informed, implicitly and explicitly, the positions articulated at various times and in different circumstances not just by Montreal's Jews, but by Protestants and Roman Catholics as well. As shall become clear, these arguments and points of principle could not always achieve both the legal and the broader constitutive democratic aims of citizenship and equality.

Canadians, Canadiens, and Jews: Constituting Citizenship in Montreal

When Jews came to Canada, they encountered public schools that were non-denominational (or denominational), common, but imbued with Christianity as an unquestioned set of values understood by the majority population to be universal.[127] When they came to Montreal, the situation was radically different, both in terms of constitutional governing norms and of structural and taxonomic practice. There was no pretence of neutrality or non-denominationalism. Montreal schools were either Protestant or Roman Catholic. They were common or public, but more importantly they were explicitly and proudly denominational. They were common schools but they were governed by confessional administrative structures, Protestant and Roman Catholic. Within this publicly denominational system, enshrined in the texts and legal practices of section 93 of the BNA Act, Jews had to seek their place.

The central question that would arise within the context of the Jewish School Question is exactly how a group, defined religiously and culturally as separate from the denominational structures that controlled public education, could in fact, and in law, find any place at all, let alone a place that would allow them to become equal British subjects and Canadians. Some have sought to claim that in broad terms the Canadian educational experience, like its American counterpart, has been characterized by liberal notions of both pedagogy and of an ideological representation of schools, which should be understood as places for the transmission and inculcation of citizenship values.[128] Will Kymlicka argues that now "it is widely accepted that a basic task of schooling is to prepare each new generation for their responsibilities as citizens. Indeed, the need to create a knowledgeable and responsible citizenry was one of the major reasons for establishing a public school system ... Citizenship education is not just a matter of learning the basic facts about the institutions and procedures of political life; it also involves acquiring a range of dispositions, virtues, and loyalties that are intimately bound up with the practice of democratic citizenship."[129]

This view of the nature and virtuous enterprise of education was one that found, in its temporal embodiment permitted by the times, a consistent voice among various elements of the Montreal Jewish communities throughout the history of battles over schooling for their children. Going to school meant for many of them becoming "Canadian," but they faced circumstances of time, place, and constitutional law that made their desire to become full and virtuous citizens, enjoying all the rights and freedoms of British subjects, an uphill struggle. They faced not just legal, constitutionally enforced, formal barriers to their claims of educational rights for their children, but also found themselves confronting political and social contexts that tended to negate their understandings of what loyalty to their new home might actually mean.

The political and legal frames that would inform and control, to a greater or lesser extent, the ways in which claims for equality and respect could be made by Montreal's Jews were ones in which the available understandings and discourses occurred in a particular and peculiar bifocal set of mutually reinforcing limits. Claims to recognition, equality, and respect that emanated from the Jews of Montreal took place at a time and in a context before multiculturalism and before cosmopolitan citizenship. They occurred in a time and a place where they were met with dominant political and ideological understandings that reinforced assertions that there were two, and only two, cultures in Montreal, Quebec, and Canada. One dominant mythology of the nature of Canada itself, advocated by many important political and legal figures within the French-Canadian elite, would assert that Confederation was a formal legal and political arrangement embodying a compact between the two founding peoples.[130] Canada was a French- and English-speaking land of two solitudes, a country where there were Roman Catholics and Protestants.[131] While the two denominations might find themselves in conflict as they struggled in their spheres of influence, they still did so within an overarching reality of a Canada that was by definition, given its two constitutive elements, Christian.[132] Whatever divided Roman Catholics and Protestants, francophone and anglophone populations of Montreal, they were united in understanding Canadian identity as informed within those categories, Roman Catholic, Protestant Christian, French- or English-speaking. There could be no primary or originary constitutive place for Yiddish-speaking Jews.

For their part, French Canadians remembered the days of a forced union with Upper Canada and the creation of Canada East and West, brought about from their perspective, in part at least, in the hope that such a union would obliterate the French population, as it would become a minority in the new Canada. From the perspective of French Canadians, official government policy within this Union aimed at their cultural obliteration. This view was not a collective, ultramontanist fantasy. It flowed from the recommendations of Lord Durham, whose report to London gave birth to the 1840 Act of Union. Lord Durham believed that "there can hardly be conceived a nationality more destitute of all that can invigorate and elevate a people, than that which is exhibited by the descendants of the French in Lower Canada, owing to their retaining their peculiar language and manners. They are a people with no history, and no literature."[133]

French Canadians were a community under siege and under constant threat of assimilation by the numerically superior English-speaking population of Canada, and by the economically dominant anglophone merchant class of Montreal and elsewhere in the province. The BNA Act, with its grant of specific powers to the provinces in section 92, and its protections of Roman Catholic schools in section 93, made available a constitutionally protected space for political and social survival. The French language and the Roman Catholic religion were absolutely essential elements of national identity, perhaps not as Canadian but as

Canadiens. Obviously there was no place for Jews within a national identity thus conceived.

Nor did these Jews fit comfortably within the Protestant minority community of Montreal with its dedication to non-denominational, but still always Protestant, education. The Scots and English merchant class of Protestant Montreal saw themselves, at many of the most important points in time within the period informed by the Jewish School Question, as besieged by the numerically superior francophone Roman Catholic inhabitants of the province. More significantly they held a fundamentally different conception of Canada and of Canadian-ness, a conception that was reflected in community institutions, especially their schools. For them, Canada was a predominantly Protestant, English-speaking country, and despite its nation state status, it was also an important embodiment of the great traditions of Britishness. Canada was part of the British Empire, and perhaps more significantly, Canadians were first and foremost British subjects. And for many, they were Protestant British subjects. At very important junctures when the Jewish School Question was occupying political space in Montreal, discourses asserting a virulent anti–Roman Catholicism, including claims that French-speaking Roman Catholics could never be truly Canadian, formed part of prominent Protestant understandings of belonging and identity in the dominion.[134] Jews obviously did not fit comfortably, if at all, within these Protestant/Christian conceptions of national and imperial identity.

Jewish pleas for equal recognition and access to all the rights and privileges of citizenship, including the right of their children to go to public school to become "Canadian" in Klymicka's virtuous sense, were invoked at a time and place in which *cosmopolitan* was a dirty word. It was not an evolving signifier for political, social, cultural, and legal taxonomies within which diversity and unity could be discovered in an ever tenuous but necessary symbiotic dialogic existence within a modern nation state.[135] Jews were cosmopolitan because that word was code for the absence of loyalty to the nation state among its Jewish inhabitants.[136] Jews were cosmopolitan because they were disloyal, and they were disloyal because they were cosmopolitan. Classic French reactionary texts in which the tropes of Jewish betrayal and their cosmopolitanism were intimately linked provided the basic codes for attacks on Jewish perfidy.[137] Quebec ultramontane anti-Semitism directly borrowed and adopted the signifiers of nineteenth-century French Jew-hatred.[138] Jews in Montreal faced these competing understandings and social practices of identity and citizenship as they made their claims to equality both generally and in the specific context of education. They were not Roman Catholic, nor Canadien, nor Protestant, or perhaps even truly British. In fact, many of the recent immigrants spoke neither English nor French, but instead lived a life of *Yiddishkeit*.[139] Their struggles for the legal and political recognition of their claims occurred at a time and in a place where the school system had been entrenched within a constitutional context that protected the rights of the members of each of the dominant Protestant and Roman Catholic solitudes, and within complicated matrices of sociological and political communities that reflected and reinforced the bi-national, bicultural notion of what it meant to be Canadian. A compact between two parties had no place for newcomers.[140]

2

Invoking Equality, Invoking Legality: Jews Constituting Their Canadian Identity

The Context of Equality

It was precisely around their understandings of equality, identity, citizenship, and justice that Montreal Jewry presented their arguments throughout the long history of the Jewish School Question. Within the Jewish community of Montreal, or more accurately within the Jewish communities of Montreal, there was never a unanimous agreement either on what the actual concrete content of these broad principles of equality, identity, citizenship, or justice might actually be at a given time and place in their history, nor was there really a community accord about how the meanings of these concepts were to be put into action over questions surrounding the schooling of their children. But it always was true, among all of the internecine disagreements, that these tropes of equality and justice, of constitutional normativity, were the ones on which everyone relied.[1] Most significant for part of the narratives that unfold throughout the entire history of the Jewish School Question is the fact that, at the most important junctures, law was invoked as the instrument through which equality was to be achieved.

This is notable for a number of reasons. First, at the most relevant times for much of the School Question, the majority of Montreal Jewry was made up of recently arrived immigrants from Central and Eastern Europe.[2] They came to the New World, fleeing pogroms, persecution, and a legally constructed and constituted practice of exclusion, discrimination, and inequality. They had left a Europe where religious minorities still struggled for equality or where the gains of recent emancipations were often still purely formal and always politically and socially fragile.[3] The long and complex battle for civic and legal equality was one for which many Eastern European Jews saw little hope of success. For them, emigration was the only way to concretize their desire to be treated as equals, as citizens.[4]

In 1921, the Canadian census recorded 45,802 Jews in Montreal, a number that grew to 57,977 in 1931, although as a proportion of the total population in the city, Jews fell slightly from 6.1 per cent to 5.8 per cent in this ten-year period.[5] In 1931, when the first set of technical, legal battles over the Jewish School Question came to an end, 45.42 per cent of Jews in the province of Quebec had come from Russia, Poland, and Romania.[6] Many of these European Jews came to Canada with specific expectations about their legal status and about their ability to carve out new lives for themselves and for their children as equal citizens. Again, this does not mean that these visions were identical among different parts of the Jewish citizenry of Montreal – Yiddish separation versus English assimilation, Orthodoxy versus Reform Judaism, Marxist versus socialist, the entire spectrum of Zionism and its opponents – these were all elements that existed in the Montreal (and other) Jewish communities at the relevant times.[7] Each had a vision of Jewishness, just as each had a view of Canada, and therefore each had nuanced conceptions of the balance to be struck between these two ideas, on how to be Canadian Jews or Jewish Canadians. No single ideology or idealization of these concepts held a hegemonic position, but proponents of each position did invoke discourses of equality, identity, and justice through law at various points throughout the history of the Jewish School Question.

One place where the Jewish struggle for equality began in Canada was at the level of official and unofficial taxonomies within which they were placed at the time of their arrival and as they sought to integrate into Canadian society. This manifested itself in both official record-keeping and communal and individual self-understandings around the always-vexed question of race/ethnicity versus religion. South of the border the normative ideal and the legal and political practice highlighted the contingent and complex constructions of the very taxonomy "race" in American law.[8] For Jews, this has historically proved to be problematic. While they could and did claim religious freedom, they still had to deal with issues arising out of this central American taxonomy. Were and are Jews a religious group or were and are they a racial or ethnic group?[9] This question would trouble U.S. immigration and other governmental officials and concern the American Jewish community for many years.[10] It continues to perplex and confound English jurisprudence to this day.[11]

Again, comparisons with the situation in Montreal and that in the United States must be made with great care and with an awareness of context and circumstance, both in terms of the legal orders at work and the taxonomical and other specificities of the situation. These two points of comparison, race and religion, and their social and legal construction become important when the focus shifts to the Canadian context and to the more specific issues surrounding the place of the Jews of Montreal within the constitutional context of the School Question. First it is clear that whatever the general position of civic and legal equality may have been for Jews in Montreal, or in Canada more generally, section 93 of the BNA Act set out an explicit constitutional barrier to equality. In Montreal, Protestant and Roman Catholic rights to establish and govern their own school system were entrenched in 1867 and protected by the Constitution thereafter. That protection clearly identified Protestants and Roman Catholics as denominational groups. While this general taxonomy did leave open several complex questions, which the courts would face over the years, it could not have been more clearly religious or more obviously exclusionary. No other religion had a constitutionally enshrined right to schools and school governance.

In the Canadian censuses of 1871, 1881, and 1891, Jews in Quebec, for the most part in Montreal, were in fact classified by religion. Their numbers increased from 549 (.005 per cent of the total population), to 989 (.073 per cent of the province's inhabitants), to 2,703 (.018 per cent of the population), in 1891, at the time of the first public crisis in Jewish education.[12] In 1901, just before of the *Pinsler* case, the Jewish population numbered 7,607, or 0.46 per cent of the total found in the census of Quebec. By 1911, there were 30,648, Jews, now reaching 1.5 per cent of Quebec residents. Jews were then classified by racial origin as well as by religion, resulting in certain slight statistical discrepancies.[13] At the same time, it is important to note that this officially sanctioned taxonomy was itself quite complex and differed somewhat from the classificatory biases of the American government project, while continuing to reflect other contemporary understandings and confusions.

As Louis Rosenberg explained, "The term 'racial origin' as used in the Canadian census does not refer to the sub-division of mankind into the Caucasian, Mongolian and Negro races, but in the words of the Official Census Reports, 'has a combined biological, cultural and geographical significance, and attempts to indicate the racial stock, country of origin and cultural background of the person designated.' The classification is comparatively simple in connection with the Danish, German, English, Jewish, Italian and other similar stocks, but is more difficult in connection with those listed as being of Austrian, Romanian, Swiss, Belgian, Russian and other stocks, where citizenship, place of birth and languages spoken are often confused with ethnic origin."[14]

Finally, of course, it is important to recognize and remember that in the contemporaneous historical context of much of the Jewish School Question, whatever the technical legal distinctions between race and religion may have been, there was a political and sociological synonymy between race/ethnicity and religion in important aspects of the debates over identity in Quebec. Roman Catholic and French Canadian, Protestant and English Canadian, were frequently invoked interchangeably, despite the cultural complexities within the groups, so that race/ethnicity and religion became themselves either interchangeable political concepts or direct identitarian tropes for each other. In the context of Montreal at the time, the idea of discursive confusion or synonymy between national, racial, and religious identity was simply part of the political narrative.

Whatever biases and contemporary constructions were in place in the Canadian and Montreal contexts, including the idea set out by Rosenberg that Jewish identity was a "comparatively simple" issue, there is also little doubt that in addition to necessary and important distinctions culturally and socially with the contemporary United States experience, it was not just the existence of section 93 that differentiated the Canadian legal experience of rights at the relevant times. Quite simply, Canada did not have a constitutional Bill of Rights, nor socially was there even a nascent rights consciousness informed by constitutional text. To some extent, however, and perhaps ironically, given the events narrated in this book, there was a rights consciousness in terms of religious practice. As shall be made clear below, Quebec Jews gained political and legal emancipation in 1832. The Quebec Act guaranteed religious freedom for the province's Roman Catholic majority.[15] Following the union of the two Canadas, the Freedom of Worship Act of 1852 further entrenched religious liberty.[16] The statute provided in its preamble that "the recognition of legal equality is an admitted principle of Colonial Legislation" and that as a consequence "the free exercise and enjoyment of Religious Profession and Worship, without discrimination or preference, so as the same be not made an excuse for acts of licentiousness, or a justification of practices inconsistent with the peace and safety of the Province, is by the constitution and laws of this Province allowed to all Her Majesty's subjects within the same."

The combined effect of these statutes was that something approaching legal equality was part of the juridical structure in relation to religion in the Canadian provinces. Reactionary elements within the Roman Catholic hierarchy would both long for a return to pre-Conquest norms and continue to insist that the church was immunized from state legal normativity.[17] At the same time, however, prominent jurists in Quebec, such as Siméon Pagnuelo, a lawyer who acted for the Roman Catholic Church in almost all its most important cases, and later a judge of the Superior Court and leading lay member of the ultramontane movement, still could, and would, recognize that the guarantees of equality and liberty afforded to Roman Catholics under the British colonial regime constituted a significant improvement over French colonial rule and that such liberties were core values of the province's legal system.[18]

Neither racial equality nor religious freedom (except insofar as education was concerned) was present, however, as a normative principle in the text of the BNA Act. Struggles for equality, justice, and recognition of minority rights all took place in a Canadian context in which legal appeals to such concepts had to be found in the common law or created by statute. A further qualifying difficulty was that the structure of Canadian federalism as found primarily in sections 91 and 92 of the BNA Act meant that different rights for different groups, or under different taxonomies, had to found in each province or at the federal level, according to the circumstances. This served as a technical legal barrier to attempts to concretize rights and more broadly and perhaps deeply as a conceptually hegemonic construction within Canadian constitutionalism. The very structures of Canadian federalism were an ideological and intellectual barrier to rights more broadly construed. As Richard Risk and Robert C. Vipond put it, "In short, ideas about federalism specified which legislatures should determine the limits about rights and, more generally, contributed to beliefs about how rights were protected. But struggles between the Dominion and provinces also obscured or preempted thinking about individual rights."[19]

This did not mean that the search for rights and equality completely foundered in Canada. The legal history of equality and rights from the period of Confederation to the adoption of the Charter of Rights is a fascinating one, in which the mixture of inventive common law evolutionary processes and political lobbying to ensure statutory embodiments of fundamental rights was at the fore.[20] Changing contexts, domestically and internationally, socially, economically, and as a consequence within legal discourse gave rise to increasingly sophisticated and compelling calls for juridically embodied civil and political rights.[21] Social democrats, trade unionists, minority groups, civil libertarians, and Protestant advocates of the social gospel, among others, formed sometimes strained political alliances to concretize legally enshrined rights.[22] Canadian Jews, individually and collectively, often played a key role in these political and juridical attempts to include in law the concrete embodiments of justice and equality, while at the same time causing taxonomical turmoil in terms of race and religion.[23]

Risk and Vipond argue that the Canadian history about rights, like that in the United States, featured lawyers as key actors in the debates over, for example, religious liberty. But they go on to assert that the Canadian experience took a separate path from the American in large part because Canadian legal elites viewed judicial review, the litigious assertion of legal rights, as "unthinkable." "They believed strongly that individual and political liberties were at once mutually reinforcing and mutually limiting. It followed that legislatures, not courts, were the appropriate bodies to determine the limits on rights, and at the same time to protect individual liberty, for they were the bodies though which political liberty was expressed."[24]

There is much to be said in support of Risk and Vipond's analysis of late nineteenth-century legal attitudes towards litigation and rights in Canada and their comparison with the American experience. Federalism did dominate legal discussion to the detriment of rights. Legislatures were called upon to settle disputes, and courts generally were not the place to seek redress. Risk and Vipond conclude their discussion of the complex history of key aspects of Canada's rights debate in the nineteenth century by stating, "Finally, perhaps religion and language seemed to be (and had been made) public issues for politicians and legislatures, not for lawyers and courts."[25]

The evolution of the Jewish School Question in Montreal, and the history of Quebec Jewry's attempt to obtain a status of equality and respect, both reinforce and contradict important parts of the Risk and Vipond thesis. Leaders among the Montreal Jewish community did in fact seek and obtain the assistance of provincial politicians and the legislature in their struggle for school equality and for respect for their rights more generally. This strategy proved to be both a success and a failure, as the discussion in the rest of this book illustrates. At the same time, these leaders, among whom were outstanding members of the Montreal legal community, did both threaten litigation and bring cases before the courts to enshrine the rights of the Jews of Quebec, in relation to schools and to issues of equality and justice more broadly understood. Montreal Jews did look to the courts as the embodiment of British justice that for them epitomized their identity as Montreal and Canadian Jews, as citizens of what was for many an adopted country, just as they looked to the provincial government and legislature for recognition of their legitimate democratic claims as citizens to equality and tolerance. But they did, perhaps unlike their counterparts elsewhere in the country, see litigation as a legitimate and possibly fruitful avenue to be explored in their struggles for recognition and equality, as they invoked core Canadian values of religious liberty against the enshrined protections afforded to Protestants and Roman Catholics in section 93.

Two cases in which Jews sought formal legal redress through the courts inform much of the narrative in this book: *Pinsler v The Protestant Board of School Commissioners*[26] and *Hirsch and Another v Protestant Board of School Commissioners et al.*[27] In *Ortenberg v Plamondon*, the Jews of Quebec City, aided by their brethren in Montreal and led in court by Sam Jacobs and Louis Fitch, lawyers who would feature prominently in the Jewish School Question, sought redress under the general liability (delict) provisions of Article 1053 of the Civil Code as the result of anti-Semitic publications, including blood libel accusations, and acts of verbal abuse and violence against Jewish individuals and property.[28] When later attempts to introduce legislation granting injunctive relief against group libel, what we would today call hate speech, failed in the face of legislative opposition from the combined forces of liberal advocates of press freedom and ultramontane Roman Catholic forces who saw a Jewish conspiracy behind the proposed law, once more the Jews of Montreal sought relief (unsuccessfully) before the courts of the province to halt another manifestation of the blood libel.[29]

Finally, and again, in relation to the School Question, they could do so only in the face of a clear legal text, section 93, which served as a constitutional and constitutive barrier to their search for true equality. When Professor George Weir, a leading authority on education and the separate school question in Canada, did not hesitate to characterize section 93 as "Canada's Educational Bill of Rights,"[30] he was simply projecting and reflecting the dominant understanding of a bi-national and bi-denominational conception of Canada and its Constitution. Section 93 served as a Bill of Rights for Protestants and Roman Catholics in those provinces where it applied, and more broadly, to be generous in reading Weir, as a Bill of Rights for public education elsewhere in the country. It was not, however, a Bill of Rights for the education of Jews in Montreal. Instead section 93 is best understood at this point as the particular embodiment of a version of the compact theory of Canada and its Constitution in both the broad and narrow senses of that term.[31] It enshrined an ideal of two founding nations but reduced them not to language, history, and culture, but to the principle of sectarianism. In the structure of Canadian federalism in Ontario and Quebec, Protestant and Roman Catholic majorities and minorities enjoyed rights to schooling. Montreal Jews litigated their part in the Canadian mosaic, just as they lobbied politicians for recognition of the justice of their claims. But they did so, always, in a constitutional context in which they had no constitutive place in the public education system. They made these pleas as otherwise fully emancipated and equal citizens, who had complete legal access to all rights of that status, except in relation to education.

Therefore, the Jewish School Question in Montreal was and is a story about rights and about the struggle for full equality. It is also a very Canadian story about rights and equality, because it takes place inside and outside the courtroom, inside and outside the corridors of political and legislative power, inside the public and the private domains of inter-communal relations. At the same time as it is situated in a broader political, social, and legal historical narrative of the struggle for civil liberties and political, civil, and human rights in Canada, the specific legal, constitutional barrier erected by the protections and guarantees for Protestant and Roman Catholic education in Montreal also places the Jewish School Question in its own specific legal, social, and political context. Not for the first or last time, this is a story about equality and rights inside and outside not just law, but other fights for equality.

Equality, Law, Politics and the Jews of Quebec: Constituting Equality

Much of the discussion in this book sets out the circumstances in which the Jews of Montreal sought to carve out new meanings within and outside a formal constitutional arrangement that excluded them from full legal participation in the school context. Likewise the dominant two nations ideology of Canadian and Canadien identities also set up discursive and narrative barriers at the social, cultural, and political constitutive levels, to full Jewish identity as Canadians in Montreal. The Jewish School Question was one where counter-narratives were available to the Jewish parents who wished to send their children to public school, but also was one where those counter-narratives always had to be invoked to combat the insistence by the constitutionally enshrined Roman Catholic and Protestant communities that their rights under section 93 be recognized and protected. These legal constitutional narratives were buttressed socially and politically by and within the broader concomitant social discourses of a bi-national, bicultural Canada, and by the simultaneous monological construction of a Quebec nation, emanating from the ultramontane elements in Quebec Roman Catholicism.[32] Jewish immigrants to Canada came to that country (if they had an image at all) with an image of a nation where equality was the norm. When the influx of Jewish immigrants to Montreal was at its apex, from the 1880s to the 1920s, this idealized vision of Canada had been concretized in a set of legal norms and practices that had slowly evolved from "a complex and at times almost unintelligible patchwork of rights,"[33] to a system of legalized formal equality and religious freedom. It is impossible to trace here the entire history of the evolution of the legal rights of Jews in Canada, but some points in time do need to be isolated and briefly explored to contextualize the Jewish School Question in Montreal more fully.

It is first important to situate even more strongly the unique status of section 93 and the issue of education in Canada and Montreal by highlighting the more broadly established practices of religious and social equality within the constitutional framework that existed at all times in which Jews were claiming educational rights of access for their children to Montreal's public or common schools. The second reason for highlighting some points of Jewish legal history in Quebec is that this history of Jewish equality in Quebec is underscored by a combination of formalized, legal constitutional practices as we understand them, and also by a set of governmental and political practices and normative behaviour that occurred at the margins of, if not outside, the technical legal boundaries of equality and citizenship. These same historical political practices, at the edge of legality and constitutional validity, but constitutive in the broader sense of the citizenship life world of

Montreal and Quebec Jewry, would also come to characterize events within, and concerning, the communities as they struggled for educational rights for their children. At certain times, practical, politically acceptable arrangements were brought into being by the parties, Protestant, Roman Catholic, and Jewish, that did not fully coincide with the demands of strict legality, but met the still often conflicting constitutive ideals and practical political and economic realities and desires of the parties themselves.

Many Jews in the British North American and Caribbean colonies had obtained some form of equality as citizens, or British subjects more precisely, under the terms of the Plantation Act (1740).[34] The statute allowed foreign-born "Protestants and others" in the colonies to become British citizens and therefore to own land and exercise other political and economic rights.[35] While the precise nature and extent of this newly acquired equality status remained in doubt, nonetheless many Jews established themselves in the North American colonies.[36] They distinguished themselves in the eyes of the authorities in London and officials in the colonies by the assistance they gave to British forces in the Seven Years War, which culminated in the British defeat of the French in North America and the conquest of Quebec. Following the conquest, the English were a demographically minority population in Quebec, surrounded by a French-speaking, Roman Catholic majority. The new local administration sought to grant key government positions to their supporters in the colony in order to ensure a solid and loyal administrative structure. Among the first appointments to such a position, as postmaster of Trois-Rivières in August 1763, was Aaron Hart, the founder of one of the most important and influential Jewish families in Quebec history.[37] One of only a few English-speakers in the community, Hart was rewarded for his loyalty to the British Crown during the war and after the victory of the British forces.[38] Three years later, in December 1766, Lazar Levy became the first Jewish notary in British North America. According to the Godfreys' account, the British authorities in London, in confirming his appointment to the commercially important and sensitive notorial position, had simply erased the words "in Christ" from his formal appointment papers.[39]

In November 1768, another Jew, John Franks, was sworn in as overseer of the chiminies for the city of Quebec. This post was particularly significant because it followed a series of destructive fires throughout the province, prompting the government of the colony to take measures to prevent further occurrences and to protect the delicate economy and its commercial infrastructure.[40] What is most important about the Franks appointment is that it again took place in circumstances that appear to have been at the margins of legality. Franks took office after swearing an oath "upon the true faith of a Jew."[41] The question of the oath of office, and the capacity of Jews to swear such an oath, would continue to serve as a technical legal bar to full emancipation of Jews in both the mother country[42] and in Quebec.[43]

While the Plantation Act had made specific provision for a Jewish oath validly made by omitting the words "upon the true faith of a Christian" (section 3), in 1766 the British Parliament had adopted the Justices Oath Act, which required that all British colonies follow the oath in force in the mother country, an oath that had to be taken "upon the true Faith of a Christian."[44] Franks's oath therefore did not comply with what must have been considered be the legally obligatory British form. Ignoring the British law, the local government in Quebec simply adopted an oath that permitted Jews in that colony to accept public office. Thus, in 1777 an immigrant German Jew, Jacob Kuhn, who had previously served in the British army and therefore could be considered loyal to the interests of the Crown in Quebec, was appointed bailiff of Montreal and later became the head of the municipal police force.[45] "The legal eligibility of Jews for office had evidently been taken for granted."[46] But more than mere assumption seems to have been at work, since the governing officials of Quebec had taken it upon themselves to fashion an oath of office that could be taken by Jews appointed to serve the British Crown. There was clearly a deliberate local practice in relation to the qualification of Jews for public office, which in its formal detail and probably in law contradicted the limits on public office in force in Britain itself. Local circumstances and political exigency had led to practices in Quebec that suited the needs of government in the province but were in all likelihood strictly illegal.

Certainly appointments such as those of Franks, Hart, and Kuhn resulted from the necessity to ensure that public offices be filled by those who would be loyal to Britain, thereby excluding the vast majority of (French, Roman Catholic) inhabitants of Quebec at the time. This is not to suggest, however, that French-Canadian Roman Catholics were excluded from important positions. For a significant time after the British victory, until the French Revolution and English fears of an American invasion, the French and English elites found plenty of room for accommodation.[47] The day-to-day administration of justice, and particularly criminal justice, was of central importance to the peace, order, and good government of the colony.[48] Prominent members of the francophone community were appointed to act as justices of the peace and played key roles in the governance of the colony, especially in the earliest days of English rule.[49] Indeed, the situation in Quebec was singular. While the legal prohibitions that flowed from the necessity of the oath of office precluded Roman Catholics from such posts in Ireland, for example, no such barriers existed in Quebec.[50] The Quebec Act contained specific provisions guaranteeing religious, political, and civil rights and privileges for Quebec's Roman Catholic majority.[51] Most significantly, section VII of the Act exempted the majority of Quebec's inhabitants from the British form and set out the terms of a specific Roman Catholic oath. The disabilities that operated in the United Kingdom itself, and in most other British colonies with large Roman Catholic populations, including the oath question, were removed by statute. But the Quebec Act made no mention of Jewish subjects who aspired to public office. A narrow, legalistic position in these circumstances might have resulted in the exclusion of Jews from government office. If Parliament had seen fit to make specific provision for exempting Roman Catholics in Quebec from the standard oath and had created a particular Roman Catholic form, it would arguably be clear that the exclusion of Jews from these special rules meant that the normal legal situation obtained and they were not eligible to hold public positions. Colonial officials in Quebec were clearly aware that the disability issue was of some moment, yet they appear to have made a specific decision to ignore strict legality when appointing Jews.

Necessity in the difficult circumstances of setting up durable and efficacious structures of government in a newly conquered territory may well have been the mother of legal invention. What is clear is that in such circumstances British officials in the colony did not hesitate to ignore strict legality and instead were more than happy to create a constitutive, if not perhaps constitutional, arrangement, in which Jews could actively participate as equal citizens of the new colony. More than being taken for granted, the eligibility of Jews for these offices seems to have been actively considered and implemented by local government officials. This was state action at the margins of legality, as the political and social narratives of the new government and its needs were given priority. However, the perils of operating such a system at the margins of formal legality would soon become apparent in the colony of Quebec as another member of the Hart family of Trois-Rivières sought public office.

Legality and the H(e)art of the Political Constitution of Quebec

The question of the legality of the oath taken by Jews in Quebec in this period would come into sharp focus in 1808. The previous year, one of the two representatives of Trois-Rivières in the colonial Assembly, John Lees, had died and an election was called for his replacement. At the public meeting where votes were openly cast, Ezekiel Hart won a plurality of votes in a three-man race and proceeded to the Assembly in Quebec City at its next session in early 1808.[52] Hart received support from all parts of the politically divided Trois-Rivières landowning community, anglophone and francophone alike. But his chief opponent, Thomas Coffin, also had strong support, including that of the powerful local political figure and Provincial Court judge, Louis-Charles Foucher, who was the first public figure to raise an objection to Hart on the grounds that as a Jew he could not sit in the Assembly because he could not take the oath in the required form.[53] Hart nonetheless travelled to Quebec City, where he swore his oath as a newly elected member in the standard form used in Quebec courthouses for Jews, with his head covered, and his hand on the Pentateuch. French-Canadian members objected to Hart's presence and brought forward a motion highlighting the legal basis for their wish to see him excluded. They asked for clarification on the form of the oath taken by Hart and immediately raised a constitutional objection, arguing that statute required that the oath be taken "on the true faith of a Christian." Inquiries were held as to whether Hart was in fact a Jew, and when French-Canadian members who knew Hart from their legal practice confirmed that he was publicly known to be a Jew, they demanded his immediate expulsion from the Assembly.[54] The governor and the attorney general objected, as did the anglophone members of the Assembly, but to no avail. On Saturday, 20 February 1808, the Assembly approved the resolution that "Ezekiel Hart, Esquire, professing the Jewish Religion, cannot take a seat, nor sit, nor vote in this House."[55]

Hart was expelled from the Assembly because he was a Jew. The majority of elected members took the position that because the imperial Parliament had set out an oath that was obligatory in the colony of Quebec, Hart was legally barred from serving. He could not, as Jew, take an oath, which required an affirmation of Christian faith, and because he could not take the oath, he could not lawfully sit. The governor, angered by the actions of the French Roman Catholic majority, dissolved the Assembly and called new elections. Hart returned to his home in Trois-Rivières and ran again in the election meant to find his replacement. The electors returned him, this time by a majority, as the member of the Assembly for Trois-Rivières. When he attempted to take his seat in the spring of 1809, the majority of members formally identified him "as the same Ezekiel Hart" who had been declared ineligible the previous year and again voted to expel him.[56]

Some of the most important factors that had already influenced the status of Jews in Quebec and would continue to inform debates in the following decades were at play in the Hart incidents. The local legal solution to the oath of office issue under which Quebec had simply ignored the imperial Parliament and gone its own way, often out of political necessity, was found wanting in the face of a majority of elected representatives who insisted on a restrictive reading of the legal texts concerning oaths of office. But this was not a simple question of legality versus illegality. The social and political circumstances of the time played equally, if not more, significant and signifying roles in the expulsion of Ezekiel Hart from the Quebec Assembly. He was elected at a time when the relations between the elected representatives and the governor were testy and tenuous. Indeed, for many French-Canadian political activists, the problem could be found in the disconnection between the promises and guarantees in favour of liberty and freedoms found in the Quebec Act and other colonial instruments and the increasingly autocratic rule of the British governor.[57] A nascent parliamentary democracy was emerging in Quebec, a parliamentary system that would be key in the political emancipation of Quebec Jews decades later. In the case of Hart's election as member for Trois-Rivières, the French-speaking, Roman Catholic parliamentary majority sought to flex its muscle by ejecting Hart, who had the support of the executive branch of government.[58] At this place and at this time, Ezekiel Hart found himself in the middle of an acute political battle between the executive and legislative branches of government, at the early stages of the struggle for responsible government.

Additionally and perhaps even more significantly, Hart, because he was a Jew, was obviously not a Roman Catholic. He was also an anglophone, or at least was seen by the francophone majority as one, despite his clear support among all parts of the local community in Trois-Rivières. His natural political allies would be among the minority English-speaking Protestant members of the Assembly who were politically more supportive of the executive powers of the governor.

By refusing a seat to Hart, the French Roman Catholic members were denying a vote to their anglophone Protestant opponents, and therefore to the governor and his policies. As a Jew, Hart found himself caught up in an early manifestation of the political and social conflicts between the Roman Catholic, francophone majority and the powerful, but minority, anglophone British Protestant population. In this case, the raw politics of the matter were perhaps formally submerged in the parliamentary discourse surrounding the affair and in the invocation of technical legality on the oath question. But whatever the political and social factors at play, strict legality was invoked by the parliamentary majority to deny Jews in Quebec their full rights as British subjects to participate in the emerging democratic institutions of the colony.[59] It was clear from the Hart affair that Jews did not enjoy the same rights as either Protestant or Roman Catholic subjects of Quebec.

But just as French-Canadian Roman Catholics dominated the Assembly at the time of Hart's election, other forces from within the majority population, liberal democrats in today's parlance, began to emerge. Influenced by Enlightenment ideals and the writings of the French *philosophes*, a more radical democratic vision was beginning, in part at least, to play a role among the elite in French Canada. Thus in 1828, a group of Montreal Jews petitioned the Assembly for legislation granting them the right to hold and maintain official records of civil status – that is registers of births, marriages, and deaths – as their Roman Catholic and some Protestant denominations could, a request that was finally passed into law.[60] In 1831, Samuel Becancourt Hart, a descendant of Aaron Hart, presented a petition to the Assembly calling for the removal of all disabilities affecting Jews in Quebec. Hart had been approached by the government of the day to become a magistrate or justice of the peace, only to see the offer revoked because British officials in Quebec had subsequently come to adopt the view that as a Jew he could not take the oath of office.[61] Hart qualified the public circumstances of this revocation of the offer by government officials as "mortifying" and added, "This is an age of liberality and universal tolerance, and in a country where a foreign Jew naturalized by a residence of seven years is admissible to every office, and in which the Petitioner is informed the disabling laws of England were never introduced. Therefore the Petitioner humbly implores the House to take his case into their serious deliberation and relieve him as well as his brethren from any disabilities they at present are subject to, by the illegal acts of the Colonial Executive."[62]

In his petition, Hart invoked arguments of equality and justice, as well as making assertions that the position of the Executive on the oath of office question, like that of the Assembly twenty-three years earlier, was in fact illegal since the restrictions imposed by the 1766 British statute on oaths of office had never been adopted in the colony. The argument by Hart and his supporters was again also a technical legal one. The specific provision of the earlier Plantation Act permitting a special form of oath to be legally taken by Jews had always been the law of the land. Because it had not been formally and specifically abrogated in the subsequent statute, it remained in force in Quebec. Hart's position was one that combined appeals to moral principle and technical legality and invoked broad Enlightenment values of rationality and equality. It also sought to invoke and highlight the illegal acts of the Executive to inspire countermeasures from the legislature. It mirrored, in an intriguing fashion, the reasons invoked by the elected representatives who had decades earlier ejected another Hart from the Assembly as a manifestation of legislative authority and supremacy over the executive branch. Hart's argument also appealed to the broader feelings among the liberal wing of Roman Catholic Canadiens, under the leadership of Louis-Joseph Papineau. For them the philosophical issue could not only serve general values of equality but also gave support to the anti-Executive feelings still abroad in the Assembly at the time. The Assembly appointed a committee to study Hart's petition in February 1831.[63] On 5 June 1832, royal assent was given to An Act to declare persons professing the Jewish Religion entitled to all the rights and privileges of the other subjects of His majesty in this Province,[64] which confirmed that Jews in Quebec were "capable of taking, having or enjoying any office or place of trust whatsoever."[65]

This brief statute, one paragraph, made Quebec, along with Jamaica in the same year, the first jurisdiction in the British Empire to offer full legal equality to its Jewish citizens, years before Westminster afforded the same rights to British Jews.[66] But this was not, as Tassé would claim several years later to his French-Canadian audience, a text that accorded political rights to Jews in a complete form.[67] In the few years following the 1832 Act, Quebec Jews once again faced a legal controversy on the question of the oath of office. The Act stated that Jews could hold any "office or place of trust whatsoever," but it did nothing to change the wording of the oath apparently required for these offices that continued to follow the British model by including the Christian faith provision. A legal argument could be made, of course, that such a subsequent general emancipation statute could be read to override the specific provisions of earlier legislation on the oath. But this was not an argument that was clearly or obviously persuasive to all those who held political power in Quebec, nor was their exact legal position in relation to the vexing oath issue clear to some prominent Jews themselves.

In 1838, two members of the Jewish community in Montreal, Moses J. Hayes and Benjamin Hart, were offered appointments as justices of the peace. Both Hayes and Hart had serious doubts as to whether they could accept the offer of these positions because of the continuing uncertainty over the oath question. They did not believe that there was legal support for an oath that would omit the phrase "upon the true faith of a Christian." Nor did they believe the substitution that had been made much earlier when Franks accepted the inspectorate of chimneys in Quebec "upon the true faith of a Jew," was legally valid.[68] They consulted a prominent Montreal lawyer, Aaron Philip Hart, who considered the matter and came to the conclusion that a Jew could not lawfully take the oath of office because the imperial statute, which imposed the wording concerning Christian faith, was still in force in Quebec.[69]

Hayes and Hart wrote a letter to the governor declining their nominations and highlighting the fact that their rejection of the appointment was the result of the legal barrier, which the oath issue raised for them.[70] The governor wrote to the colonial secretary in London seeking redress in the matter through an Act of Parliament dealing once and for all with the oath question in the colony. The position eventually adopted in London and communicated to the colonial officials was that the matter was one not for them but for the local authorities in Canada to deal with.[71]

The issue was then referred to the legislature for the next stages of the affair. A special committee was appointed and heard evidence on the oath question.[72] After carefully analysing the issues, the committee found that the 1832 Act had removed all barriers that might have been in place to obstruct Jews from holding public office in Quebec. It declared that the oath question was no longer a legal obstacle to public office for Quebec Jews. Moreover, the committee offered a clear declaration that the significance of the oath question had been exaggerated. The true sanction of the oath, it found, was to be discerned and discovered "in the religious faith of the man who takes it. If in using a prescribed form, he declares that the oath is taken under the sanction of a faith which is not his own, there ceases to be any oath whatsoever, and from too minute and verbal adherence to the Statute, its substance and end is wholly frustrated and annihilated."[73]

In the end, the special committee rejected the technical and formalistic reading of the legal situation offered by Hayes and Hart and their legal advisor and decided upon a path that was in keeping with the emancipatory spirit of the 1832 Act. No further legislative intervention was required, because there was no overriding legal obligation to include a reference to the Christian faith in any oath sworn by a Jew upon taking public office. The solution that was, from London's perspective, a matter for the colony alone, was in fact found in earlier Quebec practice that had allowed the substitution of Jewish for Christian in the oath without any requirement of confirming legislation.[74] This, the committee pointed out, had already been done in at least one instance elsewhere in the province by simply substituting the word *Jew* for *Christian* in taking the oath, and no challenge to his position had been forthcoming. Hayes and Benjamin Hart became justices of the peace soon thereafter.[75] Moses Judah Hayes later became chief commissioner of police in Montreal.[76]

Quebec Jews had achieved legal equality in the 1832 Act, and they then concretized that equality by participating in the social, political, and legal life of the province. Jews were free to practise their religion and to hold public office, as were the demographically dominant Roman Catholics and economically superior Protestant population. They had achieved this emancipation by actively participating in the political and legislative processes of the colony and by appealing to the dominant understanding of equality of the time. They had constructed a constitutive narrative for Jewish emancipation that had emerged from a state of political necessity and marginal legality following the conquest, to one that had full legislative sanction. They had suffered and benefited from historically contingent circumstances that pitted the Executive against the legislature, and French-Canadian Roman Catholics against anglophone Protestants. In the interstices of the majority and legally enshrined minority, they had found a place to narrate their equality and freedom.

But they did not figure in section 93 of the BNA Act. As the Jewish population grew, the one area of formal legal inequality, the right to education, would come to occupy an increasingly important place in communal life and in the often difficult and always delicate relations between Montreal's Jews and the two founding nations of Canada.

3

Schools, Taxes, Jews, Catholics (and Protestants): The Origins of the Jewish School Question

Constituting Jewish Education in Montreal

The dual national ideal, which informed both Protestant and Roman Catholic thinking, particularly on the question of education, posed many problems for the Jewish population of Quebec. The constitutive and constitutional process that led to formal equality for Jews always involved the two dominant interlocutors as active participants. The presence of a significant third force in the province, and particularly the increasing numerical fact of the Jewish population in Montreal, forced French and English, Roman Catholic and Protestant communities, to deal with the bi-national foundational myth in often complex, and sometimes obscurantist, ways. In the late nineteenth and early twentieth centuries, waves of Jewish (and other) immigrants to the port city of Montreal upset the traditional discourses and narratives of identity as articulated by the two founding nations.[1]

This three-way, often even more pluri-vocal, discussion about the nature of identity, British, Jewish, Canadien, and later Canadian, meant, to some extent at least, that the construction of ideas and understandings of citizenship could take place in terms that did not seek to submerge all groups into a melting pot of a single collective national identity, but instead allowed groups to seek to place themselves as subjects and citizens, while maintaining their more explicitly ethnic or religious selves.[2] This complex political and constitutional context in which Montreal

Jews found themselves also meant that many aspects of the social and political infrastructure that one might find beginning to emerge elsewhere in Canada as parts of the seemingly natural role of the state were, in practice, placed in the hands of the two dominant groups in civil society. Schools obviously were divided along denominational lines, and the role of the state, in theory at least, was explicitly and pragmatically circumscribed by section 93 and by the dominant ideology and political influence of the Roman Catholic Church. Other institutions such as social welfare, health care, and, of special importance to the Jewish community, aid to immigrants were also in the hands of denominationally ordered groups.[3] While these highly developed church-based social infrastructures would have the long-term effect of retarding the development and emergence of the welfare state in the province of Quebec, it did mean that community groups were involved in the construction of the social and welfare institutions that gave meaning to their own constitutive narratives.[4] Ironically, perhaps, the dominance of the bi-national foundational myth created political, social, and semiotic interstices into which the Jewish communities in Montreal could insert themselves. "This challenge enabled – even required – Jews to establish autonomous organizational structures, parallel to those of the French and English but lying outside the constitutional framework. Jews founded synagogues, newspapers, charitable and social-action institutions of all sorts, and eventually schools."[5]

Both the synagogues and the social welfare organizations founded by the Jews for communal aid would come to play central roles in the evolution of not just the Jewish population of Montreal, but in the Jewish School Question in particular. While the establishment of communal organizations and the creation of collective identities were common phenomena in the Jewish diaspora, in Montreal they took on a particular and specific significance because of the existing parallel confessional structures of welfare and education.[6] This communal privatization of education and welfare would be the structural arrangement into which the expanding Jewish community had to fit. As the population of Jews in Montreal grew from the handful of merchants and professional men and their families who had come to Quebec with the conquering British army, the educational needs of the younger members of the community became ever more pressing. As already noted, the Canadian census reports that the Jewish population, most of whom lived in Montreal, grew from 549 in 1871, out of 1,191,516 residents recorded as living in the province; to 989 in 1881 (when the number of provincial inhabitants was 1,358,653); to 2,703 out of 1,488,535 in 1891, and finally to 7,607 in 1901, out of 1,648,898 persons in the Province of Quebec.[7] In the earliest part of this post-Confederation period, the burden of educating young Jews fell largely on their families and the synagogues.

Again, this is not the place to trace the entire history of the Jewish communities of Montreal or indeed of the primary religious places of worship in the city.[8] For purposes of the discussion of the Jewish School Question, it is sufficient to identify the first synagogue of Montreal, Shearith Israel, which would be known as the Spanish and Portuguese synagogue, and Shaar Hashomayim, which would come to be known at the time of the events that arose in relation to schooling as the English, German, and Polish synagogue (or variously the German synagogue or the German and Polish synagogue).[9] Shaar Hashomayim was formally founded by statute following a petition by several members of Shearith Israel in the mid-1840s.[10] However, the congregation did not begin to function until some time between 1858 and 1860, when an entirely different group from Shearith Israel simply took advantage of the existing legislation to found a new and active synagogue.[11] Once again, Jews were constructing community and constituting themselves in the shadow of legislation and perhaps at the margins of strict technical legality, but whatever the situation may have been, the English, German, and Polish synagogue became one of three main players in the first iteration of the Jewish School Question.

This chapter traces the beginnings of the Jewish School Question in Montreal during the second half of the nineteenth century. In the earliest days, the two main synagogues provided basic educational facilities, both religious and secular, to the children of members. The same period marked the beginning of the more formalized institutional arrangements of Roman Catholic and Protestant educational infrastructures in the city of Montreal. The growth in Jewish populations, the emergence of a Protestant public, common educational system, and the financial difficulties experienced by the synagogues in providing a full curriculum to their children combined to mark the first stages of formal relations between "Jewish" education and "English" education. This era was also characterized by the clearly articulated desires of Jewish community members to ensure that their children were equipped with the educational and social skills necessary to participate fully and equally in the economic and political life of Montreal. Education gradually became the key to this process of integration, more particularly education within the anglophone culture at the core of the Protestant

School Board. At the same time, Jewish leaders remained attached to ideas and ideals of community membership and to ensuring that Jewish children still received an appropriate Jewish education. The tensions between the pull and attraction of secular English education and the desire to maintain a distinct Jewish identity played themselves out in complex ways, from the provision of learning in synagogue schools, to the special place of Hebrew instruction for Jewish students. Economic difficulties and a rising school population also led the Protestant and Roman Catholic educational officials in Montreal to seek new and more effective mechanisms for financing schooling in the city. This led to a statutory regime under which Jews were free to choose to pay taxes into either the Roman Catholic or the Protestant system.

The discussion that follows sets out the evolution of the Jewish School Question in these early years in which the tensions, conflicts, and possible synergies between English and Hebrew/Israelite education manifested themselves in parallel with the emergence of a more firmly entrenched Protestant and Roman Catholic school system and growing diversity among Montreal's Jews. This chapter, then, explores the first historical manifestations of the Jewish School Question, as complex issues of communal identity, belonging, class, finance, and the ability of Jews to find constitutive moments between the dominant Roman Catholic and Protestant school systems emerged. A recurrent theme throughout this book first comes to the fore here – the Jewish School Question in Montreal was never either a single question, nor was it ever simply a question for Jews alone. The constitutional reality of section 93 and the constitutive reality of the political and social contexts of identity formation in nineteenth-century Montreal would always mean that Roman Catholics, Protestants, and Jews would seek some kind of accommodation in which rights and inter-communal relations would be asserted, negotiated, and concretized both inside and outside formal legality.

Synagogues, Schools, and the Jews of Montreal

This era was characterized by the first influx of Jewish immigrants from Eastern Europe into the port city of Montreal. These Jews brought with them different cultural and religious practices, and therefore different understandings about what it meant to be Jewish. They also brought their own Yiddish language. This not only carried with it important consequences for the cultural and political developments in the history of Montreal Jewry, but it also meant that the education of their children, who when they arrived spoke neither English nor French, imposed specific burdens and needs. This multicultural diversity within Montreal Jewry led to the creation of communal welfare organizations that soon challenged the dominance of the principal synagogues as representatives of the Jewish communities. The emergence of the Young Men's Hebrew Benevolent Society, soon to become the Baron de Hirsch Institute, would play a key role in providing basic instruction to the children of newly arrived Jews. In addition, the institute brought together a group of Jewish professionals and businessmen who saw education in the city's Protestant schools as the key to the "Canadianization" of the immigrants, and therefore to the progress of the impoverished newcomers. This political voice, which sought to articulate a new vision of Jewish equality and educational rights, would play a vital role in the evolution of the Jewish School Question.

At the same time, the legal and economic structures of education in Montreal were significantly altered. A new school tax system, based on real estate valuations, emerged. A series of complex financial battles, set out in what follows, ensued, more specifically around the cost to the Protestant system of educating the children of poor, non–real estate-owning Jews. This financial issue about the real cost of educating Jewish children in the Protestant school system would be a recurring theme throughout the history of the Jewish School Question and its different iterations from the late nineteenth to the late twentieth centuries. In this particular timeframe, ironically perhaps, a key development occurred in the school tax question, not in the Protestant school structures, but between opposing elements in the Jewish community itself. The narrative that unfolds below will show how the wealthy Jews of one Jewish congregation attempted to carve out for themselves an educational system based in their synagogue and grounded in a special financial arrangement with the Roman Catholic School Commission.

Although records from this period are incomplete, it would appear that the first functioning school for Jewish students began in 1854 at the Spanish and Portuguese synagogue.[12] On 23 April of that year, the trustees of the synagogue approved in principle the idea of establishing a "Jewish school." They planned to visit each family of synagogue members to determine if there were enough children to justify the immediate opening of the school.[13] A circular was drafted outlining the reasons behind the decision to create a school for the community.[14] The school was to be entitled the Montreal Hebrew and English Educational Institute. The very denomination of the proposed school embodied the vision of education held by the trustees of what was at the time the Jewish establishment in Montreal. The Spanish and Portuguese was still the only synagogue and was therefore the unquestioned spiritual home of Montreal Jewry. In the words of the circular, the trustees did "not deem it requisite to advance anything here as to the necessity of education and the importance of combining a religious with a secular training."[15] The school, as its title indicated, would be both Jewish and English, and the children educated, according to the wishes of their parents, "as God-fearing Israelites as well as intelligent members of society, and that their Hebrew and religious studies, as is but too often the case, should not be deemed of secondary importance."[16]

It is clear from the expressed intentions of the trustees that the school was always meant to have a distinctly Jewish, or in the preferred signifiers of the time, Hebrew or Israelite, character. The influence of the rabbi, Abraham De Sola, cannot be understated in this early context. Appointed as rabbi of the Spanish and Portuguese synagogue in 1847, Abraham De Sola was a man of great scholarly repute. He was professor of Hebrew and Oriental literature at McGill University and became the first Jew to receive an LLD from that institution so important to Protestant Montreal.[17]

The educational circular made it clear to all future students and their families that the rabbi would serve as superintendent of the school, be actively involved in teaching, take charge of boarding arrangements, etc. The curriculum, which would be under the jurisdiction of a soon to be constituted educational committee of the synagogue trustees, would include "the Jewish Religion, Hebrew, English, French, German, Spanish, Portuguese, Latin and Greek languages, Mathematics, Book-Keeping, Geography, History, Sacred and Profane."[18] Therefore it would serve the fundamental purposes of religious instruction as well as providing the bases for students leaving school as "intelligent citizens." Spanish and Portuguese were included, no doubt because the synagogue followed the Sephardic or Portuguese minhag, despite the fact that, De Sola perhaps excepted, the members of the congregation were almost exclusively of Ashkenazi origin. The curriculum as a consequence reinforced the community identity of the members of the congregation as Jews, as well as the institutional identity of the synagogue itself as Spanish and Portuguese.

But the school also had profane goals. Not only would students obtain the knowledge of disciplines necessary for the formation of well-rounded and intelligent citizens, but also the study of French, in addition to its cultural value more broadly, would ensure, as would bookkeeping, the ongoing economic survival of the Jewish community in Montreal. From the 1840s to the 1870s, that community would be made up predominantly of merchants in a number of fields, retailing jewellery and fancy goods, tobacco and dry goods, and clothing manufacturing. Most were small businesses, but they managed to survive and some to prosper in a cultural and economic environment in which they were outsiders, but where there was little if any evidence of blatant and crude anti-Semitism.[19] The synagogue school began operation and, while records are scarce, by 1874, the nascent Protestant School Board had agreed to find a competent teacher once the number of pupils reached forty, providing that the board had inspection rights over the "English branches" of the curriculum.[20]

Records of the educational endeavours of the English, German, and Polish synagogue after its founding in 1858 are even more difficult to find. Nonetheless David Rome reports that a school existed in 1870, and the Protestant board minutes record both a request for support received from the English and German school and a visit by Protestant educational representatives to that school.[21] In 1874, when the Spanish and Portuguese synagogue school entered the orbit of the Protestant School Commission of Montreal, albeit partially, representatives of the two synagogues met to investigate the possibility of expanding and changing the nature of Jewish education in Montreal by founding a "Jewish free school," which had been under consideration at the Portuguese synagogue since 1871.[22] The proposed school would be open, unlike the Spanish and Portuguese school, to Jewish children of both sexes. The joint committee established by the two congregations to investigate the terms for the establishment of the proposed free school also included recommendations for equal membership on the Board of Trustees between the two synagogues and that school be indeed free, with no fees being charged or accepted. Most controversially, and fatally, the joint committee recommended that "the Hebrew Language be taught according to the German pronunciation only."[23]

The Spanish and Portuguese members of the committee were deeply troubled by this insistence from their co-religionists that only one tradition or minhag be followed. Montreal businessman David Ansell, from the Spanish and Portuguese congregation, had been appointed as chair of the joint committee but found himself in the embarrassing position of being unable to vote for the overall recommendations, which he favoured, because of the minhag question that excluded the Spanish and Portuguese Sephardic traditions and Hebrew pronunciations. Ansell was an English-born merchant, active in synagogue and community affairs, who would come to play a key role in the early years of Jewish education in Montreal.[24] On 13 October 1874 he wrote to the president of the Portuguese congregation, "I knew that our views were liberal and that we did not want to force upon them the adoption of our Minhag, and I felt that it was both bigoted and disrespectful on their part to urge the adoption of this last clause."[25]

The motion establishing the German minhag was carried by weight of numbers over the objections of the Portuguese synagogue's representatives. It was accompanied by clear declarations from those present from the English, German, and Polish congregation that they would never accede to the use of the Portuguese minhag. Ansell concluded that "amalgamation is hopeless, there would be endless petty bickering and trouble arising, and I have to resign the wish I so fondly held, that we should be able to complete the Establishment of a School for United Jews at our next General Meeting."[26] Ansell then proposed the establishment of a school for the Portuguese synagogue and any members of the German English congregation who might wish to attend.[27] A free school to be governed by a school committee of five "Gentlemen who are members of this Congregation" and the officiating minister of the synagogue as an ex officio member was created.[28]

Ironically perhaps, Ansell left the Portuguese congregation soon after this clear split on the educational issue and he next figures in the Jewish School Question as a member of the English, German, and Polish synagogue. The *Semi-Annual Report of the Treasurer of German and Polish Synagogue for the Term ending April 2nd 1882* indicates that the synagogue had spent $234.50 on its school.[29] David Ansell, as chairman of the Board of School Commissioners, reported that the board had proceeded to

> inform every family in the city announcing the intended opening of the School on the 21st Oct. last. The School opened with 25 children on the day above mentioned, since which time the number has increased to 33 day and about 25 afternoon scholars.
>
> The system of education adopted is such as to fit the pupils for the sphere of life in which they are likely to move. It comprises Hebrew and English reading and writing, history, Geography, Arithmetic and sound moral and religious training. In some instances a disposition to cultivate the more advanced branches of education has been shown by the pupils.[30]

While the two synagogues understood the importance of both religious and secular education for their children, they had been unable to find common ground upon which to establish a single Jewish free school for all Jewish children in Montreal. Instead, at this foundational stage in the development and self-understanding of Montreal's Jews and the ideals of education, identity, both religious and secular, and schooling remained fixed in the doctrinal separations of the competing minhag. Each school sought to establish a curriculum that was at one and the same time Jewish and profane. Each congregation saw school as a place where traditional Jewish identity could be maintained and reinforced, while preparing their children as Jews to enter the broader social and economic world in Montreal. Not for the last time, however, the Jewish inhabitants could not come together to agree on a single common position in relation to the schooling of their children. The constitutive narratives of Jewish Canadian identity in Montreal at this moment were complex and multiple, and would become only more so.[31]

Around them, the broader social, economic, and political world into which they wished their children to enter was changing. The Jewish population was rising rapidly and the numbers of children in need of schooling was also growing. The institutional capacity of the two synagogues to meet these needs was already being tested. Moreover, the increase of population also meant a demographically more complex Jewish community, or Jewish communities, was beginning to emerge in Montreal.[32] Schools directly tied to the two oldest synagogues would not necessarily appeal to newly arrived immigrants, many of whom more readily identified with their fellow immigrants, with whom they shared language, culture, recent history, and often geographic origins, rather than with the English-speaking mercantile elite of the two synagogues.

Finally, the most important and significant social and political changes taking place concerned the institutionalization of the Protestant and Roman Catholic school systems in Montreal. If synagogue-based education was becoming more and more difficult to maintain and manage, some form of modus vivendi would soon need to be found between and among various parts of the Jewish communities of Montreal and the dominant educational structures of the bi-national powers. Already, from the earliest days of the two synagogue schools, the Protestant School Board was not only contributing financially to the English curriculum, but it was also insisting as a quid pro quo that it exercise a supervisory, quality-control jurisdiction over those parts of profane, secular education being offered in the two Jewish schools.

Schools, Synagogues, and Taxes: Jewish Schools, Protestant Schools, 1880–1884

As Elazar, Brown, and Robinson have pointed out, this process of negotiating roles and identities for themselves had been opened up for Montreal's Jews by the reality of Canada's political and constitutional structures. "Throughout its history, then, Canadian society (and its fundamental laws) have promoted self-conscious Jewish identity and autonomous organization by providing 'space' for Jews to act. At first, that space was negative: interstices between the two founding peoples who made up the Canadian polity constitutionally."[33]

In the context of the Jewish School Question, the most significant autonomous organization would be the Young Man's Hebrew Benevolent Society (YMHBS), Canada's first non-synagogal Jewish society. Founded by a group of concerned young Jews in 1863, the YMHBS had as its object "to assist and grant temporary relief to needy and indigent persons of the Hebrew Religion."[34]

One of the main actors throughout the history of the YMHBS and its role in the evolution of the early history of the Jewish School Question was David Ansell. When preliminary and exploratory meetings were taking place about the desirability of forming such a society, Ansell was delegated to approach the Spanish and Portuguese synagogue for its support. While in agreement in principle, Shearith Israel made it clear through its representatives that they would prefer to establish a similar welfare organization under the auspices of the synagogue. In his later account of the formation of the YMHBS, Ansell attributed the increasing complexity of communal organizational structures to the rivalry between the Spanish and Portuguese and the English, German, and Polish synagogues, a rivalry that in his view extended to "each congregation trying to secure any new immigrant that arrived in Canada for their synagogue."[35] The constituent members of the YMHBS had a distinctly broader concern for the social and economic well-being of their newly arrived co-religionists and decided to form an organization outside the structures of the two principal congregations.[36]

Life was not easy for newly arrived Jewish immigrants, or for the welfare organization. In his account of the early years of the YMHBS, Ansell wrote, "For many years we pegged along as best as we could."[37] The mass influx of Jewish immigrants from Eastern Europe in the early 1880s and the continuing flow following Russian pogroms later in the decade soon taxed the meagre resources of the group. They turned to the European philanthropist Baron de Hirsch, who provided the society with an original gift of $20,000.[38] In honour of the generosity of its benefactor, the group would change its name to the Baron de Hirsch Institute, under which moniker it would come to figure prominently in the history of Jewish education in Montreal.[39] As part of its mission to assist newly arrived Jews, in 1890 the institute established a school, with day and evening classes.[40] Part of the curriculum was meant to permit adults to acquire both practical skills and language abilities to allow them to prosper in their new country. More importantly, another part of the schooling efforts of the Baron de Hirsch Institute was to provide basic education for the children of immigrants. In addition to teaching them English, the school also covered the traditional pedagogical subjects of an ordinary common school curriculum.

As the early difficulties of the Jewish School Question were about to manifest themselves, there were three main actors representing various parts and interests in the Jewish community: (1) the Spanish and Portuguese synagogue, Canada's oldest, and an institution with a long, if somewhat sporadic, history of educating Jewish children, (2) the English, German, and Polish synagogue, with a shorter history of Jewish education but a congregation dedicated to the project of schooling, and (3), most recently, the YMHBS/Baron de Hirsch Society, which existed outside the formal constitutional synagogal structures that had served until then as places for the creation of Montreal Jewish identities but had a Jewish identity of its own. It also had a particular vision and philosophy of education that would come to embody the ideal of schooling as a way to "Canadianize" Jewish immigrants. At the Baron de Hirsch School, "education, above all, was their 'passport' into the new life they sought for themselves and their children."[41]

Three schools, each representing a somewhat different vision of Jewish identity and the place of primary education were in place or would be soon. As always, the three Jewish educational institutions stepped into a formal constitutional bi-confessional environment of schools determined under section 93 and the complex administrative and again bi-confessional structures of Quebec education, of Protestant and Roman Catholic School Commissions in the city and committees at the provincial level within the Council of Public Instruction. As is often the case, the key motivating or instigating factor in the complex set of legal and political narratives that would erupt periodically under the guise of constitutional and constitutive discourse, as the Jewish School Question, was money, or more specifically, school taxes.[42]

The 1869 Education Act had brought about significant changes to the financial system of education in Montreal. For some time, the Roman Catholic School Commission had had insufficient support for its schools from the church itself, which instead focused its educational efforts and resources on the private *collèges classiques*.[43] Frustrated by this lack of backing, the Roman Catholic school commissioners had approached the provincial government to urge the introduction of a system of school taxation in the city. At the same time, the politically powerful Protestant minority, wishing to protect its position, agreed in principle to a taxation system, but convinced the government to adopt one based on real property and the declared religion of the owner. While many Roman Catholic politicians were prepared to reject the government proposal because of the perceived unfairness of the system in which Protestants held disproportionate property wealth, they withdrew their objections when it became clear that the tax solution was part of a larger legislative scheme, the ultimate purpose of which was to further entrench the separation of the denominational educational structures. At this point, many Roman Catholic voices argued that Protestants were justified in their claims that they did not wish to support Roman Catholic education, just as Roman Catholics were justified in making the same arguments and in ensuring a more completely divided system of school governance and taxation. The church apparently remained largely silent on the tax question at this time because episcopal officials saw an opportunity to gain further control of education by creating a new dynamic on the Council of Public Instruction that would ensure independence for their schools from any oversight by Protestants and government officials.[44]

A new system of school taxes on real estate was created, and the system itself was in fact based on the identification of property owners as Roman Catholic, Protestant, or neutral. Roman Catholic and Protestant taxes would go solely to the relevant board, while the division of neutral taxes would be more problematic. Jews as "persons not belonging to the roman catholic or protestant faith" were included in the neutral panel.[45] The actual tax rate varied according to the panel, in part because there were far more Roman Catholic inhabitants of Montreal. Therefore a higher per capita rate would be required in relation to the lower number of Protestants. Corporate rates would always be different from personal rates of taxation. However, the repartition of neutral funds, which would continue to vex Protestant and Roman Catholic educational relations for many years, contained one clear apparent injustice. Jews who were classified as neutrals identified educationally with the Protestant system, and most students who attended common schools did so under the jurisdiction of the Protestant board. If their tax monies were to go on a pro rata basis to each of the two systems, the Roman Catholic schools would receive tax support while not really educating Jewish students, and Protestant school officials would not receive an amount of neutral tax revenue that would accurately reflect the presence of Jewish students, even at this early stage in Montreal's educational history. A compromise that suited Protestant and Jewish officials but did not please Roman Catholic representatives was reached, nonetheless. In 1870, the school tax issue was again amended by statute.[46] This single statutory measure would have a profound effect on the evolution of the Jewish School Question. It would give rise to a series of events in which the payment of school taxes under a single provision of a provincial statute would have as important, significant, and long-lasting consequences on the constitutive narratives of Montreal Jewry as section 93.

Under section 9 of the 1870 Act, "any person belonging to the Jewish persuasion, and owning real estate in either of the cities of Quebec or Montreal, shall be entitled, upon his delivering to the city treasurer a request in writing to that effect, to have his property inscribed, at his option, upon either of the panels, number one or number two."

For the first time, Jews were recognized and identified in specific terms as participants in the common school system of the province of Quebec, or at least of the two major cities. Not all Jews were recognized, since the entire system of school taxation was grounded in the ownership of real estate. The significance of this idea would become clearer and more nuanced as the story of the Jewish School Question unfolded. At this stage it is simply sufficient to highlight this official constitution of Jews as part of the common school equation in provincial statutory language. Most obviously, the clear and intriguing limit on this constitutive manoeuvre was bound in a still more important constitutional normativity, which insisted on a Protestant and Roman Catholic duality. Jews were perhaps constructed in education law as no longer always neutral or as "non–Roman Catholic, non-Protestant" as the terminology would evolve, but they were recognized only in order to then constitutively disappear. The overarching and constitutionally entrenched duality of the school system was moved to another level, but it could never lose its defining role. Jews were free to choose, but they were not free to choose to be Jews, an unknown and unknowable category in the world of section 93. They were free to choose, within the limited and limiting context of the legal structures regulating school taxes in Montreal, to be members of Panel 1 or Panel 2, to be Roman Catholics or Protestants, for school tax purposes. But once again, in the new statutory regime there was still room to move in interesting and important ways, for the purposes of social and collective self-identity for some members of the Jewish community of Montreal. In the interstices of sub-constitutional law and legal discourses in the field of primary education, Jews, or real estate-owning Jews, had some formal identity and freedom of action, and those forms of identity would manifest themselves in important ways within these constitutionally limited margins of manoeuvre.

For the most part, Montreal Jews chose to be Protestants, for a number of reasons that would become clearer as the educational narrative in the city unfolded. But the choice to become Protestant for the purposes of school taxes in the earliest period following the 1870 statute itself led to some obvious problems. The law permitted the payment of the tax monies to the Protestant panel and then the distribution of those monies to the Protestant board. There was no specific mention of the education of Jewish students or of the existing Jewish schools. In early 1871, Reverend De Sola approached the Protestant board to seek funding for the synagogue school from Jewish tax monies. The board at this point adopted a technically correct and narrow approach, which it would repeat on many more occasions. It decided that taxes paid by Jewish owners of real estate "should be distributed simply in accordance with the provisions of the school law, and without any special arrangements between the several congregations and this Board."[47] At this stage, the Protestant school authorities had no real desire to engage with disputes or issues between different sections of the Jewish community and found a simple solution in the "provisions of the school law." As time passed, the board would, as we have seen, relax the purse strings and pay an annual subsidy to the synagogue school, although the latter was never completely satisfied with the amount it received or the terms and conditions imposed by the Protestant education officials.[48]

The Protestant board soon decided that this temporary solution, relying on rigid legality flowing from the silence of the provisions of the school law on the right of Jewish taxpayers to have access to their tax monies for the education of their children, was simply unfair. The statutory scheme placed some of the Jewish taxpayers of Montreal in a difficult and unjust position. The board resolved "to offer as a regular subvention to the schools of the Jewish persuasion recognized by the Board the same rate per pupil at which the pupils in the City Schools are now chargeable."[49]

However, the grant was not without condition. The monies were to be expended "for the purposes of general education under the supervision of the Board." The Protestant educational officials clearly at this stage still insisted that they would have no truck with subsidizing religious education outside their own constitutionally enshrined schools. Further monies might be made available upon request and according to need. More significantly, however, the offer was made subject to the Jews "inscribing their property on the panel number two, Protestant School tax."[50]

The solution upon which the Protestant board decided was at once principled and pragmatic – characteristics that would often inform Protestant-Jewish educational dialogue in the years to come. The board saw the obvious unfairness in the legal framework that allowed Jews to choose to pay their taxes to one or the other of the Protestant or Roman Catholic school panels but was silent on what happened to those monies. Any unfairness was of course exacerbated by the fact that only two denominational school boards had a constitutional existence. At the same time, however, the Protestant board was unwilling to subsidize any form of Jewish religious instruction, since this would mean not just permitting the introduction of a specifically Jewish presence in the Protestant system, but a subsidy from what were legally always Protestant tax revenues to a non-Protestant religion. When push came to shove, Protestant officials' generosity and compromise came up against the immoveable force of section 93 and the constitutional entrenchment of Protestant education. The board also insisted on supervisory powers over the general education offered in synagogue schools. Finally, and most importantly for subsequent events, it demanded that the monies distributed for Jewish education, or more precisely the education of Jews, should come primarily from the Jewish community itself; hence its position that the offer to pay the synagogue schools at the same rate per student as the city school system was conditional on Jewish participation in the Protestant tax panel. This idea was obviously one that appeared at first blush to be a simple and fair quid pro quo. At the same time, the idea was grounded in practical circumstances that were changing rapidly. While it might have been possible to ensure compliance with enrolling Jewish taxpayers in Panel 2 when the limited number of holders of real estate who were Jews could be identified through the two main synagogues, the Jewish community was expanding, and loyalty to the original congregations would be replaced by more complex communal arrangements. The assumptions of a relatively homogeneous Jewish community in Montreal would soon be belied by demographic reality. The payment of Jewish taxes would eventually become far more complex for Protestant and Jewish educational officials alike.

Nonetheless, the relationships between the Protestant board and the Jewish communities continued to flourish. For many, the connection appeared to be a natural outgrowth of political, financial, and even theological attitudes of the parties. The financial arguments are well known and would continue to be a point of both common concern and friction between the parties. The two groups also saw themselves as sharing a common opposition to the dominant Roman Catholic hierarchy and the strengthening ultramontanism that targeted both Protestantism and Judaism, theologically and politically. Moreover, with important exceptions and caveats, they shared a cultural affinity and love of learning. Each saw education not just as an end in itself, producing a degree of literacy, central to the Jewish and Protestant ideals of textual study, but perhaps more significantly, both groups voiced the idea that education played a key role in the creation of loyal and patriotic citizens and subjects. Most (but not all) of the support for common public schools in the early days of the British colony of Quebec had come from Protestant groups, influenced largely by New England educational practices. When the project failed and schools were divided along denominational lines, the ideals and beliefs in the direct link between education and citizenship remained within Protestant minds and practices. While many of these more liberal attitudes would also have to confront the insistence by powerful voices that Protestant schools would have to remain Protestant, and that the presence of significant numbers of Jews would challenge this core and defining characteristic of the educational system, broad ideas about citizenship (and equality), the importance of education, and the general spirit of ecumenism, which by necessity informed multi-denominational Protestant schooling in Montreal, would frequently combine in the minds of Protestant Montrealers to allow for a Jewish presence in their schools.[51] In these early days, as the Protestant board grew in importance, the presence of Protestant Jewish or Jewish Protestant synagogue schools appears to have posed only practical questions of governance, regulation, and finance.

In June 1877, the Protestant Commission, in discussions with the English, German, and Polish synagogue, took a vital step in Montreal's education history and agreed to welcome Jewish children into Protestant schools "in common with Protestant children" and to provide facilities in one of its buildings for afterhours Hebrew instruction.[52] In a letter to the representatives of the German and Polish Jews, the board "acknowledges as unquestionable the right of children of Jewish parentage to all the privileges of its public schools, while as heretofore, the school tax of persons of the Jewish persuasion continues to be paid on the Protestant panel."[53]

The board recognized the right of Jewish students to be exempted from religious instruction in Protestant schools, but at the same time declined any responsibility, "even by mere implication," for Hebrew instruction that it believed to have a "specifically religious character." There was, of course, a long tradition in Britain and in colonial America of Protestant Hebraists studying the language, and of Hebrew instruction in universities and theological faculties.[54] But Protestant school officials eschewed any idea that learning the Hebrew language in elementary school had any value beyond the strictly confessional limits of Jewish life. Once again, the Protestant board's position was a combination of pragmatism and principle, recognizing the specific Jewish character of students and allowing them to be exempted from Protestant religious instruction, while at the same time resisting the entry of Hebrew into the mainstream Protestant curriculum. And once again, the position of the board appeared to function in the shadow of the law.

They recognized that Jewish students had rights and privileges in Protestant public schools, rights that must flow generically from general notions and principles about the purposes of public schooling, since there appears to have been be no specific binding legal text giving these rights and privileges to Jews specifically. The 1832 statute granted Jews access to all rights and privileges, but that statute and those rights would have to be understood, interpreted, and applied in the shadow of the constitutional norm of section 93, which insisted on enshrining the educational rights of only Protestants and Roman Catholics. Likewise the 1849 statute relating to schooling had established a right to an education for all pupils aged between five and sixteen, provided their father paid the monthly fee or they were declared indigent.[55] But that statute also confirmed the rights of the religious majority and the dissentient minority to schools (section 18). These provisions were largely repeated in the 1861 Act, but again with a clear emphasis on the divisions between commissioners and trustees, religious majorities and dissentients.[56]

There was no clearly articulated social, let alone legal, position on the common school within a denominational dualistic structure. Jews apparently had some rights in relation to schooling, but no one was very sure about what that meant. Some Jews paid school taxes into the Protestant panel, and the Protestant board agreed to distribute these Jewish monies to the synagogue schools. But the only officially constituted schools in Montreal remained those that were Protestant or Roman Catholic. Jewish schools had no lawful status within the constitutional structures of Canada and Quebec, nor did they have any status in provincial statute, which created common and dissentient schools for Roman Catholics and Protestants throughout Quebec, and Protestant and Roman Catholic schools in Montreal. Protestants believed generally in the value of education, and Jewish parents were keen to see their children receive both religious and secular instruction. The rights of Jewish children to a Protestant education or to an education in Protestant schools appears to have been assumed, and the exact nature and extent of those rights then subjected to negotiation, compromise, and agreement, largely outside any formal juridical frame governing those rights, partly at least because there does not appear to have been a formal legal framework in which one could find a basis for those rights. But in 1877 in Montreal, whatever those rights might have been, they were contingent on the financial, fiscal arrangements under the panel system of school tax payments. Jews had these educational rights in Protestant schools as long as they continued to pay taxes as fiscal Protestants.

The school of the Spanish and Portuguese congregation continued to function and to receive a proportion of tax monies from the Protestant board. A Jewish synagogue school was receiving a direct subsidy for the teaching of general subjects under the supervision of the Protestant board, while other Jewish children had the right to attend Protestant public schools. A hybrid system within the bi-denominational constitutional educational structures had emerged in which Jews attended both private Jewish synagogue schools and public common Protestant schools. The system functioned as a result of political negotiations between the two main synagogues and the Protestant board. Those negotiations took place within a legal framework in which Protestant education was constitutionally protected and enshrined more practically by statutory measures relating to administration and governance. But at least partly as a result of the legal arrangements on school taxes, and the interstitial recognition of some kind of ersatz status for Jewish taxpayers, Jewish schools taught Jewish students under the broad overview of the Protestant School Board, while other Jews had gained rights and privileges, however contingent, within the Protestant school system itself.

In late 1877 and early 1878, some members of the Jewish community, as well as the Protestant board, sought to explore the possibility of creating a system of truly common education, but these efforts were unsuccessful. The two synagogue schools continued to function with the financial support of the Protestant board.[57] Despite the ongoing belief among members of the Protestant board, and some in the Jewish community, that the "the course most conducive to [Jewish children's] thorough education" would be to attend the schools of the Protestant board, the compromise system of synagogue schools, supported and to some extent supervised by the Protestant authorities, remained in place.[58] Monies from Jewish taxpayers would be allocated first to the education of Jewish students in the two schools, and Hebrew instruction, which remained problematically religious in the minds of most of the Protestant board, would now be subsidized by the board from the same tax monies, in Protestant schools.

While the system continued under the terms set out by the Protestant board in January 1878, with support and supervision of the secular aspects of the synagogue schools and a desire to place more Jewish students within the normal Protestant school system, practical difficulties soon emerged. It was increasingly complicated to obtain accurate accountings of exactly how much had been paid in taxes by members of each congregation, since they paid taxes as individuals to the city and were not identified as belonging to one synagogue or the other on the tax roll. There were further issues on the cost per pupil and the number of students actually enrolled in the German and Polish school. Finally, it was difficult to obtain information about the numbers of students studying Hebrew.[59]

Each of these problems was, to some extent at least, attributable to the tenuous nature of the overall arrangement struck between the Protestant board and the Hebrews. It was clear that the concordat was situated in the shadow of the law but was not governed by strict legality. It was arguable that the Protestant board was not bound to admit Jewish students (since the system of bi-confessionality did not make any formal legal space for Jews), or anyone who was non-Protestant or non–Roman Catholic for that matter. Yet the Protestant board strove with some consistency to do the right thing in its deployment of Jewish taxes. Indeed, they continued to adopt the broader position that the best, if not only, long-term solution to the Jewish School Question had to be found in the incorporation of Jewish students into the general Protestant educational structure. Protestant school officials appeared to have stood on strict legality only insofar as by doing so they somehow created an incentive for the synagogues and their schools to fit within the broad structures of the Protestant system.

But whatever its complications and difficulties, the system of compromise and contract with the Jewish community was grounded not just in this complex legal structure and status. It also still depended on the representative character of the two synagogues. The conception of Montreal Jewry that obtained in the city and among Protestant and Roman Catholic authorities was still intimately linked to religious organization, perhaps unsurprisingly, given the denominational essence of common schools in Montreal. Moreover, the difficulties experienced in gaining adequate information on the number of students, or the numbers taking Hebrew instruction, were often related to the ever-changing character and sometime fragility of the synagogue schools, particularly that of the German and Polish synagogue, as administrative structures evolved and synagogue membership became more fluid. An institutional arrangement, whatever its legality, could only ever be as solid as the institutions involved.

The Protestant board allocated $1,031 to what they described as "the Portuguese Jews" for 1878. Because the German and Polish synagogue had not replied to regular requests for information on student numbers, the Protestant board voted to strike off their school from the list of approved and subsidized schools.[60] The threat had its desired impact. The information was passed on from the synagogue and the next day, the board voted to provide $300 to the "Polish Jews." They also agreed that they would take financial responsibility for the salary of an approved English teacher for the German and Polish school. If the children of the synagogue were sent to city schools instead, the board voted to make the same amount available towards the expense of Hebrew classes.[61]

Again the solution reached in 1878 was extraordinary. Schools run by Jewish synagogues received money from Jewish taxes paid to the Protestant board. The Protestant board also took on the payment of a qualified secular teacher in the German and Polish synagogue school and offered a subsidy for the teaching of Hebrew to Jewish students in Protestant schools. A modus vivendi had been achieved in which schools that could be classified only as Jewish and were supported by Jewish taxes, existed within and under the broad aegis of the Protestant

School Board of Montreal, while at the same time increasing numbers of Jewish students attended common Protestant schools, where they were also able to maintain their distinct religious and ethnic identity through the provision of after-hours Hebrew instruction. Once again, a kind of institutional narrative space had opened up in which the Jews of Montreal essentially created the contexts and stories of their own collective existence, all in the shadow of section 93.

On 13 February 1879, not only did the Protestant board make available monies for the salary of an English teacher for the Spanish and Portuguese school, as it had for the English and German synagogue, it reached an even more remarkable decision at this meeting. "The Rev Dr Stevenson reported the result of the interview with Rev Dr De Sola, whereupon it was resolved that a power of veto shall be given to each Jewish Congregation in regard to the appointment of any child from its own number to a Commissioners' Scholarship, but no power of appointing a substitute."[62]

Education in Montreal was funded not just from panel taxes on real estate, but from fees charged to students and their families. Fees and thus the burden of immigrant families increased as students advanced from primary to secondary schools, making higher education unaffordable for poor families. In reality, support through scholarships was the only way for impoverished families, Protestant and Jewish alike, to give their children access to better educational opportunities. The board now adopted a position that permitted direct involvement by the two synagogues in the selection of scholarship holders. Although there was no power of nomination or substitution, the veto afforded to the two Jewish congregations involved them directly in awarding scholarships to Jewish students to pursue secondary education within the Protestant school system. By implication, there was no idea that Jews could not compete for and be awarded scholarships from the Protestant board for further study in the Protestant school system (a situation that would be radically reversed at the time of *Pinsler*).[63] The rights afforded to the Jews of Montreal in this single aspect of school governance were carefully circumscribed, but they were rights in some form. They were limited in essence to a veto over the proposed award of a scholarship to a Jewish student. They were rights afforded to each synagogue, the two of which continued to occupy a hegemonic position in Jewish interactions with the Protestant board. At the same time, the right was couched in terms that recognized the independence of each synagogue, which had sole power over students from its congregation. Within this construction of synagogue Jewry by the Protestant board, there was a pragmatic recognition of the distinct and different identities of the Spanish and Portuguese congregation and the congregation of English, German, and Polish Jews. These veto rights on the awarding of scholarships, however limited, did once more create an opening into which Jewish narratives about education in the public school system had a constitutive place. At the same time, the idea that Jews should possess any such rights in relation to the administration or governance within the Protestant school system in Montreal was extremely problematic in legal, constitutional terms under section 93 and would be a sore point in the subsequent manifestations of the Jewish School Question.

Payments from the board to the synagogue schools continued until 1880. The next year, however, the Protestant board began to experience financial difficulties, as a consequence of broader economic conditions in Montreal and the ever-expanding numbers of students. Debates and discussions with the Roman Catholic board and the City of Montreal continued over the division of neutral panel, corporate taxes. The growing number of students placed increasing strains on the boards' infrastructures, and the general economic climate was not good.[64]

At the same time, the budget for Jewish education in the Protestant schools was being stretched more and more. In 1881, for example, the Protestant board received $2,132 from the Jewish taxes paid into the Protestant panel. Of that amount, more than half went already to its own budget towards the cost of educating Jewish students in the common schools.[65] $1,100 was payable to the two Jewish schools based in the synagogues. In 1881, the Protestant board announced that it could and would no longer subsidize synagogue schools. Although they would continue informally for a few months, the arrangements with the Jewish congregations came to a formal end, after final discussions with representatives of the Jewish bodies, on 27 June 1881.[66]

The change in circumstances and the end of the brief existence of a type of Jewish school within the Protestant school system of Montreal, or at its margins, came at a time of upheaval at the Spanish and Portuguese synagogue. Abraham De Sola, the long-serving rabbi of Shearith Israel, passed away in early June. His eldest son, Meldola replaced him as *hazan*, becoming the first Canadian-born rabbi in the country.[67] Earlier, as his father's health began to fail, Meldola had begun to play an active role in the life of the synagogue. He served as a lay reader beginning in 1876 and carried most of the relationship with the Protestant board at the time of his father's death.[68]

The Protestants sought what was, in their eyes, a more definitive and suitable solution to the question of Jewish students in the Protestant system. This desire for a real and lasting resolution was in large part due to the ongoing financial hardship suffered by the Protestant board as a result of economic downturns that adversely affected its tax base in commercial Montreal. They wanted to consolidate and rationalize not just their revenue and expenses, but also the entire school infrastructure.[69] For some time, the assimilation of Jewish students into the mainstream Protestant schools had been their preferred solution and they continued their efforts in this direction.

First and foremost, the Protestant education officials revisited earlier proposals for accommodating Jewish students in the common schools. They proposed that Jewish students be admitted to the board's schools on the same terms as Protestant children, except that they would be exempt from religious instruction.[70] The board undertook to appoint a teacher of Hebrew, to be chosen by the congregations, and to set aside a room in one school, chosen as convenient by the congregations for teaching the language, at a time least likely to cause disruption to ordinary instruction. Again, the proposal was made contingent on the continued payment of Jewish taxes into the Protestant panel. A copy of the proposal was sent to David Ansell and to Meldola De Sola as representatives of the two synagogues on educational matters. Ansell replied, rejecting the proposals, while the Spanish and Portuguese congregation offered a conditional acceptance.[71] They agreed in principle to integrate all Jewish students into the common school system of Montreal but wanted some changes to the Protestant proposals. The older synagogue wanted their teacher of Hebrew, Mr Jacoby, selected for the post at a salary of $300 per annum, with an extra $100 payable if he taught Hebrew for two hours every Sunday, and supervision of the teaching of Hebrew to be in the hands of the two congregations. They also insisted that Hebrew be taught for two hours per day. They further demanded that Jewish students and the Hebrew teacher be excused from school attendance on Jewish holidays.[72] While education would no longer take place in the synagogue, essential elements of Jewish instruction and religious observance became part of the key demands of the oldest synagogue.

Negotiations continued throughout the autumn, as the English and German synagogue, seeing the writing on the wall, joined the discussions. The two Jewish bodies sought to maintain a Jewish space within the educational system in Montreal, battling to maintain their own schools and seeking exemptions from Protestant religious instruction for Jewish students attending common schools, as well as Hebrew instruction, and claiming the right for Jewish students to be absent from school on holy days. These issues of accommodation would continue to haunt and inform the Jewish School Question in subsequent iterations, but the most significant struggle at this moment was over the Protestant board's insistence that the synagogue schools must close. A payment of $300 to the German and Polish Jews was authorized by the Protestant board, but only on condition that it be made "in quittance of all claims upon the school tax."[73] The Spanish and Portuguese synagogue closed its school and its students began attending the British Canadian School operated by the Protestant board.[74] A number of Jewish students also attended the Ann Street School. In reply to De Sola's complaint that these students received no Hebrew instruction, the board replied that it had agreed, per its original letter on the matter, and on terms accepted by the Spanish and Portuguese congregation, to pay for Hebrew teaching in only one school, and that was being done in the British Canadian School.[75]

The space for Jewish constructed common education was rapidly contracting, if not disappearing. While the German and Polish synagogue kept its school, its continuing existence had always been perilous, and the Protestant board insisted that the school could make no further claim on school taxes paid by Jews. The Protestant board became increasingly frustrated with what it saw as the English, German, and Polish congregation's failure to supply the information on the number of enrolled pupils, etc., and more and more convinced that the time to end all support of the school had come.[76]

The teaching of Hebrew, so long a key element in the education of Jewish children in the synagogue schools, was now limited to a single Protestant school. Still, Hebrew was taught, and the rabbi exercised supervisory jurisdiction over that particularly Jewish aspect of life in Protestant schools in Montreal. In fact, the Protestant board respected exemptions for Jewish holidays. The space for some kind of emancipated Jewish existence within the dominant school cultures was restricted, but it still existed. A distinctly Jewish presence in the common schools was embodied in the Hebrew-language classes, paid for by the Protestant school authorities, albeit from Jewish taxes paid into the Protestant panel. But even that small area for a distinctly Jewish identity in Montreal public schools would be subjected to significant change.

Shearith Israel's leader complained that his members paid 84 per cent of the total Jewish school tax, but they did not receive a pro-rated contribution from the Protestant board. The location of the British Canadian School was not suitable for the children of the congregation who lived in the western part of the city and had too far to travel. This meant that a significant proportion of Jewish students there came not from the Spanish and Portuguese synagogue, but from the German congregation, who lived closer in the city's east end. This large number of German Jews, because they followed a different minhag, seriously disrupted the Hebrew education of those Spanish and Portuguese congregation children who managed to attend the lessons. Given the significant payment from the congregation's members to the Protestant panel, De Sola pointed out, should they withdraw, the board would be in deficit if it continued to subsidize the German school at the present rate. The Spanish and Portuguese synagogue sought a fair solution to its claims, which asserted a re-establishment of some form of special status for that synagogue and its children within the Protestant school system.[77]

The Protestant board again adopted a recommendation that repeated their earlier position of principle that they would "refuse to subsidize separate Jewish schools."[78] Once again, provided the Jewish school taxes were paid to the Protestant panel, the board now agreed to grant $600 for the salary of any teacher of Hebrew agreed upon by the two synagogues. This withdrawal of the subsidy placed the English, German, and Polish school on its last legs. The board offered to split the $600 for a Hebrew teacher between the two congregations if they could not agree on single teacher, continuing to make available the British Canadian School as had been its practice, and offering facilities in another school under the board's jurisdiction for Hebrew instruction.[79] As in the 1874 debacle over the founding of a Jewish Free School, differences in the minhag and disagreement over the correct pronunciation of the Hebrew language stood in the way of Jewish unity on the educational question. The Protestant board had offered $600 for a single Hebrew teacher, or $300 each for two, if the Jewish congregations continued to be divided on the minhag question. It also offered further accommodation for the teaching of Hebrew in its schools. This time the disagreement between the Jewish officials occurred not just in circumstances involving free discussions between the two synagogues, but within a context in which the Protestant School Board and the issue of tax panel payments of Jewish real estate assessments came to play increasingly significant roles. Any issue of community unity was no longer about establishing a Jewish free school in Montreal as a real locus for Jewish identity in the education system. Instead it was now limited to a more narrow question of the small room for manoeuvre left for Jewish schools in the world of Montreal Protestant education. The once-grand dream of a Jewish free school had given way to a period of relative autonomy for the two schools from the synagogues within the Protestant system, to the point where the Spanish and Portuguese school had closed, the English, German, and Polish school was on the verge of collapse, and debates returned to the minhag as put into practice in a room in a school run by the Protestant School Board. In addition, the cleavages within the Jewish community also took on socio-economic and spatial aspects. The longer-established members of the Spanish and Portuguese synagogue lived in the wealthier western parts of Montreal, while the vast majority of the city's Jews, including its growing immigrant population, lived in the east. Because taxes continued to be assessed on real estate, the members of the older synagogue paid the vast majority of Jewish school taxes, while the majority Jewish population lived in rented accommodation and paid no school tax.

The Spanish and Portuguese congregation accepted the latest terms of Protestant equanimity and declared their intention to nominate Meldola De Sola as Hebrew teacher. On 18 April, the English, German, and Polish synagogue also agreed and informed the board that it sought to appoint F. Cohen as teacher of Hebrew, thus splitting the original $600, in compliance with the terms of the Protestant offer. At the same time, two other matters complicated the situation. The more recently established Reform congregation of Temple Emmanuel intervened, requesting that it be able to have a "voice in the election of Hebrew teachers."[80] The Protestant board was now put on notice that the two oldest synagogues could no longer make a legitimate claim to represent the entire world of Montreal Jewry. The age of comfortable arrangements and agreements was soon to end, as the Jewish communities of Montreal sought a voice outside the hegemonic two-synagogue system, which had heretofore prevailed. The second and immediately more important complication came to the fore. The Spanish and Portuguese congregation now sought the payment in full of the $600 for De Sola, to which it believed the board had agreed.[81] Protestant officials insisted that $600 was all they could afford. It repeated its original offer that the amount had been clearly intended to be the entire sum made available for Hebrew instruction in the Protestant schools of Montreal and that this had been made clear in its earlier correspondence with the synagogue officials. The first figurative shots in the battle over the Jewish School Question were fired in rapid succession by the Spanish and Portuguese congregation and the Protestant board.

On 30 June 1886, a letter was submitted to the board from the Spanish and Portuguese synagogue formally announcing its withdrawal, or more precisely the withdrawal of members of its congregation as individual taxpayers, from the Protestant tax panel. The Protestant board responded by cancelling all existing agreements with the Jewish synagogues. The English, German, and Polish synagogue was informed that no subsidy for the teaching of Hebrew for the forthcoming year would be received from the Board of Protestant School Commissioners. Moreover, the board declared that it could make no firm or formal commitments "to any course of action respecting the education of Jewish children," while remaining open to any representations on the matter.[82] The period in which Jewish schools and Jewish students had a place under the umbrella of the Protestant board, for all the difficulties and negotiations that had characterized it, with the progressive narrowing of any particularly Jewish space in the education system, had come to an end, in part at least because the limited resources of the Protestant School Board could not be made available to satisfy the demands of the competing minhag on the pronunciation and teaching of Hebrew.

The withdrawal of the wealthy Jewish taxpayers, who were members of the Spanish and Portuguese synagogue, also put an end to any pretence that Jewish children had some right to education independent of fiscal arrangements. The contingent and fragile nature of Jewish rights in the Jewish School Question could not have been clearer.

Catholics and Jews, Jews and Jews, and Protestants: School Tax and the Jewish School Question, 1886–1890

The School Board and trustees of the Spanish and Portuguese congregation took their fate into their own hands by relying on their legal rights under the 1870 statute. They approached the Roman Catholic School Board, and after negotiations with that board, agreed to switch their school tax allocation from the Protestant to the Roman Catholic panel. In return, the Roman Catholic board would return 80 per cent of the amount received directly to the Spanish and Portuguese congregation.[83] The Spanish and Portuguese school was again up and running, with administrative and financial support this time from the Roman

Catholic School Commission, albeit in the form of monies derived from Jewish taxpayers. As for the rest of the Jewish school children in Montreal, they were "by way of doubtful consolation" left to the charity of the Protestant School Board that had seen a radical reduction in its receipts of Jewish tax monies.[84]

At this point, the Spanish and Portuguese congregation was able to carve out for itself a space of self-governance in school matters by relying on the technical legal possibility, left open by provincial statute, of choosing the Roman Catholic panel. This they could do because of their position as the spiritual home of the wealthiest Jewish property-owners in the city. Indeed, as David Rome pointed out, half of the $4,500 paid by Jewish property holders into the school tax coffers of Montreal came from two individuals, members of the Spanish and Portuguese congregation.[85] The combination of wealth and the unique choice open to Jewish taxpayers under the law of the period allowed for part of the Jewish communities of Montreal to make their own normative world in which education of their children could take place in a specifically and self-consciously Jewish environment. As for the rest of Montreal's Jews, the lack of wealth among the ever-expanding immigrant community meant that the ways in which they could create their own constitutive narratives were distinctly more limited. For other participants in the dialogic system of constructing Montreal's common school system, things were also different. The Protestant board saw a simultaneous fall in income and an increasing demand from newly arrived immigrant Jewish families for access to schooling. For the Roman Catholic board, which also struggled for adequate revenue, they educated very few, if any, Jewish students, while at the same time collecting 20 per cent of most of the Jewish taxes as a kind of administration fee.

While the new system of Roman Catholic Jewish education in Montreal experienced a few teething problems over the timing of the return of the tax monies to the synagogue, it functioned well for the parties directly concerned.[86] The *Report of the Roman Catholic School Commissioners for the Year 1888–89* indicates that they received $2,193 from the City of Montreal via "la taxe des Juifs Espagnols et Portugais de 1888," of which $1,754.40 was returned to the synagogue.[87] For the next year, 1889–90, the Roman Catholic Commission received $2,164.40 and returned $1,731.52.[88] In the year 1891–2, the amounts totalled $2,256.80 and $1,805.44,[89] and for 1892–3, $2,894.50 and $2,605.05.[90] In other words, both the Roman Catholic Commission and the Spanish and Portuguese congregation school were in a clearly better and more advantageous position than either had been when the Jewish taxpayers of Montreal had selected the Protestant panel. The children of parents who attended the Spanish and Portuguese synagogue received an English education and Jewish schooling supervised by the rabbi, including Hebrew instruction in which the proper pronunciation was taught.

Things were slightly more difficult and complicated for the Protestant board, however. At one level they had little to complain about. They had themselves insisted on strict legal formalism as a foundational principle in their attempts to enforce compliance from the two synagogues on increasing Protestant board control and supervision on school matters. The members of the Spanish and Portuguese congregation had likewise simply acted in accordance with the freedom of choice afforded to them under the 1870 statute. Indeed, the idea of allowing Jewish taxpayers to enter into the Protestant or Roman Catholic system of education more broadly had originated in the days prior to Confederation from perhaps the pre-eminent Protestant educator in Quebec, Sir John William Dawson.[91] Dawson served as principal of McGill and was for many years a commissioner of the Protestant School Board and a member of the Protestant Committee of the Council of Public Instruction. He was a firm advocate of separate schools and saw the Protestant educational system in Quebec as an essential barrier against Roman Catholic clerical dominance of life in the province.

Speaking to an audience of teachers at the McGill Normal School in 1864, Dawson had stated, "On behalf of that portion of our population which is non-catholic, but not Protestant, I would say, that it might be left at liberty to avail itself of the provisions either of the Protestant or Catholic system at its option; and it would be necessary, in order to avoid difficulty, that its rights in the matter should be recognized."[92]

There was in 1864 an awareness of the presence of non–Roman Catholics and non-Protestants (i.e., Jews) in Quebec before Confederation, and a recognition that they had rights that needed to be protected. More significantly however, the proposed recognition was simply that they be made to fit into the bi-denominational school structure. From Dawson's point of view, there was no place for truly common schools, nor for non–Roman Catholic, non-Protestant schools. The 1870 statute did nothing more than give a concrete legal footing to Dawson's ideas that Jews should fit by their own choice and election into either of the two denominational, common educational systems in the province.

But whatever the formal legal rights under the statute, and whatever essential problems would always flow from the bi-confessional educational system in Montreal, the Protestant board now encountered significant practical issues. They were still faced with increasing numbers of Jewish students from immigrant families who wished to attend the common schools, and for whom *common* meant Protestant and English-speaking schools. Likewise, at some level, and despite the necessary complications and difficulties, strong elements within the Protestant educational elite would continue to consider it a matter of basic Christian principle that the Protestant schools should welcome all non-Catholics.[93] The Protestant board had suffered a serious loss in revenue with the defection of the Spanish and Portuguese congregation, but conversely there had been little if any diminution in the number of Jewish students within the Protestant school system in Montreal. In 1888, 172 children of Jewish parents attended Protestant schools.[94] The number of students in the Spanish and Portuguese school seems to have been fixed at around 25–30 throughout most of this period of Roman Catholic Jewish education.[95] Yet the Protestant board received almost the same amount from remaining Jewish taxes as the Roman Catholic board collected for its administration of Spanish and Portuguese congregation taxes.[96] The issue of fiscal equity now manifested itself in almost crisis terms within the Protestant educational structure in Montreal.

The Protestant School Board no longer supported Hebrew teaching in its schools. It had decided that it would treat all Jews as Protestants and admit them to its schools provided their parents had paid taxes into the Protestant panel or, if they were not taxpayers, they were members either of the English, German, and Polish synagogue or Temple Emmanuel. The board issued instructions to all headmasters to satisfy themselves that Jewish students met these conditions and to report that information to the board.[97] The Protestant board continued with its traditional practice of associating its Jewish students with formal and limited synagogal structures. It also put into place a practice that recognized a correlation between paying taxes and the right to attend Protestant schools.

Whatever complex matrix of affiliation, tax panel choice, and Christian charity and duty that might have informed Protestant School Board practice and policy, the pressure of numbers also began to be felt in other ways in the Protestant system. Previously, there had been arrangements for the release from school of Jewish students on holy days. In 1888, the board received information from the two rabbis of the English, German, and Polish synagogue and the Reform temple indicating that there were seven or thirteen such holy days in the coming school year, depending on which rabbi's view they took. Faced with a theological dispute between the rabbis on the question of Jewish religious obligation, the board simply decided to abandon its practice and determined that it would henceforth not recognize or sanction any absence by Jewish students for religious observance.[98] The increasing number of Jewish students in Protestant schools in Montreal led in this instance to a reduction in Jewish educational rights. They could no longer absent themselves on high holy days; they received no Hebrew instruction; and they could attend Protestant schools only if their parents paid school tax on real estate holdings or they were members of the two other dominant synagogues, Shaar Hashomayim and Temple Emmanuel.

The burden on the Protestant board continued to grow with the number of Jewish students increasing from year to year, and indeed from month to month, with the arrival of immigrant ships into the port of Montreal. Tax revenues from Jewish real estate owners still predominantly vested in the Roman Catholic panel. As a result, the Protestant School Board approached the provincial government and the Protestant Committee of the Council of Public Instruction in order to bring about a legislative change that would result in increased revenues. In effect, they sought to legalize the religious identity of corporate real estate holders by requiring all corporations or legally registered companies to place an annual declaration with the School Board identifying the members of these bodies as Protestant or Roman Catholic.[99] The proposal also included a redefinition of *Protestant* to include "every person not belonging to the Roman Catholic religion" ("toute personne n'appartenant pas à la religion catholique romaine").[100] For the first time, at the behest of the Protestant committee charged with the education of Protestants throughout the province, came the proposal that Jews, as non–Roman Catholics, should be legally considered, at least for school tax purposes, as Protestants. The Protestant position, if accepted, would result in a net increase in tax revenues for the Protestant board, because most commercial enterprises owning real estate were controlled either by Protestants or, in a few cases, Jews.[101] It would also, potentially at least, provide a legal basis on which Jews could place a claim for full emancipation as Protestants in the common school system of Quebec. This was not to be.

The religious leader of Quebec, Cardinal Taschereau, voiced his strong objections during a meeting of the Council of Public Instruction, claiming that all education monies in the province should, in justice and fairness, be distributed in proportion to the number of students being educated. This would not be the last time that such a proposition would be heard in debates over school taxes. But at this point, the debate between the Protestant and Roman Catholic Committees of the Council of Public Instruction took another turn, resulting in a "highly regrettable misunderstanding between the Catholic and Protestant members of the Council" ("un malentendu fort regrettable entre les membres catholiques et les membres protestants du Conseil").[102] The secretary of the Protestant Committee reported that the cardinal's proposition had been put on the second day of the meeting as an amendment to the Protestant motion concerning corporate selection. The minutes compiled by the Roman Catholic Committee's secretary, on the other hand, reported that the cardinal's motion had been put and approved on the first day of the meeting, 18 April 1888. On 29 November the Protestant Committee wrote to the premier protesting against the Roman Catholic version of the meeting and the votes that they claimed had not taken place, because the original Protestant motion had been withdrawn. The premier, Honoré Mercier, replied on 10 December 1888 that he had investigated the matter, had received an affirmation from the secretary that the minutes had been signed on the day in question, and further that the cardinal himself had confirmed the version contained in the minutes. He concluded, "In these circumstances, with the respect due to your members and to you, I must consider the minutes as written to be correct."[103]

On 15 May 1889, the Protestant members of the council refused to vote to adopt the minutes that had been drafted by the Roman Catholic secretary and that reported that the council had carried the Taschereau motion. After heated debate, the meeting of the council approved the minutes with the cardinal's motion as reported by the Roman Catholic secretary, with the vote split exactly on denominational lines. As a result of the acrimony, the council would not meet again for eight years, and the two committees would simply go about their own denominational business.[104] No legislative changes were forthcoming, since the cardinal's move to propose the pro-rated system had been presented as a response to the Protestant proposal in relation to corporate taxes. The Roman Catholic Committee in fact preferred the legislative status quo.[105] According to Croteau and Gagnon, in the eyes of the Roman Catholic elite, the most important fact in the educational system was the embodiment of denominationalism at all levels, including in the separate Committees of the Council of Public Instruction, in the 1869 Act. From this politico-theological perspective, the division of tax monies in Montreal was of less importance than the ability for the Roman Catholic hierarchy to continue to reproduce a native elite class through their subsidies to the private *collèges classiques*. The education of the popular classes, again according to Croteau and Gagnon, was of secondary importance, and the battle over pro-rated payments for elementary education in Montreal was never one that they sought to carry through.[106] As always, the Jewish School Question took place in a complex set of circumstances, many of the most important of which had little to do with Jews, but concerned central interests of Protestants and Roman Catholics.

For a majority of Jews in Montreal, meanwhile, in the time of large waves of immigration, the earlier Jewish interstices in the education system that had allowed for some forms of autonomy and self-determination, and for some attempt to build a Canadian Jewish education in the shadows of section 93 had virtually disappeared. The Protestant School Board had failed to push through changes that would have given it a stronger and more reliable financial footing because of the opposition of the majority Roman Catholic membership on the Council of Public Instruction and the Roman Catholic clergy's own priorities in educational matters. The majority of Jewish students in Montreal now attended Protestant common schools, but technically only if they were taxpayers or members of the two synagogues officially recognized by the Protestant board. Again, the arrivals of heterogeneous Jewish migrants would soon, if it did not already, mean the end of any idea that two synagogues could be said to represent the Jewish community. Moreover, these Jewish students now existed in the common school system as Protestants, or at least as Protestants who could prove they were the right kind of Jews to the satisfaction of the headmasters. The Protestant board also stood firm insofar as the direct relationship between Jewish tax monies and admission to the Protestant common school system was concerned. Only if taxpayers of the Jewish community, not members of the Spanish and Portuguese synagogue, continued to select the Protestant panel would Jewish students be permitted to attend Protestant schools.[107]

In December 1890, the Young Men's Hebrew Benevolent Society opened its free day school in premises that they had been able to purchase, thanks to the gift from Baron de Hirsch.[108] The building offered accommodation for the destitute, distressed immigrants, and orphans.

It also housed the school that offered day tuition in Jewish and general studies to the children of the immigrant community and night classes to teach English mostly to adult migrants. This was the Baron de Hirsch Institute, the first Jewish non-synagogal building in Canada.[109] Another Jewish educational organization was about to enter the fray and to redefine the constitutive limits of the Jewish School Question.

The Baron de Hirsch School welcomed almost two hundred children in its first year of operation, but it could not benefit from school taxes, paid only to support public, common institutions, and was financed entirely by money from the institute fund. The chair of the school committee, David Ansell, made it clear in his annual report that he considered the present system of distributing Jewish taxes to be fundamentally unfair: "Surely a school giving instruction to over 200 poor children has some claim to a portion of these taxes. The committee ask, that the Board should as early as possible take decisive and active measures for the purpose of remedying this undoubted injustice and wrong."[110]

Ansell's ideas would be echoed in the annual report of the Protestant Board of School Commissioners.

> The Protestant Board of School Commissioners educates about 80 per cent. of the Jewish children attending day schools, and receives about 20 per cent. of the Jewish tax, and the Spanish and Portuguese synagogue educates about 20 per cent. of the children and receives 80 per cent. of the tax, out of which a commission of 20 per cent. is paid for collection to the Roman Catholic Board of School Commissioners. The Protestant Board naturally does not see the justice of educating so many for such a small per centage of the returns, and is now taking legal advice as to the rights of Jewish children to admission to Protestant schools. The Board is aware that the whole Jewish community, with the exception, of course, of the Portuguese Synagogue, is dissatisfied with the injustice of the present distribution of the tax.[111]

The issue of the place of Jewish students in the Montreal common school system now had a full list of protagonists. The Baron de Hirsch Institute school welcomed large numbers of Jewish children and received no money from the tax panel, because under Quebec law and section 93, it was neither a Protestant nor a Roman Catholic school. The Spanish and Portuguese school, by its own estimate, welcomed at most sixty-three students, while the Protestant schools had hundreds of additional Jewish students. The Roman Catholic board simply collected the Spanish and Portuguese tax monies and returned them to the synagogue after taking their fee, while educating virtually no Jewish students. The potential actors in the constitutive narrative(s) of Jewish Montreal's identity/identities within the educational context now included the two denominational boards, the oldest synagogue and the wealthiest Jewish taxpayers, and the Baron de Hirsch Institute, as well as the Roman Catholic and Protestant School Commissions. Competing images of Jewry, of collective identity and mutual aid, of what it meant to go to school in Montreal and to be a British subject enjoying equal rights were all parts of the narrative construction of the life world of Montreal Jews, Roman Catholics, and Protestants at this moment in time. And hanging over the various versions of the story, the epic of Montreal Jewries, was the sword of Damocles that was section 93 of the BNA Act. The Protestant board sought legal advice on the question of admitting Jews into common schools.[112] This was the complex legal and political world into which the Jewish students of Montreal entered, mostly against their will. The collective narratives of law and politics, economics, fiscal arrangements and statutory schemes, fairness and its different meanings, intra-communal and inter-communal dialogue and dissension were about to play themselves out in ways that would often involve plot twists unexpected by the authors of the great constitutional narrative of this chapter in the Jewish School Question.

4

Jews and Roman Catholics, School Taxes and Protestants: The First Jewish School Question

Debates, Dialogue, and Controversy in the Jewish School Question

At this point, the parameter of the Jewish School Question was clearly circumscribed. In order to ensure the proper education, secular and Jewish, of their children, members of the Spanish and Portuguese synagogue had made use of their fiscal clout and the legal choice to opt into the Roman Catholic panel left open to them under the existing statutory regime. The poorer, majority Jewish population, including the expanding immigrant groups, depended on the Christian generosity of the Protestant board and the social welfare operation of the Baron de Hirsch Institute and its school, to provide their children with schooling. The two denominational school systems, Roman Catholic and Protestant, as well as the provincial government would become key players in the dialogic process of constituting the rights of Montreal's Jews to send their children to school. Not for the last time, this discussion underscores the centrality of non-Jewish actors to the solution of the Jewish School Question in Montreal.

Originally, the two primary participants in this phase of the Jewish School Question would be the school boards of the Spanish and Portuguese synagogue and the Baron de Hirsch Institute. It appeared that an intra-Jewish solution to the issues and controversies around the question of the distribution of Jewish taxation for educational purposes was a possibility, but even at this stage, all of the relevant actors, including the Protestant and Roman Catholic School Boards, were also involved at key points. This chapter traces the discussions, disagreements, negotiations, settlements, retractions, threats, and compromises that characterized attempts to resolve the Jewish School Question in the last decade of the nineteenth century. It sets out the conflicts between the two main Jewish institutional protagonists, the Spanish and Portuguese synagogue and the Baron de Hirsch Institute. The former sought to maintain its special arrangements with the Roman Catholic School Commission, while the latter attempted to obtain what it saw to be a just and equitable solution and more commensurate divisions of Jewish taxes. Each Jewish party attempted to retain or create a space for self-constitution. The Spanish and Portuguese congregation and their school representatives continued to claim that they, as the most significant Jewish taxpayers, should and could assert a right to control those taxes for the education of their children. They would continue to defend the centrality of Hebrew-language instruction to any settlement. The Baron de Hirsch Institute made other constitutive claims about Jewish identity and the role of education, as well as about the rights of all Jewish children. Because they educated the vast majority of arriving immigrants and provided the pedagogical support allowing these children to enter the Protestant school system, they maintained that justice demanded they receive a greater share of Jewish taxes for the education of Jewish children.

At the same time, financial concerns would inform the involvement of the Roman Catholic and Protestant school systems in the Jewish School Question. While the Roman Catholic School Commission profited from its administration fee arrangement with the Spanish and Portuguese synagogue taxpayers, it sought broader justice in a new and what it saw as a fair distribution of school taxes generally. Meanwhile, the Protestant Board of School Commissioners asserted its own claims in relation to the financial shortfall and broader injustice it continued to suffer in the cost of educating increasing numbers of Jewish children and the minimal Jewish taxes coming to it because of the absence of the wealthiest Spanish and Portuguese Jews. Claims of fairness, justice, equity, and rights to community self-constitution and to educational identity would originate from Roman Catholic and Protestant school officials and from different parts of the Jewish communities, each invoking the same narrative tropes and jurisprudential appeals for what were mutually opposing ends.

This chapter exposes and analyses these narrative dynamics and explores the ways in which the various institutions asserted and acted upon their claims to educational rights. It also sets out the vital role played by the provincial government, first in facilitating dialogue between and among the parties, and then when dialogue appeared to have become impossible, in imposing the threat of legislative intervention to settle the matter legally. Once again, the discussion that follows will highlight the legal and extra-legal dynamics that were always at play in the evolution of the Jewish School Question in Montreal and give concrete examples of how the parties to the discussions and debates managed complex dynamics of self-constitution and "rights talk" inside and outside the strict limits of the constitutional norms set out in the rigid terms of section 93.

1891–1892

At the meeting of the Board of the Baron de Hirsch Institute on 11 January 1891, the school committee requested more money to keep the school running. David Ansell personally offered to contribute $100 if the board and the school committee could commit to pursuing a firmer funding base for the school. It was then announced that negotiations were taking place with the view of amalgamating the Baron de Hirsch School with that of the Spanish and Portuguese synagogue. If that were to eventuate, of course, the immigrant children would gain access to a school funded from substantial Jewish tax monies now being paid into the Roman Catholic board.[1]

Any optimism about the coming together of the Jewish communities on education proved unrealistic. The Baron de Hirsch representatives had gleaned the clear impression that there was really no interest in any form of amalgamation at the Spanish and Portuguese synagogue and that other avenues would have to be explored in the near future.[2] Among the suggestions put forward at the institute was to call a mass meeting to advise the public about the current situation, but the committee wanted a more private solution to the issue and pursued further contact and talks with representatives of the Spanish and Portuguese congregation. In addition to meetings between the two groups, a direct mail campaign to the eleven taxpayers from the Spanish and Portuguese congregation who had opted to switch to the Roman Catholic panel was undertaken. The fate of education for Jewish children in Montreal was still dependent on the vast financial resources of these few taxpaying members of the oldest synagogue. A letter, signed by the president and honorary secretary of the Baron de Hirsch Institute, Harris Vineberg[3] and S.W. (Sam) Jacobs,[4] was sent to each of the individuals who had transferred their tax monies to the Roman Catholic panel in order to support the synagogue's school for their own children.[5]

The Spanish and Portuguese school, which held classes in the basement of the Stanley Street building where the synagogue was then located, taught 25–30 students. An additional 250 Jewish students attended Protestant schools in the city, and the institute had a further 168 pupils. This meant that the vast majority of Jewish school taxes supported an infinitely small percentage of the Jewish students in Montreal. "All persuasive means have been employed but without avail."[6] A solution was in the hands of the individual Spanish and Portuguese taxpayers.

The Protestant board was threatening to end its admission of Jewish students, and a crisis loomed. The institute, having failed with the institutional embodiments of the school tax arrangement and the official structures of this part of Montreal Jewry, made a direct approach to the small number of individuals upon whom the question of Jewish taxes really rested.

> We now appeal to you personally, to assist us in avoiding this calamity, and in doing justice to the whole community, and we call upon you in the common sense of humanity, and in the interests of the poor of your Religion, to see that these children are not by any act of yours deprived of that little education afforded them, and of thereby becoming good and useful citizens, and to this end we would ask you, to withdraw your School Tax from the Roman Catholic Panel, where it does little good, and replace it in the Protestant Panel, and thereby allow the continuance and encouragement of the cause of the education of Jewish children, now so auspiciously commenced and carried on …
>
> And in the name of the poor, the Society will feel grateful, and your knowledge of having done good will be your reward.[7]

The personal appeal constructed an impressive counter-narrative about the state and nature of the Jewish community in Montreal, about duties and obligations of solidarity with impoverished fellows, and about the essential role played by education in the formation of "good and useful citizens." It sought to place the debate about taxes and schools in Montreal both within the concrete world of economics and power and then to move beyond that to a sense of citizenship more broadly understood in terms of the full and free exercise of all rights inherent in the status of British subjects in Canada. At the same time, the institute also appealed to the wealthy members of the Spanish and Portuguese synagogue's sense of Jewish solidarity. The letter constructed a narrative of broad communal understanding and identity as Jews. It set out in its appeals to the wealthiest Jews in Montreal a sense of community that transcended the walls of the synagogue or debates about the minhag and replaced those narrow concerns with attempts to appeal to a broader communal ideal of solidarity and long-standing Jewish traditions of charity and self-help. It asked for a mitzvah that would be both its own reward and that concretized these ideals of community. Ironically of course, as would always be the case in the Jewish School Question, the good deed, tikkun olam, could really occur only in a legal context that was explicitly bi-denominational and from which Jews would always technically and lawfully be excluded.

In a moment of Canadian constitutional irony, this impassioned appeal to a sense of Jewish community and solidarity had to be made in terms of requesting a change in payments of tax monies from the Roman Catholic to the Protestant panel. The emerging majority within the Jewish community on educational matters, embodied in the membership of the Baron de Hirsch Institute, clearly saw the future as intimately linked to the presence of Jewish children in the Protestant school system. On the other hand, the members of the Spanish and Portuguese synagogue had, with the administrative structural assistance of the Roman Catholic School Commission, carved out for their children a Jewish educational system in which Hebrew instruction and religious teaching were key elements. The apparent intransigence of the Protestant School Board on the teaching of Hebrew, that it had previously accommodated, and its growing insistence on matters of administrative jurisdiction over Jewish schools had driven the most powerful Jewish taxpayers of Montreal away from the Protestant system. Meanwhile the hundreds of Jewish children in that system and those receiving their Canadian education at the Baron de Hirsch School suffered.

While the few wealthy taxpayers of Shearith Israel did not opt into the Protestant panel at this juncture, there was some slight movement in the negotiations between the two parties. The Spanish and Portuguese School commissioners confirmed that they would offer some of the tax monies to the institute school if they received a written request. However, some institute members were wary of reaching any accord with the Spanish and Portuguese Commission. They were fully aware not just of the recent historical relationship between Jewish educational institutions and the Protestant board, but also of the fact that the Protestant schools still welcomed more Jewish students than either the synagogue or the Baron de Hirsch Institute. In reality, the interests of large numbers of Jewish students lay with the Protestant board. Members of the institute urged caution in reaching any arrangement with the Spanish and Portuguese synagogue that did not take into account the interests and concerns of the Protestant School Board. Even while they were not yet a direct party to the discussion, the Protestant board were present in spirit at the talks between the two Jewish groups.[8]

A committee on the tax question was formed by the Spanish and Portuguese School Commission, and the institute empowered the president "to appoint a Committee to meet their Committee."[9] The institute put forward a demand for $450 for school purposes from the Spanish and Portuguese synagogue's portion of Jewish school taxes. The synagogue school proposed that it would take thirty students from the institute and make some payment from any surplus remaining at the end of the school year.[10] Despite the earlier promise to meet a request from the Baron de Hirsch Institute favourably, the subvention was refused, just as a significant wave of Russian Jewish refugees fleeing pogroms was settling in Montreal.[11] Neither the synagogue school nor the Baron de Hirsch Institute could agree with the other side, and the situation worsened.

The Baron de Hirsch Institute decided to raise the political stakes of its conflict with the authorities of Canada's oldest synagogue. They invited a new partner into the narrative over Jewish school taxes by directly petitioning the provincial government. While there was no minister of education to whom they could turn, since the earlier abolition of that post, the provincial government was still concerned with educational matters, from the perspective of the Treasury, which always made monies available for education from the general fund when local school taxes were insufficient.[12] More importantly, the powerful Cabinet office of the provincial secretary had general carriage of educational matters in government. In addition, of course, each member of the provincial legislature represented ridings in which electors had a keen interest in the education of their children. Throughout this period politicians also always sat as members of the Roman Catholic and Protestant Committees of the Council of Public Instruction.[13]

The Baron de Hirsch Institute made a direct plea to this new interlocutor, who, while lacking direct control over the administration of education, nonetheless had great powers of moral suasion, backed up by the threat of legislative intervention. The Spanish and Portuguese synagogue joined battle and approved making available whatever sums would be necessary for legal and other expenses in dealing "with the present controversy with Baron de Hirsch Institute School."[14] For its part, the institute submitted a written brief on 4 May 1892 and sent a delegation to meet with the Cabinet officials in Quebec on 18 May.[15] Given the seriousness of the issues at hand, a second meeting, this time attended by representatives of the Spanish and Portuguese congregation, was set for 25 May.[16]

The written submission or memorial from the Baron de Hirsch Institute contained an iteration of the factual and historical background and current circumstances of the education of Jewish students in Montreal and on the tax question.[17] In addition, the memorial quite openly attacked the claims of the Spanish and Portuguese congregation, questioning their enrolment figures and slamming claims that the synagogue school was a free school open to all, in part because its Stanley Street location was simply too distant from the homes of immigrant Jews in the east end of the city to make attendance practically possible. More significantly it criticized the Spanish and Portuguese school by invoking the terms of the broad spirit of the education legislation of the province. The Jews of the Baron de Hirsch Institute did not want Jewish schools; they claimed the right to a public education for Jewish students in the common schools of the province. Perhaps with a small sense of irony once again, the institute brief argued that the legislative scheme governing the schools of the system was "framed for the education of the masses, and not for the benefit of any particular individual or Congregation." The Spanish and Portuguese school "is a Sectarian School, under the charge and control of a particular Congregation, and under the superintendence of its Minister."[18] The specific proposal now being put forward was for the creation of a separate Jewish school tax panel, the funds from which would be distributed according to the number of Jewish students attending established city schools. Looming in the background was the legal issue, already raised in some circles within the Protestant educational community, that support for denominational schools, especially Jewish denominational schools, could not pass muster under provincial legislation or under the guarantees of Roman Catholic and Protestant schools, and only Roman Catholic and Protestant schools, under section 93. The argument for pro-rated distribution, similar to the argument about the division of neutral panel tax revenues previously advanced by the Roman Catholic authorities when tax changes had been mooted some years earlier, was approved by representatives of the different congregations that had now emerged in the city, as well as other Jewish communal bodies.[19] The community again seemed divided, this time between the Spanish and Portuguese synagogue and everyone else.

A further set of interlocutors entered the fray. The leading organs of the anglophone press covered the story and were used by the two main Jewish protagonists, the Baron de Hirsch Institute and the Spanish and Portuguese synagogue, to convey their message. In its coverage of the first institute delegation's memorial and visit to Quebec, the *Montreal Star* reported the reactions of "prominent member of the S. and P. congregation that the Institute was unwilling to meet and discuss things on amicable terms. Their demands, said he, amounts to about communism. Our congregation supply 90 percent of the taxes and yet they claim an equal distribution. If communism is to be established by law we must submit; but until it is established we want to be treated as other bodies are.'"[20] Clearly the appeal to good morals and community sense of the Spanish and Portuguese taxpayers that had been invoked in the Baron de Hirsch letter was being met, in part at least, by a counter-narrative about freedom, property ownership, and individual and corporate liberty, as the school tax question became a matter of public, or at least journalistic, interest. The same newspaper in its editorial of 23 May described the actions of the Spanish and Portuguese synagogue, in league with the Roman Catholic School Commission, as being "in violation of the spirit of the laws."[21] The *Gazette*, for its part, saw the institute's complaint as invoking basic principles of fairness and urged government equality in its treatment of Jewish children. It believed that the proposal for a Jewish tax panel and the distribution to schools according to the numbers of Jewish pupils was the most practicable solution, but also read the request as one involving the creation of "a third series of schools." For the *Gazette*, "the readiest way of providing it, outside of existing schools, which it seems do not find it convenient to do the work, is on the lines suggested."[22]

The Baron de Hirsch submission in fact did not advocate payment of Jewish taxes to a new series of schools,[23] nor perhaps even the creation of a new panel, but instead referred to payments to "all properly established schools in the city."[24] This was a deliberately vague formulation, but the only properly established schools in the strictly legal sense were those common schools under the jurisdiction of the Roman Catholic or Protestant School Boards, at least in the meaning of being entitled as such to receive tax money. Private schools could exist, but in law they had no claim on school taxes paid to support common schools. The Spanish and Portuguese synagogue school and the English, German, and Polish school had always existed in the shadow of the law when they received tax money originally from the Protestant board. Throughout the history of its relations with the two synagogue schools, the board had insisted on supervising the common or English curriculum, so an argument might have been made that each school somehow fell under the aegis of the Protestant board, which exercised sufficient control over the secular parts of the curriculum to allow the school to be characterized as Protestant. But such an argument would have been merely a de facto description of some effects of the arrangements between the synagogue educational authorities and the Protestant commissioners, and not necessarily an operating de jure classification of the schools. As a matter of the educational statutes of the province and the overarching narrative of section 93, Jewish schools had no existence recognizable by law as public or common schools entitled to receive subventions from tax monies.

While the Protestant board's support of different Jewish schools at the two main synagogues may have been just, fair, and practically necessary, it was support that had been given at best with the colour of law, but almost certainly outside the legal structures of a strictly bi-confessional common school system. A fortiori, the position of the Roman Catholic board at the time was more clearly outside the limits of strict legality. It made no claim, nor did it offer any pretence, of supervisory jurisdiction over the curriculum of the Spanish and Portuguese synagogue school. It acted simply as a conduit, charging an administrative fee for money paid as school tax by members of that congregation, back to the school. Support for the Baron de Hirsch School would likewise cause the same legal issues to arise, since any subsidy would necessarily involve paying tax monies for what was, juridically, private, non-common education. Whatever the fairness and justice of such an arrangement, or the practical desirability of supporting the educational desires of newly arrived immigrants, those concerns always risked being trumped by overarching statutory positivism and constitutional normativity. The construction of the narratives of self-determination and educational advancement for Jewish pupils within the hermeneutic frames of the Jewish School Question always revolved and evolved around, but not always inside, the limits of strict legality.

The Protestant Committee of the Council of Public Instruction also took cognizance of the submission from the Baron de Hirsch Institute. As a matter of principle, the committee resolved that it did not believe that it could or should intervene in what it characterized as a dispute "between the different Jewish synagogues," but it did add that it accepted the principle of a pro-rated distribution of Jewish taxes according to the number of students enrolled in the city's schools.[25] The Roman Catholic Committee's earlier adoption of the same pro-rating principle would have applied to all students in common schools, resulting in losses for Jewish and Protestant students alike. The Protestant committee's resolution now meant that the legally established school governance structure of the province was firmly behind the principle of equitable distribution of Jewish school taxes argued for in the Baron de Hirsch memorial for the education of Jewish students. The Spanish and Portuguese taxpayers had right and legality on their side insofar as the text of the statute permitted them to elect to pay into the Roman Catholic panel, but the claims of the Baron de Hirsch Institute resounded more clearly with broader understandings of the rights of children to an education and to a basic equitable demand that school taxes should go to the schools that were actually educating students.

The case of the Spanish and Portuguese synagogue was presented to the assembled provincial Cabinet by their solicitor and for the Baron de Hirsch Institute by their counsel, Maxwell Goldstein.[26] The arguments from each side rested on the stark conflict between the Spanish and Portuguese synagogue's assertion of its absolute right to reach an agreement with the Roman Catholic board as a matter of law, and the broader appeals of the institute's lawyer to principles of fairness.[27] Before the formal reply from the provincial government had been received, the Spanish and Portuguese school representatives sought to reach what for them was a fair settlement and made another offer to the Baron de Hirsch Institute School. They proposed that the synagogue school would welcome between 100 and 125 students currently attending the Baron de Hirsch School.[28]

On 6 July the provincial secretary wrote to the parties concerned and indicated that no change in legislation was envisaged because this was a "special case."[29] He added, however, that the view of the government was that the current situation in Montreal was not acceptable, because "the distribution of the Jewish school taxes are not as equitable and fair as they should be." He added, "We expect that this will suffice to call the attention of the interested parties to those facts."[30]

The provincial government made it clear that the delicate balance of provincial education practices embodied in statute would not be altered in order to accommodate what was a fundamentally intra-Jewish dispute. It also insisted that the technical legal right for Jewish taxpayers to opt into either the Roman Catholic or Protestant tax panels would not be altered. But the provincial secretary also made it clear that the government had been moved to accept the pleas of the Baron de Hirsch Institute for greater fairness, and by implication at least, it rejected the strict legal positivism of the Spanish and Portuguese argument. Once again the proposed solution was one that sought compromise and negotiation without imposing any firm reference to an unchanged legal framework. In this instance, the two Jewish parties were effectively told to sort things out equitably between themselves. Dialogue and agreement between the parties were preferred to any idea of a heavy-handed legislative intervention, which would no doubt would have reopened the hornet's nest of the broader claims and disputes between the Roman Catholic and Protestant educational communities.

The institute rejected the synagogue's offer to accept more students, seeing it as a simple modification of the previously rejected proposition. More significantly, the proposal was characterized as a delaying tactic and concrete evidence that the Spanish and Portuguese officials were recalcitrant, even when the provincial government had clearly rejected their argument.[31] The Baron de Hirsch position was clear: an intra-Jewish solution was required, and the approaching school year, with ever-increasing numbers of Jewish immigrant students coming to the institute's school, demanded speedy action. The government expected the parties to reach a mutually acceptable agreement, and further inaction would be construed not just as obstreperous by the institute, but could be seen as "an attempt to ignore the instructions of the Government."[32]

Ansell may have been pushing the rhetorical limit in referring to governmental "instructions," but he and the Baron de Hirsch Institute members were clearly frustrated by the synagogue's inaction and delay. The government had given its moral backing to the institute and the majority of the Jewish population in Montreal, but it had clearly been unwilling to intervene more actively in what it categorized as a limited communitarian dispute to be settled by the Jews of Montreal. The stick of legislative change had been clearly taken out of the debate by the government, leaving Ansell with the weapons of rhetorical flourish and moral suasion against the fiscal power of the Spanish and Portuguese taxpayers and their existential and communal position about the centrality of a Jewish education for their children, however few.

The synagogue simply repeated its offer to increase its intake of students but added an offer of a $500 payment to the institute school as a final settlement of the dispute between the parties.[33] The offer to take a number of students from the Baron de Hirsch School had been consistently rejected as mere window dressing by Ansell and his colleagues. The proposal of a minimal subsidy, couched in tentative and conditional terms, and carrying with it some idea that it would settle the dispute once and for all, was equally unacceptable because it did not, in the eyes of the institute, go to the underlying issue of the fundamental unfairness of the Spanish and Portuguese position on school taxes. Because they characterized this as a negative response from the Spanish and Portuguese synagogue, the institute resolved to approach the government once more.[34] The institute still recognized that any lasting and equitable solution to the tax issue would have to involve the Protestant School Board that continued to receive an ever-increasing number of Jewish students into its schools.

The Protestant School Board was a silent partner in the negotiations between the Baron de Hirsch Institute and the Spanish and Portuguese synagogue. As both a practical matter insofar as the educational institutions attended by Jewish students was concerned, and as a matter of principle for parts of the Jewish community and their ideas of the benefits of common school education for their children, the real and long-term solution still resided in Jewish pupils making their way into the Protestant school system of the city. Indeed, the primary school of the Baron de Hirsch Institute worked explicitly with the intention of providing Jewish immigrant children with the language and academic qualifications that would permit them to enter mainstream Protestant education to develop the skills for future employment and the broader cultural context permitting them to become true and productive British subjects. With no further reply from the synagogue school authorities forthcoming, and the school year bringing 220 children to the Baron de Hirsch School, Ansell wrote to the provincial Treasurer, J.S. Hall,[35] furnishing all correspondence in the matter and again castigating the Spanish and Portuguese committee's inaction, which he characterized as being both against the government's wishes and evidence of the simple desire by the Spanish and Portuguese congregation to keep as much of the school tax for their own benefit as possible. Ansell underlined to the minister that the institute had attempted to act in accordance with the government's wishes and had offered a compromise in that spirit. He urged provincial intervention in protecting the interests of justice and the rights of the majority of Jews in Montreal.[36]

More Dialogue, Still More Inaction: Governments, Schools, Synagogues, and the Jewish School Question

The Spanish and Portuguese officials reiterated the previously rejected offer to enrol additional students in their school and upped the final monetary amount to $800. While moral and political pressure were being brought to bear from Quebec City, the two sides could still not reach an agreement that would satisfy their competing visions of right and their conflicting understandings of the central values of Jewish education.

The provincial Cabinet secretary again wrote to both the institute and the Spanish and Portuguese synagogue representatives expressing official exasperation with the lack of progress in Montreal. The government has "exhausted all possible means of conciliation and the time afforded has been sufficient for you to reach an agreement."[37] If an agreement were not forthcoming in the near future, the letter added, the government would be required to study the legality of any and all arrangements under which the Protestant and Roman Catholic School Commissions might give any public monies at all to schools that were neither Roman Catholic nor Protestant. The ominous shadow of section 93 and its supporting framework found in provincial education legislation now loomed over the discussions between the two sections of the Jewish communities represented in the school tax debate. In the form of a thinly disguised threat from the provincial government indicating that any money given to any Jewish school might be questionable in legal terms, the discourse and dialogue now moved from compromise and agreement between the parties, to invocations of a legal metanarrative by organs of the state in which Jews would inevitably be the losers. Again, this idea of using the law was presented by the government not as a normative set of rules that tied its hands, but as a conditional warning meant to give a further incentive to all parties to reach an amicable arrangement. Such an arrangement, inevitably involving the disbursement of tax monies for some form of Jewish education, or more precisely perhaps for the education of Jewish children, in the very terms of the government's own threat, might be illegal, but it would be acceptable if the community could come to such an agreement.

The Spanish and Portuguese congregation was still unmoved and continued to seek to protect its own deeply held understanding of Jewish identity and control over the education of their children. They addressed a letter to Hall asking for his intervention and assistance. His reply of 28 October was instructive not just of the attitudes that often lie just below the surface throughout the Jewish School Question, but also of the same exasperation found in the earlier correspondence from the government to the two parties: "Now, however, I suppose the law will have to take its course as you people are not able to agree. It would have been much better for you people to have consented to pay one thousand dollars which the other people were willing to accept. I have done all I could but it will probably result in neither party getting anything."[38]

This letter was perhaps an even clearer indication that the provincial government's legal view was that all subsidies from tax monies paid outside the Roman Catholic or Protestant systems were unconstitutional under section 93 and illegal under the statutory bi-confessional system of education established by statute in Quebec. Once again, however, a compromise between the Jewish parties, "you people" and "the other people," would have the constitutive and magical effect of making the law disappear from the equation as far as the government appeared to be concerned. Strict legality was not as important for any of the parties, at this point at least, as finding an amicable and durable solution to the Jewish School Question. Rights and right were understood in terms of strictly positive legal normativity and more broadly under conceptions of justice and fairness outside the limits of constitutional and legislative legality. The government still left the door open to the parties to reach an amicable, if illegal, settlement, failing which law would be used, and neither part of the Jewish community could foreseeably benefit from such an occurrence.

After failing in attempts to enter into direct dialogue with Roman Catholic education officials about the Jewish taxes they received, the Baron de Hirsch School Committee once more approached the provincial government for help. At the further urging of the provincial secretary, they agreed to accept the $800 offer for the current year as an interim measure, "thus giving the government an opportunity to legislate in the future for a fair and equitable distribution of the tax."[39] The institute committee wrote to the Roman Catholic board and to the provincial secretary indicating their acceptance of the sum of $800 and seeking payment thereof, and the Spanish and Portuguese synagogue in turn communicated with the Roman Catholic board to ensure the transfer of funds.[40]

The Roman Catholic board offered the final piece in a puzzle that still remained somewhat complex and slightly obscure. The secretary of the Roman Catholic School Commission, W.E. Archambault, notified the Spanish and Portuguese school secretary that the board would now take only 10 per cent of the Jewish taxes as their administration fee.[41] Presumably the 10 per cent difference would or could be made available to the Baron de Hirsch School. In the language of the day, the Roman Catholic board secretary stated that they were acting to reduce the amount they took "in order to favor the charitable dispositions of your Commission which desire to aid your countryman of the Baron Hirsch Institute."[42] At some fundamental level it was impossible for the Roman Catholic board to think of the Spanish and Portuguese congregation as anything other, or more than, Jews. For the Roman Catholics of Montreal, the members of Shearith Israel were aiding their "countrymen," despite the fact that most students of the institute were immigrants and all members of the Spanish and Portuguese leadership came from Canadian families and were native-born or British subjects. There was no place in the nation as far as Roman Catholic elite understandings went, for Jews; they were a different country.

But even after the payment had been made to the Baron de Hirsch Institute School, the two Jewish parties were far from any mutual understanding. Despite the recorded objections of both the institute and the provincial secretary, Gershom De Sola continued to record the $800 payment as "final." The official position of the Spanish and Portuguese synagogue was that the dispute was now over. The institute leaders again felt compelled to memorialize their long-standing position to the recalcitrant members of Shearith Israel.[43] The government likewise sought to defeat any assertion from the Spanish and Portuguese synagogue that $800 settled the issues of rights and justice between the parties. The assistant provincial secretary, "by command of the Honorable Provincial Secretary," indicated that the government considered the $800 subsidy as valid for one year only. It was unable to "accept the conditions mentioned." The government's position was still, as it had always been, one that favoured a definite settlement of the question by the Jews of Montreal for the years to come. It insisted that the Spanish and Portuguese School Board confirm the unconditional nature of the $800 payment.[44] Indeed when the synagogue school officials objected, the provincial secretary advised them in no uncertain terms that the government's stance was unwavering and that it had always been clear that the $800 solution was and would be considered by them as an interim answer to be put into place while a long-term solution was found.[45] "I regret to state to you that we will take energetic measures to force a settlement on the basis adopted by the Executive Council if you do not accept it forthwith and voluntarily."[46]

While negotiations continued at a molasses-like pace, the daily realities of educating Jewish students, especially immigrant Jewish children, did not disappear. The Baron de Hirsch School Committee announced that the Protestant School Board had undertaken to accept all Jewish students, provided they could speak English. In order to facilitate language instruction to prepare students to enter the common school system, the Protestant board offered to subsidize the salary of a teacher in the night school at $1.50 per night for a maximum of eighty nights.[47]

Several years after the Spanish and Portuguese synagogue had left the Protestant panel and entered its agreement with the Roman Catholic board, the situation still remained in flux. Even the temporary truce was in tatters. As more and more Jewish immigrants continued to arrive in Montreal, they were educated largely in the Baron de Hirsch School, but in reality, this was meant in most cases as a way station on the road to entry into the Protestant common school system. Students stayed at the Baron de Hirsch School until they had acquired the basic English-language and academic skills to matriculate in the Protestant system or could join the work force. At this point, at the end of 1892, the Protestant board was at best a silent partner in the dialogue over Jewish school matters, but it was encouraging the Baron de Hirsch endeavour by subsidizing the teaching of English. In principle, the government had given support to the position of the institute on the repartition of school taxes and had threatened both sides with a drastic legal solution, which would have removed all tax subsidies from Jewish schools. The Spanish and Portuguese School Board, in the eyes of the institute and the government, maintained its self-centred and narrowly legalistic position, but one that it considered essential to the proper Jewish education of its children. Everyone talked about justice, but it seemed a scarce commodity over which rhetorical, political, and legal battles took place, while the situation for the average Jewish student remained unchanged.

1893: Jews, Protestants, Roman Catholics, and the Jewish School Question

As the two parties within the Jewish community, with the ongoing involvement of the government, attempted to break the impasse that had ended the year, some dissension and discontent over the slow and unclear progress of these efforts to guarantee a solution to the Jewish School Question began to emerge. The leaders of the B'nai Jacob congregation, the Romanian congregation, and the Austro-Hungarian congregation began to express demands that the parties solve the issue equitably, failing which they too would make demands for funding for their schools. B'nai Jacob had been founded in 1886 and was known in Yiddish as the Russishe Shul or the Russian synagogue. Beth David was formed two years later in 1888, and was known the Rumaninishe Shul, or Romanian synagogue.[48] The Austro-Hungarian synagogue, Shaare Tefilah, was somewhat younger, apparently having been founded in 1892.[49] The diversity of the Montreal Jewish community was threatening to upset the delicate balance of power between the Spanish and Portuguese officials and the Baron De Hirsch Institute. A solution to the school tax issue was becoming ever more urgent. Talks continued, but the $800 final payment seemed to have become an idée fixe for the synagogue officials, just as the hope of legislative intervention had become for the institute.[50]

Having looked at the figures provided by the synagogue, Provincial Secretary Hall wrote again to Meldola De Sola and urged greater generosity from the congregation. He appealed to both the rabbi's sense of justice and to the fact that the Spanish and Portuguese position had little political support:

> I have looked into this matter again, and after making further enquiries, I have really come to the conclusion that you ought to do differently with these people to what was done last year. I have no doubt that your own sense of justice when appealed to will see that they are educating a much larger number of people than you are in your school. I would suggest therefore your giving $1300, or if you are afraid of a shrinkage in the tax, undertake to pay one-half of what you got from the City this year and the future. To do this I think the whole matter can be disposed of and settled. It is to be hoped we wont have the trouble we had last year, but they are quite determined, and they have quite a number of members supporting them, to bring legislation, if necessary, to put the matter right.[51]

The provincial government was still attempting to broker a direct settlement by appealing to principles of justice, while at the same time threatening possible legislative intervention. While he did not indicate what legislation "to put the matter right" might actually entail, it was clear that Hall's unwavering position was that any legislative solution would not be to the benefit of the Spanish and Portuguese school. He also made it clear, as had the government the previous year, that an amicable settlement between the parties was the preferred solution.

The trouble was never-ending for the provincial government, and, it might be added, the hundreds of Jewish school children in Montreal whose education was constantly in peril as the Spanish and Portuguese School Board continued to do battle with the school committee of the Baron de Hirsch Institute and indirectly with the provincial government. Meanwhile the Protestant board continued to subsidize English instruction for the night school at the institute.[52] The Protestant School Board became more involved in the matter as the year progressed and in October named a committee to deal with matters arising from the question of educating Jews in the Protestant system and the intimately related issue of Jewish school taxes.[53] The Protestant officials met with the government and the Roman Catholic board. The previously private arrangement between the Roman Catholic Board of School Commissioners and the Spanish and Portuguese school, as well as private communal negotiations between the synagogue and the institute, now involved not just the government, and to a lesser extent the Roman Catholic board as a conduit for the majority of Jewish taxes, but now both confessional school bodies were engaged in a parallel attempt to come to an overall and now public solution. What had previously been treated fundamentally as a private intra-Jewish matter, in which the government really did not wish to formally intervene, unless compelled to do so, was rapidly becoming a matter for the involvement of the official structures of school governance in the city of Montreal. Once again the constitutive spaces for all forms of Jewish self-determination in the realm of education appeared to be rapidly closing, as new narratives of Jewish Roman Catholic or Jewish Protestant education came into play.

The Roman Catholic board now appointed a committee to investigate the matter and considered proposals resulting from the approach of the Protestant School Board. Official structures were being put into place to seek an end to the crisis of the Jewish School Question, which now involved the bi-denominational school-governing bodies of Montreal. By this time, matters were also becoming further complicated. The Protestant board was not just exasperated, it was divided, with a vocal minority of members wishing to hand responsibility for Jewish education over to the Roman Catholic board, on the basic ground that Jews were not Protestants and therefore were not really of concern to the Protestant commissioners, who were legally in charge only of Protestant education in the city. The majority of the board nonetheless felt that a better solution was in the offing. The government had urged a solution but none had been reached.[54] The majority of the board also made their position clear to the provincial political authorities who were in favour of a pro-rated distribution of Jewish tax money between the two denominational boards in Montreal. They pointed out to the government that the Protestant board had spent $20,000 educating Jewish students over the preceding years and that if the current system continued, they felt within their rights, based on legal opinions they had obtained, to refuse to admit any Jewish student whose parents did not pay school tax. The Protestant board was once more giving voice to the more restrictive understanding of Jewish educational rights in Montreal, under which taxes and access to schooling were intimately linked. The position would, of course, exclude the vast majority of Jewish immigrant children, whose parents still lived in rented accommodation, from any right to education. In addition, the Protestant board's legal argument, its implied invocation of section 93, also indicated to the government that a political solution that would proceed along the existing line of educating Jewish students in the Protestant school system of Montreal would be eminently preferable to positive legality. The government got the message. John Hall again made clear its desired solution but also underlined that the Protestant and Roman Catholic boards, as the only lawfully constituted school authorities, had to be party to any agreement.[55]

The Demise of Jewish Roman Catholics: The End of the Jewish School Question, 1893–1894

Almost a full year after the urgings from the provincial secretary to the parties to find a solution to the matter, the Roman Catholic school officials in Montreal began a process that would eventually end the first set of battles in the long campaign over the Jewish School Question.[56] The board first invoked its sense of the legalities that in fact operated and exercised an important, if often unarticulated, influence over the question. It also set out an understanding of the equities of the situation. Thus it declared, in all legal logic, as had the Protestant board earlier but less formally, that Jews who paid into the Roman Catholic Panel 1 were to be considered, for school purposes, as Roman Catholics, and that, as a logical extension, the Spanish and Portuguese school was, "in reality" (*en réalité*), a school falling under the jurisdiction of the Roman

Catholic School Commission. The Jews of the oldest orthodox synagogue in Canada were, for school purposes, Roman Catholics. Such was the legal logic and transformative and truly jurisgenitive power of section 93, when combined with private arrangements over school taxes, situated as a key constitutive rhetorical device in the narrative of Jewish identity and identities, and school rights in Montreal for its Jewish populations. Thus, just as it had been possible to mount an argument that the schools of the Spanish and Portuguese and English, German, and Polish synagogues – where the English curriculum had been supervised and inspected by Protestant officials, and instruction had been given by duly qualified English teachers – were somehow Protestant, Roman Catholic officials now took the analysis one step further. Because the members of the Spanish and Portuguese synagogue paid into the Roman Catholic school tax panel, and those juridically Roman Catholic taxes supported the synagogue school, the school itself and the taxpayers from the oldest synagogue in Canada, were, for educational purposes at least, Jewish Roman Catholics.

The Roman Catholic board then concluded that the most equitable solution would be for Jewish school taxes to be "divided according to the population" (*divisée suivant la population*), the solution first proposed by Cardinal Taschereau and subsequently reiterated in different contexts in subsequent years by the Baron de Hirsch Institute submission to the provincial government. But then, the Roman Catholic board returned to the bi-confessional structure of the school system and decided that what was good for the Jewish goose was certainly equally fair for the two Christian ganders. All school taxes in Montreal, they concluded, following the system proposed for Jewish taxes, should in essence and in justice be divided according to the population. A pro-rated distribution of school taxes was in essence just and equitable for all. The Roman Catholic proposal again was not just for a pro-rated distribution of Jewish taxes, it was also a call for a more radical solution involving the simple pro-rated distribution of all monies raised from real estate valuations for school tax purposes. The result would be that the numerically dominant Roman Catholic population would receive much more from school taxes than the smaller but wealthier Protestant community. Again, the Roman Catholic proposal would have the potential effect of recreating a specific Jewish tax system, perhaps even a third panel, in which the taxes of that denomination would follow its population. On the other hand, if the logic of the outline argument were followed, it would de-denominationalize taxpayers of Protestant or Roman Catholic origins, put their money in a single pot, and then divide it according to the population ratios of the city. A less radical version of this proposal would apply only to the remainder of the third or neutral panel tax revenues, derived largely from corporate real estate assessments. Jews would benefit, Roman Catholics would benefit, and Protestants would be the big losers. Jews might gain in the sense of again finding themselves with a separate identity (albeit a unique and overarchingly simplistic Jewish identity) under the logic of one version of the Roman Catholic proposal. But the majority of Jewish school students would also end up losing under historical and continuing arrangements and sociological realities, because Protestant schools would suffer a severe blow if the taxes were divided according to this scheme. The Protestant school system would be financially devastated by such a move. Jewish students, who were merely tolerated by some elements within the Protestant educational authority, would no doubt be the first to suffer. Once again in Montreal, justice in the school context always played itself out within a complex matrix of political, economic, ethnic, and religious discourses that sometimes had unintended consequences, and in which, more often than not, Jewish educational interests were submerged in more acute constitutional and constitutive narratives of Protestant and Roman Catholic identities as the two constitutionally enshrined religious groups.

At year's end, the returns in the annual report of the Baron de Hirsch Institute indicate the receipt of $800 from the Spanish and Portuguese congregation and city taxes for the day school, and $216 from the Protestant Board of School Commissioners for the night school.[57] While the battles raged, the school managed to survive and the students to receive an education setting them on a path to lives as good and useful citizens. And while the Protestant, Roman Catholic, and Jewish educational representatives did battle in relation to broader concerns over fiscal arrangements, the Baron de Hirsch School muddled along under a series of ongoing, temporary, and legally suspect arrangements with the Spanish and Portuguese synagogue, the Roman Catholic School Commission, and the Protestant board, all under the watchful eye of the provincial government.

In its communications with the Spanish and Portuguese synagogue, the Roman Catholic board now highlighted that it been informed that other Jews, German and Polish, had begun paying into the Roman Catholic Panel 1. As a result, given its position, announced in its December 1893 resolution, that a pro rata distribution of all tax monies was the best and most equitable method of proceeding, it would henceforth hold all Jewish tax monies unattached on its books in order to permit a disposition according to these considerations of the justice of the matter. More importantly still, they resolved to withhold any and all tax monies from the Spanish and Portuguese school unless and until they received not only the details concerning the number of students in the synagogue school, but also evidence that the Spanish and Portuguese authorities "have fulfilled the obligations they have contracted with the assent of the Board towards their coreligionists the German and Polish Jews."[58] The school board now deployed the fiscal stick of payments into the Roman Catholic panel as a threat and incentive for the members of Shearith Israel to do justice to their co-religionists. In addition, as their Protestant counterparts had done and were continuing to do, the Roman Catholic School Commission now reasserted their position as guardians of their part of the bi-denominational educational structure of Montreal.

They resolved that from 1 July the agreement between the board and the Spanish and Portuguese Jews would come to an end, and that thereafter any Jewish taxes paid into the Roman Catholic panel would be "distributed for the instruction of Jewish children in the manner the Board may think proper." Ten years earlier, Shearith Israel had struck a deal with the Roman Catholic board in order to preserve their position in relation to their taxes, to maintain a Jewish educational institution in Montreal. The Spanish and Portuguese congregation and their school now confronted the juridical reality that Jewish taxes were constitutively and constitutionally under provincial statute and section 93, always only ever capable of being classed as Protestant or Roman Catholic taxes. They found themselves in the position not just of seeing the arrangement coming to an end, but indeed of having any control of taxes coming from their congregation vest in the sole discretion of the Roman Catholic School Board. Throughout most of the life of the agreement, the Roman Catholic Commission had been content to receive its administration fee and had left the rest of the money to the Spanish and Portuguese taxpayers and their school. Now they had come under pressure from the provincial government and the Baron de Hirsch Institute. They found themselves on the wrong side of the moral equation as far as every other participant in the Jewish School Question process was concerned. At the same time, the whole issue of school tax distribution was bubbling away in conflict at the provincial level between the Roman Catholic and Protestant School Boards. Any idea that an intra-Jewish solution was even institutionally possible was now beyond anyone's contemplation. As always, there was some interstitial space for some types of Jewish self-constitution, but the overarching social, political, economic, and legal dynamic always meant that the answer to the Jewish School Question could only ever really be found within the broader and more complex relationships between the two nations at the heart of Quebec identity.

Nonetheless the two bodies at the centre of the Jewish community continued to meet in an attempt to hash out a mutually satisfactory financial arrangement, and they reached a tentative settlement of $900 per year for four years to be paid to the Baron de Hirsch School, subject only to the agreement of the Roman Catholic school commissioners.[59] Gershom De Sola wrote to the Roman Catholic Board of School Commissioners informing them of the resolution of the question of Jewish school taxes reached by the Spanish and Portuguese school and the Baron de Hirsch Institute. But the situation of Jewish taxes for education in Montreal was now clearly beyond the control of the Jewish communities.

The Roman Catholic board notified De Sola that they could not accept his assertion that an intra-Jewish solution had ended any controversy or issue about Jewish school taxes and the relationship with the board. Nothing had changed from the Roman Catholic board's position enunciated in its earlier resolution.[60] In the meantime, the Baron de Hirsch Institute, anxious over the financial position of its school, pressed the Spanish and Portuguese synagogue for payment of the first agreed instalment, while the synagogue continued to meet Ansell's increasingly frantic demands with the stonewall of Roman Catholic refusal to comply with the terms of the intra-Jewish agreement, which, in their view, went against their already announced position on Jewish school taxes.[61]

The Roman Catholic School Board had, temporarily at least, withdrawn their threat to treat Jewish taxes as purely Roman Catholic and cooperated in implementing the practical arrangements that at this point allowed both the Spanish and Portuguese school and the institute school to receive subventions from Jewish tax monies. The Baron de Hirsch annual report of 1894 indicates that the school committee received $800 from the Spanish and Portuguese congregation "from City School Taxes" and a further $46.50 from the "Roman Catholic School Commissioners from City School Taxes."[62]

By September and the start of the new school year, the Roman Catholic board called an end to these temporary arrangements. It reverted to its December 1893 position on the proportional payment of Jewish taxes based on enrolments and reasserted its legal rights as one of the two legally constituted governing organisms for public schools in Montreal. It wrote to the Baron de Hirsch Institute confirming its willingness to adopt the proportionality rule in its payments to schools with Jewish students, but only if the schools "were placed under the control of their Board."[63] Again the legal framework of education in Montreal, under which only two denominational common school systems were properly constituted, would preclude any idea of a Jewish school with any form of independence. Just as the Protestant board had increasingly insisted on a supervisory role over Jewish schools, along with the payment of Jewish taxes into the Protestant panel, now the Roman Catholic School Commission pressed for its rights under section 93 to treat the schools that received tax monies for the Roman Catholic panel as Roman Catholic.

This demand appears to have involved far more than mere supervision of the English curriculum, which had operated in the earlier days of synagogue schools under their agreements with the Protestant School Board. The Roman Catholic board insisted on nothing less than the entry of the Baron de Hirsch School into the Roman Catholic school system as a quid pro quo for access to Jewish taxes to support its students. Under such an arrangement, the students at Baron de Hirsch would be even more clearly Jewish Roman Catholics than students of the Spanish and Portuguese school had been under the 1884 agreement, and they would certainly be more Jewish Roman Catholic than students in the other public schools would be Jewish Protestants. In the common Protestant school system, despite continuing disputes over such matters, they could expect some degree of relief from attendance on holy days and exemption from religious instruction. Under the Roman Catholic proposal, the school would be a Roman Catholic school under the jurisdiction of the Roman Catholic School Board. No detail was given at this stage of the Roman Catholic ultimatum as to how the curriculum, including religious instruction, would be implemented. Nor, it appears, did the Roman Catholic board propose further subsidies at this point to the Baron de Hirsch School. It promised only pro rata payments from Jewish taxes in the Roman Catholic panel. Jewish taxes would be used to pay for a Roman Catholic school. Finally of course, the underlying philosophy and operating structure of the Baron de Hirsch Institute school had always been to prepare those students who wished to pursue their education to enter the public Protestant school system, which was perceived to be more clearly British and Canadian, in ways that were central to the acculturation philosophy of the institute, than the Roman Catholic schools would ever be.

The Roman Catholic offer was really no offer at all in the broader context of the Baron de Hirsch School and its institutional aspirations. By seeking to gain access to Jewish taxes paid into the Roman Catholic panel, the institute had been hoist on its own pedagogical petard. The Roman Catholic School Board stood on its legal rights over common schools. For them, while Jewish taxes would continue to be identified as such, more broadly and more importantly, they would be considered Jewish taxes paid into Roman Catholic schools. The natural and legal evolution of the 1884 arrangement by the Spanish and Portuguese Jews now had the real potential of turning more and more Montreal Jews into Roman Catholic Jews.

The institute tried to fight back by turning to the threat of litigation. The law firm of Carter and Goldstein, acting for the Young Men's Hebrew Benevolent Society, had served a notice of protest on the Spanish and Portuguese Jews, Shearith Israel, demanding immediate payment of the monies owed to them under their agreement. The notice, or *mise en demeure*, was also served on the Roman Catholic School Board demanding that they retain $900 out of the Jewish school tax, pending the outcome of the litigation in the matter.[64] Two could play at the formal legal game, although the institute's claim to access monies in the Roman Catholic tax panel, even Jewish money, was, to say the least, as previous government threats had indicated, constitutionally problematic.[65] Gershom de Sola asked the Roman Catholic Board for $800 rather than $900 and insisted that the payment would bring an end to claims from the Baron de Hirsch Institute, a demand that was reluctantly accepted. Representatives of the majority of Montreal's Jews had tried dialogue and pleas to elected officials. They had written to individual members of the Spanish and Portuguese congregation appealing to their conscience and sense of communal solidarity and charity. They had sought direct intervention of the Roman Catholic board, only to find themselves faced with the prospect of having their school fall under its direct control. Finally, as they would in the future, these Montreal Jews invoked, or at least threatened to invoke, the power of the courts in their battle for equality and justice.

Because of its increasingly complex controversies with the Roman Catholic school commissioners, the school board of the Spanish and Portuguese synagogue requested a meeting with the Protestant School

Board "upon the subject of Jewish education," to which the Protestant representatives agreed.[66] The Spanish and Portuguese congregation decided to again place its school under the Protestant board. The formerly Roman Catholic Jews of Shearith Israel were about to become Protestant Jews once more. They agreed to pay their school taxes into Panel 2, the Protestant panel, and to place their school directly under the Protestant board, accepting its course of study. When faced with falling under the jurisdiction of the Roman Catholic board, the Spanish and Portuguese congregation decided that Protestant jurisdiction was preferable to Roman Catholic sovereignty. The school would remain as a free school but would henceforth also admit Christian children. But the central importance of proper Jewish education, that had always been at the heart of Shearith Israel's position, was also part of the proposed compromise.

Biblical instruction, which was part of the core Protestant school curriculum, would be based in the Old Testament. Hebrew would be taught by a teacher to be named, and the teacher's salary of $600 would be paid by the Protestant board. This marked a practical return, in relation to the insistence of the congregation on the teaching of Hebrew, to the status quo ante at the 1884 split. The Spanish and Portuguese congregation had not only regained the right to Hebrew instruction but they had managed to extract control over that instruction and the payment of the salary of the Hebrew-language teacher from Protestant coffers. Likewise, in a return to the system that had been operating in the Protestant school system, despite a series of disagreements and ongoing controversies, Jewish students would be exempted from school attendance on a number of holy days, to be agreed at a later date. Jewish children would also be allowed to attend the schools of the Protestant public education system. All other Jewish taxes paid into Panel 2 would be used to educate Jewish students in the Protestant schools, and the Protestant board would assume the current lease on the Spanish and Portuguese school and continue the contractual arrangement with the caretaker.[67] The Protestant board approved an agreement on the terms set out by the synagogue. But this apparent solution would be short-lived.

The next day David Ansell and Maxwell Goldstein addressed the Protestant board as representatives of "the Hebrew community of the city excepting the congregation of the Spanish & Portuguese Synagogue."[68] Positioning themselves as carrying this broad and democratically representative mandate, they proposed an arrangement remarkably similar to the one to which the Protestant board had just agreed with Shearith

Israel. The Baron de Hirsch School would come under the control of the Protestant board, as a free school; a teacher of Hebrew to be named by the Baron de Hirsch Institute would be part of the deal; and the Protestants would take over the rental of the school. The Protestant board listened intently to the representatives of the Baron de Hirsch Institute and the Hebrew community of the city. They were presented with a historical and documented account of the Jewish tax issue, including the intra-Jewish disputes to which they had not been a party. The board considered that record as exposed to them by Ansell and Goldstein and took particular note of the institute's insistence on the express wishes of the provincial government about the kind of solution it found desirable. The Protestant Board of School Commissioners then immediately rescinded its recent resolution concerning the agreement with the Spanish and Portuguese synagogue, in order enable themselves to deal with the whole question of Jewish education at a subsequent full meeting of the board.[69]

The Roman Catholic School Board's resolve to regain control over the entire amount of Jewish taxes, to distribute them more equitably, and to reassert its jurisdictional rights over schools in the educational system of Montreal supported by monies from the Roman Catholic panel had driven the Spanish and Portuguese synagogue back to something resembling its pre-1884 situation. Its insistence on Hebrew instruction had been met with an argument for parity by the Baron de Hirsch Institute in an echo of debates that had been taking place in relation to Jewish education in Montreal since the 1870s when the issue of competing minhag had divided the Spanish and Portuguese and English, German, and Polish synagogues in their failed attempt to create a Jewish free school. The Spanish and Portuguese congregation now saw its position and its wishes vindicated but then almost immediately rejected by the Protestant board. It also found itself completely isolated from its former ally in the Roman Catholic board, with whom it had ended its agreement, thanking them for the "courteous and liberal manner" in which that Roman Catholic officials had conducted themselves, but indicating that it was unable to accept the terms under which the Roman Catholic board wished to continue their relationship.[70] The Roman Catholic board's position was, in their view, contrary to the preferred governmental solution and apparently against the interests of the Hebrew community of Montreal.

The Protestant board decided that a solution to the Jewish School Question, and its intimate connection with the broader school tax issue, would be better dealt with under a global agreement with Roman Catholic school officials.[71] The Roman Catholic board referred the matter to the provincial level, seeking the advice of the Council of Public Instruction on the legality of any arrangement between the two confessional school boards in Montreal.[72] Once again, the constitutive fate of Montreal's Jewish schoolchildren rested not in their hands, nor in the hands of bodies representing the Jewish communities, but in those of provincial educational authorities. Practical arrangements for the education of Jewish students in Montreal depended upon the legal determination of the fate of an accord over Jewish taxes between Roman Catholic and Protestant School Boards. But the Baron de Hirsch School Committee was reasonably happy with the plan proposed by the two boards in Montreal. The vast majority, if not the virtual totality, of Jewish students were educated in the Protestant school system or in their institute school. Almost no Jewish students attended Roman Catholic schools, and only a few were enrolled in the Spanish and Portuguese school, which was on the verge of collapse or Protestant takeover. Any pro rata arrangement would mean that almost all Jewish taxes would come to the Protestant panel. Whether money would then be provided to the Baron de Hirsch School depended on it becoming a Protestant school.[73]

But at this stage, legality prevented the compact between the boards. Provincial authorities insisted that, legally speaking, only two denominational school systems existed in Montreal, and no arrangement outside that framework could be considered lawful. On 31 October, Meldola De Sola and other members of the Spanish and Portuguese congregation met with the Protestant board and submitted a revised formal proposal to bring their school under the Protestant system. Again, their taxes would go to the Protestant panel. Under this version, however, they offered to close their school, which, in reality, was in irreparable financial difficulty as a consequence the Roman Catholic board's position on the distribution of tax monies and the continuing small enrolment numbers. They also insisted on the engagement of a Hebrew teacher, nominated by the synagogue, at an annual salary of not less than $800. Either party giving notice before 1 June of any given year could end the agreement.[74] Once again, the members of Shearith Israel were insisting not just on the centrality of Hebrew to the proper Jewish education of their children, but on the subsidization of that teaching by the Protestant School Board as an essential condition to their re-entry, and the re-entry of their tax contributions, into the Protestant school orbit. For their part, David Ansell and Maxwell Goldstein simply submitted a written request for $1,500 from the board for their school as the appropriate pro rata amount owed to them from Jewish taxes. The Protestant board took both matters under advisement and instructed the treasurer to make inquires of the city government about the amount of Jewish taxes paid into Panels 1 and 2, as well as the amount of Hebrew tax remaining in the neutral panel.

The Protestant board met again on 24 November. A letter from the provincial attorney-general to the Council of Public Instruction declaring that any arrangement between the two boards in Montreal concerning the pooling and pro rata distribution of Jewish tax monies would be illegal, was tabled. The idea of a joint Protestant/Roman Catholic method of dealing with the Jewish School Question was now off the legal and political agenda. Yet in radically reduced form, a Protestant/Jewish arrangement that still allowed a self-governing Jewish school to receive Protestant tax money was apparently legal, or practical enough. They then resolved to accept the 31 October proposal of the Spanish and Portuguese synagogue to place their taxes into the Protestant panel and send their children to Protestant schools, and agreed to the appointment of a Hebrew teacher to be named by the synagogue and to be paid $800 per annum. Such a teacher would be subject to the supervision of the principal of the school and the Protestant inspector appointed by the provincial superintendent of Protestant education and would, of course, be subject to the general regulations of the Protestant School Board of Montreal. The Baron de Hirsch Institute School was granted $1,500, provided that its attendance records were sent to the Protestant Board and that it was subject to inspection by Protestant authorities.[75]

The Spanish and Portuguese school was no longer,[76] its students would be absorbed into the Protestant school system. Their only remaining piece of separate Jewish presence and relative autonomy could be found in the nomination of the only Hebrew teacher following their minhag.[77] The Baron de Hirsch School, on the other hand, continued to exist; it was still governed by a school committee constituted entirely by Jews. It was subject to reporting obligations in relation to attendance, since its subsidy from the Protestant board was calculated and dependent on its teaching certain numbers of Jewish students. It was equally liable to inspection by Protestant authorities, yet it still sat legally outside the official Protestant system of school governance, on the margins of dependence/self-determination and of (il)legality. Of course, the school run by the institute continued to function according to the particular educational philosophy under which it had begun. Its aim was to produce scholars capable of entering the pedagogical mainstream of Protestant education, where they would not just complete their schooling, but also would become useful British subjects and fully equal inhabitants of Montreal. While it still constituted an island of significant Jewish control over Jewish education in Montreal, the institute school embodied a particular, and not universally accepted vision of the nature and function of Jewish education in Montreal. For the time being, however, the school committee of the institute hoped that "the difficulty which had so long existed would now be set at rest."[78]

On 14 December 1894, Gershom De Sola wrote to the Protestant School Board advising them that on the previous day the school board of the Spanish and Portuguese Jews had unanimously voted to name Reverend Meldola De Sola as Hebrew teacher, a nomination accepted the same day by the Protestant School Board.[79]

5

Taxes, the Rabbi, and the Schoolboy: Section 93 and the *Pinsler* Case

Narrating Protestant and Jewish Education in Montreal

The arrangement with the Roman Catholic School Board had come to an end. The school taxes of the members of the Spanish and Portuguese congregation and the supporters of the Baron de Hirsch Institute now were paid into Panel 2, the Protestant panel. The Protestant board subsidized the Baron de Hirsch School, and the Shearith Israel School was permanently closed. The problem of Hebrew instruction appeared to have been dealt with, and the Jews, for educational purposes, now fell within the remit of the Protestant School Board. The Jewish School Question had been settled, again with a much-restricted space for Jewish autonomy or self-definition, but with Jewish students now part of the common education system.

But, as Gerald Tulchinsky in his history of the Canadian Jewish community points out, the first crisis around Spanish and Portuguese congregation school taxes and the education of Jewish students in Montreal, had, in fact, awakened a sleeping dog: "The Protestant board were now more conscious of what they came to view as a growing 'injustice' – having to educate a rapidly growing number of Jewish children without adequate compensation from school taxes on Jewish-owned property."[1]

The following discussion highlights the ways in which the Protestant School Board and the Jewish communities struggled with the financial and existential realities of the accommodation and agreement that had been reached as the Spanish and Portuguese taxpayers had come back to the Protestant panel, and the Baron de Hirsch School had been brought more fully, but not completely into the Protestant educational orbit. The chapter traces developments as the financial question that already troubled the Protestant board as it assumed more and more of the burden of educating poor Jewish students manifested itself at two levels. The first issue that was a constant niggling aggravation for Protestant school officials was the so-called special treatment enjoyed by Rabbi De Sola as Hebrew teacher for Jewish students in the Protestant system. The Hebrew-language question had always been central to the idea of maintaining a Jewish cultural and religious identity, especially for those associated with the Spanish and Portuguese synagogue. Now it would become an issue of significance for Protestant educational officials, and not just on the question of De Sola's salary. The Hebrew-language issue now became an existential touchstone for Protestant school leaders, and for their understanding of what a properly Protestant education was. The presence of increasing numbers of Jewish students began to raise the issue of just what a Protestant school system should and could look like, if, as in some schools, the majority of students were Jewish. Jewish educational rights, which had enjoyed a continuing if tentative recognition in Montreal, despite occasional formal reversions to the duality of the denominational system by both Protestant and Roman school officials, would come to clash with some essential understandings about the nature of Protestant education, the real right guaranteed by section 93. This chapter elucidates how and why the Jewish School Question came to be a Protestant school question.

The second point of conflict that ran alongside the existential, self-constitutional conflicts between the rights of Jewish students to attend school and Protestant section 93 rights was the now familiar financial issue. For the Protestant School Board of Montreal, expansion in the system was hampered and threatened by the burden imposed on Protestant schools as a result of the shortfall between the cost of educating Jewish students and the amount of Jewish taxes actually received from the panel. This chapter explores the twin existential crises that arose for Protestant education in Montreal, as a result of practices enshrining, however tentatively, the long-standing Jewish claims to educational rights and equality. These competing rights claims, to education by Jews and to Protestant education under section 93 by Protestants, would come to a head and result in the *Pinsler* case, addressed in later parts of the chapter. The discussion concludes with a brief description of the legal aftermath to that case, in which the Quebec legislature would attempt to enshrine both tax equity for Protestant schools and Jewish educational equality as "honorary Protestants." The chapter highlights how particular issues, such as the Hebrew teacher's salary, always embodied much broader questions of collective rights and religious identity, how demands for recognition and status were articulated within and outside strict legal norms, and how ongoing financial crises in Protestant education also consistently gave rise to claims of existential core values, of the rights of Protestants to Protestant schools. Finally the chapter demonstrates once more how solutions to these competing rights claims often exceeded or went outside the strict parameter of positive legality.

Taxes and the Rabbi, 1895–1900

The legislation in place for the City of Montreal was clear. School tax was derived from the owners of real estate. The legislation specifically excluded tenants from its operation and banned owners from seeking to impose any school levy on tenants under any general provision relating to taxes in a lease agreement.[2] At this time, most Jews in Montreal were immigrants, of more or less recent vintage, and they were renters. The argument, which would be consistently raised and invoked by the Protestant board, was that the effect of this demographic reality was that they, or Protestant taxpayers, were compelled to educate Jewish students at a cost that was never met by Jewish taxes.

The first sign of trouble arose very early in the post-truce period. The Spanish and Portuguese School Board wrote to the Protestant board requesting the first half of Meldola De Sola's yearly salary as the Hebrew teacher.[3] On 27 May 1895, the Protestant School Board met and decided that while it would continue to employ De Sola as the teacher of Hebrew, it would reduce his salary from the original $800 to $500 for the next school year. Once again, the offer was conditional upon the continuing payment of Jewish taxes into the Protestant panel.[4] E.W. Arthy,[5] the secretary of the Protestant board, wrote to Meldola De Sola, notifying him of the offer of continuing employment at a reduced salary. Arthy added that even that reduced rate was "the highest paid to any person in the service of the Board."[6]

The Spanish and Portuguese School Board unsurprisingly rejected the Protestant offer, insisting that the original arrangement, under which they had left the Roman Catholic panel and opted back into the Protestant school tax system, had included a promise that the Hebrew teacher's salary would be $800. As a result of what they considered to be a breach by the Protestant school officials, the synagogue sought to terminate the contract at the end of its current year.[7]

Several months into the agreement that had ended the first series of key disputes over the education of Jewish students in Montreal, the deal appeared to have come undone again, as it had at the time of the Spanish and Portuguese decision to opt into the Roman Catholic panel, over the question of the salary to be paid by the Protestant Board to Meldola De Sola for teaching Hebrew.

The cancellation was being explained away as an instance of the Spanish and Portuguese congregation simply protecting its rights by relying on the formal conditions set out in the arrangement between the parties. The $800 salary was a fundamental term of the contract. By offering only $500 for the next year, the Protestant board had in fact misunderstood the essential meaning of the agreement, thereby reneging on its undertakings.[8] The financial difficulties facing the system of Protestant education at the time in Montreal, the shortfall between collected Jewish taxes and the real cost of educating constantly increasing numbers of Jewish students, and the growing exasperation, frustration, and anger felt by certain members of the Protestant board at the cost of subsiding the highest teacher's salary in the entire Protestant school system in Montreal in the form of $800 to the Shearith Israel rabbi, were the real concerns of the Protestant educational authorities with whom the synagogue was in dialogue.

The Spanish and Portuguese position showed little regard, if any, for the broader questions, or for the necessary consequences the dispute might have on Jewish schoolchildren, except insofar as they believed that Hebrew instruction was central to the proper education of young Jews. They refused to be moved and as had been their wont, insisted on the rights they saw as enshrined in the agreement. The discourse from the Jewish side was one of contract, of binding undertakings, and of the centrality of Hebrew to the Jewish identity of their children. The concerns of the Protestant School Board were equally deep. For them, any idea that in the context of the Jewish School Question, a contract was limited by the rules of privity, was far from acknowledging the complex political, social, and financial circumstances in which the contract actually operated and within which the parties negotiated. A key part of that context was the troublesome place of Hebrew-language instruction in a Protestant school system.

The Protestant board had also received a reply from David Ansell concerning their subsidy to the Baron de Hirsch School. Ansell indicated that the institute considered the matter to be unsettled because a condition of the offer of support from the Protestant board had been the continuation of the practice of Jewish taxes being paid into the Protestant panel. When the Spanish and Portuguese synagogue threatened to withdraw, the Baron de Hirsch Institute felt that a condition precedent to the offer of a subsidy, albeit one beyond their control, had not yet been met. By construing the conflict in contractual terms, the Spanish and Portuguese congregation once again appeared to hold in its hands the fate of the Baron de Hirsch Institute School, and therefore the education of a significant number of Jewish children who were strangers to Shearith Israel. Under the rules of contract law, the Baron de Hirsch Institute was outside the legal parameter but directly affected by the terms of the agreement and the dispute over the meaning of those terms. The apparent privatization of the dispute now removed from the institute's hand any real ability to create a narrative space for itself or for the hundreds of Jewish students it was educating for entry into the Protestant system. Only by invoking the problem caused by the dispute as a condition precedent to its own bargain with the Protestant board could it begin to seek a space for the enrichment of its students' social life. Contract law was now being used as an instrument, both positive and negative, in the constitutive struggle of Montreal Jewries, as the parties wrestled for control of the situation of Jewish students. After more deliberations, however, the Protestant board wrote to Meldola De Sola announcing that the agreement would remain in effect for another year, at the $800 rate.[9]

However, the Spanish and Portuguese School Board did not consider the matter closed. They insisted that the previous correspondence meant that the Protestant board had changed the nature of the agreement into "a yearly one, requiring special renewal each year." The Shearith Israel Board wished to return to the original agreement that they characterized as "an agreement continuing from year to year until terminated by notice from either Board." Not only would this guarantee the continuation of the $800 salary, but also it would "avoid the necessity of annually reopening the discussion of the Jewish School question."[10]

In an ironic twist, the Shearith Israel officials now positioned themselves as the party seeking a permanent solution to the Jewish School Question. They did so by characterizing the contract as a continuing one, renewed automatically every year unless and until one party or the other indicated in writing its intention to withdraw from the agreement. While apparently happy to renew the contract at the $800 salary for the next year, the Protestant Board was not willing to give up what it saw as its rights to terminate or alter the arrangement as circumstances required at the end of each twelve-month period.[11] Arthy apprised Gershom De Sola of the board's insistence and unwillingness to cede its right to an annual review and renewal of the contract. For the Spanish and Portuguese congregation, the nature of the disagreement was not over whether either party, upon giving proper notice, could terminate the contract. Instead, the point of contention was whether the agreement required a formal renewal by the parties each year, as the Protestant Board apparently wished, or conversely, whether the agreement was, in the absence of the required notice of termination, simply automatically renewed on the same terms. The synagogue had lived up to its promises by having its members switch to the Protestant panel. The Protestant Board of School Commissioners had received its entire payment of Jewish taxes but had handed over only little more than half of the Hebrew teacher's salary. Again, the Spanish and Portuguese School Board shifted the moral ground. It wanted an end to the problem, it had lived up to its side of the bargain, and any ongoing issue on the Jewish School Question was now entirely due to the Protestant board's attempts to change the rules of the game and its failure to honour its undertakings.[12]

The Protestant Board now invoked its own version of the justice of its position. It wrote "that the total amount of the City School Tax levied upon Jewish properties is and always has been insufficient to meet the cost of educating the rapidly increasing number of Jewish children in attendance in the schools controlled and subsidized by the Board, and that consequently a considerable loss accrues to this Board under the present arrangement."[13]

Not only was the Protestant Board highlighting its precarious financial situation in relation to Jewish students, a theme to which it would return throughout this phase of the Jewish School Question and beyond, but it was at least implicitly putting paid to the Spanish and Portuguese argument that it was the party holding the superior moral ground in this dispute. Even more, perhaps, than the general point about the equities in the broad context of the education of Jewish students in the Protestant school system highlighted by the cross-subsidy issue, the board was underlining another fact to which it had previously referred. The $800 paid to De Sola for teaching one subject, Hebrew, to a limited number of students, was the highest salary paid to any employee of the

Protestant board.[14] Again the hermeneutic was one in which there was a clear narrative competition over the justice and equities of the matter. There was another set of discourses, once again pitting the special status of the rabbi and Hebrew instruction against broader issues of the education of large numbers of children from the Jewish population of Montreal. The Jewish School Question in Montreal was always a question both for Jews and about Jews, and the conflict between the two narrative perspectives would structure the ways in which competing constitutive stories of the issue would be told and understood.

The accounts of the Protestant board confirm a payment of $744 to "Rev. M De Sola, Teacher of Hebrew." In comparison, the same accounts indicate that "Mr H.H. Curtis, Director of French," received $332, the next highest amount.[15] Not for the first or last time, matters appear to have been settled by private negotiation and arrangement on terms satisfactory to the two principal protagonists, the Protestant School Board and the Spanish and Portuguese congregation. But the Baron de Hirsch School also benefited from the end of hostilities, however temporary. Its accounts show that it received a subsidy of $1,500 from the Protestant School Board.[16] The financial records of the Protestant board indicate that for next year, it provided $2,040 to the Baron de Hirsch Day School and $744 to Meldola De Sola.[17]

Over the next few years, the Jewish School Question entered a period of tranquillity. While occasionally there were issues concerning the status or circumstances of Jewish students in Montreal's Protestant schools, they were dealt with pragmatically. For example, in February 1895, a situation arose at Dufferin School, a Protestant school in which the majority of students were Jewish.[18] The parents of these children sought to have them excused from the instruction in the New Testament that was part of the Protestant curriculum. This matter had presented itself to the Protestant School Board before and had been dealt with by a definite engagement to exempt Jewish students from such instruction upon a written request from their parents.

The problem of absence was exacerbated for the Protestant educational officials by the fact that at the Dufferin School, the question of exemption was not a matter of excusing one or two students from attendance. Instead the vast majority of students sought to be excused. In order to deal with the absence of such a large number of students from the classroom during the daily period in which the Bible was taught, the Protestant board decided to ask Rabbi De Sola to attend at the school for twenty minutes each morning to conduct Hebrew classes for those exempted from New Testament study.[19] The board was meanwhile considering a more permanent solution to the problem: the creation of Jewish schools in which the Jewish students would be assembled and educated away from their Protestant schoolmates.[20] The issue of the disruption caused by releasing Jewish pupils from Protestant religious instruction was a concrete manifestation of the more fundamental issue, for the Protestant School Board, of how to maintain a system in which the schools were Protestant when the clear majority of the students were Jews. In the mind of many educational officials, a Protestant school in which most students were exempted from Bible study and instead were about to receive Hebrew lessons no longer looked or felt like a Protestant school. To deal with the synergy of practical concerns and an emerging existential identity crisis, the Protestant School Board was now seriously contemplating a segregated common school system in which Jews and Protestants would be taught separately, in separate schools, albeit within the overall governance structures of the Protestant education system. The space for Jewish self-constitution, or for the choice of how Jewish children would be educated in the schools of Montreal was again rapidly diminishing. While the Jewish children would still be attending common schools, they would be sitting in classrooms only with other Jews. The ideal held from its very beginnings by the members of the Baron de Hirsch Institute that entry into the Protestant school system would be the first institutional stage of the acculturalization for Jewish immigrant children, on their way to becoming full and useful British subjects, was in danger of becoming a pipe dream. At the same time, the issue of continuing Protestant subsidization of Jewish students was on the minds of the commissioners of the Protestant School Board.

The board's Committee on Jewish Education reported that it had submitted the question of its power to segregate Jewish students into a separate building to the attorney general and that a reply was awaited. They also proposed that the provincial government provide a subsidy to each of the two official boards in Montreal for the education of non-Protestant, non–Roman Catholic students, to an amount that would be the equivalent of the actual cost of educating Jewish students. If Jewish taxes would not suffice to educate Jewish students, the burden needed to be shifted from Protestant taxpayers to the state.[21]

The Protestant board nonetheless approved the continuation of the "existing arrangements with the Jews." The subsidy to the Baron de Hirsch Day School was set at no more than $2,000.[22] In 1897, the Baron de Hirsch Day School had received $2,795.20 from the Protestant board and Meldola De Sola his full salary as teacher of Hebrew of $800.[23] In a matter of five years, the support granted to the Baron de Hirsch School had increased significantly, although it did fluctuate. When it first received a subsidy from the Roman Catholic board and the Spanish and Portuguese synagogue, this had amounted to $846.50.[24] In 1895, the school received $1,500 from the Protestant board.[25] The Protestant School Board was seeking to cut back on the subsidy to the Baron de Hirsch School and was now using a flat rate, rather than providing an amount based on the actual enrolment figures. In 1898, the Baron de Hirsch School reported revenue from the board of $2,795.20,[26] but in 1899, the $2,000 cap was imposed.[27] The Protestant board was slowly reducing once again the room for manoeuvre and self-definition open to Jews within the school system, by cutting back on its subsidy to the remaining Jewish school. At the same time, it was contemplating the creation of its own de facto Jewish schools within the system of common public Protestant education in Montreal.

Indeed, in October 1898, the board wrote to David Ansell with its preferred solution. It would sell the Dufferin School building to the Young Men's Hebrew Benevolent Society for $50,000: $30,000 in cash and the remainder through the assumption by the YMHBS of the existing $20,000 mortgage. The Protestant board would guarantee a subsidy of $3,000 for three years to the Baron de Hirsch School. Under the proposed arrangement, there was, at one level at least, the possibility of some return to an era and a place where Jewish students would be educated in schools administered by Jews. But of course, this would still exist under the broad umbrella of the Protestant board in the sense that the school would continue to depend on the subsidy of $3,000, which was guaranteed for only three years. The more general ideal of a place for Jewish students within the common schools as part of their Canadianization was nowhere to be found in the Protestant scheme, nor was there any emphasis on the board's historical opening of its doors to Jewish pupils. The Protestant plan would lead to permanently separate Jewish schools. This was clearly anathema to the founders and directors of the Baron de Hirsch Institute. Theirs was a charitable organization, founded to assist immigrants upon their arrival with the longer-term goal that such assistance would give them the skills and knowledge they would need to succeed in their adopted country. Its founders always saw the school as a stepping-stone on the way to entry into the educational mainstream of the city's Protestant common school system and as the first step on the way to active participation as citizens in the immigrants' adopted Canada.

The Protestant board now sought to isolate and segregate the Jewish school population and to make the Jewish communities responsible for the exercise. Among the other conditions, the board insisted that the sale of the building would be valid only if it continued to be used as a school for Jewish children; that the YMBHS relieve the Protestant board from any responsibility for the teaching of Hebrew; that all Jewish school taxes continue to be paid into the Protestant panel; and finally that the Spanish and Portuguese congregation "intervene in this agreement and signify their acceptance of it."[28] Clearly the Protestant board was aiming to create a separate Jewish school, in which there would be only Jewish students, and where Jews would take over responsibility for what many members of the board had always thought was at its core a purely confessional subject, Hebrew. They wanted the two main representative Jewish bodies to agree to the creation of such a Jewish school and to guarantee the ongoing payment of Jewish taxes into the Protestant panel. Finally, while this would in fact constitute a contractual arrangement between the Protestant board and the Jewish communities' representatives, the board also insisted that it would be valid only if approved by the provincial government. The arrangement once more would look like a private contract, but in practice it would be a private agreement sanctioned by the state. The Protestant board clearly remembered that a few years previously, an attempt to deal with the Jewish School Question through an arrangement with the Roman Catholic board for dividing Jewish taxes had been subjected to legal objections from the provincial attorney general on constitutional grounds. It now wanted government approval for what amounted to a reorganization of the Protestant common schools in Montreal and the creation of separate Jewish Protestant schools.

The Jewish communities and their representatives continued to resist segregation. While there was at this point a degree of de facto segregation, this was, to a greater or lesser extent, the practical consequence of demographic patterns in Montreal.[29] The Protestant School Board continued to seek a global solution, in terms of obtaining a significant direct subsidy to cover the shortfall between the costs of educating Jewish students and the amount of Jewish tax paid into Panel 2. But the authorities of the Baron de Hirsch Institute sought to refute the argument at its root. The principal of the School, W.H. Baker, in his report of January 1899 pointed out that there were 330 students enrolled in his school, which received, as we know, $2,000 from the Protestant board. The Protestant board claimed that there were at the time around 700 other Jewish students in its common schools and that the shortfall in taxes was approximately $15,000 per annum. After examining the figures presented to the board, Baker pointed out that the calculations used by the board, taking into account the amount paid in school fees for each student, worked out at a cost of $31 per head for Jewish students, while the same board calculated its general educational costs per student at $17. In other words, the very basis for claiming that an injustice was being forced on the Protestant board was an absurdity as far as the Baron de Hirsch officials were concerned, after an examination of the Protestant board's own figures.[30] It was ridiculous for the Protestant board to claim that in practice it was nearly twice as costly to educate a Jewish pupil as it was to provide schooling for a Protestant student, even after accounting for some differences caused by the early education of recently arrived students and issues of language instruction and remedial learning. In fact, these elements of the cost of educating Jewish students were paid for from the now fixed subsidy to the Baron de Hirsch Institute School. No other obvious costs, except again for the De Sola salary, were evident from the Protestant board's calculations.

However, the Protestant board did not retreat from their position, insisting that their figures were accurate. Even using a cost per student of $19.38, they argued that they had received only $4,519 in Jewish taxes in 1898. They spent $2,000 on the 358 students at the Baron de Hirsch School and the remainder on the 349 students who attended Protestant schools. This they claimed resulted in a loss of $10,951.68 to the Protestant board above what they had received in taxes from Jewish contributions to the Protestant panel.[31]

While these figures do show a loss, they do not appear to manifest the deficit claimed by the Protestant board, who paid only $2,000 to the Baron de Hirsch Institute for the education of 358 students. If the real cost of educating them was indeed $19.38 per student, this meant an annual loss to the Baron de Hirsch School of $4,916.56. For the rest of the 349 students, this would mean a cost of $6,763.62 to the Protestant board, set against remaining tax revenue of $2,519, or a loss of $4,244.62. According to Baker, the Protestant board said that there were no Jewish free students in their schools, which would have meant that Jews paid $5 per student per year, or an additional $1,745 to the Protestant board, leaving the board with a Jewish deficit of just under $2,500 per annum, a far cry from the almost $11,000 it claimed. Even if the subsidy of $2,000 were added to the Protestant debit side, this left the board with a shortfall of almost $4,500, not far from that of the Baron de Hirsch School. On such accounting debates did the fate of the Jewish school children come to depend.

But if, at the time, the Protestant board could not obtain a full victory for their demands on the financial front, or succeed in their attempts to sell the Dufferin School and set it up as a separate institution for Jewish students, they invoked and deployed other strategies.[32] They still sought the complete segregation of Jewish students into a separate school building. And when that failed, the Protestant School Board continued to chip away at those elements of a specific Jewish presence in their common schools. First among these was, unsurprisingly, the continuing subsidization of the teaching of Hebrew.[33] "The language appeals to nothing in the proper train of Canadian children. It is not the language of commerce. It is employed for the purposes of inculcating the religious tenets of the Jewish system. It is to enable the Jewish pupils to take part in religious services in the synagogue."[34]

The teaching of Hebrew, at least at the elementary school level, was anathema to the very idea of Protestant education, however fluid and non-sectarian that conception might have been.[35] Moreover, the payment of $800 per annum, still the highest in the Protestant system, to the rabbi Meldola De Sola continued to grate. The provincial attorney general had apparently expressed doubts over the constitutional validity of the practice of the Protestant board subsidizing what could be characterized as Jewish educational instruction within a school system that was legally constituted as Protestant.[36] Nonetheless the board continued to honour their undertaking. This accommodation of the needs and desires of at least a part of the Jewish population in Montreal continued to exist, by common accord, in the shadow of legality, and despite the ongoing doubts of some members of the Protestant board about the desirability of such a practice, not just in a strict legal sense, but in the more fundamental existential sense of what it meant to have Protestant schools.

Despite these persistent fissures in the relationships central to the arrangement, which had brought an end to the first Jewish School Question, David Rome has written positively about the state of education at this time: "By 1900 the Jews of Montreal had their own schools, maintained in part out of tax funds. In the state of public education at the time, with the Protestant Board a relatively young body, it suited the commissioners to subsidize existing schools instead of convening all pupils into the city schools of the Board; not the least, the Board was thus retaining the social traditions built around these local institutions."[37]

While it is true that the Baron de Hirsch Day and Night Schools continued to function as essentially Jewish schools, Rome's assessment was perhaps overly rosy. The Spanish and Portuguese School had been closed for several years. The subsidy from tax monies from the Protestant School Board to the Baron de Hirsch School had been capped, and the Jewish School operated with extremely limited funds. Protestant officials continued their agitation with the provincial government over what they saw as the unjust formula for the distribution of monies from the neutral tax panel.[38] At the same time, the Board was seeking a way of segregating Jewish students within the common school system, and to get out of the arrangement under which it had agreed to maintain the teaching of Hebrew.[39]

At the Baron de Hirsch Institute, officials continued to struggle to put their educational policy into practice in such circumstances. While they were Jews, and they did have a deep attachment to their religion and the social practices of their communities, leaders like David Ansell and Maxwell Goldstein did not want a permanent separate Jewish school, either within the Baron de Hirsch structure or under the jurisdiction of the Protestant School Board. That is why the Institute School Committee reported with pride that one of the school's former pupils had not only entered the common school system but had been awarded a scholarship to the high school, and that others had finished first or won prizes in the public schools.[40] It is why they praised the teaching staff for their dedication and skill in achieving the school's primary aim: "the intellectual development of the pupils committed to their care, and with an earnest desire to make them good, useful, and loyal citizens of the country of their adoption."[41]

Finally, it was why the Baron de Hirsch School Committee appointed a special committee, headed by Maxwell Goldstein, to study "alleged discrimination of the Protestant Board of School Commissioners against the Jewish pupils in their schools."[42] Those Jews associated with the leadership of the Baron de Hirsch Schools did not want anything other than to give to the children of Jewish immigrants to Montreal equal access to the experience of public schooling, which would allow them to become "loyal citizens." They wanted equal rights for Jews within a constitutional structure enshrining Protestant and Roman Catholic education. They were about to be disappointed by law.

The Turn of the Century and the Turn of the Constitutional Screw: Jewish Children and Section 93

Events in the first five years of the twentieth century put the Jewish School Question into a new political and more specifically legal framework. In the previous years, with ongoing reluctance, the Protestant School Board had welcomed increasing numbers of Jewish schoolchildren into the common schools under their jurisdiction.[43] The presence of this distinct cohort of pupils was, in the view of the board, the source of many disruptions to the pedagogical processes of Protestant education in Montreal. In at least one school, Jews were numerically dominant, a fact that in itself challenged the Protestant nature of the Protestant school. For many, Hebrew had no place in a Protestant elementary school curriculum. Moreover, the continuing subsidization of Hebrew-language instruction within the denominationally Protestant school system was under close questioning on the matter of its very legality. Finally, the Protestant board continued to insist that it was paying more to educate Jewish students than it was receiving from Jewish taxes.

The Protestant Board soon took the position that it would no longer grant scholarships to Jewish students.[44] The policy was implemented at the beginning of the 1901 school year. The Jewish community, or at least one set of voices that represented the views of those who had long been concerned with the issue, expressed their outrage, in terms that had been, and would remain, central to much of the fundamental discourse of the Jewish communities of Montreal in educational matters. They demanded justice and equality. They sought Jewish school rights. On 5 July 1901, the *Canadian Jewish Times* published an impassioned plea for the Protestant board to rescind its position and to treat Jewish students as equal to their Protestant classmates.[45] Founded in 1897 by Samuel W. Jacobs and Lyon Cohen, the *Jewish Times* was the first English-language Jewish newspaper in Canada. It played a key role in publicizing the position of an important section of the Jewish community on all matters, but it was specifically vocal on the School Question: "Besides they cannot violate the fundamental principle of the British constitution which regards all subjects as equal before the law, no matter what may be their race, color, creed, or nationality. We take our stand on this principle and will not allow the matter to rest till justice is done to our Jewish pupils."[46]

As Jews had done since their earliest days in the colony of Quebec, they asserted their right to be treated as equals. They used the rhetoric of justice and equality within a legal framework, because this was the basis for their understanding of their rightful place in the polities of Quebec and Canada. They constituted and asserted themselves as citizens by invoking basic principles of equality found in the British constitution. They used the language of the time, which reflected the view of Canadian identity as part of the empire abroad among the English-Canadian elite and was therefore also likely to resonate among members of that elite who were in charge of the Protestant education system in the city. In addition, underlying all this invocation of British constitutional principles of equality before the law, in this particular context, was a belief that Protestant schools were, for Jewish parents, the embodiment of those very values and the institutional framework in which their children were to gain access to being fully and truly equal.

The Protestant School Board did not see it that way. In an interview with the *Daily Witness*, E.W. Arthy again highlighted the litany of Protestant grievances: Jews still retained the legal option to pay into either the Protestant or the Roman Catholic panel: Jews could and did send their children to Protestant schools, where they were taught the same curriculum and paid the same fees; there was a significant shortfall in Jewish taxes to support the education of their children; and the Protestant board continued to pay $800 a year to De Sola and to support the Baron de Hirsch School. Scholarships were meant to support poor Protestant students. They were necessary to ensure equality for poor Protestants within a school system that was at its core Protestant. Neither Jews nor Roman Catholics could make a claim on these monies. Arthy and the Protestant Board had come a long way since the time when the Spanish and Portuguese and the English, German, and Polish synagogues had been given a veto by the Protestant board over the nomination of Jewish scholarship holders.

For the Protestant School Board, their schools were Protestant schools, and specific separate identities could not be tolerated if they were to remain as such: "As soon as the Jews are willing to come in as Protestants, and give and take exactly what the Protestants do they will be treated in exactly the same way. But so long as certain Jews continue to make bargains with the board for the teaching of Hebrew in elementary classes and threaten to withdraw their children if it is not taught, they cannot expect more than they are getting."[47]

Arthy combined several arguments, which again came down to a basic Protestant existential understanding of the essential nature of a Protestant school system, aggravated perhaps by what the Protestant

School Board experienced or understood to be a form of pushy Jewish parochialism, by members of the Spanish and Portuguese synagogue. The idea of a specific Jewish presence in the Protestant system called into question this core character of their schools as Protestant. He argued that the issue of equality was really one for the Jews to consider, since their ongoing insistence on special treatment through the teaching of Hebrew set them apart, and indicated in fact that they did not want real equality. In part, of course, Arthy's argument was with the Quebec legislation that continued to allow Jews, as a matter of law, to opt into the tax panel of their choice. But it was also intriguingly aimed at Jews who would seek to use their legal right as a bargaining tool in negotiating with the Protestant board. "Certain Jews continue to make bargains," perhaps because that was, for the Protestant Arthy and some of his fellow school officials, what Jews did anyway. They made self-interested bargains and used legal remedies as a bargaining chip. After all, Shylock was a Jew. The underlying anti-Semitic tropes that frequently underpinned key parts of the Jewish School Question became more evident as the debates continued.[48]

Whatever Arthy's personal views, however, it was clear from his interview in response to the *Jewish Times* article that the real problem, from the Protestant board's perspective, was the obdurate and ongoing insistence by the wealthy members of Shearith Israel not just on ensuring that Hebrew was taught to their children, but that it was done in the Protestant schools, and that it was taught by their rabbi, who continued to receive an inordinately high salary for doing so. The majority of Jewish students in the Montreal Protestant school system were being made to pay the price for what was seen, both by some on the Protestant Board and not a few Jews within the Baron de Hirsch circle who had lengthy experience with what they saw as Spanish and Portuguese special pleadings, as the position of a privileged few. The children of the members of the Spanish and Portuguese congregation, still the wealthiest owners of real estate, would have no need for scholarships to pursue their studies beyond the elementary schools. The children of immigrant Jews who lived in rented accommodation, and whose parents were in low-income jobs, needed this support to continue their education. Inequality was not just a question for the Protestant board. The class divide between and among members of the Jewish communities of Montreal was also significant.

For the editors of the *Jewish Times*, the injustice of punishing the many for the sins of the few, perceived or actual, still smacked of injustice.[49]

Again, the paper pointed out that teaching Hebrew and paying a salary to the rabbi of the Spanish and Portuguese synagogue was not accepted by "nine-tenths of the Jewish supporters of the Protestant schools."[50] Moreover, the money spent on the Baron de Hirsch School was in fact a benefit to the Protestant board and its schools because, if the immigrant students were not taught there, they would have to be accommodated elsewhere in the Protestant system. The Protestant commissioners were unmoved. The next step was litigation.

In November 1901, Samuel W. Jacobs, representing Paul Pinsler, acting as legal guardian for his son Jacob, sought a writ of mandamus to compel the Protestant board to issue a commissioner's scholarship to Jacob based on his results in the board's examinations. In fact, this was a test case, meant to establish the parameter, under existing school law in the city, of the rights of Jewish students.[51] The positions of the two sides, if there were only two sides, were fixed and certain and mutually exclusive. Cohen and Jacob's paper again highlighted the central constitutional and constitutive importance of the case, whatever amicability existed in fact in the relations between the parties: "The educational status of the Jew who is a British subject in this country is precisely the same as that of any other subject of His Majesty King Edward. In attempting to fix the status of the Jew otherwise the Protestant Board of School Commissioners assumes a power which none but the yarliament [*sic*] of Great Britain can exercise."[52]

As the co-founder of the newspaper, Jacobs had the advantage of presenting his argument in the press before it reached the courts. But more significant perhaps for a fully contextualized understanding of the Jewish School Question was the continuation of the legal argument founded in ideas and ideals of citizenship, belonging, and equality. For Jacobs and the Jewish community behind Jacob Pinsler's claim to his commissioners' scholarship, this case went directly to the nature and real content of the right to equality won by Quebec Jews in 1832 and maintained through ongoing political and legal struggle since then. The rhetoric of the *Jewish Times* also reflected anglophone Canada's understanding of itself as part of the empire, and of the empire as both the seat of ultimate power and the source of liberty. From this perspective, Jacob Pinsler was the ideal plaintiff. He was Jewish, but he was Canadian-born. His father and mother had come to Canada in 1885, and Jacob, their eldest child, had been born in the province of Quebec.[53] His father, Paul, was a British subject, and Jacob was a Canadian-born British subject, vested with all the equality rights that followed this status.

Pinsler's supporters highlighted their criticism of the Protestant position according to which a private bargain about the teaching of Hebrew, insisted upon by a wealthy minority of Montreal's Jews, was being used as a bludgeon against innocent Jews who had nothing to do with the contract and who saw no merit in the institutionalization of Hebrew instruction in the Protestant school system.[54]

The Jewish community representatives involved in the case had turned to the courts because they had faith that the courts would render British justice and recognize their right to equality. They did not reckon with section 93 as the constitutional embodiment of a distinctly unequal set of political, social, and legal arrangements in the educational field. More importantly at this stage, perhaps, the reliance on the courts evidenced the end of a long period in which the issues surrounding the rights of Jewish children had been dealt with, if not settled, by a series of public and private arrangements between the communities and the duly constituted educational and political authorities. There had been a thirty-year period in which the synagogues, the Protestant and Roman Catholic boards, the Baron de Hirsch Institute, and the provincial government had negotiated, pressured, cajoled, agreed, withdrawn from contracts, paid taxes under their legal rights, etc., all in what became, with each set of bargains and discussions, increasingly problematic in the strict legal sense. Yet there had been a modus vivendi without recourse to litigation. As Risk and Vipond argued, the idea of litigating over such issues was perhaps simply not Canadian.[55] The turn of the new century witnessed the blooming of a different attitude, as many Montreal Jews now turned to the courts to concretize their right to equality.[56]

But while litigation did now come to play a central role in the Jewish School Question, and law would provide an increasingly certain and concrete frame within which constitutive social and political dialogue would have to take place, recourse to judicial institutions did not bring the pre-existing dynamics of dialogue to a complete halt. The friendly litigation continued to wind its way through the delays of the legal process, and the Protestant School Board still dealt with representatives of the Jewish communities on matters of mutual interest. The Protestant board approved a one-time grant of $22 to the Baron de Hirsch Night School, just before considering the report from its lawyer about the status of the *Pinsler* litigation.[57] The Baron de Hirsch School Committee reported at the end of 1902 that they had continued to receive the $2,000 annual subsidy from the Protestant board, as well as an allowance of $28.58 for books for the night school, pending the outcome of *Pinsler*.[58]

More significantly, the Protestant board had received firm and unambiguous advice from their lawyers that they could not lawfully support the teaching of Hebrew with tax monies administered by them for Protestant education. Hebrew was a Jewish subject, and the school system was Protestant. Any subsidy paid to support a Jewish subject within the denominational school structures of the province was a fundamental attack on the Protestant nature of education protected and enshrined in section 93. The board resolved to terminate their arrangement with Meldola De Sola, as they were permitted to do, under the terms of the contract, by giving notice in writing before June.[59]

The Spanish and Portuguese congregation and leadership did not sit idly by. While the contract with De Sola came to an end, the congregation approached the Protestant Committee of the Council of Public Instruction about the possibility of including Hebrew as an optional subject in the curriculum of the Protestant schools in Montreal, and throughout the province. The Protestant committee received the application and after original support for the idea from the bishop of Quebec, it decided to delay its decision pending consultation with the Spanish and Portuguese congregation, other synagogues, and the Protestant Board in Montreal.[60]

The Baron de Hirsch Institute rejected the proposal from the Spanish and Portuguese synagogue. David Ansell, the author of the institute's reply, argued that if the synagogue wished to teach Hebrew to its children, it should do as other Jewish bodies in the city did and arrange for instruction in the synagogue itself.[61] The Baron de Hirsch Institute, he added, taught Hebrew in its school, but that teaching was funded privately and was not supported by the subsidy received from the Protestant board. Ansell ended his response to the Protestant committee in Quebec both with a plea for continuing support, but also with an unequivocal indication of the educational philosophy behind his school. He wanted a place to teach immigrant children "to enable them to earn a livelihood for themselves and become useful members of society and true and loyal Canadian subjects."[62]

Given its long-held belief that such instruction was problematic and contrary to the Protestant nature of its schools, combined with a legal opinion that such instruction was in any event illegal, and buttressed by the backing of the Baron de Hirsch Institute, the Protestant School Board resolved to reject any change to its curriculum along the lines suggested by the Spanish and Portuguese congregation.[63] It was finished with Hebrew. Faced with the opposition of the Protestant School Board, and the clear objections of the Baron de Hirsch Institute, seen to represent the dominant opinion on the matter among Montreal's Jewish communities, the Protestant Committee of the Council of Public Instruction rejected the Spanish and Portuguese request and adopted a motion stating, "Given that it has been proven before this Committee that those who are requesting the teaching of Hebrew in the Protestant Schools of this province are a small minority of the Jews of Montreal, and that the great majority are clearly opposed to the proposed teaching, as a result, this request cannot be agreed."[64]

The Spanish and Portuguese congregation and its rabbi had been isolated from the majority of Jews in Montreal. While they battled over the broad constitutional and legal principles that governed the place of Jewish students within the common schools of Montreal, the Baron de Hirsch Institute School, as a representative body of Montreal's Jewish communities, had aligned itself with the Protestant board on the Hebrew instruction issue. While their reasons for arriving at the conclusion that Hebrew instruction had no place in the Protestant school system may have been different, the two bodies had once more come together and reached an accord, again in the pending shadow of the law and the looming decision in the *Pinsler* case.[65]

The Court Speaks: Law, Politics, and the Jewish School Question, 1903

On Valentine's Day, 1903, Justice Davidson of the Quebec Superior Court delivered his judgment in the case of *Pinsler ès qual. v The Protestant Board of School Commissioners*.[66] The message was not a sweet one for the Jewish communities of Montreal.

The judge reviewed the regulations of the Protestant board, formally in effect since 1892, which had declared that its schools were open to all Protestants and to non-Protestants who were owners of city real estate and to "all Jews, except to those belonging to the Spanish and Portuguese Synagogue."[67] In 1897, all references to the rights of Jews to attend Protestant schools had been removed from the regulations, as Protestant policy on the question evolved. In 1900, a further amendment limited admission to all children of Protestant parents and the children of all those who paid into the Protestant panel taxes owed on their real estate.[68] Jews and Roman Catholic students were apparently admitted, "where there is room." Davidson confessed that the Protestant regulation applying to non-Protestants and to the children of non-taxpayers was "absolutely incapable of clear interpretation."[69] However, he was able to glean from the hermeneutic morass that Jacob Pinsler had the right to enter the Protestant school system up until 1897, but that from 1900 "those in his position were only admissible by the grace of the commissioners."[70] Likewise he had been eligible for a scholarship in the school year 1899–1900, but not in the following year.

The judge then proceeded to an exhaustive examination of the history of school legislation in the province of Quebec and of the special provisions relating to school taxes in the city of Montreal.[71] He concluded, unsurprisingly, that the system of education in the province and the city had, at all relevant times, been divided along denominational lines between Roman Catholics and Protestants. He found that neither Protestants nor Roman Catholics in Montreal were free to shift their taxes to the other panel. That right extended only to Jews by the clear language of the legislation. But since the days of the split with the Spanish and Portuguese congregation, those taxes had not been sufficient to cover the actual cost to the Protestant board of educating the majority of Jewish students. The judge accepted without further inquiry the figures provided by the Protestant board that by 1900, 1,153 Jewish students were being educated in the Protestant system, while the board received only $11,016.24 in Jewish taxes and school fees. This left the board with a deficit of $23,435.40 in relation to Jewish pupils. "The action of the board in 1900 in amending their rules as to make the reception of all children save those of resident Protestants, or of actual school tax contributors, a matter of grace, instead of right, resulted from acute want of accommodation and the distressing load upon revenue."[72]

Davidson emphasized that he was also "glad to be able to say that the controversy is wholly free of race or religious prejudice."[73] Except of course, it could never be free of the "race or religious prejudice" that had been instituted as constitutional principle in section 93 of the BNA Act and then reaffirmed in the provisions of the statutory regime governing common schools in Montreal, and finally in the regulations of the Protestant School Board of Montreal. The exclusion embodied in the most recent version of the regulations of the Protestant board did not target Jews. It excluded Jews who did not own real estate, or those few who did not pay into the Protestant tax panel but who had opted for the Roman Catholic system. Of these, the latter category existed in theory but not really in practice at the time.[74] The real target of exclusion was those Jews who did not pay school tax because they did not own real estate. In other words, the practical effect of the regulation was to exclude, as a matter of law, the children of the vast majority of Jews in the city, who, like Paul Pinsler, British subject, father of Canadian-born children, lived in rented accommodation.

For Davidson the ideal of equality embodied in the 1832 statute, which emancipated Quebec's Jews, was not of any legal moment in the case. The constitutional and constitutive arrangements of the denominational, common school system in the province of Quebec and in the city of Montreal gave rights to Protestants and to Roman Catholics, in "their structure and spirit."[75] It was, according to the judge, "possibly" the case that a Jewish taxpayer who opted for the Protestant or Roman Catholic panel, as he was entitled to do, gained the right to access to that school system, but it was clear that a non-taxpaying Jew did not have any right "to have his children admitted to the public schools."[76] Paul Pinsler had no rights because he did not pay school tax; Jacob Pinsler could attend the Protestant school system only "by grace and subject to whatever conditions the commissioners choose to impose, inclusive of non-eligibility for the scholarship in question."[77] Nowhere in Quebec law did Jews have a right to attend public schools or to receive an education.

The legal answer was clear. The Montreal public school system was open as of right to Protestants and to Roman Catholics. It might be open to the children of a Jewish taxpayer who had selected to pay into Panel 1 or 2 in Montreal, but Davidson did not give a clear or final view on that question. What was certain was that access to public education for the majority of Jewish children in Montreal was subject to the conditional grace of the Christian school officials. The Jews of the city had turned to the courts because they believed in the principles of British justice. As a British subject, Paul Pinsler believed that his son was equal before the law. The plaintiffs in this friendly lawsuit had sought out the redemptive power of the British constitution and its basic norms of equality in which they had invested so much, and which they saw as the informing ethos of public education. They had not counted on the juridically powerful and insular nature of the 1867 Canadian federal compact as embodied in section 93, the entire history of Quebec schooling legislation since the 1840s, and the regulatory power of the Protestant School Board of Montreal.

But Justice Davidson did not close the door to future and further dialogue in the matter. He recognized both the demographic reality and the fundamental issues of fairness that were abroad in the case and had become even more acute as a result of his decision. More than 10,000 Jews, and the continuing arrival of other immigrant property-owning groups who were neither Roman Catholic nor Protestant "create problems which did not exist when the foundations of our present educational system were laid. Their solution by the legislature, if this judgment correctly interprets the law, has become of pressing importance."[78]

The real problem was whether a solution to the Jewish School Question in Montreal could be found now that one side in the debate had law on their side, and the other only appeals to justice.

"Honorary Protestants": The Legislative Solution to the Jewish School Question

Reaction was swift and reasonably unanimous. Most accepted that Justice Davidson's decision was legally correct, but they also recognized the difficult practical consequences of that decision. The *Montreal Gazette* published the judgment in full and added editorially, "This is not a proper situation. There should be some public school, and it should be efficient, to which any child, Jew or Gentile, could gain admittance as a matter of course and without any one having the right to question him or her. The Legislature may have to give the matter its consideration."[79]

The Jewish communities organized quickly in response to the judgment. Despite claims by Sam Jacobs that the legislature was unlikely to act until a final judicial determination of the matter by the Privy Council, the vast majority of the Jewish representatives sought a quicker remedy to the School Question than a lengthy and expensive appeal to London.[80] The Board of Governors of the Baron de Hirsch Institute met on 18 February in order to ensure "taking concerted action to maintain and secure the rights of all Jewish parents to have their children at the public schools, on an equal basis with those of other creeds."[81] Following that meeting, a Jewish Educational Rights group was founded. For the first time in the history of the Jewish School Question, the principal bodies of Montreal Jewry had come together. The group included the Spanish and Portuguese congregation, represented inter alia by Clarence De Sola,[82] the brother of Meldola and Gershom, with the idea of presenting a united political front on the Jewish School Question.[83]

While there was broad agreement that the effect of the *Pinsler* judgment had to be overturned, and that a political solution was the best method, there was a wide range of views and proposed solutions on the table and in the minds of the Jewish community over issues of schooling and especially taxation. Indeed, there were also early murmurings about Jewish representation on the Protestant board. As they tried to grapple with the difficulties that the litigation solution had imposed on them and on their children, the Jewish communities of Montreal opted for a pragmatic approach and put aside deeper issues. A committee was appointed to meet with the Protestant board, and a delegation of twenty was named to travel to Quebec City to speak with the government. Among those chosen to go to the capital were individuals representing a broad section of the Jewish communities of Montreal and having a long history of involvement in educational matters. They included David Ansell, Maxwell Goldstein, Sam Jacobs, Lyon Cohen, Clarence and Meldola De Sola, and Rabbi Hirsch Cohen.[84]

"For the first time the entire Jewish community was represented" at a meeting with the Protestant Board.[85] They sought to bring the entire Jewish educational question within the remit of the Protestant school system and offered their support for any attempt to increase school taxes to give the Protestant board a better revenue stream. They also agreed to renounce their statutory right to opt into either Panel 1 or 2 and instead promised to put all Jewish taxes permanently within the Protestant panel. The majority sought to fix themselves to the Protestant system as a united Jewish community.[86] Goldstein underlined that the Jews of Montreal did not wish to change the religious character and constitution of the Protestant school system. He insisted on this in his presentation to the Protestant board. The Jews of Montreal asked only to be treated as Protestants for school purposes and to benefit from a conscience clause excusing their children from Christian educational lessons.[87] They made no further claims and would not seek to challenge or question the foundationally Protestant nature of the school system.

After the Jewish representatives withdrew, the board resolved that the Davidson judgment had created a situation with a "glaring anomaly and injustice which deprives so large and respectable an element of our population as the Hebrew people of their rights as regards elementary education should be removed."[88] They declared their "readiness to co-operate with our Jewish fellow citizens in seeking remedial legislation as will remove this inequality."[89] The Jewish communities had united behind a single vision of the rights of their children as best placed in the Protestant common schools. They had declared their intention to renounce their legislative right to choose the panel into which their taxes were paid and to tie themselves permanently to the Protestant panel. They did not and would not challenge the existing denominational character and governance structure of the schools as Protestant. Instead they asked only for the renewal of the historical but sporadic practice of a conscience clause for Jewish students on questions of religious instruction in the schools. The *Pinsler* litigation, which had ended to their detriment, had served as a positive impetus to seek continued dialogue with the Protestant board and consequent legislative reform to enshrine the rights of Jewish children to a public education. Any idea of Jewish autonomy within the school system, but for the limited idea of the conscience clause, had been foreclosed by the *Pinsler* judgment and the consensus behind the political solution within the Jewish communities. The narrow and potentially insular constitutive moment of *Pinsler* had, with the Christian grace of the Protestant board, which recognized the injustice of the result, been reshaped by dialogue into what appeared to be a move towards a permanent legislative enshrining of the right of Jewish children to attend Protestant common schools.

But there was a but. The Protestant board made it clear that the tax and financial issues that had been the foundation of the crisis at the moments leading up to *Pinsler* still had to be dealt with. They recognized that the pro rata system that had been proposed previously by Baron de Hirsch representatives (and was favoured by the Roman Catholic educational authorities in relation to all neutral panel monies), as a matter of logic and equity, had an obvious appeal. However, such a solution would not help the financial situation of the Protestant system. Indeed with the rate of immigration into the port city of Montreal only likely to increase, the financial burden in educating poor immigrants would only grow and become more acute for the board. In the absence of a single common school system, the board concluded, it would assist the Jews in their appeal to government, but would only agree to a solution that dealt adequately with their financial situation more permanently and thereby ensured the continuing protection of Protestant school rights in Montreal.[90] Any real solution to the Jewish School Question would require special consideration from the provincial government and would necessarily involve the protection of the rights of the Protestant school system as a Protestant system, a sine qua non of the board's agreement to cooperate with the Jewish attempts to seek legislative redress.[91] The Jewish School Question could be understood only in the broader contexts of the bi-denominational constitutional character of Montreal's common schools and the practical financial issues surrounding the education of increasing numbers of Jewish immigrant children within the Protestant school system.

The combined forces of the united Jewish communities of Montreal and the Protestant School Board of Montreal had no difficulty in convincing the government of the necessity of legislative change.[92] However, the terms of that legislation again had to be the product of negotiation and dialogue, and those discussions always had to maintain the position of the Protestant system and the rights and powers of the board, ultimately protected by section 93. The draft bill passed by the lower House, the Assembly, and about to be presented to the upper chamber, the Legislative Council, contained a specific conscience clause provision. The board originally objected, not to the actual content of the clause, but to its inclusion in the legislation. As far as they were concerned, such a matter was one at the heart of local school governance and needed to be part of the board's own regulations.[93] The constitutional guarantee of Protestant educational autonomy, in their view, demanded that such issues remain in principle within the control and remit of local Protestant school authorities. The Protestant board finally agreed to include not just a conscience clause, but to allow Jewish students to be absent from school on obligatory religious holidays, to not schedule tests or examinations on religious holidays, and to create a system in which official representatives of the Jews would provide the board with a list of such holidays.[94]

On 25 April, assent was given to An Act to amend the law concerning education, with respect to persons professing the Jewish religion.[95] The statute applied throughout the province. Jewish taxes would be paid into Protestant school systems, except where there were no Protestant schools in existence (section 2). The special option for Jews to select the school tax panel was abolished (section 3). Most significantly, notwithstanding any other legislative provision, the Act set out that "persons professing the Jewish religion shall, for school purposes, be treated in the same manner as Protestants, and, for the said purposes, shall be subject to the same obligations and shall enjoy the same rights and privileges as the latter" (section 1).

And

> After the coming into force of this act, the children of persons professing the Jewish religion shall have the same right to be educated in the public schools of the province as Protestant children, and shall be treated in the same manner as Protestants for all school purposes.

No pupil of the Jewish religion can, however, be compelled to read or study any religious or devotional books or to take part in any religious exercises or devotions, to which the father or in his default the mother or tutor or person having the care or maintenance of each pupil shall object. (section 6)

Jewish parents were to be Protestants "for school purposes," as were their children. The 1903 Act transformed Jews into ersatz "honorary Protestants" within the educational system in the province. It did not, as had the 1832 statute, give them equality with other subjects. Instead, it made them into something they were not – Protestants of a limited type – in a move made necessary by the bi-denominational constitutional and legislative framework governing education in Quebec, and in Montreal more specifically. But this "rather inelegant compromise," as Michael Brown put it, did mean that as far as the common schools in the province were concerned, Jews now enjoyed the same rights as Protestant subjects/citizens, whether they paid school taxes or not.[96] Indeed, they enjoyed a further legislative right of exception on questions of religious instruction within the common Protestant schools of Montreal, as the conscience clause remained in the statute itself. The constitutive struggle over the Jewish School Question seemed to have come to an end. While the legislative fiction of making Jews into "honorary Protestants" had been necessary to arrive at the solution, it was a solution agreed to by the representatives of Montreal's Jewish communities and by the Protestant board. The bond of the Jews of Montreal with the Protestant School Board now was cemented not just within a firm legal, legislative framework, but through a solid working relationship and accommodation and solidarity over the financial questions that had always underscored the overarching frame of battles over Jewish educational rights.[97]

But of course, in the messy world of compromise, dialogue, and negotiation, informed by a complex social, historical, and political context relating to the taxonomies of religious faith, fractures would begin to appear as the parties sought to give concrete and contextualized meaning to the terms and conditions of the arrangement and to fit those narrative understandings within their own institutional, political, and social normative orders. In October the question of the practical implementation of the regulations concerning absences for Jewish holidays arose and gave early notice of fissures in the relationship. Arthy requested guidance from the board on how the absences of Jewish students on such holidays were to be classified and memorialized bureaucratically within the broader system of recording attendance in Protestant schools. The board decided that such absences would be entered as an absence like any other, and that such absences would enter into the overall calculation of a student's attendance record, and that such absences would therefore have to be communicated to the parents in the monthly report from the school.[98] Jewish students numbered 617, 332, and 156 in three schools alone. By not recording these absences of such significant numbers of pupils on Jewish religious holidays, schools would either be creating a false record of the number of students in attendance on any given day, or by recording them, their overall attendance figures would be dramatically affected. The problem, it would seem, was bureaucratic and practical and had nothing to do with anything other than the proper maintenance of records for running an efficient Protestant school system.

But the real problem here was yet another manifestation of the Jewish School Question and the effect of the demographic realities of Jewish population density in Montreal.[99] Dufferin School had an overwhelming number of Jewish students. In 1903, the school population was 800 pupils, of whom 600 were Jews. For thirteen days a year, the number of Jewish holidays recognized by the board, "the work of the whole school practically stopped."[100] One solution was raised in the discussions once more: building separate schools for Jews and Christians. Six months after the legislative embodiment of school equality for Jews as "honorary Protestants," some Protestant educational authorities saw Montreal's Jews as again creating more bother than they were worth. The conflict between the two legal rights for Jews upset the way in which this particular school, and the two others like it with large numbers of Jewish students, managed the daily running of a normal curriculum when up to three-quarters of the pupils were absent. Crucially for the Protestant School Board, the situation at Dufferin School challenged the Protestant character of the schools themselves. Protestant pupils were in the minority in schools that were formally, legally, and administratively, as well as existentially Protestant. Separation and segregation were seriously considered as options within the Christian grace of the Protestant School Board. When it was pointed out during discussions that such a solution was probably illegal under the very clear terms of the 1903 statute, another return to the past was suggested. Perhaps a tacit agreement could be reached with the Jewish community for such separate schools.

At the same time, the Protestant board was seeking changes to the school tax situation by increasing the rates due on assessments of real property.[101] Part of their justification for doing so was the ongoing deficit in relation to Jewish students and Jewish taxpayers. They presented their arguments in a public circular on the tax question. The allegation that Jews were responsible for the continuing financially precarious state of the Protestant school system in Montreal offended many in the Jewish community and led to a belief among some at least that the Protestant board were acting in bad faith after their agreement to the terms of the recent legislative change.[102] Not only was the view that continued to single out Jews as a separate category of taxpayer and student in the school system, when the statute granted them full equality as Protestants, contrary to the letter and spirit of the law, it also evidenced a particularly narrow-minded vision of education in the common schools. For many in the Jewish community, the benefits to Jewish students of an education in the Protestant system went beyond financial issues: "The education now given them will result in securing for the future a highly intelligent, active and invaluable class of public spirited citizens. This alone will be a splendid return for the money spent in their education."[103]

Again, competing narrative understandings of the place and function of education in the essential self-definition of the different groups at the heart of the Jewish School Question came to the fore in the practical context of the life worlds and self-definitions of the groups, all under the frame of apparently narrow considerations of the taxation system for school financing. The law and its limitations, permissions, prohibitions, and textual embodiment of formal equality were not necessarily capable on their own or in isolation of determining the content of those narratives, nor would they inevitably fix those self-constituting meanings for either group, Jewish or Protestant. Law would not, because it could not, stand in the way of more dialogue and discussion. The practical constitution of communities in the broad political and cultural sense, was, in the many sub-contexts of the Jewish School Question in Montreal, a living process and an often messy one at that. Nothing here was carved in stone. The Protestant board focused on an ongoing financial crisis and the disruption caused to school governance by the presence of significant and often overwhelming numbers of Jewish students in some schools. More fundamentally, some other members rejected the 1903 solution and insisted in proclaiming their belief that the very presence of Jewish students was inimical to the essential Protestant nature of their schools. On the other side, the Jewish community, speaking at the time with one voice, at least publicly, was still articulating a vision of education and equality, now embodied in statute, which had been consistently part of the narrative of the Jewish elite in Montreal associated with the Young Men's Hebrew Benevolent Society. The two groups were constructing essentially parallel, not intersecting, narratives of the social, religious, and political identities that underpinned their positions. The world of law and the processes of constituting political and legal identities, for Jews and Protestants alike, would grow ever more complex.

Perhaps other legal constitutive ironies flowing from the *Pinsler* case, its apparent resolution, and the legislative construction of Jews as "honorary Protestants" should be mentioned to place both the case and its sequelae in a fuller context. The judgment indicates in obiter that Jewish taxpayers would have the right to send their children to Protestant schools. The first level of juridical irony exposed by *Pinsler* is that nowhere in the school legislation operating in Quebec on a province-wide basis, or in Montreal in particular, was there a specific right granted to Jewish children to attend school. The entire structure of the legislative scheme was couched in terms of school taxes and the rights of dissentients and majorities to form their own schools, and in Montreal, for the creation of both Protestant and Roman Catholic educational systems. Taxpayers were granted rights in terms of electing commissioners or trustees in the province's schools (but not in Montreal) and were legally obliged to pay taxes into the common or dissentient school systems, or again in Montreal, into the Protestant or Roman Catholic panel. Provisions of the 1849 and 1861 statutes had embodied the rights of the children of taxpayers, or indigents in some cases, to attend school from the ages of five to sixteen, but always and only within the informing context of common and dissentient schools, the religious majority and minority.[104]

School boards had rights and duties, and majority and dissentient taxpayers had rights and duties, including the right to send their children to the school system into which they paid their taxes. As with many other elements of Quebec's education system and the Jewish School Question, there was an unarticulated and generally accepted presumption about the rights of Jewish taxpayers, albeit without real or clear delimitation of that right, its source and extent, that appears to have operated throughout, as a directing social norm, but in the absence of a specific and clear legal rule. Indeed, Justice Davidson's hesitation about any declaration that the children of Jewish taxpayers had the right to attend school can be traced to this awkward silence in school law in the province.

The second juridical irony that needs to be addressed briefly is the flip side of the right to education. Throughout most of the period of the events surrounding the Jewish School Question, Quebec had no compulsory education law. This meant that not only did children not have a clearly established right to an education, their parents and guardians had no duty, in the legal sense at least, to send their children to school. While this is not the place to rehearse the entire social and political history of debates over compulsory schooling in Quebec, some points should be emphasized briefly. First, it is important to note that arguments about the benefits to be derived from compulsory education were not absent from the province's political discourse. Proponents highlighted the benefits of education, literacy, the creation of an educated workforce both as a more sophisticated and engaged polity, and, for the province's economic development, the battle against delinquency, all of which formed parts of similar debates in other jurisdictions.[105]

Supporters of compulsory education were found not just among Protestant officials, although they were consistent and vocal advocates of school attendance laws.[106] *Rouge* elements among the Roman Catholic francophone population also supported legislative intervention in order to promote the welfare and progress of the French-Canadian working class, whom they portrayed as being held back by clerical control over education and by a cultural distrust of education beyond the primary level.[107] A burgeoning francophone industrial and commercial bourgeoisie joined in the campaign for greater state involvement in education and in favour of compulsory education.[108] However, opposition to compulsory education legislation was deeply embedded among the Roman Catholic episcopate and formed a key element of their ideological and political battle with government attempts to interfere with church-based education

For the church hierarchy, schooling and decisions about attendance were within the ken of the *bon père de famille* in consultation with the local priest. Education was, and had always been, in this ideological and theological position, a matter for *la famille et l'église*, but most definitely not for *l'état*.[109] Compulsory schooling laws were understood in this political frame as an attempt by the state and secular officials to create a slippery slope of interference in the religious life of family and church, and as such, they had to be resisted ferociously.[110] As a result of unrelenting church opposition, successive governments in the province under the Liberal Party simply decided that discretion was the better part of valour. If the government had to do battle or engage with the church on matters of broad social importance, it left education to one side and concentrated on those other matters.[111]

As a result of Roman Catholic episcopal opposition, and decisions by successive provincial governments to ignore difficult and controversial educational issues, Quebec became the last province to adopt compulsory school attendance laws, in 1943. Marshall argues, convincingly I believe, that such legislation became possible at this time because of the political position and new-found power of the labour unions. Social welfare reform, including mandatory educational norms, had long been a demand from Quebec unions, and in a war economy, their political clout had finally begun to match that of the church.[112] In this move to social welfare reform more broadly and in relation to school attendance legislation, Protestant education officials joined the unions, and once more liberal elements of the francophone bourgeoisie also supported the change.[113] This combined with the election of the more reform-minded, if not entirely *rouge*, Godbout Liberal government, which already had significant support from French-Canadian industrialists. Moreover, Roman Catholic school officials in Montreal had undertaken a greater social welfare role during the Depression, as poverty struck the French-Canadian community. One result of that expanded role had been a gradual realization of the importance of school attendance for the general welfare of the children.[114] The gradual lessening of clerical influence had begun, even among Roman Catholic school officials, and with it the Compulsory School Attendance Act became a reality.[115]

As in many other manifestations of the Jewish School Question, the issue of a right to education was in legal flux, but its existence had formed the core and crux of Jewish assertions, Protestant acquiescence, and provincial legislative adoption of the legislative solution to *Pinsler*. Rights, duties, obligations existed as part of the constitutive and constituted reality of Jews, Protestants, and Roman Catholics in the Montreal educational system, but they existed in the shadow of formal constitutional legality as embodied in section 93. Each group narrated a constitutional existence in what Tully articulates as "the negotiation and mediation of claims to recognition in a dialogue governed by the conventions of mutual recognition, continuity and consent."[116]

6

Promises, Promises: "Honorary Protestants" in Protestant Schools

The Realities of Life as "Honorary Protestants" in Montreal

Despite the apparent truce between the Montreal Jewish communities and the Protestant School Board following the 1903 statute, trouble continued to bubble to the surface as the ground rules for the new relationship were being worked out. Jews and Protestants had not only to reach practical agreements on a number of issues, but for each, the consensual arrangements also took place within a new informing legal framework, and more importantly as part of the ongoing narrative construction of their own self-understandings. The post-*Pinsler* world of education in Montreal was more than one of concrete legal obligations and rights. It was once again a time and place where they sought to give life to the collective narratives of Jewish and Protestant identities and public schooling. The promise of concrete educational equality that accompanied the 1903 Act constituting the Jews of Montreal as Protestants for school purposes had to be worked through in relation to the ongoing issues: Jewish holidays and school absences; the role of the Baron de Hirsch School within the framework of educating Jewish immigrants on their way into the Protestant common school system; debates over the continuing segregation of Jewish students; the emerging problem of Jewish teachers; and finally, growing calls for full equality for Jews as Protestants for educational purposes, that is, for Jewish representation on the Protestant School Board.

This chapter sets out the ways in which each party to the new world of Jews as "honorary Protestants" sought to concretize the meaning of that ideal within the practical realities of Protestant education. The narrative as it unfolds demonstrates that ideas of accommodation, of maintaining some form of Jewish identity within the Protestant schools, while safeguarding the core Protestant nature of Protestant schools, soon brought the representatives of the two communities into conflict. While a general ecumenism in Protestant theological and social practice within the educational system recognized without difficulty the principle that Jewish students should be permitted to absent themselves from religious instruction crafted to instil Protestant values in Christian students, that principled sympathy was stretched to its limit, and often to the breaking point, in relation to Jewish claims that students could and indeed were obliged to absent themselves from schools on a number of holy days. The regulations of the Protestant School Board recognized Good Friday and Easter Monday, as well as ten days at Christmas as holidays. In addition, they permitted absences on "obligatory religious holidays."[1] The extent of this right afforded to observant Jewish students would be determined by annual negotiations between Jewish representatives and the commissioners. The discussion in the following sections highlights the frictions that arose when the idea of Jews as "honorary Protestants" crashed up against assertions that Jews still had rights as Jews to religious observance. This sense of friction and often even resentment about Jewish students receiving special treatment again called into question the Protestant character of Protestant schools with large Jewish student numbers. Tensions would grow more acute as the Baron de Hirsch School closed and the Protestant Board of School Commissioners took over responsibility for educating the entire Jewish student population in Montreal.

Finally, as the chapter unfolds, another narrative about Jewish rights begins to emerge. Jewish parents now paid their taxes into the Protestant panel. Their children attended Protestant schools. Quebec law had granted them equality with Protestants for school purposes, or at least that was an understanding of their status. For them, ideals of fairness, equality, and democracy, embodied in the principles of the 1832 statute and the 1903 legislation, meant that Jewish teachers had the right to jobs in the Protestant schools. More significantly, these same principles of citizenship and belonging, of the equality of all British subjects, also led them to demand Jewish representation on the Protestant Board of School Commissioners for Montreal. The chapter highlights the demands, the political controversies, and failed legislative attempts to deal with yet more issues under the broad rubric of the Jewish School Question. From the City Council of Montreal, to which Jews were now being elected, to the provincial legislature in Quebec City, Jewish Montrealers sought what they considered to be their fundamental rights as citizens, and Protestants fought back, defending the right of Protestant schools to be Protestant, run by Christians, as guaranteed by section 93. The evolution of the Jewish School Question once again highlights the ways in which each party continued to evoke both self-constituting norms and appeals to rights embodied in broader political and indeed juridical principles of equality, citizenship, and constitutional law, however contradictory and mutually exclusive their competing narratives.

Holidays, Exemptions, and Teachers: Jewish-Protestant Relations after 1903

Many Protestant school officials, from teachers and principals, to members of the school board, continued to put into place practices that resulted in the de facto and almost de jure segregation of Jewish and Protestant pupils in schools within the common education system.[2] The segregation, although still explained and justified by Protestant school officials in terms of the disruption caused by absences from school on religious holidays, and from the classroom during periods of religious instruction, in fact had little to do with Jewish religious observance.[3] It was clear from the very beginning that most Jewish parents did not exercise the right to have their children opt out of Protestant, New Testament instruction. They simply appear to have taken "it for granted that attendance at these schools involved this concession of conscience to accommodation."[4] Not only was this concession made by Jewish parents to allow their children to fit into the normal daily existence of Protestant school pupils, but it should also have had the effect of removing one ground invoked throughout by Protestant school officials to justify segregation.[5] No longer were segregated schools simply based on the demographic facts of Jewish settlement in the area demarcated roughly by Park Avenue and Saint-Denis Street. Throughout the period of mass Jewish migration to Montreal, the Protestant Board constructed a distinct policy of segregation in its schools, and that segregation was not solely the result of Jewish residential patterns. If 95 per cent of the student body of Baron Byng High School, Fletcher's Field of Duddy

Kravitz fame, was Jewish, this did not mean that the Jewish students came from the immediately surrounding area. In fact, the population of Baron Byng was consciously constructed by the Protestant School Board to be Jewish. The student population of Baron Byng was also deliberately constituted in this fashion, not just to segregate Jews, but in order to permit a concomitant change in the student body of the high school on University Street from 65 per cent Jewish to 80–85 per cent Protestant.[6] School populations were deliberated manipulated by the Protestant School Board in order to ensure the de facto existence of separate and distinct Jewish and Protestant schools.

In reality, the root problem was one that no statute by itself could remedy. The issue was constitutive and constitutional in a broader sense than that allowed by mere legislation or other legal technique. The policy of deliberate segregation was almost certainly motivated in part by a form of anti-Semitism abroad through much of the period and that would manifest itself in the context of the evolving dynamics of the Jewish School Question. In addition to a broadly embedded anti-Semitic feeling, the Protestant reaction to the practical consequences of the 1903 Act was the reflection of the world view of the Montreal Protestant communities.[7] The presence of increasing numbers of Jewish students in Protestant schools quite simply, again, called into question the Protestant nature of the educational system itself.[8] Parents complained that their children could not receive a Protestant education if they were surrounded by Jewish pupils all day.[9] While the Protestant school system in Montreal avoided sectarianism by eschewing theological battles between and among Anglicans, Presbyterians, Baptists, and other denominations, it was still always Christian and Protestant, in clear opposition to the Roman Catholic system. Such was the core constitutional and constitutive dynamic of Quebec public schooling.[10] It was one thing to create a legal fiction for purposes of school taxes and attendance rights that Jews were to be treated as Protestants for educational purposes, but it was another entirely to ensure that the schools remained Protestant when Ferguson sat next to Finkelstein in the classroom. The legal fiction of Jews as "honorary Protestants" clashed constitutively with the reality of strongly held sentiments of Protestant self-understanding. This was not a case of violent exclusion or withdrawal, or indeed of peaceful departure by independent or autonomy-seeking collectivities from statist constitutional normativity.[11] Instead what was going on in Montreal was a constitutional world in which law and identity coincided for both Roman Catholic and Protestant religious groups, but where at the same time it excluded the third group, the Jews. Montreal Jews sought to be included within the constitutive life as British subjects, enjoying full rights, but the law, and the legal guarantees of the denominational essence of public schooling in Montreal, excluded them from full emancipation and concrete equality in education, except through the legal fiction "honorary Protestants." The link between the community life world and legal right was always a tenuous one for Montreal's Jewish students and their parents. For Jews as Protestants for school purposes, the technical legal exclusion was then reinforced in practice by the insistence by many Protestants that the school system remain at its core Protestant. While there may have been doubt, uncertainty, and occasional conflict about what a Protestant school might have looked like, there was growing agreement that it did not look like a school full of Jews.

Many of these fundamental issues of community self-definition came to a fore over the hiring of Jewish teachers in the Protestant school system. To some extent, this was a problem of the Protestant board's own making. Because of the practice of creating separate Jewish classes, and in some instances of schools that were predominantly Jewish, the board found itself faced with the practical issue of who was going to teach Jewish students. One reasonable answer, a response consistent with the move to segregation and one situated within the logic of the board's own practices, seemed to be Jewish teachers, but the board had historically refused to hire qualified Jewish normal school graduates. As a result of the natural progression of Jewish students through the Protestant system, further education as teachers had become an attractive career choice, especially for young Jewish women in the female-dominated profession. More and more Jewish girls attended MacDonald College, the new McGill normal school, and graduated with the expectation of becoming schoolteachers.[12] Could the Protestant School Board of Montreal hire non-Protestants as members of its teaching corps, charged with conveying the fundamental principles of Protestant education?

Records show not only that they could, but that they had done so already. In October 1905, after David Ansell had submitted, according to the agreed practice, the list of Jewish holy days for the year, Sarah Gordon, a teacher at Mount Royal School, applied for a leave of absence on those holidays.[13] In order to honour its agreement with the Jewish communities' representatives and its obligations under the 1903 statute, and at the same time to maintain as zealously as was permissible, the Protestant character of its schools, the board "ordered that arrangements should be made for the transfer of Miss Gordon to the staff of Baron de Hirsch School as soon as convenient."[14]

Not only would Jewish students be segregated within the Protestant system, but the awkward case of Sarah Gordon would be dealt with in the same way. The Jewish teacher would instruct Jewish students. But while such a solution might have worked in the isolated case of a single Jewish teacher, the broader question of the growing number of unemployed or underemployed Jewish female graduates of the Protestant teacher-training system would not go away. The realities of the divisions of the school population and the Protestant Board's hesitation compelled some Jews to advocate a solution to the teacher question that at the same time affirmed the idea of segregation. Members of the Protestant School Board viewed contact between Protestant pupils and Jewish teachers as undesirable and as putting in danger the Protestant nature of the educational system. Prominent members of the Jewish communities continued to argue that the appointment of Jewish teachers was required to concretize in full the spirit of the 1903 Act. In an apparent attempt to adopt a conciliatory position, the Jewish representatives were willing to take cognizance of the fact of Jewish separation within the Protestant system and to adapt their claims to that situation. Jewish teachers could be engaged to teach Jewish students. Bowing to demographic reality and Protestant School Board practices of segregation, together with the board's intransigence on the hiring of Jewish teachers, Jewish representatives pushed a position on the hiring of Jewish teachers that reinforced the Protestant board's policy and practice of segregating Jews within the school system. Such were the self-constituting compromises that Montreal Jews were virtually compelled to make in their struggle to deal with the realities of the application of the idea and ideal of being treated as Protestants for school purposes. At a core existential and constitutive level, there was little honour in being treated as "honorary Protestants."

In addition to asserting the general justice claim, these spokesmen (and they were men) also pointed out the necessary contradiction in the Protestant position. If they wished to segregate Jewish students, why not follow through on the logic inherent in their position? Their acceptance of segregation was almost complete on the question of hiring young Jewish women who were graduates of normal school: "Granted that the mere contact between Jewish teachers and Protestant pupils would be 'undesirable,' why not have them teach in the schools where 95 per cent. of the children are Jews? Surely the presence of Jewish teachers in schools such as the Aberdeen or the Dufferin could scarcely destroy any 'Christian character.' However, such is the acknowledged policy of the Board that, although many capable young Jews take Protestant Normal School diplomas, no Jewish teacher has a chance of employment under any circumstances in the Protestant schools, in which 37 per cent. of the scholars are Jews."[15]

Finally, in 1913, the Protestant School Board decided that it could hire Jewish teachers. Again the decision appears to have been a consequence, in part at least, of ongoing conflict and controversy over different aspects of the Jewish School Question. Earlier in the year, a grade six teacher at Aberdeen School, Miss McKinley, had made a disparaging remark about her Jewish students.[16] She had apparently said that Jews were dirty and that the school had been very clean when she first arrived, but with the Jewish students in attendance, it had become a dirty place. The pupils reacted by staging a walkout. They marched to the Baron de Hirsch Institute and to the offices of the *Keneder Adler* (*Canadian Eagle*), the Yiddish-language newspaper with a strong claim to represent the views of the majority of Montreal's Jewish community.[17] They returned to school after a half-hearted apology by the teacher was issued following the intervention of the Baron de Hirsch representatives.

The concession of the Protestant School Board on the question of Jewish teachers did not arise in a vacuum. It came after several years of agitation and argument from the Jewish communities and their representatives. The claims for equal treatment, as Protestants for school purposes, had met with hostility and resentment by the Protestant board at what they perceived to be attacks on the Christian character of their schools. It followed a short-lived student protest against what might be called the insensitivities of Protestant teachers (or it might be labelled simple anti-Semitism). Jews were asserting the full extent of their rights as Protestants for the purposes of education under their liberal interpretation of the spirit and intent of the 1903 legislation. The Protestant board was pushing back against these pressures, relying not just on the law and the overarching framework of Quebec legislation and section 93 of the BNA Act, but also on a different interpretation of the foundational spirit of the agreement that had informed the 1903 Act. For them, the statements by Maxwell Goldstein during the negotiations following the *Pinsler* decision, assuring them that Jewish demands for access to the Protestant school system were in no way influenced by a desire to change the fundamentally Protestant and Christian character of the school system, provided a basis upon which they could meet Jewish demands for a fuller version of school equality.

Although the Protestant board had finally agreed to hire Jewish teachers, as always, conditions were attached.[18] They proceeded, but not without legal assurances that the board could do so without violating its fundamental Protestant character, and firm minuted reassertions of that identity.[19] The board's lawyers advised that the hiring of teaching staff was a matter of pure administration within the discretion of the board and therefore within their legal powers. The commissioners then agreed that, given the ever-increasing number of Jewish students in its schools, it would consider hiring duly qualified Jewish teachers on a case-by-case basis. It would ensure that, when such teachers were employed, "it shall be arranged by the principal of the school that every Christian pupil in their classes shall receive instruction in the study of the New Testament from a teacher of his own faith, and shall attend the customary religious exercises so conducted."[20] For its part, the Protestant board also insisted "that as far as possible the Jewish women teachers be placed only in classes composed of Jewish pupils."[21]

These battles over holidays, segregation, and the hiring of Jewish school teachers took place in the shadow of other, perhaps larger, conflicts, first over the status and very existence of the Baron de Hirsch School, and second over the increasing agitation among the Jewish community on the question of Jewish representation on the Protestant board. If Jews were Protestants for educational purposes and paid their taxes into the Protestant panel and sent their children to Protestant schools, then it followed as a matter of principle, not the least of which was "no taxation without representation," that Jews should be named to the Board of School Commissioners. While this argument was not without apparent merit in terms of justice, it did raise two further complications. First, it was questionable, to say the least, that Jewish school commissioners, members of the Protestant board, could pass muster under guarantees of a Protestant school system under section 93. Politically and socially, as a matter of the relationship between the Protestant School Board and the representatives of the Jewish communities, such claims to rights to representation clearly flew in the face of the assurances given by Maxwell Goldstein to the board during their attempts to thrash out an acceptable agreement dealing with the Jewish School Question following the decision in *Pinsler*.

All of these battles would soon give rise to a feeling in parts of the Jewish communities in Montreal that the great experiment of Jews as "honorary Protestants" was not working and could never work. Jewish students were still being segregated, the communities had to struggle for years to convince the Protestant board to hire fully qualified Jewish teachers, and the result of Jewish female educational success was a policy to place them only with Jewish students. For increasing numbers of Jews in Montreal, the clear answer was the creation of a third school board in the city of Montreal, a Jewish Board of School Commissioners. If the Protestant School Board wanted separate Jewish schools, so be it. This group, whose voice would be found in the *Eagle*,[22] was made up largely of Yiddish-speaking, more recent immigrants, for whom their political and religious frames for Jewish identity and public schooling were both intimately linked and under constant threat in the ever-reluctant Protestant school system. They would become the downtowners of later debates.[23] Their opponents, the uptowners, were the more assimilated, English-speaking Jews who lived mainly outside the Jewish residential areas of the city's east end. The long-time proponents of Jewish educational rights, members of the Baron de Hirsch Institute, and those primarily responsible for the negotiations that had led to the 1903 pact after the *Pinsler* case, would find a voice in the Jacobs and Cohen–owned *Jewish Times*.[24]

The Baron de Hirsch School: The Demise of Jewish Protestant Education in Montreal

The Baron de Hirsch School had played a vital role in the education of immigrant Jewish children and in the unfolding dramas surrounding the Jewish School Question. Subsidized in part, both during and after the Spanish and Portuguese synagogue split, by the Protestant School Board, it had served as an introduction to schooling for the children of newly arrived immigrants and, for those who wished to pursue their education, as a feeder school into the Protestant system in Montreal. By taking up the pedagogical needs of a cohort of students who possessed neither the academic background nor the English-language proficiency, both qualities required to succeed in the educational mainstream, it had relieved the Protestant School Board of a significant burden.[25] It had also done so, for much of its existence, at a cost to the Jewish citizens of the city who supplemented the shortfall between the actual costs of the school and the varying subsidy provided by the Protestant board.[26] Following the 1903 statute, however, the idea of a separate Jewish school became more and more intellectually problematic, since all Jewish students were now, by statute, Protestants for educational purposes. In practical terms, however, the raison d'être of the Baron de Hirsch School still made sense. Eastern European Jewish immigrants continued to come to Montreal, and few, if any, of their children spoke English or had sufficient educational backgrounds to gain immediate entry into the Protestant school system. The number of foreign-born in the population of Montreal had risen from 4,111 in the period 1896–1990, to 10,741 for 1901–5, and then to 18,872 between 1906 and 1911.[27] The question to be resolved by the Baron de Hirsch Institute and the Protestant School Board was how to make the school operate effectively in the new legal and practical landscape following the *Pinsler* decision and the 1903 Act.

The Protestant board put its views into a draft agreement between itself and the Baron de Hirsch Institute.[28] The board would provide and pay the salaries of fully qualified teachers to staff the school, the premises for which would be provided by the institute. The Baron de Hirsch School would be open to two classes of students. It would accept Jewish students whose knowledge of English was insufficient to "profit by instruction given in that language," and Jewish students who wished to attend the Protestant schools but who had yet to obtain sufficient academic standing to enter the fourth grade in the Protestant system. The school would be required to supply monthly attendance reports to the Protestant board and to be, as before, open to inspection by Protestant officials. Students in second and third year would be expected to follow the normal course of study within the common Protestant education system and to pass standard examinations in nominated subjects.[29]

Some details remained to be worked out on maintenance fees and on students who lived too far from the institute's school to allow regular attendance there. Principal Baker of the Baron de Hirsch School again wrote to Arthy explaining that another influx of mostly Russian Jewish immigrants came with the arrival of each steamer in the port of Montreal and that as a consequence, the school was under pressure because it had too few teaching staff available, especially those with necessary language skills, and was operating under severe space constraints.[30] Student arrivals did not follow the schedule of the school year. Children and their parents simply showed up at the institute school in numbers after the arrival of each ship from Europe. The institute welcomed these students because that was its self-ordained function, but it suffered severely in terms of money and physical space with each passing month.

Despite these practical problems, the Baron de Hirsch School continued to function as the first educational port of call for immigrant Jewish children and as a jumping off point on the way to the Protestant common school system. At the same time, the physical infrastructure of the Protestant system itself was under increasing stress. A class from the Dufferin School was moved to the library of the Baron de Hirsch Institute, a move made possible, of course, by the continuing program of segregating Jewish students and Dufferin School's de facto status as a Jewish school.[31]

The resources of the Baron de Hirsch School were now under constant pressure as the Protestant Board continued to refuse admission to the common school system to Jewish students who did not speak English. This situation and the policy adopted by the Protestant board created a new category of student, not legally recognized by the 1903 statute, but one identified in the three-year agreement between the board and the institute: non-English speaking Jews, for whom the institute was entirely responsible in practice.[32] While providing assistance to immigrant Jews had always been the main goal of the Young Men's Hebrew Benevolent Society from the time of its founding, the extra burden was becoming financially untenable. The school had lost or given up power over the hiring of staff and the curriculum, as it became increasingly subject to the control of the Protestant board. While such a move towards greater involvement in the school by the Protestant board was perfectly consistent with the broad principles of the 1903 Act, and ultimately with the historic aspirations and pedagogical philosophy of the Baron de Hirsch School, the Jewish community provided the school building and the teaching expertise in non-English language instruction to the immigrant population. Under this strain and mounting pressure on its limited resources, the Baron de Hirsch Institute finally decided that, as the expiry of the original contractual period approached, it needed to renegotiate the terms of that agreement on a basis more practical and practicable from the institute's perspective.[33]

The Protestant board's response to the institute's claims was unambiguous. It decided that it no longer needed the Baron de Hirsch Institute School. It could now accommodate all Jewish students in the ordinary Protestant schools of the city. As a result, it would also no longer require the services of the teachers employed at the Baron de Hirsch School after the end of the current school year. The Baron de Hirsch School, as a Jewish Protestant institution that had enjoyed a unique status in and at the margins of the Protestant School Board, like the synagogue schools before it, was now teetering on the brink of extinction.

The Protestant school commissioners had decided to fully incorporate Jewish students into the mainstream educational system.[34] But it would incorporate only those Jewish students who were fit for the ordinary course of instruction. Following the opinion of its legal advisors, the board had clearly decided that it had no legal obligation to admit any student who did not speak English.[35] The board was eventually prepared to accept even students who did not speak English provided the parents were willing to allow them to follow the ordinary course of instruction.[36]

The Protestant commissioners now simply refused to meet with representatives of the Baron de Hirsch School. Because they were accepting all Jewish students into the common schools, there was nothing to discuss between the parties.[37] Once more, dialogue and discussion were replaced by a monopolistic assertion of jurisdiction by Protestant school officials. The Baron de Hirsch Institute now could really welcome only those students who did not possess sufficient English-language skills or whose parents did not wish them to attend Protestant schools, or who felt that they were not ready to attend them.[38] The Baron de Hirsch School opened and welcomed 200 students in the new school year. On 20 October, the Protestant board wrote to the institute, insisting that there had been an apparent misunderstanding, since they had believed that the institute wished to continue to provide separate schooling for immigrant children under its own auspices and without any involvement of the Protestant board. If that were not the case, the Protestant Board would be happy to open its schools to all children presently enrolled in the Baron de Hirsch School.[39] Seeing the writing on the wall, the institute accepted.[40] The Baron de Hirsch School was no more.

The period of détente and co-existence between the institute and the Protestant board had come to an end with the unilateral decision of the Protestant school officials to end the three-year agreement. The halfway house position of the Baron de Hirsch School, which had operated for many years under a general supervisory jurisdiction of the Protestant board but with a clearly Jewish governing structure, had given way to increasing control under the 1904 contract, until the last remaining Jewish-controlled school that had a form of semi-independence from the public common schools of Montreal, had finally proved too difficult and too expensive to manage for the Jewish communities, and too unruly and awkward for the Protestant board. No private/public arrangements were necessary, because the law had established a formal framework of equal rights within which Jews were now Protestants.

The Baron de Hirsch Institute now ran two schools, a Hebrew school with 148 students across two sessions per day, Monday through Thursday after public school hours, and a night school teaching 131 students, divided into three classes.[41]

Despite the closure of the school, the school committee of the Baron de Hirsch Institute continued to lobby the Protestant School Board on behalf of Jewish students. It ran a campaign in conjunction with the *Eagle* to ensure that Jewish parents knew that they had the right to send their children to Protestant schools, and identified individual students who had not been admitted by Protestant school principals.[42] Even in the absence of formal contractual arrangements, and in the shadow of the legal equality enshrined in the 1903 statute, the institute still placed itself as the public protector of Jewish educational interests and rights within the Protestant common school system. It continued to see its role and mission of seeking to invoke and ensure the constitution of Jewish educational equality as a way of enriching the life and prospects of members of the community. Mere statutory guarantees were not enough. Experience supported the view that Protestant school officials were often less than wholehearted in meeting Jewish demands for educational equality, and the institute officials were there to ensure compliance within the Protestant educational system.

The idea of formal equality in educational matters, of Jews as "Protestants for school purposes," also began to give rise to other claims for real, substantive equality. If Jews were Protestants, and Jewish taxes went to support the Protestant School Board, then basic constitutional principles of British democracy must, in the eyes of a growing number of Montreal Jews, have compelled the Protestant board to recognize the inherent justice of demands for Jewish representatives on the Board of Protestant School Commissioners. The limits of the constitutive and constituting narratives of the Jewish School Question were about to be put to the legal and political test.

Jewish Protestants and the School Board: Democracy Lite and the Jewish School Question

The discursive and political battles over the issue of Jewish representation on the Protestant School Board did not arise solely as matters between representatives of a united Jewish community and a unified Montreal anglophone Protestant elite. As the debates over possible Jewish representation on the school board raged, parts of the Jewish community used the ensuing political and legal stalemate to reassert claims for separate Jewish schools and for a separate Jewish School Commission.[43] These claims would not diminish until the 1930s. Moreover, these original political attempts to change the governance structure of the Protestant School Board in Montreal themselves did not originate solely within the Jewish community, or uniquely as a result of Jewish sentiment about the idea of "no taxation without representation," or some invocation of the foundational norm of equality on which their vision of the British Empire was founded. There was, in fact, a growing, if still minority, discontent among liberal elements within the Protestant community about the unrepresentative character of the Board of Protestant School Commissioners in Montreal.

The norm for school governance, both for common and dissentient schools throughout the province was that taxpayers in the school district elected local commissioners and trustees.[44] While certain members of the local community, most notably women, were disenfranchised under this system, the structure did permit significant local involvement in electing officials who had quite extensive powers of taxation and broad governance authority over local education.[45] In Montreal, however, since the structures of the educational system had been concretized in the 1869 legislative regime, the provincial government appointed three of the six Protestant commissioners and the Montreal City Council selected the other three. This meant that the clergy and the liberal professions were always well represented on the board, while teachers, women, working-class citizens, the business community, and of course non-Protestants were not represented. From 1894, on the Roman Catholic side, the archbishop named three of the nine commissioners in Montreal.[46]

Many members of the more liberal elements of the Montreal Protestant community wanted to exercise the same electoral rights enjoyed by their cousins outside the city. At other historical junctures, members of the Montreal Protestant community, including the school board itself, had come to believe that elected commissioners would be more likely to protect Protestant interests than those whose nomination would be in the hands of governments in Montreal and Quebec City, governments controlled by the Roman Catholic majority, although in practice systems of relative autonomy in relation to denominational schools had belied these fears.[47] Many Protestant officials held two mutually reinforcing fears about a popularly elected school board. First there was a belief that education would become politicized in the sense that individuals pursuing a political career would seek a seat on the school board as a steppingstone to other elective office. Such individuals would prioritize their own careers over the pedagogical and broader educational needs of the school system. Second, a turn to elected officials would run the risk of sectarianism, as numerically dominant Protestant churches could come to control a school board that had always sought to govern by compromise and to avoid interdenominational strife by insisting on a broad and inclusive Protestant view of education.

For the majority of the Protestant population of Montreal, and for the members of the school board, all of these issues and concerns faded into the background when faced with the idea that an elected board could allow for the possibility of Jewish electors and Jewish members. For them, as always, the primary concern was in maintaining a Protestant Board of School Commissioners that would be, in its essence, Protestant. Any dilution of this fundamental constitutive element of the board was anathema. The nomination process had worked to ensure not just the absence of sectarianism, but that the Protestant character of the board was unchallenged. Any Jewish presence would operate a fundamental change to the defining character of the school board. Finally, and again, the board also rejected and continued to reject the basis for claims to Jewish representation. Over and over they invoked the shortfall in Jewish taxes against the actual cost of educating Jewish students in the Protestant school system. At the height of this first stage of the struggle for Jewish representation on the Protestant board, in 1908, there were 4,374 Jewish students in Protestant schools. The board argued that the cost of educating a single student was $28.95 per annum. Therefore in round figures, the burden imposed by Jewish students was $120,000, while Jewish taxes amounted to only $30,000. It cost Protestant taxpayers $90,000 to educate Jewish students. On what principled basis did this situation warrant representation on the board?[48] If there were taxation without representation, there was more importantly taxation without covering the costs of education. Jews may have been Protestants for educational purposes, but they were, as far as the Protestant School Board was concerned, both a separate accounting category and an ever-increasing financial burden on real Protestant taxpayers. Such for the Protestant School Board were the stakes once again in arriving at any answer to the Jewish School Question.

In 1906 C.B. Carter, the member of the Legislative Assembly from the St Antoine Ward,[49] introduced a private member's bill calling for the election of all members of the Protestant School Board, and including

Jews among eligible voters and candidates.[50] Gerald Tulchinsky has argued that Carter's intervention was "largely Jewish in origin, and represented a further drive by a militant group to secure full civil rights, to eliminate all barriers to Jewish participation in the civic and political life of the community."[51] Putting aside the description of Sam Jacobs, Maxwell Goldstein, and others as a "militant group," Tulchinsky appears to have come to this conclusion in the absence of careful historical analysis and by failing to properly periodize the series of debates that arose around the question of the election of members to the Protestant School Board. There had always been part of the Protestant community that had sought to achieve more democracy in school governance generally, and to limit clerical control of education more specifically. Tulchinsky seems to ignore or elide this historical context. Moreover, the bills dealing with the franchise in Montreal education issues were introduced by Carter, and later by John Finnie.[52] While Finnie in particular represented the electorate of St Laurent with a significant Jewish presence, neither man could be said to be so totally lacking in agency or his own political agenda and beliefs that he acted as a simple stalking horse for Jewish interests. The evolution of attempts to introduce elections for Protestant and Roman Catholic school commissions took place over several years, and only later in the process did the Jewish community become involved. David Rome more accurately asserted that there was simply "no reason to believe that there was any Jewish initiative behind, or support for, the 1909 Finnie bill."[53]

Even more significantly, in 1909, a subsequent version of the Finnie bill concerning the Protestant commission was accompanied by the second effort of Godfroy Langlois, member for the Third District from Montreal, seeking an elected Roman Catholic school board.[54] Langlois was a proponent of *laïcité* and a long-suffering *rouge*, a social and political liberal, or in relative terms, a radical presence within the Liberal Party and a thorn in the side of the dominant accommodationist wing of the party that sought to maintain a peaceful and non-confrontational relationship with the Roman Catholic Church.[55] At this point at least, there was significant if minority support for fundamental change to school governance mechanisms in Montreal among elements of both the Protestant and Roman Catholic political elite. Jews appear to have had nothing to do with these specific attempts at democratizing Montreal educational administration.

In a study more nuanced in its timeline, Jean-Philippe Croteau observed, as did David Rome, that at the time of the first Carter bill in 1906, there was little, if any, reaction or involvement from the Jewish community or its leaders.[56] When Langlois first introduced proposed changes to the Roman Catholic system in 1907, the Jewish community was quite obviously uninvolved, given its formalized legal status within the Protestant system. The leading historian of Montreal Jewry, David Rome, again pointed out that at the time of the first Finnie and Langlois measures, a complex array of forces was in fact at work in debates over the future of education in Montreal.

> The business community wanted more modern, practical schooling for a better trained work force; anti-clericals wanted to limit church control of education; those who appreciated a more literate approach wanted a system of public libraries; the international labor unions and democrats generally wanted representative and elective government in schooling as everywhere else; government may have wanted the schools, and other social institutions under its control; conservatives were afraid of revolutionary change; they saw the hand of the Masonic Loge de l'Emancipation everywhere; some Liberals who held these views saw the school issue as a means of strengthening their group within the party; the church was vulnerable, under attack.[57]

There was, therefore, no concrete evidence of any Jewish involvement in the introduction of the early measures to ensure elected school boards in Montreal and significant historical contextual indications that the issue was of interest to members of the non-Jewish Montreal communities. But the Protestant board immediately assumed that the bills were little more than concrete manifestations of a Jewish plot. They issued a circular to the community explaining that the religious character of the education was "the distinctive feature of the schools of this Province."[58] Allowing Jews to vote and sit on the school board would be disastrous. "The immediate effect of this change would be to place the Protestant Schools under the administration of a body not distinctly Christian in its character and composition. The ultimate consequences of such a change must be both far-reaching and revolutionary."[59]

The Carter bill failed to progress because of clear and vocal opposition from the Protestant board. Langlois was convinced to withdraw his proposal as the result of a promise from the premier, Lomer Gouin, that the government would study the question and reintroduce legislation in the next session, covering not just the Roman Catholic Commission but the Protestant board as well. In addition he promised support for two of Langlois' other interests, the establishment of lay technical schools and a public library in Montreal.[60] Gouin knew full well that any attempt to establish elected public school boards in Montreal would be doomed to failure because of the power of the denominational school systems and that the Protestant and Roman Catholic education officials would unite to kill any attempted change.[61]

While there was obviously strong and growing Jewish interest in the question of representation on the Protestant School Board, Tulchinsky appears to have gone too far in asserting that it was the "only" real interest in change to the system. Many elements in Montreal, from both dominant religious denominations, had their own reasons for wanting to move to elections, while others had equally strong reasons for opposing any change to the status quo. Other interests, other political concerns, other constitutive discourses were always at play. And again, other elements of the School Question boiled and bubbled away at the same time: segregation and discrimination, the refusal to hire Jewish teachers, and of course, the constant complaint that Jewish students were being subsidized at enormous cost and to the detriment of their own children, by Protestant taxpayers.[62]

Dr Finnie introduced another bill in March 1909. In his speech to the Assembly, Finnie asserted that the main reason behind his desire to see elected school commissioners in Montreal was to increase "the presence of men of thorough business experience on the Protestant School Board."[63] Moreover, he highlighted the school tax issue, but from a slightly different perspective. He argued that businessmen would bring greater acumen to school expenditures and that this would be especially necessary if the board was successful in its attempts to raise the rate for school taxes. In addition, he stated that basic democratic principles, which operated throughout the province outside Quebec City and Montreal, throughout Canada, and in the United States, demanded that those who paid taxes should have some say in how they were spent. If the clergy, as they asserted, found it an assault on their dignity to have to run for elected office, Dr Finnie stood ready to amend his bill to allow for some number of clergy to be appointed, as was the current case. He concluded by arguing that the issue of school governance had been "a vexed question for years" and that he had received many letters from leaders of the city's Protestant community urging him to introduce his legislation.[64] Nowhere in Finnie's speech was their any mention of the rights of Jewish taxpayers.

In response, the spokesman for his opponents, P.S.G. Mackenzie, not only attacked Finnie's assertion that there had been significant agitation and support for the bill among the Protestant community, but went on to elaborate what was for him the heart of the matter.[65] Finnie's proposal that Jews be deemed to fall within the definition of Protestant for purposes of the bill was a threat to Protestant schooling. He stated in by now familiar terms, "The educational system of the Province is absolutely Christian in character, Christian safeguards are embedded in the very rock of our Constitution. But yet, in this bill, the word Protestant is to include Jewish. This portends an innovation which should be carefully considered in a Christian country. It is opposed to the country's base. I have nothing personally against the Jews, but in such classification I see a grave danger to Christianity."[66]

Putting aside the idea of Christianity as a duality between Protestants and Roman Catholics, an ideal belied by the arrival in numbers of Greek and Syrian Orthodox immigrants in Montreal at around this time, the assertion by Mackenzie once more went to the awkward and troubling question raised by the increasing numbers of Jewish immigrants. If Canada truly was a Christian country with special, constitutional, and constitutive bases in the two majority faiths, Protestantism and Roman Catholicism, the rights of Jews in all domains would always be fundamentally fragile and contingent. Statements such as those of Mr MacKenzie simply brought the fragility, as a matter of law, if not politics, of the status of Jewish residents and citizens once more into the bright light of day. As Mackenzie also highlighted, it was not just the country in general terms that was Christian, but this was especially the case of the educational system, the Christian character of which was enshrined in very specific terms in the text of the country's constitutional document, the BNA Act. For Mackenzie and Protestant Montrealers, the danger was clear and present. "Suppose that the Jewish population of Montreal exceed the Protestant, then they would have control of the whole Protestant population of Montreal. That is the danger that I see in this measure."[67]

The situation that already obtained in several Protestant schools in Montreal might soon become a demographic reality in the city as a whole. Jewish residents were moving from the Main, in the east end of the city, into more central parts of Montreal, while many Protestants were establishing themselves in the suburbs, outside the city limits. Democracy, in the form of an elected school board, could easily lead to Jewish domination. That Protestants should control the whole Jewish population was ordained and concretized in the constitution of the country itself. That Jews should control the fate of Protestants was abhorrent and un-Canadian.

When the Carter bill had been presented in 1906, the Presbytery of Montreal had objected on the familiar grounds that any elected element in which Jews were allowed to participate would destroy the basic

Christian character of the Protestant schools. Now some of its members saw an increased danger with the growth of the Jewish population and began to agitate for an end to the current arrangement embodied in the 1903 Act under which Jews were "honorary Protestants." In Protestant terms, they echoed calls from some parts of the Jewish communities of Montreal and urged the creation of a new, separate, third school system for Jews.[68] In some Protestant quarters, the point of exasperation was fast being reached. Many Jews were becoming equally frustrated with a system in which each seemingly final resolution to the Jewish School Question was almost immediately belied in the practice of the Protestant School Board. In the aftermath of *Pinsler*, the accord between a united Jewish community and the Protestant Board of School Commissioners, leading to the 1903 Act, had been followed by de facto segregation of Jewish students, debates over absences on holy days, and the controversies that were soon to emerge over hiring Jewish teachers. Now democracy was being portrayed as a Jewish threat to the Protestant way of life and the 1903 Act was being called into question. Jewish pride and Jewish self-identity were being put to the test by the Protestant board's recalcitrance in recognizing the validity and justice of Jewish claims to representation.

The *Jewish Times* expressed the views of the members of the Jewish community who had long battled for educational rights within the Protestant system. They came to demand equality, not as ersatz Protestants, but as non–Roman Catholic British subjects. They wished only to exercise their rights as British subjects, equal to all other British subjects, and to send their children to school with all other non–Roman Catholic Canadians. For them the division was clear. They had no place in the Roman Catholic school system that was subject to overwhelming clerical control. By implication, they also had no place in a Roman Catholic, francophone, nationalist Quebec society. They wanted, as always, to be Canadian, and the only way to achieve that in the educational system was within the Protestant schools, but as equals.[69] If secular, national schools were beyond the current state of political and legal imagination, they sought a constitutive place within the society of which they were equal and otherwise fully emancipated citizens.

> A broader principle than that signified by the term Protestant will have to be accepted and acted upon. We do not deny that the Protestant Commissioners have shown a commendable spirit towards us. We are not ungrateful for the advantages we enjoy as citizens of a free country, but we are British and the fact

of not being Protestant does not deprive us of the right to have a voice in the disposition of the taxes to which we contribute. The justice and constitutionality of the bill are unquestionable. We are glad to accept it as an act of justice in keeping with British principles.[70]

The rhetoric and the communal self-understandings of the main opponents in the debate, the Protestant communities and their educational representatives, and the members of the Jewish communities who had been involved in the 1903 settlement, were constructed as mirror images. Each invoked a set of constitutional principles upon which their communal existence depended and within which the hermeneutic of the collective self-understanding took place. For the Protestants, section 93 and the entire legislative history of education law in the province set them apart as one of the two privileged and protected groups at the very point of the creation of the Canadian nation state. Protestants had guaranteed control of their schools, and those schools were, and must always be Protestant. For those members of the Jewish community involved in the ongoing struggle for educational equality, the anomalous position of Jewish students and taxpayers was starkly and obviously contrary to the principles of British constitutional justice and freedom, and to the formal legal equality guaranteed to Quebec Jews in the 1832 statute. As British subjects, they must be allowed to educate their children and to participate in decisions about that education, on a fully equal footing. The Jewish community representatives expressed happy surprise at the introduction of the Finnie bill, while the Protestant educational hierarchy would continue to create a narrative of a Jewish conspiracy originating from the time of the Carter bill in 1906. According to the Protestant telling, the story of attempts to find a means to ensure elected representation on the school board started with a broken promise by the Jews. When Maxwell Goldstein, speaking for the united Jewish community after the *Pinsler* decision, had accepted the terms of the agreement, which would come to be enshrined in the 1903 Act, he had clearly stated that the Jewish community recognized and always would recognize the fundamental Christian character of the Protestant school system. He had assured the Protestant board members that Montreal's Jews would never attempt to bring that character into question. Yet as far as the Protestant educational officials were concerned, that promise proved to be an empty one. Following the 1903 agreement, "definite steps were taken by the Hebrew population, before three years had expired, to revolutionize the whole system of management of the Protestant schools of Montreal and to introduce Jewish representatives on the Protestant school Board."[71] Jewish perfidy hid behind their claims to equality and a democratic franchise.

Another bill, introduced by Finnie in 1909, simply repeated the scene, once more in the eyes of the Protestant educational and religious establishments, endangering the very nature of Protestant existence in the province and the city of Montreal. This time, a different aspect of the essential character of Quebec Protestantism would come to the surface. A delegation from the Jewish community, Maxwell Goldstein, Sam Jacobs, and Lyon Cohen, travelled to Quebec City to meet with the government and Protestant educational officials.[72] Jacobs told the legislators that Jews had no desire to dominate the school board and as far as they were concerned, the Assembly was free to insert any safeguards it wished in the legislation. Jewish demands were grounded in simple requests for justice and equality as British subjects.[73] The Protestant representative, James Barclay, a commissioner since 1902, explained the board's unremitting opposition to any attempt to modify its essential Protestant character. Education within its schools had to and would remain Protestant. The case for him was clear. Jews were not Protestants. He was reported as having said, "The Jew is my brother, but so is the infidel my brother, and so is the thief my brother. I would not entrust the education of my children to a thief."[74]

Barclay's reiteration of some of the basic tenets of a Protestant theology was unsurprising and as a simple, abstract statement of dogma, not at all shocking. In the context of the meeting with government representatives, one might have expected some moderation, but his expression of that theology in such blatantly anti-Semitic tones was also unsurprising. The tenor of Protestant complaints about a Jewish presence in the school system had always been one in which anti-Semitism was present just below, and occasionally above, the surface. Indeed, Barclay had given voice to ideas that had come close to breaking through, even in the friendly litigation in the *Pinsler* case. The entire proposition of that litigation from the Protestant side had been that they had absolute discretion insofar as Jewish students were concerned, and that Christian grace was the only basis on which Jewish students could attend common schools in Montreal. Such grace would compel Barclay to forgive and to accept and to love the infidel, the thief, and the Jew, as his brother, but it would not really extend to allowing Jews to enter positions of power within the school system. As far as Barclay and many other Protestants were concerned, the 1903 Act was perhaps the ultimate embodiment of Christian grace and charity by the Protestant communities of Montreal, who had acquiesced to the characterization of Jews as Protestants for school purposes. This acquiescence, however, could never be seen to be, because it was never intended to be, an act of grace informed by any ideas of political or legislative powers of transubstantiation. Jews were and always would be Jews. They could be loved and forgiven, they could be Protestants for educational purposes, "honorary Protestants" at best, but they could not vote or make decisions that might affect Protestant children. Despite vigorous responses from prominent Jews, the Protestant board did not resile from the underlying principles that had structured Barclay's assertions.[75]

Dr Finnie persisted in his attempts to democratize Protestant school governance in Montreal. He presented different versions of his bill in successive sessions of the Assembly, including in subsequent versions, as he had promised in 1909, provision for the appointment by the government of clergy as members of the Montreal board.[76] Constant and regular opposition from the broader Protestant community and the Protestant clergy in particular doomed each attempt to failure.[77] The idea of equality for Jewish citizens had come up against a roadblock constructed from constitutional text, Protestant recalcitrance, and the inherent narrative limits of Christian grace and charity.

Montreal City Council, Jews, and Protestants: Political Failure on the Road to Democracy

As the Finnie bills headed to their inevitable defeat, session after session and year after year, elements in the Montreal Jewish communities began to deploy a different two-part tactic in their efforts to gain representative status on the Protestant board. In 1911, in a speech at McGill University, Maxwell Goldstein proposed that the city council and the provincial government consider changing the types of individuals they named to the Protestant board. He urged them to reduce the number of clergymen, and to begin appointing women, businessmen, teachers, and Jews. This proposal did not seek to change the system from appointed to elected commissioners, but rather to broaden the representative nature of appointed officials. The appeal was couched in terms asserting general principles of fairness and inclusivity, and at the same time it invoked modern ideas of competence and ability, echoing the *rouge* Langlois and the Carter/Finnie arguments. Educators and businessmen had a clearer stake in modern schooling than did the Protestant clergy, while democratic principles still demanded representation by all concerned groups in school governance.[78]

While the post-*Pinsler* issues of segregation, release for holy day observance, the hiring of Jewish teachers, and demands for Jewish representation constituted a central part of the political (and legal) context of Jewish attempts to forge a lived equality as British subjects in Montreal, another case at the core of Jewish rights arose, this time in Quebec City. The well-known case of *Ortenberg v Plamondon* was making its way through the Quebec legal system.[79] The province's Jews attempted to use legal means to bring a halt to a virulent anti-Semitic campaign, led by ultramontane elements in the provincial capital.[80] What is worth our attention here is the summation offered by Sam Jacobs in his pleading for the Jewish plaintiffs, because it shows how Quebec and Montreal Jews used all the elements and avenues available to them in their struggle for full equality. Jacobs reminded the court that the 1832 emancipation statute was for the province's Jews "our Magna Charta."[81] The plea for damages in *Ortenberg v Plamondon* formed part of the same principled assertion as Jews had invoked in 1832, and since then, before the legislature to ensure the realization of their equality rights. Likewise, Jacobs underlined that when the decision in *Pinsler* had been handed down and their equality rights were put in jeopardy, the Jews had recourse to the legislative branch. "There has not been a single act referring to Jews and giving them, from time to time, greater measures of civil rights, which was not passed unanimously by the Legislature of Quebec."[82]

In this instance, as the Jewish population sought to invoke the general liability provisions of article 1053 of the Civil Code, to bring an end to attacks invoking the infamous and pernicious blood libel and other anti-Semitic canards, the plea for equality was being made before the courts. When that had failed, Quebec Jews sought their civil rights, successfully, before the legislative branch. In addition, it is clear that the School Question was understood to be part of the broader fight for equality and civil rights by Montreal Jewry. They had been blocked in *Pinsler* but achieved their goal with unanimous legislative approval in the 1903 Act. Litigation, legislation, and negotiation were all available means to the end of equality and full respect for Jewish rights. Litigation was to some extent a final step, but the Jewish population always conceived of British justice and the rights of equality that were inherent in their citizenship rights as British subjects in a holistic fashion.

While Jews were agitating for fully concretized equality rights as they understood the guarantees of the 1903 agreement and statute, many in the Protestant educational and broader communities had a different understanding of the post-*Pinsler* school situation. For them, the 1903 agreement had been accompanied by assurances from representatives of the Jewish community that they would not seek to call into question the Protestant nature of the Protestant schools of the city. Claims to representative status by Jewish political and community figures put those assurances into question and led some Protestant officials to begin a plan for the removal of any Jewish presence from their schools.[83] These educational officials saw that the compromises of the 1903 statute, of Jews as "honorary Protestants," had led only to further complications and more significantly to a situation that endangered the Protestant essence of their schools. Protestant recalcitrance on the representation issue led to heightened Jewish political agitation for membership on the board and a growing belief in parts of the communities that Jewish independence in educational matters was preferable to constant struggle with Protestant school officials.

In 1912 the Protestant School Board had indicated its willingness to sell the school buildings already occupied by a majority Jewish student population – Aberdeen, Alexandra, Dufferin, and Mount Royal – in the event of the creation of a separate Jewish school system in the city. The Protestant board sought to maintain the fundamental Christian character of its schools and of the system of educational governance as its primary aim. Elements within the Protestant educational establishment continued to see merit in Jewish arguments that a separate Jewish school system might be a practical solution to all of the aggravation, disputes, and annoyances that had come to characterize the Jewish School Question. The growing numerical influence of foreign students not only agitated Protestant school officials, but also caused significant concerns among Roman Catholic authorities in Montreal and at the provincial level.[84]

At the same time, the Jewish community began both to demand its place in the political realm and to establish its own formal educational structures. The first Yiddish-language school, the Maylender Shul (the Mile End School), became the first institutional embodiment that would further inspire the movement for Jewish education in the 1920s and 1930s debates over a separate Montreal Jewish school system, alongside the Protestant and Roman Catholic boards.[85] At around the same time as Goldstein was appealing to a broad coalition of interested parties to join in the struggle for a more representative Protestant School

Board, others decided to turn to electoral politics as the path to Jewish equality. In 1911, the United Hebrew Political Society was founded with the aim of electing Jews to political office.[86] The *Jewish Times* began an editorial line urging leading Jews to seek elected office. The Jewish communities had failed in their efforts to gain representatives on the school board, and on the two bodies that named commissioners, the provincial government and city council. Up until now Jews had made no communal effort to seek office. The time had come to unite claims of Jewish rights with the practical deployment of Jewish votes.[87] The editorial appeal met with almost immediate success. In 1912 Abraham Blumenthal became the first popularly elected Jewish alderman in Canada.[88] He almost immediately began asserting the rights of Jews to be represented on the Protestant School Board.[89]

Another Montreal Jew, Louis Rubenstein – Canadian, American, and world figure-skating champion, Jewish community activist, and benefactor – joined Blumenthal on the council two years later.[90] Rubenstein served as acting mayor on many occasions. Lyon Jacobs also joined the council in 1918[91] and would become the youngest acting mayor in Montreal history.[92] With strength in numbers and concrete evidence of their increased electoral power in the city, the Jewish communities redoubled their efforts for representation on the Protestant School Board.

Following the 1916 municipal elections, both Blumenthal and Rubenstein were re-elected, but a sitting councillor who had been on the Protestant School Board had lost his seat. Blumenthal proposed that Rubenstein be named to one of the two vacancies on the Protestant School Board.[93] For Montreal Protestants, there was a clear danger. With the two Jewish votes, a Roman Catholic, mischievous majority on the city council could conceivably ignore the wishes of the Protestant community and name Rubenstein to the Protestant board. The churches presented a united front to the city council. The Anglican Synod and the bishop of Montreal declared, "The vacancy in the Protestant School Commission [should] be filled by appointing an Alderman who is a Protestant, and protests against any other than a Protestant, however well qualified in other respects he may be, and would urge the injustice to the Protestant ratepayers of the City of Montreal of any other appointment than that of a Protestant."[94]

The opposition from the Protestant community, carefully couched not just in constitutional terms, but in constitutional terms that would recall to the minds of the Roman Catholic francophone members of the city council that their rights were also protected by section 93 in the compromise between the two founding peoples, scuppered Rubenstein's appointment, at least temporarily.

The next year another vacancy occurred on the Protestant board, and again Rubenstein was nominated.[95] Those opposed to Jewish representation immediately moved that the vote on Rubenstein's nomination be delayed in order that the City Law Department advise the council on whether, under the British North America Act, the provincial legislation establishing Protestant education in the province, and the 1903 Act, "the Council may appoint a person professing the Jewish religion on the Protestant Board of School Commissioners and whether the latter may hold such a position." The referral to the city's lawyers was approved.[96] On 29 May, the attorneys reported back to the council, indicating that the nomination of a Jew to the Protestant School Board was ultra vires. A Protestant councillor was appointed to the board.[97]

Once more, in the face of united Protestant opposition aimed at maintaining the distinct Christian character of the common schools in the city, a Jewish attempt to achieve what they perceived as simple justice failed. Not only did the competing narrative of a properly constituted Protestant school system carry the day, but once more, after *Pinsler*, the legal edifice of section 93 and a complex set of provincial statutes and administrative structures in both Quebec City and Montreal proved to be an insurmountable obstacle to full Jewish emancipation in the educational context. Jews may have been legislatively defined as enjoying the rights of Protestants for school purposes, but in practice that status as ersatz "honorary Protestants" was clearly limited to allowing Jewish students to attend often segregated classes within the Protestant system and compelling Jewish taxpayers to place their money into the Protestant panel. Any idea of a broader interpretation of Jews as "honorary Protestants" and equal citizens was rejected as contrary to the constitutional norms of section 93 and the constitutive self-understanding of Montreal's Protestant communities.

Where law and politics failed, negotiation and discussion came once more to the fore.[98] At a meeting with the Protestant board, Maxwell Goldstein reiterated his 1903 promise and declaration that the Jewish community had no desire to upset or change the Christian character of the Protestant school system. While he declared, in accordance with the dominant uptown view, and echoing Bram De Sola's remarks a few years earlier at McGill University, that the best solution would be the creation of a system of national schools – that is, public schools – with no denominational character at all, he argued to the Protestant representatives that he and the Jewish community could do nothing to change the legal and constitutional character of schooling in Montreal.[99] Instead he once more invoked basic principles of justice and British fair play, calling upon the Protestant representatives to recognize the fundamental equality principle informing Jewish desires for a place on the school board as citizens and as taxpayers.[100]

The Protestants were unmoved. They made it clear to the Jewish delegation that they "would never consent to hand over to Jewish administration and control the splendid educational system"[101] and that they would continue to fight any attempt to ensure Jewish representation as contrary to the constitutional rights of the Protestant population. The Protestant board was willing to continue under the terms of the 1903 Act, but if the Jewish community was unhappy with that arrangement, the Protestants of Montreal would co-operate with them in their efforts to establish a separate Jewish school system.[102] They then addressed Goldstein's invocation of British fair play by highlighting once more their version of the history of the Jewish School Question. When the Jewish community had been unable to educate their children on their own, the Protestants of Montreal had welcomed Jewish children into their schools. They had consented not just to equality in the 1903 Act, but also to the granting of special privileges for Jewish students on matters of religious instruction and the observance of holy days.[103] Moreover, the large numbers of Jewish students in Protestant schools not only jeopardized the Christian character of those schools, but severe financial hardship was still being imposed on the board and on Protestant taxpayers. In the end, the Protestant board reiterated that their insistence on maintaining the Christian character through Protestant control of the schools "is no lack of British Fair Play, but a reasonable precaution in the interests of self-preservation."[104]

The narratives of the two communities passed like ships in the night. For the Jewish representatives, fairness and justice demanded that they be represented on the governing body of the school system to which they paid taxes and to which they sent their children, to be educated as British subjects in Canada. For the Protestant board and the broader Protestant community, their schools were, and must remain, Christian. They were essential to their communal self-definition and to the perpetuation of their presence as a linguistic and religious minority in the province. The schools had always served as a bulwark permitting Protestant existence and flourishing against French-Canadian clerical domination of education. Those protections had been enshrined in the

Canadian Constitution. Now those same schools were under threat from within. Christian grace and charity had been granted to the Jewish community by the Protestant School Board, which not only had taken in Jewish students whose community could not pay for their education, but had granted them special religious dispensations from otherwise compulsory parts of the curriculum.

But no further accommodation could result from this exemption. The Protestant board insisted on their autonomy and authority in school administration and relied on legal formalism to further delimit the actual extent of Jewish religious freedom within the school system. They changed, or reinforced, depending on one's point of view, curricular demands. Because of the requirement of the Council of Public Instruction that the subject form part of the Protestant curriculum, Jewish students would receive the average mark in the class for the subject "New Testament Scripture." They would not be permitted to take an alternative subject.[105] They were treated as Protestants for educational purposes and given full rights to attend common schools under the board's jurisdiction. A line in the interest of the self-preservation of Protestant schools as Protestant schools had to be drawn and maintained. If the Jews were not happy with their current status as Protestants for school purposes, they were free to seek government approval for their own school system.

Not all Protestants necessarily shared the more radical vision of the future, and some even recommended that two Jews be allowed to sit on the school board for a trial period of ten years. However, such compromise was quickly shouted down by voices more experienced in dealing with the Jewish School Question. After the 1916–17 city council affair, the Anglican Synod in Montreal had adopted the emerging view that the only practical solution to the problem was the establishment of a separate system of Jewish schools in the city of Montreal.[106] For educational purposes, the "honorary Protestants" could stay together in Jewish classes taught by Jewish teachers, or they could create their own school system.

At the same time, the social and political context was becoming more hostile to the increasing flow of Jewish immigrants into the city. Incidents of physical violence against Jews were recorded throughout the period.[107] Roman Catholic anti-Semitism, in its nationalist variant was becoming more and more widespread. Any liberal voice among the majority population, especially in educational matters, was subjected to vicious and sustained ultramontane attacks.[108] The future of the

Jewish School Question would be decided in a series of constitutive discourses in which Jews would play only a part. The constitutional structure of education in Montreal, with its confessional duality, would make some place, however begrudgingly, for a set of discourses about Jewish schools and Jews in schools, but that set of tropes would always be overdetermined by other sets of rhetorics about national identities, the Christian character of Canada and of Quebec, and the essential fact that section 93 left very little room for the formal political or legal creation of a space for the public education of Jewish citizens in Montreal.

7

Jews, Protestants, and Taxes (Again): The Jewish School Question in the 1920s

Demography, Sociology, and the Jewish Communities of Montreal in the 1920s

This chapter traces the development of the Jewish School Question through a series of crises in the 1920s. The period was one of economic and social upheaval, and of demographic change within the city of Montreal and beyond. In Quebec the 1920s also saw the emergence of a public discourse of blatant and increasingly virulent anti-Semitism, a discourse often supported by elements within the hierarchy of the Roman Catholic Church. The discussion that follows traces how these demographic changes and the anti-Semitic attitudes abroad in society led not just to a series of conflicts about the Jewish presence itself, but also, again, how the Jewish School Question came to be a focus for these broader social and political concerns. It briefly traces the place of other immigrant groups within these broad political and legal concerns around the educational structures of the city's schools and unsurprisingly discusses in some detail the re-emergence of fiscal crises as the apparent impetus for the latest iterations of the Jewish School Question.

The period that followed the Jewish representation conflicts of the late 1910s was one of continuing demographic and social change in the city of Montreal in general, and more particularly within the Jewish communities.[1] In 1921, 93.7 per cent of all Jews in Greater Montreal lived within the city limits. The 42,817 Jews of the city constituted 6.7

per cent of the population. The next-highest totals were in the neighbouring cities of Outremont (1,195/9 per cent) and Westmount (1,002/5.7 per cent).[2] In the next decade, to the census of 1931, the year in which this part of the Jewish School Question would be resolved once again, the Jewish population of Montreal began their inexorable move westward. While the city population grew to 48,724 Jews, the Jewish percentage of the overall population fell to 5.9 per cent. In the municipalities of Outremont and Westmount, the Jewish populations grew to 6,783 (23.7 per cent) and 1,1780 (7.3 per cent).[3] For the period of the 1920s, the significant number of Jews in the city of Montreal proper would concern the Protestant School Board and lead to the next crisis in the city's schools.

The Jewish population was still concentrated in the St Lawrence ghetto, in the city's east end.[4] Such population concentrations were and are, of course, not unknown in the history of immigration. In Montreal, in addition to the general phenomenon of immigrant clusters, throughout its history, the city has seen characteristically segregated housing areas along linguistic and ethnic or national origin lines. Thus anglophones and francophones have been associated with certain areas of the city, as have more specific subgroups, such as the city's Irish populations.[5] Population density had already played a role the evolution of the Jewish School Question for the Protestant School Board. But the existence and growth of the ghetto also concretized important social changes in the lives and needs of the Montreal Jewish communities.[6] The large increase in numbers of Yiddish-speaking Eastern European Jews would challenge the social, cultural, and political dominance of the traditional anglophone Jewish elite.[7] The dynamics of the downtowner versus uptowner debates would play a significant role in the Jewish School Question, as would the import of Jewish religious practices from Eastern Europe, accompanied by a new set of Jewish religious officials who would make claims of representative status that again would challenge the authority of the traditional, established synagogues.[8]

In addition, the social composition of the communities underwent rapid change. More and more Jews became part of the working class and participated in political movements alongside their comrades.[9] At the same time, their children experienced the deprivations of the working-class poor in Montreal, and the Jewish community, like other working-class immigrants, suffered from juvenile delinquency and youth unemployment, and child labour issues in increasing numbers.[10] As it had always been, education was still identified as a way of improving the lives of these children and their families. But the immigrants also brought with them conflicting ideas of religiosity and secularism, as well as all the divisions and disputes that had characterized the European left. To demonstrate their freedom from archaic religious practices, anarchists in Montreal held a Yom Kippur Ball, a secular party on the highest holy day, the Day of Atonement, when observant Jews pray, contemplate repentance, and attend synagogue, fifteen years after the phenomenon had occurred in London and New York.[11] Labour and Socialist Zionists, like their comrades in Europe, fought not just between themselves but also with the religious authorities within the communities.[12] Jewish education, as a separate idea of cultural or religious schooling to supplement Canadian secular education, competed with ideals of a complete and self-contained Jewish education, secular or religious, in People's schools, Peretz schools, Talmud Torah, etc.[13]

But again, the debates over the Jewish School Question in this period would occur in contexts that were not uniquely Jewish. In the broader educational field, the 1920s were a time of financial difficulties for both denominational systems, as the population of Montreal grew not just with Jewish immigration, but also with an influx of rural French-Canadians seeking employment.[14] It was also a time of financial and structural difficulties for the provincial Protestant system as rural schools continued to be seriously under-resourced, and as Protestant populations also moved – problems that had surfaced earlier and would trouble the Protestant system in the interwar period.[15] Within both denominational systems, local communities and other groups lobbied for more representative membership at the provincial level on the two Committees of the Council of Public Instruction. Women, teachers, and working-class organizations all made serious attempts to challenge the male, clerical, and professional elite memberships of the two committees. Objections were made to the practice of nominating sitting politicians to the governing bodies, often revisiting older concerns about the politicization of education. While Protestant women did gain some small measure of success, most of the other pleas for representative educational governance fell on deaf ears.[16] The world of education administration into which the Jewish School Question would re-emerge from 1920 to 1932 was not one of peace and tranquillity. Nor, as this chapter will demonstrate, was Quebec society, more broadly speaking, without its fundamental disputes. Immigrant communities, particularly Jewish immigrant communities, were seen to pose a threat to Quebec's national identity. In this atmosphere, virulent anti-Semitism would become increasingly manifest and it, in turn, would inform many interventions into the Jewish School Question. The chapter also highlights how the arrival of other significant immigrant minorities, whose children needed education, would raise particular questions about Quebec society, and in the specific context of a dual Roman Catholic/Protestant educational matrix, it would bring into the harsh light of day the often artificial and unsatisfactory nature of Protestant/English, Roman Catholic/French social and educational narratives.

Outside the educational domain, other interests would instigate debates and changes, intervene in the political and legislative realms, and turn the issues of the Jewish School Question into concerns over Protestant and Roman Catholic identities and power, and such debates, as in early iterations of the Jewish School Question, ultimately decided the outcome of the issues that would directly affect the minority Jewish community.[17] These interventions and dynamic interactions would occur in the school context, but they would not necessarily be concerned primarily with the place of Jewish children in the city's common school system. For many French Canadians, and especially for the intellectual class, for example, the broader area of social, cultural, and political concern was the phenomenon of Jewish immigration *tout court*. This influx of new arrivals upset even more the delicate balance between the two solitudes at the core of the dominant dualist visions of Canadian identity.[18] The rising number of Jews threatened to directly challenge the Christian character of Quebec. More particularly, the ideal of a French-Canadian national identity as a Roman Catholic community was under threat as French Canadians, especially in Montreal, were surrounded by Protestants and increasingly by Jews.[19] The immigration question would figure prominently in French-Canadian nationalist discourse and politics in the 1920s, and it would manifest itself in increasing public anti-Semitism.

Many of the messages of French-Canadian anti-Semitism came from the francophone elite and from within the educational establishment. Max and Monique Nemni, in their intellectual biography of Pierre Elliott Trudeau and his time at the *collège classique* Brébeuf, a hotbed of Jesuit-influenced French-Canadian nationalism and training ground for the future elite of Quebec, detail Trudeau's authorship of a one-act play with strong and undisguised anti-Semitic elements.[20] John English also highlights Trudeau's involvement with nationalist politics and his ready adoption of the anti-Semitism that was part of the *air du temps* in these educational circles.[21] Unsurprisingly perhaps, in his own *Memoirs* Trudeau was silent about such incidents and attitudes, which of course he would transcend.[22] What is of interest is that, at the time, Trudeau's attitudes, formed to a large extent in a particular elite Roman Catholic educational environment, serve as but one reflective example of the manifestation of the dominant ideals of a French-Canadian nationalism of which anti-Semitism was a core element.

But as with the School Question, any debate about anti-Semitism in Quebec in the period under review in the rest of this chapter must be placed in a more nuanced context. As the noted historian of Quebec Jewry and intercultural relations, Pierre Anctil, explains, "Any study of antisemitism in Quebec in the interwar period has to take into account a number of factors that have little to do with either Jews or Judaism."[23]

The anxieties of cultural and social identity among Canadiens grew as regional, rural Quebec was depopulated, as French-Canadian farmers left to seek employment in larger urban centres, and those collective existential worries caused by immigration were acute. However, Anctil points out that the earliest manifestations of clear anti-Jewish bias were to be found in the anglophone Protestant communities of Montreal. In 1913, only 6.8 per cent of students at McGill University were Jewish. By 1924–5, that figure had risen to a quarter of the freshman class. In arts, the number reached 32 per cent, and in law, 41 per cent.[24] Jewish students had benefited from their status as "honorary Protestants" for educational purposes under the 1903 statutory regime and now were beginning to seek further advantages through higher education. McGill instituted a *numerus clausus* by requiring higher grades from Jewish university applicants than those demanded of Christians.

But if both French and English Canadians, Protestant and Roman Catholic, in Montreal voiced and concretized anti-Semitism in broader social and economic contexts, it was in debates over the Jewish School Question that the complex set of constituting narratives of Jewish, Roman Catholic, and Protestant identities and community self-definitions would come to the fore. Most significantly, this is the point in the history of the Jewish School Question that Roman Catholic anti-Semitism began to figure in the debate in a specific way. Ultramontane elements used Jewish claims for equality to launch broader attacks on the Jewish peril, on the influx of immigrants, on Jewish communists, and above all on the threat that these Jews posed to the very existence of Quebec, of Canada for Canadiens, who were, of course, Roman Catholics. Protestant anti-Semitism would not go away, and it would be quite visible in the Jewish School Question in the 1920s, but it was the turn to ultramontane, public anti-Semitic discourse that marked out the 1920s, followed by the rise of a *fascisant* ultramontanism in 1930s, as a particular and important phase in the Jewish School Question.

Once again, the dynamic interactions would construct themselves in narratives situated and constituted at the margins of legality and at the very heart of legal discourse. Jewish Montrealers would invoke law to construct a positive place as equal citizens, and at the same time Protestants and Roman Catholics would use law as a constitutional bulwark of exclusion and self-protection. The jurisprudential shield of section 93 would once again be deployed in attempts to define the educational realm as one in which equality existed for only the two founding nations. In the shadows of this legalized discourse, politics provided the ground for attempts to find a third way in which narratives of, and demands for, Jewish equality rights and full emancipated status could be given some kind of concrete form.

Beyond the Jewish School Question: Non–Roman Catholic Non-Protestants, and Montreal's School System

But even before these debates could take place, other voices emerged, and they too would seek a place in the constitutive and constitutional discourses of the Jewish School Question. Jews, obviously, were not the only immigrants to seek a better life in Canada. Among the groups that had established themselves in Montreal as the nineteenth century came to an end and the twentieth began were Chinese, Greek, Italian, Ukrainian, and Syrian/Lebanese communities. They too had children and they sought to educate them in the ways and mores of their new country, while at the same time keeping the languages and traditions of their homelands alive.[25] Mordecai Richler offers a trenchant assessment, from the perspective of the Jewish students, of the situation at Fletcher's Field High School, his fictionalized version of Baron Byng: "For making their way in the world his first students had also graduated from the streets of cold-water flats that surrounded FFHS to buy their own duplexes in the tree-lined streets of Outremont. In fact, that morning as Mr MacPherson hesitated on a scalp of glittering white ice, there were already three gentiles in the school that is to say, Anglo-Saxons; for Ukrainians, Poles, and Yugoslavs, with funny names and customs of their own, did not count as true gentiles."[26]

It is not possible to do justice to these complex histories of Montreal immigration, but their voices, and their very presence, were part of the debates in the first third of the twentieth century as the Jewish School Question became, for some at least, a question of non-Catholic non-Protestants, that is of all groups who did not fit within the constitutional duality of Quebec educational rights. Like the Jews before them, at least some of these groups had to look for ways to ensure access to common schools in Montreal, while not fitting into the category Protestant or Roman Catholic. Others, who could be placed within the operative religious taxonomy of Quebec education, nonetheless also exposed the fractures and fissures that occurred when social, cultural, and political reality rubbed up against historically sterile legal categories.

Some of these immigrant groups fit the dominant paradigm because they could be classified as Protestant or Roman Catholic. Many within the Chinese community, while maintaining communal cultural practices that would be classified generally, and not always accurately, as Confucian, did formally convert to Protestantism or Roman Catholicism. Some had been converted by (mostly) Protestant missionaries before they had left China, while others converted in Montreal as a result of the efforts of domestic Christian missionaries.[27] Thus, for the Chinese populations of Montreal, the real question was not whether they could attend the common schools,[28] since they met the religious test, but whether and how the two common school systems would deal with maintaining traditional customs and, in the school context, with giving instruction in English (or French) as well as in the native tongues of the immigrants.[29]

At this stage in the diaspora, Ukrainian immigrants were mostly Roman Catholics. The problem for them again was in seeking Ukrainian-language instruction within the Roman Catholic school system and in dealing with suspicions among the church hierarchy that the community was under communist influence.[30] As with the Chinese, the educational issue was constructed in terms of maintaining cultural identity and the native language within the established denominational school system. For the Roman Catholic School Commission, the presence of and the demands for instruction in the native languages of these immigrant groups would pose practical and ideological difficulties. While concessions to the long-established Irish Roman Catholics could be and had been made to fit within the dominant paradigm of the two founding peoples,[31] ideas of multiculturalism and multilingualism were still unimaginable. In Montreal, for the Roman Catholic Church and the members of the school board, the French language was an essential part of the Franco-Catholic national identity, which the church and its schools were meant to safeguard.[32] The idea of Roman Catholic instruction that was in neither French nor English was almost incomprehensible to local education officials.

Similar concerns also played a significant role in the place of Italian Roman Catholic immigrants to Montreal. Not only did they wish to educate their children in a way that would maintain their ethnic, national identity as Italian, but they also wanted to educate their children in English, rather than in French. Italian immigrants saw themselves at this historical juncture largely as immigrants to North America, rather than to Canada or Quebec or Montreal.[33] Their family and local networks from the home country among other Italian immigrants spread across Canada and into the United States. Therefore they saw their children's future in the broader continental context and they realized that English was the North American language.[34] In addition, during the economic crises of the 1920s and 1930s, the Roman Catholic educational and social services infrastructures experienced serious and severe financial strain. As a result, many Italian immigrants "converted" to Protestantism in order to have access to a seemingly better-funded but still enormously strained social welfare system and to schools that were not only financially better off, but whose language of instruction was English.[35]

Other groups fit precisely into the emerging non–Roman Catholic, non-Protestant category, most notably the Greek and Syrian immigrants to Montreal. Each was Christian, but neither was Protestant nor Roman Catholic. While the Greek community would later split along political and theological lines, they were always predominantly members of the Greek Orthodox religion.[36] As with many immigrant communities to Montreal, at this time and later in the twentieth century, they saw that English-language education offered greater opportunities for their children, and they sought entry into the Protestant school system as a result. At the same time, they also established Greek day schools to allow their children to be educated in their parents' native tongue and in the tenets of the family's Orthodox religion.[37] Like the Italians and Jews, Greeks in Montreal would engage in delicate and sometimes troubled struggles with the two dominant communities, as they sought out a place in the social, economic, linguistic, and political structures of Montreal that would permit them to participate as citizens, while at the same time maintaining and concretizing their cultural identities and practices, which were not Roman Catholic or Protestant, French or English.[38]

The first group of Syrian (or Syrian-Lebanese) immigrants to Montreal came from the same region along the Syrian-Lebanese border and were all members of the Syrian Greek Orthodox religion, although again theological divisions did manifest themselves.[39] Because they came from an area within the French sphere of influence, many members of the community already had a facility in French and might have sent their children to schools within the Roman Catholic system. During the early days of the crisis that would emerge as the Jewish School Question in 1921 and 1922, the Syrian Orthodox community of Montreal arranged to hire a lawyer and had lobbied the Quebec government so that their situation would be taken into account in any settlement of the crisis or change to the educational arrangements in the city. As they made clear in their petition and in subsequent meetings with provincial and school officials, they were not Roman Catholic and saw themselves as excluded from that system on religious (but not linguistic) grounds. Because their taxes went to the neutral panel, the Protestant School Board had begun to refuse to allow their children to attend Protestant schools. They sought in their pleas and negotiations either to be allowed to pay their taxes into the Protestant panel or to have a separate panel for themselves.[40] As the Jewish community had many years earlier, the Syrian community pleaded with the superintendent of public instruction to remedy the situation in which they found themselves because they wished to "allow for their children the education which would make them into citizens for the greater good of the country."[41] Narratives of citizenship and belonging once more surfaced in the educational realm, but as usual they came from immigrant communities who wanted their children to become Canadian. Meanwhile the Protestant and Roman Catholic systems saw these non–Roman Catholic non-Protestants as troublesome interlopers who did not even pay their school taxes into Panels 1 or 2.

The problem of non–Roman Catholic non-Protestants in the Protestant school system had been simmering for some time. The 1914–15 report of the Board of Protestant School Commissioners enumerated the presence in Protestant schools of 26 "Greek Catholics,"[42] a number that was reduced to 18 the following year.[43] By 1922, it had risen to 511.[44] In 1915, the Council of Public Instruction considered reports from both the Protestant and Roman Catholic boards in Montreal indicating that the presence of "Italians, Polish, Ruthenian and others" was causing significant concern to both common school systems.[45] As time passed, the Protestant board began to present the problem as a broad one of all non–Roman Catholics non-Protestants. In doing so, they deliberately submerged the specificities of the historical Jewish case, the 1903 statute, segregation of students, discrimination against qualified Jewish candidates for teaching posts, and the spectre of separate Jewish schools, under a broader concern over all groups that posed a series of essential questions to the two solitudes enshrined in the exceptional text of section 93.[46] Of course there was validity to claims by these groups to equality as British subjects wishing to send their children to public schools, and especially for the Greek and Italian communities, alongside Montreal's Jews, these events would serve in part at least to consolidate political and social movements within the communities.[47] Despite Protestant claims to the contrary, however, by the beginning of the 1920s, the problem was still essentially the Jewish School Question and not the non–Roman Catholic, non-Protestant problem.

From Bad to Worse: Jewish Students, Jewish Taxes, and Protestant Schools

Reports from the Protestant Board of School Commissioners from the period following Dr Finnie's failed attempts to create a system of elected commissioners highlighted the demographic facts that would give rise, in the early 1920s, to the next concrete phase in the Jewish School Question. In 1911–12, there were 9,830 Protestant students enrolled in the board's schools, and 6,858 Jews.[48] Jews had also succeeded, as Protestants for the purposes of education, in winning a number of Commissioners' Scholarships. From Aberdeen School the winners were Aidinger, Becker, Benjamin, Friedman, Ginsberg, Hornstein, Klineberg, Lewis, Louis, Meyerovitch, Rapaport, and Shraga. From Dufferin School, Cohen, Hirshorn, Hoffman, Kaufman, Schultz, Shultz, and Weiner won Protestant School Board scholarships.[49] In the 1914–15 school year, the Protestant numbers had grown to 12,131 and the Jewish students to 9,642.[50] The following year, the number of Protestants was relatively unchanged, but the number of Jewish children in Montreal's Protestant schools was now 10,027.[51] Protestant numbers had risen to 18,597 by 1922–3, while there were now 11,974 Jewish students.[52] Although there were significant numbers of Jewish students in the Protestant schools in raw numbers, the actual ratio of Protestant to Jew was in fact changing slightly in favour of the Protestant population. At the highest point, there had been .82 Jewish students for each enrolled Protestant, but by 1922–3 that had fallen to .64. In 1924, for example, eleven Protestant schools in Montreal had a majority Jewish student body, whereas by 1928 that number had been reduced to nine, all of which were in the ghetto.[53]

For the Protestant School Board, however, the more important consideration was that because Jewish students continued to come from immigrant and working-class backgrounds, their families did not pay school tax because they did not own real estate. As far as the Protestant school officials were concerned, the great 1903 experiment of the alchemical change of Jews into "honorary Protestants" continued to be a financial failure. The school tax system, as the Protestant Board had insisted at the time of the 1903 statute, had to be changed and Protestants relieved of the burden of subsidizing the education of Jewish students. In addition, the ever-present problem of the Protestant character of a school system with such a substantial minority of Jewish students continued to trouble Protestant school officials in Montreal.[54] The Jewish ideal of "sharing the lifestyle, educational system and social ideals of an open, democratic nation," to be achieved in this context by attending public schools, was now confronted by the constitutional peculiarity of Canadian education under section 93, and the social and psychological reality of Protestant fears about the loss of the Christian identity of their schools.[55]

The Protestant School Board of Montreal sought to bring about significant changes in the ways in which minority populations, but particularly Jews, were dealt with within the common schools of Montreal. In order to do so, they demanded the abolition of the 1903 Act and changes to the school tax system, the most important of which would be a stipulation that the Protestant board have a first claim on the funds from the neutral panel to make up for the shortfall between the actual cost of educating Jewish students and the amount received under the arrangement by which Jewish taxes were paid into the Protestant panel. After several years of growing frustration and some aborted attempts to bring about those changes, the Protestant educational establishment of the province and the city finally managed to gain enough political momentum to draft legislation to deal with the problems facing Protestant education in Montreal.

With the Reverend Rexford in the chair, the Protestant Committee of the Provincial Council of Public Instruction met on 26 May 1922.[56]

Among the legislative proposals that came out of the meeting was the idea of a first charge on the neutral panel to meet the cost-revenue differential for Jewish students, calculated on the basis of a cost per annum of $60 per student (section 3(2)). Each of the two school boards would be required to file an annual report on the number of "Jewish and other non–Roman Catholic non-Protestant children" enrolled (section 4). The proposal called for the distribution of the remaining neutral panel funds on the long-debated pro rata basis. And to avoid double counting, notwithstanding the 1903 Act, Jews would not be classed as Protestants for this purpose (section 5). After 1 January 1923 (although the proposed Act was meant to come into effect on 1 May 1923), the Montreal Board of Assessors was to place a distinctive mark – a *J* – as an indication next to the name of each Jewish taxpayer (section 7). Finally, section 8 would allow the lieutenant governor in council, the government, after 1 July 1924, to repeal the 1903 Act insofar as it applied to the city of Montreal.

The Protestant Committee of Public Instruction, at the behest of the Protestant board in Montreal, sought to get rid of the legal fiction of Protestant Jews within the educational system in Montreal and to replace it with a system of strictly identifying Jewish taxpayers, ensuring that it would receive, via its first charge on Panel 3, full compensation for the cost of educating Jewish students. While there was a mention of other non–Roman, Catholic non-Protestant students in section 4, it was clearly the aim of the Protestant educational establishment to return to a version of the pre-*Pinsler* situation in Montreal. The 1903 Act had guaranteed not just a system of the payment of Jewish school taxes into the Protestant panel, but the rights of Jewish children to attend Protestant schools as Protestants. The thrust of the proposed legislation was to remove those rights and to once again treat Jews as Jews for educational purposes.

But even that did not go far enough for the Protestant School Board in Montreal. They decided that they now wanted to create a new system under which Jews would not be treated as Jews at all, but instead would fall under the new catchall non–Roman Catholic, non-Protestant rubric.[57] They demanded the immediate repeal of the 1903 Act, the payment of all taxes by non–Roman Catholic, non-Protestant (now including Jewish) proprietors of real estate into the neutral panel. The consequence of that reclassification would then be that the education of non–Roman Catholic, non-Protestant students would become the first charge on the neutral panel, from which payments would be made to the two systems based on the number of these non–Roman Catholic, non-Protestant pupils present in each. Finally all students falling into the new taxonomy of Montreal education would have the right to attend the common school, Roman Catholic or Protestant, of their election. Delegates of the combined Protestant committee and the Protestant school board had met with the provincial government on 9 November. The case that the Protestant community, itself a minority within Quebec, had been forced to subsidize the education of other minorities for several years was put forcefully to the premier.

While it was understandable that these minorities turned to the Protestant system because they wanted their children educated in English, this choice by Jews and by other groups, especially at this point Orthodox populations, had imposed significant burdens on Montreal's Protestants. First, the school tax rate was higher for the neutral panel and the Protestant panel than it was for Roman Catholic taxpayers, again simply because there were far more Roman Catholic taxpayers in the population, allowing the tax burden to be spread. Second, the extra cost of educating minority students had come from limited resources, which meant that the real victims in the case were the Protestant students in Montreal who were deprived of a valuable Protestant education. The Jewish School Question was, from their perspective, really a Protestant School Question under which Protestant children suffered irreparable harm under the burden imposed on the school system by the presence of large numbers of Jews, or as they now wished to describe them, of non-Protestant, non–Roman Catholic students.

The school board was on the horns of a dilemma. The Protestant tax rate was already higher than the Roman Catholic rate, so that any further increase would be politically untenable and would again impose a burden on Protestant taxpayers to subsidize the education of non-Protestants. It was also unfair that in a dual confessional school system only one of the denominations was faced with the real cost of educating these minority groups. Almost without exception, non-Protestant, non–Roman Catholic students attended or sought to attend the Protestant schools of Montreal. Finally, the Protestant committee and board representatives emphasized to the premier and his Cabinet colleagues that any necessary changes could be considered only if the legislation contained provisions "safe-guarding ... the rights secured to the Protestant minority by the Act of Confederation to conduct, under their own management, a system of schools which are Christian and Protestant."[58]

Once again constitutional protections were available to the minority Protestant population, but other, lesser minorities were without such legal safeguards. Indeed the thrust of the Protestant position throughout 1922 had been to return to the status quo ante, to abolish the statutory regime of 1903, which had granted Jews a type of equality by insisting that they be considered Protestants for school purposes. The revocation of the statutory and fragile rights of these "honorary Protestants" was now the focus of Protestant pleas. Protestant officials now insisted that all non–Roman Catholic, non-Protestants should pay taxes into the neutral panel and attend institutions in either of the common school systems. At least there appeared to be some implicit recognition that the children of these non–Roman Catholic, non-Protestant taxpayers might be free to attend school without having to rely on the Christian grace of the two commissions, and that they had some right to do so. But all of these statements came from a Protestant board that continued to segregate Jewish students and refused to give much more than lip service to the idea of hiring Jewish teachers.[59]

The Protestant Committee of the Council of Public Instruction received another report from the special committee dealing with non–Roman Catholic, non-Protestant children.[60] The real issue at hand, the cause of Protestant aggravation, was the presence of almost 15,000 Jewish students in the Protestant school system.[61] But despite objections voiced by Maxwell Goldstein on behalf of the Jewish community, the government had agreed to enact legislation that incorporated many of the previous suggestions from the various Protestant bodies.[62] A new category – non–Roman Catholic, non-Protestant, and non-Jewish taxpayer – was created, and those in that group would pay into the neutral panel. Their children could attend schools in either of the denominational systems, and the cost of their education would come from a charge on the neutral panel determined at the rate of $60 per student. The Protestant board would receive the same amount from Jewish tax monies and then any remainder from the neutral panel. The Jewish taxpayers would have the mark *J* placed in government records, as their European brethren would experience only more than a decade later. Finally, the statute would include provisions permitting the government to abolish the 1903 Act after 1 July 1924.[63]

The Jews had won a temporary reprieve. The 1903 Act remained in effect, at least temporarily, so that they remained Protestants for school purposes, although they were now Protestants for educational purposes against whose names city tax assessors would enter the letter *J*. The other minority immigrant groups now had a legislatively mandated right to send their children to the schools of their choice, and the Protestant and Roman Catholic boards would each gain a further slice of neutral panel taxes on the pro-rated basis that had long been mooted in discussions between the two groups. But the insistence of the Protestant board on maintaining the Protestant character of its schools, and the ongoing complaints about the financial burden posed by Jewish (and non–Roman Catholic, non-Protestant) students were ominous. The Act respecting the education of non–Roman Catholic, non-Protestant children of Montreal, embodying the agreement, did little to assuage concerns.[64] The preamble indicated not just that Jews continued to constitute a problem, but that any such problem would always be solely understood in the framework of the dual confessional system: "Whereas, since 1903, the population of non–Roman Catholic non-Protestant children has increased very largely, and their education has become a heavy burden upon the resources of the Protestant School Board of the city of Montreal; and Whereas it is recognized by Roman Catholics and Protestants alike that a remedy must be applied to the situation thus created ... "

The apparent gains of 1903 were now shown in all their fragility. The 1922 statute provided for the repeal of that emancipatory law by the government in a little over a year. Jews were still free to attend Protestant schools, but the constitutional and constitutive frame had shifted. The dominant discourse of Protestant and Roman Catholic systems of common schools had been challenged by the growing number of Jewish students and by the arrival of other non-Jewish immigrant groups who again simply asked for equality in educating their children as British subjects in Canada. But full equality was constitutionally unknown and unknowable in the common schools of Montreal. Jews were equal only because of the legalistic taxonomical trickery operated by the 1903 Act, a mystical legal transformation that now was clearly under threat. Everyone else, more recently arrived, without the growing Jewish political influence, which came with large numbers, fell into yet another ersatz category, unknown to constitutional discourse and yet firmly grounded in the semiotics of dual confessionality. They were "non": non-people for educational purposes, non–Roman Catholic, non-Protestant. Then they were changed from "non" to neutral for the always-important purpose of school taxation. Still they had a right to choose which school system to attend.

But the principal issue remained the very existence of Jewish school rights within the common, Protestant educational system. The eighteen-month delay until the possible repeal of the 1903 Act was meant to provide a period in which the two parties could return to past practice and reach an amicable and mutually acceptable agreement.[65] But the problem was that a significant portion of the Protestant educational establishment, although not all of the actors on the Protestant side, saw the 1923 Act not just as a victory for their desire to maintain and further concretize the position of Protestant schools in Montreal, but as the first step in a process which would lead to the repeal of the 1903 Act.[66] For many influential voices within the Protestant community, the final abolition of the 1903 Act, presaged in the 1922 law, was really the most important provision of that statute. It laid out a clear timetable for the restoration of full Protestant control over the Protestant school system. For them, the constitutional and constitutive normative baseline was to be found in the text of section 93 and in the pre-1903 structure of provincial school legislation. Those legal texts had constructed the reality of the Protestant school system as a system for and by Protestants. Non–Roman Catholic non-Protestants, including Jews, simply had no place in the dual denominational narrative of identity and belonging in the province's and the city's school systems. School tax revenues were important, but Protestant schools for Protestants were existentially vital.

Jews, Protestants, and the Constitutive Reality of Law and Politics, 1922–1923

Two developments in the history of Montreal Jewries would coincide with this latest manifestation of the Jewish School Question, and each would have profound effects on the ways in which the issues were placed in the public domain, debated, and used to inform broader constitutive discourses of Jewish identities within the dynamics of a political, social, and economic context dominated by the two solitudes. Following on the electoral success in earlier Montreal council elections, the first important development was the election of Peter Bercovitch as a Liberal member of the provincial Legislative Assembly. The second vital event was the creation of the Jewish Community Council, the Va'ad Hair.

Peter Bercovitch, the son of Romanian immigrant parents, was born in Montreal in 1879. He graduated in law with degrees from McGill and Laval universities and was named king's counsel in 1911, the youngest lawyer in Canada to gain that title at the time.[67] Most significantly, he became the first Jew to be elected to, and take his seat in, the Quebec Legislative Assembly in 1916.[68] In 1923 he was the only Liberal to maintain his seat on the Island of Montreal. Throughout his career, he represented the interests of Montreal's Jewish communities, ensuring the passage of legislation to validate Jewish marriages and to permit all rabbis in the Jewish communities to maintain registers of civil status, a right already granted to other denominations in the province, but only to some Jewish congregations and to rabbis who were British subjects.[69] While he came to be seen as the Jewish representative in the Assembly, Bercovitch was more generally an active and influential member of the Liberal Party. To a great extent, his efforts on behalf of the Jewish community could have succeeded only because he was very well regarded by his fellow parliamentarians, and particularly by the Quebec premier, Louis-Alexandre Taschereau. Like Sam Jacobs in Ottawa,[70] and his more recent colleague in the Quebec Assembly, Joseph Cohen,[71] Bercovitch always had to tread a careful line between general party and government interests, as was his duty as a Liberal member, and his clear vision of the rightful place for Jews in Quebec and Canadian society. He was an ethnic member, but he served both sets of interests with distinction and tenacity.[72] He would play a key role in the evolution of the Jewish School Question throughout the 1920s and early 1930s.

The second key development in the history of Montreal Jewry, at the time when the Protestant School Board was adopting strategies to be rid of its obligations to the Jews of the city imposed in the 1903 Act, was the creation of the Va'ad Hair, the Jewish Community Council.[73] Founded in 1922 by a group of Orthodox Jews, led by Hirsch Wolofsky, the publisher and editor of the *Eagle*, the Va'ad sought to become a unifying voice for Orthodox Jewry, not just in Montreal, but also in Canada.[74] Coming out of the downtown community, but with establishment figures of uptown Orthodox Jewry such as Lyon Cohen among its leadership, it saw itself as a unified body representing the wishes and interests of those in the Jewish community who felt that the Jewish establishment in the city, the uptowners, had failed to properly take into account their needs and concerns. One of the main tensions between the two groups was over the School Question, underlying which were the more basic constitutive debates and splits over the place of schooling in Jewish communities. The uptowners would persist in the belief of a "republican" ideal of citizenship through schooling in the public school system.[75] On the other hand, many Orthodox Jews believed that education was and should be a matter of religious (male) training.

On many other subjects, including ideas of citizenship and belonging, however, the Orthodox community leaders and rabbis were far from united.[76] In addition, traditional religious views conflicted internally with the secular tendencies within the downtown community, represented by left-wing branches of the political spectrum and of divisions within political Zionism, whose members saw Jewish cultural, linguistic, and political education as essential to citizenship, but not necessarily to Canadian citizenship. For them, education was meant to serve in the formation of ideal Zionists, future citizens of an Israel still idealized and yet to come.

The Va'ad would become an important player in the School Question in the 1920s and early 1930s as it presented itself as the new voice of the Jewish Orthodox, immigrant majority. However, it would also soon be racked by internal divisions, over intra-Orthodox theological issues, between Orthodox and secular ideals of Jewish identity, and most well known, over its failed efforts to establish itself as the sole arbiter of *shechita* (ritual slaughter) and of kashrut generally.[77] From its earliest days, it presented itself to the provincial government as the authentic voice of the majority of Montreal Jews. It objected to the 1922 statute, agreed to by Goldstein, Nathan Gordon,[78] and Michael Hirsch,[79] as the Jewish Educational Committee representatives, who came out of the historically central role played by the Baron de Hirsch Institute in representing Jewish educational interests.[80] Already the Jewish community was divided in the face of a concerted Protestant effort to put an end to the arrangements set out in the 1903 Act.

The revanchist elements in the Protestant educational community continued their plans to end the arrangement and guarantees of equality enshrined in the 1903 Act. They aimed to take back the Protestant common schools for Protestants. While they were preparing to introduce legislation in the Quebec Legislative Assembly that would allow them to achieve this goal, the Protestant board met with representatives of the Jewish communities on 18 October 1923. Nathan Gordon and Maxwell Goldstein spoke for the uptowners. Gordon underlined that it was impossible to determine exactly how many Jews were represented by either group, but he did highlight that he and Goldstein, with the support of Peter Bercovitch, who was unable to attend due to illness, did represent the views of "a very large and influential section of Jewish ratepayers, organizations, and incorporated companies."[81] Somewhat ironically, perhaps, the group that had a few years earlier railed against claims from the Spanish and Portuguese synagogue that it represented the biggest taxpayers in the Jewish community, the Baron de Hirsch group, the uptowners, now made similar claims to legitimize their views in front of the Protestant board in opposition to the Orthodox Va'ad.

Gordon and Goldstein underlined to the school board that the groups they represented were essentially content with the present system and wished to maintain the arrangements under which Jewish children frequented the Protestant schools of the city. Again, Goldstein argued for a return to the traditional mechanisms of dialogue and negotiation between the parties to settle any outstanding differences, none of which "could not be amicably solved."[82]

The downtowners were less accommodating, although they did thank the Protestant board for its historic role in educating Jewish children. For them, however, the time had come for a new system of educational governance in the city, one that included separate Jewish schools and a separate Jewish tax panel. Their chief spokesperson was Louis Fitch. Fitch had been admitted to the Bar in 1911 and had joined the law firm of Sam Jacobs. Fitch was a staunch Zionist and a prominent member of the downtowner community. At the height of this crisis in the Jewish School Question, Fitch would be narrowly defeated by Peter Bercovitch in a provincial election.[83]

His fellow Jewish lawyer, Michael Garber,[84] and Rabbi Hirsch Cohen[85] joined him as downtowner representatives and as the spokespersons for the ideal of a separate Jewish school system. The Protestant School Board took note of the presentations and promised to give them its full consideration.

Its full consideration consisted of drafting legislation to be introduced before the Assembly repealing the 1903 Act. After consulting with the Protestant Committee of the Council of Public Instruction, less than a month after meeting with the representatives of the Jewish communities, the board gathered on 16 November 1923 to discuss and approve a draft bill dealing with the issue of "the education of non-Protestants and non–Roman Catholics."[86] At this point the board was still invoking the rhetorical taxonomy that denied any existence to Jews as a separate category in Montreal school politics, preferring to simply lump the entire mass of the population that did not belong to one or the other of the dual denominations protected by law. The draft discussed and approved by the board contained provisions repealing the 1903 Act and requiring all non-Protestant, non–Roman Catholic taxpayers to pay into the neutral panel, from which their monies would go to either of the two officially sanctioned boards. Gone at least was the indication *J*, to be replaced by *N*, in all official tax records.

Again, while the substantively significant provisions of the Protestant proposal dealt with the ongoing problems of proper division of school taxes, especially from the neutral panel, making this a piece of legislation apparently aimed at financial issues, the introductory sections of the bill made the real nature of the legislation apparent. They called for the maintenance of the dual confessional system as the core principle of educational law in the province and insisted that non-Protestant, non–Roman Catholic citizens could send their children to schools of either denomination as a privilege. Without doubt, this was a return to the situation confirmed by Justice Davidson in *Pinsler*, where the law appeared to indicate that Jews (and now others) attended the public common schools in the city of Montreal as a matter of Christian grace and solely as the result of the goodwill and beneficence of the Roman Catholic and Protestant school commissioners. Absent was any articulation of the previously informing principle that non–Roman Catholic, non-Protestant children had a right to attend school. The Protestant School Board sought to end the existing set of legal arrangements set out in the 1903 Act and to return to the *Pinsler* rules. It sought to do so through legislative means, thereby rejecting any notion that it should or could engage in dialogue with representatives of the Jewish communities. Indeed it had simply ignored both sides of the Jewish community and instead had proceeded along its obviously predetermined path to reclaim Protestant schools for Protestants. A situation in which law framed a broad parameter within which both sides acted and attempted to influence the other, on questions such as segregation of students, or the hiring of Jewish women teachers, had previously obtained in Protestant/Jewish relations. Within that apparently rigid legal frame, narrative and hermeneutic flexibility had permitted the creation of an ongoing dialogic process of self-constitution for both Protestants and Jews in the educational context. Now the new Protestant recalcitrance led to the school board using law as a blunt tool to return to exercising the power and the grace, which they saw as their proper right and duty.

The problem in Montreal in 1923 was that different sets of narrative constructions were now competing for hermeneutic dominance in an atmosphere in which dialogue had no apparent place. The Protestant narrative sought to privilege, maintain, and protect the position within the educational system of the city, which was their right, guaranteed by the BNA Act and a historical series of provincial legislative measures. The 1903 Act was for them an anomaly that had radically disrupted the dominant constitutional narrative of two nations and two denominations at the centre of the school system. The creation of an ersatz equality for Jews as Protestants for school purposes had upset this delicate and vital historical balance and compromise between the two founding nations. This legislative fiction had then been concretized in the non-fictional world of Aidinger, Becker, Benjamin, Cohen, Friedman, Ginsberg, Hoffman, Hirshorn, Hornstein, Kaufman, Klineberg, Lewis, Louis, Meyerovitch, Rapaport, Schultz, Shraga, Shultz, and Weiner, winners of scholarships and leading their classes in a Protestant school system.

For the uptowners, some way to assuage the Protestant feelings of existential threat had to be found in order to ensure the continuation of a system that allowed Jewish children to receive a Canadian education.[87] For them, even with the problems of segregation of Jewish students, etc., a Protestant, English education for Jewish children was the principal way to ensure the proper acculturation of Jewish pupils as British subjects. They abhorred not just the idea of being rejected by the Protestant common school system, but also the notion of creating a segregated, Jewish school system in which the influence of Orthodox rabbis would do battle with the ideals of Socialist Zionists. They had always pursued a narrative of Jewish emancipation and Canadianization that was now directly challenged by Protestant revanchism and by different versions of political and religious Jewish separatism.

For the downtowners, the uptown vision was both un-Jewish and anti-Jewish. For Orthodox believers who saw a direct and necessary connection between religion and education, like their Roman Catholic and Protestant counterparts, the ideals of acculturation propounded by the uptowners, were really ideals that would lead inevitably to assimilation and the loss of specific Jewish identity. The left element in the downtowner group shared the critique of the uptowners' arguments, while seeking to promote through education a secular Zionist attitude among the children of the Jewish communities. This could not be achieved within a Protestant school system, nor could it be achieved within an overly religious, Orthodox educational system. Despite the efforts of leading and respected members of the Jewish community of Montreal to bring the sides together throughout 1923, uptowners and downtowners remained as divided as Jews and Protestants.[88] While the downtowners sought to achieve a form of legal equality with Protestants and Roman Catholics through the creation of a separate Jewish school system, foundational issues and conflict over questions of cultural, religious, and political Jewish identities were always part of broader debates for this part of Montreal Jewry.

The narrative worlds that separated all the parties in this manifestation of the Jewish School Question were profoundly divided along the lines of distinct claims to the right to education and competing and complex ideals of citizenship. There was little if any common ground. Instead, each sought its own mode of creating a legal world that would concretize its normative vision, but one from which all other normative claims would be excluded. The problem was one created within, and caused by, an originary constitutional moment in section 93, which was, in its essence, exclusionary in religious terms. As far as the uptowners and their claims were concerned, the Protestant return to *Pinsler* was a legalized assault on their self-understanding of belonging and equality, which as a community they had achieved in the Quebec statute of 1832, and then in the school field in 1903. They were not a minority community seeking to withdraw from the majority life world of associational autonomy or collective self-definition. Instead they were a minority group being shut out of the broad community of citizens because of a constitutional provision that gave special and exclusionary status and power to Roman Catholics and Protestants. The downtowners' broadly shared notion was of a different sort of equality, an equality of groups within a constitutional system and set of constitutive narratives that privileged and entrenched denominational identity as a fundamental legal, cultural, and political value. If Protestants and Roman Catholics could and did have their own schools, then equality demanded that Jews be given the same rights.

The desire to return to a state of *Pinsler*-era existence, in which the Protestant schools were constitutionally and constitutively Protestant, was equally understandable. From the perspective of a firmly and honestly held belief in the centrality of a Protestant identity within the political, social, economic, educational, and legal life worlds of Quebec and Canada, their argument resonated historically and juridically. But that perspective and that self-understanding dangerously excluded Jews (and others) from the constitutive process of common education. While the history of the Jewish School Question to this point had been characterized by compromise, dialogue, and discussion, by room to manoeuvre for Jews within the constitutional structures, often at the very margin of, if not outside, strict legality, this space for communal self-definition was being eliminated by intractable Protestant claims. It was leaving room only for radical separation of the communities in the form of a downtowner ideal of a Jewish school system. David Rome described this period in somewhat positive terms when he wrote, "The months of 1923 and 1924 were the period of the great debate in Canadian Jewish history, a debate within the community, with the Protestants, with the Catholic church and with the provincial government; a debate that was conducted on a remarkably high level of political and social intercourse."[89]

The difficulty with Rome's assessment is that insofar as the Protestant Board of School Commissioners was concerned, there was no real intercourse. They had made up their minds to win back the Protestant schools for Protestants. They had promised to take the positions offered by both uptowners and downtowners into consideration, and then proceeded to follow a path upon which they had already embarked, a path towards the reassertion of absolute Protestant control over the Protestant schools of Montreal. They had also, according to both Michael Garber and Michael Hirsch, as Harold Ross reports, a great deal of confidence that the law would support their right to return to the *Pinsler*-era position and to recognize their right to exclude Jewish students if they wished.[90]

The danger of the Protestant board's position was that its reliance on the constitutionally exclusionary taxonomy of section 93 would, simply by brute force of law, exclude Jews and other non-Protestant, non–Roman Catholic students from the public school system of Montreal. The rest of this episode of the Jewish School Question would unfold in a narrative world in which law would, in fact, allow for some form of reconciliation, but in unexpected ways, which would disappoint some, delight others, and be greeted with resignation by still other parties.

The Jewish School Question, 1923–1925: The Political and Legal Crisis and the Commission of Nine

From the Protestant perspective, Jewish interventions had changed nothing. The numerical position of Jews in the Protestant schools of Montreal posed an imminent and ongoing threat to the system as Protestant. There was no further room for dialogue and agreement. A return to the constitutional source of section 93 was in order.[91]

The 1923 report from the Protestant School Board indicated that Jewish students accounted for approximately 38 per cent of enrolments in the city school system controlled by the board, 11,974 out of a total of 31,391,[92] figures that changed little the following year (11,557 Jewish students to 18,857 Protestants).[93] The Protestant board in Montreal persisted in its efforts to operate a fundamental change in the system of education in the city, especially insofar as the schooling of non-Protestant, non–Roman Catholic students was concerned, because of the ongoing financial issue of what it saw as gross underfunding to the detriment of Protestant ratepayers and their children, and because of the existential threat to Protestant education.

Dr Rexford suggested that the simple presence of such large numbers of Jewish students meant that Protestant parents felt that they had to send their children to private schools for a proper education. Protestant flight from the city's common schools was invoked, but Rexford provided no evidence that this phenomenon was real. He also continued to argue that the absence of Jewish students on Jewish holy days caused serious disruption and pedagogical difficulties for the students themselves through time lost. The ever-present question of Jewish teachers also caused tensions between the Jewish communities and the Protestant board, but more significantly for Rexford, "Many of them being from a foreign population speak English imperfectly, and even Jewish parents, in bringing their children to the Protestant Schools, often ask that they shall be placed under Gentile teachers. Moreover in mixed classes it does not seem reasonable to place Christian children under direction of these Jewish teachers."[94]

The real problem was never one of school finances, of a Protestant subsidy for the education of Jewish students. It was the problem caused by and for the Protestant School Board members in the simple presence of Jews in Protestant schools. They caused disruptions; their very existence as students brought the Protestant educational system into disrepute; and the Jewish teachers did not even speak proper English, despite having graduated from McDonald College, the bastion of English Protestant educational training in Quebec. It was not reasonable to place Protestant students under the direction of Jewish teachers. Of course the converse was not true, since it was perfectly natural that in a Protestant school system attended by Jewish students, they should be under the direction of Protestant teachers. Again, the real difficulty was not with the obvious Christian anti-Semitism to which Rexford and other Protestant educators would give voice throughout this period (let us remember Barclay's theologically structured equivalence between a thief and a Jew, for educational purposes). Instead the core problem was that Rexford and his colleagues could not see, or even imagine that it was possible to take offence at such a statement of logic and reason. The Protestant school officials proceeded to introduce the bill repealing the 1903 Act.

But the Protestant Board of School Commissioners did not speak univocally for a united Quebec Protestant community. The provincial Protestant Committee of the Council of Public Instruction did not agree that such radical legislative measures were called for immediately. It passed a resolution indicating that the financial issue had been dealt with to its satisfaction by the earlier legislation, which had adjusted the payments from the neutral panel for both Jewish students and those falling under the rest of the non-Protestant, non–Roman Catholic classification. It continued, "In consideration of the fact that various conferences with interested individuals, and with representatives of interested bodies, have shown that questions involving grave principles have not been satisfactorily adjusted, it is not advisable or expedient that any change be made at the present time in the legislation now affecting the education of non–Roman Catholic, non-Protestant population."[95]

For some in the Protestant educational structures within the province, there was still a notion that further dialogue might bring a negotiated solution to the dilemmas that divided the parties to the debate about what was still in the political and social reality of Montreal in 1923, the Jewish School Question, despite the occasional persistence of the non–Roman Catholic, non-Protestant nomenclature. At the same time, the downtowners and uptowners were struggling for position within the Jewish communities, and they often appeared to be as closed to discussion as the Protestant board.[96] The Protestant board's bill had been introduced into the Assembly in late December 1923 and had its second reading in January 1924, before the Protestant committee's resolution.[97] At the same time, Lyon Cohen's efforts, as president of the Va'ad Hair, to reach a unified Jewish position by bringing together the Jewish Community Council, the downtowners, and the uptowner body, the Jewish Educational Committee, as well as the two leading Jewish legislators, Sam Jacobs and Peter Bercovitch, did not bear fruit.[98] The Protestants urged Jewish representatives to allow the bill to pass and promised to appoint a subcommittee to deal with the question of Jewish students after the law was in place. Once it became clear that there was no possibility of an agreement, between Jews and Protestants, among the various Jewish plans, or between the Protestant School Board and the provincial Protestant Committee of the Council of Public Instruction,

Premier Taschereau proposed setting up a special commission to study and report on the matter.[99] The premier referred the bill to committee and voiced his objection to the legislation.[100]

In a time-honoured move within Canadian politics, the government created a commission with the power to investigate the educational governance structures on the Island of Montreal.[101] The commission would be equally constituted by Roman Catholic, Protestant, and Jewish members. The Jewish School Question would now receive formal institutional consideration. Before the commission was named, the Jewish Community Council wrote to the provincial authorities claiming its right to be represented on the Jewish committee and put forward the name of Louis Fitch as its preferred candidate.[102] It failed to get Fitch on the commission, but the downtowner voice(s) would be represented. The so-called Commission of Nine was composed of three Roman Catholic representatives, the commission chair, Lomer Gouin, Victor Doré,[103] and Aimé Geoffrion;[104] three Protestants, Arthur Currie,[105] E.W. Beatty,[106] and W.G. Mitchell;[107] and three Jews, Michael Hirsch, Samuel W. Cohen,[108] and Montreal Alderman Joseph Schubert.[109] A fourth unofficial member of the Jewish committee, who carried out the bulk of the research for the commissioners, was the secretary, Abraham J. Livinson.[110] Each denominational committee had its focus. The Roman Catholics considered the question of extending the powers of the Montreal Roman Catholic School Commission to deal with difficult issues of school finances and governance within the Roman Catholic system.[111] The Protestant committee, in addition to considering the Jewish School Question, had to look at the extremely indebted and impoverished school board in the suburb of Verdun, as well as rationalizing school governance through greater centralization, along lines similar to those being addressed by the Roman Catholic commissioners. Suburban growth had resulted in a spread of populations throughout greater Montreal, with the creation of new schools and a loose framework of governance that left much to be desired, with multiple levels of decision-making, and related inefficiencies. Of course, the Jewish committee would focus solely on the Jewish School Question.

The community council continued to voice its objections over the unrepresentative nature of the appointees. Suggestions were made that Alderman Schubert be asked to resign because he represented only a small section of the "radicals" among the complex downtowner left. For the Va'ad Hair members, the vast majority of Orthodox Jews, parents of most of the schoolchildren affected by the commission's work, and its ultimate recommendations to the provincial government, were without representation, while the minority uptowners had the majority of the Jewish commissioners.[112]

Members of the Jewish communities spoke to the first public meeting of the denominational committee, addressing their experiences, their hopes, and their fears.[113] Some spoke in favour of maintaining the 1903 statute, but with Jewish representation on the Protestant board, and a just proportion of appointments of Jewish teachers.[114] Others, like the principal of the Montreal Hebrew Free School, favoured a separate Jewish school system, in large part because of the desire to see Jewish children receive a Jewish education.[115] In subsequent meetings, similar voices for and against the creation of a separate Jewish school system continued to be heard, and the communities were clearly no closer to resolving the central conflict at the heart of the divide in Jewish Montreal.

The Jewish commissioners held private meetings on 3 and 4 September, at which they discussed the continuing controversies of Jewish teachers and the Protestant board, and of student segregation as practised by the board. Peter Bercovitch attended the second meeting, and discussion soon turned to the Protestant assertions that the 1903 Act was unconstitutional. Bercovitch stated that if these doubts persisted, a reference to the courts was a possibility.[116] The real stumbling block in the minds of all three Jewish commissioners remained the attitudes of the members of the Protestant School Board of Montreal. Protestant officials still rejected any notion that the government would have any influence over their decisions about how to govern the Protestant schools of Montreal. They continued to oppose the elected government of the province, the Jewish communities of Montreal, and their own Protestant Committee of the Council of Public Instruction.

Following the last of the public meetings, where once more the only thing to emerge was further evidence of an insurmountable divide within the Jewish communities, the Jewish commissioners continued to meet in order to prepare for the public hearings of the commission as a whole. They maintained their attempts to collect the information that was meant to serve as the basis of their final report. Livinson wrote to a number of Jewish organizations in the United States and the United Kingdom, as well as to the educational authorities in most Canadian, U.S., and British cities, in order to ascertain what the accepted practice was on releasing Jewish students from attendance on holy days.[117] In the end, the Jewish commissioners compiled "about 50 volumes of historical publications and statistical authorities."[118] None of this convinced the Jewish Community Council. Fearing that their views would not play a role in the final report from the Jewish commissioners, they wrote again in November 1924 to Gouin and Taschereau, once more complaining that the majority of the Jewish commissioners, Hirsch and Cohen, did not represent the views of the majority of the Jewish population of Montreal.[119]

However, having been notified of the views expressed by the more recalcitrant elements of the Protestant community, the Jewish commissioners focused more on the Protestant contention about the constitutionality of the 1903 Act. Any claim for Jewish representation on the school board or any other Protestant educational body at this stage rested, legally at least, on the idea of Jews as "Protestants for school purposes" embodied in that statute. Jewish representation had always been presented as the logical extension of that synonymy, but legal advice from the Protestant board's lawyers had historically rejected this idea. The legal department of the City of Montreal had previously indicated that the appointment of non-Protestants to the Protestant School Board was not legally permissible. If the basic ideal of equality between Protestants and Jews embodied in the 1903 legislation was open to constitutional challenge as contrary to section 93 – as the Protestant School Board now maintained – then a major constitutional monkey wrench was about to be thrown into the machinery of the Jewish School Question. The commissioners sought legal advice.[120] Meanwhile, as law loomed, the time had come to hear what everyone else thought. The Commission of Nine began its public hearings on 30 September.[121]

The chair of the Protestant Board, Creelman, was the first to address the commission.[122] He established the board's position quickly and unambiguously, in terms similar to those he had used in his brief discussion with Jewish representatives: "The attitude of the Board is that we presented a Bill to the Legislature last year, and we are still behind that Bill, and hope to see it carried at the next session."[123] That finished his three-paragraph statement to the commission. After answering a series of questions about the financial arrangements concerning Jewish students under past and current statutory tax regimes, Creelman admitted that the most recent legislative changes, which resulted in the charge on the neutral panel to meet the difference between Jewish taxes and the actual cost of educating Jewish students, had put an end to the financial difficulties and to issues of an unjust Protestant subsidy for the cost of educating Jews.[124] However, he did add that there were still unresolved problems with Jewish students in Protestant schools, chief among them the question of Jewish holy days. The chaos caused by having seven

Jewish holidays in the period of twenty-three calendar days, as was the case in the current school year, and the effects of which Creelman had personally investigated before appearing in front of the commission, simply caused too much disruption. This problem was what had led the board to adopt a policy of segregating Jewish students, a policy that had worked to the benefit of the Protestant students. But again the real crux of the board's position was that the schools under its jurisdiction were in danger of no longer being Protestant schools.[125]

Creelman then reiterated that the board would be happy only with the repeal of the 1903 Act and the elimination of the unconstitutional idea that Jews were Protestants for school purposes.[126] Indeed, under questioning from the commissioners on the status of Jewish students under the board's proposed new legislation, Creelman asserted that since the 1903 Act was unconstitutional, it would not matter whether one spoke of rights or privileges, since the Jews could have no rights under an Act that was unconstitutional.[127] Clearly the Protestant board would be content only with a return to the principles enunciated by Justice Davidson in *Pinsler*, under which Jewish students entered the Protestant school system on sufferance and thanks only to Christian grace and charity, little of which was in evidence in Creelman's defiant presentation.

The dialogue was proceeding along parallel lines and did little more than confirm the idea that had informed Tashereau's decision to create the commission in the first place, that there was little agreement between Protestant and Jew, or between Protestant and Protestant, or between Jew and Jew. This was confirmed when H.M. Marler, MP, spoke on 2 October, the second day of the commission's hearings.[128] He appeared in his private capacity as a "Protestant rate-payer of the City of Montreal," but Marler was also a respected federal member of Parliament, a prominent Quebec anglophone Protestant, and a member of the Quebec Protestant Committee of the Council of Public Instruction.[129] His position was strong and clear: "There are Protestants in the City of Montreal who do not believe entirely in the way the Chairman of the Protestant Board of School Commissioners has spoken before this Commission. That speech, to my mind, (and I say it advisedly) is full of intolerance, and if it is full of intolerance, and the various other members of the Board are following their Chairman like a lot of docile sheep, then they are equally intolerant."[130]

Marler dismissed all issues raised by Creelman as matters that could be easily dealt with through the historically accepted and successful practices of discussions between and among all interested parties. He attacked any notion that there was any barrier in the 1903 Act to Protestant religious instruction in the Protestant schools of Montreal. He underscored the board's reluctance to look at any option but the total repeal of the 1903 law and highlighted the fact that the more representative Protestant Committee of the Council of Public Instruction had refused to proceed along those lines.[131]

Dr Rexford, he of "our educational problem" and chair of the Protestant Committee of the Council of Public Instruction, addressed the commission.[132] Rexford shifted the focus from those who had criticized the attitude of the Protestant Board by pointing out the Jewish attempts to change the Protestant school system to their advantage by getting Jewish representation on the board, from the Finnie bills to the Montreal City Council debates on appointing a Jewish councillor to the Protestant School Board in 1916–17.[133] The Jewish School Question, he implied, was the creation of the Jews themselves and their attempts to subvert Maxwell Goldstein's 1903 promise that the Jewish community respected the Protestant denominational character of the Protestant Schools and had no wish, desire, or intention to change that reality. He therefore reverted to what had become the real central issue: how could the Protestant schools of Montreal remain Protestant with the increasing numbers of Jewish students and in the face of unending Jewish demands for representation on the board itself?[134] Segregation was only natural in a system in which Jews were treated not just as equals, but as students who enjoyed special privileges in relation to absence on holidays.[135]

The competing Protestant voices expressed very different understandings of the questions and of the principles at stake. The difficulty for the commission remained unchanged from the day of its inception, because the terms of the debate had not moved. There was no single answer to the Jewish School Question that would or could satisfy Protestants and Jews, or Protestants and Protestants and Jews and Jews, and the Roman Catholic viewpoint had not yet been articulated. Some Jews and some Protestants came together to advocate the creation of a separate Jewish school system in Montreal as the only way forward. For the Jews who accepted this position, the question of whether there would be secular Zionist, national schools, or Orthodox religious schools was a problem for the future and one for the constituent members of the Jewish communities to resolve as Jews among themselves, just as Montreal's Roman Catholics and Protestants made similar decisions for themselves. For other Protestants and Jews, the modus vivendi of compromise and mutual respect, which they saw as having always informed the Jewish School Question, still presented the best way out of any current difficulties or disagreements. There was no need to revisit the basic principles of Jews as Protestants for school purposes embodied in the 1903 Act. Practical issues flowing from the implementation of the statute, questions of segregation and of hiring more Jewish teachers, for example, were simply difficulties that could be discussed and resolved by the goodwill of all concerned.

Worryingly for the Jewish representatives of the uptowner point of view, not only was there a potentially dangerous convergence of political views between the hardline Protestants of the school board and the downtowners on the separate school issue, but the threat of litigation to determine the validity of the 1903 Act featured more and more prominently in the Protestant argument. The Jewish communities of Montreal were now threatened with a legal system that, if the Protestant interpretation were correct, would be lethal to its aspirations of equal citizenship, of no taxation without representation, and of the ideals of British justice, on which both uptowners and downtowners explicitly and implicitly relied.

The Jewish Educational Committee and the community council were at radically opposed points, with one insisting on the elaboration of a plan for Jewish representation within the Protestant school system and the continuation of the broad spirit of the 1903 Act, and the other claiming that Jewish schools were a necessity because the key idea of Jewish identity, however complex, could never be met in a Protestant school system. The majority of Protestant School Board officials clearly no longer wanted Jewish students in Protestant schools.[136] The Commission of Nine was now vested with the unenviable task of sorting out the mess.

8

Jews, Protestants, Roman Catholics, and the Law: The Jewish School Question Goes to Court

The Commission of Nine and the Shadow of the Law

When the commission met on 22 October 1924, Samuel W. Cohen presented a plan, which at the time had the support in principle of some of the other members of the commission. That plan called for the creation of an Island-wide body to be known as the Protestant Metropolitan Financial School Commission, which would fix school tax rates and on which Jews would be represented.[1] Schubert presented a separate scheme for Jewish schools. The divisions in the Jewish community now manifested themselves in the split in the commission itself. However, the real sticking point came quickly to the fore. Despite the Jewish commissioners' insistence that a finance committee or commission was not the same as a school board, which would remain in place, Mitchell expressed the first doubts about the plan's constitutional validity. Beatty saw this as an attempt to get Jewish representation "by a detour."[2] While none of the Protestant members spoke in favour of Schubert's plan for a third panel, they still rejected any idea that Jews should have representation on any Protestant board, commission, or committee.

Schubert insisted that he had 60 per cent of the Jewish population behind him.[3] It did seem evident at the time that the Hirsch/Cohen plan for continuing with the current arrangements of Jewish students in Protestant schools, with a form of Jewish representation on the newly proposed financial body, and possibly on the provincial Council of Public Instruction, was one that came from the uptowner faction, which, while politically and economically powerful, now represented a minority position within Montreal Jewry. At the same time, however, the Protestant members of the commission now opposed both the idea of third panel and a separate Jewish school system. They wanted to have their constitutional cake and to eat it too. They would maintain the constitutionally sanctioned duality of Montreal common school education and in doing so insist on excluding any idea of Jewish self-determination in educational matters. Once again, the issue came down to irresolvable splits in the Jewish communities and an evident divide between the forces in the Protestant community. While neither the uptowners nor the Protestant members of the special commission wanted separate Jewish schools, they could not agree on the fundamental issue of Jewish representation. For those whose views were expressed by Hirsch and Cohen, this was a sine qua non of any resolution to the Jewish School Question. While they sought to maintain the 1903 Act's provisions insofar as Jewish students were concerned, they also insisted that the necessary implication of treating Jews as Protestants for school purposes carried with it a right to Jewish representation on school governance bodies. Increasingly, however, even for the Protestant members of the Commission of Nine, the representation issue fell under the exclusionary protections offered to Quebec Protestants in the BNA Act. Protestants had a right protected since 1867 to govern Protestant schools, and in 1867 Protestants had been Protestants, not ersatz creatures of a legislative compromise that made Jews "Protestants for school purposes."

The commission finally confronted the looming shadow of section 93 head on.[4] The members discussed the 1831–2 statute granting emancipatory equality to Quebec's Jews, the BNA Act, and the legal opinions obtained by the Protestant School Board. As Mitchell put it, "The law of 1831 only gave Jews political rights, not educational rights."[5] The confederative compromise of 1867 had made a clear distinction for the Protestants between political equality and the special status afforded to them under the BNA Act provisions relating to education. For the Jewish representatives Hirsch and Cohen, the idea that Jews could constitute 40 per cent of the student body of Protestant schools, that all Jewish taxes went into the Protestant panel, and they still could not be legally represented on the governing body of the school system was an affront to them as fully equal British subjects. The idea of a split between political equality under the 1832 Act and educational inequality under section 93 was anathema to them. The commission had decided that it could not proceed without getting legal advice on the question of the place of Jews under section 93 and the constitutionality of any proposals for Jewish representation from the leading Montreal lawyer of his era, Eugène Lafleur.[6] In the meantime, the uptowners of the Jewish Educational Committee sought their own legal opinion from another eminent Canadian lawyer, Wallace Nesbitt.[7]

Lafleur gave a broad reading to the 1903 Act. He found that the underlying principle that Jews "shall, for school purposes, be treated in the same manner as Protestants" could not be read as being limited to Jewish students' rights to attend Protestant schools. Instead, he argued, the idea of equality enshrined in the legislation was that contained in the uptowners' position that in all educational matters, from the appointment of teachers to membership on the school board, Jews were Protestants.[8] However, after a careful review of the situation of Protestant education at the time of Confederation in 1867, Lafleur concluded that the legal system had afforded to the Protestant communities "the most complete control, both financial and pedagogic, of their own schools, and could not be called upon to share that control with members of any other religion."[9] By granting rights and privileges to Jewish students and by extension to Jews in terms of representation, the 1903 Act had "effected a complete revolution in the status of the Protestant community" and had "very materially diminished, and from the Protestant point of view, prejudicially effected" their rights and privileges.[10] In other words, the 1903 Act was unconstitutional, and as such, even the consent of the Protestant board in 1903 could not save the statute. Lafleur found that any idea that the Protestant board might be compelled to hire Jewish teachers would be equally unconstitutional, as would any attempt to create a commission on financial matters with non-Protestant membership. Likewise, in his opinion, Jewish membership on the Council of Public Instruction would adversely affect Protestant school governance and would therefore also be unconstitutional. Even the appointment of Jews as advisory members of the provincial council would, in Lafleur's view, "violate the principle of absolute autonomy which the Protestants enjoyed at the time of Confederation."[11]

However, what Lafleur failed to address in this part of his opinion was that his understanding of "absolute autonomy" and the fixing of rights in 1867 should have led him to a more considered approach to the Council of Public Instruction question. The structure of the council, with its Protestant and Roman Catholic committees, was in fact created post-Confederation. The Protestant and Roman Catholic committee structure became enshrined as denominationally separate bodies only after 1867. The status of the council therefore was arguably not one fixed at Confederation and over which the Protestant education system enjoyed any absolute rights in terms of Lafleur's own analysis. In addition, of course, the Council of Public Instruction constituted Protestant and Roman Catholic sub-committees, each of which had functioned relatively independently, but nonetheless together constituted the council. The council was a creature of the provincial government and, as constituted, it always had a Roman Catholic majority. On occasion that majority could and did impose its will over the objections of the Protestant sub-committee. On the basis of Lafleur's opinion, the real problem would not have been the presence of Jewish advisors or members on the council. Instead, the very existence of such a body where a Roman Catholic majority could, in theory, decide broad issues affecting the Protestant school system should have been considered an unconstitutional infringement on the absolute autonomy enjoyed by Quebec and Montreal Protestants over school matters.

In a second, supplementary legal opinion to the commission, Lafleur noted that the system of education protected in the BNA Act was a religious and not a racially determined one. Therefore in answer to the question from the commission of whether "a member of the Jewish race can be appointed a member of the Protestant School Board," he highlighted the now well-known confusion caused by the religious and racial taxonomies present in the commission's query. A Jew who converted to Protestantism could be named to the board, but a "member of the Jewish faith" could not.[12] Nor could the word *Protestant* in section 93 ever be interpreted to include Jews. He further opined, in response to specific queries from the commission, that the provincial government could lawfully appoint a committee of representation and recommendation on which there would be Jewish representatives, because that would not affect Protestant authority over Protestant schools. In answering Schubert's specific question about the legality of a third school system, Lafleur expressed the view that section 93 of the BNA Act gave sole jurisdiction over education to the provinces, subject to the provisions concerning the rights of Protestants and Roman Catholics. Insofar as the creation of a third school system would not affect those rights, it would be a valid exercise of general provincial legislative powers under section 93.

Wallace Nesbitt was of a different opinion. He believed that, if it could be shown that Jewish schools existed before 1867, they would simply fall under the broad rubric of dissentient found in the 1861 education statute. He rejected Lafleur's view of the historical position of school law in the province and insisted that at Confederation the understanding of dissentient found in provincial statutes did not refer expressly to any specific denomination or creed. It referred only to those who were of a religious faith different from the majority, not to those of a Christian faith different from the majority. In Montreal there were no dissentient schools so, for Nesbitt, this meant that as common schools, a fortiori, there were no Protestant schools protected by the fixing of rights in the 1867 Constitution.[13] According to Nesbitt's reading, the historical analysis revealed that the real changes to denominational – Protestant and Roman Catholic – school systems occurred under the 1869 Act and subsequently. Because these laws were not in place at the time of Confederation, they could in no way be invoked in any constitutional analysis. The 1903 Act was valid. Jews could be named to the school board and the grant of complete educational equality to Jews in that statute was fully within the lawful remit of the provincial government.

The commission had to face other issues, such as the Roman Catholic commissioners' question of further consolidation of the city's schools under the Roman Catholic board, and Protestant concerns over the Verdun financial crisis.[14] These were discussed at its final meeting on 22 December.[15] The Roman Catholic commissioners recommended to the government that the jurisdiction of the Roman Catholic School Board be extended to include more school districts that had not yet fallen under its remit.[16] The Protestant commissioners recommended that in order to deal with the Verdun case, the government create a broader jurisdiction for the Protestant School Board, which would now include Montreal, Verdun, Lachine and Dorval, Coteau St Pierre (Montreal West), Westmount, St Laurent, Mount Royal, Sault aux Recollet (Montreal North), Pointe aux Trembles, and Montreal East.[17] All of this was dealt with without difficulty and with the members of the commission happy to leave the proposals up to each of the denominational subcommittees' expertise. The reorganization of Protestant and Roman Catholic school administration on the Island of Montreal was best left to Protestant and Roman Catholic officials. But the real question was, as it had always been, what about the Jews?

The Protestant commissioners again recited the history of the Jewish School Question and concluded that, in light of all the evidence received, the current two-denominational school system should be maintained; Jewish claims of "no taxation without representation" ignored the Jewish right to elect provincial members of the Legislative Assembly and Montreal aldermen, who decided on nominations to school board positions (as long as the decision did not involve appointing a Jew); and that the 1903 compromise offered a "proper and commendable" model for proceeding, but that because of its constitutional failings, it should be repealed and replaced with a new statute that would ensure Protestant control over Protestant schools and clearly define the rights of non-Protestants and non–Roman Catholics.[18]

In its final recommendations the commission highlighted the lack of agreement between the Protestant and Jewish members over the way forward.[19] The Commission of Nine therefore went over what common ground could be found. The maintenance of the dual school system seemed to be agreed by all parties, except Schubert, and subject only to their demands for representation being met, by Hirsch and Cohen. They did unanimously recommend that any change be delayed and that the government seek a judicial opinion from the Court of Appeal and, if necessary, from the Privy Council, on the entire issue of the rights of Jews in the province's educational system.

The commission's report also included the majority Jewish report from Hirsch and Cohen and a minority report from Schubert.[20] The majority report contained the plan presented by Hirsch and Cohen early on in the deliberations for the creation of a new financial body for Montreal's Protestant school system on which Jews could have some membership. They hit out at the Protestant commissioners' decision to hold off on any commitment until the legal issues had been settled and declared that they could not bind the Jewish community to staying with the plan. They reported "that they may have to extricate themselves and their children from the humiliating position of inferiority in which they have been, and are being placed as regards the Schools of the Island of Montreal."[21] Even uptowners were being confronted by the stark choice left to them by Protestant School Board recalcitrance – the possibility that if the Protestant officials in Montreal remained unmoved, Jews would have to seriously consider abandoning their preferred option and plan for the creation of an independent Jewish School Board.

Schubert presented his dissenting view, calling for the creation of a separate system of Jewish schools, splitting the present Protestant panel into two divisions, the Protestant or Christian, and the Jewish. This would address the issue of non–Roman Catholics and non-Protestants who, like the Greeks and Syrians, were Christian, and would place such groups more firmly within the Protestant ambit while allowing Jews to create their own school system. Schubert even acknowledged the changing and dynamic nature of Montreal's demography, earlier echoed in some of Lyon Cohen's attempts to create a compromise between the uptowner and downtowner factions. His proposal was that Jewish control be exercised over schools with a majority Jewish student body, and that Protestants control majority Christian schools. Arrangements would be subject to annual adjustments in discussions between the Protestant/ Christian and Jewish boards. He also assimilated into his dissenting proposal the Hirsch/Cohen plan for a central financial authority.[22]

The Courts, Jurisgenesis, and the Constitution of Canada and Canadians

The government of Louis-Alexandre Taschereau was not long in taking up the recommendations of the Commission of Nine. They issued an Order in Council on 3 February seeking an advisory opinion from the Court of King's Bench, then the Court of Appeal for Quebec.[23] The government asked the Court for its opinion on a number of questions:

1. Is the 1903 Act constitutionally valid?
2. Under the Act, could Jews be appointed to the Protestant board and is the board obliged to appoint Jewish teachers?
3. Can the provincial government pass legislation appointing Jews to the Protestant board, or the Protestant Committee of the Council of Public Instruction, or as "advisory members of these bodies"?
4. Can the provincial government pass legislation compelling the Protestant board to hire Jewish teachers?
5. Can the government pass legislation implementing the Metropolitan Financial Commission and appoint Jews to it?
6. Can the government pass legislation creating schools for non–Roman Catholic non-Protestants?
7. Assuming that the 1903 Act is unconstitutional, do Jewish children attend the Protestant schools (a) as a matter of grace; (b) as a matter of right; and (c) can the province force the Protestants to accept children professing the Jewish religion under such conditions?[24]

Leading members of the Quebec Bar presented the arguments to the

Court. Peter Bercovitch and future Canadian prime minister Louis St-Laurent acted for Hirsch and Cohen.[25] Charles Laurendeau[26] and George Campbell[27] appeared for the Protestant board.[28] Louis Fitch and Michael Garber represented Alderman Joseph Schubert.[29] Antonio Perrault[30] and Aymé Lafontaine[31] argued on behalf of the Roman Catholic School Commission. When the Court rendered its verdict, the case took on the designation it would carry throughout the litigation's history: *Michael Hirsch and Samuel W. Cohen v The Protestant Board of School Commissioners and the Catholic Board of School Commissioners and Joseph Schubert, and the Attorney General*.[32]

Even in the official designation of the case, the traditional antagonists were placed in positions of legal conflict, reflecting the philosophical, political, and theological differences that had always characterized much of the Jewish School Question. The uptowners, Hirsch and Cohen, pleaded for the legality of the 1903 Act and for its logical extension, which this section of Montreal Jewry had long asserted, to include Jewish representation as part of the rights of British subjects enjoyed by Jews in Quebec since their emancipation in 1832. They largely repeated the technical legal argument advanced in Nesbitt's advice that the statutory history of Quebec education law, prior to and at the time of Confederation had enshrined a system of common schools in Montreal.[33] Following the Privy Council in *Maher v Town of Portland*, the only rights that would be legally cognizable would be those rights enshrined and embodied in law, rather than in practice or demographic happenstance.[34] Since the rights of Protestants to Protestant schools governed by Protestants were in fact enshrined in legislation only after Confederation, the overarching principle of equality should lead to the conclusions that the 1903 Act was valid and that Jews enjoyed representation and other rights necessary to concretize their general equality with all citizens of the province. The final set of questions about the rights of Jewish students need not be answered, because the statute of 1903 was constitutionally valid.

The Protestant argument mirrored the opinions offered by Lafleur. Indeed their factum reproduced large parts of his opinion to the Commission of Nine. At least since 1841, Protestants had enjoyed the right to govern their schools as Protestant schools free from interference from any other denomination. "Education in the Province was before Confederation entrusted by law exclusively to Roman Catholics and to Protestants, and it is manifest that the legislator wished that education within the Province should be Christian in character."[35]

The questions before the Court therefore answered themselves as far as the Protestant position was concerned. The 1903 Act was ultra vires. As had been its practice, the board was free to hire Jewish teachers, but as a matter of pure administrative discretion. Likewise, Jewish students attended Protestant schools at the sole discretion of the Protestant board. They had no right to attend, just as Jews had no rights to representation. Political equality rights were irrelevant because such rights, wherever enshrined, "do not include the special rights or privileges in relation to education now under discussion, and are therefore inapplicable to the present case."[36]

Fitch and Garber for Alderman Schubert limited themselves to the simple assertion, supported by both Nesbitt and Lafleur, that the provincial legislature had the constitutional authority to create a separate school system in Montreal for Jews and that the creation of such a system would not in any way interfere with the rights or privileges of Protestants or Roman Catholics.[37] The Roman Catholic position insisted on the educational autonomy of each of the two denominational school systems and more generally on the idea that the entire system of education in Quebec schools had been essentially Christian at the time of Confederation. As such, any third school board would adversely affect the rights and privileges enjoyed by both Roman Catholics and Protestants at the time of Confederation. It would create a fundamental breach in the Christian character of all Quebec education.[38]

There were no surprises. Each side's political, social, and theological world view had been translated into the technical arcana of legal argument about the state of educational rights in Quebec in 1867. Equality, separation, rights, and privileges for the Christian character of education in Montreal – each ideal was articulated in an attempt to call upon law's constitutive power to concretize the social and political aspirations of the different groups in the case. Again this was a debate about identification and belonging, and about identification and separation.[39] The uptowners wanted to identify at once as Jews and as full British subjects, and the only way for them to do this was to argue at one and the same time for equality, indeed for the continuation of the Jew as Protestant legal fiction, and to concomitantly urge their recognition as a separate and distinct group. The downtowners had other complex and often competing ideas about identity and belonging, and for all their class, political, theological, and secular/religious divisions, they simply wanted a set of autonomous community structures, including schools, in which the formation of Jewish identities could occur on an footing equal with Protestants and Roman Catholic citizens.[40] And, of course, many Protestants wanted to be Protestants, free from the pernicious influence of Jews with their different values and social mores. While the downtowners and the Protestants sought separation and autonomy in order to engage in constitutive self-definition, the uptowners put forward a more complex set of arguments about constituting themselves as equal British subjects, within a system of schooling that placed its primary self-definitional emphasis not on constituting citizens, but on constituting Roman Catholic and Protestant citizens. The Roman Catholics, for their part, insisted on the profoundly Christian character of education in the province.[41] Education was a matter for the church and the family, but not for Jewish religious officials or parental authority. They resisted any measure, such as the emergence of a third, Jewish school system, which would call the Christian centrality of education in Quebec into question and would violate the underlying normativity of denominational educational structures enshrined since 1867 in section 93.

The Court proceeded to confirm the hopes of some, and dash those of others.

After having reviewed the legislative history of the province's educational system, Justice Greenshields concluded that the Roman Catholic board's assertion that education in the province had always been Christian was the only logical and accurate conclusion to which he could come. Greenshields's adoption of a position that the core characteristic of Quebec education was found in this absolutist Christian taxonomy led him to a conclusion, which would appear in other manifestations of subsequent argument as the case made its way through the judicial hierarchy. For him, if all schools had to be Christian, the logical next step was that any attempt by the province to create a third system of education would by definition come into stark and inescapable contradiction with that core Christian identity of the province's schools, as long as that Christian identity was understood as Protestant and Roman Catholic. (There could be no room for post-1867 Greek Orthodoxy, for example, or for the emergence of groups that might define themselves as Christian, but also identify as opposed to both Protestants and Roman Catholics, such as Jehovah's Witnesses.) On this view, not only were Roman Catholic and Protestant schools enshrined in the Constitution of 1867, and the autonomous rights of the two denominations protected, but also the entire education system of the province had been frozen into this denominational duality. Any other type of schooling would be "subversive of the whole recognized established and fundamental principles of education as recognized in the Canadian Constitution of 1867."[42]

The dynamic of section 93 and its guarantees of Protestant and Roman Catholic autonomy in school matters meant that the broader provincial jurisdiction over education in section 93 had no real role to play. The invocation of this general power to create Jewish schools would have the inevitable and ultra vires consequence of adversely affecting denominational rights. This ideal of a Christian educational structure, which was in fact a Protestant and Roman Catholic structure, left him in the awkward position of having to declare that while non-Protestant and non–Roman Catholic children "should" be accepted into schools, the provincial legislature could not compel either denomination to accept such students. Greenshields returned to the Christian grace of *Pinsler* to deal with the rights that were not rights in an enforceable sense, of Jewish and presumably all non-Protestant, non–Roman Catholic children who wanted a public education.[43] These children were "entitled to a secular education" in either the Roman Catholic or Protestant schools, however that could be managed within an inexorably Christian, denominational defining structure, but the legislature could not create a third system, nor in Greenshields's own logic, could the government compel either system to accept children of any other religion. In light of Greenshields's own argument and logic, the idea that Jewish children were entitled to an education was not an entitlement at all because neither school system could be compelled by law to accept educational Others.

The other anglophone judge, Flynn, answered all the questions in line with the unanimous finding of the Court that the 1903 Act was ultra vires, until he came to the issue of the rights of Jewish school children. He believed that it was possible to create a separate Jewish school system in a way that would not violate the rights of Roman Catholics and Protestants under the BNA Act.[44] He did not accept the Greenshields's notion that the school system was irreducibly Christian. On the rights of Jewish children to attend Protestant schools, Flynn simply cited the conclusions of Justice Davidson in *Pinsler*, confirming that the Protestant board could decide as a matter of Christian grace to permit Jews to attend their schools, and stating, in terms that could not be more ambiguous, that Jews who paid real estate taxes "possibly" had a right to send their children to school.[45]

Justice Tellier likewise found that the 1903 statute was unconstitutional. For him, the simple legal fiction assimilating Jews as Protestants for school purposes "causes prejudice to the rights and privileges of Protestants."[46] Likewise he confirmed the holding in *Pinsler* that Jews had no right to attend Protestant schools.[47] Significantly, however, he also found that, under its general jurisdiction, the provincial government, which had powers in matters of education under section 93, subject only to the limitations imposed in relation to denominational rights established in law in 1867, could create a third school system.[48] While no non–Roman Catholic non-Protestants had any constitutionally guaranteed right to a separate school system, a privilege reserved for the two founding denominational groups, the provincial legislature had every power to create such a system, and its establishment would not adversely affect any right or privilege of the Roman Catholic or Protestant citizens at the time of Confederation.[49] Tellier rejected Greenshields's contention that among the rights enshrined in section 93 was the right to maintain a strict Christian educational duopoly in Quebec, and in Montreal in particular.

After a detailed review of the legislative history relating to education in the province, Justice Rivard likewise found that the 1903 Act could not pass constitutional scrutiny. He also accepted the argument put forward by Greenshields, reflecting the position of the Roman Catholic Board of School Commissioners that the entire history of Quebec law in the matter indicated that all common schools in the province had a Christian character.[50] "A law which would give to non-Christians the right to separate schools, neither Catholic nor Protestant, would be contrary both to the spirit and the letter of all our school legislation, and would create a situation against which militates the essential character imprinted in our public education, and which would cause harm to the right of Christians, under the Constitution, to teach the children in the province of Quebec."[51]

Of course, it is impossible to find the word *Christian* in section 93. Protestant schools and the educational institutions of Roman Catholics are protected Christian schools, just as non-Protestants, non–Roman Catholics, or Jews are unknown categories in the constitutional text. Perhaps even more significant in Rivard's judgment, since it is a theme that would be picked up in other discussions of the Jewish School Question, are his comments about what could be expected of immigrants when they came to Canada and what those immigrants themselves could and should expect. For the judge, immigrants naturally fell under the protections offered by Canadian law, but at the same time they must be deemed to have come to the country and have been satisfied by the protections offered by those laws. If the country offered common schools that were Protestant or Roman Catholic, then immigrants must have accepted this as an essential term of the implied immigration contract. If there was a problem, they must deal with it by establishing a system of private schools where their interests could be better protected.[52] This then was the constitutive narrative offered by one justice of the Court of King's Bench. The public common schools in Quebec were Christian. Accept this or pay for your own educational system. Of course, Schubert and the downtowners wanted nothing more than to pay for their own educational system, only they wanted to do this out of public tax monies. For Rivard, this was not acceptable. The public school system was Christian, while a private system could be anything the individual or group wanted. The idea of citizenship on offer here was one of passive acceptance by the minorities (or a minority) within the system created by the majorities and enshrined in the Constitution. Quebec was founded by two nations, and no one else had a substantive, constitutive contribution to make. Any other group outside the founding duality had to make its way through an acceptance of the inevitable concretization of that duality in the school system as the only type of public education available in Montreal. Jews apparently had a legal duty to pay school taxes, but they needed to find other revenues to pay for their own schools, since those taxes went to support the public, Christian system.

Yet Rivard admitted not just that Protestants could, as an act of grace or favour, allow Jews to attend their schools, but that in some cases the Protestant board had a legal obligation to admit any Jewish students in cases where their parents had "by some means provided for in law, opted, or are deemed to have opted for Protestant schools (except that regulations issued by the competent authority for the administration of the schools and in order to protect the Christian confessional character of education must be observed)."[53] What Rivard offered was a return to the system apparently approved, however uncertainly, by Justice Davidson in *Pinsler* that Jewish school taxpayers had a right to send their children to Protestant schools. As Rivard's opinion would have it, in the rest of the province outside the cities of Quebec and Montreal, where there existed either common schools alone, or common and dissentient schools, Jewish children could attend common or dissentient schools, depending on their father's election under the general school law. In Montreal, Rivard returned to a tax situation that had existed for some time, especially under the first crisis of the Spanish and Portuguese synagogue taxpayers and the Jewish School Question, in which Jews would be entitled to select the panel into which they paid. In such cases, the children of these taxpayers would be entitled as matter of law to attend the Protestant schools if they had paid into the Protestant panel. The 1922 Act had placed non–Roman Catholic, non-Protestant taxpayers into the neutral panel with the option to attend either of the common school systems, but it had excluded Jews from this taxonomy. But because the 1903 Act was now unconstitutional, Rivard felt that the best solution was to read the 1922 statute as if Jews now fell under the non–Roman Catholic, non-Protestant classification.[54] As with *Pinsler*, however, the case of non-taxpaying Jewish families would apparently remain subject to the Christian discretion of the school boards. Of course the proposed legislation, which the Protestant School Board had every intention of introducing once the litigation had come to an end, would have rendered both *Pinsler* and Rivard's opinion moot. Under the Protestant scheme, Jews, like all non-Protestant, non–Roman Catholic taxpayers, would place their taxes into the neutral panel and could therefore no longer claim a right to have their children educated in Protestant schools. Their entry would be subject again to the Christian grace of the denominational school administrators. Under the proposed Protestant scheme, obligations to pay school tax still existed as a matter of law, but there was little room for a concomitant right to attend denominational schools. The remaining ambiguity was over the question of the rights of Jews outside Quebec City and Montreal to attend schools, and Rivard's view did little to clarify this matter.

Justice Létourneau adopted the general view about the Christian denominational nature of the schools of Montreal and found that the 1903 Act could not meet the appropriate constitutional standards. He waffled on the right of Jewish children to attend schools by insisting that the state provided education for all children, while also asserting that the common schools were fundamentally Christian. Any non-Christian attending those schools had to comply with the rules and regulations of the school and not upset the normal functioning of the schools. He answered "yes" to all parts of question 7 and without further elaboration shared the opinion of Rivard, leaving open several questions and failing to provide any real clarity.[55]

No one had particular reason to be completely happy with the outcome of the reference to the Court of King's Bench. The judges had unanimously agreed that the 1903 Act was unconstitutional, to the pleasure no doubt of the Protestant and Roman Catholic School Boards. As a consequence, they had clearly indicated that no idea of Jewish representation, even of the consultative kind, could be contemplated within a system of education that was denominational and Christian. However, they had disagreed on the right of Jewish children to attend the common schools of the province. Some answered the question by referring to the confusing *Pinsler* decision, which had left the fate of non-taxpaying Jews in the hands of Christian grace, while others read the 1922 statute in a way that once again would include Jews in the broader non–Roman Catholic, non-Protestant group but was equally tax-based. At the same time, some in their number believed that, outside of Montreal, Jews could in fact declare themselves to be dissentient and obtain the right to attend Protestant schools, as long as they did not interfere with the Christian character of the schools.

Hirsch and Cohen and the uptowner faction were no doubt the most disappointed. In effect, their entire case had been defeated. All the judges of the Court of King's Bench had agreed that, as a matter of constitutional law and principle, Jews were excluded from any concept of equality in educational matters. Joseph Schubert and the downtowners convinced some of the judges that, if it saw fit, the provincial legislature, with its general powers under section 93 in the field of education, could create a separate system of Jewish schools, but again this view was not unanimous. While winning on most points, the two school boards still contested the idea that Schubert's plan could go ahead, preferring the Greenshields/Rivard position of an exclusionary complete Christian educational duopoly.[56] Likewise in areas outside the cities of Quebec and Montreal, the idea expressed by some judges that Jews could belong to the religious majority or be dissentient, which had not been seriously addressed in great detail, did not sit well within the broad ideological and theological understandings of the dual confessional system argued for by the two school boards.

But the message by the editors of the *Revue du Droit* conveyed to the francophone legal professional elite was that the Court of King's Bench decision had confirmed in no uncertain terms that the province's schools were denominational and Christian.[57] In a subsequent issue, the same journal, a key organ of the province's Roman Catholic lawyers and notaries, gave further evidence of the position then current among the Canadien elite on the school question.[58] There, Léo Pelland, an ardent conservative Roman Catholic social and legal activist, made clear his support for the opinion expressed by Rivard as the best embodiment of Roman Catholic jurisprudence.[59] Indeed, even a passing comment from Greenshields that the 1841 educational statute had imposed an obligation on the state to provide a secular education to non–Roman Catholic, non-Protestant students, was attacked by Pelland as "equivocal and dangerous" because it came perilously close to the idea of the state "*maître d'école*."[60] This was anathema to the dominant ideology of Quebec Roman Catholicism, which had always maintained that the parental role was the key to the provision of education for children in the province. The necessary consequence, of course, was that a *bon père de famille québécois* would turn to the church to ensure that his children received a proper moral, Roman Catholic education. The idea of a Jewish family's authority over their children's education had no place in the public law world of section 93 in Montreal. A third panel again posed a dangerous challenge to the school as a Christian institution, founded and fundamentally meant to ensure the survival and flourishing of the natural organism, the family.[61] Therefore from the Quebec Roman Catholic perspective, the essential recognition in the Court's opinion that all schools in Quebec were denominational was challenged by any notion that common schools also had, or had had, a duty to educate non-Christians. No one was perfectly satisfied with the divided opinion of the Court of King's Bench.

An appeal to the Supreme Court of Canada was inevitable, and by now the arguments were familiar.[62] Nesbitt joined Louis St-Laurent in the case.[63] Unfortunately, once again, the Court confirmed the King's Bench opinion that the 1903 Act was clearly unconstitutional, if given the reading offered by Hirsch and Cohen. The Court rendered a unanimous opinion.[64] Writing for the Court, Chief Justice Anglin again canvassed the legislative history and found that in Montreal, both the Protestant and Roman Catholic schools were common schools as a matter of law. Because this was the case, there were no dissentient schools in the city.[65] He also confirmed the idea that Jews could not, insofar as education law was concerned, be considered as Protestants simply because they were not Roman Catholics. The term *Protestant* had a wide meaning but it applied only to those Christians who had split from Roman Catholicism during the Reformation or who fell broadly under the Western Christian rubric. Thus not only were Jews not Protestants, but Greek and Syrian Orthodox citizens could not be considered as Protestants either. Moreover and more importantly, the system of Quebec education, with common and dissentient schools, had always been denominational. This meant that any reliance on *Maher v Portland* as urged by Nesbitt could not stand. The common schools of New Brunswick in that case were public, non-denominational institutions, while in Quebec, common schools were always either Roman Catholic or Protestant. Despite the arduous efforts of many Protestants, some French-Canadian progressives, and the colonial administration, the idea and ideal of a common public school system in Quebec had been defeated by the political power and intransigence of the Roman Catholic Church.[66] There had never been, at least at the time of Confederation, a non-denominational common school system in Quebec.[67] In 1867, however, one important distinction, outside of Montreal and Quebec, did obtain. Dissentient schools had the right to exclude students on the basis of religious faith. Common schools did not.

Because the schools of Montreal were all common schools, and because the current state of law had to be presumed to have been in the minds of those who negotiated the BNA Act and section 93, and in the mind of the British Parliament when it passed the Act, "it follows that in the city of Montreal every child between the ages of five and sixteen years resident within the municipality retained the right conferred by the Act of 1861 to attend any school under the control of the Commissioners, whether Catholic or Protestant; and the correlative obligation to receive and provide for them incumbent upon both bodies of Commissioners likewise remained unimpaired."[68]

For the chief justice, at the relevant historical legal juncture there was and had always been a clear distinction between common schools and dissentient schools. This constitutional and constitutive distinction was not that they were not both denominational, since in Montreal there had only ever been Protestant or Roman Catholic common schools. Instead the vital legal point was that common school commissioners had never had the right to exclude students on the basis of religion, whereas the 1861 Act had clearly granted that right to dissentient school trustees. Since religion was now out of the equation, as far as the students within the common school system were concerned, he then was led to construct the question as a relevant consideration in terms of individual rights and correlative obligations. The analysis offered here by the chief justice was based on individual students and not on their adherence to any religious creed. Likewise he was unwilling to accept the idea that the composition of the Council of Public Instruction was enshrined and limited to Roman Catholics and Protestants. He pointed out that the 1861 Act was silent on the denomination of its members, and as a result it was in a different category for section 93 analysis.[69]

Therefore, given this legal historical survey of the educational system, and the key importance of the distinction between common and dissentient schools on the issue of attendance rights, Anglin took a more subtle and nuanced approach to Jewish rights and their relation to the 1903 statute. Insofar as the Act purported to treat Jews as Protestants in rural communities with a dissentient Protestant school, it was ultra vires. As far as the city of Montreal was concerned, the provision was legally unnecessary, since Jews, like anyone else, had always had the right to attend a common school.[70] However, exactly where one might find the origins of this legal right to a common school education remained obscure, given the vague references to various statutes. Nonetheless, for the Supreme Court this meant that nothing in the Act on the attendance issue could be said to adversely affect Protestant rights in their Montreal schools because they had never had the constitutional right to exclude Jewish students, nor had their Roman Catholic counterparts. However, for the Supreme Court, the situation in rural communities could adversely affect the Roman Catholic majority if the tax provisions of the Act were allowed to stand. Because the majority school would be the common school, which Jewish students had a right to attend, and the Protestant school would be a dissentient school that Jews had no right to attend, in those communities where the confessional dynamic reflected the broad demographics of the province, the payment of taxes to the Protestant system by Jewish ratepayers who could not send their children to Protestant schools would unduly burden the Roman Catholic school system and adversely affect their rights and privileges protected by law in 1867. Otherwise this would mean that Jews would pay taxes under the 1903 Act to the local dissentient Protestant school but would have the legal right to attend only the common, Roman Catholic school. The Protestant system would be unjustly enriched and the Roman Catholic conversely impoverished.

Ordinary statutory construction would allow some provisions of the 1903 Act to stand as long as they were interpreted to exclude any legislative intent to permit Jewish representation on the Protestant board.[71] If one read the statute to do anything other than declare the rights of Jewish children to attend common schools and to make consequential changes to tax arrangements, as Lafleur had long contended, the statute would be unconstitutional in its entirety, because it would interfere with the rights of the Protestants of Quebec to exclusively control their school system in all matters "financial and pedagogic."[72] Finally, the creation of a separate school system, not Roman Catholic and not Protestant, would be within the legislative power of the province as long as it did not impinge on the rights and privileges of the two established denominations.[73] Therefore Anglin did not accept the position advanced by the Quebec judges, Greenshields and Rivard, and insisted upon in the Roman Catholic board's pleadings, that the mere act of creating a third school system would damage the core and monopolistic Christian character of Quebec education, with its concomitant duopolistic Protestant and Roman Catholic structure.

Again, the Court both gave and took away. It confirmed the failure of Hirsch and Cohen's vision of Jewish representation as taxpaying equals on constitutional grounds. The schools of Montreal were common schools, but in Quebec at the time of Confederation, common schools had been denominational schools. The only factor that distinguished Montreal (and Quebec City) schools from those of the rest of the province was that instead of having a common school system and a dissentient school system, it had two common school systems. But again, those common schools were denominational, and in the Quebec constitutional context that meant Protestant and Roman Catholic. Jews were not and could not be Protestants and therefore they had no right to interfere by being represented in the administration of the Protestant school system by Protestants. At the same time, the Court also confirmed Schubert's contention that the province could create a separate Jewish school system under its general jurisdiction in educational matters under section 93, and that it would not *per se* prejudice the Roman Catholic and Protestant educational structures. Hirsch and Cohen did obtain some clarity about the rights of Jewish children to attend Protestant schools in Montreal.[74] That right existed not because of the 1903 Act but because all children had the right before Confederation to attend common schools in the province.

For the Roman Catholic and Protestant Boards, the judgment was less than ideal, because it clearly overturned the *Pinsler* precedent and took away any discretion or Christian grace concerning Jewish children's right to attend common schools in Montreal. While most of the 1903 Act was now rendered unconstitutional or read down in such a way as to be inoperative in important ways, the Protestant board had lost what it had always assumed, and what had been confirmed by Justice Davidson, was its ultimate right to exclude Jewish students from

Protestant schools. On this point they had won the battle in *Pinsler* but lost the war in their attempt to rid themselves of the 1903 Act. The Roman Catholic board was also now in a position where it would be obliged, if the Supreme Court decision stood, to admit Jewish students to its schools as of right. More significantly, it had lost the constitutive, existential battle over the question of the uniquely and solely Christian character of all Quebec schools. The creation of a third school system was now constitutionally permissible. For the Roman Catholic School Commission and for the church hierarchy whose views it echoed, the creation of a third independent school system was the first breech in the bulwark that ensured that education was a matter for the family and then for the church. It was the first step towards the creation of a system of public, state, secular schools that would remove God from the classroom.[75] The Privy Council beckoned.

Jews, Protestants, and Roman Catholics in London: The Privy Council and the Jewish School Question

The government of Quebec had already passed the special legislation required to permit appeals from these provincial matters to the Supreme Court and to the Privy Council.[76] Two years after arguments had been filed before the Supreme Court, on 29 November 1927, the four-day hearing of the appeal to the Privy Council in the case of *Michael Hirsch v The Protestant Board of School Commissioners of the City of Montreal et al* began.[77] In their oral argument and in their written submission, counsel for the appellants expended some effort to extend the meaning of *Protestant* in Quebec legislation relating to schools to include Jews, based at least in part on the lack of definition of the term in any legislation, and the differences between and among many groups that might fall under the term's broad meaning. But the idea was rejected almost out of hand by the Privy Council.[78] Once again the key question was whether the 1903 Act, which assimilated Jews as Protestants for school purposes, was unconstitutional because such an assimilation caused harm to Protestant rights over Protestant schools as they had existed in 1867. Indeed, for the Protestant board, the existential crisis of Protestant education in Montreal was acute. "The issue … is … whether the whole right of Protestant control is to be endangered. Jewish children now constitute forty per cent. of the school population. A few years ago they were only twenty per cent. If the future has in store anything like the experience of the past, it is a matter of a very few years before the Jews, on the basis of population, would be entitled to elect more School Commissioners to the Protestant Board than the Protestants themselves, and the Protestant and even the Christian character of the their school system might be destroyed."[79]

Any claim of right made by Quebec Jews in virtue of the guarantee of equality in the 1832 Act could not pass legal scrutiny because the test for membership on the Protestant School Board was, and had always been, a religious one. The Jews were in no worse position than the Roman Catholic majority of the province, who were likewise excluded by law from being represented on the Protestant School Board.[80] Of course, this argument ignored the other reality, that the Roman Catholic people of the province were represented on their own school boards while Jews were not, and much of the legal argument sought to prevent them from ever possibly having their own schools.

Significant energy was expended, especially in the argument of the Roman Catholic board, in asserting once more and with force the central plea for the recognition of the essential duopoly of the educational system and attacking the Supreme Court's decision supporting Schubert's claim that a separate third school system could be established within the ambit of the province's general constitutional powers over education. They again asserted the constitutional status of the Christian nature of the Quebec educational system that had convinced Greenshields and Rivard on the Quebec Court of King's Bench, but not the Supreme Court.[81] The Roman Catholic submission also claimed that the creation of such a third system, which would necessarily result in a change of the current distribution of tax monies paid by non–Roman Catholics, non-Protestants, and Jews, especially sums designated to the neutral panel, would by definition adversely affect both the Protestant and Roman Catholic School Boards, by diminishing the total amount of tax monies available to them to carry out their educational programs.[82] In other words, they had a right to Jewish taxes, but Jews did not. Schubert simply replied that while Protestant and Roman Catholic education was enshrined in the Constitution, "no particular scheme whereby such revenues are derived is a fundamental right or privilege."[83] Indeed, the history of education law in the province was one of an ever-changing set of fiscal arrangements without any idea that a particular system of financial support for schooling in Quebec had been forever fixed in 1867. Once more, battle was joined, and the rights of Jews, as British subjects as the uptowners had always insisted, in the educational system of Montreal were to be determined by the Privy Council.

The Privy Council rendered public its advice to the King on 2 February 1928.[84] Viscount Cave examined the most relevant statute, the 1861 Act, and declared that at the time of the BNA Act, there were two different educational systems in the province, those in the so-called rural areas and those in Montreal and Quebec City. In the rural areas, there were common schools run by commissioners, and in some instances, where a minority professing a religion different from the majority desired their creation, dissentient schools run by trustees. At Confederation, dissentient schools clearly fell under the definition of religious schools of a "class of persons" protected by the provisions of section 93. On the other hand, schools run by commissioners had been and still were common schools governed by these commissioners elected by voters who need not all be of the same faith. The religious character of most common schools in 1867 and thereafter had been a matter of demographic circumstance, as was the case in New Brunswick, in its mirror image, in *Maher v Portland*. In each instance, section 93 did not protect or enshrine the rights of the members of these denominations because of "an accident" to which their denominational nature was attributed.[85] The Constitution protected rights enshrined by law and not any practice created by mere demography.

In Montreal, however, the statutory regime at Confederation had not created common and dissentient schools, but instead Protestant and Roman Catholic schools. Both were common schools. For the Privy Council, as for the Supreme Court, Montreal's schools were common schools whose character was denominational. They were controlled by a "class of persons," Protestants and Roman Catholics, whose rights were protected by the Constitution. The Supreme Court of Canada had emphasized the common character of Montreal's dual system and therefore granted rights of attendance to all. The Privy Council focused on, and gave more rhetorical significance to, the denominational character of the schools, which as a direct consequence enshrined rights and privileges of discrimination and exclusion as a matter of constitutional principle.

For all the turmoil and upset caused by the Spanish and Portuguese synagogue's decision to opt for the Roman Catholic panel, by disputes over the Protestant subsidy to support the education of Jewish students, by Meldola de Sola's insistence that he be paid the highest salary in the Protestant school system, by the segregation of Jewish students, and the controversies over absences on holy days, or the hiring of Jewish teachers, even after *Pinsler* had given the Protestant Board a relatively clear legal statement of its rights, each of these incidents that had been at the core of the Jewish School Question had been discussed and debated between and among the parties. Government-sanctioned arrangements had created law in the broadest constitutive sense between the parties. Now in *Hirsch*, the minority Protestant community insisted on defending and entrenching its rights that its previous representatives had negotiated away in their constitutive dealings with the Jewish community and the government in 1903. Now they were joined by the Roman Catholic majority, who wished to see its associational right of self-determination in the educational field protected again by destroying any legal claim from the minority Jewish community. Faced with this opposition, the uptowners had striven to reassert equality and British justice within their relationships with the Protestant representatives, while the downtowners had seen an opportunity and perhaps a necessity to produce their own form of associational constitutional self-identity within a system of Jewish schools.

Viscount Cave did not openly echo Anglin's emphasis on a liberal reading of the statute, or of the dominance of the common over the denominational, in the characterization of the Montreal school system. However, despite this rhetorical shift to, and insistence on, the denominational character of Montreal's schools, the Privy Council adopted the consequence that flowed from their common status and confirmed the general principle enunciated by the Supreme Court. Any claim of Jews to join dissentient schools outside the two cities of Montreal and Quebec was impossible to countenance for the Privy Council, as it had been for the Supreme Court. These dissentient establishments were unquestionably denominational schools, the rights over which inhered in the relevant denomination at the time of Confederation. Likewise, the common schools of Montreal, which were denominational in the same sense as the rural dissentient schools, were permitted to exclude and reject any attempt by Jews to representative status in the governance of the city's schools. They were still Protestant and Roman Catholic schools, and therefore any claim to some right of a voice in administration by anyone who did not belong to the denomination was unconstitutional. One of the rights and privileges recognized by law at Confederation had been the autonomy of each of the two denominations in matters of school administration. No right to engage with denominational schools in terms of governance could be envisaged for anyone who did not share the denominational allegiance of the relevant school board.[86]

Alderman Schubert emerged triumphant once again. Viscount Cave stated unambiguously that the provisions of section 93 in no way froze the educational structure along the same denominational lines as those that might have existed in 1867. The constitutional text protected the rights of two "classes of persons," Roman Catholic and Protestant, but at the same time gave broad and general legislative power over education to the provincial government. To accept the thesis set forward most prominently by the Roman Catholic board that section 93 had enshrined the uniquely Christian character of Quebec education flew in the face of the nature of provincial power in the field of education, but more significantly, it sought to create a new class of persons, Christians, who had no legal right to schools in 1867. There had been no Christian school commissioners or trustees in 1867. Roman Catholics had rights, and Protestants had rights, but collectively as Christians they did not.[87]

Despite the general expression of an understanding of the Protestant and Roman Catholic schools of Montreal as at one and the same time denominational and as common, Viscount Cave did not in any detail address the issue of the rights of Jewish students to attend the Protestant schools in Montreal, the issue that had been central to the Jewish School Question since the last days of the nineteenth century. Instead the Privy Council preferred to reply to the question in the same terms as had the Supreme Court. Viscount Cave had clearly discussed the representation issue and rejected any notion that the Jews could play a part in administering Protestant schools, but on the question of whether Jewish children attended Quebec schools as a matter of legal right or by the Christian grace of education officials, he chose to confirm the opinion of the Supreme Court. He had stated unambiguously that Jews could have no claim to a right to attend dissentient schools in rural areas, again the same position adopted by the Supreme Court. He simply concurred in the answer given to the question by Chief Justice Anglin on Jewish students' right to attend common schools in the city.

After this final appellate ruling, it appeared that Jews were excluded from representation on the Protestant School Board, or on any kind of special committee, which might have been created under the Hirsch/Cohen plan presented to the Commission of Nine. But the uptown supporters had found confirmation of their right to attend the common schools of the city of Montreal as students, a right they also held in common schools throughout the province, but not in relation to any dissentient school. In addition, Schubert had prevailed in his claim that the provincial government was empowered to create a separate system of Jewish schools if it so wished. The battle between the uptowners' vision of full integration of Jews within the Protestant school system as the path to belonging and citizenship still confronted the downtowner pleas for a separate Jewish school system.[88] Each had won before the Privy Council. Law could be used to concretize both the uptowner and the downtowner visions of the place of education in the construction and constitution of Jewish identities in Montreal. But within the political and social power struggle in the Jewish community, the uptowner position had a growing, stronger claim to democratic legitimacy than just a few years earlier. Louis Fitch had run against Peter Bercovitch in the elections of May 1927 and had made the *Yiddishkeit* claim to separate Jewish schools a central focus of his campaign. Bercovitch, a long-time and vocal supporter of the uptowner position, emerged victorious in St Louis, as did Joseph Cohen, also a Liberal and uptowner supporter, in the St Lawrence riding.[89]

The Roman Catholics had failed in their broad contention that a Jewish school system would destroy the essential Christian character of the Quebec school system and that therefore any Jewish school system must be unconstitutional.[90] Their response was quick and to a large extent unchanged and unbending. They now insisted on staking a new extra- or almost supra-legal claim. Their analysis relied on statements in all three decisions confirming the legislative power of the province to create a separate third school systems for non-Christians. Those judicial pronouncements had inevitably set out a position with the effect that provincial legislative power over education was itself limited by the rights of the existing Protestant and Roman Catholic schools, a simple reiteration of the text of section 93. The Roman Catholic position started again from the premise of their defeated legal argument that all common schools in Quebec were Christian and the creation of any new system would be subject to that limit, that is, a constitutional impossibility after the decisions in *Hirsch* from the Supreme Court and the Privy Council.[91] The ultramontane elements in the church had not given up hope simply because the courts had issued judicial pronouncements about the meaning of a constitutional text. They would do everything possible in the political domain to ensure that the rights of the founding nation of Quebec would not witness the destruction of their history and their educational heritage by allowing the creation of a separate Jewish school system.[92] A Jewish *bon père de famille*, naturally, had to maintain control of his children's education. He could do so by sending them to Christian schools, Protestant or Roman Catholic, or to private schools.

But he could not be permitted to destroy the Christian common schools of Quebec, no matter what the Supreme Court and Privy Council might have declared.[93] Viscount Cave had left no doubt that Christians were not a protected class under section 93, but this was no longer simply a legal issue, if it had ever been. For many prominent Roman Catholic legal and theological officials, the question of Quebec's Christian educational heritage was an existential one, an issue of basic national values, a question of the province's overarching and foundational political and social identity.

Finally the Protestant board had won its main claim keeping Jews from its governance structures, but it had lost its other clear aim of confirming the principle enunciated in *Pinsler* that Jewish students attended Montreal schools as a matter of sufferance and Christian charity. The repeal of the 1903 Act, their unrelenting campaign goal throughout the 1920s, was now meaningless on the issue of Jewish students in Protestant schools. Much of the 1903 Act creating the legal fiction of Jews as "honorary Protestants" for school purposes had been declared unconstitutional insofar as the broader governance and representational issues were concerned. But since the right of Jewish children to attend Protestant schools, as common schools, did not depend on the 1903 legislation, the Protestant Board could not return to the ideal of the *Pinsler* era when they had the right to exclude Jewish students. What that meant in practice was murky, but the legal principle had been established and the Protestant School Board had lost.

For the Jewish communities, they now faced a dilemma. Insofar as the legal right to school attendance was concerned, the uptowner view had prevailed. On the separate school question, Schubert and the downtowners had also triumphed. Jewish students could attend Protestant schools as they had been doing for many years, or the Jewish communities could unite and ask the government to create a new school system for Jewish children. For all parties, the law, as embodied in the Privy Council advice, had given and the law had taken away. As in previous iterations of the Jewish School Question, the political and social realms would now play the key role in structuring the arrangements for Jewish education in Montreal. Law, in its constitutional guise, would again simply set a hermeneutic framework within (and perhaps outside of) which other constitutive narratives would shape the relations between and among Protestants, Roman Catholics, Jews, and the state on the Jewish School Question.[94]

9

Jews, Protestants, and Roman Catholics: Two Crises and the Jewish School Question, 1928–1931

Law, Politics, and the Solution to the Jewish School Question

Following the opinion of the Privy Council, the Jewish School Question once more entered a political phase. The general parameter of the issue in constitutional law terms had been set: a separate Jewish school system could be established under the province's general jurisdiction over education, and Jewish children in Montreal had a right to attend the common, Roman Catholic and Protestant, schools of the city. Therefore, between downtowners and uptowners within the Jewish communities, nothing had been settled. As the discussion that follows elaborates, each of the two parties would come to the table armed with rights.[1] The Roman Catholic educational representatives and their legal elite continued to insist that Rivard had expressed the only acceptable view of the whole matter: the school system of the province, and indeed the province itself, was fundamentally and essentially Christian. The 1832 emancipation of Quebec Jews meant nothing in a context in which political rights were distinguished from and trumped by educational rights. Protestant opinion continued to be divided between those who sought a continuation of the old system of dialogue and compromise and those who insisted that, because the Jews had now won the right to their own school system and the Protestant Board had lost its *Pinsler* rights of exclusion, the only way to maintain the Protestant character of Protestant schools was to advocate, along with the downtowners, the creation of the third school system in Montreal. This chapter explores the political, legal, and social dynamics that would lead, again not without conflict and controversy, to a series of legislative interventions culminating in the appointment of a Jewish School Commission, the sole function of which would be to negotiate yet another agreement with Protestant school officials. Once more, the narrative unfolding here is one of conflict and compromise, of legal victories and political defeats, and after all of this, a practical if ultimately unsatisfactory compromise that would guarantee Jewish children's right to attend Protestant schools in Montreal, while at the same time stymying any hope that Jews could begin either to enjoy a form of educational autonomy or assert and concretize their long-standing claim that full emancipation and political, legal equality of life as "honorary Protestants" had to include the core right to be part of the administrative structure of the school system in which their children were being educated. The chapter is about law and politics, compromise, and the end of one vision of Jewish educational autonomy in obeisance to the political reality of life in Quebec in the 1920s and 1930s.

The Protestants, the Government, and the Uptowners

Less than a month after the opinion of the Privy Council in *Hirsch*, H.M. Caiserman, who was now the chairman of the Separate Jewish School Committee, wrote to the Jewish Educational Committee to arrange a joint conference of the downtown and uptown school committees. The goal was to agree on "plans for a harmonious activity for the education of the Jewish children of Montreal" that could be put into place.[2] The Jewish Educational Committee uptown representatives preferred to act according to what had become their normal practice. They arranged to meet with the Protestant School Board and the provincial government to achieve a political settlement to their own satisfaction, just as they had after *Pinsler*. Following several months of talks with the Protestant board, the Jewish Educational Committee and the Protestant representatives arranged to meet jointly with the provincial secretary, Anathase David.[3] At that meeting on 18 October, the Protestant board members were joined by Michael Hirsch, Peter Bercovitch, and Joseph Cohen.[4] Clearly, the Jewish Educational Committee at this stage had the ear of the elected Jewish representatives in the provincial Assembly, and of the government. Perhaps even more importantly, they had the ear of the Protestant School Board.[5]

Among the points upon which the Protestant school officials agreed was the creation by the provincial government of a five-member Jewish Educational Committee, which would be entitled to make representations "to any School Board or educational authority where the interests of the Jewish people are involved."[6] In addition the board agreed that, as a matter of administration, they would look favourably upon suggestions that school facilities be made available after hours for religious instruction of Jewish children. They felt that the nature of this question was not appropriate for inclusion in legislation, and it should be left to the discretion of subsequent school boards and the Jewish community as matters of purely local administration and discussion.[7] They also sought a continuation of the system under the 1922 statute according to which Jewish taxes would pay for the education of Jewish students, with a first charge on the neutral panel to make up any shortfall.[8] Because the Protestant School Board of Montreal had no involvement in the appointment of members of the Protestant Committee of the Council of Public Instruction, at this stage they preferred not to make any representations on the question of Jewish representation on the Committee or the Council.[9]

The Court of King's Bench had decided unanimously that the appointment of Jews as advisory members of the Protestant School Board was unconstitutional, while the Supreme Court and Privy Council decided that more detail on the duties and powers of the proposed advisory members would be required for the question to be answered. All judges were convinced that a body such as the finance committee proposed by the Hirsch/Cohen plan would constitute an undue infringement on the absolute autonomy of the Protestant and Roman Catholic School Boards in running their schools. Significantly, the Protestant proposal was clearly delimited by this legal frame. It insisted that the Jewish Educational Committee would be empowered only to make representations to the relevant board (including the Roman Catholic board as the proposal stood). It therefore could not possess any decision-making power. That would rest solely with the denominational school authorities. Moreover, the Protestant board had also insisted, in its description of the procedures to be followed for the presentation of such recommendations from the Jewish representatives, that they would have to approach the board with an application to meet, which would be considered by the appropriate school authority. Therefore even the decision to have a discussion would remain solely and absolutely in the hands of the Protestant or Roman Catholic School Board.[10]

The Protestant position was clearly aimed at maintaining respect for the opinions of the courts and ensuring the continuation of the constitutionally protected Protestant absolute administrative authority over Protestant schools. In this case, the Jewish advisors would be members of a separate body created by the government and not advisory members of the Protestant commission, thereby avoiding the constitutional issues flagged particularly by the Court of King's Bench. In attempting to reach another compromise with the Jewish communities, the Protestant Commission was willing to do so only in terms that enshrined its absolute autonomy guaranteed by the BNA Act. At the same time, many of its proposals offered a return to the situation, as it had existed in the early 1920s before the Commission of Nine and the *Hirsch* litigation. The Jewish Educational Committee agreed in principle with the Protestant position.[11]

However, the Jewish Educational Committee still wanted to push its representative agenda. They believed they now had judicial authority on their side, which would permit Jewish membership on the Council of Public Instruction. Because the division of its membership into Protestant and Roman Catholic committees had been the result of a post-Confederation legislative change, the argument posited, as first voiced in some legal opinions to the Commission of Nine, that it fell within the general remit of the provincial legislature over educational matters to decide on the actual constitution of the Council of Public Instruction. Despite its previous statement that it would not venture an opinion on the possibility of Jewish membership on the council because the composition of that body was outside its competence, when faced with Peter Bercovitch's insistence on Jewish membership at the meeting with Anathase David, the Protestant Board of Montreal stated that Jewish persistence on this question would cause them to withdraw from all negotiations.[12] In order to preserve the ongoing talks, Bercovitch agreed to give his support to the Protestant recommendations but reserved the right to introduce the question of Jewish representation during the legislative process, should that become necessary.

The Protestant Board provided Michael Hirsch with a number of documents outlining the current state of the school taxes received from the neutral panel. The education committee needed this information not just to prepare its position in relation to maintaining the 1922 statutory arrangements, as the Protestant board's resolution sought, but also to have complete financial details at hand to address ongoing downtowner assertions that there would be enough Jewish tax money available to permit the government to establish a separate Jewish school system.[13] On 20 December, members of the Jewish Educational Committee met at the home of Lyon Cohen with Cohen and Caiserman.[14] There was still some effort aimed at finding a common Jewish communal position on the School Question.

Cohen suggested a modification to the proposal on the subject of Jewish education. Instead of after-hours use of Protestant school facilities, he argued that in schools with an 80 per cent Jewish student body, Jewish subjects would be better taught during parts of the normal school day. Cohen sought to create a system in which Protestant schools within the Protestant school system would become de facto Jewish schools in which religious education would be part of the normal daily curriculum. The committee approached the board with Cohen's idea. While identifying several practical concerns with any such arrangements, the board again stated that this entire question appeared to be a matter of administration, which could form part of the representations to the Board of Protestant School Commissioners by the soon-to-be appointed Jewish Educational Committee.[15] The official Protestant position at this time was that it would consider further and ongoing discussion with the government-endorsed Jewish educational representatives once the official structures had been put in place following legislative amendments. Of course this would constitute a return to the way of doing things that had obtained for several years before the revanchist elements of Protestant school government had had their way on the board. At the same time, the idea of using regular school hours for Jewish subjects carried with it potentially dangerous echoes of past manifestations of the Jewish School Question. The issue of Hebrew instruction had caused anxiety and friction over a number of years in the Protestant schools. Release time for Jewish students excused from Protestant religious instruction had also been a sticking point for those who saw this as a disruption and as a version of special treatment for Jewish students in a Protestant school system. The Protestant commitment to engage in dialogue with the soon-to-be-created Jewish Educational Committee sat uncomfortably with the recent history of the board's positions on these Jewish questions and with the realities of the implementation post-*Pinsler* of the legislative scheme under the 1903 Act.

It also sat oddly with the ideas announced tentatively and generally in the court decisions in *Hirsch* that the common Roman Catholic and Protestant schools of Montreal had a duty to provide Jewish students with a *secular* education. The courts had contemplated the issues that might arise in a common school system in which the Roman Catholic or Protestant denominations formed core parts of the schools' identity and where religious instruction was an essential part of the curriculum. Constitutionally and practically these schools had to negotiate the perilous path between their denominational core identities and their status as common public schools. The courts had indicated that the common schools would have to provide an education to Jews, or to non–Roman Catholic, non-Protestant students, an education that would avoid such religious or denominational parts of the curriculum, but they had not considered Jewish demands for Jewish education in those common schools. In all likelihood, on a reading of the judicial pronouncements in the *Hirsch* cases, there could be no legal obligation imposed on the denominational school authorities to acquiesce to such requests, since instruction on Jewish subjects surely would prejudice the denominational Protestant or Roman Catholic character of the schools themselves, as understood by the school authorities and as enshrined and fixed into constitutional place in 1867, a view confirmed several years earlier by provincial and Montreal municipal legal authorities during the controversies over the teaching of Hebrew. But at this stage the Protestant School Board did not appear to stand on its constitutionally protected rights and interests. Instead, there was evidence of a desire to institute a viable solution for Jews and Protestants without a final and silencing recourse to strict legal constitutional discourse. Instead, the board was anxious to obtain formal agreement from the Jewish Educational Committee so that all parties could meet with the provincial secretary to discuss the terms of legislation embodying the parties' understanding. The years of the Commission of Nine and the wending journey of the *Hirsch* case to its final destination in London had created yet more uncertainty. The Protestant school authorities simply wanted a legislative end to the matter, but not necessarily one that would adhere strictly to all of the judicial pronouncements in the case.

The three parties – the Protestant board, the Jewish Educational Committee, and the provincial government – met on 14 January 1929. The Jewish uptowner representatives made it clear to the provincial secretary, David, and to the Protestant representatives that while they agreed broadly with the Protestant written submission and memorandum, they also supported Bercovitch's position, reserving his right to address the issue of Jewish representation on the Council of Public Instruction by way of an amendment to any proposed legislation, if that proved necessary. The Protestant representatives noted the Bercovitch position and expressed their likely opposition. Nonetheless, they urged the provincial secretary to accept the memorandum as an expression of the broad agreement between the parties and to introduce legislation concretizing the common position between Protestants and Jews.[16]

Meanwhile the Separate Jewish School Committee continued its agitation and mustered support among the downtowner population and its various constituent political, cultural, and religious bodies. Those Jewish bodies, "autonomous organizational structures" that had been created by the communities in the interstices left by the bi-national character of Montreal, often formed in the shadow of that overarching constitutional framework, now came to the fore of the debate over school rights for Jews.[17] Throughout January, February, and March, downtowner representatives addressed the provincial government, in person and in writing, and continued mass meetings including the "Conference of Synagogues, Labour Unions, Sick Benefit Societies, Loan Syndicates, and Cultural Societies" in English and Yiddish, in support of separate Jewish schools and all rights recognized in the Privy Council decision.[18] Taschereau replied to Caiserman, "The Government is now giving its best consideration to this most difficult matter."[19] There was evidence of movement and some indications that parts of the Jewish community and the Protestant Board were in broad agreement. Just as it had in the 1910s and 1920s, however, the representation issue was proving a stumbling block to any final settlement.[20] There was also evidence that the downtowner faction, with significant popular, institutional support, was mustering its forces, buttressed by the Privy Council's view, in favour of a third Jewish School Commission for Montreal.

Jews, Protestants, and Roman Catholics: The 1930 Statute, *la loi David*

The government in fact saw little room for manoeuvre "in this most difficult matter." It was placed in an unenviable position. While the courts had recognized some school rights for Jewish students, they had blocked all hope for Jewish representation in the direct governance of Montreal's schools and had done so by confirming the almost absolute educational autonomy enjoyed by the two dominant denominations in the province.[21] The law provided a framework within which possible solutions could be worked out, but the social and political spheres evidenced little more than complexity and discord. It became clear as time passed that the split in the Jewish community was as raw as ever. It was also obvious that both Protestant and Roman Catholic school officials continued to have problems with the proposals for legislative change being mooted at the time. For the Protestant representatives, the idea proposed by Bercovitch for Jewish representation on the Council of Public Instruction was anathema. At a specially convened meeting in Montreal on 3 January 1930, the Protestant Committee of the Council of Public Instruction heard the legal opinion of Eugène Lafleur on the matter. Following Lafleur's advice that the BNA Act had given Protestants and Roman Catholics "the full and undisturbed control of their respective educational establishments," it reasserted its disapproval of any attempt to impose a different membership, the effect of which would be to deprive Protestants of their basic right to educational self-determination. Finally it underlined the fact that the currently mooted idea of Jewish membership on the Protestant panel not only adversely affected Protestant self-governance, but it left Roman Catholic educational autonomy intact, thus upsetting the reciprocity of rights and privileges of the two denominational systems.[22]

The Protestant School Board of Montreal wrote to Premier Taschereau on 10 January expressing its opposition to the appointment of Jewish representatives and outlining the terms of the agreement between the board and the Jewish Educational Committee in which the Protestant authorities had expressed the same view.[23] While still anxious to reach an accord with the Jewish community "in an atmosphere of goodwill," the Protestant School Board would not budge on the question of Jewish representation.[24] The board itself reasserted its claim that the appointment of any non-Protestant "would be an infringement of the rights of the Protestant minority in this Province to direct and control their own schools."[25]

The Protestant Committee of the Council of Public Education[26] then sought legal advice on the constitutionality of an appointment of a Jewish member. Aimé Geoffrion offered a nuanced reading of the *Hirsch* case. First he stated that it had been clearly established that because it was a post-Confederation body, an appointment of Jewish members to the Council of Public Education was legally permissible. He then went on to point out, however, a further stumbling block, one that had already featured in legal reactions to the Privy Council opinion. The courts had insisted that no Jew could be appointed to the Protestant Board in Montreal or Quebec, or to the Protestant Board of Examiners, nor could Jews join in the creation of a dissentient school outside the two cities.

For Geoffrion, the question had not been considered by the courts in relation to the nature and functions of the Protestant Committee of the Council of Public Education. Even though the denominational nature of the divided Protestant and Roman Catholic committees of the council was a post-Confederation development, this did not in and of itself settle the constitutional debate. If it in fact exercised powers that at Confederation had been exercised by local school authorities, which were denominational and protected by section 93, then any legislation that changed the composition of the council and gave any of those powers to non-Protestants and non–Roman Catholics could run afoul of the constitutionally entrenched rights of those denominations. He gave the example of the power vested in clergy to select books for moral and religious instruction for local schools in 1867. Since those powers now rested with the council and the Protestant committee, the committee in fact exercised roles reserved exclusively for Protestant school officials at Confederation. The question was not the time at which the body had been created, but the time at which the functions had been reserved to Protestant jurisdiction. Any change granting non-Protestants any power in such matters would be unconstitutional.[27] Geoffrion's view was replicated in another letter of legal advice to the committee from Eugène Lafleur.[28] Whatever the hypothetical situation of the constitutional status of the Council of Public Education might have been, what was clear was that the province's Protestant educational officials were arming themselves for a potential further round of legal challenges if Jewish representation became a part of the government's legislative response to the *Hirsch* opinion. Montreal public opinion leaders among the Protestant community also echoed concerns about the legality and the appropriateness of Jewish representation in a Protestant educational institution.[29]

Following the Protestant committee's resolution in early January, other Jewish voices were again making themselves heard.[30] Caiserman on behalf of the Separate School Committee wrote to Taschereau declaring not for the first time that in the face of such opposition by the Protestant authorities, any idea of Jewish membership on the Protestant Committee of the Council of Public Instruction was moot. The only possible way forward, unsurprisingly, according to Caiserman, was the creation of a separate Jewish school system in which Jews, like all other citizens of the province, could exercise their right to equality in full.[31]

The third influential actor, after the Jewish communities and the Protestant educational establishment, was now about to enter the scene.

The Roman Catholic Church was broadly opposed to the creation of a third panel for a number of interconnected reasons flowing from its fundamental belief in the Christian character of Quebec education, and thence its fear that the creation of a new panel would be the first step on a slippery slope to a state-based system of secular education. In late February and early March 1930, the Roman Catholic hierarchy expressed its growing concerns, as part of its general opposition to many of Taschereau's attempts to deal with the political and social problems affecting the province in the 1920s and 1930s.[32] David Rome would later qualify the correspondence emanating from the church hierarchy as "border[ing] closely on the imperious."[33] The Roman Catholic Church and educational hierarchy objected to the idea that legislation of such importance would not have been sent to the Council of Public Education for consultation.[34] Archbishop Cardinal Rouleau wrote two letters to Premier Taschereau, and some of his remarks were repeated and expanded upon in a speech given by Mgr Georges Gauthier at St Joseph's Oratory in Montreal.[35] The church spokesman complained that the government had spent its efforts bending to Protestant susceptibilities and surrounding the Jews with "an absolutely unjustified sympathy." Was it not time, he asked, that the government take account of the Roman Catholic majority and not adopt any measures that would completely upset the educational system that had served as a safeguard and security for them?[36] Taschereau explained that the problem the government faced was serious, and any failure to deal with the issue would inevitably result in continuing agitation and social tumult. The government did not wish to find itself forced to withdraw its legislation because of opposition from the episcopate, on whose shoulders the responsibility for the following social and political unrest would lie. He suggested that a conference between the church and the government would have been a better way of dealing with any remaining disagreement than public correspondence and speeches at the most prominent Roman Catholic edifice in Montreal.[37] As had been the wont of Taschereau and other provincial (and federal) Liberal leaders, the idea was to settle controversies with the church out of the public eye. The government was faced with difficult issues between Jews and Protestants in Montreal, and the vociferous involvement of the Roman Catholic hierarchy was the last thing it needed.

The meeting took place at the cardinal's palace in Quebec City on 21 March involving the cardinal and three of his bishops, Taschereau, and David. It ended in an agreement that the proposed legislation would permit the creation of a Jewish school commission that would be subject to the control of the superintendent of public education. Further consultations with the Roman Catholic cardinal resulted in a drafting change clarifying and reinforcing the idea that the superintendent would remain under the obligation to act in conformity with instructions received from the council.[38] In other words, through its domination of the Roman Catholic Committee of the Council of Public Education, the Roman Catholic Church would continue to closely supervise any possible Jewish educational body through its ability to guide the actions of the superintendent. It was also clear that any idea of a Jewish presence on the Council of Public Education would never gain acceptance either from the Protestant committee or from the Roman Catholic hierarchy. The leadership of the Roman Catholic Church was now reasonably content that its position and that of Roman Catholic schools were protected, even if it had lost the principled battle over the Christian essence and duality of the province's schools as a legal principle.[39] At some level, throughout the ongoing controversy over Jewish schools, the government attempted to circumvent the clerical opposition by dealing with the highest-ranking Roman Catholic in the province, Cardinal Rouleau, and sidelining Mgr Gauthier of Montreal. Gauthier was a noted "blue" (*bleu*) or arch-conservative and no friend of Taschereau or David. Even after the cardinal suffered serious injuries in a car accident and was sent to convalesce in a Dominican convent in Massachusetts, David continued to correspond with him in an effort to gain episcopal approval for the government's proposed solution to the school question.[40] Meanwhile, in Montreal, Gauthier's other contribution to the Jewish School Question was to engage a young Montreal journalist as a quasi-official spokesperson and publicist for the ultramontane elements in the church's ongoing struggle against a separate Jewish school system. That journalist was Adrien Arcand, a notorious anti-Semite who would become the leading Canadian spokesperson for fascism and Nazism in the lead-up to the Second World War.[41]

The government now had little choice but to act. The views of the Jewish communities were still opposed; the Protestants sought a political solution where the legal answers from *Hirsch* were less than satisfactory, and the limits of Protestant autonomy remained unclear; the Roman Catholic hierarchy defended the Christian character of education, largely to prevent any hint that a state-based educational structure had any place in Quebec. The government turned to Bercovitch to draft appropriate legislation. Bercovitch gave notice of a bill that would create a separate Jewish school commission and would mandate Jewish membership on the Council of Public Instruction, despite the legal opinions that armed the Protestant committee's opposition to such a measure.[42] Bercovitch had maintained throughout the negotiation phase that he reserved the right to opt for Jewish representation in legislation, and his draft bill now embodied that position. Political and legal issues that divided not just Jewish opinion within the communal factions, but also Protestants and Jews, and Roman Catholics and Jews, therefore clearly remained to be resolved. Some Jews still held out for Jewish representation on the Council of Public Education.[43] Neither the Protestant nor the Roman Catholic committee would tolerate such a move, and they had significant legal advice to support their view. The Protestants would never consent to having Jewish members on their committee, no matter what the Privy Council may have indicated was constitutionally permissible.[44]

Roman Catholic officials meanwhile insisted throughout that the Council of Public Education had to be maintained as a Christian educational body. The Roman Catholic authorities could not countenance the creation of a third committee, because that would fly in the face of their entrenched belief that the province and the province's schools were profoundly and inescapably Christian. Jews could not sit with Protestants and Roman Catholics and decide educational policy and practice for Christians. Meanwhile, of course, the government, some Protestants, and the Jews represented by the Separate School Committee among the downtowners saw only one way out of the impasse that continued to block any change to educational governance, which might be seen to fully accommodate the courts' opinions in *Hirsch*. They wanted and insisted upon a separate Jewish school system in Montreal. David intervened and inserted changes to the bill, largely as a result of the insistence of Roman Catholic officials. The bill that would become known as the *loi David*, then proceeded to the Legislative Assembly.[45]

Bercovitch explained that he had never supported a separate Jewish school system, but that the practices of segregation put into place by the Protestant School Board had created a ghetto in the school system that did little to advance the British ideals of equality and citizenship that access to the Protestant schools had originally promised to Jewish children. Both he and Cohen expressed the view that Jewish educational equality had to be fully concretized or else they would reluctantly support a separate Jewish school system. This was the last chance for the government to fully realize the promise of the 1832 Act.[46] On 4 April

1930, An Act respecting the education of children of the Jewish faith on the island of Montreal, always known in the French Canadian press as the *loi David*, received royal assent.[47] The Jewish School Question was over.[48]

The legislation provided for the appointment by the government of a seven-person Jewish School Commission of Montreal, all of the members of which would be "members of the Jewish faith" (section 1). The commission was given the same powers as the Roman Catholic and Protestant Boards of School Commissioners (section 10), but it was given only advisory powers at the level of the Council of Public Instruction, with which it could meet only by invitation, reflecting the original position adopted by the Protestant educational authorities (section 11). The superintendent of public education (formerly public instruction) was given sole jurisdiction at the provincial level over all matters concerning the new Jewish commission and Jewish education generally. At the insistence of the Roman Catholic Church hierarchy, the superintendent was made specifically subject to instructions from the Council of Public Instruction and its denominational committees (section 13). In effect, at its strict textual level, the 1930 *loi David* embodied the positions adopted by the Protestant School Board of Montreal and the Protestant Committee of the Council of Public Instruction, as well as confirming the insistence of Roman Catholic authorities that any Jewish presence within provincial educational governance structures be subjected to an overarching Christian supervisory and limiting control embodied in the role of the superintendent of public education. Enjoying what it saw as the legislative embodiment of its victory in its long struggle, the Jewish Separate School Commission wrote to Premier Taschereau on 17 April with a list of its nominees for the newly established Jewish School Commission.[49]

But of course, the Jewish School Question was unsurprisingly far from over. Section 16 of the Act provided that instead of creating separate Jewish schools, the commissioners would be empowered to enter into an arrangement with a local school board for the education of students of the Jewish faith. Section 17 created a separate Jewish school municipality for the City of Montreal from 1 April 1931, "failing an agreement between the Protestant Board of School Commissioners of the City of Montreal or the Montreal Catholic School Commission previous to April 1st, 1931." Again, the long-standing question for Montreal Jewry, which had divided opinion in important parts of communities, as to whether the School Question would be resolved by a deal with the

Protestants or by the creation of a separate Jewish school system was back on the table, despite the fact that many parties had hoped that the 1930 Act, after *Hirsch*, would put an end to the conflicts once and for all.

The Jewish School Commission would always be the subject of controversy. In May 1930, the provincial Cabinet announced the membership of the commission.[50] Samuel Livingstone was named as chair.[51] Nathan Gordon, Herman Abramowitz, Edgar Berliner,[52] Max Wiseman,[53] A.Z. Cohen,[54] and Michael Garber made up the rest of the commission. Five of the seven Jewish school commissioners had close connections with the uptowner community and the Jewish Educational Committee, and only two were connected with the downtowner Separate School Committee.[55] Nathan Gordon and Michael Garber had served as opposing lawyers throughout the crises of the 1920s for the uptown and downtown factions. Rabbi Abramowitz had served the Shaar Hashomayim synagogue since 1903.[56] While the commission was entitled under the statute to negotiate with the Protestant board, feeling was still strong across the Jewish community that Jewish equality had to be respected. Important elements within the uptowner constituency believed that Bercovitch and Cohen had given voice to the bottom line on the Jewish School Question. If the issue of Jewish representation could not be adequately addressed in discussions with the Protestant board, then perhaps the time had come for the Jews to go their own way. If the Protestant Commission would not yield, then a separate school system had to be created. "There is no denying of the thought that under certain mitigating circumstances it might be more advantageous to cooperate with the Protestant Board, but we cannot permit any member of the Commission to sell out Jewish rights for a mess of potage."[57]

In September, four months after the appointment of the seven Jewish school commissioners, the superintendent of public education wrote to the Roman Catholic and Protestant School Boards in Montreal inquiring whether any arrangement, as permitted under the 1930 Act, had been entered into with the Jewish School Commission. The Protestant board replied that "no negotiations have been entered into" and that the board was continuing to operate in the same manner as it had in previous years.[58] The superintendent, Cyril Delage, noted the absence of any agreement concerning the education of Jewish children to the Roman Catholic committee of the Council of Public Education on 20 September. The Roman Catholic committee continued its self-defined role in overseeing the evolution of Jewish school question and passed a resolution requiring a further report on the same subject from the superintendent in February 1931. That resolution was moved by Msg Gauthier and seconded by Antonio Perrault as the Montreal Roman Catholic ultramontane faction continued to agitate against the third panel. The motion was met with an amendment proposed by Justice Martineau that the original motion might be seen as suggesting that the Roman Catholic committee was asserting a right to supervise Jewish schools, which it could not legally have. Even the Roman Catholic committee was not able to adopt a unanimous view on its own role in the Jewish School Question. However, the amendment was ruled out of order by the chair as the more conservative elements of the Roman Catholic hierarchy held sway.[59] As had always been the case throughout the history of the Jewish School Question, the ultimate solution, either legally or politically, lay outside the control of the Jewish communities themselves.

Delage would eventually have something to report. On 4 December 1930, a notarized agreement was signed between the Protestant Board of School Commissioners of the City of Montreal and the Jewish School Commission of Montreal.[60] On 8 December, the *Montreal Gazette*, somewhat prematurely, announced the end of the Jewish School Question.[61] The Protestant representatives on the Council of Public Education recommended the passage of the legislation required to give full effect to the agreement between the parties. However, the Protestant committee added two important caveats to its resolution. First, it insisted, unsurprisingly, on the conformity of any such legislation with the Privy Council opinion in *Hirsch*, a subtle reminder to the government that the Protestant communities of Quebec would not agree to any adverse impact on their school system arising from legislation in relation to Jewish schools or to the education of Jewish students. Second, on a point that would become much more significant in the years to come, it insisted that the legislation governing the education of Jewish students include agreements with other municipalities that had significant Jewish populations but did not fall under the jurisdiction of the Protestant School Board of Montreal. Otherwise those educational districts would not be bound either by the agreement as it stood or by subsequent enabling legislation, which limited itself to the City of Montreal.[62]

The Protestant committee was concerned with the situation in the adjoining but independent municipalities, and school boards, of Outremont and Westmount.[63] In Outremont, the Roman Catholic schools were the common schools and the Protestant School Board was dissentient, run by trustees. In Westmount, however, with its anglophone majority, the Protestant schools were the common schools. This meant, at the time, that Jewish children in Westmount attended Protestant schools as of right, as they attended common schools as of right throughout the province outside the cities of Montreal and Quebec.[64] In the case of Outremont, however, under *Hirsch*, Jews had no right to attend dissentient schools and could do so only with the Christian grace and consent of the trustees. Therefore, as far as the Protestant committee was concerned, Outremont's Protestant school officials had to be brought into the arrangement with the Jewish school commissioners and covered by the confirming legislation. The matter was also acute, as the Protestant committee probably well knew. Outremont bordered the ghetto. As the Jewish population shifted and moved ever westward, Outremont became their first destination. In the city of Outremont, the Jewish residents had numbered 1,195 and constituted 9 per cent of the citizenry in 1921 as the Jewish School Question erupted in Montreal. By 1931, as the deal was being negotiated between the Montreal board and the Jewish commission, the number of Jews had grown to 6,783, almost a quarter (23.7 per cent) of the total population.[65] Jewish students numbered 1,192, while there were 1,369 Protestant children enrolled in the city of Outremont dissentient schools. The deficit between tax income and expenditure for the education of Jewish students in the Protestant schools of Outremont was claimed to be over $41,956 for the school year 1931–2.[66] Under pressure from central Protestant education officials in Quebec and the Protestant School Board of Montreal, the trustees of Outremont's Protestant schools advised Delage that an agreement had in fact been signed with the Jewish School Commission.[67]

The parties to the principal agreement between the Montreal Protestant officials and the Jewish School Commission had agreed that all Jewish children would attend Protestant schools in Montreal and that "all Jewish children shall be subject in all respects to all the rules and regulations of the Protestant Board applying to Protestant children and shall receive the same treatment and be subject to the same obligations and enjoy the same advantages in all respects as Protestant children" (paragraph 2).

Paragraph 3 ensured that Jewish children would attend Protestant schools in the regular school district in which they lived and that "there shall be no division or separation of Jewish children from Protestant or other children." Jews were free from participation in religious or devotional exercises or study to which their father or legal guardian objected (paragraph 4). The question of absence for holy days figured in paragraph 5. No loss or reduction of marks would result from absence for two days of the New Year (Rosh Hashana), one day for the Day of Atonement (Yom Kippur) and four days for the Tabernacles (Sukkot). The Protestant board would consider Jewish teaching candidates eligible for appointment or promotion without ceding any of its rights or powers over all general matters of school administration (paragraph 6). The agreement would come into effect on 1 July 1931 and would run for fifteen years (paragraph 8). It would remain contingent on the passage of legislation by the provincial government providing for the appropriate distribution of funds to support the cost of educating Jewish children (paragraph 10).

The uptowner vision had held sway, to some extent at least. Jewish children would attend Protestant schools as equals. Segregation into the school ghettos decried by Bercovitch and others since the 1903 Act would come to an end. Once more the Protestant board had agreed to hire and promote Jewish teachers. Jewish religious liberty was protected in terms of freedom from religious education in the schools, in conformity with the finding in *Hirsch* that the common schools were legally obliged to provide a secular education to Jewish students. Religious liberty was also maintained with respect to Jewish observance on holy days. However, despite its best efforts, the Jewish School Commission was unable to extract any concessions from the Protestant board on Jewish religious instruction in Protestant schools.[68] On the religious front, the schools remained essentially and irredeemably Protestant, as section 93 and the courts throughout *Hirsch* had confirmed, and had legal opinion since the days of the Hebrew teaching controversy.

In effect, the agreement marked a return to the vision of the Jewish Education Committee at the time of the 1903 Act.[69] Law in the shape of the *Hirsch* case had played a framing role, but pressure from the government in Quebec City and the combined efforts of the Jewish and Protestant commissioners had led to an agreement acceptable to most parties. Downtowners had lost the political battle once again,, in large part because they continued to be divided among themselves and were financially impoverished.[70] They had also lost because the other powerful political forces involved, Bercovitch and Cohen, the government, the Protestant board and committee in Quebec, and the Roman Catholic committee all wanted a deal between Jews and Protestants. None of those other actors in the dramas of the Jewish School Question shared the political, religious, and philosophical dreams of the downtowners for a separate Jewish school system. Protestant support for a separate

Jewish system had always been lukewarm, largely tactical, and contingent on the realization of other political and social goals in the questions of school finance and maintaining the Protestant character of Protestant schools. Some Jewish representatives wanted the arrangement because it had always been their goal to have Jewish children become Canadians, socially and culturally, in Protestant schools. Many Protestants wanted it because they strived more broadly to create a solid coalition of anglophone forces against the Roman Catholic francophone majority, but also because they felt that such an arrangement would be more consonant with their Christian duties.[71] Roman Catholic officials wanted it because they abhorred the very idea of a third panel as an affront to the Christian nature of Quebec and its education system, and as a sign of creeping secularism and state interference with the church's essential role in education. The downtowners had lost their struggle for separate Jewish schools. The uptowners had lost their attempt to ensure Jewish representation.[72]

Protestants, Jews, Roman Catholics, and Anti-Semites: The 1931 Statute and the Jewish School Question

While the Roman Catholic Committee of the Council of Public Education maintained its watching brief over events concerning the Jewish School Commission, the ultramontane press in the province was not quiescent. From the time of its introduction in 1930, the *loi David* had created an uproar in Roman Catholic newspapers and journals and among leading figures associated with Roman Catholic conservatism.[73] The overarching theme was familiar: the creation of third school system was the first step towards state control of education and was a direct attack on the Roman Catholic majority, its practices, its faith, and its traditions.[74] But what characterized the press and other attacks on the *loi David* was the virulent anti-Semitism of the attempts to undermine the new educational statute.[75] When the mayor of Montreal, Camilien Houde,[76] a major political challenger at the time to the Taschereau government, called for the repeal of the statute in October 1930, this was seen by some as an indication of the power of the anti-Semitic press to influence popular politics.[77] In fact it was merely one salvo in a discourse that had characterized certain elements within Quebec politics for some time.

The period of the 1920s and early 1930s was a time of great social, economic, and political upheaval in Quebec. The early part of the

1920s had witnessed another influx of European immigrants to Montreal, not the least of which was another wave of Jewish incomers.[78] Again, French Canadians were leaving rural Quebec to seek employment in the city, with all its potentially corrupting influences.[79] In the later years of the decade and into the 1930s, the world financial crisis of the Great Depression had a severe impact on the province's economy. Unsurprisingly, many elements among ultramontane Roman Catholics looked for a scapegoat and found one in the growing Montreal Jewish community.[80] Jews were taking French-Canadian jobs; they were clannish and gave the first choice of jobs in Jewish factories to their fellow Jews; most of the unrest caused by strikes was being fomented by Communist Jews who sought the overthrow of Quebec society;[81] Jews were foreign and they were unchristian.[82] Their very presence posed a severe and ongoing threat to French-Canadian identity as a Roman Catholic society and nation.[83] The Jewish School Question provided plenty of fodder for Roman Catholic anti-Semites, led by Adrien Arcand and his allies.[84] But the School Question was not the only instance serving as an excuse for the manifestation of Jew-hatred in the province and in the city of Montreal during this period.[85] Publications such as *Le Goglu*, *Le Chameau*, and *Le Patriote* filled their pages with anti-Semitic outbursts, including the vicious blood libel. Political and social bodies such as *Jeune Canada* and the *Société St Jean Baptiste* coupled Quebec nationalism with anti-Semitism.[86] City-controlled newspaper kiosks in Montreal carried signs declaring "Buy Your Papers from French Canadians. Don't Buy from Jews."[87] In 1934, interns at Notre Dame Hospital would go on strike when Sam Rabinovitch was appointed to the staff of a French-Canadian Roman Catholic hospital.[88] When Roman Catholic officials decided that Sunday observance was a key element of French-Canadian Roman Catholic identity, they sought not just to enforce the law on the subject, but to remove the exemption that Quebec Jews, unlike their brethren elsewhere, had won for religiously observant co-religionists for whom Saturday Sabbath was essential.[89]

The Sunday League (*La Ligue de Dimanche*) of the Roman Catholic Church launched a concerted propaganda campaign against Sunday work.[90] While at first their actions targeted large commercial pulp and paper mills in rural Quebec, run by anglophone Protestants, their attention soon turned to the unfair competition of small Jewish businesses that remained open on Sundays while their French-Canadian equivalents closed out of respect for the Lord's Day and the law.[91] Soon the legal elite of ultramontane Roman Catholicism joined the battle, and the pages of the *Revue du Droit* began to echo calls for the respect of the holy day and of the law.[92] In addition to a concerted campaign of prosecutions against Jewish businesses that remained open on Sunday, the Roman Catholic activists sought to remove the Jewish exemption from the Quebec statute altogether.[93] When the Court of King's Bench ruled that an amendment to the 1907 law was within the constitutional remit of the provincial government, the writing was on the wall, and Roman Catholic revanchism gained a victory by having the Jewish exception removed from Quebec law.[94]

In such a political, legal, and social environment, it was hardly surprising, then, that when the legislature of Quebec was called upon to consider the statutory enactment required to sanction the agreement between the Jewish school commissioners and the Protestant School Board, Roman Catholic opposition to a separate school system and the contempt in which the *loi David* was held would manifest themselves in a concerted campaign openly conducted in anti-Semitic terms. While church officials continued to insist on the central Christian character of the school system of the city and the province, the gutter press, led by Arcand, proceeded to attack the special privileges afforded to Jews under the statute of 1930. Now that a new legislative enactment was required to confirm the agreements in Outremont and Montreal, elements within the church began once more to campaign in favour of re-establishing the previous duopoly in public education by removing any legal trace of the Jewish School Commission.

David and Taschereau consulted with episcopal officials on the nature and content of the proposed Act, but they did not discuss the proposal at all with the Jewish School Commission nor, it would appear, with Cohen or Bercovitch, each of whom had always proved himself a loyal Liberal. The Protestant and Roman Catholic Committees of the Council of Public Education were consulted, and each in turn gave its approval to the proposed legislation.[95] An Act respecting the education of certain children in Montreal and Outremont was introduced in the Quebec Assembly by Anathase David on 24 February 1931.[96] Both Jewish members spoke out against the government's bill, an extraordinary show of opposition to their own party's official position. Bercovitch attacked the removal of the rights that had been given to the Jewish School Commission in the previous statute but which were now reduced to supervising the implementation of the contractual arrangements. Even though he personally had never favoured the establishment of a Jewish school system and had publicly and forcefully spoken out against the inevitable ghettoization that would result from such a system, he saw the removal of such rights as an affront to the broader equality claims of the Jews of Montreal. Cohen also objected to the bill, which, he argued, was based in an erroneous notion that the basic rights of Jews could simply be negotiated away.[97] The objections were for naught. The bill became law on 4 April 1931.[98]

The first two paragraphs of the statute simply stated that the notarized agreements between the parties in Montreal on 4 December 1930 and in Outremont on 20 January 1931 were "confirmed, ratified and validated." To a large extent, this marked again a return to the old way of doing things in relation to the Jewish School Question. Private arrangements were worked out in the shadow of the law, and the legislature in this instance stepped in to give the private contracts between the parties, the Protestant boards in Outremont and Montreal and the Jewish School Commission, a public affirmation and a concretized embodiment as statute law rather than as a mere notarized agreement. The power of the two associational groups, the Protestant boards and the Jewish School Commission, to create a set of legal arrangements for the two communities, both of course creatures of statute themselves, was then affirmed by the government, as the public and the private took on this unique shape as an answer to the Jewish School Question.

The Jewish School Commission was confirmed in its "perpetual succession" (section 2 (2)). However, the scope of its power was cut back from what had been granted in the 1930 statute. In effect, the two most important of the Jewish School Commission's rights and powers under the original 1930 statute, to establish a separate Jewish school system and to consult with and advise the Council of Public Education, however limited in scope, were simply eliminated. Instead its right of perpetual succession was restricted to "carrying out the present act and the agreements mentioned in section 1 thereof" (section 2 (1)). In Outremont, Jewish taxpayers were moved to the Protestant panel (section 8), and in Montreal, Jewish taxpayers were given the same rate of assessment as Protestants, and their names were to be marked with a *J* by city tax assessors (section 7). Non-Protestant, non–Roman Catholic taxpayers were to be treated as neutrals, and the cost of their education would come from the neutral panel as a charge (sections 10a and b). The rest of the neutral panel taxes would be distributed on a pro rata basis to the Roman Catholic and Protestant School Boards (section 10c). For the purposes of calculating the population under section 10c, Jews would be included with the Protestant cohort.[99]

The statute constituted a new, old set of arrangements and dynamics within the broader context of the Jewish School Question. Many of the statutory elements could be recognized as versions of previous measures dealing with a Jewish presence in the Protestant school system. Jews were treated as Protestants for purposes of neutral panel distribution, indicating an iteration of the taxonomy of the 1903 statute, but for a much more limited school purpose. The *J* for Jew mark on city tax records made an unfortunate return. The idea of the taxation and payment of non-Protestants and non–Roman Catholics in the school system from the neutral panel likewise marked a return to the 1920s statutory regime. Unfortunately, in the view of many Jews, including some uptowners who saw the existence of the right to Jewish educational autonomy as an essential fallback protection in case of any further or future Protestant recalcitrance, the most significant change was the removal of any right for Jews, or for the Jewish School Commission, to establish a separate school system, even in theory. That power had been removed and the Jewish commissioners now had a simple supervisory jurisdiction and function over the implementation of the Outremont and Montreal school contracts. The Roman Catholic Church had emerged victorious, as the 1931 statute marked a return to the dual confessional system of public schooling in Quebec. At the same time, voices from the ultramontane and even fascist right of the church still bemoaned the Taschereau government's concessions to "the Jews."[100]

Jews had negotiated the right to attend Protestant schools in Montreal, a right they had under the *Hirsch* opinion in any event. The sole gain lay in the fact that the Jewish School Commission had negotiated a similar right with the dissentient board in Outremont, a result encouraged by the government and the Protestant Committee of the Council of Public Education. This was an almost natural result of the demographic reality of Jewish population movements westward on the island of Montreal. Everyone got what they wanted except for the Jewish communities of the city, now constituting a population of some 48,486 individuals.[101] The downtowners had lost politically what they had gained legally in *Hirsch*, the right, with provincial government approval, to establish a separate Jewish school system. While the right remained in theory, events in 1931 indicated that it would stay at that level. Political forces that were much more powerful provincially than a politically diverse east end Montreal Jewry had aligned against the downtowner dream of a separate Jewish school system. The uptowners had been joined in effect by the Protestant educational officials, the government, and especially the Roman Catholic Church, each for its own reasons and each for its own political purposes.[102] With these forces mustered against them, the downtowners could never have hoped to concretize the legal right to separate Jewish schools.

On 12 April 1931, representatives of the Jewish communities, the Jewish school commissioners, Bercovitch, and Cohen attended a public meeting. Following his report on the events leading up to the passage of the 1931 Act, Samuel Livingstone, as chairman of the Jewish School Commission, called upon his colleagues to resign en masse because they had been stripped of virtually all their powers. Three days later, the resignations of the seven members of the Jewish School Commission were handed to Premier Taschereau.[103] The commissioners made it clear that the legislative changes imposed by the government in relation to the terms of the commission's mandate had left them with no choice: "The recent legislation places the Jews of Montreal in a position which is intolerable, unfair, and contrary to the tradition of the Province of Quebec, which recognizes equality for minorities and majorities. As a protest against the injustice and indignity of the recent legislation, the Jewish School Commission of Montreal resigns."[104]

Taschereau merely acknowledged the letter of resignation and issued a public statement indicating that the future of the Jewish School Commission was largely a matter for internal discussion and settlement by the Jewish communities themselves.[105] While politically Taschereau was no doubt correct in his assessment, legally speaking he was wide of the mark. The 1931 statute provided for the "perpetual succession" of the Jewish School Commission.[106] It also confirmed the appointment of the president and six other members of the commission under the 1930 statute until 1 May 1935, with the possibility of their removal for cause at any time prior to that by the lieutenant governor in council (section 2 (3)). According to the statute, reappointment of the Jewish School Commission would occur at the expiry of the term of office of the current commissioners, and such appointments would be made, again for a five-year period, by the lieutenant governor in council (section 3). Most significantly, section 6 provided that "the Commission shall not be dissolved through one or more vacancies amongst its members or the disappearance of all its members. Any such vacancy or vacancies shall be filled by the Lieutenant-Governor in Council."

As a matter of law, then, the resignation of the entire commission did not have the effect of destroying the Jewish School Commission of

Montreal as a legal entity. While as a matter of politics, Taschereau and the government of the day may have preferred that the Jewish communities come forward with a plan for the ongoing activities of the commission, or indeed for them to let matters lie, legally speaking it was always in the government's power to reconstitute the commission with new members.[107] In the end, it simply did nothing and the Jewish communities likewise decided that the death of the Jewish School Commission after the betrayal of their hopes and desires, not to say their collective belief in social, political, and legal equality, was the only solution. However, the solution was not a solution in many senses, either legally according to the terms of the legislation itself, or politically and socially in a broader constitutive context. Now the situation was one in which the Protestant School Boards of Montreal and Outremont again had almost total power over the Jewish School Question. They were bound by the terms of their agreement, but the other party to that accord no longer had any practical existence or power to supervise the contract. Once more Jewish taxpayers paid for the right to send their children to Protestant schools, and once more they had no say over that education. The 1931 statute enshrined not just much of the system that had obtained since the *Pinsler* era, but it also affirmed the distinction between Jewish political equality under the 1832 Act and Jewish educational inequality under section 93.

As Pierre Anctil has written, the fifty years of negotiations and compromise over the Jewish School Question, from the first crisis arising out of the Spanish and Portuguese tax migration to the Roman Catholic panel, and the fate of the majority of Jewish school students in the 1880s, to the 1931 Act, had led only to a situation where "Jewish children had the right to attend schools in classes where the teaching personnel were in a very large majority foreign to their traditions, and in an administrative context where their parents were deprived of any right to representation."[108] The uptowners had gained the formal legal recognition of their right to educate their children in the Protestant school system in the hope of obtaining access for them to what they had always understood as a concrete British and Canadian identity, but at the cost, imposed by the foundational legal violence of the Canadian constitution and section 93, and by the political reality of a Roman Catholic domination of Quebec educational politics, of any claim to a right to equal representation as citizens within a school system that remained irredeemably bi-denominational. The downtowners had lost any chance to create a separate school system for Jewish children, a right formally recognized in law, because of the political realities of Quebec's educational system.

On the other hand, David Rome offered a more optimistic view and preferred to characterize the evolution of the Jewish School Question at this historical juncture as a series of victories for the downtowner communities, even in the face of defeat on the substantive question.

> The down town had passed through an important experience. They had fought a legal battle and a constitutional war, had won it on its merits, and had lost it through the imposition of political force majeure ...
>
> How they were able to organize, to study the complex political and legal Canadian issues, arrive at proposed solutions, submit memoranda, negotiate with the government, send delegations to the cabinet, defend their positions before the press, the public, the Protestant Board and the highest Courts and compete with experienced, influential men of the community – how they were able to accomplish these tasks is part of the mystery and wonder of recent Jewish history.[109]

The downtowners, the immigrant Jews of Montreal's early twentieth-century, *Yiddishkeit* Montreal, according to Rome's reading of the deeper text of constitutionalization as a political hermeneutic process, had profited politically and socially as a result of their engagement within the Jewish School Question. What they had lost in the strictly technical and narrow sense of the right to separate schools, they had gained more broadly in the generation of communal and collective understandings of Jewish identities, or at the very least, a concretization of the discourses surrounding the complexity and necessity for political and social struggle over competing visions of those identities. They had engaged within political and legal realms where they played an active role in the generation of consequent political and legal norms, often against powerful interests within their own Jewish communities. In other words, they had become Canadianized as they struggled with the exclusionary nature of Canadian citizenship in the educational realm in Montreal. And finally, as David Rome also points out, the Jewish community, which had always manifested a certain preference for a public, secular school system, had vigorously and publicly set itself against the realities of Quebec common schools as denominational.[110] They had consistently framed the hermeneutic of common schools in Montreal in terms that would triumph in the long run and in another uniquely Quebec way. But before the triumph of linguistic separation over denominational distinctiveness would come to characterize Quebec public education, other iterations of the dual confessional system and the Jewish School Question would arise.

Jews, Protestants, and Roman Catholics: The School Question after 1931

Neither the Jewish School Question nor other manifestations of Quebec anti-Semitism disappeared with the Jewish School Commission. The Rabinovitch affair in a number of Roman Catholic hospitals would erupt. Various municipalities including the city of Montreal would pass resolutions calling on the government to reject any attempt by Jewish refugees from Europe, fleeing Nazi oppression, to come to Canada.[111] Camilien Houde continued his race-baiting form of Franco-Canadian populism.[112] Prominent Roman Catholic theologians persisted in advising their readers that Jews simply had to understand that there were two peoples in Canada, the English and the French. French Canadians had discovered and colonized the country and the English had conquered it. Canada was in its foundational essence Christian.[113] By coming to live in Canada, Jews had come to a Christian country, and they simply had no right to make demands on the founding peoples that would in any way damage the Christian character of the country.[114] The entire history of the Jewish School Question had confirmed this. Jewish attempts to characterize their plight along the same lines as claims made for Roman Catholic or French-language schools outside Quebec were ample evidence that Jews simply did not appreciate their difference in Canada. French-Canadian Catholics were *chez nous* everywhere in the country they had discovered and colonized. They had rights. Jews did not.[115] The 1931 Act had simply been the manifestation of the basic and fundamental truth of the bi-denominational character of Quebec and of its school system. Grouping Jews in schools of their own would have been consistent with this vision, as long as such schools remained under the jurisdiction of the Protestant School Commission.[116]

While Roman Catholic thinkers and politicians continued to invoke the Jewish School Question as a concrete manifestation of disaster avoided by the devoted actions of the church to protect and defend the vital Christian identity of the nation against unwanted and foreign influence, the practical issues of Jewish education again became a matter for the Protestant authorities to manage. In October 1932, the provincial statistician requested official confirmation of the numbers of Jewish students in Montreal schools. Through the assistant director of Protestant education in Quebec, the school board confirmed that for the school year 1931–2, there were 11,010 Jewish students in all schools, of which 2,250 were in grades eight to eleven.[117]

In September 1936, the fixed cost of $75 per annum per Jewish student under the 1931 Act, pursuant to which all charges on the neutral panel were calculated, came to its statutory five-year term. While the agreements between the Protestant education officials and the Jewish School Commission ran for fifteen years, the tax arrangements for the neutral panel had a five-year limit. The director of public education wrote to the Protestant board warning them of the legal lacuna it now faced. "Consequently, no provision is at present made, to my knowledge, for the cost of educating children professing the Jewish faith, attending the Protestant schools in the city of Montreal, during the present session."[118]

The Protestant school system was already aware of the expiry issue. In fact, in January 1936, a meeting of the Protestant Central School Board had passed a resolution confirming its desire and willingness to continue with the arrangement under the statute of $75 per student, from year to year unless the parties decided otherwise. The Roman Catholic board passed a similar resolution on 24 March and the Protestant Board of School Commissioners adopted the agreement by resolution at its meeting on 27 March. On 2 April, the Protestant board wrote to the Montreal City Finance Department notifying them of the two boards' willingness to continue with the arrangement that had come into effect under the 1931 Act. City officials agreed to continue the arrangements based on the twin resolutions, but in the absence of a proper provincial legislative mandate.[119] Once again, Jewish education in Montreal occurred in the shadows of strict legality, if not plainly outside positive legal norms.

The board formally apprised the provincial director of Protestant education of the arrangement after having received the 11 September warning from Quebec City.[120] The provincial official was concerned that the agreement might not be legal, absent a legislative approbation, and wrote to the attorney general asking his advice on 21 September.[121] No fundamental legal obstacle was found and the practical administrative arrangement agreed by each of the denominational boards was put into place. Once more in the long history of the Jewish School Question in Montreal, the actual practice of educating Jewish students and finding a financial framework in which to do so were issues dealt with in ways that manifested a practical embodiment of a desire by all sides to arrive at solutions with which the communities could live. The law of the parties, in this case the Protestant and Roman Catholic educational officials in Montreal, with the accord of the City Finance Office, had been put into place by a set of formal and informal arrangements. In fact, there were resolutions and agreements between the denominational school officials, and then between them and the city officials who collected and disbursed the school taxes from the neutral panel. There was technically no legislative framework in place once the five-year period had expired, but the education establishments and the city government dealt with the issue in a semi-formalized way, without reference to the legislative branch. Indeed the record appears to indicate that had not the director of Protestant education brought the matter into the public domain by writing about the expiry of the legislative mandate, the parties would have been happy to continue their arrangement without involving provincial officials at all. Deals were made in the shadow of the law, or in the absence of law in the limited, technical sense, and the parties created law between and among themselves, again a familiar way of dealing with issues throughout the saga of the education of Jewish students in the common schools of Montreal.

What is perhaps most interesting about this small episode in the history of the Jewish School Question in Montreal is that one voice was clearly absent from the negotiations and from the final arrangements. After events in 1931, there was no place for the Jewish communities. The constitutive arrangements about the education of Jewish children in the Protestant schools of Montreal took place with the active involvement of local and provincial governments, and the Protestant and Roman Catholic School Boards. The absence of Jews from educational self-government was the bizarre and yet necessary result of the legal processes, which had begun in this instance with the Commission of Nine and carried on through the *Hirsch* litigation, afterwards encountering the political and social realities of the 1930 and 1931 Acts. Jews had won the right to separate schools and to attend the Protestant (and Roman Catholic) common schools of Montreal, but they had been defeated in their attempts to obtain a right to representation on any Montreal school commission or on the Council of Public Education. After its brief and troubled existence, they had even lost the Jewish School Commission and its right to address Jewish educational issues at the invitation of the Council of Public Education. The BNA Act, Protestant and Roman Catholic denominational self-protection, and the way these factors manifested themselves within the political realities of Quebec and Montreal had killed any hope of Jewish participation in dialogue about the education of Jewish children in the public common school system of Montreal. Jews paid taxes into the Protestant educational system and their children attended Protestant schools. Beyond that, the Jewish School Question was a matter for everybody but the Jewish communities of Montreal.

10

The Protestant Jews of Ste Sophie and La Macaza: Constituting School and Community in Rural Quebec

The Legal Frame of Public Education in Rural Quebec

This chapter offers a brief interlude from the struggles surrounding the Jewish School Question in Montreal to recount the legal and social history of the Jewish Protestant schools in the two Laurentian communities of Ste Sophie and La Macaza. In those small outposts, Jewish settlers established a Jewish life in rural Quebec. They struggled with the brutal winter climate of the province and the harsh and unforgiving soil of the mountainous regions north of Montreal, but they constructed a full Jewish existence for themselves and for their children. As part of this Jewish world, the settlers who came to these areas established schools. These schools existed for some years as Jewish schools, within the context of the dual confessionality of public education in Quebec, with an almost exclusively Jewish student body, Jewish teachers, and Jewish administrators. In the same period, the dream of Jewish participation in the education of Jewish children in the common schools, so dear both to the uptowners and downtowners of Montreal throughout the 1910s and 1920s, was a brief lived reality for the Jews of Ste Sophie and La Macaza. It was, as was so often the case in Montreal, a lived reality that occurred in the shadow of legality, if not as examples of outright and blatant illegality tolerated and approved by provincial educational authorities. The unique governance structure of these Jewish schools was the only viable accommodation to the distinct physical, geographical, and demographic realities of each locality. These schools were embodiments of the triumph of common sense and practical necessity over strict legalities. Throughout their relatively short existence, they manifested the power of local communities to give effect to their political and social desire to educate their children, and to do so through a process that was jurisgenitive and strictly illegal at its heart.[1] These two Jewish schools in rural Quebec were concrete manifestations of communal constitutionalization outside the boundaries imposed by a legal system, which, in its formal embodiment, could not deal effectively with the reality of its citizen-subjects. After a brief examination of the legal provisions that should have applied in these two cases, this chapter offers a concise history of Jewish agricultural settlement in Canada and in these two Quebec municipalities. It then turns to an examination of the available archival records of these rural Jewish Protestant schools.

The education law of the province of Quebec established two kinds of schools outside the cities of Quebec and Montreal. The norm was for the creation of a common school, administered by commissioners. In areas with a minority religious group, those who did not share in the majority's views were permitted to establish their own dissentient schools, administered by trustees.[2] In essence, the common school was always by dint of demography one that reflected the religious views of the majority population, but it was legally a common school. The dissentient school was by definition strictly denominational. "In any school municipality, any number of proprietors, occupants, tenants or rate-payers professing a religious belief different from that of the majority of the inhabitants of such municipality, may give, in writing, to the chairman of the school commissioners, a notice by which they inform him of their intention to withdraw from the control of the school commissioners, in order to form a separate corporation under the administration of school trustees" (section 123).

Dissentients were granted exemptions from general prohibitions on sending their children to schools outside the school municipality in which they resided (section 120). They could unite with another school municipality either as a complete consolidation of dissentient schools, or for the purpose of sending their children to a dissentient school in situations where parents did not wish their children to attend a common school controlled by those of a different religious belief, but where there were not enough members of the religious minority to establish a separate and viable dissentient school (section 131 and following). In any school municipality where population growth or movement changed the relationship between dissentient and majority groups, the former could organize themselves as the new majority and establish a "corporation of school commissioners" (section 127). The former majority could likewise declare themselves to be dissentient by following the notification rules applicable for such declarations (section 128). In addition to the collective interest of the dissentient religious minority, individual rights were protected under the statute. Any individual professing a religion different from the majority was entitled to declare himself a dissentient or, conversely, cease being a dissentient by complying with the notice requirements of the law (section 139).[3] However, the dissent had to be genuine and could come only from someone who professed a religious belief different from that of the majority.[4] In a similar fashion, and consistent with the broader societal understanding that education of children was in the first instance a matter for the *bon père de famille*, the declaration of dissidence or of adhesion to the majority was a matter strictly for the taxpaying father. The religion of the children was legally irrelevant.[5] Matters of public interest, the administration of the schools, the system of taxation for education, and the right to vote in school elections for commissioners or trustees all followed the common/dissentient school matrix. In areas where only common schools existed, all taxpayers who were otherwise qualified could vote in elections for school commissioners. In areas with the dual system, dissentients could not become school commissioners or vote in commission elections, and the converse applied to members of the religious majority (section 145 and following). The only other qualifications on voting rights were property ownership and the payment of all school contributions (section 148). Within their respective realms, common school ratepayers and dissentient groups had a high degree of autonomy and electoral power. Unlike the situation in Montreal, their fellow taxpayers elected school commissioners and trustees.[6]

From the earliest days of Quebec school legislation establishing common and dissentient schools, the courts of the province had to deal with a series of disputes about the limits and parameter of the divisions within the education system along the lines of religious faith. In 1865, in a dispute over the status of a non-resident dissentient taxpayer – someone who owned property and paid tax in the school municipality but who lived in another district – the Court was clear that the entire philosophy of the education legislation was to ensure peace and harmony between religious majorities and minorities through the application of a generous and liberal interpretation of the statute, an interpretation and judicial attitude that would ensure religious liberty.[7] In this case, the common school commissioners sought to collect taxes from the defendant because his property could not be considered to belong to a resident who had declared his dissent. The Court rejected the argument by insisting that once a dissentient school corporation was in existence, it was "religious belief alone" that determined who fell under the jurisdiction of the dissentient school trustees and was subject to their tax powers.[8] Similarly, despite the existence of legal mechanisms for the establishment of a dissentient school system, the courts were willing to recognize the legal existence of minority schools in the absence of official declarations of dissent and by oral evidence proving the long-term presence of dissentient schools and the payment of taxes to support such schools.[9]

But the denominational system in the provincial school system was strictly limited to a single case of dissent.[10] There could not be multiple denominational schools within the public framework of Quebec's educational structures. Most obviously this situation related to the many Protestant denominations in the province. At the local level, Protestants had a right to form a dissentient school municipality, but only one. There could not be separate Anglican, Presbyterian, and Baptist dissentient schools in a single municipality. This understanding of Protestant as a collective legal category was confirmed in the interpretive provisions of the 1899 Act. While the substantive provisions relating to the establishment of dissentient schools refer only to religious minorities or to religious belief different from that of the majority, the definition offered in section 25 clearly established and confirmed the dual denominational character of the education system. "The words 'religious majority' or 'religious minority' mean the Roman Catholic or Protestant majority or minority, as the case may be."

Because the statute allowed for the creation of dissentient schools only by a religious minority in relation to a religious majority, and because these terms were restricted to Roman Catholic and Protestant, a second dissentient corporation in a municipality would be impossible, as the Court in *Cushing* decided. Likewise, it would appear that in a wholly Protestant municipality, with, for example, an Anglican majority and a Presbyterian minority, the latter could not create a dissentient school because as far as the statute was concerned, they would always be part of the Protestant majority.

The only question remaining in relation to this legal framework for schooling outside Montreal was that of Jewish residents of the province's rural communities. The provisions of the 1903 Act were incorporated into the 1909 Revised Statutes of Quebec and again in the 1925 Revision. The core principle was that Jews would, "for school purposes, be treated in the same manner as Protestants, and, for such purposes, shall be subject to the same obligations and shall enjoy the same rights and privileges as the latter."[11] Jewish students enjoyed the right to be educated in Protestant schools "as Protestant children," with the exemptions from religious instruction (section 581). Therefore it would have been possible to construct a legal argument according to which the assimilation of Jews as Protestants "for school purposes," "enjoy[ing] the same rights and privileges" as Protestants, meant that in rural localities with Protestant common or dissentient schools, Jewish taxpayers could vote in elections and indeed could stand for office as commissioners or trustees, because in the dual denominational system, they were legally Protestants. On this interpretation of the statute, redolent of the uptowner view in Montreal, they were part of the religious majority or minority, according to the circumstances. As Jews, they would have been excluded from this taxonomy and would enjoy no such rights to dissent or to establish their own schools, because it was beyond dispute that only Protestants and Roman Catholics had such rights. But because they were "Protestants for school purposes," they arguably enjoyed these voting and representative rights.

Of course, the *Hirsch* case put paid to any such arguments.[12] The Privy Council stated in unambiguous terms that rural dissentient Protestant schools were protected by the provisions of section 93 at the time of Confederation, and that Protestants enjoyed complete and absolute control over those schools. Insofar as the 1903 Act could be read to assimilate Jews to Protestants in such cases, it was clearly unconstitutional.[13] While common schools were not denominational in the same legal sense as dissentient schools in rural communities, there was no doubt at all that Jews did not have the right to send their children to dissentient Protestant schools, to vote in elections for trustees, or to stand for election as trustees. Those rights were reserved to Protestants, and Jews were not Protestants. In areas without dissentient schools, for example, all taxpayers, Protestant and Roman Catholic, were free to vote and to stand as school commissioners. Only when a dissentient system existed did Protestant and Roman Catholics gain separate rights of voting, taxation, and representation. This meant that Jewish children could attend common schools no matter what the religious beliefs of the majority population might have been, just as they could attend either Roman Catholic or Protestant common schools in Montreal. Presumably, although this was not decided, Jewish taxpayers would also retain a right to vote for commissioners and indeed to present themselves for election as school commissioners, because the common schools did not have a legally recognized denominational character. No religious qualifications existed as far as common schools outside Montreal and Quebec City were concerned. The idea of a religious majority and a religious minority, defined in terms of Protestant and Roman Catholic, had apparent legal significance only for the process of dissent and its consequences. For common school purposes in rural communities, in the absence of the 1903 Act, large parts of which would be found to be unconstitutional, Jews were simply taxpayers.

Jews in the Country: Ste Sophie, La Macaza, and the Jewish Colonization Experiment

Just as much of the story of the Jewish School Question in Montreal took place in the broader context of massive Jewish emigration from Europe, so too the history of Jewish education in Ste Sophie and La Macaza was influenced in fundamental ways by the waves of Jewish immigrants fleeing Europe in search of safety and a better life. While outbreaks of pogromic violence often had direct influence on decisions to leave home, many Jewish immigrants to Canada came to escape overwhelming poverty. Of course, that poverty was attributable in large part to the anti-Semitic orderings of social and economic life in Eastern Europe. This massive and apparently inescapable material deprivation, combined with state-sanctioned violence against Jewish populations, led wealthier and more secure Jewish philanthropists in Western Europe and the Americas to seek ways of aiding their brethren. A major influence on these philanthropic endeavours was an understanding that it would serve little purpose to assist Jews from Russia and other Eastern European countries to flee their homes, if they then found themselves enduring deprivation and poverty in their new countries. While this was in fact an all too common story of immigration to the large urban centres such as Montreal or New York, those seeking to aid the cause of Jewish emigration and immigration engaged in serious efforts to avoid precisely this outcome.

Among the principles in the basic philosophy of Jewish philanthropy and communal aid at the time was an idea that the best way to avoid moving from one type of poverty in Europe to a new type of deprivation in Canada was to encourage newly arrived Jews to take advantage of the natural riches of Canada through agriculture.[14] Jews could escape poverty and become key actors in, and contributors to, their new country through productive farming.[15] Although the final tally of successful Jewish farming settlements in Canada was small, each attempt at establishing these communities marked moments of self-definition for Jewish immigrants in their new country.

The key organization in the international effort to encourage and support Jewish agricultural efforts was the Jewish Colonization Association (JCA), founded and supported by Baron de Hirsch, with local agents in the United States, Canada, South America, particularly Argentina, and in parts of the Middle East.[16] Earlier efforts had taken place among Canadian Jews to assist Jewish agricultural colonization in order to bring groups of Jews to Canada who could settle together, avoiding isolation, and create strong Jewish communal bonds.[17] As was the case with Jewish education in Montreal, the singular efforts and contributions of Baron and Baroness de Hirsch gave the financial support necessary to concretize and expand efforts to bring Jews to different parts of the world and to create colonies of Jewish farmers who would become integral parts of the local economy and society.[18] The Jewish Colonization Association in Canada was formed and for many years had a close association with the Baron de Hirsch Institute in Montreal, including sharing many of the same leading personalities.[19]

While colonization efforts often struggled with poor soil and harsh weather, Jewish colonists did enjoy success in the Canadian west in particular, with the settlement of New Hirsch, Saskatchewan, being perhaps the best known and remembered. Less well known, perhaps, are the colonies established in Quebec. In 1904, Ste Sophie and La Macaza became Jewish agricultural communities in that province.[20]

Ste Sophie is situated in the Laurentians about sixty-five kilometres from Montreal, near St Jerome, and in the vicinity of the other small settlements of St Lin and New Glasgow. Irish immigrants originally settled the area, and when the Roman Catholic Church created the parish of Ste Sophie in 1851, the congregation was composed of sixty-three anglophone and eighteen francophone families.[21] In 1863, the village of New Glasgow, with its anglophone Protestant population, became an independent municipality, the smallest in Canada, and it virtually cut Ste Sophie in half.[22] At the turn of the twentieth century, Jewish settlers arrived in Ste Sophie. While the official town history indicates that relations were generally peaceful, it also notes that in 1919, the local council passed a resolution, on behalf of Protestant and Roman Catholic inhabitants, condemning the fact that Jews continued to work, even slaughter young cattle, on Sunday.[23] This is but one indication of the ongoing hostility encountered by Jews, not just in Montreal, but also throughout the province. It was also perhaps a strong influencing factor in the Jews' decision to establish their own school in Ste Sophie. In the early 1920s, the community turned to the poultry industry for their livelihood, creating large egg-production concerns and a slaughterhouse. The products were sold in Montreal for the most part. Some farmers supplemented their income by renting out accommodation to summer visitors who left the crowded city in search of fresh country air.[24] While the Jewish population of Ste Sophie has declined precipitously in recent years as parents and children left for a variety of reasons, during the period from early settlement to the end of the school crisis in Montreal with the adoption of the 1931 Act, there was a vibrant and relatively successful Jewish community in the hamlet.[25]

The village of Ste Sophie had its first school sometime after the parish was founded in 1851, although many of the precise details of the village history are still obscure.[26] The Sainte-Sophie de New Glasgow School Commission was in charge of local education from the founding of the first schools, indicating that there was a common school, which, in all likelihood, was predominantly Roman Catholic. The names of the presidents of the commission from 1914 to 1930 are French Canadian, and the secretary-treasurer position was held by John Joseph Carey in 1914–15 and by Alfred Carey from 1915.[27] The village school in New Glasgow was anglophone and dissentient.[28] Wilfrid Laurier, who would become the first francophone prime minister of Canada, was sent by his father to this school in order to learn English and to appreciate the culture of the other solitude.[29] In the Paisley district of Ste Sophie, a local school existed and was under the general jurisdiction of the majority commission. This was the part of the village nearest the Jewish farms, and until 1916 the Jewish children attended this school.[30]

The village of La Macaza is situated farther to the north from Ste Sophie, approximately 170 kilometres from Montreal. Farming conditions there were much harder for the Jewish immigrants, and many colonists moved several times in search of better land. The population was dispersed to some extent along several kilometres of often-impassable roads, and as a consequence the Jewish population fell within two different school districts, Canton Marchand–La Macaza and Ascension, sometimes known as "Little Judea."[31] In 1916–17, on the north shore of the La Macaza River, the Jewish community of the village built a school.

The histories of the Jewish schools of La Macaza and Ste Sophie share several important points. These schools were really Jewish schools. The students were Jewish, and the teachers and administrators were Jewish. More significantly, the schools themselves became sites of community constitution. While education remained at the core of the institution, the actual functions of the schools and of the administrative bodies charged with running them frequently slipped over into the religious and secular lives of the communities. In La Macaza, the school building also served as the synagogue, as required.[32] In Ste Sophie, the school board often spent much of the time at its meetings discussing issues such as hiring a shochet and issuing sanctions against members of the community who did not comply with the ritual slaughter practices approved by the school board. In other words, the Jewish schools of Ste Sophie and La Macaza really were foundries of citizenship for the entire community. The strict limits of institutional competence, which might have operated in Montreal between the Va'ad Hair and the Protestant School Board, simply disappeared as the schools in these small communities became truly jurisgenitive bodies. All matters of self-government, from religious ritual to hiring schoolteachers, were essential to the communities' notions of identity as Jews, and to the schools as Jewish schools. No artificial jurisdictional divide could stand in the way of basic associational self-government as the Jews of rural Quebec constituted themselves into viable and vibrant social, cultural, religious, and political communities. The legal regime of common and dissentient schools gave way to a deeper foundational dynamic of Jewish self-constitution, all with the active participation of provincial education officials.

Ste Sophie: The Jewish Protestant School

Even before the Jewish farmers of Ste Sophie sought to form a school for the secular education of their children, they tried to ensure religious instruction for them. In 1911 they had approached the authorities of the Jewish Colonization Association in Montreal with a request for $20 per month to help pay for hiring a shochet and a Hebrew teacher for the community. The Jewish farmers themselves would make up any shortfall in salary and expenses.

Two years later, the farmers of Ste Sophie approached the JCA for support for the erection of a school building to provide for an "English education" for the children of the community. Again the farmers promised to make up the difference in actual costs of the building by themselves. Once the building was erected, the colonists stated that they would request financial support to hire a teacher. As the Montreal JCA explained to the ICA, "Your Committee would point out that the nearest school, which is under Roman Catholic administration, is six miles from the centre of Ste Sophie colony, and it is therefore practically impossible for the children to avail themselves of same. Further the curriculum in this school is in French, and the language of the Jewish children is English."[33]

Even after the building had been erected, however, the Jewish parents of Ste Sophie faced a fundamental difficulty. They wanted their children to receive "an English education," which in the constitutional, constitutive, and statutory framework of Quebec education really meant that they wanted their children to receive a Protestant education, or at least an education under the auspices of the Protestant educational authorities. Two sets of problems presented legal obstacles to their ability to create a viable, legally constituted school for their children. First, they were Jews. While the 1903 Act was on the books, they might have safely believed that they were legally considered to be Protestants for educational purposes, so that they could in all legality constitute themselves as a Protestant School Board. Of course we know now, after *Hirsch*, that their interpretation was faulty, but at the time it was perhaps understandable that they would rely on the equivalence established in the statute.

However, the second problem was slightly more complex and much less ambiguous legally. The Jewish settlers appear to have believed that because of its independent village status, New Glasgow and the Ste Sophie colony were in different school municipalities. However, in fact both were in the Ste Sophie parish and therefore fell within the Ste Sophie school district. The New Glasgow School already existed and it was a dissentient school. Under Quebec law, the Jews of Ste Sophie could not constitute a second dissentient school board in the same district.[34] The creation of a separate school district would therefore be impossible for Jewish taxpayers, even if they were Protestants for educational purposes. When they sought to issue a declaration of dissent according to the legal requirements, they indicated that they dissented from the Ste Sophie School Commission but added that they wished to join the dissenting board of Scotland. But because there was an existing dissentient school system in Ste Sophie (the New Glasgow Protestant school), the Department of Public Education advised the notary acting for the dissentients that they could validly join the Protestant Board of Scotland only if their property were annexed to the territory of the Scotland school municipality under the operative provisions of the law.[35]

The director of Protestant education in Quebec City pointed to this legal fact in a letter to the community and suggested that the best option for the Jewish colonists would be to associate themselves with the New Glasgow dissentient school.[36] Wanting their own school and reluctant to align themselves with a physically distant school board, the Jews of Ste Sophie met with the local school inspector, who also consulted with the Protestant dissentient trustees. The inspector came to the conclusion that the l'Archigan river, which ran between Ste Sophie and New Glasgow, constituted a logical physical border between the two areas, and one that was more obvious to common sense than the artificial divisions between the ecclesiastical parishes of St Lin and Ste Sophie on which the existence of the New Glasgow dissentient board was dependent.[37] Against the strict legal requirements for the erection or recognition of school municipalities, he recommended to Protestant officials in Quebec City that the Jewish farmers be permitted to establish a separate school board. The official in charge of Protestant education within the provincial government, George Parmalee, "was not entirely happy with the legal ramifications of the Ste Sophie arrangement and nor was he comfortable with the prospect of a Protestant Board comprised entirely of Jews."[38] Given the clear evidence that the Jewish residents of the Ste Sophie colony insisted on their own school board, Parmalee reluctantly suggested that they petition the government to establish a new, separate school municipality "for Protestants only."[39] The Jewish residents submitted a petition to the government in May. An Order in Council created the new school municipality in July. MacLeod and Poutanen highlight the fact that Parmalee drew the line at any reference to a Jewish school. The new district would be a separate one, run by a board of Protestant school commissioners under the name "Scotland" for the new school municipality.

What was perhaps most interesting about this stage of the new Protestant school in Scotland, besides the fact that it was Jewish, was that the residents proceeded to form their school under sections 96 and following of the Education Act. Under these provisions, the lieutenant governor in council was entitled to "erect school municipalities" upon the request of interested parties, and such erections could be made to "apply only to the Roman Catholics or Protestants, as the case may be, comprised within their territory" (section 97). The creation of such Order-in-Council schools would later create controversy and constitutional difficulty in the suburban areas of Greater Montreal. In essence the question here would be whether, under the legislative provisions governing education, there were not two, but three types of schools in Quebec: common schools, which, after *Hirsch*, were not denominational; denominational dissentient schools; and Order-in-Council schools, which were clearly denominational, since by definition they were erected for one or the other of the two religious beliefs recognized within the legal framework of the educational system of the province. On the one hand, it would have been possible to assert that the provisions for the creation of new municipalities for school purposes were simply the embodiment of administrative measures meant to ensure flexibility in dealing with population shifts or other demographic changes that would have the need for a reordering of school borders as a consequence. If this were the case, then in the first instance the new municipality would be a common school, because no other school would exist in that district. If this view were not correct, however, and Order-in-Council schools were neither dissentient nor common, this would raise difficulties insofar, after *Hirsch*, as attendance rights were concerned. If they were not dissentient, but common schools, Jews might well also have had the right to the representative status they appropriated for themselves in Ste Sophie.

The statute was not helpful on these questions. Section 104 provided that the taxpayers in the newly erected municipality had to elect their school commissioners in the normal manner prescribed by law, as the Jews of Ste Sophie did. Arguably the designation of the officials as commissioners must be seen as some clear indication that the school in the newly erected Order-in-Council municipality was to be considered a common school, since dissentient schools were run by trustees. The newly erected municipality of Ste Sophie was created for Protestants only, clearly an impossibility once it came into existence, if it were a common school, since common schools were open to all. Again this inherent legal contradiction in relation to Order-in-Council schools provided some credence to an argument that such institutions were a third, sui generis type of school within the statutory structures of Quebec education law. MacLeod and Poutanen describe the Ste Sophie Scotland school as dissentient, but since it was created as the only school in a new school municipality, it seems difficult, if not legally impossible, to accept such a designation as a legal matter.[40] Dissentient schools could exist only in circumstances in which members of the municipality who did not share the religious belief of the majority declared their dissent in the form recognized by the statute. Withdrawing and creating a new school municipality under the Order-in-Council provisions was not legally identical or statutorily equivalent to declaring dissent within the same municipality. The Jews of Ste Sophie could not declare such a dissent, since there was apparently no majority but themselves in the new Scotland school municipality. The school in Ste Sophie was Protestant in law and Jewish in fact, but it was never a dissentient school. In any event, the JCA paid $40 for legal expenses in relation to the establishment of "a separate school Municipality from the provincial government for our Ste Sophie Colonists."[41] In Ste Sophie, then, a Jewish Protestant school existed, run by Jews, for Jews, erected by Order in Council for Protestants only.

Again, the solution to this iteration of the Jewish School Question outside Montreal was established by a set of discussions, negotiations, and arrangements involving local Jewish actors, the local Protestant school inspector, the trustees of the dissentient Protestant school in New Glasgow, and the provincial director of Protestant education. The new school municipality was created because of the need of the local citizens and, despite Parmalee's insistence on adherence to parts of the school law in relation to the ban on dual dissentient schools in the same district, the whole process of creating the Scotland Jewish school, while receiving the official sanction of the provincial government, owed much more to the jurisgenitive aspects of the social and associational life of the Jews of the Ste Sophie colony than it did to strict compliance with technical legal norms found in Quebec's provincial statutory regime governing educational structures in the province. Such an arrangement would have been unimaginable in Montreal, for a number of reasons, both legal and political, but in rural Quebec, Jewish Protestant schools became a reality.

The surviving Minute Books of the "Ste Sophie Protestant School of Scotland," as the Jewish citizens called themselves, provide important insights into this jurisgeneration as it continued once the formal and informal constitutive process of creating a school municipality had been completed. Indeed the centrally Jewish nature of this Protestant school is confirmed by the fact that many of the minutes recorded by the school secretary-treasurer were written in Yiddish. At its first recorded meeting, the board refers to itself as the trustees of the school, indicating that local understandings of their position within the legal structures and technical nomenclature of Quebec education law were at odds with strict legal formalism.[42] At its next meeting, on 19 August 1914, the board got down to the business of school governance and fixed the tax rate.[43] It then dealt with the legal process under the Education Act, acknowledging the receipt of a report from the school inspector and granting full authority to the secretary to comply with the requirements imposed by the representative of provincial educational authority.[44] As the school became a concrete reality, the board hired teachers, purchased firewood, sought funding from the provincial superintendent of education, and sought to create pedagogical arrangements of teaching of an "English" and a "Hebrew" curriculum.[45]

On 21 January 1919, a general meeting of the taxpayers was held at which it was decided "for the welfare of the municipality that a Law Comitee [*sic*] should be appointed." The purpose of the committee was to collect unpaid school tax. Unsurprisingly, the procedure adopted by the board was not strictly in keeping with the legislative provisions governing the assessment and collection of these taxes. In essence it was the best practical solution to the ongoing problems caused by unpaid taxes in the small school community, but strictly speaking it was also illegal. The Education Act set out a system under which the local council performed normal tax collection (section 373), failing which the secretary-treasurer of the school board was vested with the power to demand payment by serving a notice on tardy or recalcitrant property owners (section 375). There was no provision for the appointment of a law committee charged with the secretary-treasurer's functions. Again, the system of collecting school taxes for the Protestant Jewish school of Ste Sophie was developed by the community, in the interests of the community, to ensure that the school could continue to function. The school was the community's school, and there was no need or apparently any desire to charge the municipal authorities of Ste Sophie with collecting taxes from Jewish taxpayers for the Jewish school. Given the history of Jewish education in Montreal and in Ste Sophie, it is not surprising that the Jewish colony created a system of self-governance outside the formal structures of the school law. The board complied with the legal requirements when it had to, such as by ensuring obedience to all the demands of the Protestant provincial school inspector. But when it deemed it necessary or expedient to do so, it simply turned to its own communal powers of self-definition and self-constitution in the interstices of the law, or indeed outside the strict legislative framework.

The school board continued to encounter financial problems, in large part because many residents simply refused to pay their school taxes. In March 1919, the regular meeting of the trustees was told not just of further recalcitrance, but that there were now insufficient funds to pay the teacher's salary.[46] The president was required to seek a loan. Ste Sophie colony was not alone in suffering severe financial hardship at the time. Largely because of endemic rural poverty throughout Quebec, these problems were a part of the normal trials and tribulations of rural school boards, especially Protestant boards with their smaller population base, in the early years of the twentieth century.[47] In finding itself in straitened financial circumstances, the Protestant Jewish school of Ste Sophie was just like many other rural Protestant schools.

As the school became part of the life of the community, it and its leaders became the de facto – and almost but never fully de jure – political and social representatives of collective opinion. They dealt with common issues that clearly went beyond the normal matters of school administration and acted largely as a local council. In addition to school finances, finding textbooks, and hiring teachers, the school board also became the quasi-official municipal government for the colony. At its meeting of 6 March 1921, for example, it discussed the ongoing problems of ritual slaughter.[48] It had been agreed that the community would hire a shochet. A set of fees had been commonly agreed and established. Part of the agreement was to give the shochet a monopoly on slaughter and to bind him to stay in Ste Sophie, which he could leave only with the consent of the board. Nonetheless some farmers either found another slaughterer or killed their own animals. This was seen as a grave contravention of community law. The board declared, "All the members that weren't present by this meeting are obliged to follow our orders & failing to obey there [*sic*] children will be sent out of Jewish school."

The board would also later develop a supplemental way of collecting unpaid taxes from members of the community. The meeting instructed the secretary to make out bills for the amounts due by individuals and to give the bills to the Hebrew teacher. The teacher would be instructed to tell the children of the debtors to advise their parents that they had three days to pay, failing which the children would be sent away from the school. The secretary and the Law Committee would supervise the payment process.[49]

Not only was there an admixture of the secular and the sacred, ritual slaughter performed according to religious law, and the functions of the school board, but the sanction for violating one was imposed on the children's rights to an education. The board adopted not just the jurisgenitively positive role it had been playing since its beginnings in the construction of a communal constitutive reality, in which the social, the political, and the religious worked in some type of harmony. Now it had also taken on a more necessarily jurispathic function, issuing orders that had to be obeyed and imposing punishment not on those who killed their own animals, but on their children. Of course this reflects the process of lawmaking described by Robert Cover in his discussions of associative communities. The process of self-definition, of creating communal forms of self-understanding, of local lawmaking in the broadest sense always entails sanctions for transgressions, because transgressions of the community's laws threaten the solidarity and cohesion necessary to that self-definition and to the very survival of the collective body.[50]

Problems with non-payment of school taxes would continue to dog the colony's board, particularly in relation to members who would not contribute to "Jewish teaching" (Yiddish and Hebrew). Some members of the farming community saw and understood the school's purpose and function in purely secular terms. They sent their children to school so that they could learn to read and write in English, to learn the skills and gain the knowledge necessary to prosper in Canada. Like some of the uptowners in Montreal, these Jews in Ste Sophie understood the role of the school as separate from any idea of maintaining or instilling any Jewish religious or cultural identity. They most commonly spoke Yiddish at home, and Hebrew was the language of the synagogue, not the English school.

Once the educational matters had been dealt with, meetings then often turned to other community concerns, and particularly the slaughtering of animals. The school board repeatedly appropriated for itself powers to impose penalties and to demand banishment over issues that in any other circumstance would obviously fall outside the ambit of any school board's jurisdiction. Yet it was clear that the community itself consented to this form of regulation and governance within its own institutional framework and constitutive processes.

Not only was there a *nomos,* which was being constructed through the institutional mechanism of the school board meetings, but the colony clearly constituted itself as a *demos*. The hermeneutic process of collectively constructing a complex and interwoven set of meanings for their existence as the school community and as the Jewish colony of Ste Sophie obviously found its institutional embodiment in the Protestant School Board of Ste Sophie of Scotland. Again, as Cover illustrates in his discussion of associational communities and their practices of collective self-identification through exclusion, the Ste Sophie School Board also had and exercised its jurispathic function. In order to regularize the slaughtering issue, which continued to arise regularly, both in terms of the board's desire to exercise control over the shochet's activities and to ensure full compliance with the shochet's monopoly over ritual killing, on 16 November 1922 the school board decided that no farmer could request, and the shochet could not carry out the killing of an animal without a "stamped note with the secretary's initials."[51] While the Va'ad Hair in Montreal struggled to gain and maintain a monopoly over ritual slaughter in the city, in Ste Sophie the Protestant School Board put into effect its own monopoly over *shechita*.

In 1931, after the resignation of the Jewish school commissioners in Montreal and the 1931 Act had ended all hope of Jewish school representation in the city, in rural Ste Sophie the Protestant School Board of Scotland formed another special committee, which had as its object "the regulation of the Jewish course of study."[52] It reinforced the parallel "English" and "Jewish" curriculum under its jurisdiction in ways the downtowners and Alderman Schubert could only ever have dreamed about. In April 1932 the school board not only continued the contract of the Hebrew teacher, but it created yet another committee, this time with the goal of providing agricultural assistance to new settlers.[53] It paid for the painting of the school building[54] and continued to struggle to ensure that all members of the community paid their school tax bill.[55] It arranged for candies to be provided at the Purim party for the children and discussed the need to hire a new Hebrew teacher.[56] It also approved a motion formally separating "English" school functions from those relating to Jewish instruction, and placing each under a separate committee.[57] Occasionally the meeting of the board was chaired by the visiting provincial Protestant school inspector, who made practical suggestions for the better management of the facilities, details of which were added to his annual report.[58]

The School Board of Scotland acted as school board, and a Jewish School Board at that, as a representative municipal council for the colony, a Va'ad Hair, and a local version of the JCA. It fulfilled all of these educational, political, social, economic, cultural, religious, and philanthropic functions under its official (and only) legal guise as a Protestant School Board. It offered the Jewish colonists of Ste Sophie a forum to become actively involved not just in questions of the education of their children, but on most matters of collective concern. It was, above all else, a cauldron for the constitutive arrangements and debates of a community actively creating its own *nomos* through a complex set of narrative practices.[59] In the view of MacLeod and Poutanen, "Ste Sophie represents a unique example of a Jewish community virtually co-opting the school-board to meet its own needs."[60] Their substantive analysis of the way in which the school board structure was taken over by the Jews of Ste Sophie and transformed into something much wider and deeper than an organization charged with hiring teachers, ensuring heating in the winter, and collecting school taxes is compelling, and accurate, as the Minute Books in English and Yiddish illustrate. Certainly it did all of those things, but it did much more. Where MacLeod and Poutanen are perhaps mistaken, however, is in their description of Ste Sophie as "unique."

La Macaza

It is important to underline that direct comparisons between the Ste Sophie experience and that in La Macaza are extremely difficult, if not impossible. The written record is much more complete for Ste Sophie because the community managed to hold on to the school Minute Books. The Ste Sophie colony was significantly larger and more financially prosperous than its neighbour to the north. The La Macaza school had a more sporadic and chequered history and was much shorter lived as a result of the diminishing population base, the economic struggles of the community, and the more physically dispersed nature of the Jewish settlement there. But this does not mean that the La Macaza experience should be ignored. For all its limitations, it is an example, this time, of a Jewish School Board, legally constituted as a dissentient Protestant board, existing in Quebec at the same time as many of the dramas of the Jewish School Question were unfolding not that far away among the Jewish communities in Montreal. It that sense, both La Macaza and Ste Sophie offer intriguing examples of "what if" in relation to the way the Montreal situation evolved. In Coverian terms again, La Macaza is another manifestation of the ways in which the tension in law between the "what is" and the "what might be" could be played out in constitutive normative practice, which brought the "what might be" to life, however temporarily.[61]

The La Macaza case, for all its documentary lacunae, brings more clearly into the light the relational dynamics that were at play in the creation of these rare Jewish School Boards that remained legally Protestant. First, there is a much more extensive record of correspondence between the provincial educational authorities in Quebec City and the La Macaza School Board, in large part because the board had a significantly more troubled existence than its counterpart in Ste Sophie. Second, the correspondence with the JCA in Montreal offers interesting and important insights into how the Jewish immigration organization actually dealt with the problems arising out of the School Question in rural Quebec and with a functioning Jewish School Board. While the Ste Sophie experience provides useful information about how a settler community constructed itself as a community within, and then outside, the official legal strictures of the dual denominational, common and dissentient school board framework, the La Macaza experience adds more of the external dynamic to the constitutive process by introducing provincial school officials, the formal application of the provisions of the Education Act, and the more intimate and direct involvement of the JCA in the school issues in that community.

The 8 September 1911 letter from the JCA to the ICA, concerning a subsidy for the hiring of a Hebrew teacher and a shochet, dealt not just with Ste Sophie but also with the education of children in La Macaza. In support of the request for financing, the JCA noted that such aid reflected "the necessity of assisting these Colonists in their endeavors to provide their children with a Hebrew education, which has the further effect of holding them together and awakening a sense of pride in the administration of their colony."[62]

Maintaining Jewish identity and community solidarity among rural colonists was essential to the projects, aims, and missions of the JCA and the ICA. A proper Jewish educational environment was believed to be key to those aims. Earlier the same year, the Montreal officials had notified London that a further sum had been advanced to permit the construction of a regular school building for the education of the Jewish children in La Macaza. Unlike the Jewish settlers of Ste Sophie, who were located in an area that had both a historical anglophone Roman Catholic presence and a contemporary Protestant population and school in New Glasgow, the Jews of La Macaza found themselves in Roman Catholic rural Quebec. Before the first establishment of the Jewish school in 1911, some Jewish children did attend the francophone Roman Catholic common school.[63] Because of the location of the colonists and their dispersal, many Jewish children lived six miles away from the nearest school. The JCA explained that the school was "under the supervision of Catholic School Trustees."[64] The characterization of the school as under Roman Catholic trustees is no doubt an error, since the school would more likely have been the common school in La Macaza and therefore under commissioners. Nonetheless, the school was in fact a Roman Catholic one, and many of the Jewish parents did not want to send their children to such an establishment. The result was that only nine of the thirty Jewish children in La Macaza were receiving any education, and that was only in non-winter months, since the roads were impassable once the snow fell.

A temporary arrangement had been made with one colonist to use a room in his house as the original school, which apparently worked well in the summer months, but again because of the distance involved for some students, attendance suffered in the winter. The new school was to be built in a position that would be more central and accessible to all Jewish settlers.[65] In 1911, the school was receiving a small subsidy from the provincial government and the JCA reported, "A Board of Trustees has been legally formed."[66] Because there was no other dissentient school in the municipality, the La Macaza Jews did not experience the legal difficulties in constituting themselves as a valid dissentient school board, as would their fellow settlers in Ste Sophie. Of course they still faced the fundamental constitutional truth that Jews had no right under section 93 to establish or to belong to a dissentient school board, Protestant or Roman Catholic. But that question would not be settled for some years until the *Hirsch* opinion of the Privy Council. In the meantime, the Jews of La Macaza were able to constitute themselves under the 1903 Act as Jewish Protestants and create a dissentient Protestant School Board, run by Jews, for Jews.

While the Jewish farmers had filed a declaration of dissent to establish their school as a dissentient Protestant school, operating in the same school municipality as the common, Roman Catholic school of La Macaza, the first Jewish Protestant school lasted only until 1914 when it ceased operation, largely because of poor attendance and the inability of the small group of Jewish farmers to maintain the school financially. In the period of inactivity of the Jewish school from 1914 to 1918, those Jewish children who did attend school again went to the Roman Catholic common school in La Macaza. According to Bélanger's account, the Roman Catholic priest at the time respected the religious beliefs and practices of the Jewish students. Bélanger recorded interviews with former students, and one French-Canadian pupil recounted that Jews were permitted to leave the room when the priest came to teach the catechism, in a way that mirrored the system implemented in

Montreal's Protestant schools, releasing Jewish students from religious instruction. On the other hand, a former Jewish student at the school recalled that the Jews learned the catechism, but they did not kneel like the other students, remaining seated instead.[67] In 1915, Reuben Belansman, who would become secretary-treasurer of the Jewish School Board, recorded in the Yiddish newspaper in Montreal, *Der Veg* [*The Way*], regular anti-Semitic outbursts from the local schoolteacher in La Macaza against "dirty Jews" and "Christ killers."[68]

Little wonder then that there was again, or still, a felt need for a Jewish school for the children of the agricultural colony. In March 1918, the superintendent of public instruction acknowledged the receipt of the renewal of dissent by resident "Hebrew taxpayers of Macaza" and advised them that they needed to contact the local inspector in order to gain his support for the new Jewish Protestant School within the local municipality.[69] The school board secretary, J. Shaner, reported to the JCA at the Baron de Hirsch Institute on the names and ages of the children then already attending the school.[70] There were thirty-one students, nineteen boys and twelve girls, ranging in age from six to thirteen. He sought instructions from them on what they should say in their letter to the inspector. The JCA indicated that they should simply indicate their dissent in the same terms as they had to the department in Quebec City, and request that the inspector ensure the payment of the relevant sums from tax revenues and general provincial funds to the dissentient school. If they did not receive an adequate response from the Protestant education official, the JCA would turn the matter over to "our Mr S.W. Jacobs, K.C. M.P. who will interview the Government in reference to the matter."[71]

Even this brief correspondence in relation to the La Macaza School illustrates some of the key institutional dynamics at play. The local board signified its continuing dissent under the law. The Department of Public Instruction acknowledged receipt of this declaration and told them they would need the support of the local Protestant school inspector. These provincial government officials displayed no qualms at all about a dissent originating from Hebrew taxpayers. Information about the regular mechanisms of obtaining their share of school monies was passed on to them, and they sought further advice from the JCA. At the same time, the school board in La Macaza functioned as a dissentient Protestant Board of School Trustees and as a Jewish school.

But the Jewish school soon ran into trouble and had to call upon the JCA to bail the board out of trouble. They had received a loan from a local man, Mr Gilet, for $250 to finish the construction of the school building. They had paid $50 and interest, but Gilet now refused to renew the loan and demanded immediate payment in full. "If a gentile – an anti-semite – favored us with a loan of $250.00 signed by the school Board then surely the Committee that consists of generous and broad-minded men will not turn down our petition."[72]

In addition to the general plea for assistance, the letter from the school board highlighted an issue of which the JCA must have been aware. The Jews of La Macaza were much more isolated than the colony in Ste Sophie. As the correspondence noted, they were surrounded by an overwhelming Roman Catholic majority. From the earliest days of Jewish settlement, the local Roman Catholic hierarchy and populations, or parts of it, had decried the Jewish presence in generally anti-Semitic terms and in supporting language invoking a vision of rural Quebec as constituted of and by *pure laine* Roman Catholics.[73] The JCA offered help but demanded certain guarantees from the members of the La Macaza community.[74]

After many months and the involvement of lawyers and notaries in Montreal and beyond, the JCA paid Gilet and took a mortgage on the schoolhouse of the dissentient Protestant School Board of La Macaza. While the Jewish parties of the JCA and the school board were attempting to reach a settlement on the loan question, the Protestant School Board of La Macaza, which had always had a perilous existence, was attempting to wend its ways through the legal technicalities of Quebec school law. In July 1920, an election of trustees had been scheduled, but the few eligible voters failed to turn up. The secretary of the board wrote to Cyril Delage, superintendent of public instruction, asking what to do in such circumstances. Delage replied that education electoral law required that official notices be reposted and the election held on 19 July, the next lawfully permitted date for school elections.[75] The law was the law and it needed to be strictly applied by the Jews who made up the Protestant School Board of La Macaza.

Non-payment of taxes and intra-communal disputes then became acute in the small Jewish colony of La Macaza, and they posed serious problems at this juncture of the life of the dissentient Protestant Jewish School. There were only eight resident Jewish families at the time, one of which had no children. The total Jewish population was merely fifty-three and they were not wealthy.[76] The conflicts dividing the few members of the Jewish community would simmer for some time, resulting in a lawsuit against Jacob Shaner for non-payment of school taxes brought by the school board under the influence of his long-term foe, Ruben Belansman. The dispute among the Protestant Jewish dissentient school electors would ultimately end in the closure of the Jewish school in La Macaza.

In addition, the limits of strict legality confronted the Protestant Jews of La Macaza. One trustee had left the area, abandoning the harsh life in rural Quebec to seek the comforts and possibilities of life in Montreal, as would many of his co-religionists, creating a vacancy. The board wanted to appoint Reuben Belansman, but as secretary-treasurer he was not entitled to become a trustee. He proposed resigning that post and appointing his daughter, a former teacher at the school, as secretary-treasurer under his supervision. The superintendent of public instruction in the provincial capital notified him that the arrangement would not work, because while women could act as assistant secretary-treasurers of a School Board, they could not hold the full office under Quebec law.[77] With the small Jewish population, and the inherent gender bias of Quebec educational law, the actual number of eligible male taxpayers who could act as trustees constantly caused difficulties for the governance of the Protestant School of La Macaza. In 1923, the board was faced with the refusal of one elected trustee to take office, contrary to the provisions of the Education Act.[78] In 1924 the conflicts in the Jewish community itself meant that members of the local community simply declined once more to show up for school board elections. Again provincial education authorities insisted that legal steps be taken to post a new notice of election and the voting be scheduled for the next lawful date, the following Monday.[79] At this second legally scheduled school election, no one showed up to vote.

Belansman, who continued to serve as secretary-treasurer after the legal impediment prevented his daughter from taking his place, explained to the superintendent of public instruction that the origins and causes of the problem were largely demographic. Most Jewish colonists had left La Macaza for Montreal as the colony struggled financially, and as they sought out surroundings in which they felt they could find a better and less isolated life among their co-religionists in the city. By the time scheduled for the 1924 school elections, only six Jewish taxpayers were left in La Macaza, Belansman himself, Messrs Kauffman, Shaner, Boxer, Rabinovitch, and Westerman. Kauffman could not read or write and therefore was ineligible to be a trustee. Shaner opposed the school board and had long been at loggerheads with Belansman. He refused to pay his taxes and was the subject of lawsuit by the board to recover those unpaid monies. As such, he was legally ineligible to serve as a trustee. Westerman came to La Macaza only during the summer months. Rabinovitch had been a trustee since the school began and no longer wished to serve. Boxer, who had been a trustee for the last three years, did not want a further term, and in any event, he spent the winter months in Montreal.[80] The Jews of La Macaza could no longer either muster enough men eligible to serve or feasibly run the school for the five or six remaining students.

Delage accepted the inevitable and instructed Belansman to file a report covering the period up to the present, have that report audited, and have the school board's books and any remaining cash sent to the department in Quebec City. If the dissentient taxpayers continued to be without a school for a full year, the commissioners of the common school could apply for the abolition of the dissentient board, and for the future payment of taxes into the common school fund. "Your few remaining children will attend, if they wish, the schools of the commissioners."[81]

Two outstanding matters remained. The case against Shaner was still before the courts and the board wished to know how to proceed. More significantly, Belansman expressed concern over the outstanding debt of $276. 55, contracted largely to the JCA, by the Protestant School Board.[82] The superintendent could not offer any advice concerning the lawsuit, but he did make it clear that the outstanding debt would have to be cleared as a matter of law. Normally the trustees were empowered under the Education Act to relieve and eliminate such a debt by a special tax levy, but this was impossible where the body entitled to raise such a tax, the Board of School Trustees, no longer existed, and where there was clearly no remaining sufficient tax base. The only solution appeared to have been to ask the majority Roman Catholic school commissioners if they would accept the debt.[83]

But the Protestant School Board of La Macaza was not quite dead and buried. On 22 September, Sam Boxer, Philip Kaufman, and Jacob Shaner, describing themselves as farmers with children in school, wrote to the superintendent of public instruction asking permission to run the school for the year. The provincial authorities gave vent to their frustration at the ongoing troubles at the dissentient Protestant School Board of La Macaza. The reply to the farmers on 23 September reiterated the history of the school elections, for which notices had been twice given but did not take place. Moreover, the provincial education official noted, "I judge that a state of quarrelsomeness exists in the municipality and this will have to be overcome before steps can be taken to appoint a Board."

While the Ste Sophie School Board had to deal with quarrelsomeness within that community, from recalcitrant taxpayers, to disobedient slaughterers, to those who wanted no part of Hebrew education, the disputes had all been dealt with by the community and within the community. There was no evidence of state interference or involvement beyond the normal aspects of an annual school inspection in the governance of the Ste Sophie School. It had existed as a quasi-autonomous institution of Jewish educational self-government. The La Macaza community, impoverished, isolated, and apparently divided, did not have the inner strength or capacity as a collectivity to exist without the involvement of the JCA and the provincial educational authorities. But still some in the community persisted in efforts to maintain the dissentient Jewish Protestant school.

On 2 October 1924, the new, or future self-described secretary-treasurer of the La Macaza Protestant School Board again wrote to the provincial authorities and explained that there was still a willingness in the community to have a school. The previous elections had not taken place because an unnamed former trustee had told the community that because there were not enough children, the school would be closed, so there was no purpose to be served by a school election. This was the only reason the eligible electors had not complied with the notices of election. However, the letter made clear there were at least ten children who needed an education, and the local community stood ready to hold elections once the Department of Public Instruction gave an indication that the school should open. Boxer, Shaner, and Kaufmann were all taxpayers who could read and write, and Boxer had in fact already served as a school trustee. The letter assured government officials that on school matters there was no discord in the La Macaza community. The school could run as before, except that Belansman would have to be replaced as secretary-treasurer, since he too had left La Macaza. Perhaps this now explained why there was no longer any discord on school matters, permitting Shaner to present himself for the trustee position in his long-time opponent's absence. On 20 October 1924, the superintendent of public instruction wrote to the provincial secretary requesting that he seek the consent of the lieutenant governor in council to appoint Boxer, Kaufman, and Shaner as school trustees.[84]

Meanwhile quarrelsomeness in fact and in law had reared its head again. Belansman wrote to the superintendent of public instruction from his new residence in Montreal reiterating that he had previously been authorized by the board to act in their behalf in the lawsuit pending against Shaner for unpaid school taxes. He was concerned that Shaner might use his new position as a trustee to scupper the suit.[85] As a matter of law, of course, if Shaner had not paid his school contributions, he could not be appointed or elected as a school trustee and the lieutenant governor in council would have named a legally ineligible trustee. The superintendent wrote to the new secretary of the new dissentient Protestant Jewish School Board in La Macaza on 23 October seeking verification that Shaner had paid his taxes and was indeed eligible to sit as trustee.

The provincial documentary record ends here, but we do know that after 1924, there was no dissentient Protestant School Board for Jews and by Jews in La Macaza. The experiment of Jewish educational self-government under the broad and flexible frame of Jews as Protestants for school purpose permitted by the provisions of the 1903 Act had come to end in that part of the province. Despite the constant insistence on strictly observing the technical requirements of the Education Act, provincial Protestant school officials and even the superintendent of public instruction, a member of the Roman Catholic Committee of the Council of Public Instruction, had proved to be flexible and accommodating of the Jewish desire for educational self-determination. The Hebrew taxpayers of La Macaza had been able to file a notice of dissent not once, but twice, as they struggled to keep the school for their children running. Even as the school was in the throes of closing, the superintendent of public instruction managed to obtain the appointment of new Jewish trustees of the dissentient Protestant School Board of La Macaza by the lieutenant governor in council. But even this degree of accommodation by the provincial authorities, and financial aid from the JCA, was not enough to save the Jews of La Macaza from internecine conflict and the harsh realities of life for poor immigrant farmers in rural Quebec in the 1920s. The La Macaza Protestant School gave the Jews of that settlement a taste of "what might be," but the "what is" of geography, demography, and economics proved too powerful.

Perhaps the summation of the experiences of the Protestant Jews of Ste Sophie can best be articulated in a broad and generous understanding of Davina Cooper's "promising spaces."[86] The Jewish School Question in these two Jewish agricultural colonies played itself out in ways that differed dramatically from the instantiations of the same issues in metropolitan Montreal. While each was geographically and temporally limited, they provided concrete manifestations and embodiments of a Jewish *nomos* and *demos* outside and sometimes formally within a constitutive and constitutional legality in which such Protestant Jewish schools should perhaps have been impossible. However briefly, the promise of these spaces was a concretization of the normative "what could be" outside the formal legal limits on what was elsewhere. The Jews of La Macaza and Ste Sophie found an institutional structure, within the Protestant educational system, that provided a space for a Jewish life world that could only be dreamt of by the downtowners and uptowners of Montreal.

11

Outremont and Beyond: The Jewish School Question Moves West

The Debate across the Mountain

This chapter traces the next manifestation of the Jewish School Question in Montreal, or more precisely in the suburb of Outremont. The issues and debates will be familiar. A Protestant school board insisted that its financial difficulties were entirely attributable to the presence of a large number of Jewish students in its schools. These echoes of the debates and controversies from the 1910s to the 1930s in Montreal were then amplified, again as they had been in the city itself, by Protestant concerns about the dangers posed to the identity of their schools as Protestant with growing numbers of Jewish students. While Protestant continued to be a broad-based and inclusive category across a number of denominations, at its existential and juridical core it always rejected the idea of any foundational Jewish claim to educational rights beyond the always problematic and questionably legal construction of "honorary Protestants." Collective existential narratives mixed with financial hardship would once more form the discursive core of the Jewish School Question, this time in Outremont.

The issue of Jewish students in Protestant schools would be articulated and put into practice though a deliberate strategy by the Protestant school trustees in Outremont of excluding the Jewish community as interlocutors. Educational officials in the dissentient school board portrayed the question of school finances, under the colour of which the controversy in Outremont would occur, as one involving only Outremont's Protestants and the provincial government. Jews might have been the cause of the problem, but the solution was to be reached without their involvement. The dialogue and inclusive compromises that had characterized the Jewish School Question from the nineteenth to the second half of the twentieth century would be replaced by a set of dual interlocutions, as the Protestant trustees negotiated with the government, and the Jewish community did the same. This changing political and cultural dynamic in the events in Outremont also resulted in a changing juridical framework. The accords under the *lois David* that had been enshrined in law, just as the compromise agreement between Jewish and Protestant leaders in 1903 after *Pinsler*, embodied in statute, would be replaced by a statutory regime in which the provincial government would play a more central and public role. The chapter highlights the ways in which the provincial government was becoming more centrally involved as a separate actor in educational matters in Quebec generally and in the Jewish School Question more specifically. Finally the chapter underscores the continuities within the Jewish School Question throughout its different iterations with a brief discussion of debates and concerns about the continuing controversies surrounding demands from within the Jewish community that Protestant school officials continue to allow Jewish students to be absent during holy days.

The 1931 Agreement and the Temporary Revival of the Jewish School Commission

The *loi David* of 1931, more properly known as An Act respecting the education of certain children in Montreal and Outremont, 21 Geo V, c 63, had led to the end of the Jewish School Commission and placed the fate and control of Jewish education in the two cities in the hands of the Protestant School Boards. Section 2 of the statute had ratified the contract between the Jewish school commissioners and the Protestant board in Outremont, and the notarized contract dated 20 January 1931 had been included in the statute as Appendix B. Jewish children had the right to attend Protestant schools in Outremont on the same terms as Protestant children, with the liberty exception relating to religious instruction, and the provisions governing the right to thirteen days of absence for holy day observance.

Many of the root causes of the next Jewish School Question that would arise over a significant period of time beginning in 1943 in Outremont were to be found in the economic and social progress of Jewish immigrants. For some in the ghetto, a move to the west when resources permitted was a step up the ladder, and the first district to the west of Park Avenue was the city of Outremont. Robert Rumilly sets out the facts of Jewish migration to Outremont, which he characterized as spreading "like an oil stain" in his official, but always ideological, history of the city.[1] The Jewish population of Outremont in 1931 was 6,793.[2] In the same census, according to Rumilly, the origins of the rest of Outremont's inhabitants were English, 5,859; Irish, 2,252; Scots, 1,782; and French, 10,553. The largest group, French Canadians, constituted only a plurality of the population.[3] However, that had been enough to have changed the Protestant schools of Outremont from common schools, administered by commissioners, into dissentient schools under trustees, a change in legal status that would have a profound and long-lasting effect on Jewish students. Once the Protestant schools became the institutions of the religious minority, Jews no longer had a legal right to attend Protestant dissentient institutions after *Hirsch*.[4] Hence the necessity that the Protestant trustees assent to their own notarized agreement in order that Jewish students in Outremont be allowed to attend Protestant schools. Ten years later, just before the next crisis marking the Jewish School Question erupted, a further shift in the city's population was noticeable. There were now 11,713 French Canadians, while the British and Irish population numbered 7,835. The Jewish population had increased by almost 2,000, to 8,745. The most important fact, highlighted by Rumilly, is that the decline in the English population, which had shifted to surrounding areas of Hampstead, Westmount, and the Town of Mount Royal, mirrored the gains in the Jewish population.[5] An indication of the rapid and recent demographic upheaval in Outremont can be found in comparative school statistics. In 1932, Jewish and Protestant students were evenly divided in numerical terms. By 1940, Outremont's Protestant schools had an enrolment of 2,440 students, of which 1,616 were Jewish.[6] Jews constituted 66.70 per cent of elementary pupils and 65.28 per cent of high school students.[7]

The other source of the Jewish School Question in Outremont could be found in an even more basic demographic reality. The total Protestant population in Quebec, including here the Jewish Protestants of the 1931 Act, had always been far below that of the dominant Roman Catholic majority. This meant again that the Protestant tax base was always much more restricted. As a consequence, Protestant schools operated from a smaller tax base and, in comparative terms, were more expensive to run than the better-funded Roman Catholic system. The financial difficulties in Outremont, which would serve as the public catalyst for the next version of the Jewish School Question, were in fact simply a manifestation of this much wider problem throughout Protestant education in the province, and therefore not really Jewish at all.

Paragraph 8 of the contract signed between the Jewish School Commission and the Protestant School Trustees on 20 January 1931, and being "deemed to have gone into effect on the first day of July, nineteen hundred and thirty," provided for a fifteen-year duration for the agreement, renewable for further similar periods, "unless notice of termination hereof shall have been given in writing ... at least two (2) clear years before the expiration of any fifteen (15) year period." The section also stated that the necessary written notice "shall have been given in writing by one Party or its successor to the other party or its successor." On 26 June 1943, the Protestant Board of School Trustees of the City of Outremont published a notice in the *Official Gazette*, dated 21 June, that the contract would be terminated on 30 June 1945.[8] The notice appeared in the *Official Gazette* because the party to whom written notice was to have been given, the Jewish School Commission, no longer existed, and there was, either in fact or in law, no successor to whom notice might have been given, as stipulated in the agreement. However, the agreement and the legislation were silent about the validity of substituting "written notice to the Party" through publication in the *Official Gazette*, and some question would remain as to whether the agreement could be legally terminated, pursuant to such notice, in 1945.

The Jewish school commissioners had resigned, following the removal of almost all aspects of Jewish educational autonomy from the first to the second of the *lois David*, but the 1931 Act had created the Jewish School Commission as a body with perpetual succession. Indeed, section 6 clearly provided that the commission remained in existence even if all of its members disappeared. It used compulsory language, "shall," to impose a duty on the lieutenant governor in council to fill any vacancy or vacancies. While Premier Taschereau had made the political calculation following the resignations of the members of the commission that the matter was to be resolved by the Jews of Montreal, the statute itself imposed a legal burden on the government to reconstitute the Jewish School Commission. That they did not do so would have lasting effects during the crises over the education of Jewish students in Outremont. The period of silence and inaction that followed the publication of the notice by the Outremont School Board was due in part to the fact that the Jewish School Commission was in a state of legal limbo, but also to the fact that nobody read or paid attention to notices in the *Official Gazette*.[9]

It was more than a year later that the Protestant Board of Outremont wrote to the provincial secretary, Omer Côté.[10] They advised him that because of "vastly changed conditions" that had arisen during the course of the agreement, the board had given the notice required in the *Official Gazette* in order to prepare the ground for a new, revised agreement to be drawn up.[11] At some level, the board also appeared to have been aware that their notice in the *Official Gazette* had been ineffective, or at least legally problematic, because they indicated to the provincial secretary that "the Jews should be notified at an early date, in order that they may have time in which to make other arrangements for the education of their children."[12] The letter from the school board indicated that the primary motivating factor behind their desire to renegotiate the arrangement was a continuing fall in revenue and a consequently rising deficit in the cost of educating Jewish students in Outremont. The alleged cause of the deficit, according to Rumilly, was to be found in the fact that at the time there were 1,795 Jewish students and only 552 Protestant students in the city's schools. By the mid-1940s, 76 per cent of the students in Outremont's Protestant schools were Jewish.[13]

At this stage, the Outremont Protestant School Board looked upon the state of affairs as one involving only themselves and the provincial government, dealing with the school tax deficit, and entailing a request for further funding from the provincial government. The agreement they sought was an agreement with the provincial government and not one with the Jews. There was clearly no intention to return to the mechanism of a notarized deal between the trustees and the Jewish community, however represented. Failing such an infusion of funds from Quebec City, the trustees sought a legal change in tax arrangements and in governance structures. In effect, once more, and as a natural result of the disappearance of the Jewish School Commission, the fate of the Jewish students of Outremont was in the hands of the provincial government and the dissentient Protestant School Board. The issues as far as these two parties were concerned appeared to have had nothing to do with the Jews, except insofar as the Jews were once more the source of the financial difficulties in which the trustees found themselves. Clearly the Protestant school trustees had no intention of communicating directly with the Jewish communities, assuming it could identify someone with whom to communicate. It left that task up to the government.

Once again, the Jewish School Question involved political elements that had little to do with Jews. As the "Memo re Education of Jewish Children in Outremont" attached to the letter to Côté made clear, the Outremont Protestant School Board was unhappy with the statutory changes, flowing from the recommendations of the Commission of Nine, which had led to the creation of the Montreal Protestant Central School Board. Not only did the Outremont school officials regret the general loss of autonomy, but they also argued that the Central School Board was constituted by members "not affected by the question of Jewish children. To them it is a matter of no special importance."[14] The Outremont board made the restoration of its full autonomy a sine qua non of the continuing presence of Jewish children in its schools. It then requested a special funding arrangement whereby the provincial government would make up the deficit imposed on the board in relation to the costs of educating Jewish children, since the neutral panel monies did not provide sufficient sums.

Most significantly, the Outremont board also demanded that Jewish children resident in Outremont now be counted "without question" in the neutral panel. Of course, they referred legally not to Jewish children, but to their taxpaying parents, but the substantive point was the key one. At this point, the Outremont board saw a renegotiation of the 1931 agreement in terms of a return to the school tax system proposed by the Protestant School Board in the early 1920s, which had provoked the Commission of Nine investigations and the *Hirsch* case. The new arrangement they sought was not a renegotiation in any real sense. Instead, the Protestant school officials in Outremont wanted to return to a system that would undo the very foundations of both the 1903 Act, and the political, contractual, and legislative aftermath of *Hirsch*. In 1931, the political thrust of the Protestant and Roman Catholic educational authorities, the provincial government, and the uptowner faction had been the entry of Jewish students into the Protestant school system, and the arrangement of the school tax system to accommodate that result. Recognizing the demographic trends on the Island of Montreal, Protestant officials had insisted that the dissentient schools in Outremont be brought under the aegis of the agreements and legislation meant in combination to offer a solution to the Jewish School Question. In addition, of course, after 1943, Quebec now operated a regime of compulsory school attendance.[15] This meant that Jewish parents were legally obligated to send their children to school, and by implication, that their children had the right to attend school. However, since *Hirsch*, given Outremont's educational history, the common school to which Jewish parents had the right to send their children was now within the Roman Catholic system. Legally speaking, in the absence of a special legislative/contractual regime for Jews in Outremont, they had no right to access the dissentient Protestant schools. Legal, educational rights for Jews in Outremont clashed formally and strikingly with their deeply felt constitutive wishes, and with many years of practical experience. The old governance and financial structures under the legislative changes of the late 1920s and early 1930s no longer met the requirements of Protestant education in Outremont, and the conditions necessary for Jewish educational rights in the broader sense of the community's own express desires were under legal threat.

Now, as the Second World War raged in Europe, the Protestants of Outremont wanted to undo the essential political compromise of 1931.[16] Elsewhere in Canada, lawyers were preparing the ground for an envisaged new legal world of post-war rights.[17] In Outremont, the entrenched rights of section 93 reinforced the ancient and still dominant constitutional and constitutive order in the field of public education. As one Jewish resident of Outremont, Mrs Ben Rothenstein, would put it in a letter to the *Montreal Star*, "As for me, I know that my husband is overseas. Should I tell him that we are keeping the home-fires burning, and he is fighting for his country so that his children should be kicked out of the public schools?"[18]

The Outremont board informed the Protestant Central School Board of its intentions, and contact was made between Lazarus Phillips, as a leader of the Jewish community, and Montreal educational officials sometime later.[19] Phillips sent the correspondence to Michael Garber, a former member of the Jewish School Commission, and now a prominent leader of the Canadian Jewish Congress.[20] The CJC would take on a representative role for the Jewish community of Outremont and would make claims to the provincial government on its behalf. Unlike the uptowner and downtowner school committees that had vied for representative status throughout the Jewish School Question of the 1920s and 1930s, the CJC could claim a broad and general mandate within Jewish Montreal's communities. Montreal's Jews, while never truly united, had come together to play a key role in the formation of the congress. With changing demographics, Jews became wealthier and more prosperous as a group, and their population was now less concentrated in the ghetto than it had been in the 1920s and early 1930s. *Yiddishkeit* culture was slowly dying out, as Jewish children graduated from Protestant schools and English-language universities.[21] The creation of the Canadian Jewish Congress, with strong representation from the remnants of the downtowner faction, brought together those who had been opponents a few years earlier to assert Jewish school rights. A separate Jewish School Board was by now consigned to the "what might have been" of Jewish history in Montreal. The CJC would become a powerful and consistent voice for Montreal Jewry during this phase of the debates over the educational rights of Jewish children.

Garber entered into contact with W.P. Percival, the provincial director of Protestant education, in Quebec City, requesting information through official channels about the Outremont request, which Phillips had passed on to him unofficially.[22] He also notified Percival about the current state of the Jewish School Commission. A.Z. Cohen and Nathan Gordon had died; Rabbi Abramowitz, Dr Max Wiseman, and Garber himself were still in Montreal; the remaining members, Samuel Livingstone and Edgar Berliner, were living in California.[23]

At this time, the echoes of 1931 were very strong indeed. Michael Garber issued a statement in the Yiddish press the same day as he wrote to the director of Protestant education. Garber claimed to be speaking as a member of the Jewish School Commission, which he asserted was still in existence because no legal effect had ever been given by the government to the resignation of its members and no successors had ever been appointed.[24] While Garber was correct that no effect had been given to the resignations by the appointment of other representatives to fill the vacancies on the Jewish School Commission pursuant to section 6 of the 1931 Act, his legal analysis – which may have been more accurately described as a political attempt to cloak his position, and that of the CJC, in the historically legitimate robes of the Jewish School Commission as a new controversy in Outremont loomed – was clearly faulty. Section 2 of the 1931 Act limited the term of office of the commissioners to five years ending on 1 May 1935. After that period, the lieutenant governor in council was to appoint members of the commission for another five-year term. Even if they had not resigned in 1931, the commissioners would have lost their mandate in 1935. Because he was not reappointed at that time, Garber was, legally speaking, no longer a member of the Jewish School Commission. Once more, however, in the Jewish School Question, what was strictly legal in the narrow sense had little to do with the processes under which difficulties would be worked through, and according to which the Jewish community of Montreal would engage in constitutive law-making, as it set out to narrate the terms and conditions of its communal life in the context of the educational issues concerning the Jewish children of the city, and of Outremont.

Garber's statement also highlighted the notice issue concerning the Outremont board's use of publication in the *Official Gazette* as a way of announcing its intention to terminate the agreement. "No Jews were ever given notice." Garber insisted that the publication in the *Official Gazette* constituted notice only to the government of the Protestant board's intentions in relation to the agreement and did not meet the legal standard for the notice in writing required under the 1931 agreement and Act. Finally, Garber advised the community that Protestant officials in Outremont had declared that they had no intention of not renewing the agreement. Their only idea was to "iron out difficulties." This version of the Protestant intention in Outremont was, of course, significantly different from the position staked out in the "Memo re Education of Jewish Children in Outremont," which had been sent to the Montreal Central School Board and the provincial secretary. The Protestant school trustees had stated a clear intention to effect fundamental changes to the agreement and to return Jews in Outremont to a status as neutrals for tax purposes previously contemplated in the 1920s.[25] Throughout this manifestation of the Jewish School Question, the Protestant position in Outremont would be obscured by the trustees' decision not to enter into direct dialogue with the representatives of the Jewish communities. The situation was exacerbated as the Protestant trustees continued to offer public statements that were at odds with the position they adopted in official discussions with the provincial government.

Garber obviously remembered the constant accusations from one side and the other during the crises of the 1920s and 1930s about the validity of the other's claim to represent Montreal Jewry.[26] He made sure that no such charges would interfere with the substantive concerns of the anxious parents of the Jewish students in Outremont, as he invoked both the historic Jewish School Commission and the status of the CJC. His main problem, he stated to Percival, was that he simply could not get any real idea of the substance of the Outremont board's desired modifications to the 1931 contract, because they refused to enter into contact or discussions with him.[27]

Percival indicated that at this stage the government wanted to maintain school board autonomy and did not wish to become further involved in the issue. The position appears to have been one in which the two parties to the 1931 agreement were meant to sort out any modifications or changes between themselves, except that one party, the Protestant trustees, would have nothing to do with the other. Percival seemed not at all concerned with the legal fact that Garber was not a Jewish school commissioner, or with the political fact that the Outremont board had been clear in its correspondence with Omer Côté that they saw the problem as one grounded in the current school tax structure over which the provincial government had the ultimate jurisdiction. The dissentient school board of its own accord could not simply place Jewish taxpayers in the neutral panel. The very nature of the 1931 arrangement under which the notarized contract had been included in the Act was but one more embodiment of the complex taxonomies of public and private that had always operated within the broad constitutive parameter of the Jewish School Question. When it came to the issues of Jewish students in Protestant schools in Montreal and now in Outremont, any idea of autonomy, for Protestants or for Jews, was qualified by legal, economic, and political realities. Percival maintained the long-standing provincial government position that in reality the matter was one for private agreement. He suggested that Garber contact the Outremont officials directly and deal with the issues accordingly.[28]

In February 1945, CJC representatives met with the three remaining Jewish school commissioners to hash out a collective position in response to the emerging situation in Outremont.[29] In addition to the congress's role in overseeing the legislative change that would appear to be the most likely result of the Outremont board's actions, the CJC also considered the idea of reviving the Jewish School Commission so that it could act as the recognized Jewish institution in educational matters. Finally, because things never really changed at the fundamental level throughout the entire history of the Jewish School Question, the CJC also tentatively considered the advisability of a separate Jewish school system in Outremont where Jewish students were in the anglophone majority.[30]

On the Protestant side of the matter, the real issues for Outremont's school trustees were again both financial and existential, as they had always been in Montreal. Some Protestant parents objected to sending their children to Protestant schools with an 80 per cent Jewish student body. The idea of "a Christian girl at school who might have four Jewish boys seated around her" was fodder for the worst anti-Semitic fears of many good Montreal Protestants.[31] Moreover, in Outremont, the school trustees felt that it was their duty to maintain the absolute autonomy guaranteed by law to ensure the rights of the 20 per cent Protestant minority in their schools. The Outremont Protestant population was diminishing, and the tax base falling. This was exacerbated by the increasing significance of Jewish day schools in Outremont and Montreal, which reduced the overall number of students in the Outremont schools and consequently the revenues received from the neutral panel, which were determined on the number of students enrolled in the school system. In addition, these Jewish educational establishments were beginning to take away qualified teachers from the public school system – a problem for some, but not all Protestant school officials who still refused to hire Jewish Teacher's College graduates.[32]

The CJC accepted that it must insist on the continuation of the 1931 agreement. It also recognized that if the proposed legislation proceeded, there would be serious community agitation in Outremont for a separate Jewish public school system, which history had taught was bound to lead to discord and division. In early 1945, the Jewish communities of Montreal and Outremont had no desire to revisit the communal battles of the 1920s and 1930s over separate Jewish schools. Even Michael Garber, the long-term ally of Louis Fitch and a key member of the Zionist left in the downtowner faction in the 1920s, had no desire to look back to the uptowner/downtowner divisions, or the political objections from Roman Catholic officials to any idea of third, non-Christian school commission in Montreal. Maintaining Jewish rights to send their children to Protestant schools was the basic community bottom line.[33] In this, they were naturally joined by the traditional view from Roman Catholic opinion, which continued to engage in the broader political arena on the Jewish School Question. According to this unwavering Roman Catholic position, Jews had no claims of right in the bi-national framework of Canada and Quebec and were therefore simply compelled to accept the dual confessional, Christian nature of Quebec education. Moreover, Roman Catholics viewed the presence of Jewish children in Protestant schools as, broadly speaking, a windfall for Protestant schools, giving them access to a growing tax base of Jewish property-owners and to funds from the neutral panel.[34] The only ones who had a problem with the current arrangement were the Protestant trustees in Outremont.

The provincial secretary had indicated, as had Percival, that the community's wish to renew the arrangement was the preferred course of the government as well.[35] Once more, the government in Quebec City aligned itself on the side of harmony and compromise in relation to the Jewish School Question, as views, which might be characterized as extreme within the Protestant educational system, came into conflict with the drive for educational equality within the always-problematic bi-denominational structures of Quebec education. In pursuit of that goal, a committee of Jewish parents and others sought to meet with the Protestant school officials as part of their role as "active participants in this undertaking."[36] The local community had taken the issue into its own hands, and any constitutive actions in relation to the rights of their children in Quebec's schools would have to involve not just the formal representatives of the Jewish School Commission or the CJC, but the members of the Jewish communities of Outremont themselves. The Outremont Protestant school trustees had no interest in dialogue with anyone outside formal government circles, including Jewish parents of students attending their schools and paying taxes for that right. The matter had been characterized from the beginning as one involving purely financial issues that would be dealt with between the board and the provincial government. As far as the Protestant trustees were concerned, the Jewish parents would simply be notified of the results of these discussions.[37] The trustees again insisted that the real problem was the ongoing deficit experienced by the board as the result of the massive presence of Hebrew students and the lack of sufficient resources in the neutral panel.[38] Little had changed since the early 1920s in this version of the Protestant position. But to some extent the openness and hermeneutic frame had shifted. Even if Jews were the source of the problem, they were now outsiders to its resolution.

The trustees also made it clear that the understanding that had come from their talks with the government was that there would be no appointment of any Jewish School Commission, and that any settlement of the matter, because it involved changes to the tax system and the makeup of the neutral panel, would be managed among the Protestant Board of School Trustees, the government, and the two Roman Catholic School Commissions within the municipal boundaries of the City of Outremont.[39] This response did not please the Jewish parents whose children constituted the majority of students in the Protestant schools of Outremont. They objected to the Protestant idea that they would be excluded from any arrangement and insisted that the provincial government could not possibly countenance an arrangement for the education of Jewish students in Outremont that would exclude Jews from participation in constructing its terms and conditions. The government had already received a delegation of Jewish representatives, including the parents, and there could be no reason why the Protestant board would not extend the same courtesy. Whether the Jewish School Commission would be reconstituted, or some other mechanism would fulfil the new arrangement, the Jewish community of Outremont, through its parental group, would not "feel themselves bound if same will have been entered into without their prior consent."[40]

At a basic foundational and constitutive level, the Protestant trustees in Outremont simply did not see the issue of a continued presence of Jewish students in their schools as being in any way a Jewish School Question. They refused to meet with the Jewish community, invoking the idea of the confidentiality of their discussions with the government. They promised to keep parents informed "through the press."[41] The old mechanisms of dialogue and compromise, where the parties met and discussed the issues in order to hammer out a compromise, simply did not suit the school trustees, who wanted to decide the fate of Jews within the Protestant schools of Outremont without the Jews.

In this case, however, the Jewish community was organized and united. It also had significant clout in electoral politics, at municipal, provincial, and federal levels, and it would not hesitate to bypass the Protestant school officials if required. It was not only the Protestant Board of School Trustees that could cut one side out of the discussion. The CJC did not resile from engaging in a publicity campaign, involving not just the Jewish community, but also public opinion in Outremont and in Montreal. There the 1931 agreement had been renewed without impediment.[42] On 14 June 1945, a public meeting of Jewish parents in Outremont was held at the Adath Israel Synagogue. Over five hundred people attended. Michael Garber presented a detailed report of the situation, a copy of which had already been sent to the anglophone press in Montreal.[43] The meeting expressed its outrage at the fact that Jewish school children were being used "as a political football in the efforts of the Protestant School Board to get better financial conditions from the Government," and formally elected a committee with broad representative characteristics to protect the interests of the Jewish parents of Outremont.[44] The Education Committee of the CJC therefore expanded its membership to include representatives of the parents and of the Outremont Jewish community more broadly to formalize the conclusions from the public meeting at the community synagogue.[45] The Education Committee would meet at the CJC headquarters and use congress facilities and press contacts, but it would have a broader, local mandate than even the CJC could have claimed. The lessons of the 1920s and 1930s battles between the uptowners and the downtowners had been learned and adapted to Outremont. The divisions and squabbles over who spoke for the Jewish community would not be part of the Jewish community's struggles for school equality this time.[46]

The Outremont Protestant Board of School Trustees was at this point politically outgunned, temporarily at least. Garber and his colleagues had learned from the 1931 Act and its history that the solution to the Jewish School Question would always be political.[47] The results might be enshrined in the technical legal framework of legislation, but the real battle was to be waged and won in the field of public opinion, and in the corridors of political power. The overwhelming feeling in Jewish Outremont was that the arrangement with the Protestant board should continue,[48] and that view had to be put to the government and to the Protestant Board.

The premier of Quebec, Maurice Duplessis, took personal carriage of the matter and arranged an interim solution of further provincial funds to all schools in the province, including the Outremont Protestant schools. The personal involvement of Duplessis raises intriguing issues about the place of the Jewish School Question and the Jews of Montreal in the broader struggles over human rights emerging at the time. Elsewhere in Canada, especially in Ontario and Saskatchewan, it is clear that Jewish Canadians played key roles in the battle for a human rights system. In Quebec, however, the issue was somewhat more complex. It is clear that since the 1832 statute, Quebec Jews had enjoyed formal equality before the law. The history of their emancipation also demonstrates the ways in which they were able to adjust to a variety of legislative norms in order to ensure that Jewish religious and cultural institutions were able to function as their Roman Catholic and Protestant equivalents did. There had been a long and ongoing battle for rights and equality, and the Jewish School Question was one very particular manifestation of that struggle.

Likewise individual Jews and Jews who belonged to organizations like labour unions, the CCF, and the Communist Party and affiliated groups had been active in broad social and political debates and struggles, many of which involved civil liberties and human rights. The years of the Duplessis regime in Quebec brought many of these issues to the forefront of political and legal conflict, as the government, under the clear guidance of the premier, used legal cudgels under various rubrics such as seditious libel and the prevention of Communist propaganda, etc. to quash dissent. Communists and trade unions were key targets for Duplessis's repression, and many Jews figured among the victims. Jehovah's Witnesses, who rejected secular authority, as well as both Roman Catholicism and Protestant churches, received the special ire of the government. Jewish lawyers dedicated to civil liberties and progressive causes helped defend these groups and individuals and subsequently led the legal attack against Duplessis. Abraham Feiner joined Frank Scott in *Switzman v Elbling*, when the infamous Quebec Padlock Law targeting premises used for the production or dissemination of Communist propaganda was declared ultra vires.[49] A.L. Stein represented Aimé Boucher against charges of seditious libel for distributing Jehovah's Witness literature.[50]

Most famously perhaps, Stein and Frank Scott represented Frank Roncarelli in his damages action against Maurice Duplessis for abuse of power. The case is rightly known as a landmark in Canadian civil liberties law, but as Eric Adams points out, contemporaneous reaction to Roncarelli's victory was highly contextualized, dependent on local circumstances, and more nuanced than one would have believed.[51] Most significant for Montreal Jewry and its struggle for full equality, however, was Scott's pleading in favour of rights grounded in citizenship. "Scott employed the language of rights and citizenship deliberately. The idea of national citizenship offered the means to attach individual rights to the legal subject, notwithstanding the absence of a formal constitutional bill of rights. The concept of citizenry rights particularly attracted Scott because it configured two constructs central to his constitutional theory: individuals holding rights and freedoms equally among fellow citizens; and a national community of citizens whose rights fell under exclusive federal jurisdiction."[52]

Scott's view of the federal ideal of rights within the Canadian confederation would eventually win the day with the introduction of the Charter of Rights and Freedoms, but unsurprisingly not in Quebec.[53] In this legal rhetoric it is not difficult to trace many narrative vectors leading to the history of the Jewish School Question specifically and the broader question of the Jewish struggle for equality in Quebec. *Roncarelli* was not the first instance in which the general delictual provisions of Article 1053 of the Civil Code had been invoked to bring the actions of the powerful under legal control in the province. *Ortenberg v Plamondon* clearly figures as the first such instance in the struggle for equality and civil rights in the province. Likewise, the ideals of citizenship and equality invoked by Scott were not pleaded here for the first time. Equality stemming from their status first as British subjects, and now in the post-war context, as Canadian citizens, always formed the core of Jewish claims throughout the long history of the School Question. *Roncarelli* can be understood then as a key point at which the legal history of the struggle for educational rights in Montreal schools becomes an important background narrative within the broader story of civil liberties in Canada. But it is also a point where the Jewish School Question takes on its own specificities and it diverges to some extent from the rest of Canadian civil rights/human rights history.

While many of the actors in key cases, such as *Switzman*, *Boucher*, and *Roncarelli*, were Montreal Jews, and while many Jewish socialists, progressives, and trade unionists joined in the struggles against Duplessis in Quebec, organized Montreal Jewry, unlike their colleagues in Toronto, for example, were particularly quiescent on this front. Montreal Jews had never hesitated to attack manifestations of anti-Semitism through litigation, when that was their best or only option. They had never ceased to lobby government and to wage publicity campaigns in order to protect their collective interests throughout the long history of the Jewish School Question, and in other areas of collective community concern. In Outremont, now, they waged political and publicity campaigns and sought the intervention of the Duplessis government. They did so with the supporting rhetoric of the foundational norms of equality and Canadian citizenship, particularly in wartime and immediately thereafter. When Montreal Jews were later asked to join others in discussions about a possible national Bill of Rights, on the other hand, they declined. "We succeeded in establishing an excellent relationship between the two ethnic groups. We dare not do anything which may hinder or undermine that relationship – certainly not for the sake of the Bill of Rights."[54]

Jews would fight as hard as they could to ensure group survival and collective rights to equality. But the corporatist structures of Quebec, Protestant and Roman Catholic, anglophone and francophone, always present in the province and at the heart of the School Question, and Jewish and other struggles over equality and identity were particularly strong under the Duplessis government. Individual Jews may have been part of the broader civil liberties struggle, but the collective representatives of the community, particularly the CJC, had reached an accommodation with the political power structures of the province, in an arrangement that protected their collective interests and one they would not endanger. The Jewish School Question in Outremont would be settled by political and social dialogue and political negotiation. Deeper claims about civil liberties and broader debates about belonging in Quebec outside the dominant dualist conception of identity would, as far as the CJC was concerned, have to wait at least until the days of the Quiet Revolution, when all aspects of belonging and identity in Quebec would be up for grabs.

Again, while his time in office was characterized by an authoritarian conservatism, many attacks on civil liberties, and endemic anti-Semitism, Duplessis's involvement in the Jewish School Question appears to have been exemplary. Throughout, the idea of competing but coexisting dual national identities in the province, and of the interstitial spaces for Jewish identity and equality would find concrete manifestations as a political solution was sought. The premier urged that in exchange for broad provincial fiscal support, the Protestant trustees accept the continuing education of the Jewish children in Outremont schools.[55] The school officials agreed to a one-year extension of the practice of admitting Jewish children, but they maintained their bottom line desire, which was in effect to ensure the Protestant character of Outremont's Protestant schools by removing Jewish students. They no longer had a serious financial claim to support their exclusionary desires. Just as had been the case in Montreal in the late 1920s and early 1930s, taxation was easily dealt with, and once it was settled, the true political, social, cultural, religious, and existential questions quickly came to the surface. The familiar ideas informing claims about the difficulty, if not the impossibility, of maintaining a Protestant education system with increasing numbers of Jewish students present in the schools would make their way into the public forum. In the absence of a more permanent understanding and enforceable agreement, and one more particularly that included active involvement of the Jewish community, trouble continued to brew.

The Jewish School Question in Outremont: Protestant Identity, Jewish Equality, and Taxes (Again)

As the provincial government took charge of the matter, Outremont's Jewish community was not pleased with the political, legal solution being put forward in Quebec City.[56] The government was proposing to extend the agreement for one to two years, while the Jewish community, which had been living with temporary solutions and the incumbent uncertainties, again was pushing for a more long-term answer, but one for the future without any return to the issues of the 1920s and 1930s.[57] It felt that if the government could deal with the province-wide problem of school finance, as the Duplessis administration had already done temporarily, the Protestant trustees would lose whatever political, financial, and moral purchase their position might have had.[58] With a provincially mandated solution to the school finance crisis, the Outremont Protestant officials would be satisfied and the Jewish School Question would cease to be a problem for them.[59] While Garber was no doubt aware that there was, as there had always been, a more profound existential malaise among the Protestant trustees over the Protestant identity of their schools when Jewish student numbers grew, the CJC presented the issue in terms that echoed the official statements of the Outremont Protestant Board itself. If this was merely a financial question, as the Outremont officials insisted, then a financial solution would make the problem of the Jewish School Question in Outremont disappear.[60]

Using statistics and information provided by the city, the CJC advised the government that in the school year 1943–4, the cost of educating Jewish students had been $177,545.92, which had risen to $194,944.07 in 1944–5. The school board derived its income from the Protestant panel, the neutral panel, and miscellaneous sources such as fees from non-residents, etc. It had received 74 per cent of its Protestant panel income from Jewish taxes in 1943–4, and over 75 per cent in 1944–5. The amount received from Protestant, non-Jewish taxpayers did not cover the cost of educating non-Jewish students. Indeed, taking the amounts received and dividing by the number of students in each group, it became apparent that the Protestant board in Outremont received $52.08 and $59.63 per Jewish student in the system and $37.46 and $37.23 per Protestant, non-Jewish student for the two school years. As its first charge on the neutral panel for educating Jewish students, the board received $59,056.57, and $59,645.07. Had the neutral panel monies been distributed on a simple pro rata basis between Roman Catholic and Protestant systems without the first charge, the Outremont trustees would have received only $34,144.65 and $34,456.81 in those two school years. According to the CJC calculations, then, the actual deficit for the board was $15. 56 per Jewish child, but $68.37 per non-Jewish child. In other words, without the Jewish students, whose presence contributed almost 80 per cent of the income of the Protestant schools, the Outrem ont Protestant Board would have been in even more serious trouble. There was a financial problem in Outremont, but it was a problem of underfunding generally, not of too many Jews. The Outremont trustees nonetheless adamantly maintained that the Jewish population was at the heart of the problem and that the issue was at its core a financial one. They asked the province to include provisions in any legislation that would attach a different, higher tax rate to Jewish properties than that charged to Protestant taxpayers.[61] Once again, the Protestant proposal for statutory reform would define the Jewish School Question by formalizing Jewish educational inequality under section 93.

But the problem was obviously not the financial one the Protestant representatives persisted in presenting to the public and to the government. The figures did not lie, and the Outremont school trustees problems were not only, or perhaps even primarily, attributable to an issue with Jewish taxes. Their problem was a problem with Jews.[62] The Protestant board in Outremont had recently instituted the practice of segregating Jewish and non-Jewish children into different classes in its schools. This practice was a clear violation of the agreement signed in 1931, which had been extended by the government until 1947, as part of its temporary solution the previous year. Segregating Jewish students was a violation of "the principles of Canadian citizenship." In a single sentence the CJC indicated the strength of feeling among Outremont's Jews, the ongoing and persistent complaints of members of Jewish communities about Protestant school administrators, and how much the situation had changed from the heady days of the downtowner school committee. "We wish to make it clear that the Jewish community will not tolerate the operation by your board of what is virtually a separate Jewish school system from which, furthermore, Jewish teachers are completely excluded."[63]

For Outremont's Jews, the 1931 agreement had enshrined the principles of equality, citizenship, and religious freedom they considered essential to their self-understanding as Jews and now as Canadians. The education of their children in the city's Protestant schools was an embodiment of the ideas and ideals of Canadian values to the city's Jewish population. In their view, the Protestant board was flaunting the agreement, the law, and the basic philosophical and political principles of democratic citizenship and equality.[64] By practising segregation, the trustees were returning to the days of the 1920s and thumbing their noses at the legal obligations to which they had voluntarily assented. They were also instituting policies and practices against which Canadians, and Jewish Canadians at that, had only recently fought and died in Europe.[65] Once again, the Jews of this part of Montreal found themselves face-to-face with the powerful legal, political, and social limits within the educational context, which ultimately had always stood in the way of their real powers of self-constitution. Equality, citizenship, and a growing understanding of Canadianness were all stymied by Protestant intransigence and the legal sterility imposed by section 93. Foundational norms of full equality meant little when confronted with a barely disguised Protestant anti-Semitism, buttressed and discursively obscured under the rubrics of the recurring themes of the financial cost of educating Jews in the Protestant system, and the absolute rights given to Protestant school autonomy by section 93.[66]

While Jews once more sat in classrooms only with other Jews, in schools controlled by Protestant officials, the matters of the 1931 agreement and the education of Jews in Outremont's schools were under constant political consideration in the provincial capital. The CJC continued to make representations to the government, always seeking to ensure that the rights, which had been obtained by Jews through many years of political and legal struggle, were not removed from any legislation that might treat the Outremont question as a purely financial matter.[67] As it would later recognize, and as it always knew, the most important parts of the 1931 Act and contracts enshrined in it had been the protection of Jewish holy day observance, the prohibition against the segregation that had been adopted routinely by the Montreal board in the 1910s and early 1920s to preserve the Protestant nature of the schools under its jurisdiction, and the right to have boards consider hiring and promoting Jewish teachers.[68] Each of these acknowledgments of Jewish specificity had allowed the community to maintain some sense of its Jewish identity within the Protestant school system while ensuring access to Canadian education and broader ideals of citizenship and equality that had always been so important, especially to the uptowner faction. The 1931 Act enshrined this delicate balance between Jewish identity and Canadian-ness in a way that had apparently met the aims of the Jewish community and transcended mere financial concerns over tax-panel disbursements. However, matters did not progress as the CJC and the Outremont Education Committee had wished.[69]

The government responded to the CJC by assuring them that the matter was again under consideration and that they "will always try to afford justice to the minority, whoever they may be."[70] In a struggle between the minority Protestants of Outremont and the minority Jews of that city, the government's stated position could not have been more ambiguous. Moreover, it did not satisfy Jewish claims.[71] The situation became clearer when the government introduced Bill 73, An Act respecting Protestant Schools in the city of Outremont. The bill provided for a five-year agreement for the education of Jewish children in Outremont Protestant schools, the arrangement to be made between the provincial secretary and the Protestant Board of School Trustees. As the Protestant board had long urged, the government would take upon itself the payment of any deficit remaining after the distribution of taxes from the neutral panel for the education of Jewish students.

The government's wish was to tread a careful line in a battle they saw as involving two minority groups, each of whom had valid claims for at least part of their arguments, and neither of whom were committed supporters of the Duplessis regime. Such apparent timidity was not likely to satisfy the Jewish community that continued to live with the ongoing uncertainty of temporary solutions. The bill did little to assuage their concerns, justified by historical experience, that Jewish school rights were always contingent, always subject to the constitutive normativity of Canada's two founding nations, and ultimately determined within the historically fixed rights granted to the Protestant minority by section 93. They had preserved what claims they had to educational equality only through discussion, negotiation, and the political actions that had informed those other discursive practices, even though many of those agreements enshrining Jewish equality fell outside the limits of strict legality. Unlike the 1880s and 1890s, or in the early 1900s around the *Pinsler* case, and certainly throughout the *Hirsch* era, the Jewish community was now politically united, at least on the School Question, more financially influential, and the time had come once again to assert the voice of solidarity. The Outremont law, which enshrined an agreement between the government and the Protestant trustees, circumvented any Jewish participation. The Jewish School Question in Outremont had apparently been settled without the Jews.[72] The statute provided for the admission of Jewish students to the Protestant schools but did not include any of the other religious liberty or free exercise provisions of the second *loi David* of 1931.

A public meeting took place on 1 May 1947 at the Beth David synagogue in Outremont. Among the speakers were prominent representatives of the Montreal Protestant ministries who supported the Outremont Jewish community's claims. Michael Garber again provided a trenchant summary of the history of the dispute since 1944 and urged the meeting to demand that the arrangement between the provincial secretary and the Protestant trustees include "our minimum

Bill of Rights" freely consented to by the boards of Montreal and Outremont in the original agreements.[73] While again expressing its thanks to the government for ensuring that any deficit in the cost of educating Jewish children would be met from the public purse, and that Jewish children could attend Outremont Protestant schools, the meeting again gave voice to the community's broader concerns. It asked for a new agreement that would incorporate the most important provisions of the 1931 deal on Jewish rights in Protestant schools, and the naming of a new Jewish School Commission to supervise the arrangement. The Jewish community sought once more to constitute itself formally and organizationally around a Jewish School Commission that would have the moral weight of unanimous sentiment among Outremont's Jews, and legal authority recognized in the 1931 statute. After all, the commission was a body of perpetual succession and had never ceased to exist.

The Jewish community insisted, again and still, on a return to the 1931 Act and its protections of Jewish religious observance and educational equality within the Protestant school system. It was joined to some extent by voices from within the Protestant community of Montreal that sought a more permanent solution in Outremont, and the implementation of a system that would mirror the relationship between Protestant school officials in that city and those on the other side of the mountain in Montreal. Garber wrote to Côté the next day, underlining once more the strength of Jewish, and growing Protestant, opinion on the matter.[74] Apparently, however, Garber had already received private assurances from the provincial secretary that any accord reached with the Outremont board would indeed contain guarantees of religious liberty and equality like those in the 1931 Act.[75] Once again, the Jewish School Question was going to be solved not by Jews, but by the government and the Protestant Board, with Jewish participation pushed into the legal and political background.[76] Nonetheless the Jewish political presence had made itself felt throughout the process. The penumbra of the agreement between the provincial government and the Protestant school trustees enshrined the "minimum Bill of Rights" on which the Outremont Jewish representatives had insisted. An agreement had been reached, often involving processes in the shadows of law and politics, and the Protestant Board and the government had achieved a happy compromise. While they were not parties to the contract, the Jews of Outremont were the substantive beneficiaries of the deal. Like that in Montreal proper, the Jewish School Question in Outremont had been resolved in the interstices of Quebec's dual denominational, constitutionally enshrined school system, in a place where Jews could and did insist on democracy, citizenship, and equality as essential and constitutive elements of their political educational struggles. If the 1832 emancipation statute was the Magna Carta of Quebec Jews, the arrangements enshrining their right to holy day absences and exemption from Protestant religious education formed the basis of their evolving educational Bill of Rights.

The Jewish School Question in Montreal: When a Solution Isn't a Solution

However, it was not long before the Jews of Outremont felt compelled once more to seek the assistance of the provincial secretary in their dealings with the Outremont Protestant School Board. This was simply the natural consequence of the political dynamic that had led to the 1947 solution of an agreement between the Protestant board and the government. The Jews were not a party to the accord, although they did derive direct and concrete benefits from its terms. But in a way it had been able to avoid under the 1931 Act, which enshrined a Jewish/Protestant understanding, the government was now directly implicated in all matters relating to the Jewish School Question in Outremont. In July, the Montreal Council of Orthodox Rabbis wrote to Omer Côté notifying him of the state of Jewish religious observance of holy days, because the Outremont school officials had apparently expressed some doubts on the matter. The rabbis explained that Jewish law prohibited children from attending school on such days. The religious authorities indicated that these holy days were identical to those incorporated in the 1931 agreement.[77]

The Protestant board of Montreal permitted the absence of Jewish students on these days, and the rabbis asked that the provincial government ensure that the Outremont school trustees do likewise. However, while instructing its principals to enrol Jewish students in unsegregated classrooms for the school year, the Outremont board was still insisting on entering into a formal written agreement that would limit excused absences to three days – two for Rosh Hashanah and one for Yom Kippur.[78] Absences for any other holy day would be granted by the board only if the majority of Outremont's Jewish parents made a specific written request for every such religious absence.[79] In a mess partly of its own making, the provincial government was now caught in the middle of a dispute between the Orthodox rabbinate and the dissentient Protestant trustees over religious questions surrounding holy day observance by Jewish students.[80] The Outremont committee had been satisfied with the provincial secretary's assurance that discrimination would not be tolerated, and with undertakings from the Protestant board about the end of separate Jewish and non-Jewish classes in Protestant schools. Together these promises were adequate substitutes for the inclusion of a non-segregation clause in the agreement itself, but Outremont's Jews were less accepting on the holy day issue.[81]

Garber again wrote to Côté, not just about the point of religious principle involved in Jewish student absence on holy days, but on specific events in Outremont's Protestant schools. Sukkot fell on 29 and 30 September, and again on 6 and 7 October. Teachers had apparently begun enforcing the agreement, as understood by the Protestant representatives but yet to be finalized by the provincial government, by telling Jewish students that they had to attend on those days under pain of losing marks or missing tests that might be scheduled. The delay between the start of the school year and the announcement of the new policy by the school principals governing arrangements for parental requests for absence on holy days such as Sukkot was too short to arrange for Jewish parents to comply with the Protestant proposal and request release for their children. Garber reminded Côté of the importance of these issues for the Jewish community, and that, given the assurances concerning non-segregation, the holy days were the last remaining roadblock to a five-year period of peace, as far as the Jewish school problem in Outremont was concerned.[82] Garber could not convince the provincial secretary, or the provincial secretary could not convince the Protestant trustees, on the question of holy days. The agreement between the government and the Protestant board of Outremont, which contained no mention of the hiring of Jewish teachers or of non-segregated classes, and which allowed for much more restricted holy day absences, was signed on 24 September 1947.[83] Newspaper reporting on the agreement incorrectly characterized it as one involving three parties, including the "Outremont's Jewish authorities."[84] Michael Garber quickly issued a statement correcting this error, insisting that only the government and Protestant board were signatories to the agreement. He also bemoaned the changes from the 1931 accord, which had been imposed over Jewish objections, and urged Jewish parents in Outremont to write immediately to the Protestant trustees requesting the excused absence of their children for Sukkot observance.[85] Jewish rights had been diminished as a result of an accord between the Duplessis government and the Protestant school trustees, but the Jewish community was still determined. It was united, organized, and resolute in pressing demands for recognition.

Of course, just as financial deficits in educating Jewish students, special tax panels, etc., had been a mere stalking horse for the real issues, which were Protestant anti-Semitic bias, and apparently profound existential doubt about their place and fate in a demographically changing Montreal and Quebec society, so was the Jewish holiday issue. In Outremont, the falling anglophone presence in the city and its schools combined with an increasing francophone, Roman Catholic presence and an expanding Jewish population. Anglophone Protestants in Outremont were falling under the irresistible pressure of social and political reality. In October the problem surfaced quickly once more as the Sukkot holidays approached.[86] The Outremont board was again digging in its heels, intimating that it might be wiling to grant no more than one more holiday, whatever parental requests it might receive under the terms of its new publicly announced policy. As they had in relation to segregated classes, the Protestant trustees indicated that, when it came down to Jewish school rights, they were more than willing to break their word.

"The Board expects Jewish children in future to attend school on holidays on which their parents do business."[87] Events now revealed the true nature of the Jewish School Question in the minds of the Protestant school trustees. Jewish perfidy was again causing trouble in the Protestant schools. The mere presence of Jewish students in the Protestant school system was disruptive, not just to good governance of the schools themselves, but the Protestant and Canadian character of those schools. By the claims themselves, Jews and other groups who sought recognition of their religious holy days in the school system attacked the dual confessionality at the core of Quebec education and of the compact of Confederation. The pretence that the issue had ever been really and fundamentally about money was as easily dismissed following the actions of the Protestant school officials, as was the notion that they had any real intention of ensuring the protection of Jewish religious rights within the Protestant school system.

Garber took the Jewish case to the general anglophone and largely Protestant public of Montreal, about what really happened in Outremont at Sukkot. Before the Jewish parents could comply with the requirement of the school trustees, imposed against their will and without their participation in negotiations, and issue a written request for excused absences, the board had presented all Jewish students with a letter urging them to attend school on the holidays, in violation of what many saw as fundamental obligations under Jewish law. In fact, no Jewish student went to school in Outremont on any of the holy days. The Protestant trustees had then presented the rabbis of the two Outremont synagogues with an ultimatum to preach to the parents that they had an obligation to send their children to school.[88] The message was unmistakable: Protestant schools did not permit absences on Jewish holidays, because they were Protestant schools. Moreover, as some comments from Protestant school officials indicated, the Jews were not only seeking special exemptions, but they were engaging in disruption that was typically devious. In Outremont in the 1940s, there could be no religious obligation incumbent on students to absent themselves from school if their parents felt free to work on the same day. The Protestants argument contained inescapable echoes of the arguments from ultramontane Roman Catholic anti-Semites in the 1920s and 1930s, when the *Ligue de Dimanche* led campaigns proclaiming that Jews were circumventing the Sunday closing law and abusing its religious exemption. That exemption was in place for observant Jews for whom Saturday was the Sabbath on which they were forbidden to work. Instead, according to the Roman Catholic argument, Jews simply worked seven days a week and cheated the system. Once more, the Jewish School Question was reduced to its core. Some Protestants did not like Jews, and they certainly did not like Jews in their school system. For the CJC, the school board in Outremont was not only violating the spirit and the letter of its agreement in relation to holy days, but despite its assurances to the contrary to the provincial secretary, it was also beginning once more to segregate Jewish students within the city's Protestant schools.[89]

But the heat of the matter eventually died down as the board changed its practices to bring them into conformity with the deal reached with the government. The plenary session of the 1949 meeting of the CJC would hear that "the committee which was charged with the Outremont school question has succeeded in stabilising the situation."[90] The Jewish School Question in Outremont had been resolved to the reasonable satisfaction of the Jewish community, thanks to the support and interventions not just of the provincial government, more particularly the premier and the provincial secretary, but to a number of Protestant clergy and theologians who had interceded on their behalf.[91] Indeed throughout the long history of the Jewish School Question in Outremont, Protestant bodies and associations had sought to intervene to temper the revanchist trustees and to propose their offices as both informal and formal intermediaries between the school officials and the Jews of the city.

In addition to maintaining its contact with the provincial government in the hope of arranging an acceptable, more long-lasting settlement, the CJC had sought the assistance of the Protestant Central School Board of Montreal, asking them to "do all in your power both financially and morally, to help find a solution for this vexing problem."[92] Early in the controversy, the Notre Dame Branch of the YMCA of Montreal wrote to Michael Garber and gave voice to an argument that echoed the position of Baron de Hirsch supporters at the turn of the century. Education was for citizenship, the letter said, and all citizens were equal. The practices of the Protestant trustees in Outremont were inconsistent with this principle, with democratic freedom, and with Christian values.[93] The Canadian Legion supported the Jewish students and condemned the Outremont board's actions in terms of some contemporary relevance. The Legion characterized the Protestant actions as "negating the very principles for which many hundreds and thousands of our Comrades have fought and died."[94] The Legion did not point out that those principles were in fact enshrined in the provisions of section 93 of the BNA Act, but their broader point – that the question of Jewish children in the schools of Outremont and Montreal posed fundamental challenges, as the Jewish community had always insisted, to Canadians' understandings of, and commitment to, equality for all citizens – was clearly taken and had broad resonance among the anglophone community in Montreal.

A prominent citizen of Outremont would later refuse to accept a nomination as a school trustee because there was a manifest divergence between the current representatives' version of Protestant, Christian principles and values and his own.[95] The Anglican Synod had clearly pointed the finger at the Outremont trustees when it condemned racial discrimination as "utterly at variance with Christian principles and productive of hatred and strife."[96] The Protestant trustees did not speak as the univocal representatives of Protestantism in the school system, in Montreal or Outremont, but they, like the Protestant commissioners in Montreal in the era of the Commission of Nine, had managed to frustrate attempts for direct discussions, rejecting overtures from the Anglican Church, the Montreal Council of Women, and the Federation of Home and School Associations to serve as intermediaries between them and the Jewish community's representatives. They had maintained their refusal to meet directly with Jewish representatives throughout the Jewish School Question.[97] But the presence of other Protestant voices eventually had an impact in Outremont and perhaps as importantly in Quebec City.

The eventual solution was also made possible because the levying, collection, and distribution of school taxes in Outremont had been placed in the hands of the Protestant Central School Board of Montreal. The influence of the central board, which enjoyed much more harmonious relations with the Jewish community and had renewed the 1931 agreement without difficulty, appears historically to have calmed the Protestant school officials of Outremont.[98] Moreover, the vexing problem of financial support for the Protestant schools of Outremont had been dealt with through this mechanism. While the Protestant board had struggled for years to convince city officials to raise its valuations on property, on which school taxes were based, the municipality of Outremont and certain Jewish taxpayers had always resisted any such politically unpopular move. Now the valuation and assessment of properties for school tax purposes had been depoliticized, and the trustees had no further reason to invoke financial penury.[99] As MacLeod and Poutanen point out, once a vague sense of normality returned to the Protestant school system, the trustees relaxed their views and policies. Without admitting that the practice allowed for the observance of the Jewish Sabbath, for example, they moved school dances from Friday to Saturday nights.

The constitutive arrangements that brought about reasonable peace and harmony in Outremont had been achieved through the intercession of a provincial government, which in reality had nothing to gain in a direct political or electoral sense from assisting the Jewish community who continued to vote for their political rivals, together with the voices of strong dissent from Protestant churches and lay organizations. The CJC and the Jewish parents were not alone in their battle to maintain the status quo by ensuring the continuing presence of Jewish students in Outremont's Protestant schools. Just as Protestant opinion had been divided in the early 1920s between the Montreal School Board and the Provincial Protestant Committee of the Council of Public Education, other political forces had voiced their opposition to the Outremont trustees' actions throughout this iteration of the Jewish School Question.

It is still worth underlining that during the whole process, unlike the various instances of the Jewish School Question in Montreal itself, the two principal parties, the Jewish community and the Protestant School Board, had almost no direct contact. Negotiations, compromise, and agreement had taken place between the government and the trustees, who proved to be particularly recalcitrant in accepting any intercession from outsiders, including the parents of the Jewish students who were subjected to segregation, and the looming threat of expulsion from the Protestant schools. Two sides were implicated directly in the Jewish School Question in Outremont, and they moved in parallel lines. The constitutive arrangements over schooling for Jewish students in Outremont had been concretized by interaction, dialogue, compromise, political pressure, and appeals to equity, fairness, and democracy, but the two parties whose identities were being constructed and institutionalized never met.

In Outremont, the Jewish School Question would be replaced in the city's political world, by a broader issue: the democratic power of an increasing Jewish electorate.[100] For many years, the Jews of Outremont had supported anglophone Protestant candidates for the municipal council. The time had come for Jews to be represented by Jewish councillors.[101] Of course, as in Montreal, Jews were free to participate in the electoral process and to take their seats in local government. However, they could not become trustees of the Protestant School Board. Section 93 and the *Hirsch* case had seen to that and had confirmed the status of Jews as non-participants in the governance of school systems in which their children were being educated, for the most part. They had political, economic, and social equality, and they remained blocked from school equality. Nevertheless, the Constitution on the School Question was no friend to Outremont's or Montreal's Jews.

12

Hampstead and Beyond: From the Ghetto to Citizenship and Equality under Law's Shadow

Democracy, Law, and Education: The Jewish School Question That Won't Go Away

This chapter sets out the details of eruptions of the Jewish School Question from the 1940s onwards. More centrally, it examines the details of the impact that increasing Jewish residential mobility, combined with broader social and political changes in Quebec, had on the number of claims to full democratic equality for Jewish taxpayers. As the Quebec and Canadian economies boomed in wartime and thereafter, Jews gradually climbed the socio-economic ladder in Montreal. The move westward from the ghetto had begun with the Jewish settlement in Outremont. Now demand for new suburban housing for growing and prosperous Jewish families created further mobility across the Island of Montreal and beyond, often into areas originally settled by Protestant anglophones and therefore with established Protestant school systems.

This led to a series of clashes at both the practical and juridical levels. Jewish parents sought to send their children to Protestant schools, a number of which had a degree of independence from the Protestant School Board of Montreal because of their historical geographical situation outside city limits and because many had a peculiar and particular legal basis, as so-called Order-in-Council schools. The discussion that follows details the legal and political debates about the nature and legal status of Protestant schools in these suburbs, more specifically in light of two claims made by Jewish parents and taxpayers about the nature and extent of their rights in the educational domain. The first set of issues surrounds the arguments about the rights of Jewish children to an education in Protestant schools outside the strict geographical and juridical limits of the City of Montreal and details the legacies of changes to the education statutes following the compromises in the early 1930s. The second series of debates and controversies arose in a context in which Jewish taxpayers insisted on the right to vote in school board elections and to stand for election as school trustees or commissioners. The issue of rights of representation had been at the heart of the Jewish School Question in the 1920s and early 1930s in Montreal. At the political level, the result had been the defeat of any attempt to establish a Jewish school system, and as a legal matter of any claim that Jews could sit on the Protestant School Board. Outside the city limits, however, a different situation appeared to exist, as, like those elsewhere in the province, school boards were elected rather than appointed. The narrative that unfolds then is not just one about Jewish democratic rights or the substantive content that had to be given to the "honorary Protestant" taxonomy; it is equally informed by the changes in Quebec society and politics being wrought in the Quiet Revolution. However tentatively and incrementally, Quebec society was beginning to throw off the hegemony of the Roman Catholic Church and to assert and proclaim the values of electoral and representative democracy. As usual, the chapter underscores the contextual nature of a Jewish School Question and of the centrality of non-Jewish actors and institutions in all significant debates under the general rubric of the Jewish School Question.

Framing the Jewish School Question inside and outside the Law

Following the settlement of the Jewish School Question, with the statutes of 1930 and 1931, the Protestant Central School Board of Montreal, now acting with greater financial resources and greater certainty of its tax base and its legal obligations, had turned its mind to the infrastructure of the Protestant school system.[1] "Now that the Jewish question may be considered as settled for some time to come, the Central Board could no longer delay the large building programme that has been accumulating during the last few years and hastened to relieve the situation in districts, where it has become severe."[2]

As part of this program, it had approved the addition of new classrooms at the Strathcona Academy and Guy Drummond School in Outremont. In the suburb of Hampstead, situated farther to the west and attracting a growing population, it approved the completion of the top story of the school begun in 1928. The decade of the 1930s, with its rising anti-Semitism in Montreal, brought with it many trials for the Jewish community, but for the most part, the School Question had entered a period of relative calm in the city's Protestant schools. An occasional legal issue would arise, particularly for isolated Jewish families outside the city limits, but generally speaking, the problems of access to education for the vast majority of Quebec's Jews in Montreal had been resolved. In the rest of the province, the 1941 revised version of the Education Act had enshrined the 1931 Act, and the consequent arrangements, which would later resurface in Outremont. The statutory scheme in the rest of the province outside the boundaries of the City of Montreal and Quebec City resorted to the 1903 formulation under which "any provision to the contrary notwithstanding, in every municipality of the province, whether governed, as regards schools, by this act or by a special act, or by this act and a special act, the Jewish religion shall, for school purposes, be treated in the same manner as Protestants, and for such purposes, shall be subject to the same obligations and shall enjoy the same rights and privileges."[3]

The next section of the statute then provided, "In every municipality in the Province, persons professing the Jewish religion shall pay their school taxes to or for the benefit of the school corporation in such municipality which is under the control of the Protestant Committee of the Council of Public Education, and if there be no such corporation, then to the sole corporation existing therein" (section 585).

The other provisions of Part X of the statute dealing with "Education as Regards Persons Professing the Jewish Faith" required Jewish property entered in the neutral tax panel to be moved, as matter of law, into the Protestant panel (which would be subject to subsequent changes) (sections 586–7), and granted the attendance rights and exemptions from religious instruction to Jewish children in language duplicating the 1903 Act (sections 588–9). In 1941, the Protestant Committee of Public Education received a request for clarification of the position on the case of a lone Jewish taxpayer in a rural municipality. That taxpayer had paid taxes into the Protestant panel but sought to transfer them into the Roman Catholic, majority panel, when the rate of taxation in the Protestant panel exceeded that of the majority.[4] Again this was a common case in rural communities with small Protestant minorities. In order to support their schools from a much smaller tax base, and without being able to rely on the wealth of a majority, quasi-monopolistic church, dissentient Protestant boards had to impose a higher rate of taxation on their property owners. W.P. Percival replied by citing the provisions of the Education Act compelling Jewish taxpayers to place their taxes in the Protestant panel, where such a panel existed.[5]

Several points of interest and importance arise from this brief correspondence. First, after the *Hirsch* opinion from the Privy Council, it was quite clear that any situation in which Jews were assimilated to Protestants in rural municipalities with dissentient schools was almost certainly unconstitutional.[6] While Jewish students had the right to attend either Roman Catholic or Protestant schools in Montreal and Quebec City because these were common non-denominational/denominational institutions at law, in rural communities the Privy Council had been clear that Jews could not attend minority Protestant schools as of right because such a legally imposed arrangement would interfere with the absolute autonomy of dissentient schools guaranteed in section 93 of the BNA Act. Yet the Quebec legislature and the Protestant school authorities had simply chosen to ignore this constitutional barrier by including the 1903 guarantees in the Education Act and extending their application to the whole province. Once again, while the Constitution provided some kind of hermeneutic horizon and formal legal framework, to be invoked and asserted as the case might have been, in practice, accommodation, compromise, and practicality dominated the real-life constitutive practices for members of the Jewish (and Protestant) communities in large parts of the province.

The second point was that Jews were granted school equality with Protestants insofar as rights to attend schools were concerned and were also afforded a large degree of religious liberty, when Jewish students were freed from religious instruction. The Privy Council in *Hirsch* had concretized these two rights in common schools.[7] Like the Supreme Court, the Privy Council had confirmed in broad terms that Jewish students had the right to receive a secular education in the common schools of the province. Again, the legislation dealing with schooling outside Montreal and Quebec City imposed obligations upon, and interfered with, the autonomous self-government of Protestant dissentient school trustees, not just by compelling them to allow Jewish students to attend their schools, but by making room for statutorily imposed exceptions for a class of students, religiously defined, from the compulsory religious instruction that had always been an essential and defining element of Protestant education for many Protestants. Again, these provisions of the provincial legislation were striking in their obvious unconstitutionality. Religious liberty for Jews in such Protestant schools could not really ever be possible, as a matter of law, since, after *Hirsch*, Jewish students had no rights at all in relation to Protestant (or indeed Roman Catholic) dissentient schools. Throughout the province, the presence of Jewish students in dissentient schools was a question within the Christian grace of trustees.[8] No provincial legislation could interfere with the absolute right of dissentient school trustees to decide whether those not belonging to the dissentient faith, Roman Catholic or Protestant, could attend their schools, without clearly violating the constitutionally enshrined protections of section 93. A dissentient school was one formed by a religious minority, most often, but not always Protestant, which sought a school system that would provide an education for their children according to the tenets of their faith. By definition and at its very core, it was denominational statutorily and existentially. There was no clearer case of the rights of a "class of persons" falling under the protections of section 93.

The third point that is also of some interest, as a matter of legal principle and of some importance in the events which that later unfold in the Jewish School Question in Hampstead and other Montreal suburbs, was the position of the Jewish taxpayer in municipalities with a Roman Catholic common school and a Protestant dissentient establishment. Under the provisions of the 1941 Act, as a matter of law, such a taxpayer was compelled to pay into the Protestant tax panel. In effect, assuming that this specific provision overcame and trumped any general provision of the statute, this meant that Jewish taxpayers actually had fewer legal rights than their Protestant counterparts. As a matter of law, Protestant ratepayers could always renounce their dissent and enter the common, majority school system. If and when they exercised this option, their school taxes followed them to the common school panel. On this reading of the statute, advanced by Percival, Jewish real estate proprietors could not. They were compelled to be Protestants, in the name of equality, but they did not enjoy the same freedoms as Protestants to accede to the majority. While few would have wanted to do so, it was not unheard of, even in Montreal, for Jewish parents to send their children to Roman Catholic schools, and for Roman Catholics to send their children to Protestant schools. In rural areas of the province, with population changes, small Protestant communities could unite into a single school municipality, but this might mean that the dissentient school was some distance from the homes of many children, and particularly in winter, travel could become extremely difficult, if not impossible. In such cases, dissentient Protestants could renounce their dissent by following the provisions of the statute, pay their taxes into the common school system, and send their children to the common school. The inequality, which was imposed upon Jews in this section of the provincial education statute, and which was meant to ensure their broader educational equality, is intriguing. Moreover, under this interpretation, it deprived Jews of the right, recognized in *Hirsch*, to attend most of the common schools of the province outside Montreal and Quebec City. By compelling Jews to be Protestants for school purposes, the Quebec legislature violated both the autonomy of Protestant dissentient schools and the basic legal right of Jews to attend common schools. Also, as in the case with which Percival had to deal in 1941, it compelled Jewish taxpayers to pay a higher rate of tax to a school board where, under *Hirsch*, they had neither a right to representation nor indeed a constitutional right to send their children.

Such were the legal and social consequences of a constitutional legal system, which, at one and the same time, imposed juridical limits on Jewish autonomy and ignored positive constitutive Jewish educational possibilities after *Hirsch*. Constitutional meaning in the broader sense, constitutive hermeneutics of understandings, compromise, and arrangement took place in Quebec in a legal framework of compulsory unconstitutionality, to which all but an occasional recalcitrant taxpayer gave their accord and consent. The government by legislating, the Protestant Committee of the Council of Public Education by insisting, Protestant trustees and Jewish citizens by complying, and the Roman Catholic population and school commissioners, by leaving the others to get on with it, all participated in a complex narration of the Jewish School Question that set the tales of power and resistance outside the strict legal, normative framework of section 93 and *Hirsch*, as they had in Ste Sophie and La Macaza, with their Protestant Jewish schools. However, all such narratives, whether inscribed formally within law or practised informally in law's shadow, were always necessarily fragile and contingent at their core. Ironically, perhaps, a combination of a Protestant regression to an insistence on strict adherence to section 93, and the Jewish struggle for equality, for a full participation in the democratic governance of their lives and their children's education, would, as it had in the 1920s, once again upset this constitutive arrangement under which Jews were honorary, but never fully fledged Protestants for school purposes. A new/old hermeneutic of justice and equality for

Jews would compete with Protestant constitutionally and legislatively guaranteed rights in the narrative and constitutional debates of the Jewish School Question in Hampstead and in other Montreal suburbs. Once again, broad and deeply embedded values of political and social equality would clash with the constitutive and constitutional barriers to full educational equality.

Geography, Demography, and Democracy: The Jewish School Question in Hampstead

Situated just to the west of Mount Royal and Montreal, for many years Hampstead had been a rural idyll in easy reach of the centre of the city. An anglophone, Protestant enclave, after the consolidations in the Montreal school governance arrangements flowing from the Commission of Nine, it had fallen under the broad administrative and financial jurisdiction of the Protestant Central School Board but remained a separate school municipality with its own local board.[9] In 1939, Louis Rosenberg's study of Jewish populations in Canada indicated that the satellite town of Hampstead had no Jewish residents.[10] Rosenberg would later report that Jewish prosperity and migration to the west of the traditional settlement in the ghetto, and indeed beyond the original westward migration to Outremont, meant that the numbers of Jewish students in Hampstead schools had risen from zero in 1940–51, to 58 in 1953, and to 195 out of 320 students by 1962.[11]

As early as 1949, parents in Hampstead were complaining to the CJC that the Hampstead elementary school was refusing to admit Jewish students. The principal of the school was interviewed by a representative of B'nai Brith and stated that the school policy was not to admit Jews or Roman Catholics. While acknowledging that there were in fact three Roman Catholic students in his school, the principal advised the B'nai Brith investigator that the policy would remain unchanged for Jewish pupils.[12]

The broader CJC Joint Public Relations Committee, which took carriage of the issue at this time, decided that instead of waiting to mount a legal challenge via a test case, the most efficacious path was to contact the Montreal Central Protestant School Board and notify them of the principal's statement of his school's policy.[13] At the same time, the CJC offices carried out a review of the situation in Hampstead and in surrounding suburbs with small, but growing Jewish populations. Their information revealed that thirty Jews attended Protestant schools in

Verdun, twelve in Lachine, and ten in the Town of Mount Royal (TMR). Jews paid taxes into the Protestant panel in those municipalities. Each of these schools appeared to fall under the provisions of section 576 of the Education Act, which gave Jews equal rights to attend Protestant schools. The reason that Jewish students were attending Protestant schools in Lachine, Verdun, and TMR, and not in Hampstead, given the presence of at least fifty-six Jews in that suburb, could be attributed only to a discriminatory policy operated by the school there and confirmed by the principal.[14]

The problem of the law and the politics of the Jewish School Question since the 1931 Act, the agreement, and the continuing renewal of the contract allowing Jewish students to attend Protestant Schools in Montreal rose to the surface. Section 589 of the consolidated 1941 Education Act made it clear that the provisions of Part X relating to Jewish educational rights did not apply "to the territory under the jurisdiction of the Montreal Protestant Central School Board." Technically, this was the area covered by the 1931 Act and the associated agreement. A special regime governed by the limits imposed by the *Hirsch* decision and the continuing contractual arrangements operated. For many administrative and financial purposes, as had been the primary aim and goal of the amendments to school structure coming from the Protestant members of the Commission of Nine, Hampstead did fall under the jurisdiction of the Central Board, but for other purposes it retained a degree of autonomy, as had the Outremont School Board. The situation as far as the law was concerned was therefore unclear for the CJC.[15] Indeed, the case was more complex than even they believed. They were aware of the possible legal argument that if Hampstead fell under the broad and general ambit of the Central Board, they would be bound by the ongoing arrangements in relation to the education of Jewish children in Montreal, even if they had been incorporated into the Central Board after the arrangements had been entered into. If they fell outside the ambit of the Central Board and retained a higher degree of autonomy, the general provisions of Part X of the Act applied to them, and the Jewish children also had the right to attend the Protestant schools of the municipality. If the legal provisions excluded them from both the agreement and the provisions of Part X of the Act – because they had not been a party to the original agreement concerning Jewish education or its renewals, or because the agreements had originally not been with the Central Board, but with the Boards of Protestant School Commissioners in Montreal and Outremont – then the provisions of section 589 would lead to the apparently absurd position that Jews in Hampstead had no rights under either Part X to be treated as Protestants for school purposes, or pursuant to the agreement with the Montreal educational authorities to attend Protestant schools. Finally of course, in an option that the CJC did not consider at the time, if Part X, were to be applied to Hampstead, depending on the history of the Protestant Board there, it might be unconstitutional.

Following still more complaints about the exclusion of Jewish children from the Hampstead school, CJC representatives met with the Protestant Central School Board to seek their advice and intervention.[16] When CJC investigations revealed that many children actually attending the Hampstead Protestant School were the children of non-residents, and one was a Roman Catholic, Louis Rosenberg stated that there could therefore be no justification for the exclusion of Jewish students whose parents lived in Hampstead and paid their taxes into the Protestant panel.[17] However, his conclusion was legally shaky. It seemed clear that the board allowed non-residents and non-Protestants to enrol. The only reason to keep out Jewish residents was because they were Jewish. But if the Protestant Board in Hampstead were dissentient, following *Hirsch*, Jewish students could be excluded without any further justification than the arbitrary decisions of the trustees. Again, if the school were dissentient, the provisions of the law under which the Jews were compelled to pay taxes to the Protestant panel were themselves liable to legal challenge. If the school was a common school, then Jewish students had a right to attend. The legal solution to the Jewish School Question in Hampstead at this point demanded a careful analysis of the history of Protestant education in that municipality, and a detailed study of the statutory provisions governing schooling there.

The CJC was informed that a Jewish entrepreneur was building a number of new homes and duplexes to meet the growing demand in Hampstead for Jewish housing. The builder, Mr Mensher, told the CJC officials that he intended to bring 72 Jewish families to Hampstead that year, to be followed by more in subsequent years, to a total of 200 new Jewish families. While he was anxious not to upset the municipal authorities, he had spoken to the principal of the school, who had insisted that the school was "parochial."[18] Now faced with the prospect of a significant influx of Jewish families, many of whom would have school-aged children and who would pay their taxes into the Protestant school panel, either under the provisions of Part X of the Education Act, or under the arrangements in place under the supervision of the Protestant Central School Board, the school officials in Hampstead and the Jewish community represented by the CJC were at a political, social, and jurisprudential impasse.

In 1924, the Protestant schoolchildren of Hampstead had no school of their own and attended the Roman Catholic School in neighbouring Côte Saint-Luc. This arrangement proved to be unsatisfactory for all parties, and the Protestant community undertook a fundraising campaign to build their own school. They had obtained a charter via Order in Council for a school to be erected, and a school municipality created, for Protestants only.[19] In all other circumstances, as the only school in a separate school community, Hampstead school would have been common, and as such, non-denominational by law. But the Order in Council establishing the Hampstead school district erected a school for Protestants only, a status normally attributed to dissentient minority establishments. Under one view, these schools were neither common schools nor dissentient, but sui generis and of a type not considered in terms of Jewish educational rights by any court. Authority on the point was scarce. In 1896, the Superior Court had ruled that the legal effect of the creation of such a school municipality for Protestants only was plain and simple. After the Order in Council took effect, there were two separate and distinct school commissions in the old single municipality. A new municipality for school purposes was created by Order in Council in which school commissioners acted for the identified Protestant residents. No declaration of dissent was required, since the new municipality had no legal relationship with the former municipality or its school commissioners.[20] That such a school was not dissentient was also evidenced by the nomenclature of governance, since it was administered not by trustees, but by commissioners.

While some in the Protestant community of Hampstead were willing, in theory, to countenance the admission of non-Protestants to their school and were keen to avoid conflict and negative publicity, at the same time they insisted that in order to do so, they had to be assured that the Order-in-Council Charter would permit them to admit non-Protestant students, or that it could be modified. In other words, the Protestants of Hampstead were standing on their ultimate legal rights, or on one version of the Order-in-Council school under Quebec law, insisting that by law the school system was Protestant and more specifically that it had been erected for Protestants only. Any dialogue or discussion that might take place could occur for them only in a narrative context bound by their legally enshrined rights. Given the turn to legality, the CJC consulted their own lawyer.[21] In the meantime, the CJC also continued to engage in other modes of dialogue and the narrative constitution of Jewish school rights in the Protestant municipality of Hampstead. They contacted the Protestant Committee of the Council of Public Education and the principal of the Hampstead School, seeking firm and official information about policy and practice in Hampstead.[22] Again, multiple parties with different interests were being pulled into complex political, pedagogical, theological, and legal debates simply because taxpaying Jewish parents wanted to send their children to the schools where they lived.

Harold Newman's legal opinion for the CJC confirmed the basic historical facts about the Hampstead School. It had been created by Order in Council in 1924, pursuant to the provisions of section 72 of the Revised Statutes, which granted to the government (the lieutenant governor in council) the power to erect new school municipalities for Roman Catholics or Protestants only.[23] He then offered the perhaps problematic view that these provisions of the province's educational statutes were "merely another application of the principle that our educational system recognizes only two groups, the Roman Catholics and the Protestants."[24] As far as a general description of the statutory and political framework of Quebec education is concerned, Newman's view was sound. However, he neglected to mention that the control of one of the two groups over the schools in a municipality where there are common and dissentient schools was considered to be a de facto matter as far as the common school was concerned, and not a legal one. As the Privy Council and the Supreme Court of Canada had emphasized in *Hirsch*, only the dissentient school in such cases was properly denominational and protected by section 93. The common school, which in most, but not all cases in Quebec would be controlled by the Roman Catholic majority, would not be a protected Roman Catholic school in the same sense. It would be, legally speaking, most significantly a common school. In this case, it would appear that the existing school municipality from which the Hampstead municipality and its Protestant population had split, Côte Saint-Luc, continued to operate as a common school, de facto under the control of the Roman Catholic population. One consequence of such a situation, it would be argued, would be that, for any Roman Catholics who found themselves resident in the new school municipality of Hampstead, the creation of that municipality for Protestants only would mean that, for school purposes, they continued to be residents of Côte Saint-Luc. In theory, such an interpretation of the Education Act provisions relating to Order-in-Council schools would mean that Roman Catholic minorities would have no need, and probably no right, to dissent. At the same time, it could also mean that Jewish residents of Hampstead also remained, for school purposes, residents of Côte Saint-Luc, with the legal right to attend the common school there, but no right to attend the Protestant school in Hampstead. Only the specific Jewish provisions of the Education Act or, more tenuously, the continuing 1931 agreements, might give them access to Protestant education.

Newman argued that the municipality of Hampstead was a rural municipality, since it fell outside the borders of the City of Montreal. In such communities, under *Hirsch*, Jewish students had the right to attend common, but not dissentient schools. Newman then asserted that the school law of the province dealt only with common and dissentient schools. The erection of a separate school for Protestants alone had the effect of eliminating dissent, although none had ever existed in Hampstead, and of creating a new common school, under the jurisdiction of commissioners.[25] Order-in-Council schools, on Newman's reading of the law, were not dissentient schools, nor would they really be considered as denominational after *Hirsch*, even though erected here for Protestants only, because, by their monopoly over education in a rural area, they became common schools. In this view, Jewish children had a right to attend Hampstead School, and the school commissioners could not refuse their admission.[26]

Newman's legal advice elides one important point about the nature of Order-in-Council schools. They were created under a mechanism that established a new, independent school municipality, separate as a matter of law from the former school municipality. The standard interpretation seemed to have been that there was no legal relationship between the two, and that therefore no declaration of dissent was required. There was no religious majority and minority situation as contemplated by the normal operation of Quebec school law. At the same time, the predominant view was also that when the Order in Council created a new school municipality for Protestants only, the Roman Catholic population was unaffected by the transformation – again they remained residents of the original school municipality that had been bisected for Protestants. This would mean, in effect, that they would continue to pay their taxes and send their children to the existing common school in Côte Saint-Luc. Therefore, they could not establish a dissentient Roman Catholic school in Hampstead, because that school municipality existed only as a school municipality for Protestants. Likewise, it also meant that one key element essential to rural common schools under the provincial statutory regime, and after the Privy Council's advice in *Hirsch*, could never apply to the Order-in-Council school in Hampstead. The only students who could attend the Protestant school in Hampstead, as of right, were Protestants. Roman Catholic students did not live in the school municipality as a matter of law. Jewish students who might have lived in Hampstead could attend only if the school were a common one, or if more broadly, the provisions of Part X of the Education Act could be said to apply to the rural school. The proper legal classification was still a legally murky legal area as Jews moved in significant numbers into Hampstead. Once more in the histories of the Jewish School Question, demographic change would drive legal controversy. Meanwhile, the CJC was growing increasingly frustrated with its inability to extract a straight answer from the Hampstead Commission. It sought further legal advice from another prominent Montreal lawyer, Émilien Brais, CR.[27]

Brais began his opinion by making clear that, perhaps unlike Newman, he had seized the difference after *Hirsch* among schools that were denominational de jure because they were dissentient, schools that were de facto denominational but de jure common schools in rural areas, and schools in Montreal that were both denominational and common.[28] He then indicated that the crucial question, upon which the matter would ultimately depend, was a firm historical determination of the situation that had obtained over the territory of Hampstead at the time of Confederation. He reviewed the legislative history of Hampstead that had been created by statute in 1914, detaching it from Côte Saint-Luc, which had itself previously been detached from Notre-Dame-de-Grâces, each of which was a rural municipality for purposes of the legislation relating to schools. At the time of the creation of Hampstead, no dissentient Protestant board existed in Côte Saint-Luc.

After reviewing the legislation, the rights of dissentient groups to establish schools different from those of the religious majority, and the changes that operated where the majority/minority relationship within a given municipality was reversed, Brais concluded that the overall effect of these provisions and the history of the various divisions of the municipal structure in this part of Montreal was to allow dissentient schools to seek a change in their status by requesting the creation of a new municipality by Order in Council. When this happened, they opted to shift from being a dissentient school governed by trustees within a municipality in which the majority had a school system run by commissioners, to a common one governed by commissioners. Yet, Brais' position became significantly less clear after this. At the time when the municipality of Hampstead was created in 1924, following the separation from Côte Saint-Luc, the Protestants of that town could simply have constituted themselves as a dissentient school within the still existing municipal school limits of Côte Saint-Luc. But they did not form a dissentient school. Instead they opted to establish a new school municipality for Protestants only, administered by school commissioners, under the Order-in-Council mechanism. However, under Brais' somewhat problematic analysis, that had been sufficient to constitute the Hampstead school as a common school for the newly created municipality. The erection of a new school municipality could not be viewed as the creation of a sui generis third type of school in the province, because nothing in the law of education could be found to support that view. In those cases where the situation obtained, the effect of such a new municipality was to eliminate the dissentient status of the former minority, which now became the majority in the newly created school municipality. Brais read the denominational characterization, for Protestants only, as simply being an indication that the change to a new school municipality did not affect the rights or status of Roman Catholics, for whom the old school boundary remained in effect. With this reading, the Hampstead School had always been a rural school and a common school. As a matter of law, then, the commissioners of Hampstead School had no right to exclude Jewish students.

The Hampstead Board of School Commissioners, faced with objections and opposition from the CJC, and increasingly from parts of the broader Protestant community as well, was forced to act.[29] At its meeting of 7 December 1951, it adopted the following resolution: "That the policy of the present Board of Hampstead School Commissioners is to approve application by any resident of Hampstead for admission of his or her child or children to study in Hampstead School, subject to the availability of space in the class rooms and to geographic location within the Greater Montreal Protestant School System."[30]

Some members of the board admitted that this constituted a reversal of their previous policy – in other words that there had been an exclusionary practice towards Jewish students – while others offered no comment on that issue.[31] The CJC kept a watching brief on the matter. It could report in September 1952 that local parents in Hampstead had received notices from the school board that their children would be admitted to the schools. "The issue, therefore, seems to be terminated."[32] The Jewish School Question in Hampstead had been settled through the application of steady moral and political pressure by the CJC, and local Jewish residents, as well as through the involvement of other voices within the broader Montreal Protestant community, to bring moral suasion to bear on the local school commissioners. Legal arguments had been mustered to buttress the political and social dynamics in the municipality of Hampstead, but the actual juridical limits of the Order-in-Council schools remained unclear. The demographic reality of an increasing Jewish presence in the town, and the obvious and growing importance of Jewish taxes also contributed to a solution, which again had left open the legal questions of Jewish educational rights, in favour of community self-constitution, by both Protestants and Jews in Hampstead, through political action, in the shadow of legality.

The Jewish community in Hampstead – through concerted action and with the occasional assistance of some elements in the Protestant education hierarchy of Montreal, and the province, and with the threat of litigation – had brought the matter to an end.[33] Doubt, frustration, anger, and law had hung over the issue of Jewish students in the Protestant school of Hampstead for over two years. The CJC and Hampstead's Jewish community had managed, as had their predecessors in Montreal, Outremont, Ste Sophie, and La Macaza, to get their children an education within the schools of the Protestant/Roman Catholic duopoly of Quebec education. Political action, lobbying, discussions, and legal threats had again proved an apparently effective political and pragmatic combination, as Jews attempted to carve out a place for themselves as self-constituting and equal citizens, within the constitutional and broader constitutive structures of a society, and a legal system that seemed designed to thwart their modest ambition of educating their children in the public schools of the province.

Unsurprisingly, the Jewish School Question was not terminated or "settled completely."[34] It simply took another form, in Hampstead and in other Montreal suburbs with growing Jewish populations.

School Elections, Voting Rights, and the Jewish School Question

The question of the admission of Jewish students to Protestant schools in the greater Montreal area had largely been settled. Through a combination of legal authority grounded in section 93 of the BNA Act, as interpreted by the *Hirsch* opinion, the compromises and refusals flowing from the 1930 and 1931 iterations of the *lois David*, arrangements, contracts, further government intervention by legislation and by contract, the threat of further litigation, and shifts in Protestant public opinion, from Montreal, to Outremont, to Hampstead, Jewish communities had been able to construct for themselves, but always in conjunction with the other key players in the hermeneutic process of constituting Quebec, a place in the educational system of common and dissentient schools, still and always dominated by the dual denominational, two founding peoples paradigm, and perhaps also always in a situation of questionable formal legality.

By 1960, Quebec had experienced significant social and economic change and was on the cusp of undergoing even more fundamental transitions. As the Quiet Revolution took hold and spread, the province began to experience a decline in clerical influence over many aspects of life, including education.[35] This transformation was accompanied socially and politically by a changing set of understandings over what democracy meant, and how those meanings and new social mores were to be translated into concrete practice and normativity.[36] One of the areas in which the question of the normative limits of Quebec's struggle for democracy in a modern, industrialized world was the question of Jewish representation in the formal governance structures of the education system. In parts of Montreal, Jewish students comprised the clear majority in Protestant schools. According to the Finance Department of the City of Montreal, by February 1961, Jewish property valuations totalled $402,659,710, while Protestant school tax property values were $145,808,560. For school taxes collected, this translated to $4,337,657 for Jewish taxpayers and $1,603,997 for Protestants. Demographic and geographic movements in populations within the city explain part of this shift. Other aspects of the explanation also lie in the increased economic prosperity of Jewish Montrealers, as the newer generations achieved social and financial success in business and the professions, due no doubt in significant part to the educational advantages of being classified as "honorary Protestants" and benefiting from the pedagogy of the Protestant school system. In the end, the most important point was that at this time, Jewish taxpayers contributed to the Protestant school system at a rate of almost four-to-one in relation to Protestant citizens, but they remained unrepresented on the Protestant School Board of Greater Montreal (PSBGM), or the Council of Public Education, which remained resolutely denominational bodies.

In 1961, the CJC Committee on the Position of Jews in the Educational System of the Province of Quebec adopted a resolution to take all necessary measures to ensure that this "conflict with the basis and accepted principles of democracy" would come to an end.[37] At this historical point, they had not only the weight of student numbers within the Protestant school system in the city and surrounding suburbs, but also the strength of the financial contribution that Jewish taxpayers were now making to the Protestant schools of the city and greater Montreal. The calls for democratic representation for Jews in the 1920s and 1930s had been met not just with objections about the essentially Protestant character of the schools, but also with the financial-burden argument about the costs of educating Jewish students. Protestant education officials had consistently played the deficit and cross-subsidy cards when faced with Jewish claims to equality and representation. The cost of educating Jewish students caused undue hardship to Protestant taxpayers, they had claimed, and the shortfall always had to be made up from the neutral panel or more directly by provincial government intervention. The situation was now radically different, and Jewish taxpayers, like citizens throughout the province calling for fundamental social and political reform on a number of other issues, were making vocal pleas for the recognition of their democratic rights.[38]

In suburban Laval, the city of Chomédy had been created by the amalgamation of St Martin, l'Abord-à-Plouffe, and Renaud. As in Hampstead, developers had transformed rural farmland into large areas of new housing for families within relatively easy reach of the city. The Protestant School Board of Greater St Martin had been created to provide educational facilities for the Protestants of the area, including Jews by virtue of Part X of the Education Act. Because Protestants were in the majority in the newly created school municipality, their schools were run by commissioners.[39] In the spring of 1961, a group of local Jewish residents decided that they should be represented on the school board, and they devised a plan to present one of their number as a candidate at the next school elections. They submitted formal election papers, supported as required by law by affidavits from school taxpayers. School electoral officials rejected their application because the chosen candidate, Harvey Grotsky, was not Protestant, but Jewish. While no religious or denominational qualification for the post of school commissioner could be found in the provisions of the Education Act, local officials relied on anti-Jewish bias. They evidenced a mistaken legal understanding that appears to have transformed the de facto Protestant majority control over the schools into a de jure requirement that commissioners be Protestant.

Despite objections from the local Jews who had begun proceedings, the CJC intervened and took carriage of the matter in order to ensure both that the best possible legal arguments were put forward, and to maintain a consistent approach to the question of Jewish school representation across greater Montreal.[40] The case was brought as a direct administrative law challenge to the decision of the election officials to reject an otherwise qualified candidate. The issue was clear. Could a Jewish taxpayer, who was a literate Canadian citizen, of the proper age, a resident of the municipality, and current in his school taxes, therefore fulfilling the legal requirements under the statute, stand as a candidate for the Board of School Commissioners? The legal debate came down again in part to the meaning of the provisions of Part X of the Education Act, which appeared to treat Jews as Protestants for school purposes, as had the 1903 Act, and to the way in which the current statute had to be interpreted following the *Hirsch* opinion. If the Board were a common school, outside of Montreal and Quebec, it would and should also have appeared that no religious qualification could be maintained, since common schools were not, and had never been as a matter of law, denominational in the strict legal sense. Indeed, under this analysis, the provisions of Part X were of no effect. But again St Martin had not been erected as a common school. Instead, it was like Hampstead an Order-in-Council municipality, created for Protestants only, raising once more the questions of exactly what legal meaning should be afforded to that phrase, and what status should be given to such school commissioners – common school, dissentient Protestant in all but name, or some sui generis hybrid i.e. a denominational school operating as the only school in a given municipality.

Faced with demands for representation from the CJC, and other members of the Jewish communities of Greater Montreal, the Protestant Committee of the Council of Public Education sought legal advice on its position. Peter Laing, QC, offered an extensive analysis of the *Hirsch* opinion and of the relevant statutory provisions. He concluded that because Protestants at the time of Confederation had the right to erect dissentient schools only in those municipalities in which they were the religious minority, they did not possess any further right at that time to erect what would later become Order-in-Council schools, or schools that were apparently both denominational and majority in character. At

Confederation, when Protestant school rights were to be determined in the context of constitutional law and any analysis of the section 93 implications, there were no Order-in-Council schools. Thus, he concluded, the board of commissioners was in fact governing a common school system. Moreover, the idea of erecting a school municipality could only ever be consistent with the idea of a common school, since under Quebec statute, dissentient schools did not operate in a separate and distinct school municipality, they merely formed a corporation of dissentients within the majority, or common, school municipality. The schools of St Martin were common schools, and in St Martin there were no religious qualifications for election as a school commissioner.[41]

Given the advice to the provincial Protestant educational body, the school board did not contest the legal action brought by Grotsky and his friends in the Jewish community against the decision to exclude him as a Jew from the list of school commission candidates. On 15 March 1962, a judgment was entered in the Magistrate's Court declaring the school election null and void and upholding Grotsky's claim that he was eligible for election as a school commissioner.[42] This time, with the assistance of the CJC, a local community had used the legal system of the province of Quebec to exercise rights, granted to them as the logical consequence of the *Hirsch* case, to be able to stand for election in common school municipalities. The Protestant Committee of the Council of Public Education had obtained legal advice confirming the rights of Jews in so-called Order-in-Council municipalities to stand for election, and by necessary implication, although this was not before the Court in *Grotsky*, to vote in such elections. The Laing opinion now echoed those obtained several years earlier by the CJC in relation to the Hampstead question. They had asserted, albeit on different legal grounds, that Order-in-Council schools were in law common schools. Outside the limits of Montreal and Quebec, and especially insofar as the historical boundaries of the City of Montreal at least were concerned, where common schools existed, Jews had the right to vote and to stand for membership on the school commission. Of course, under *Hirsch*, they still and always had no such rights in Montreal or in those areas where Protestant schools were properly dissentient.

In addition, another factor, outside the control of either the CJC or the PSBGM, meant that further negotiations over Jewish school issues, especially about the electoral franchise in other school municipalities, would be further delayed. Faced with growing demands for fundamental change in the educational system, whose traditional structures had been so essential to the construction of the historical bi-denominational Christian identity of Quebec, the provincial government had created a royal commission to examine the myriad and complex issues involved in a fundamental rethinking of the province's school system.[43] The commission would take its name from its chair, Mgr Alphonse-Marie Parent, the vice-rector of the Université Laval. In addition to its chair, the commission consisted of Sister Marie-Laurent de Rome, a philosophy teacher; Gérard Filion, director of *Le Devoir*; Professor Jeanne Lapointe, of the Université Laval; Paul Laroque, the secretary of Aluminum Limited; John McIlhone, of the Montreal Catholic School Commission; David Munroe, director of the Institute of Education at McGill University; and Professor Guy Rocher, head of the Department of Sociology at the Université de Montréal.[44]

One of the most significant aspects of the Quiet Revolution in Quebec had been the move to undertake fundamental changes to the educational system of the province. Driven in part by the changing socio-economic context, there was also abroad a feeling that the traditional classical training provided by Roman Catholic institutions to the majority of French-Canadian students at the secondary and post-secondary levels was ill-suited to the formation of business leaders for the modern world. If francophone Quebeckers were to be able to compete for a place in the economy of the province alongside the traditional anglophone elites, the educational system had to change. Concern over the suitability of the education system was also part of a wider set of debates, which took place in the broader context of the time, where many in the province sought to diminish the role of the church outside the strictly religious domain.[45] One of the changes, now part of this social and political movement, was a growing demand for a secular, public school system in the province.[46] Such a public school system had long been pushed by a number of groups, including the Federation of Home and School Associations during the Outremont crisis, and had of course long featured in the Jewish community, as an ideal to which they aspired, at least since the days of Bram De Sola's call for a system of "national schools." However, the ideal remained beyond reach, given the constitutional legal structure and the political realities of the times. Behind the idea of a common, non-denominational education system was a fundamental shift in Quebec society, which resulted in a widespread call for the democratization of all of the province's public institutions. The issue for the Jewish communities of their continuing disenfranchisement in school elections fit comfortably within the political and discursive matrix of the times in the province, as part of the Quiet Revolution, if not within the constitutional imaginations of Protestant school authorities.[47]

In August 1961, the CJC had again entered into contact with the PSBGM, to discuss the Jewish School Question and to address its proposed submission to the Parent Commission. The CJC saw these discussions and meetings with the PSBGM as a simple manifestation of the ongoing relations that had always existed between the Jewish community and the Protestant school officials in Montreal. For them, this dialogue was part of the constitutive arrangements of Jewish communal life in the educational field. The existence of the relationship and the continuing formative dialogue between the two groups meant that the CJC did not want to make public submissions to the royal commission before having informal exchanges with the PSBGM on what the CJC always considered to be questions of mutual concern for the Jewish and Protestant communities.

Jewish students in Protestant schools now accounted for 30 per cent of the student body across the system, and as much as 80 per cent in Outremont. From this factual and financial basis, the CJC put forward the fundamental complaint that had troubled Jewish Montreal since at least the 1920s, if not before. Given the facts of Jewish enrolment, the accounts of Jewish tax monies, combined with the legislative and contractual arrangements according to which Jews paid taxes into the Protestant panel, the absence of Jewish representation on the PSBGM, and the Council of Public Education, the democratic deficit was acute. The CJC urged the PSBGM to join it in seeking changes to the current legislative arrangements, to ensure some measure of Jewish representation. It also sought to emphasize the growing importance of Jewish day schools in Montreal. Increasing numbers of Jewish parents were opting for this form of combined Jewish and secular education for their children.[48] Students in the Jewish day schools in Montreal followed the Protestant school curriculum, Protestant inspectors inspected the schools, and these students could transfer automatically to the mainstream Protestant school system. This type of arrangement was not limited to Jewish educational establishments and their close relationship with the Protestant school system. Such arrangements were spreading throughout the educational infrastructure of the province. The Council of Public Education could recognize private schools for the purpose of funding students. Later a system of formal affiliation with Protestant or Roman Catholic schools would be put into place.

Whatever the legal regulatory context that would operate at any given time, the CJC wished to ensure support from the PSBGM for its position that students in these Jewish schools should be eligible for the new system of public grants available to students who attended approved private educational institutions. In addition, it urged the Protestant authorities to support its efforts either to revive the Jewish School Commission or to have the CJC recognized as the authoritative body on educational matters for the Jewish community. Experience from the crises of the 1920s and 1930s in Montreal, the 1940s and early 1950s in Outremont, and even the more recent Chomédy and Hampstead battles had taught the Jewish communities the importance of an organizational structure in which they could present a unified position. Such a single voice had to be maintained when significant change on the educational governance front was in the cards.[49] But above all, the CJC emphasized its intention to argue for no change in the basic structure of Quebec education. The CJC still maintained the formal position, which had been adopted from the beginning by uptowner spokesmen and throughout the history of the Baron de Hirsch School, through the Outremont case. The vast majority of Jewish students would continue to be educated in the Protestant school system. Jews still wished to be "honorary Protestants" for educational purposes. While they recognized the philosophical merit in arguments about the creation of a system of real public common, non-denominational schools in the province, as they always had, the Jewish communities equally recognized that a constitutional amendment to section 93 was not an immediate or foreseeably realistic political possibility.

The CJC continued these themes in its brief to the royal commission. It made clear its commitment to the current bi-denominational school system in the province, not because Jewish Quebeckers did not favour a single common school system as a matter of principle, but because they recognized the "special circumstances which obtain in the province of Quebec" would make such a radical change legally, politically, and socially impossible at the time.[50] But the CJC made it clear that its position on Jewish representation had to be heeded. Within the complex political, social, religious, and legal constitutional realities of Quebec's school system, a constitutive place for Jews had to be found. "The salient fact remains that this is an inexcusable violation of even the most basic tenets of democracy."[51] The fate of Jewish children and their parents as full Canadian citizens should not be contingent on an agreement renewable in Montreal and Outremont after a number of years, or frozen in the historical situation between Protestants and Roman Catholics in 1867. Absent a fundamental constitutional change with the unimaginable abolition of section 93, the basic ideas of democratic government and basic equality for all had to lead to a formula for Jewish educational representation. Political equality would always be less than complete as long as fundamental inequality reigned in the educational domain.

The CJC also announced in its brief that it had been engaged in negotiations with the PSBGM and the Protestant Committee of the Council of Public Education, and that a number of interim measures, pending an amendment of the Constitution, had been agreed for consideration by the royal commission.[52] These would include representation of Jews on the PSBGM and consideration of participation by Jewish representatives on the Council of Public Education on matters that would not infringe upon the pre-Confederation rights of Protestants. The CJC also suggested that the commission recommend the re-institution of the Jewish School Commission, a body that, while in fact not operating, still existed as matter of law in "perpetual succession" and whose membership could be (re-)constituted by the lieutenant governor in council.

The CJC brief contained and repeated many of the themes and tropes that had appeared in Jewish arguments and assertions about the Jewish School Question for over eighty years. The idea of education was intimately linked to the ideals of citizenship, democracy, and representation, which Jewish taxpayers were claiming as their right, and which formed the broader ideological foundations of the Quiet Revolution. Jews sought only equality within a system that would continue to recognize religious liberty on the question of absence from school on holy days and would recognize the right of Jewish day schools to receive government subsidies, just as Roman Catholic and Protestant private institutions did. They would happily remain essentially within the Protestant system and urged again and ultimately only recognition of Jewish citizens' rights to formal and actual equality. These were familiar arguments, which would have found support, in many respects, from the Baron de Hirsch Institute under David Ansell, or from Peter Bercovitch and Joseph Cohen in the 1920s and 1930s. While the political, social, and economic circumstances of Quebec had undergone important and revolutionary change from the days of the influx of Jewish immigrant schoolchildren to the Baron de Hirsch School, the principles of the arguments in the Jewish School Question had remained relatively constant. Legal arguments had been mustered with varied success, political and social arrangements had been hammered out, broken, renegotiated, modified, and put into place, often in the form of provincial legislation. The Jews of Montreal had found a space for themselves in the interstices of the two dominant cultures and Roman Catholic and Protestant religious groups, and in the shadows of a constitutionally entrenched, legally protected, bi-denominational school structure. But for Montreal's Jews that structure still remained a stumbling block to the realization of dreams of full equality and democratic participation in the education of their children.

Of course, the CJC was not the only body interested in the broad remit of the Parent Royal Commission, or indeed in the more narrowly construed Jewish School Question. Obviously the Protestants of Montreal and Quebec more widely had a direct interest in continuing Jewish assertions about their right to membership on, and voting for Protestant School Boards.[53] Roman Catholic educational officials and prelates had long insisted on the bi-national, bi-denominational character of Quebec identity, and of the core character of the province's school system, and the church could not easily abandon such an ingrained and deeply held philosophy, even as the majority Roman Catholic population moved away from active religious practice.

The Council of Public Education, which had not met for a half-century as a joint body of Protestants and Roman Catholics, was now brought together to consider the implications of the Parent Royal Commission. It considered matters of general importance, but it focused on the revived non–Roman Catholic, non-Protestant issue, and a series of related questions concerning their new power to recognize independent schools and to subsidize fees for students in those schools. Unsurprisingly, the council argued strongly for the status quo insofar as its own existence and membership were concerned, and more basically for the continuation of the denominational system of common and dissentient education in the province.[54] It urged a just and fair solution to the non–Roman Catholic, non-Protestant issue but emphasized that such a solution would have to respect the constitutionally enshrined rights of Protestant and Roman Catholic communities. The council continued to follow up the issue of non–Roman Catholics and non-Protestants at subsequent meetings because, in part, some of the same questions were raised in relation to Protestant and Roman Catholic students. As it stood, neither the Protestant committee nor the Roman Catholic committee could legally pay the annual fees for students who attended independent schools attached to the other committee.

In other words, while the council and its constituent committees had the power to subsidize students who attended recognized private schools, the system of payments to students had functioned solely along traditional denominational lines. Independent schools were still labelled as Protestant or Roman Catholic. The traditional bifurcated taxonomy still dominated, with the effect that the Roman Catholic committee could not subsidize the fees of Roman Catholic students who attended Protestant independent schools, and the converse obtained for the Protestant committee.[55] The Protestant committee likewise could subsidize only Jewish students in Montreal and Outremont, considered as Protestants under the contractual arrangements in place. The council sought solutions to each of these problems, caused in part by the hegemonic bi-denominational structure of the educational system alone, and otherwise by the fact that in a bi-denominational system, third parties who were and had always been "non," sat uncomfortably at best within that system, if at all. Some began to doubt that the council could be considered to be an institution well adapted to the rapidly changing and increasingly pluralist Quebec society.[56]

The royal commission would not make its final submission to the government until 1966. For the CJC and the Jews of the Montreal region, this further delay in reaching agreement on Jewish taxpayer voting and representation rights would be simply unacceptable. While the royal commission considered the evidence and gathered its facts for its final report to the government, the Jewish School Question continued to unfold around the City of Montreal proper.

School Elections, Jews, and Protestants: The Jewish School Question and Electoral Democracy in Hampstead

In 1962, 195 of the 320 children attending Hampstead School were Jewish.[57] By 1966, CJC estimates were that 75 per cent of the students in Hampstead School were from Jewish families.[58] Jewish parents paid a substantial proportion of the school taxes that kept the school functioning. However, while their children now attended the school without hindrance, Jewish parents were kept off the electoral roll for school board elections.[59] Once more the questions of democracy and electoral justice emerged in the context of the Jewish School Question. Because the Hampstead board was historically a rural one, although it fell under the general administrative and financial jurisdiction of what was now the Protestant School Board of Greater Montreal, it retained significant autonomy. Not the least important manifestation of this independence was that, unlike in the City of Montreal proper, in Hampstead the school commissioners were elected just as they had always been and were in other rural school municipalities throughout the province. But Jewish taxpayers, who supported the school and whose children by the mid-1960s constituted the great majority of students, were denied a democratic say in the governance of their children's education. By 1965, there were early signs of discontent and agitation among Jewish parents and at the CJC over what was seen and understood as yet another example of anti-Jewish bias by Hampstead officials. The refusal by the school board to allow Jewish parents to vote in school commission elections was an embodiment of the concrete lack of equality for Jewish citizens in educational matters.[60]

While in the Montreal crises of the 1910s, 1920s, and early 1930s the question had been the right of Jewish representation on the Protestant board in Montreal and the Council of Public Education in Quebec City, the first manifestation of the debate in Hampstead figured around the electoral franchise. This had never been a concern in Montreal, because of the absence of elections for school boards in the city. While representation would come to the fore in Hampstead and other parts of the Montreal suburbs, the first set of debates were on the fundamental issue of Jewish taxpayers' right to vote for school commissioners in Hampstead.

On 6 April 1966, Perry Meyer, a law professor at McGill University, a Jew, and a resident of Hampstead, at the behest of the CJC, wrote to the secretary-treasurer of the School Municipality of Hampstead. Meyer pointed out that he paid school taxes and that therefore both he and his wife, parents of three school-age children, were qualified under the law to be entered onto the municipality's electoral roll. Because Hampstead was a common school municipality, he stated, the board had no right to engage in religious exclusion.[61] Four other Jewish taxpayers joined Meyer and asked to be entered on the roll. The PSBGM consulted its lawyers and sought a legal opinion on the validity of the request from the taxpayers.

J. Palmer Howard, legal adviser to the Protestant Board of Greater Montreal, replied. He traced the history of the territory from the formation of the Notre-Dame-de Grâce (NDG) School Commission in 1876, as a common school board controlled by Protestants, to the breakup of the large NDG Board into Westmount, a common school controlled by Protestants, and Coteau St Pierre, another Protestant-controlled common school. Much of the rest of the original NDG territory was absorbed into Montreal proper. The western part of NDG became Côte Saint-Luc and was controlled by a Roman Catholic common board. Finally, as we know, Hampstead was detached as a school municipality for Protestants by Order in Council only in 1924.

Howard concluded that Hampstead fell into the general territorial jurisdiction of the PSBGM. In his view, Jews in Hampstead now paid taxes into the neutral panel and not the Protestant panel. Section 589, which excluded the Jewish school equality provisions from any territory under the PSBGM, applied to Hampstead because it was under the jurisdiction of the Montreal Central Protestant School Board or its successor. Jews had no claim to be treated as Protestants for school purposes in such circumstances, as both the statute and *Hirsch* confirmed, except in accordance to the agreements from the time of the *lois David*. While recognizing that the question was obscure and awaiting judicial determination, Howard offered the view that the board in Hampstead as a creature of the Order-in-Council mechanism was clearly denominational, and possibly or probably dissentient, or legally equivalent thereto. Therefore, in his opinion, Jewish taxpayers were ineligible to vote. They could vote in the common school elections, but not for a dissentient board. Despite the Laing opinion to the Protestant Committee of the Council of Public Education, and court decision in *Grotsky* some four years previously, indicating that Order-in-Council schools should be treated as common schools and offering an arguable legal case to counter the Howard/Protestant School Board position, the CJC decided to forego legal action or further efforts until the next year, but Hampstead's Jewish population was growing increasingly restless and anxious to resolve the issue of their exclusion from the electoral roll.[62]

Before the electoral roll for the next school elections would have been finalized, the CJC again approached the Protestant School Board in Montreal and asked them to consider acting to change the fundamental issue of disenfranchisement of Jewish taxpayers in Hampstead, and other similarly situated suburbs of Montreal, such as TMR and St Laurent.[63] In their plea to the Protestant board, the CJC appealed not just to the board's "interest in fair play and equity," but also to a set of legal arguments underlining the lack of justice for Jewish taxpayers. For the Jewish representatives of the CJC, the current disenfranchisement of taxpayers resulted both from erroneous legal interpretations of *Hirsch* and the status of Order-in-Council schools, and from the problem posed by section 589 of the Education Act, which removed the application of Jewish educational equality in Part X from schools under the jurisdiction of the Montreal Protestant Board, where a series of quasi-public contracts had been in effect since the early 1930s, despite the fact that the Jewish School Commission no longer existed. That statutory provision had been amended to take into account the change to the Montreal Protestant Central Board, but not its current embodiment, the Protestant School Board of Greater Montreal. The CJC therefore asked the PSBGM to join them in seeking the repeal of section 589, a legislative change that would have granted Jews statutory equality with Protestants everywhere in the province. However, as the CJC themselves recognized, there were significant legal difficulties with their argument, which would not be solved by the simple repeal of a single provision.

The repeal of section 589 would have had the effect of merely making the rest of Part X of the Act – with its guarantees of religious liberty and equality for Jews, as Protestants for school purposes – applicable to Hampstead, as a school board subject to the PSBGM. But that result would have had serious constitutional consequences. Such a repeal would also make all of the section on Jewish school equality – Jews as Protestants for school purposes – applicable to all Protestant schools in Montreal. *Hirsch* had made it clear that, insofar as the 1903 Act could be read to grant Jews access to Protestant dissentient schools in Quebec, it would clearly be unconstitutional. Some Protestant School Boards in Montreal, such as Outremont, were dissentient boards. The proposed total repeal of section 589 could not constitutionally have given Jews any rights in relation to those schools. Likewise, the old issue of exactly what a school municipality for Protestants only, erected by Order in Council, meant in legal terms had never been litigated since the *Stephens v Longeuil* decision in the 1890s. *Grotsky* was a Magistrate's Court case in which the Protestant commissioners had not contested the issue.

The CJC also had opinions from Newman and Brais, finding, for different reasons, and based in distinct and opposed interpretations of the statutory regime and the constitutional framework, that this did not affect the status of the Hampstead school in the common/dissentient school dichotomy of the legislative scheme governing Quebec education. Howard's legal view was that Hampstead was dissentient or some variant thereof, and Jews had no legal claims to representation. Only if the Protestant Board of School Commissioners governed a common school system would the Jewish taxpayers have a right to vote in school elections, since all non-dissentient taxpayers had such a right under general education legislation, a system that had been in place outside Montreal and Quebec for common schools for many years. The PSBGM and Hampstead board's legal position at this point was that, as an Order-in-Council school established for Protestants only, Hampstead was either a purely denominational Protestant school, or one legally equivalent to a Protestant dissentient school, or outside the application of Part X of the Education Act because it fell broadly under the jurisdiction of the Protestant board in Greater Montreal. The municipality had its origins in a decision by Protestant taxpayers to leave the Roman Catholic Côte Saint-Luc common school municipality, and as such was the legal equivalent of a declaration of dissent, under a different statutory mechanism.[64]

The Hampstead case also raised other important issues that had yet to be litigated in relation to the Jewish School Question. As Brais had made clear in his opinion on the school admission question, the real issue would have to begin with the state of education over the Hampstead territory in 1867. Until the historical facts were elucidated, a definitive answer would be impossible to find. Finally, the other remaining issue was the legal, constitutional fate of the area, and neighbouring Côte Saint-Luc more particularly, under section 93. They had been incorporated into Montreal after 1867, as the city expanded its borders though amalgamation with formerly rural suburban areas. The Supreme Court in *Hirsch* had declined to express a view on the matter because the issue was not before them. The Privy Council had acted in a similar manner but it did state, "It is clear that no post-Union annexation of territory could deprive any class of persons of the protection afforded to them by s 93 of the Act of 1867."[65]

Of course, such an historical determination and legal position on post-Confederation amalgamations would not directly assist the Jewish residents of Hampstead, because they were not a "class of persons" protected by section 93. However, it might have had an indirect impact if it were found that the schools of the area were historically common. Again without a more careful constitutional analysis, the franchise rights of Jewish taxpayers in Hampstead remained subject to potentially serious legal roadblocks. Only if the Protestant Board of School Commissioners for Hampstead really were a board of commissioners, governing a common school, could the Jewish taxpayers make any kind of claim to a right to vote. In the years since *Hirsch*, the Quebec courts had been confronted with problematic cases in relation to schools, both common and dissentient. Jehovah's Witnesses, for example, professed a religious doctrine that condemned both Roman Catholicism and the mainstream Protestant churches.[66] While the courts of the province might have been willing to consider Jehovah's Witness students as Protestant for school purposes, notwithstanding their theological rejection of Protestantism, the same could not be said of Jews, despite their legislatively mandated status as "honorary Protestants." All the courts in *Hirsch* had insisted that Jews could not be considered to fall under any cognizable legal doctrine that would treat them as Protestants. Only the Education Act pretended to do that, and it was constitutionally suspect, to say the least. Therefore, Jews could vote as taxpayers, regardless of religion, only in common school elections.

While the PSBGM took the matter under advisement, yet again, the local Jewish community continued to act on several interconnected fronts. While the CJC sought to establish a firm legal basis for any future actions and continued to place significant importance on its dialogue with the PSBGM, Hampstead Jews persisted in presenting demands that they be entered on the electoral roll.[67] The CJC now had a list of almost ninety Jewish taxpayers who had made explicit demands to be included on the electoral roll in Hampstead and whose requests had been rejected because they were Jews and not Protestants.[68] The CJC now instructed lawyers to file formal objections to the exclusions of Jewish taxpayers, which would be the first step in subsequent legal proceedings under Quebec electoral law.[69] Nonetheless, CJC opinion on the tactical question was still divided. Some Jews saw merit in the PSBGM position, largely because other school boards in the greater Montreal region, such as St Laurent and TMR, faced similar issues and legal questions, and waiting for a more definitive settlement seemed to be the best possible solution in the long run. Others felt that the Hampstead case had simply gone on long enough.[70] Nonetheless, the CJC maintained the importance of arriving at a unified view and then making its position clear and public in ongoing negotiations with Protestant educational authorities. Historical experience had always underscored the importance of Montreal Jewry speaking with a common voice on the Jewish School Question.

Hampstead was a long-standing case of clear injustice from the Jewish communities' perspective, and the CJC asserted that the easiest solution would simply have been for the PSBGM to seek a legislative amendment to ensure equality for the Jewish taxpayers there.[71] Moreover, the situation was becoming more acute because Hampstead taxpayers, like Jews elsewhere in greater Montreal, were now seeking not just to vote, but also to stand for election as school commissioners.[72] At the same time as they sought to bring pressure on the PSBGM to introduce legislative changes to enfranchise the Jews of Hampstead, the CJC had finally begun litigation against the commissioners of Hampstead School.[73]

But the litigation simply hung as a shadow over ongoing talks and developments elsewhere on related matters. Legislative intervention was being considered. Jews in other Montreal suburbs were experiencing similar problems. Jewish democratic claims were beginning to come to the surface throughout greater Montreal, in large part as a manifestation of the democratic urges unleashed as part of the zeitgeist of the Quiet Revolution. Nothing had ever really been resolved via the courts in the entire history of the Jewish School Question, and this latest instance would be no exception.[74]

13

TMR, St Laurent, Côte Saint-Luc: Democracy, Law, and the End of the Jewish School Question

Demography and Democracy: Equality, Citizenship, and the Jews of Montreal

As negotiations continued between the CJC and Protestant educational officials, and as Perry Meyer and his Jewish friends and neighbours tried to get themselves on the electoral roll in Hampstead, Jewish citizens in the suburb of TMR also sought to exercise their electoral franchise. The Jewish school population there had grown from 143 out of 1,586 students in 1954 to 613 out of 2,048 by 1962, a significant percentage of the student body.[1] The Protestant Board of School Commissioners of the Town of Mount Royal governed a system in a school municipality created by Order in Council in 1919. Like Hampstead and St Martin, then, there was a board of school commissioners, not trustees, and the school municipality was one erected for Protestants only. The constitutional and legal status of such creatures of statute and executive action once again came to the fore.

The PSBGM continued to insist, as they did for Hampstead, that such schools were legally dissentient. Therefore no Jew could vote or be elected to the commission, which was in its essence and inexorably Protestant.[2] A new opinion offered by Peter Laing, QC, to the Protestant Committee of the Council of Public Education in 1961 supported the current PSBGM view.[3] For Laing, because these municipalities had been erected for Protestants only in Montreal, they differed from rural areas, such as Chomédy/St Martin, whose situation he had also addressed. TMR and Hampstead were to be considered denominational, as were all boards in the city. Therefore Jews were not eligible to vote or to become members of the commission. Unlike St Martin, which lay outside the borders of the City of Montreal, TMR was within the boundaries of Montreal where Protestant schools existed only for Protestants. Thus according to Laing's analysis, Order-in-Council schools outside Montreal took on the character of common schools, while those erected in Montreal, whatever the juridical extent of that geographical category might have been, became denominational schools. Except, of course, that in Montreal, after *Hirsch*, Protestant and Roman Catholic schools were at one and the same time denominational and common. Again the exact and precise characterization of these Order-in-Council schools appeared to escape the best Protestant legal minds of the time, but they were unanimous on the result. No Jews. The same issue would also arise when Jewish taxpayers in suburban St Laurent joined in demanding electoral and representative rights from local Protestant school officials.

While Jewish taxpayers in Hampstead, TMR (and St Laurent) pressed claims for representative rights, other developments were continuing to take place in the broader context of the Jewish School Question. The Parent Commission had placed education in Montreal at the top of the political and social agendas. With debate about the possible de-confessionalization of the school system, or at least the creation of other governance structures for education becoming part of the political horizon, the CJC again began to contemplate the possible re-emergence of the Jewish School Commission. It was anxious to avoid the debates and divisions of the past by insisting that it, or a broad representative body within the Jewish communities, and not the government, nominate members to such a commission.[4] And as always, the Jewish School Question entered a mix of other interests, and other political dynamics, of which it could ever only be a part. In July 1964, the PSBGM had again approached the CJC to contemplate joint action on the legislative front. The issue at first was not the question of Jewish electoral rights, but instead one that marked a return to the 1920s in Montreal, and the 1940s, and 1950s in Outremont, but with an ironic twist. The question was one of school taxes.

Once more in the history of the Jewish School Question, which more often than not had been a Protestant School Question, the tax issue was being invoked in debates about the position of Jews in the province's educational system. Again, the issue arose in the broader context of Protestant and Roman Catholic relations.[5] The Roman Catholic School Commission was suggesting a simplification of the school tax system, resulting in the pooling of all taxes from the three panels, Roman Catholic, Protestant, and neutral, to be accompanied by a distribution based on a pro rata calculation of student numbers.[6] In the past, the Roman Catholic Commission had made similar arguments for a pro rata distribution. This proposed general pooling and pro-rated distribution would clearly benefit the numerically superior Roman Catholic Commissions throughout the province and have a conversely negative effect on the Protestant school system. In addition, according to the PSBGM, Jews would suffer. First they attended Protestant schools, so they would necessarily feel the effect on that system if the suggested change went ahead. Second, but for Montreal and Outremont where by agreement Jewish taxes went into the Protestant panel, in the rest of the province, Jewish taxes had been paid into the neutral panel for some time and then distributed almost exclusively to the Protestant schools attended by Jewish students.[7] While the Protestant system benefited from this distribution generally, the Protestant board took the view that if the Roman Catholic proposal were adopted, the Montreal and Outremont agreements would end, as the government would legislate for the entire province, and it would suffer losses of over $3 million as a result. In response, the Protestant officials were now willing to negotiate with the CJC to ensure the payment of Jewish taxes into the Protestant panel to counter the Roman Catholic proposal. As a result, the Protestants would now put on the table the reconstitution of the Jewish School Commission to ensure some form of Jewish representation on Protestant boards.[8] The combination of Roman Catholic political pressure on the government on the distribution of taxes and the economic power of Jewish taxpayers had now compelled the Protestant educational authorities to countenance Jewish representation within, or at the margins of, the administrative structures of their school system. The core existential arguments about maintaining the Protestant nature of their school system and its administrative structures had now apparently given away significantly to overwhelming demographic and fiscal realities.[9] Constitutionally enshrined guarantees of absolute Protestant autonomy over Protestant school administration that had always been the buttress and final bulwark against full claims of Jewish equality seemed to yield to an even deeper existential crisis for Protestant education. Without Jewish taxes, Protestant schools would no longer be financially viable.

In October of the same year, T. Palmer Howard again contacted the CJC, insisting that they appoint a lawyer as liaison with the PSBGM, so that the two groups could work on a full and complete brief on the payment of Jewish taxes into the Protestant panels throughout the province, and on the related matter of Jewish representation, everywhere but in Montreal and Outremont. When pressed on the matter, he simply stated that while *Hirsch* would bar any Jewish rights in those two school systems, a solution was possible for other parts of greater Montreal, although he refused to elaborate further.[10]

Howard welcomed the appointment of Samuel Godinsky, QC, as CJC liaison with the PSBGM, and declared, "I see no reason why a completely legal and all embracing solution cannot be worked out, and I shall strive to this end. It is my intention to discuss with Mr Godinsky the problems of Jewish representation and the problems of school taxation … These problems are distinct and separate, but the more one looks at both of them, the more one reaches the conclusion that they are not entirely separable."[11]

Now the issues of taxation and representation were inextricably bound together, as they had been from before the Commission of Nine, through *Hirsch* and would be throughout the 1960s in greater Montreal. Faced with the potential loss of $3 million in Montreal, the PSBGM was now willing to consider the possibility of Jewish representation on boards where Jewish taxpayers were demanding their democratic rights. But at the same time as they were holding out the possibility of a solution to the representation problem to the CJC, Howard and the PSBGM were advising those same boards that Order-in-Council Protestant School Commissions were irredeemably Protestant, and that Jews attended them only through Christian grace, as they had at the time of *Pinsler*. They continued to adopt this legal view, while claiming to the CJC that there was a legal solution to the problem of Jewish representation. Ironically, then, Howard was offering a different view, based in large part on Peter Laing's earlier memorandum, to the PSBGM and to local boards around Montreal, but outside the city's expanded limits, as he entered talks with the CJC.[12] As had been the case in Outremont, this appears to have been another instance in which Protestant officials were telling each party what they thought they wanted to hear.

Howard now put forward the opinion that it was the specific provisions of Part X of the Education Act itself, limiting the equality rights for Jews in school matters to schools outside the PSBGM, that stood in the way of Jewish representation in Hampstead and TMR. Outside the area of Montreal proper, such as in St Laurent, the question arose only in relation to the status of Order-in-Council schools. Howard now adopted the view put forward by Laing that these schools were post-Confederation creations and therefore not protected as denominational by section 93, although he would later offer a different analysis. Based in part on the holding in *Stephens v Les Commissaires d'Écoles de la Paroisse de Longeuil* – that a change from a dissentient school board to the creation of a new school municipality by Order in Council eliminated any existing dissent – Howard accepted the contention that this made such schools common schools.[13] This then served as the basis for his contention in his communications with the CJC that a solution to the issue could be found legally.

But of course, the argument was still open to the same analysis that Howard and Laing had signed off on not so long before, according to which the creation of a specifically denominational school, for Protestants only, led to the logically consistent and possibly legally persuasive position that they were exclusively Protestant, and more akin to dissentient schools than to common schools, especially in Montreal. Indeed, insofar as reliance was had on *Stephens*, the argument now advanced by Howard seemingly would have to be limited to areas in which there had been a Protestant dissentient school and taxpayers had left one municipality in order to become a Protestant Order-in-Council school, as was the case in St Laurent. This was certainly not the case in all areas surrounding the city of Montreal in which there were now Order-in-Council schools and where those school municipalities found themselves with significant Jewish populations. For example, in Hampstead, or more precisely Côte Saint-Luc, there had never been a dissentient Protestant school.

In addition, Howard asserted that in his view such schools were common schools and that the provisions of Part X of the Act, making Jews equal to Protestants for school purposes, would apply. But such an argument was a belt-and-suspenders position, since if the schools were common schools, all taxpayers, regardless of religious affiliation, were and had always been able to vote, stand as commissioners, and send their children to such schools. This general position obtained in any common rural school, that is, ones outside Montreal and Quebec City. Part X was redundant in such cases, unless it was to be read as taking away these rights, which Jews held along with all taxpayers, and limited them to attending Protestant schools. In all cases where there were dissentient Protestant schools, Part X would have clearly violated the law as set out by the Privy Council in *Hirsch*. The reading now proffered by Howard and the Protestant educational officials of Montreal would have meant that Part X of the Education Act had been unconstitutional, or at least inapplicable, if those provisions could be read down to a constitutionally valid core. Only if Order-in-Council schools were sui generis would the question of Part X become relevant. Legal certainty was in short supply.

Finally, Howard's opinion was made more problematic by his view that Order-in-Council schools were common schools and that in such an instance a dissentient Protestant school could be established. Under clear precedents in the province and a plain reading of the Education Act and its predecessors, this could not be the case. Protestants had always been a single class of persons enjoying rights to their schools, including most importantly the right to dissent. But such a right existed only in cases where the minority was of a religion different from that of the majority, that is, under the dual taxonomy where Roman Catholics and Protestants were in such a numerical relationship. Dissident Protestants had no right to form a dissentient Protestant school in relation to a Protestant majority. In areas such as Hampstead, for example, where there was a school municipality for Protestants only, no Protestant taxpayers could legally dissent. He or she might have been able to mount some kind of argument supporting withdrawal from the Protestant to a separate municipality and to send her or his children to the neighbouring common Roman Catholic school system of Côte Saint-Luc, which had remained unchanged for Roman Catholic residents after the creation of the Order-in-Council school municipality of Hampstead. However, on the clearest reading, such a right in the statutory scheme seemed to have existed only where there were common and dissentient schools in the same municipality. Similarly, it was difficult to construct an argument granting some right to establish a dissentient school to Roman Catholic residents of Hampstead. These citizens would not in fact have been residents for school purposes of Hampstead. They remained, on the most common and broadly accepted view of Order-in-Council schools, residents of the Côte Saint-Luc school municipality. Any idea that the legal situation of Order-in-Council schools was clear and unambiguous was not just naive, it was belied by legal opinion commonly held by Protestant school officials and their lawyers. Howard's assurances that there was a simple solution to the question of Jewish representation flew in the face of legal complexity, the entire history of the Jewish School Question, and the still dominant dual confessionality of

Quebec education, not to mention the more than occasional juridical ambiguity asserted by Protestant legal officials, and the ever-present spectre of section 93.

Whatever the constitutional and statutory complexities that remained, Howard was now apparently willing to put forward an argument on the basis of which Jews could legally vote in Protestant School Board elections and stand for office in those elections. Again, constitutional legal formalities may have formed a broad framework within which the Jewish School Question was formulated, discussed, and played out, but the real and concrete constitutive practices for the Jewish communities, and for their Protestant, Roman Catholic, and governmental partners were constitutive at a very different normative level. The formal and substantively important dialogue in this instance took place between T. Palmer Howard and Samuel Godinsky. The parties recognized that equity demanded that Jews have representative and electoral rights, and that there was urgency to the matter for the Protestants and Jews alike.[14] That urgency was a result of a combination of now synergistic elements – the provincial climate in which democratization was an emerging and overarching norm: Jewish demands for equality in educational matters, and the looming political and fiscal crisis resulting from Roman Catholic lobbying of government over school taxes. Roadblocks could be found in the constitutional arrangement after *Hirsch* and the ethical and legal obligations imposed on the PSBGM to maintain the essentially Protestant nature of its schools. The discussions between Howard and Godinsky canvassed a number of possible legal changes, including the amendment or repeal of the provision of Part X of the Education Act limiting Jewish school equality to areas outside the PSBGM area, or of repealing all Orders in Council creating schools for Protestants only. It seemed at this point that Howard (or the PSBGM) was unwilling to stand fully behind his recent jurisprudential change of heart on the common school question for Order-in-Council schools, at least insofar as the problematic legal analysis could serve as the basis of a new constitutive arrangement between Protestant educational authorities and representatives of the Jews of the Montreal region.

On the basis of long experience, and recognizing that such legislative changes would never be immediate, the parties contemplated a series of measures that could be implemented more quickly. They recommended the re-institution of the moribund but still legally existing Jewish School Commission to act as a commission at large under the PSBGM, an idea that soon disappeared, most likely because it had been clear from the deliberations of the Parent Commission that further confessionalization of school governance structures was not likely to feature in future legislative change.[15] When the political mood was one in which most believed that the dual confessional system of Protestant and Roman Catholic schools was largely responsible for the crisis in Quebec public education, the addition of another confessional element embodied in a revived Jewish School Commission went against the tide of opinion. Instead, the PSBGM placed a public announcement in the *Montreal Gazette* announcing its intention to introduce a private bill at the next session of the legislature in order to permit, inter alia, "increasing the number of members of The Protestant School Board of Greater Montreal so as to provide for Jewish representation on the Board."[16]

The bill was introduced and entered into law unproblematically, if not entirely constitutionally, on 15 July with effect from the first of that month.[17] After consulting with the CJC, the government named five Jewish school commissioners, who sat not as the reconstituted Jewish School Commission of 1930 and 1931, but as statutory members of the PSBGM.[18] Jews in Montreal now had appointed representatives on the Protestant governing body by virtue of the political intervention of that body, and the passage of a legislative enactment concretizing the negotiations between Howard and Godinsky. While the old Jewish School Commission continued its life in limbo, as a legal body with perpetual succession, the CJC had obtained two major victories. Through years of political engagement, it had managed to realize the long-held dream of Jewish membership on the Protestant School Board. It had also established itself, as no other group had really been able to do since 1903, as the representative embodiment and spokesperson for the Jewish community and its interests, although an occasional dissenting voice could still be heard.[19]

Of course, this was far from being a total victory. At the same time that Jews achieved membership status by appointment on the PSBGM, they were still being denied the same rights in several Protestant school boards in surrounding areas. They could not be enrolled on the list of eligible voters, nor could they stand for election in those municipalities. The local boards were supported by legal opinions from Howard, who again appears to have abandoned his earlier view that Order-in-Council schools were common schools, in favour of a constitutional interpretive scheme that kept Jews from participating as equal citizens throughout the greater Montreal area. Ironically, perhaps, it seems quite clear, as it must have at the time, that the appointment of five Jews to the PSBGM was blatantly unconstitutional. To all intents and purposes, the PSBGM was the legal successor of the Protestant School Board of Montreal and was treated by all parties as such. All courts in the *Hirsch* case had declared any idea of Jewish membership on that body, or any other similar body, including the financial committee proposed by Cohen and Hirsch, to be a clear violation of Protestant rights enshrined in section 93 of the BNA Act. Jews were still being barred by Protestant legal argument from school governance in various suburbs, under the same section 93 norms of Protestant educational rights, while by almost certainly unconstitutional legislation they were granted the representative status in Protestant schools in Montreal for which they had so long struggled.

During the Howard/Godinsky negotiations and the subsequent legislative process, the PSBGM had consented to the naming of the five Jewish commissioners. *Hirsch* had made it abundantly clear, however, that Protestant consent to the 1903 Act could have no bearing on the constitutionality of any statute adversely affecting the rights or privileges of the Protestant school system in Montreal. Apparently $3 million in Jewish tax money, and the threat arising from Roman Catholic attempts to get their hands on a high proportion of that $3 million, alongside basic principles of justice, equity, and fairness, of course, could override constitutional concerns about fundamental Protestant educational rights in Montreal. There is no small irony in the fact that the same PSBGM that ignored and blatantly violated the constitutional rules in relation to its own constitutive make-up now insisted on the strict application of those same rules for other Protestant Boards in the Montreal area. Meanwhile, in St Martin, an Order-in-Council municipality where the *Grotsky* case had stood unchallenged for several years, two Jews now sat on the Protestant School Board.[20]

While political compromise, changing social attitudes, and the economic reality of Jewish school tax dollars had combined to allow Jewish representation after many years of struggle, this did not mean that section 93 was dead and buried or that the Protestant educational officials of Montreal and Quebec would not continue to insist on their constitutional rights.[21] Successive attempts by the provincial government to impose new educational regimes grounded in the emergence of linguistic nationalism, or to create new systems of school finance, the effect of which might have been a reduction in the taxing power of local school boards, were met with concerted invocations of constitutional rights guaranteed to Protestants under the BNA Act.[22] Jews were perhaps more solidly "honorary Protestants," but Protestants were still Protestants, and not Roman Catholics for educational purposes.

The political and fiscal compromise of the post–Parent Commission era once more demonstrated that the Jewish School Question had little to do with Jews and almost nothing to do with the law. The PSBGM and the provincial government engaged in a constitutive change that was clearly unconstitutional. Yet the political and economic interactions between the Jewish communities and the Protestant officials had led to a conclusion where Jewish demands from the early part of the century had finally been met sixty years later. In the narrow sense, once again the government had played a constitutive and unconstitutional role in facilitating the self-constituting dynamic of Jewish/Protestant relations in the school context. Whether it was legal or not, Jews could now sit on the Protestant School Board in Montreal.

While the CJC found a sympathetic ear from the local school commissioners on representation and voting questions, the Protestant officials still claimed that their hands were tied and, under the current state of the law, they could not permit Jewish taxpayers to vote in school elections. They suggested that a joint committee be established to find a way out of the impasse, but the Jewish community of TMR, for example, did not accept either the legal argument or the offer of joint discussions. Instead they brought legal proceedings to compel the inclusion of their names on the list of eligible electors for the next school commission elections.[23] In the meantime, the school commissioners attempted to convince the PSBGM to seek an amendment to the law to bring the general school equality provisions to bear for municipalities and commissions under the broader administrative and financial administrative remit of the PSBGM.[24] Other school boards under the PSBGM joined in the TMR request, as did some local governments.[25] In April 1968, 1,700 Jewish and non Jewish taxpayers of TMR petitioned the minister of education to end the situation that was "contrary to the elementary rights of citizens."[26]

While Jewish citizens across Montreal continued their struggles for the right to vote and to stand in school board elections, the Parent Royal Commission had delivered its recommendations to the provincial government.[27] In its most relevant findings for the Jewish School Question, the commission recommended the maintenance of Protestant and Roman Catholic schools, with the creation of a third non denominational option, a possible first step towards public schools, properly so called. It also argued for non-denominational school commissions, which would nonetheless have the legal obligation to provide a confessional education to those who wanted it. It further recommended the recognition of rights of students to withdraw from religious observance and instruction in denominational schools to which they had been admitted, and to be given an equal opportunity to receive an appropriate education. It urged an end to the power of the committees of the Council of Public Education to recognize schools as Protestant or Roman Catholic.[28] Overall, the Parent Commission's recommendations reflected the difficult and complex political and legal constitutional framework of Quebec's educational structures. Most experts believed that the time had come to de-confessionalize the province's education system and to move to a linguistically based governance structure. To a large extent, this idea fit into the secularization of Quebec society that had been a key element of the Quiet Revolution. It was also consistent with broader and emerging understandings of national identity grounded in language and the move away from a denominationally defined notion of Quebec as a distinct society.[29] Moreover, it was in keeping with notions of educational best practice and the recognition of the increasing importance of schooling for social and economic progress in the province. However, section 93 presented an insurmountable constitutional barrier to any such change. The potential consequences of implementing these recommendations were so complex and raised such a variety of political and legal questions that the government created another group to consider how, in fact and in law, these recommendations might be put into effect. The Council for Educational Restructuring on the Island of Montreal was created under the chairmanship of Joseph Pagé, former deputy minister of education and vice-chair of the Montreal Roman Catholic School Commission.[30] Democracy in education for the schools of Quebec, and especially those on the Island of Montreal, was a long, complex, and onerous process.

In the pursuit of a long-term solution to the Jewish School Question in those areas of greater Montreal where the problems of voting rights and rights of representation were still undecided, the PSBGM sought to amend the Education Act provision that made Part X inoperative for schools under its jurisdiction.[31] On its face at least, such an amendment would not violate the *Hirsch* limits, because it would still not permit Jewish membership on a school board in Montreal, which the case had clearly declared to be unconstitutional, nor would it apply to the dissentient board in Outremont. Its proposed inclusion of all other schools would allow for Jewish representation in effect by an implied admission that, in law, Order-in-Council schools were common schools. At the same time, however, the proposal ignored the potential difficulties surrounding the application of such a scheme for Jewish equality in school districts that had existed in 1867 as denominational. The Privy Council had clearly been of the view that the rights to denominational autonomy of any such school were frozen and guaranteed by section 93. With its large Jewish population and an untouchable dissentient Protestant Board of School Trustees, Outremont stood as a stark reminder that the full equality for Montreal's Jews was perhaps a constitutional impossibility.

No amendment to the Education Act was forthcoming as the government continued to consider more wide-ranging changes, and once again the Jews of TMR were not permitted to vote in the elections concerning the running of the schools attended by their children. They had the support of the local Protestant Board of School Commissioners and of the PSBGM. They also had the support of the CJC. Still, Part X of the Education Act – which embodied a version of the *Hirsch* protections of Protestant rights and privileges in education, but in other aspects provided Jewish education rights as "honorary Protestants" – stood as an apparently insurmountable legal barrier to the democratic flourishing of the municipality's Jewish taxpayers. Jews in nearby communities like Hampstead were involved in the same fight. But the necessary partner in this dialogue, the provincial government, felt that it could not act because it wanted to deal with the issues of Montreal's educational system as a whole. As always, the Jewish School Question occurred in a larger context, in which Jewish voices and interests were only part of a broader and more complex political and social mix.

Part of that social and political matrix had been the long-awaited Pagé report, on the future administrative structures of Montreal's common public school system(s). In October, it had handed in its recommendations, which included the creation of a governing committee in each school, made up of the parents of the children attending the school. The school committees in each school commission area would together form an electoral college to choose half of the members of the commission, the other half to be elected by local universal suffrage.[32] The government's own committee, which had followed its own royal commission, was now recommending a fundamental change to school governance in Montreal, one that would bring Montreal common schools into line, in part at least, with their homologues elsewhere in the province and subject them to a limited electoral review. Democracy was in the air, but not yet for Jews.

Ville St Laurent: More Demands for Equality, Less Democracy for Jews

In the suburb of Ville St Laurent, as in Hampstead and TMR, Jewish numbers had also increased with population movements westward across the Island of Montreal. In 1954, there had been 1,502 students in St Laurent schools, of whom 27 were Jews. By 1962, of the 5,103 students, more than 25 per cent, or 1,447, were Jews.[33] Two different issues served as catalysts for the Jewish School Question that rose to the surface in St Laurent, as the difficulties in Hampstead and TMR were wending their way through the complex narrations of the Jewish School Question in other parts of suburban Montreal.

In 1966, changes to the school tax system in St Laurent had come into effect.[34] There, as in other parts of the province outside Montreal itself, Jews paid their taxes into the neutral panel, and their children attended the Protestant school system. The tax rate for the Protestant and neutral panels was the same. However, in 1965, the annual tax year for the neutral panel, but not for the Protestant panel, was changed from the calendar year to a fiscal year from 1 July to 30 June, and for the first year the measure was made retroactive to 1 July 1964. The result was that the retroactive assessments affected Jewish taxpayers, but not Roman Catholics, or especially Protestants. Jewish taxpayers experienced this as a discriminatory measure, which had the effect of taxing them more highly than their Protestant fellows for the same services and in retroactively piling injustice on injustice.[35] Local and provincial tax and government officials dismissed the claim of discrimination, describing the change as a mere fiscal adjustment, which had its effect only once, in the first year of the change, and then only for six months. They claimed that the matter was of little practical importance, resulting in an average retroactive extra payment of around $14. The local Jewish community continued to protest what they saw as an example of anti-Jewish prejudice. Despite the intervention of the CJC and the PSBGM, which passed a resolution highlighting the discriminatory nature of the retrospective change to the tax year, the government remained unmoved.[36] While the CJC recognized the strength of feeling of the Jewish taxpayers and the importance of the principle at stake, they adopted a position that minimized their involvement in efforts to achieve a change to the tax issue.

The CJC acted in the hope that once the first six months of the re-adjusted tax year had passed, the matter would go away. In addition, they pointed out to members of the St Laurent Jewish community that the congress was engaged in a number of significant matters affecting the Jewish community more broadly, including its endeavours in TMR and Hampstead to gain voting rights for Jewish taxpayers, and their efforts to gain recognition for Jewish day schools as institutions eligible for government subsidies. In the end, the CJC pointed out, the discrimination against Jewish taxpayers would, and did, reach its natural end once the current school tax year came into effect and the retrospective period had run its time.[37] A one-off payment of $14 per Jewish taxpayer simply paled in comparison to the struggle over the fundamental discriminations still operating against Jews in the school system. They noted that Jewish taxpayers elsewhere in Montreal suffered a similar ignominy, if not a greater one, when their names were marked with a *J* on the tax roll.[38]

But just as taxation in unfair circumstances was almost by definition likely to raise the ire of Jewish residents in St Laurent, the same broader issue of taxation and the absence of representation was also boiling over there, as it was in Hampstead and TMR. In November 1968, the Protestant School Commission of St Laurent held a public meeting to discuss the issue of non-Protestant, non–Roman Catholic representation on local school boards.[39] Several weeks later, the St Laurent Board wrote to T. Palmer Howard asking for his legal advice on Jewish voting rights and representation in relation to their commission.[40] Howard corrected his client's description of the commission as dissentient, pointing out that as a matter of law, as an Order-in-Council school municipality, they were denominational because they had been erected "for the Protestant rate-payers only," but they were not dissentient under the law.

Unsurprisingly, he concluded that, if the commissioners were correct in their claim that theirs was a dissentient board, Jews had no right to vote or to be represented. This was clearly the case under both a constitutionally constrained reading of the provisions of the Education Act and what all the courts in *Hirsch* had established. If the board were denominational but not dissentient, Palmer also consistently maintained his position that, as the law stood, Jews had no rights to representation or to vote, a somewhat more problematic legal conclusion for schools outside Montreal (or Quebec City) that, legally speaking, could not be denominational and also a view from which on other occasions he had resiled.

A legal opinion produced for the CJC took an entirely different view. From the same attorneys who had acted in the *Grotsky* matter and who were also representing the taxpayers of Hampstead and TMR in their attempts to gain the same rights now being sought in St Laurent, this advice contained little constitutional surprise. As had Howard, the lawyers for the CJC recognized that if the St Laurent commissioners' assertion that they were a dissentient board was correct, nothing short of a constitutional amendment could give Jewish taxpayers any rights.[41] If the board were not dissentient, the lawyers adopted their traditional view, and one Peter Laing had earlier supported in his opinion to Protestant officials, that such post-Confederation Order-in-Council commissions, outside Montreal itself, were non-denominational common schools. In effect, as a rural board, one outside Montreal and Quebec City, the schools under its jurisdiction would be common schools, unless it was created as the result of a declaration of dissent as required by the law. However, the situation was in fact and in law somewhat more complex. The original Protestant board in St Laurent had been dissentient, under the governance of school trustees. According to the CJC lawyers, its petition of 1951 seeking to establish an Order-in-Council municipality constituted the legal erection of a new school municipality under commissioners. The legal consequence of the successful erection of a new municipality under formerly dissentient Protestants was to eradicate any trace of lawful dissent, as the *Stephens* case had held. The lawyers for the CJC insisted that dissentient rights had been lost when a new school municipality was created.

Unlike Hampstead or St Martin, where no such dissentient school had existed before the Order in Council, the situation in St Laurent was arguably significantly different on the facts. In one view, the existing dissentient school had simply changed its legal identity by the Order in Council but had maintained its dissentient status, or one proximate to it, by remaining for Protestant ratepayers only. Indeed, the other option that might have been open at the time, although the commission gave insufficient detail, was that available under the statute, which allowed a dissentient school to petition to become the common school where that population had subsequently become the majority, and for the former majority to exercise its right to dissent. But this mechanism would have meant that the Protestant School would clearly have become a common school, which all students could attend. To maintain its Protestant status, the St Laurent Commission had sought to create a new Protestant municipality and had in no way wished to give up any of its dissentient Protestant rights. This was the school commission's position. By refusing to become a common school and opting for the creation of a new Order-in-Council municipality for Protestants only, the commissioners had manifested their intent to remain a denominationally restricted Protestant school. On the other hand, the CJC lawyers asserted that, within a majority or common school municipality, the Order in Council had turned a formerly dissentient school system into a new municipality in which it was the majority or common school.

Again, the only legal authority on the question did not really settle the matter. *Stephens v Les Commissaires d'Écoles de la Paroisse de Longeuil* involved an attempt by the common Roman Catholic School commissioners to collect taxes from a Protestant resident after the erection of a new school municipality for Protestants only, largely on the basis that the taxpayer had not filed a declaration of dissent.[42] In ordinary circumstances, a Protestant taxpayer who had not filed a declaration of dissent according to the modalities set out in the Education Act would have been considered as a member of the majority and therefore would have been liable to pay taxes into the common school system. In *Stephens*, the Court found that the erection by Order in Council of a new municipality for Protestants only meant that a new school municipality had been created, and that as a consequence, all declarations of dissent had been legally erased, because they were no longer necessary. Thus, the case established the principle that a new school municipality, which had no juridical relationship with the previous common school district, was established by the Order-in-Council mechanism. However, it did not decide the question as to the exact nature – common, denominational, sui generis, etc. – of the newly erected school municipality, because it had not been faced with it.

In and around Montreal, legal uncertainty, unaided by Protestant legal advice, which changed with the wind, continued to dog the claims of Jewish taxpayers to what they considered to be their basic democratic right to vote, and to participate in the running of the schools attended by their children, just as their Protestant and Roman Catholic neighbours did. As always, however, the Jewish School Question in Hampstead, TMR, St Laurent, and Montreal would not be resolved in the courts, nor would it be resolved, *strictu sensu*, as the Jewish School Question. There were other actors, from the PSBGM to the provincial government, and other school bodies in Montreal whose participation would once again be key to the ongoing struggle for Jewish rights in the Quebec educational context.

Protestants, Jews, Democracy, and Law: The PSBGM's Jewish Members

The PSBGM was still reluctant to act in an all-encompassing way on Jewish rights. For the CJC and the Jewish taxpayers of suburban Montreal, waiting for democracy to come had already taken several years. They still had no definitive answer to their demands for equality. However, the provincial government, acting on the Parent Commission's recommendations for changes to the educational governance structure, had now created the Ministry of Education, bringing schooling in the province back into the heart of government, after many years of handing responsibility over to the Council of Public Education, with the heavy influence of the Roman Catholic episcopate and the provincial secretary. It had also followed up on other recommendations and modified the Council of Public Education in name and in composition. It had now become a unified Superior Council of Education, composed of sixteen Roman Catholics, four Protestants, and one non–Roman Catholic, non-Protestant member.[43] As a post-Confederation body, the council had been technically open to such changes since *Hirsch*, although the two denominational committees had always opposed any such modifications in membership and had threatened legal action to prevent any fundamental interference by non–Roman Catholics or non-Protestants. But times had changed in the broader political and social context of the province, and the first "non" member took his place on the new Superior Council. In this instance, it was Perry Meyer of Hampstead, who became the first Jew on the council, a very long time after Michael Hirsch and Peter Bercovitch had campaigned so hard for such an appointment.[44] Meyer could now have a voice in setting educational policy for the entire province, but he could still not vote in his local school elections or run for office as a school commissioner in his own home of Hampstead. Such were the constitutional and constitutive ironies of the Jewish School Question in Quebec in the early 1960s of the Quiet Revolution and its aftermath.

Meanwhile, a legal committee had been formed by the PSBGM to deal with the question of Order-in-Council schools, which the Protestant educational and legal officials recognized to be different from both dissentient schools and Montreal common but denominational schools.[45] The PSBGM continued to insist on its constitutional and legal analysis, which characterized such commissions as denominational but not dissentient. They existed as schools for Protestants only, and as such, while they were the only school in the erected municipality, dissent from them was impossible. In other words, the Protestant legal position now accepted the view that, because these were Protestant schools and for Protestants only, Roman Catholic taxpayers continued to live within the school municipality from which the Protestants had been removed when the new Order-in-Council school municipality had been created. Since these Roman Catholics were not and apparently never could become part of the new municipality, there could never be any need for them to dissent. At the same time, of course, since Protestants as a whole were the only group of persons vested with a right to dissent from Roman Catholic common schools, Protestants could not make a declaration of dissent from a Protestant board; the Order-in-Council schools could not be considered as common schools. They were not dissentient schools, although they shared many of the rights of such schools, in particular the right to administrative autonomy and to refuse admission to non-Protestant students. No statutory change could take away the rights of autonomy that denominationally Protestant schools enjoyed at the time of Confederation, a position like that of Order-in-Council schools. The legal stance and its consequences were clear for the PSBGM, although as even the lawyers pointed out, there may well have been policy and other considerations that might be argued to operate in the context of the difficult question of Jewish rights in such school municipalities. However, the opinion on the legal issues was clear, at least until they changed their mind. The Jews of St Laurent had no right to vote in school elections or to stand as candidates for the position of commissioner in such elections.[46]

The Protestant Board of St Laurent was still anxious to find a practical and inclusive solution to the matter, but the legal opinion from the PSBGM held great weight for them. They were also now faced with a potential lawsuit, like the one in Hampstead, challenging the electoral roll.[47] The CJC suggested that the board adopt the position of the St Martin Commission some years earlier in the *Grotsky* case and allow the action to proceed unchallenged. However, the board was greatly influenced not just by the weight of legal opinion in its favour, but also by the idea that such a decision on their part might be seen legally as an abandonment of the denominational character of the commission and its schools. They feared that such a concession embodied in a decision not to contest the Jewish legal case against the commission could, in and of itself, turn them into a common school. The matter was placed in the hands of the lawyers, who sought to move the case, by prerogative writ, from the lower court where school electoral matters were normally handled, to the higher jurisdiction of the Superior Court, from which an appeal to the Court of Appeal would lie. The legal representatives on both sides clearly wanted a more definitive determination from a higher court on the question of Order-in-Council schools.[48] In August 1969 the matter went to the Superior Court on the technical issue of the availability of a writ of evocation to bring the case to that court from the Provincial Court.[49] In February the matter went to the Court of Appeal. If an appeal to the Court of Appeal from the Provincial Court ruling on the merits of the challenge to the electoral roll were possible, as a matter of law the prerogative writ would be unavailable. The existence of an alternative, effective remedy would preclude access to a prerogative writ, under general principles of administrative law.[50]

The Court of Appeal rejected the attempt to bring the matter before the superior jurisdictions, on the grounds that elections were held every year. Any Provincial Court decision would not be binding on any subsequent year's election. Attorneys for the CJC suggested that this might mean that further talks with the school board would now be possible, since the underlying message from the procedural decision was that because future rights were not at stake, they could allow Jews to vote without being bound at law by the decision in relation to any future situation. Therefore, as a matter of law, such a decision to allow Jews to vote while talks proceeded would not turn the Protestant system into a common school municipality.[51] The case went back to the Provincial Court for hearing, and the matter dragged on for some time, until other developments led to its being postponed sine die, with the permission of the presiding judge.[52]

Meanwhile and still, while five Jews sat on the PSBGM and the debates in Hampstead, TMR, and St Laurent continued, the municipality of Côte Saint-Luc had also entered the fray.[53] City council had approved a resolution calling on the PSBGM to ensure that Jewish taxpayers in all municipalities had the right to vote and to stand for office in school board elections.[54] Over 90 per cent of the students in the municipality were now Jewish, and the same proportion of revenue in the Protestant schools was received from Jewish taxpayers.[55] The PSBGM, including its five Jewish commissioners, would have to consider the matter, as would the provincial government, to which the council resolution had been forwarded.[56] Unfortunately for the Jews of Côte Saint-Luc, they could not achieve the same rights that would eventually be granted to the Jews of Hampstead and St Laurent. At the behest of the PSBGM and the CJC, the amendment to the Education Act, so long sought as a means to end the discrimination and inequality in local school boards outside the city, was passed, granting electoral rights to the tens of thousands of Jews who had been denied these basic constitutive elements of democratic citizenship.[57] However, the legal changes left the Jews of Côte Saint-Luc in legal limbo. The statutory amendment did not affect them. For the PSBGM, only the limited modification of the Act had been possible. Any attempt to simply abrogate the provision limiting the Jewish equalities in school matters to areas outside Montreal proper would have left the entire idea of Jewish equality in school matters open to a section 93 challenge. Such a general change to the statutory regime governing education in the province would have amounted essentially to a return to the situation that had obtained under the 1903 Act, without any attempt in the legislation to pay even lip service to *Hirsch* and the clear limits imposed by section 93 on modifications to the system of Protestant school governance. While the Jewish members of the PSBGM continued to seek a total repeal and the CJC continued to lobby to that effect, the PSBGM majority stood their constitutional and constitutive ground.[58]

As it had always intended, the PSBGM pursued and ultimately achieved a change to the operative provision, now section 580 of the Act,[59] to limit its restrictions on Jewish equality to the City of Montreal, and Outremont (and Verdun).[60] This amendment rather than repeal strategy had been pursued by the PSBGM against the objections of the Jewish commissioners, who supported the outright elimination of the provision, but that was not to be.[61] The Jews of Côte Saint-Luc, where the municipality had been swallowed up in Montreal's westward expansion, would still find themselves victims of the democratic deficit imposed by the operation of section 93 and the temporally frozen protection of Protestant educational rights and privileges in Montreal.

Côte Saint-Luc had previously been part of the suburban municipality of St Pierre but had been annexed to Montreal by Order in Council. In 1941, the Protestant School Municipality of Coteau St Pierre and the dissentient school municipality of Côte Saint-Luc had been amalgamated as a dissentient Protestant board. The attorneys for the Roman Catholic School Commission had then filed an objection with the Department of Education, indicating that the dissentient board had been illegally constituted because two thirds of Protestant taxpayers had not signed the notice of dissent, as required by law. The Protestant tax panel therefore received only monies from those Protestant taxpayers who had actually signed the dissent. To remedy the problem, Coteau St Pierre petitioned the department to annul the unification with Côte Saint-Luc. The Protestant taxpayers then filed a valid form of dissent in 1951, and a properly constituted dissentient school board was established. That school board then requested a union with the Protestant School Board of Montreal, which agreed to the amalgamation.

At that time, the population of Côte Saint-Luc comprised 49.2 per cent Protestants, 45.4 per cent Roman Catholics, 3.1 per cent Jewish, and 2.3 per cent "other." The more recent influx of Jewish families, the majority status of Jewish students in the schools, and the fiscal reality that Jewish taxes kept the Protestant schools afloat did nothing to change the constitutional and constitutive character of the school system as unchangeably Protestant. The Jews of Côte-Saint-Luc were considered to be within a school municipality of the City of Montreal and living in the area under the jurisdiction of the Protestant School Board. For school purposes and as matter of constitutional and constitutive framing, Côte Saint-Luc therefore fell under the jurisdiction of the Protestant Board of School Commissioners of Montreal and its successor bodies, to which even the most recent amendment to the Education Act did not apply. While Côte Saint-Luc had its own municipal government, it did not exist as a separate school municipality.[62] Again, standing on its constitutional and constitutive rights, the PSBGM had sought and obtained a legislative amendment, which would be in strict accordance with the opinion in *Hirsch* that Jews had no representative rights in relation to the Protestant School Board of Montreal, or to the dissentient board of Outremont (and Verdun). This continuing narrow but strict adherence to *Hirsch* deprived the Jews of Côte Saint-Luc of full equality.[63] And of course, one might wonder at the legal chutzpah of the PSBGM, in all likelihood illegally constituted now that it had Jewish members, asserting constitutional principle, the effect of which was to deny rights to the Jewish taxpayers of Côte Saint-Luc.[64] Nonetheless, the Jews of Côte Saint-Luc had no right to vote in school elections because they were Jews and not Protestants. The CJC could celebrate the victory in extending voting rights for Jewish taxpayers in Hampstead and TMR, each of which seemed to move in and out of the PSBGM legal orbit under Part X at will, and St Laurent. Their co-religionists in neighbouring Côte Saint-Luc still suffered, as did the Jews of Montreal, now legally restricted in its geographic reach, along with those in the historically protected suburbs of Outremont and Verdun, from a basic inequality, enshrined, as it had always been, in the provisions of the Canadian Constitution, section 93 of the BNA Act.[65]

Protestants, Jews, Democracy, and Law: The PSBGM's Jewish Members Redux

As it had throughout the long history, and various iterations of the Jewish School Question in and around Montreal, the law continued to serve as a formal constitutional framing mechanism, which was invoked when it suited the interests of one of the many parties, including the Jewish community, in the broader context of the political and social relations between and among the relevant constituent groups. A classic case of law as limit arose with the question of the Jewish quota on the PSBGM in 1972. The probably unconstitutional statute, which had given Jews representative rights for the first time on the broad governing body for Montreal Protestant schools, had limited the number of Jewish commissioners to five, who were named by Order in Council for different periods. The municipality of Westmount – a common Protestant board, like other local school boards in Montreal, common, dissentient, and Order-in-Council – had the right to have a representative on the PSBGM, which, in its various institutional embodiments since the organizational reforms arising out the recommendations of the Commission of Nine, had served as the site of collective Protestant school governance. In 1972, Mrs S.L. Kaplan had been elected as the Westmount representative on the Montreal body. Mrs Kaplan was Jewish. Her election therefore brought the number of Jews on the PSBGM to six, five appointed by the government, and now one from the Westmount School Board. It was accepted by all parties, without further inquiry or question, that the limit of five Jews was the definitive numerical maximum Hebrew presence on the Protestant board. By common accord, the constitutive and legally constitutional framework for the PSBGM still limited the full equality of Jewish Montrealers by a *numerus clausus*.

No one sought to argue that, because she was a representative from Westmount, Mrs Kaplan's presence on the board was of a different legal type, and that therefore she sat, not as a Jew, but as the representative of that school board. Such an argument could have been made and perhaps should have been made, but it seemed to have been beyond the political and legal imaginations of those involved. The Protestant members of the board saw Mrs Kaplan as a Jew, and the Jewish members, along with the CJC, did as well. Perhaps this was unsurprising, given that Jewish claims to representation had always been made in denominational terms, and Protestant objections to those claims had also be voiced in similar language. Indeed, the whole structure of Montreal common school education had historically been – and in the 1970s continued to be – constructed and constituted foundationally in denominational terms, because section 93 and the historical reality of religious rights in Montreal's schools demanded one and only one frame of reference. Jews sat on the PSBGM as Jews in a Protestant system. The very legal fact of Jewish representation had been rendered by statute in this same overarching hermeneutic frame. The Protestant School Board was still a denominational board, albeit now one with a Protestant and Jewish membership. After much debate, pleading, and negotiation over which of the other Jewish members should resign to make way for Mrs Kaplan, Samuel Godinsky, who had been at the heart of the negotiations with the Protestant officials that had led to Jewish membership on the PSBGM in the first place, resigned to allow the Westmount representative to take her seat.[66] The idea of denominational identity, which, from the beginning, had defined the structures and essence of Montreal public schools, with the ineffable distinction between Roman Catholics and Protestants, had now had a direct and ironically negative impact on the Jews of Montreal. By defining the membership of the PSBGM as Protestant or Jewish, the law had created a situation in which all Jewish members of the PSBGM could only ever be defined as Jews. The idea of democratic representation from local Protestant boards on the PSBGM was overridden, or subsumed by the Jewish quota on the board, as a whole. The CJC had simply accepted this legal fact. The shadow of section 93 continued to prevent the full flowering of the democratic impulses that had informed significant efforts by Montreal's Jewish communities to achieve equality in educational matters, and that, more broadly, had been a key impulse in the transformation of Quebec society during the Quiet Revolution. Law continued, ultimately in the context of Quebec education, to serve as a crucial impediment to democracy and equality in terms of citizenship understood outside narrow religious categories.

The next year, the Quebec legislature passed statutes confirming the confessional nature of the province's educational system, while at the same time introducing universal suffrage into school elections.[67] After many years of campaigning from citizen groups, seeking democratic governance in the school system throughout the province, the ideal had become reality.[68] The law still required voters to be classed as Roman Catholics or Protestants for electoral purposes, including all non–Roman Catholic, non-Protestant voters.[69] But once that selection had been made, all Canadian citizens over the age of eighteen were free to participate in school board elections, as voters and as candidates.[70] The change insofar as Jews were concerned was sweeping, since they were no longer considered a special case. Now, as had been the proposal in the 1920s introduced by the Protestant board with the support of Roman Catholic school officials, they were considered to be non–Roman Catholic, non-Protestant. This status, while again still one imposed by the dual denominationality framed by section 93, gave them the option to select between the two founding religious categories, for all school purposes, including elections. In some intriguing way, this perhaps marked a partial return to the situation that had obtained at the time of, and had given rise to, the first Jewish School Question, when Jews in Montreal had been given the option of choosing the panel into which their taxes would be paid, and the members of the Spanish and Portuguese synagogue had opted to become Roman Catholic Jews for a brief period. But the context was now significantly different from what it been when the Baron de Hirsch Institute had engaged in its struggle to prevent the Shearith Israel taxpaying elite from barring access to education to the city's poor Jewish immigrant children. The long battle for enfranchisement had now come to an end with the introduction of this form of universal suffrage. Of course, such changes were also almost certainly, if not blatantly, unconstitutional insofar as they granted electoral rights to Jews, or any other non-Protestants, in Montreal to elect Protestant (or Roman Catholic for that matter) School Commissioners.

By allowing non-Protestants to vote in elections for Protestant schools in Montreal and schools elsewhere that had been dissentient, the Quebec legislature was clearly affecting rights and privileges enjoyed by the Protestant "class of persons" at the time of Confederation. The CJC had always understood that real school equality, including total enfranchisement of Jewish citizens, could legally take place only with the repeal of section 93 of the BNA Act.[71] The PSBGM had also always clearly grasped this point, as their continuing legal advice to Order in Council schools had consistently highlighted. The recent changes, advocated and achieved by the Protestant educational authorities, to section 580 of the Education Act, maintaining restrictions on Jewish equality only in Outremont, Verdun, and the narrowly defined area of the Protestant School Board of Montreal, had been explicitly drafted in that way in order to maintain a formal, legal respect for the constitutional limitations imposed by section 93, as interpreted in *Hirsch*. The naming of Jews to the PSBGM had probably been unconstitutional in terms of the Privy Council's opinion in that case. The introduction of a new system of universal suffrage, which permitted Jews to vote in elections, which would include dissentient Protestant schools and Protestant schools in Montreal however narrowly defined, was also most likely unconstitutional. But the Quebec government, Protestant and Roman Catholic educational authorities, the CJC, the province's Jews, and the people of Quebec generally agreed that universal suffrage and elected school boards were of major democratic import for Quebec.[72] The Quiet Revolution's impulse towards full and concrete equality had long since replaced the anti-democratic sentiments that had led to the rejection of the Finnie and Langlois bills sixty-five years earlier. That the changes were most likely technically unconstitutional seemed to be of little consequence to all parties. Once more, the Jewish School Question was part of a much broader political and pedagogical context. And again, the Jewish School Question was one to which a political and social solution – and not necessarily a legal, constitutional one – would be found. With this statutory amendment creating universal suffrage for school elections in Montreal, whatever its technical legal status as a matter of constitutional law, Jews had finally achieved the equality they had struggled for, inside, outside, and around the political and jurisprudential edges of the constitutional and constitutive framework of section 93. Seeking to invoke technical illegality at this point would perhaps have been to ignore an underlying truth of the Jewish School Question. With all its contradictions and complexities, with the vagaries of law in context, the historical reality of the Jewish School Question had always been more broadly constitutional and constitutive. Protestants, Roman Catholics, and Jews; teachers, students, and school administrators; clergy, community leaders, bureaucrats, and elected officials – everyone had engaged in struggles through which they had constituted themselves and their communities, sometimes inside, sometimes outside, and often alongside, the formal limits of constitutional law.

14

Constituting Canada and the Jewish School Question in Montreal, *fin*

(Not) Moving On: The Modern Jewish School Question

By the mid-1970s, then, the Jewish School Question had been settled, albeit perhaps not in full accordance with the constitutional text. In 1974, the *J* designation was finally removed from tax assessments in Montreal.[1] Jews in Quebec could vote in school elections, be candidates for the position of school commissioner, and sit on the PSBGM and the Superior Council of Education. They could send their children to any common public school in the province. They could do all of these things because the still-powerful Protestant minority and the Roman Catholic majority of the province had seen fit to accommodate demands for democratic equality within the complex evolving dynamics of Quebec social structures and political mechanisms. From the days of the Quiet Revolution, for many citizens of the province, the existential and social definitional quality of denominational adherence had become less significant. Quebec Jews had been able to achieve this end to the Jewish School Question because Protestants and Roman Catholics echoed Jewish demands for democracy on the educational front. All parts of Montreal's populace now sought greater and more direct community control over the education of their children. The Jewish communities had also been able to achieve school equality because throughout the 1950s, 1960s, and into the 1970s they had presented a united voice. While local Jewish communities occasionally clashed with the centralized strategic needs of the CJC, there had been essentially a single Jewish voice and a single Jewish position on the key issues.

Of course, and again, the Jewish School Question did not disappear. It simply took on other guises. Some were familiar. While the PSBGM and the CJC continued discussions on Jewish representation and a democratic franchise in Montreal school elections, the CJC also had to continue to approach Protestant school officials over the right of Jewish teachers to be absent from school on holy days.[2] Other changes operated at more fundamental levels within Jewish Montreal and the political environment of Quebec.

Ironically, the period from the 1950s, which had marked the emergence of a unified voice in the Jewish communities' struggles for school rights and educational equality, also brought with it significant changes in the constitutive make-up of those same Jewish communities. The first major change was the influx of significant groups of Hassidic Jews to Montreal. These groups added to the mix in debates about the nature of Jewish identity/identities, which had always formed an important part of the life world of Jewish Montreal.[3] Their particular views on the relationship between the religious and the secular would often bring them into conflict with their French-Canadian neighbours in Outremont, where Hassidic groups established themselves.[4] Disputes arose over the creation of an eruv,[5] and today battle lines are still being drawn over such vital neighbourhood issues as traffic and parking on holy days.[6] In the world of schooling, similar disputes, often involving gender and education, would lead to many years of debate and conflict with government authorities.[7]

The other significant change to affect Montreal Jewry and to add further complexity to the Jewish School Question in Montreal to this day, was the arrival, again from the 1950s, of significant numbers of Sephardic Jews from North Africa.[8] Religiously and culturally Jewish, they also came from familial and collective experiences as people deeply embedded in the francophone cultures of Algeria, Tunisia, and Morocco.[9] Unlike their Ashkenazi predecessors, many North African Jews wanted their children to be educated in French.[10] In Montreal, where language and religion had been intimately linked for so long, this caused several years of conflict and difficulty, not just in the Sephardic community's relationships with the two dominant groups of Canadian bi-denominationalism and bilingualism, but with their anglophone fellow Jews on the CJC.[11] Arrangements had to made for Jewish, francophone education within the Roman Catholic school system, and later within the

Protestant system as well. The Jewish communities of Montreal had to adjust their self-identity as anglophone within the dominant matrix of cultural politics in Quebec.[12] Likewise, francophone Quebeckers had to rethink their identity as foundationally Roman Catholic, as Jews who spoke French and who lived and thrived in francophone culture became part of the province's complex demographic, social, political, and cultural reality.[13] Montreal Jewry continued to shift and change, yet around them the formal constitutional legal context remained static until 1997.[14]

Old Wine in New Bottles: Goodbye to Section 93

Whatever demographic changes occurred, whatever cultural and communal existential elements structured the self-constituting dynamics of Montreal Jewries, section 93 nonetheless remained in place.[15] It still inevitably constituted a constitutionalized roadblock to advances in Quebec society and its educational system. On the Island of Montreal in particular, the complex demographic situation, with its linguistic complications and increasingly diverse ethno-cultural make-up, led to increasingly vocal demands to restructure the schools along language lines – demands that had been heard consistently since the early days of the Quiet Revolution in the 1960s and had formed part of the political dialogue in the province since the Parent Commission. Still, however, the situation remained juridically fixed in 1867, and advances in Montreal's educational system were still stymied by the provisions of section 93.[16] The Protestant community offered two-fold resistance to any proposed move to linguistic school governance. T. Palmer Howard, long-term legal representative of the Protestant Board of School Commissioners, with significant drafting assistance from F.R. Scott, had produced a careful report.[17] After reiterating the standard defence of Protestant educational rights as guaranteed by section 93, the Protestant advocate recognized the practical and political significance of the argument in support of linguistic school structures. However, the Howard Report made it clear that if the dominant legal taxonomy were to shift from Protestant to anglophone, fundamental assertions of rights would not disappear from the constitutive political and legal discourse. The English-speaking minority could never consent to the creation by legislation of a school system that did not have constitutionally enshrined protections against majority attack. The terms of the debate may have shifted much more in favour of a consensus on language as the key signifier of identity in education, but this did not mean that constitutional rights would not be in play.

When the Quebec government attempted to change the overall tax system for education and put in place a system of grants from the province, the Supreme Court found that many parts of that scheme adversely affected the rights that local school boards had enjoyed at the time of Confederation, both to receive proportional grants and to levy local taxes.[18] The provincial government attempted a more fundamental change, to move from denominational school structures to linguistic ones, a reform again from the times of the Parent Royal Commission and the Pagé Committee. At the time, such a restructuring of Quebec's educational system reflected the dominant identity politics of Quebec more than the Protestant/Roman Catholic dichotomy. Nonetheless, the fundamental guarantees of the right to dissent and of the denominational character of schooling in Montreal continued to stand in the way of sweeping change.[19] In one of its most important structural embodiments – the system of public education for its citizens – Quebec society was impeded by a constitutional legal structure frozen in 1867 and the historically dominant bi-confessionality that failed to reflect the political and social realities of an increasingly secularized and linguistically polarized (not to mention multi-, pluri, or inter-cultural) Quebec.[20] At the same time, efforts to introduce deep and fundamental changes to the constitutional system of the Canadian federation, through the complex process of patriating the constitution, met with political, cultural opposition from provincial governments in Quebec, which sought a greater constitutive embodiment of Quebec identity and autonomy in any new Canadian constitutional arrangement.[21]

Throughout this telling of the stories of the Jewish School Question in Montreal, section 93 has been omnipresent. At various junctures, both Roman Catholics and Protestants invoked its letter and its spirit in order to guard and protect their educational rights, while Jews in the periods of *Pinsler* and *Hirsch* sought alternative interpretations in order to concretize the promises of British citizenship and the equality found in the emancipatory text of the 1832 Act. At other times, the penumbra of section 93 informed and limited every attempt to find accommodations, arrangements, and agreements to put an end to each of the disputes that together make up the complex history of the Jewish School Question. That penumbra was ignored on occasion, as practical provisions were put into place to put an end, however temporary, to the conflicts that arose over the presence of Jewish students and Jewish parents in Montreal's educational worlds. But Montreal's Jews, Protestants, and Roman Catholics always knew that, in the end, section 93 stood as a constitutional barrier on the path to complete Jewish equality and emancipation and to any foundational, constitutive reordering of education in Montreal.

It is not my goal here to trace in detail the story of the struggle for a new set of constitutional arrangements, a struggle that still informs Canadian politics today. Instead I offer only a brief summary to underscore the events and contexts that led to the final constitutional and constitutive determination of the Jewish School Question. The story of patriation is already well known.[22] The Supreme Court of Canada held that the complex Westminster constitutional rules and conventions governing Canadian constitutional law permitted the bringing home of what would become the Canada Act.[23] Prime Minister Trudeau acted swiftly to ensure that the U.K. and Canadian Parliaments could fulfil the requirements for the Canadianization of the Constitution, including the incorporation of the Charter of Rights and Freedoms.[24] Quebec remained recalcitrant, despite the fact that its claim to a veto over any attempt to modify, including to patriate, the Constitution had failed to convince the highest court. The political struggle over the constitutive ideals of the Canadian federation within and outside Quebec did not end with legal defeat.[25]

Efforts were made to bring Quebec into the constitutional fold, culminating with the political failures of a rewriting of the constitutional text to include recognition of Quebec as a "distinct society" within the Canadian federation at Meech Lake[26] and at Charlottetown.[27] There are many explanations for the failure of the constitutional amendment process, not all of which are attributable to intransigence by the governments of Quebec.[28] Issues of First Nations' place in the Canadian idea, struggles over equality of gender and multicultural identity, and the perception that the amendment process emanated from political elites and lacked democratic legitimacy rose to the fore of political debate. Assertions of other forms of regional identity led to other provinces advancing a claim similar to Quebec's insistence on its veto right and to attempts to create a different amendment formula for the Constitution. And as always, Quebec's insistence on a set of constitutional and constitutive demands doomed the process.[29] When the nationwide referendum meant to affirm the deal hashed out in Charlottetown went down to defeat, what Peter Russell called "mega constitutional politics" came to an end.[30] For Russell, it was time to return to more traditional Canadian constitutional processes. "There are a myriad of ways in which the Canadian federation can be made to work more efficiently and responsively without risking the heavy politics of formal constitutional amendment."[31]

While the idea of a return to business as usual, to political dialogue and compromise was perhaps a common sense approach to the disappointments and failures of the constitutional moments of Meech Lake and Charlottetown, the basic constitutional and constitutive fact that has informed this book remained in place. Section 93 still governed the educational system of Quebec, and Quebec's place in the Canadian confederation continued to trouble the nation's constitutional identity.[32]

The election of a Parti Québécois government in 1994 led the next year to a hard-fought referendum campaign on independence/sovereignty and resulted in a win by federalist forces.[33] The narrowness of the victory did little to assuage Quebec nationalists or to put federalist sentiment at ease. The federal elections that followed resulted in a further divided and regionalized Canadian political landscape nationally, including the loss of some electoral power by the Bloc Québécois.[34] While the state of the Canadian federation remained politically complex and Quebec's place in it was always still in doubt, the simple and daily realities of government and governance still faced provincial and federal governments. In Quebec, one issue that again played a central role in the political and social arenas was the ongoing reform of the province's educational system. Among concerns about the province's schooling, ranging from problems with primary and elementary schools and strong evidence of regional and socio-economic inequality in the education system, to the rapid increase of numbers in the province's universities and difficulties in building a continuing education system to cope with changing workforce demands, the issue of section 93 and confessional schooling again appeared as part of the core political and social program in Quebec.

Following the Supreme Court's mixed response to the provincial scheme attempting to institute linguistic boards, and the clear obstacles presented by the historical right to dissent and the specificities of denominational rights in Montreal, the province was looking for a way around the section 93 impasse.[35] As broader political debate and controversy swirled on educational issues, the Quebec Ministry of Education commissioned another report on school structures, this time from the Advisory Committee on the Establishment of Linguistic School Boards, headed by Patrick Kenniff, who had been a law professor at

Laval, a deputy minister in the provincial government, and rector and vice-chancellor of Concordia University, and was perfectly at home in both French and English. The title of the advisory committee indicates the narrow brief it received, but it did engage in an in-depth consultation and in 1994 produced its report.[36] Once again, the Kenniff Report, as it was known, recommended the establishment of a province-wide system of dual school administration and governance on the basis of language. The report recognized that the implementation of such a system would confront the two well-known constitutional hurdles under section 93. First, the right to dissent outside the boundaries of Quebec City and Montreal was enshrined in the legal interpretive history of the text of the BNA Act. The advisory committee suggested that legislative limits be placed on this right, in effect eliminating future dissent, although it appears that it was fully aware of the potential legal challenges to such an arrangement.[37] For Montreal and Quebec City, the report urged the government to replace the existing structures with linguistic, English- and French-language school boards, which would then incorporate "denominational committees to which certain powers would be delegated, in order to meet the requirements of the Canadian Constitution and the decision of the Supreme Court of Canada."[38] The proposal aimed to deal with section 93 by creating a more complex administrative structure under which the existing Protestant and Roman Catholic School Commissions would be rolled up into the new English and French systems and be reconstituted as committees of each linguistic school system. Again, such a proposal would clearly have been open to a constitutional challenge, given the historically strong idea of denominational educational autonomy reflected in judicial interpretations of the guarantees of section 93. Moreover, the governance structure put forward by the Kenniff Report was clunky and full of potential duplication and demarcation debates over the scope and breadth of the committees' roles and jurisdiction. Finally, and perhaps most significantly, the presence of two denominational committees at the heart of the linguistic school system did not assuage the belief of many proponents that secularization had to be a core element of Quebec's new educational arrangement. The politics of language, religion, and education were complicated and section 93 did not help matters. A further study of schooling in the province was commissioned. The Estates General on Education conducted yet another broad review of Quebec's school system and confronted the problem of section 93 head on.[39]

Again the political dynamic in play was complex. However, it seems clear that two principle motivating factors were at hand in this latest attempt to deal with the bi-confessional education structure in Quebec. First, there was the omnipresent and now long-standing desire to arrange education along linguistic lines, as a more accurate and true reflection of the sociological structures of the province. For the Parti Québécois government in particular, the idea of a Quebec identity formed along language lines was a core political and ideological value, in line with other legal and governmental arrangements dealing with its basic belief in Quebec as a nation. Second, the longer-term dynamic of Quebec education and social reform, dating at least from the days of the Parent Commission, was increasingly prone to *laïcité*, of bringing an end to clerical and religious dominance of education in the province. The move to a complete de-confessionalization of Quebec public schools had long been blocked by section 93 and broader issues of constitutional reform in the province. For the Estates General, the de-confessionalization of schools was of primary importance in the broader process of separating church and state in the province, a process begun with the Quiet Revolution and enshrined provincially in the principles set out in the Quebec Charter of Human Rights and Freedoms.[40] Linguistic school structures, the removal of any vestige of clerical or denominational control of school governance, and education as a core part of national identity and socio-economic progress and equality formed the basis of the government's ideological program. The Estates General now called upon the Quebec government to take all necessary steps to remove the anomaly that was section 93. While scholars criticized the Estates General Report on a number of grounds, it was clear that the document had grasped the constitutional nettle. This report exhorted those with the power to do so, to reorganize Quebec education along lines more appropriate to the approach of the twenty-first century by getting rid of the legal text that froze the province's schools in the nineteenth.[41]

The lessons of Meech Lake and Charlottetown were clear. Mega constitutional reform was not on the national or provincial political horizon. The Quebec government had narrowly lost the sovereignty referendum and had no taste for another round of foundational, constitutive struggles. The federal government no doubt wished to bring Quebec back inside the broader national constitutional framework, but it could practically do so only by following what Edward W. McWhinney characterized as the "politics of little steps."[42] "The obvious way – the logical way

– to proceed to constitutional change today in the absence of any popular national consensus in support of total revision of the constitution is to concentrate on specific change in response to specific problems. This was clearly Prime Minister Chrétien's preferred approach."[43]

One such specific problem was the reform of education in Quebec. Foundational change to the province's education system and the formation of linguistic school boards had not only been a long-standing issue for successive provincial governments, but the very idea of Quebec constructed and constituted in linguistic terms was central to the heart of the Parti Québécois and at the core of its educational platform. Prime Minister Jean Chrétien's view of Quebec as a "distinct society" and of the importance of bringing Quebec into the emerging constitutional fold informed federal openness to dialogue and change. At the same time, the provincial government continued to reject the legitimacy of the 1982 patriation and of the Constitution Act, including the Charter. The dilemma was obvious. A constitutional amendment was required to get rid of section 93, which had been an insurmountable obstacle. But the provincial government had always specifically and actively opposed any idea that the Constitution in its present form was a valid normative instrument.

A further practical hurdle also presented itself in addition to the ideological push and pull in the positions of the Quebec and federal governments. The question was how to change section 93 without going through the process of "mega constitutional politics." Part V of the Constitution Act itself contained formal provisions dealing with "Procedure for Amending Constitution of Canada." Again this is not the place, nor is it necessary, to cover the complexities of constitutional amendment in this or any other legal text in Canada.[44] Despite lingering questions about the exact meaning of the provisions, the most obvious choice was to proceed under section 43 of the Constitution Act. "An amendment to the Constitution of Canada in relation to any provision that applies to one or more, but not all, provinces ... may be made by proclamation issued by the Governor General under the Great Seal of Canada only where so authorized by resolutions of the Senate and the House of Commons and of the legislative assembly of each province to which the amendment applies."

This bilateral amending provision could remove the obstacle of section 93 as it operated in Quebec through the agreement of the National Assembly and the two houses of the federal Parliament.[45] A detailed study by the historian of Quebec education, Jean-Pierre Proulx, and the constitutional scholar José Woehrling, originally commissioned by the provincial Liberal shadow minister for education, had detailed the case that an amendment to section 93 under the bilateral process was both desirable and permissible.[46] This then moved debate beyond the complexities and impossibility of complete constitutional change and offered a clearer and more precise way of gaining a linguistic school system without the confusing governance structures that had informed the Kenniff Report. There was intellectual and political support for changing the constitution by abrogating section 93. In principle, Quebec was already in agreement to make this change to finalize the deconfessionalization of its school system, and the Proulx-Woehrling study gave them a juridically sound and politically acceptable way to achieve this goal without engaging in constitutional meta-politics. The Estates General had urged action, and the government had begun the process of constitutional change.[47] Leaders of the Roman Catholic Church were still seeking firmer guarantees about the protection of private denominational schools under any new organizational structure within the province, and leaders of some Protestant denominations shared those concerns and advanced others about the delicate and fraught issues within Quebec's political domain about protections for, and the continuing vitality of, Quebec's anglophone communities.[48] As the Howard Report had presaged, when the terms of the debate shifted from denominationalism to language, they did not eliminate the political concerns of the minority. Instead the locus of the necessary constitutional guarantees for minority survival simply shifted from religion to language. The debates surrounding moves towards a new non-confessional system of public education in Quebec had never reflected anything approaching unanimity.[49] At public hearings of the National Assembly education committee, francophone Protestants had expressed concerns about maintaining their Protestant identity in the new linguistic system, where they would clearly be in the minority.[50] Other voices from the anglophone community expressed worries about the long-term effect of Quebec language legislation on the viability of an English-language school system and sought guarantees of their communal survival in any future legislative framework.[51] Others spoke in favour of the change, arguing that the time had come to establish the primacy of French-language instruction in the province's schools. Some groups reiterated long-standing positions that the current confessional system was a block to true democratic and modern school governance and education.[52] Political compromise was on the agenda, and the idea confirmed by legal experts and politicians alike that both the federal Charter and future provincial legislation would protect broader anglophone and allophone rights appeared to have paved the way for a Quebec consensus on procedures to remove section 93 from the educational landscape.

For its part, the federal government was content to accept the applicability of the bilateral amendment procedure. The minister of intergovernmental affairs, Stéphane Dion, informed the House that the two governments had agreed on the appropriate amendment mechanism and that no apparent legal obstacles stood in the way.[53] However, the minister also stated that the unanimous vote of Quebec's National Assembly did not indicate that there was total agreement within Quebec society. After underlining the fact that the Quebec government had guaranteed the ongoing existence of denominational schools for those who wished to send their children to them, Dion also indicated that the federal Charter of Rights and Freedoms would always protect religious freedom and linguistic rights in the province, despite Quebec's penchant for invoking the "notwithstanding clause" as part of its broader rejection of the legitimacy of the Constitution, and an embedded cultural understanding among some Quebec jurists that the Charter itself was an obstacle to national flourishing.[54] On balance, for the federal government, support of the people of Quebec for the change to linguistic boards was long-standing. Foundational constitutional protections were in place for both language and religion. Dion was convinced that the constitutional amendment should proceed. "To conclude, the government is of the view that the proposed constitutional amendment we have received from the National Assembly falls within the class of bilateral amendments provided for in section 43 of the *Constitution Act, 1982*. The government believes that this amendment should be passed expeditiously, in accordance with parliamentary procedure, for it will have positive consequences for Quebec society, including both of its linguistic communities. Quebec society has reached a consensus on a constitutional issue that touches upon the vital issues of schooling language and religion."[55]

Later that year, the government appointed a special joint committee of the Senate and House of Commons to consider the matter, as required under section 43 with its condition of the approval of the two federal chambers.[56] The joint committee decided that it was not a mere rubber stamp for what appeared to be the clear will of the federal and provincial governments. There may have been a consensus that the time to de-confessionalize the schools had come, and that section 93 was a relic of Victorian visions of Canada, but consensus was not unanimity, and strong voices from within Quebec and from minority francophone populations elsewhere in Canada still objected to the constitutional change. It held its own hearings and received evidence, in order to determine whether Ottawa should adopt the proposed amendment. Among the issues addressed and upon which the joint committee focused was the federal test that should be applied when faced with a provincial request to amend the Constitution. It was evident that there was a consensus in Quebec on de-confessionalization and had been since at least the days of the Parent Commission. The National Assembly had given its unanimous assent to the abrogation of section 93. But the joint committee was aware that political arrangements in provincial legislatures did not necessarily reflect or embody a core idea of protecting the rights of potentially vulnerable minorities. It chose to adopt the approach suggested by Patrick Monahan in his testimony that it assure itself that the "majority of minorities" affected by the proposed amendment be in agreement.[57]

One important minority affected by any move to modify the system of education in Quebec was the Jewish community. Joe Rabinovich, chair of the CJC Education Committee for Quebec, articulated the complexities of the position of the province's Jews.

> It's twofold, and one is connected to the other. In principle we are in agreement with the attempt or the desire of the Quebec government to amend the constitution as proposed, provided that if they extend the rights of confessionality at the school level to Catholics and Protestants, these same rights must be extended to other religious minorities.
>
> This has been our position from day one. As we move toward the 21st century … the BNA Act of 1867 reflected what were the standards in 1867. The 21st century in Quebec is not what it was in 1867. The school system in Quebec must reflect the new Quebec in terms of the changing face of Quebec. We believe one step towards this is the amendment of this section to remove what I'll call a privilege of Protestants and Catholics which must have been needed in 1867. It's not now.[58]

The concern again was not with the idea of abolishing the privileged position of Roman Catholics and Protestants in education under the Constitution. Quebec Jews had always articulated arguments about this anomalous situation, informed by broad concerns for equality and the rights of their children. What bothered the CJC representatives was not the abrogation of section 93. Rather, it was the substance of the proposed provincial legislation de-confessionalizing the province's schools. There they saw an attempt to grant rights and privileges to the two historical denominations by expressly permitting the continuing existence of Protestant and Roman Catholic systems, while once again putting the Jewish communities and their schools in a position governed by potential legislative silence and inequality.[59] The CJC had sought assurances that the rights of minority religions would not be adversely affected under provincial legislation. In the end they were convinced that the rights guaranteed under the Canadian Charter and the province's larger framework for private school funding would protect Jewish interests under the proposed linguistic system. Indeed, as David Sultan, CJC community relations officer, pointed out, the arrival of North African Jews in Montreal in the late 1950s and early 1960s meant that Jewish Montrealers had experienced both French- and English-language schooling and were able to speak about the move to a linguistic system with a foot in both dominant camps.[60] Despite its reservations about certain matters pertaining to provincial education policy more broadly, the CJC assured the joint committee that the Jewish communities of Quebec, and anglophones and francophones more broadly, "unequivocally" supported the creation of linguistic, non-denominational public schools in the province.[61]

While some doubts remained, the joint committee reported, "Overall it appears that, although some witnesses expressed their concerns with respect to the proposed amendment, there is a consensus in Quebec society supporting this change."[62]

While evidencing a remarkable degree of agreement and cooperation between federal and provincial authorities, the process also embodied the wider conflicts and discord that characterized Canadian constitutional politics at the time. Quebec cooperated in bringing about the amendment to the constitutional text that had stood in its way to a linguistically defined identity within the province's schools. It had also used the formal process of constitutional amendment to voice its fundamental opposition to the constitutional ideal more generally. When the National Assembly passed the appropriate resolution authorizing the governor general to amend the Constitution, it did so with the proviso that "such amendment in no way constitutes recognition by the National Assembly of the *Constitution Act, 1982*, which was adopted without its consent."[63]

In an unsurprisingly Canadian solution to the problem of section 93, Quebec refused to recognize in principle the text upon which the entire legal, constitutional, and constitutive process relied. It rejected and used the constitutional mechanism simultaneously. Nonetheless, the constitutional gymnastics of bilateral amendment had one lasting and key effect. The Jewish School Question in Montreal had come to an end.

The final change, the ultimate resolution of the traditional manifestations of the Jewish School Question, would become possible only in 1997, with the adoption of section 93 A of the Constitution Act that stated simply, "Paragraphs (1) to (4) of section 93 do not apply to Quebec."

Constituting Law, Constituting Quebec: After Section 93

One simple sentence removed the shadow of illegality that had hung over all legal arrangements in education, under which Quebec Jews had managed to achieve the full equality rights promised to them since 1832.[64] In Quebec, the amendment marked the end of constitutionally enshrined denominational education and its long-awaited replacement by a system of French- and English-language schools and administrative structures.[65] This did not end social, political, and cultural struggles in the province or more specifically in Montreal itself. However, it did confirm the emphasis that had increasingly characterized sociological and political inquiry and debate since the 1960s on linguistic identity and a quest for some version of equality within those identity structures and Quebec society more generally.[66] The real cleavages in Quebec politics now centred clearly and explicitly on language, not religion. The embattled minority was no longer Protestant; it was clearly anglophone (and allophone to a lesser extent).[67] The constitutional hermeneutic imposed by section 93 had been replaced with a different form of discourse that more accurately reflected the political realities of life in Quebec, as it had in the 1920s and 1930s, where the Jews would feature and became a debate about national identity, but this time without primacy given to an overarching and hegemonic Roman Catholicism. At the same time, religion did not magically disappear from Quebec society or from versions of Quebec identity overnight. A glance at the cross that continues to sit atop Mont Royal and overlooks the city or at the crucifix in the chamber of the National Assembly identifies the still strong semiotic cultural presence of a Roman Catholic/Québécois synonymy, even if that relationship is more complex and multi-variant as a social and political phenomenon than it was through most of the time of the Jewish School Question.

However, the abrogation of section 93 did bring with it important legal, social, political, and social changes. It became part of the fundamental shift in the rhetorical vectors of Quebec politics, from Roman Catholic nationalism to Québécois demands for independence or sovereignty. For many Montreal Jews, this resurgent nationalism, which had culminated in Parti Québécois electoral victories and the narrow loss in the independence referendum for sovereignist forces, simply resulted in a rebranded version of anti-Semitic nationalist politics.[68] For them, an ethnically/racially structured hermeneutic about all those who were not *pure laine* francophones in Quebec had always been deeply embedded in the majority culture.[69] Not a few Jewish Montrealers saw francophone Québécois nationalism as a rebranded Jew hatred and prejudice, which had informed Jewish/Roman Catholic, and now Jewish/francophone Québécois relations.[70] Many Jews decided that their stay in Quebec had come to an end, or would soon do so. Emigration to English Canada became a serious option for a community that had become established in Montreal through decades of self-constituting political and legal struggle.[71] The rhetoric separating the majority from this minority was ratcheted up, as it became increasingly clear that a set of new negotiated dialogues and social attempts to create new spaces for minorities within a dominant Québécois social and political space would be difficult.[72]

Within that dominant culture, hegemonic Roman Catholicism had been replaced not just by a francophone nationalist self-identity, but also by an increasing desire in important parts of the community for a linguistic and uni-cultural hegemony. The emerging multicultural, multi-religious, immigrant dynamic within the province and in Montreal in particular was now upsetting that desire. The question of the space for these groups, and individuals from these groups, available in the majority society took rhetorical shape within the legalized and constitutionalized discourse of "reasonable accommodation."[73] A government commission was established. At public hearings, the worst versions of anti-Semitic and other racial and religious vilification were voiced, as were more reasoned ideas for a future multicultural Quebec. The commission reported and recommended a Quebec version of French secular republicanism (*la laïcité*) for the province.[74] Later, the minority Parti Québécois government would seek to introduce a Charter of Secularism/Charte de Laïcité.[75] One provision of the proposed Charter would have meant that no public servant could wear any form of dress indicating membership in a particular faith. Section 5 provided, "In the exercise of their functions, personnel members of public bodies must not wear objects such as headgear, clothing, jewelry or other adornments which, by their conspicuous nature, overtly indicate a religious affiliation."[76]

No civil servant, no schoolteacher, for example, could wear an obvious religious symbol, such as a *kippah*. Premier Pauline Marois, who had been minister of education during the section 93 abrogation debates, insisted at the same time that the crucifix would remain in the National Assembly as a cultural and historical symbol of Quebec identity. But no observant Orthodox Jew could be a judge in the province whose primary ethical and legal values were shrouded in the cloak of *laïcité*. As with the Bouchard/Taylor Commission, debate around the Charte was heated and often nasty. Incidents of anti-Muslim and anti-Jewish aggression were recorded, and once more the idea of a multicultural and tolerant Quebec citizenship was put to the test of public discourse rife with anti-Semitism and other forms of racial and religious hatred.[77] Marois was defeated in the next provincial election, and the Charte has entered political limbo until, perhaps, another Parti Québécois government.

No commission, no solution proposed by such a commission or embodied in a legal text, no Charter could ever concretize or give voice to all the contradictory hopes, wishes, and constitutive self-identities being asserted in Quebec in the twenty-first century.[78] Many of these battles appear to be taking on a more obviously juridified existence. Multicultural rights, and the respect for religious minorities in schools, long the core of the Jewish School Question, have taken on a litigious aura. Release time for religious observance for Jewish teachers is no longer a matter for negotiation between the school authorities, the teachers, and the Baron de Hirsch Institute, or the CJC. Instead, courts now decide how the claims of the school to administrative discretion, union rights to negotiate a collective agreement, and the teachers to religious freedom are to be balanced and accommodated within constitutional normative discourse.[79] Now that the state in Quebec has taken over the common public schools of the province, issues of collective identity and discursive practices between and among educational officials and members of minority communities have been replaced by an ever more firmly imposed state-centric ideal of those identities.[80] This then means a further turn to litigation as members of those communities seek to protect themselves, by an invocation of rights in a world of Charter of Rights and Freedoms litigation, from a dominant social, political, and cultural construction within the educational environment.[81]

Again, it is worth noting that the democratization of Quebec education, the removal of clerical control, and the institution of a system of state, common public schools, so long desired by the uptowners and later by the general Jewish populations in Montreal, has led to the loss or radical reduction of a social space in which minority communities could attempt to negotiate their own constitutive understandings of the nexus between education and citizenship. The failed reforms of the 1840s in Quebec had aimed at this institutionalization of governance and citizenship within the educational domain, as had earlier attempts to create a system of public schools.[82] Quebec Jews had long constructed their appeals to educational justice in terms of equality and their rights as British subjects and Canadian citizens. Now the victory enshrined in the abrogation of section 93 has been coloured by a shifting constitutional and political landscape. The formal constitutionalization of rights with the Canadian Charter of Rights and Freedoms marked the end, or in the best case, a radical narrowing of the spaces for the types of community-based constitution that had always characterized the socio-legal history of the Jewish School Question.[83]

But again and typically, the concrete, political end to the Jewish School Question, as it had emerged since the 1880s, had come well before the Canadian and Quebec polities achieved a textual, formalized constitutionalized victory in 1997, and before the discourse over minority rights became more formally constitutionalized and juridified. Since the 1970s, Montreal's Jewish communities had managed to achieve a level of equality in the shadow of legality. Section 93 was then still the defining constitutional text, but it stood in the background throughout the struggles for school equality in the second half of the twentieth century. While the PSBGM had insisted on the centrality of constitutionally enshrined, section 93 Protestant school rights in relation to dissentient and Order-in-Council schools, eventually they had simply backed away from asserting these rights in relation to claims for Jewish equality. They faced a new economic reality that without Jewish taxes, Protestant education could not survive. The government had passed appropriate legislation, with the approval of both the Protestant and Roman Catholic educational establishments. These statutory provisions, which in all likelihood would have failed constitutional scrutiny under *Hirsch*, collectively embodied and enshrined full Jewish equality in educational matters in Quebec. Elazar, Brown, and Robinson again have argued, "Throughout its history, then, Canadian society (and its fundamental laws) have promoted self-conscious Jewish identity and autonomous organization by providing 'space' for Jews to act. At first, that space was negative: interstices between the two founding peoples who made up the Canadian polity constitutionally."[84]

While there is a historical strength to this argument on the Jewish School Question in Montreal, especially insofar as the formation of Jewish community and welfare groups is concerned, perhaps a slight change of emphasis is more accurate. The Jews of Montreal did not carve out school rights, for themselves and their children, in the interstices between Roman Catholic French Canadians and Protestant anglophones. They dealt directly with these two groups and found a place for themselves, however tentative and however problematic, for the most part within the Protestant school system. They engaged in lobbying, politics, debate, protest, litigation, and negotiations, all within constitutional and constitutive structures and dynamics controlled by these two groups. They made themselves part of a complex, legal, and political hermeneutic process and exercised to the fullest extent possible the limited political power available to them within this broader bi-partite dynamic to advance their communal interests. That they sat awkwardly in a dual national, denominational, political, and educational structure was a simple fact of constitutional and self-constituting life for the Jewish communities of Montreal. In practice, they were always able to educate their children within the common school system, and in the earliest days of the Jewish School Question, with some degree of Jewish educational autonomy. *Pinsler*, *Hirsch*, and section 93 all posed roadblocks and hurdles to be overcome, in order to achieve the full educational equality of Jews as British subjects and later as Canadian citizens in Quebec, since the 1832 statute first recognized their legal emancipation. The Jews of Montreal managed to overcome these constitutional roadblocks, in many cases by convincing the two main groups in Quebec society that strict adherence to constitutional legal principle would not only result in a basic injustice for tens of thousands of citizens, but also the political and social unrest and uncertainty likely to arise from such constitutional certainties were more trouble than technical legality was worth. While framed by law, the Jewish School Question had always been a social and political issue, solved by politics within the complex sociology of evolving Quebec society. In the interstices of the dominant religious duality of Quebec identity, Jews sought out equality and full democratic citizenship as subjects of the British Empire, as Canadians and as inhabitants of Quebec. And of course they sought to do so in terms that allowed them to maintain and concretize their complex and sometimes conflicting understandings of themselves as Jews. They carried out their struggles inside, outside, and in the shadows of strict legality as they and the Protestant and Roman Catholic communities constituted themselves within often mutually exclusive self-understandings of their constitutional identities.

Another product of the Protestant educational system of Montreal, a graduate of Westmount High School and grandson of Lyon Cohen, the founding president of the Canadian Jewish Congress, perhaps best summarizes the contingent, interstitial, and narrative struggles in the construction of identities throughout the history of the Jewish School Question.

> There is a crack in everything
> That's how the light gets in
> – Leonard Cohen, "Anthem"

Notes

Chapter 1

1 Roderick MacLeod & Mary Anne Poutanen, *A Meeting of the People: School Boards and Protestant Communities in Quebec, 1801–1998* (Montreal & Kingston: McGill-Queen's University Press, 2004).

2 Mordecai Richler, *The Apprenticeship of Duddy Kravitz* (Toronto: Penguin Modern Classics, 1959) at 8. Richler repeated his "S" as a dollar sign story from his school days in the Introduction to *The Street* (Toronto: McClelland & Stewart, 1969) at 11.

3 (1903) 23 CS 365.

4 Glen Eker, *Index of Jews Resident in the Province of Quebec According to the 1861 to 1901 Censuses of Canada* (Toronto: Ontario Genealogical Society, 2004) at 57.

5 *Ibid* at 172.

6 Robert C Ellickson, *Order without Law: How Neighbors Settle Disputes* (Cambridge, MA: Harvard University Press, 1991).

7 "Opting Out of the Legal System: Extralegal Contractual Relations in the Diamond Industry" (1992) 21 J Legal Stud 115.

8 Robert L Tsai, *America's Forgotten Constitutions: Defiant Visions of Power and Community* (Cambridge, MA: Harvard University Press, 2014).

9 Robert Cover, *Justice Accused: Antislavery and the Judicial Process* (New Haven, CT: Yale University Press, 1975); Cover, "*Nomos* and Narrative" (1983–84) 97 Harv L Rev 4; Cover, "Violence and the Word" (1985–86) 95 Yale LJ 1601.

10 Peter Berger, "The Mission of Quebec Ultramontanism: A Luhmannian Perspective" (1985) 46 Sociological Analysis 37; Nive Voisine, *Histoire du catholicisme québécoise: le XXe siècle*, tome 1, *1898–1940* (Montreal: Boréal Express, 1984); Nadia Fahmy-Eid, *Le clergé et le pouvoir politique au Québec: Une analyse de l'idéologie ultramontaine au milieu du XIXe siècle* (Montreal: Hurtubise HMH, 1978); Jacques Monet, "French Canadian Nationalism and the Challenge of Ultramontanism" (1966) 1 Historical Papers 41.

11 The British North America Act is officially known and cited as the Constitution Act, 1867 (UK), 30 & 31 Vict, c 3, reprinted in RSC 1985, App II, No 5. However, because this book covers a specific historical period and the relevant actors at the time referred to the British North America or BNA Act, the common contemporary appellation will be used throughout.

12 The two colonies of Quebec and Ontario were united as Canada East and West under the provisions of the British North America Act 1840 (Act of Union), 3 & 4 Vict, c 35.

13 Quebec Act, 1774, 14 Geo III, c 83, ss 5 and 6.

14 Bernard Hyams, "The Colonial Office and Educational Policy in British North America and Australia before 1850" (1990) 2 Historical Studies in Education 323.

15 Bruce Curtis, *Ruling by Schooling Quebec: Conquest to Liberal Governmentality – A Historical Sociology* (Toronto: University of Toronto Press, 2012); Louis-Philippe Audet, *Le Système Scolaire de la Province de Québec*, 4 vols (Quebec: Les Éditions de l'Érable and Les Presses Universitaires Laval, 1951–52).

16 Curtis, *supra* note 15 at 331.

17 See, e.g., *The First Annual Report of the Central Auxiliary Society for Promoting Education and Industry in Canada* (Montreal: Herald Office, 1827).

18 Robin Bredin, *Struggling with Diversity: The State Education of a Pluralistic Upper Canadian Population, 1791–1841* (PhD Thesis, Department of Theory and Policy Studies in Education, University of Toronto, 2000) [unpublished].

19 Anthony Di Mascio, "Educational Discourse and the Making of Educational Legislation in Early Upper Canada" (2010) 50 History of Education Quarterly 33.

20 Franklin A Walker, "The History of Ontario Separate Schools: Sources and Problems" (1988) 55 Historical Studies 7; Michael F Murphy, "'Catholic Schools for Catholic Children': The Making of a Roman Catholic School in London Ontario 1850 to 1871" (1997) 63 CCHA Historical Studies 59.

21 Lorna R McLean, "Education, Identity, and Citizenship in Early Modern Canada" (2007) 41 Journal of Canadian Studies 5.

22 For the background of Confederation debates, see generally, Donald Creighton, *The Road to Confederation: The Emergence of Canada, 1863–1867*

(Toronto: Macmillan Canada, 1964); John KA Farrell, "Roman Catholic Influences Supporting Canadian Confederation" (1969) 55 Catholic Historical Review 7.

23 Alexander Tilloch Galt was of Scottish descent, but was born in London on 6 September 1817. He came to Canada as a young man and was a successful businessman and entrepreneur. He was elected at various times to the Legislature to represent Sherbrooke and achieved both high-level office and esteem. He was a strong proponent of Confederation but also a fervent protector of the anglophone Protestant minority of his adopted home in the Eastern Townships, and in Quebec more generally. He was knighted and died in Montreal on 19 September 1893. "Galt, Sir Alexander Tilloch" in Dictionary of Canadian Biography Online, <www.biographi.ca/en/bio/galt_alexander_tilloch_12E.html>.

24 Creighton, *supra* note 22 at 399; Thomas Jr White, *The Protestant Minority in Quebec in Its Political Relations with the Roman Catholic Majority: A Letter to Sir Alexander Tilloch Galt* (Montreal: Dawson Brothers, 1876).

25 Robert M Stamp, *The Historical Background to Separate Schools in Ontario* (Toronto: Ontario Department of Education, 1985); Walker, *supra* note 20.

26 Creighton, *supra* note 22 at 410; Robert Nicholas Bérard, "The Dartmouth Schools Question and the Supreme Court of Nova Scotia" (2005) 28 Dal LJ 199.

27 Mélanie Lanouette, *Penser L'Éducation, Dire Sa Culture: les écoles catholiques anglaises au Québec, 1928–1964* (PhD Thesis, Université Laval, 2004) [unpublished]; Sherry Olson & Patricia Thornton, "The Challenge of the Irish Catholic Community in Nineteenth-Century Montreal" (2002) 35 Social History 331.

28 Mélanie Lanouette, "L'école confessionnelle comme lieu d'expression identitaire des communautés linguistiques de Montréal, 1940–1960" (2006) 37 Documents pour l'histoire du français langue étrangère ou seconde 161.

29 Robert Choquette, *Language and Religion: A History of English-French Conflict in Ontario* (Ottawa: University of Ottawa Press, 1975); John Zucchi, *The View from Rome: Archbishop Stagni's 1915 Reports on the Ontario Bilingual Schools Question* (Montreal & Kingston: McGill-Queen's University Press, 2002).

30 Choquette, *supra* note 29; see Chanoine Charron, *La Langue Française: De quelques raisons de garder notre langue française* (Montreal: L'Oeuvre des Tracts, 1928).

31 [1917] AC 62; [1928] AC 363.

32 [1892] AC 445.

33 [1917] AC 62, 69.

34 *Ibid.* For a more recent iteration of related issues, see, *AG of Quebec v Quebec Association of Protestant School Boards et al*, [1984] 2 SCR 66.
35 [1928] AC 363, 366.
36 *Ibid.*
37 *Ibid* at 376.
38 *In the matter of the reference re the Education Act, SQ 1988, c 84*, [1993] 2 SCR 511; *Greater Montreal Protestant School Board v Quebec (AG)*, [1989] 1 SCR 377; *Greater Montreal Protestant School Board v Quebec (AG)*, [1989] 2 SCR 167.
39 See also *The Protestant School Board of Greater Montreal et al v AG of Quebec*, [1989] 1 SCR 377; *AG of Quebec v Greater Hull School Board et al* [1984] 2 SCR 575.
40 *City of Winnipeg v Barrett* [1892] AC 445; *Brophy v AG Manitoba*, [1895] AC 202. For a contemporary legal account, see Edward Meek, *The Legal and Constitutional Aspects of the Manitoba School Question* (Toronto: Hunter, Rose, 1895). The Manitoba school issue became a *cause célèbre* throughout the country, as it raised basic questions of both religion and language, two linchpins of struggles over Canadian identity. See, e.g., Jean DesPrairies, *Une Visite dans Les Écoles du Manitoba* (Montreal: Librairie Saint-Joseph, 1897), for a contemporary "French Canadian" account; see FC Wade, *The Manitoba School Question* (Winnipeg: np, 1895). On the eventual political compromise, see Stephen T Rusak, "The Canadian 'Concordat' of 1897" (1991) 77 Catholic Historical Review 209.
41 Gerald John Wheeler, *Confederation Law of Canada: Privy Council Cases on the British North-America Act, 1867* (London: Eyre & Spottiswoode, 1896), 338.
42 *Ibid* at 339.
43 *Ex parte Renaud*, 14 NBR 273 (1873); 3 RCLJ 93, (1873–1875).
44 Gordon Bale, *Chief Justice William Johnstone Ritchie: Responsible Government and Judicial Review* (Ottawa: Carleton University Press, 1991), 141–2.
45 Wheeler, *supra* note 41 at 366.
46 *Ibid* at 367.
47 Mark Heerema, "Newfoundland Religion in Term 17 (3) of the Newfoundland Act and Its Challenge to the Current Discourse on Freedom of Religion in the Public Sphere" (2005) 14 Dal J Leg Stud 111; John Edward Fitzgerald, "'The True Father of Confederation'?: Archbishop EP Roche, Term 17, and Newfoundland's Confederation with Canada" (1998) 14 Newfoundland Studies 188; Ki Su Kim, "JR Smallwood and the Negotiation of a School System for Newfoundland, 1946–48" (1995) 11 Newfoundland Studies 53.

48 See, generally, Roger Magnuson, *The Two Worlds of Quebec Education during the Traditional Era, 1760–1940* (London, ON: Althouse, 2005); Andrée Dufour, *Histoire de l'éducation au Québec* (Montreal: Boréal, 1997); Henry Milner, *The Long Road to Reform: Restructuring Public Education in Quebec* (Montreal & Kingston: McGill-Queen's University Press, 1986); Louis-Philippe Audet, *Histoire de l'enseignement au Québec*, 2 vols (Montreal: Holt Rinehart, Winston, 1971); Louis-Philippe Audet & Armand Gauthier, *Le Système Scolaire du Québec* (Montreal: Beauchemin, 1967); Louis-Phillippe Audet, *Le Système Scolaire de la Province de Québec*, 4 vols (Quebec: Les Éditions de l'Érable & Les Presses Universitaires Laval, 1951–52).

49 *Report of Committee of the Council on the Subject of Promoting the Means of Education* (Quebec: Samuel Neilson, 1790).

50 *A Letter: Most Respectfully Addressed to the Roman Catholic Clergy and the Seignors of the Province of Lower Canada Recommending the Establishment of Schools* (Quebec: J Neilson, 1810); Charles Mondelet, *Letters on Elementary and Practical Education* (Montreal: John James Williams, 1841); Curtis, *supra* note 15; W Dutton, *An Address to the Protestant Inhabitants of Canada on the Dangerous Character of the Education Act of 1846* (Montreal: JC Beckett, 1849).

51 Allan Greer and Ian Radforth, "Introduction," in Allan Greer and Ian Radforth, eds, *Colonial Leviathan: State Formation in Mid-Nineteenth-Century Canada* (Toronto: University of Toronto Press, 1992) at 3–16, 7.

52 Bruce Curtis, "Class Culture and Administration: Educational Inspection in Canada West," in Greer & Radforth, *Colonial Leviathan*, *ibid* at 103.

53 Curtis, *supra* note 15.

54 *Ibid* at 429; Jean-Pierre Proulx (with Christian Dessureault & Paul Aubin), *La genèse de l'école publique et de la démocratie scolaire au Québec: les écoles de syndics (1814–1838)* (Ste Foy, QC: Les Presses de l'Université Laval, 2014).

55 Magnuson, *supra* note 49 at 51; Roger Magnuson, "The Public School Myth: Quebec Education 1875–1960" (1987) 22 McGill Journal of Education 29.

56 An Act to repeal certain Acts therein mentioned, and to make further provision for the establishment of Common Schools throughout the Province, 4–5 Vict, c 18; Pierre Carignan, "La place faite à la religion dans les écoles publiques par la loi scolaire de 1841" (1982–83) 17 RJT ns 9.

57 An Act to repeal certain Acts and to provide in a more efficient manner to elementary education in Lower Canada, 9 Vict, c 28.

58 Robert Sellar, *The Tragedy of Quebec: The Expulsion of Its Protestant Farmers* (Toronto: Ontario, 1907); Edward McChesney Sait, *Clerical Control in Quebec* (Toronto: Sentinel, 1911); Mark McGowan, "Rethinking Catholic-

Protestant Relations in Canada: The Episcopal Reports of 1900–1901" (1992) 59 Historical Studies 11; JR Miller, "Anti-Catholic Thought in Victorian Canada" (1985) 66 Canadian Historical Review 474. On colonial, including Quebec, Protestant anti-Catholicism, see generally John Wolfe, "Anti-Catholicism and the British Empire, 1815–1914" in Hilary M Carey, ed, *Empires of Religion* (Houndsmills, Hants: Palgrave Macmillan, 2008) at 43.

59 JI Little, *The Other Quebec: Microhistorical Essays on Nineteenth-Century Religion and Society* (Toronto: University of Toronto Press, 2006).

60 9 Vict, c 28, s 42.

61 *Ibid*, s 45.

62 *Ibid*, s 43.

63 An Act to amend the school law of Lower Canada, 12 Vict, c 50, s 18.

64 An Act to amend common school laws, and further to promote elementary education in Lower Canada, 14 & 15 Vict, c 97, s 9.

65 An Act to further amend the common school laws, and further promote elementary education in Lower Canada, 19 Vict, c 14.

66 *Ibid*, ss 14ff. See generally, Louis-Philippe Audet, *Histoire du Conseil de l'instruction publique de la province du Québec 1856–1964* (Montreal: Éditions Leméac, 1964).

67 On the council generally, Audet & Gauthier, *supra* note 48; Montarville Boucher de LaBruère, *Le Conseil de l'Instruction Publique et Le Comité Catholique* (Montreal: Le Devoir, 1918).

68 An Act to amend the school laws of Lower Canada, 22 Vict, c 52.

69 An Act respecting provincial aid for superior education and normal and common schools, Consolidated Statutes of Lower Canada, 1861, c 15 & 16; Pierre Carignan, "La raison d'être de l'article 93 de la Loi constitutionelle de 1867 à la lumière de la législation préxistante en matière d'éducation" (1986) 20 RJT ns 375.

70 Ss 34ff; ss 54ff.

71 Ss 128ff.

72 An Act to amend the law respecting education in this province, 32 Vict, c 16.

73 S 24.

74 An Act to further amend the law respecting Public Instruction, 39 Vict, c 15.

75 For a study of the brief history of the ministry, see Keith D. Hunte *The Ministry of Public Instruction, 1867–1875* (PhD Thesis, McGill University, 1964) [unpublished].

76 Code de l'Instruction Publique, 1888, Art 39.

77 Audet & Gauthier, *supra* note 48 at 35.

78 Audet, *supra* note 66 at 80ff.

79 Onésime Gagnon, *Cultural Developments in the Province of Quebec: Minorities' Rights and Privileges under the Educational System* (Toronto: University of Toronto Press, 1952).

80 Mary Anne Poutanen, "'Unless she gives better satisfaction': Teachers, Protestant Education, and Community in Rural Quebec, Lochaber and Gore District, 1863–1945" (2003) 15 Historical Studies in Education 237; Ruby Heap & Alison Prentice, "'The outlook for old age is not hopeful': The Struggle of Female Teachers over Pensions in Quebec, 1880–1914" in Michael D. Behiels, ed, *Quebec since 1800: Selected Readings* (Toronto: Irwin, 2002), 313; Marta Danylewycz & Alison Prentice, "Teacher's Work: Changing Patterns and Perceptions in the Emerging School Systems of Nineteenth- and Early Twentieth-Century Central Canada" (1986) 17 Labour 59; Danylewycz & Prentice, "Teachers, Gender, and Bureaucratizing School Systems in Nineteenth-Century Montreal and Toronto" (1984) 24 History of Education Quarterly 75; Nadia Fahmy-Eid & Micheline Dumont, eds, *Maîtresses de maison, maîtresses d'école: Femmes, famille et éducation dans l'histoire du Québec* (Montreal: Boréal Express, 1983); Jean-Pierre Charland, *L'entreprise éducative au Québec, 1840–1900* (Ste Foy, QC: Les Presses de l'Université Laval, 2000), 274.

81 Anne Drummond, "Gender, Profession, and Principals: The Teachers of Quebec Protestant Academies, 1875–1900" (1990) 2 Historical Studies in Education 59.

82 Eric W Sager, "Women Teachers in Canada: 1881–1901: Revisiting the 'Feminization' of an Occupation" (2007) 88 Canadian Historical Review 201.

83 Normand Renaud, "Le collège classique: la maison d'enseignement, le milieu d'études, les fins et les moyens" (1981) 14 Études littéraires 415; Claude Galarneau, *Les Collèges classiques au Canada français: 1620–1970* (Montreal: Fides, 1978).

84 Patrice A Dutil, "The Politics of Muzzling 'Lucifer's Representative': Godfroy Langlois's Test of Wilfrid Laurier's Liberalism, 1892–1910" (1993) 28 Journal of Canadian Studies 113; see MP O'Connell, "The Ideas of Henri Bourassa" (1953) 19 Canadian Journal of Economics and Political Science 361, for a study of a self-identified ultramontane *rouge*. See also David Rome, *The Jewish Biography of Henri Bourassa*, 2 vols (Montreal: National Archives, Canadian Jewish Congress, 1991).

85 Yvan Lamonde, *The Social History of Ideas in Quebec, 1760–1896* (Montreal & Kingston: McGill-Queen's University Press, 2013); Voisine, *supra* note 10, 240.

86 Margaret Westley, *Remembrance of Grandeur: The Anglo-Protestant Elite of Montreal 1900–1950* (Montreal: Libre Expression, 1990), 63ff.

87 *Report of the Protestant Board of School Commissioners for the City of Montreal, 1847–1871* (Montreal: Gazette, 1872).

88 *Protestant Public Schools, Montreal, Province of Quebec, Dominion of Canada* (np: Montreal, 1878) at 4.

89 *Ibid* at 5.

90 The High School of Montreal began as a private academy and came under the jurisdiction of the Protestant Board in 1870. It was a primary training ground for the Anglo-Protestant elite and also included prominent members of the Jewish community among its alumni. Elson I Rexford, I Gammell, & AR McBain, *The History of the High School of Montreal* (Montreal: High School of Montreal, ca 1950); Anon, "Project for the Establishment of an Academy to Be Called the High School of Montreal," 24 March 1842, <https://archive.org/details/albertatest_01397>.

91 See Magnuson, *supra* note 48 at 121–23; Robert Gagnon, *Histoire de la Commission des Écoles Catholiques de Montréal: Le développement d'un réseau d'écoles publiques en milieu urbain* (Montreal: Boréal, 1996).

92 *An Account of the Schools of the Schools Controlled by the Board of Catholic School Commissioners of the City of Montreal* (Montreal: CO Beauchemin & Son, 1886), (prepared for the Indian and Colonial Exhibition, London, 1886).

93 *Ibid* at 7.

94 Brian Young, *George-Étienne Cartier: Montreal Bourgeois* (Montreal & Kingston: McGill-Queen's University Press, 1981).

95 Mildred A Schwartz, "The Social Make-up of Canada and Strains in Confederation" (1977) 111 Canadian Public Policy 458.

96 PA Dutil, "The Politics of Progressivism: The Gouin 'Coup' Revisited" (1988) 69 Canadian Historical Review 441.

97 Wendy Johnston, "'Contestation et continuité': les comités confessionnels et la gestion des écoles publiques au Québec (1920–1945)" (1995) 48 Revue d'histoire de l'Amérique française 403.

98 Canadian Jewish Congress Charities Committee National Archives [CJC], PSBGM January 1871–November 1919, Education – History and Chronology, 1846–1989, Special Meeting of the Protestant Board, 17 October 1871.

99 *Ibid*, 10 February 1881.

100 Walter P Percival, *Across the Years: A Century of Education in the Province of Quebec* (Montreal: Gazette, 1946); WAF Hepburn et al, *Report of the Quebec Protestant Education Survey* (Montreal: Montreal Protestant Central School Board, 1938); John Adams, *The Protestant School System in the Province of Quebec* (London: Longmans, 1902).

101 Ruby Heap, "Urbanisation et éducation: La centralisation scolaire à Montréal au début du XXe siècle" (1985) 20 Historical Papers/Communications historiques 132.

102 Jean-Pierre Proulx, "L'évolution de la législation relative au système électoral scolaire québécois (1829–1989)" (1998) 10 Historical Studies in Education/Revue d'histoire de l'éducation 20; Guy Bourassa, "La Structure du Pouvoir à Montréal: Le Domaine de l'Éducation" in Pierre W Bélanger & Guy Rocher, eds, *École et Société au Québec: Eléments d'une sociologie de l'éducation*, vol 2 (Montreal: Hurtubise HMH, 1970) at 259.

103 Johnston, *supra* note 98.

104 Will Kymlicka and Wayne Norman, "Culturally Diverse Societies: Issues, Contexts, Concepts" in Will Kymlicka and Wayned Norman, eds, *Citizenship in Diverse Societies* (Oxford: Oxford University Press, 2000) at 1.

105 Martha C Nussbaum, "Teaching Patriotism: Love and Critical Freedom" (2012) 79 U Chicago L Rev 215; Michael Hand, "Should We Promote Patriotism in Schools?" (2011) 59 Political Studies 328; Katheryne Mitchell, "Education for Democratic Citizenship: Transnationalism, Multiculturalism, and the Limits of Liberalism" (2001) 71 Harvard Educational Review 51.

106 The literature is vast and complex. For good, general introductions to different perspectives, see e.g. Kwame Anthony Appiah, *Cosmopolitanism: Ethics in a World of Strangers* (New York: WW Norton, 2006); Charles Taylor, ed, *Multiculturalism: Examining the Politics of Recognition* (Princeton: Princeton University Press, 1994); Will Kymlicka, *Politics in the Vernacular: Nationalism, Multiculturalism and Citizenship* (Oxford: Oxford University Press, 2001); Kymlicka, ed, *The Rights of Minority Cultures* (Oxford: Oxford University Press, 1995).

107 Michel Rosenfeld, *The Identity of the Constitutional Subject: Selfhood, Citizenship, Culture, and Community* (London: Routledge, 2010), 279.

108 James Tully, *Strange Multiplicity: Constitutionalism in an Age of Diversity* (Cambridge: Cambridge University Press, 1995) at 201.

109 Of course, the experience of Jewish immigration to the United States differs markedly from that in Canada in a number of important aspects relating to the development of the communities in their new environments. See Stuart Schoenfeld, "The Jewish Religion in North America: Canadian and American Comparisons" (1978) 3 Canadian Journal of Sociology 209; Jonathan D Sarna, "Jewish Immigration to North America: The Canadian Experience (1870–1900)" (1976) 18 Jewish Journal of Sociology 31.

110 Robert M Seltzer & Norman J Cohen, eds, *The Americanization of the Jews* (New York: New York University Press, 1995).

111 Joel Perlmann, *Ethnic Differences: Schooling and Social Structure among Irish, Italians, Jews and Blacks in an American City, 1880–1935* (New York: Cambridge University Press, 1988).
112 Stephan F Brumberg, *Going to America, Going to School: The Jewish Immigrant Public School Encounter in Turn-of the-Century New York* (New York: Praeger, 1986); Alan Wieder, *Immigration, the Public School, and the 20th-Century American Ethos: The Jewish Immigrant as a Case Study* (Lanham, MD: University Press of America, 1985).
113 Jeffrey S Gurock, *Jews in Gotham: New York Jews in a Changing City, 1920–2010* (New York: New York University Press, 2012); Ruth Jacknow Markowitz, *My Daughter, the Teacher: Jewish Teachers in the New York City Schools* (New Brunswick, NJ: Rutgers University Press, 1993).
114 Gurock, *supra* note 114 at 32.
115 For one version of the counter-narrative, see Melissa F Weiner, *Power, Protest, and the Public Schools: Jewish and African American Struggles in New York City* (New Brunswick, NJ: Rutgers University Press, 2010).
116 Gil Ribak, *Gentile New York: The Images of Non-Jews among Jewish Immigrants* (New Brunswick, NJ: Rutgers University Press, 2012); "'They are slitting the throats of Jewish children': The 1906 New York School Riots and Contending Images of Gentiles" (2008) 94 American Jewish History 175.
117 Tracy L Steffes, *School, Society, & State: A New Education to Govern Modern America, 1890–1940* (Chicago: University of Chicago Press, 2012).
118 Steven K Green, *The Bible, the School, and the Constitution: The Clash That Shaped Modern Church-State Doctrine* (Oxford: Oxford University Press, 2012); Benjamin Justice, *The War That Wasn't: Religious Conflict and Compromise in the Common Schools of New York State, 1865–1900* (Albany, NY: SUNY Press, 2005); Noah Feldman, "Non-sectarianism Reconsidered" (2002) 18 JL & Pol'y 65; Diane Ravitch, *The Great School Wars: A History of the New York City Public Schools* (Baltimore, MD: Johns Hopkins University Press, 1970).
119 See Claris Edwin Silcox and Galen M Fisher, *Catholics, Jews and Protestants: A Study of Relationships in the United States and Canada* (New York: Institute of Social and Religious Research & Harper and Brothers, 1934). On the later "alliance" of Roman Catholics and Jews to reconstitute American constitutional discourse, see Kevin M Schultz, *Tri-Faith America: How Catholics and Jews Held Postwar America to Its Protestant Promise* (New York: Oxford University Press, 2011).
120 Kent Greenawalt, *Does God Belong in Public Schools?* (Princeton, NJ: Princeton University Press, 2005).

121 Kent Greenawalt, *Religion and the Constitution*, 2 vols (Princeton: Princeton University Press, 2006); Paul Horwitz, *The Agnostic Age: Law, Religion, and the Constitution* (New York: Oxford University Press, 2011).

122 *Rogers v Bathurst School District No 2*, 1896 CarswellNB 9. The case was reprinted in pamphlet form in *Bathurst School Case: The Judgment of His Honor, Mr Justice Barker Delivered in the Supreme Court in Equity of New Brunswick, 17 March 1896* (St John: J & A McMillan, 1896).

123 *Ibid* at 8.

124 *Ibid* at 13.

125 Paul Bowlby, "Canadian Social Imaginaries: Re-examining Religion and Secularization" in Solange Lefebvre and Lori G Beaman, eds, *Religion in the Public Sphere: Canadian Case Studies* (Toronto: University of Toronto Press, 2014) at 25.

126 *Ibid* at 37.

127 Luigi G Pennacchio, "The Defence of Identity: Ida Siegel and the Jews of Toronto versus the Assimilation Attempts of the Public School and Its Allies, 1900–1920" (1985) 9 Canadian Jewish Historical Society Journal 41; Shmuel Shamai, "Jewish Resistance to Christianity in the Ontario Public Education System" (1997) 9 Historical Studies in Education 251; Martin S Sable, *Keeping the Faith: The Jewish Response to Compulsory Religious Education in Ontario's Public Schools, 1944–1990* (DEd Thesis, Department of Theory and Policy Studies, University of Toronto, 1999) [unpublished].

128 Paul Douglas Axelrod, *The Promise of Schooling: Education in Canada, 1800–1914* (Toronto: University of Toronto Press, 1997); Ronald Manzer, *Public Schools and Political Ideas: Canadian Educational Policy in Historical Perspective* (Toronto: University of Toronto Press, 1994).

129 Kymlicka, *supra* note 107 at 293.

130 Ramsay Cook, *Provincial Autonomy, Minority Rights and the Compact Theory, 1867–1921* (Ottawa: Queen's Printer, 1969). While the idea is perhaps less popular or accepted today, it refuses to go away, especially insofar as the idea of Quebec as a "distinct society" still informs constitutional discourse. Paul Romney, "Provincial Equality, Special Status and the Compact Theory of Canadian Confederation" (1999) 32 Canadian Journal of Political Science 21.

131 See the great Canadian novel, Hugh MacLennan, *Two Solitudes* (Toronto: Macmillan, 1945), for the cultural resonance of this idea of Canada and Quebec.

132 Daniel J Elazar, Michael Brown, & Ira Robinson, "Issues and Contexts: An Introduction" in Daniel J Elazar, Michael Brown, & Ira Robinson, eds,

Not Written in Stone: Jews, Constitutions and Constitutionalism in Canada (Ottawa: University of Ottawa Press, 2003) at 6–8.

133 *Lord Durham's Report: An Abridgement* (Ottawa: Carleton University Press, 1982) at 150.

134 Kevin Anderson, "'[T]he Cockroaches of Canada': French Canada, Immigration and Nationalism, Anti-Catholicism in English-Canada, 1905–1929" (2015) 39 Journal of Religious History 104.

135 Natan Sznaider, *Jewish Memory and the Cosmopolitan Order* (Cambridge: Polity, 2011).

136 Eleonore Kofman, "Figures of the Cosmopolitan: Privileged Nationals and National Outsiders" (2005) 18 Innovation 83.

137 Édouard Drumont, *La France Juive* (Paris: Marpon, 1885); Jules Ménard, *La France au pillage: Le juif, les cosmopolites, les accapareurs, la haute banque internationale, les ouvriers étrangers, les traîtres et les complices* (Rennes: L Ragigois, 1898).

138 RP Archambault SJ, *Sous la menace rouge: L'accroissement de la population cosmopolite de Montréal* (Quebec: L'Oeuvre des Tracts, 1936).

139 Rebecca Margolis, *Jewish Roots, Canadian Soil: Yiddish Culture in Montreal, 1905–1945* (Montreal & Kingston: McGill-Queen's University Press, 2011); Hershl Novak, *La Première École Yiddish à Montréal, 1911–1914*, Pierre Anctil, trans (Sillery, QC: Septentrion, 2009); Irving Massey, "Public Lives in Private: Ida Maza and the Montreal Yiddish Renaissance" in *Identity and Community: Reflections on English and Yiddish, and French Literature in Canada* (Detroit: Wayne State University Press, 1994) at 46.

140 Gerald Tulchinsky, *Taking Root: The Origins of the Canadian Jewish Community* (Hanover, NH: Brandeis University Press/University Press of New England, 1993) at xvi.

Chapter 2

1 Daryl J Levinson, "Parchment and Politics: The Positive Puzzle of Constitutional Commitment" (2011) 124 Harv L Rev 659.

2 The 1911 Census records, for example, that of the 47,861 foreign-born Jews in Canada, 33,930 had come from Russia, 5,334 from Romania, and almost another 4,000 from Austria-Hungary. Department of Trade and Commerce, Census and Statistics Office, *Special Report on the Foreign-Born Population* (Ottawa: Government Printing Bureau, 1915) at 32, table 16.

3 Rainer Liedtke & Stephan Wendehorst, eds, *The Emancipation of Catholics, Jews and Protestants: Minorities and the Nation State in Nineteenth-Century Europe* (Manchester: Manchester University Press, 1999).

4 David Aberbach, *The European Jews, Patriotism and the Liberal State 1789–1939* (New York: Routledge, 2013); Pierre Birnbaum & Ira Katznelson, eds, *Paths of Emancipation: Jews, State and Citizenship* (Princeton: Princeton University Press, 1995).

5 Louis Rosenberg, *Canada's Jews: A Social and Economic Study of Jews in Canada* (Montreal: Bureau of Social and Economic Research, Canadian Jewish Congress, 1939) at 31. The work has been republished as Morton Weinfeld, ed, *Canada's Jews: A Social and Economic Study of Jews in Canada in the 1930s* (Montreal & Kingston: McGill-Queen's University Press, 1993). All references are to the original version.

6 *Ibid* at 76–80.

7 Annie Polland, "'May a freethinker help a pious man?': The Shared World of the 'Religious' and the 'Secular' among Eastern European Immigrants to America" (2007) 93 American Jewish History 375.

8 Ian Haney López, *White by Law: The Legal Construction of Race* (New York: New York University Press, 2006).

9 Eric L Goldstein, *The Price of Whiteness: Jews, Race, and American Identity* (Princeton: Princeton University Press, 2006); Karen Brodkin, *How Jews Became White Folks and What That Says about Race in America* (New Brunswick, NJ: Rutgers University Press, 2002).

10 Joel Perlmann, "Views of European Races among the Research Staff of the US Immigration Commission and the Census Bureau, ca 1910" (2011) Levy Economics Institute of Bard College, Working Paper no 648; Eric L Goldstein, "Contesting the Categories: Jews and Government Racial Classification in the United States" (2005) 19 Jewish History 79–107.

11 Didi Herman, *An Unfortunate Coincidence: Jews, Jewishness, & English Law* (Oxford: Oxford University Press, 2011).

12 Rosenberg, *supra* note 5 at 10–11, 20.

13 *Ibid* at 8–11. *Pinsler v The Protestant Board of School Commissioners* 23 CS 365 (1903).

14 Rosenberg, *supra* note 5. Rosenberg's comments mirror official government determinations that "racial origin" was a useful, if incomplete, category for the classification of immigrant groups. Dominion Bureau of Statistics, *Illiteracy and School Attendance in Canada* (Ottawa: FA Acland, King's Printer, 1926) at 64. For contemporaneous related debates among members of Montreal's Jewish communities, see Gordon Dueck, *The Salamander and the Chameleon: Religion, Race, and Evolutionism in the Anglo-Jewish Press, 1897–1914* (PhD Thesis, Department of History, Queen's University, 2000) [unpublished]. As Christopher points out, the use of the category "religion" in census data has a long and complex history in the British Empire, although

its use in early Canadian censuses appears to have been unproblematic and indeed necessary for a number of reasons. Anthony J Christopher, "The 'Religion' Question in British Colonial and Commonwealth Censuses 1820s–2010s" (2014) 38 Journal of Religious History 579–96.

15 An Act for making more effectual Provision for Government of the Province of Quebec in North America, 14 Geo III, c 83, (1774), s 5.

16 An Act to repeal so much of the Act of the Parliament of Great Britain passed in the Thirty-first year of the reign of King George the Third, and Chaptered Thirty-one as relates to Rectories, and the presentation of Incumbents to the same, and for other purposes connected with such Rectories, 14–15 Vict, c 175, 1852.

17 Louis-Adolphe Paquet, *Le Droit Public de l'Église* (Quebec: La Compagnie de l'Événement, 1909).

18 Siméon Pagnuelo, *Études Historiques et Légales sur la Liberté Religieuse en Canada* (Montreal: CO Beauchemin & Valois, 1872).

19 Richard Risk and Robert C Vipond, "Rights Talk in Canada in the Late Nineteenth Century: 'The good sense and right feeling of the people'" (1996) 14 LHR 1; Mark R MacGuigan, "Civil Liberties in the Canadian Federation" (1966) 16 UNBLJ 1.

20 See generally Ross Lambertson, *Repression and Resistance: Canadian Human Rights Activists, 1930–1960* (Toronto: University of Toronto Press, 2005); Lambertson, *Activists in the Age of Rights: The Struggle for Human Rights in Canada* (PhD Thesis, Department of History, University of Victoria, 1998) [unpublished]; James W StG Walker, *"Race," Rights and the Law in the Supreme Court of Canada: Historical Case Studies* (Waterloo, ON: Wilfrid Laurier University Press/Osgoode Society for Canadian Legal History, 1997); Constance Backhouse, *Colour-Coded: A Legal History of Racism in Canada, 1900–1950* (Toronto: University of Toronto Press/Osgoode Society for Canadian Legal History, 1999); Dominique Clément, *Canada's Rights Revolution: Social Movements and Social Change, 1937–82* (Vancouver: University of British Columbia Press, 2008). A careful study of each volume will also reveal the complexities of taxonomic constructions of Jews, race, and religion.

21 Eric M Adams, *The Idea of Constitutional Rights and the Transformation of Canadian Constitutional Law, 1930–1960* (SJD Thesis, Graduate Department of Law, University of Toronto, 2009) [unpublished]; Adams, "Canada's 'Newer Constitutional Law' and the Idea of Constitutional Rights" (2006) 51 McGill LJ 435; Christopher MacLennan, *Toward the Charter: Canadians and the Demand for a National Bill of Rights, 1920–1960* (Montreal & Kingston: McGill-Queen's University Press, 2003).

22 George Egerton, "Entering the Age of Human Rights: Religion, Politics,

and Canadian Liberalism" (2004) 85 Canadian Historical Review 451; see Carmela Patrias & Ruth A Frager, "'This is our country, these are our rights': Minorities and the Origins of Ontario's Human Rights Campaigns" (2001) 82 Canadian Historical Review 1, on the existence of an undercurrent of anti-Catholicism, even within the human rights activist communities; Ross Lambertson, "'The Dresden Story': Racism, Human Rights and the Jewish Labour Committee of Canada" (2001) 47 Labour/Le Travail 43.

23 Irving Abella, "Presidential Address: Jews, Human Rights and the Making of a New Canada" (2000) 11 Journal of the Canadian Historical Association 3; James W StG Walker, "The 'Jewish Phase' in the Movement for Racial Equality in Canada" (2002) 34 Canadian Ethnic Studies 1; Carmela Patrias, "Socialists, Jews, and the 1947 Saskatchewan Bill of Rights" (2006) 87 Canadian Historical Review 265; George Egerton, "Entering the Age of Human Rights: Religion, Politics, and Canadian Liberalism, 1945–50" (2004) 85 Canadian Historical Review 451.

24 Risk and Vipond, *supra* note 19 at 2–3.

25 *Ibid* at 31 (footnote omitted).

26 23 CS 365, (1903).

27 [1928] AC 200; [1926] SCR 246; 31 R de J 440, (1925).

28 35 CLT 262 (1915).

29 *Abugov v Ménard*, Cour Supérieure, District de Montréal, no. 106465, 3 September 1932, (unreported).

30 George Weir, *The Separate School Question in Canada* (Toronto: Ryerson, 1924), 22ff.

31 James Cappon, "The Principle of Sectarianism in the Canadian Constitution" (1905) 4 Can L Rev 303.

32 Robert Leroux, "'La nation' and the Quebec Sociological Tradition 1890–1980" (2001) 26 Canadian Journal of Sociology 349.

33 Sheldon J Godfrey & Judith C Godfrey, *Search Out the Land: The Jews and the Growth of Equality in British Colonial America 1740–1867* (Montreal & Kingston: McGill-Queen's University Press, 1995); Louis Rosenberg, "Some Aspects of the Historical Development of the Canadian Jewish Community" (1961) 50 American Jewish Historical Society Journal 121. See also Benjamin G Sack, *History of the Jews in Canada: From the French Régime to the End of the Nineteenth Century*, vol. 1 (Montreal: Canadian Jewish Congress, 1945); Abraham Rhinewine, revised and enlarged by Isidore Goldstick, *Looking Back a Century: On the Centennial of Jewish Political Equality in Canada* (Toronto: Kraft, 1932); Martin Wolff, "The Jews in Canada" (1925–26) 5 American Jewish Year Book 154.

34 An Act for naturalizing such foreign Protestants and others therein mentioned, as are settled in His Majesty's colonies in America, 13 Geo II, c 7; AH Carpenter, "Naturalization in England and the American Colonies" (1904) 9 American Historical Review 288.

35 Holly Snyder, "Rules, Rights and Redemption: The Negotiation of Jewish Status in British Atlantic Port Towns, 1740–1831" (2006) 20 Jewish History 147; Montague S Giuseppi, ed, *Naturalizations of Foreign Protestants in the American and West Indian Colonies* (Baltimore: Clearfield Genealogical, 1995). More generally, see Abigail Green, "The British Empire and the Jews: An Imperialism of Human Rights?" (2008) 199 Past and Present 175.

36 Andrew C Joseph, "The Settlement of Jews in Canada" (1893) 1 Publications of the American Jewish Historical Society 117.

37 Denis Vaugeois, *Les Premiers Juifs d'Amérique, 1760–1860* (Sillery, QC: Septentrion, 2011); Raymond Douville, *Aaron Hart: Récit Historique* (Trois-Rivières, QC: Éditions du Bien Public, 1938).

38 Godfrey & Godfrey, *supra* note 33 at 98.

39 *Ibid* at 98–9.

40 *Ibid* at 93 and 100.

41 *Ibid* at 93.

42 For contemporaneous accounts of the debates, see e.g. John Elijah Blunt, *A History of the Establishment and Residence of the Jews in England with an Enquiry into Their Civil Disabilities* (London: Saunders and Benning, 1830); Charles Egan, *The Status of the Jews in England* (London: R Hastings, 1848); Israel Abrahams & S Levy, eds, *Macaulay on Jewish Disabilities* (Edinburgh: Ballantyne, Hanson for the Jewish Historical Society, 1910). For later historical accounts, see e.g. Henry S Henriques, *The Jews and the English Law* (Oxford: H Hart, 1908); MCN Salbstein, *The Emancipation of the Jews in Britain: The Question of the Admission of the Jews to Parliament, 1828–1860* (Madison, NJ: Fairleigh Dickinson University Press, 1982); generally on the legal history of oath controversies, Enid Campbell, "Oaths and Affirmations of Public Office under English Law: An Historical Retrospect" (2000) 21 J Legal Hist 1.

43 The idea of the oath of office and its intimate link to ideals of citizenship also played a key role in Jewish emancipation in France. Lisa Moses Leff, "The Jewish Oath and the Making of Secularism in Modern France" (2013) 58 Leo Baeck Institute Year Book 23.

44 7 Geo III, c 9.

45 Sack, *supra* note 33 at 63.

46 Rhinewine, *supra* note 33 at 17.

47 F Murray Greenwood, *The Legacies of Fear: Law and Politics in Quebec in the*

Era of the French Revolution (Toronto: University of Toronto Press for the Osgoode Society for Canadian Legal History, 1993).

48 Donald Fyson, *Magistrates, Police, and People: Everyday Criminal Justice in Quebec and Lower Canada, 1764–1837* (Toronto: University of Toronto Press for the Osgoode Society for Canadian Legal History, 2006); more generally, Fyson, "Between the Ancien Régime and Liberal Modernity: Law, Justice and State Formation in Colonial Quebec, 1760–1867" (2014) 12 History Compass 412.

49 *Ibid* at 23ff.

50 Fyson, *Magistrates, supra* note 48 at 73–6.

51 An Act for making more effectual Provision for Government of the Province of Quebec in North America, 14 Geo III, c 83, (1774).

52 See generally Joseph Tassé, "Droits Politiques Des Juifs en Canada" (1870) 7 Revue Canadienne 409; and Vaugeois, *supra* note 37.

53 Vaugeois, *supra* note 37 at 143–5; Benjamin Sulte, "Les Miettes de l'Histoire" (1870) 7 Revue Canadienne 426.

54 Quebec, Assembly Debates, February 1808.

55 *Ibid* at 144.

56 Quebec, Assembly Debates, 19 April 1809 at 106, 122.

57 Janet Ajzenstat, "Canada's First Constitution: Pierre Bédard on Tolerance and Dissent" (1990) 23 Canadian Journal of Political Science 39.

58 Sulte, *supra* note 53 at 435ff.

59 There is perhaps no small irony in the historical fact that the primary impetus for an elected assembly in Quebec had originated among the anglophone Protestant community. See *An Account of the Proceedings of the British and Other Protestant Inhabitants of the Province of Quebeck in North-America, in Order to Obtain an House of Assembly in That Province* (London: B White, 1775).

60 Lower Canada, Assembly, Journal, 13 December 1828ff. Petition of Jews of Montreal for the right to maintain registers of births, deaths and marriages and to hold sufficient land to erect thereon a place of worship, and a habitation for a minister of worship, 9 Geo, IV, 4 December 1828.

61 *Petition for Equality of Jews Under the Law, Submitted by Samuel Becancourt Hart to the Legislature of Lower Canada in 1831*, Canadian Jewish Congress National Archives, Community Files, Trois-Rivières, ZD.

62 *Ibid*. Julius J Price, "An Unpublished Letter of Aron Ezekiel Hart" (1918) 26 Publications of the American Jewish Historical Society 256; "Proceedings Relating to the Expulsion of Ezekiel Hart from the House of Assembly of Lower Canada" (1915) 23 Publications of the American Jewish Historical Society 43.

63 Assembly, 1 Will IV 1831, c 102.
64 1 Will IV 1831, 102, CAP LVII.
65 In 1857, George Benjamin of Belleville, Canada West (Ontario), became the first Jew to sit as a member of an elected legislative assembly. Sheldon Godfrey & Judith Godfrey, *Burn This Gossip: The True Story of George Benjamin of Belleville, Canada's First Jewish Member of Parliament, 1857–1863* (Toronto: Duke & George, 1991). Henry Nathan of Victoria, British Columbia, became the first Jew to sit in the post-Confederation federal Parliament from 1871 to 1874. Martin Woolf, "The Jews of Canada" (1925–6) 27 American Jewish Yearbook at 169–70.
66 Mordechai Arbell, *The Portuguese Jews of Jamaica* (Kingston, Jamaica: Canoe, 2000); Swithin Wilmot, "Jewish Politicians in Post-Slavery Jamaica: Electoral Politics in the Parish of St Dorothy, 1849–1860" in Jane S. Gerber, ed, *The Jews in the Caribbean* (Oxford: Littman Library of Jewish Civilization, 2014) at 261.
67 Tassé, *supra* note 52 at 425: "[N]otre législature provinciale leur accordait ces privilèges dans toute leur plénitude dès 1832."
68 Sack, *supra* note 33 at 110–13.
69 *Ibid* at 112.
70 *Ibid* at 111.
71 *Ibid* at 112–13.
72 4 Will IV Appendix (G.g).
73 *Ibid*, 28 February 1834; Jeremy Bentham, *"Swear not at all": Containing an Exposure of the Needlessness and Mischievousness, as well as Antichristianity of the Ceremony of an Oath* (London: R Hunter, 1817).
74 When the two Canadas united, the legislature quickly formalized the ideal of equality in other cases and included a form of oath that was neutral. An Act to secure to, and confer upon, certain inhabitants of this province, the civil and political rights of natural born British Subjects, 4–5 Vict, c 7, 1841.
75 David Rome, *On the Jews of Lower Canada and 1837–38* (Montreal: Canadian Jewish Congress National Archives, 1983) at 80–3.
76 Irving Abella, *A Coat of Many Colours: Two Centuries of Jewish Life in Canada* (Toronto: Lester & Orpen Dennys, 1990) at 39; Sack, *supra* note 33 at 131–2.

Chapter 3

1 Danielle Gauvreau, Sherry Olson, & Patricia Thornton, "The Harsh Welcome of an Industrial City: Immigrant Women in Montreal 1890–1900" (2007) 40 Social History 345; Michael D Behiels, *Quebec and the Question of Immigration: From Ethnocentrism to Ethnic Pluralism, 1900–1985* (Ottawa:

Canadian Historical Association, 1991); Sylvie Taschereau, "L'histoire de l'immigration au Québec: une invitation à fuir les ghettos" (1988) 41 Revue d'histoire de l'Amérique française 575.

2 Daniel J Elazar, Michael Brown, & Ira Robinson, "Issues and Contexts: An Introduction" in Daniel J Elazar, Michael Brown, & Ira Robinson, eds, *Not Written in Stone: Jews, Constitutions, and Constitutionalism in Canada* (Ottawa: University of Ottawa Press, 2003) at 7.

3 Yolande Cohen, "Immigrant Aid in Quebec 1867–1939: Gender, Religion, and Ethnicity" (2012) 52 Québec Studies 5.

4 Dominique Marshall, *The Social Origins of the Welfare State: Quebec Families, Compulsory Education, and Family Allowances, 1940–1955*, translated by Nicola Doone Danby (Waterloo, ON: Wilfrid Laurier University Press, 2006).

5 Elazar, Brown, & Robinson, *supra* note 2 at 6.

6 Tobias Brinkmann, "'We are brothers! Let us separate!': Jews and Community Building in American Cities during the 19th Century" (2013) 11/10 History Compass 869.

7 Louis Rosenberg, *Canada's Jews: A Social and Economic Study of the Jews in Canada* (Montreal: Bureau of Social and Economic Research, Canadian Jewish Congress, 1939) at 10ff, table 5.

8 Wilfred Shuchat, *The Gate of Heaven: The Story of Congregation Shaar Hashomayim of Montreal, 1846–1996* (Montreal & Kingston: McGill-Queen's University Press, 2000); Esther I Blaustein, Rachel A Esar, & Evelyn Miller, "Spanish and Portuguese Synagogue (Shearith Israel) Montreal, 1768–1968" (1971) 23 Transactions of the Jewish Historical Society of England Session 1969–1970, 111. Shearith Israel was originally known as the "Corporation of the Portuguese Jews of Montreal," 9 &10 Geo IV, c 75; 9 Vict, c 96 and "By-Laws of the Corporation of the Portuguese Jews of Montreal, Revised and Passed the 1st day of Nov., 1857." The name was changed to the Corporation of Spanish and Portuguese Jews "Shearith Israel" in 1890. 53 Vict c 85.

9 An Act to amend the charter of the Corporation of the German and Polish Jews of Montreal, 2 Ed VII, c 95, (1902), creating "the Congregation of English, German and Polish Jews of Montreal."

10 An Act to amend the Act of Lower Canada therein mentioned, extending certain privileges to persons of the Jewish persuasion, 9 Vict, c 96, 9th June 1846.

11 Shuchat, *supra* note 8 at 17–20.

12 For a general overview of this period in Jewish education in Montreal, see David Rome, *The Drama of Our Early Education* (Montreal: Canadian Jewish Congress National Archives, 1991).

13 CJC, Spanish and Portuguese Archives, Min. Book I, Trustee Meetings, 1854, CJC Archives, Collection Shearith Israel, folder 1832.

14 Circular, CJC, *ibid*, folder 1854.

15 *Ibid.*

16 *Ibid.*

17 Arthur Daniel Hart, "The Late Dr Abraham De Sola" in *The Jew in Canada* (Montreal: Jewish Publication, 1926) at 86.

18 Circular, *supra* note 14.

19 Gerald Tulchinsky, "'Said to be a very honest Jew': The RG Dun Credit Reports and Jewish Business Activity in Mid-19th-Century Montreal" (1990) 18 Urban History Review 200.

20 CJC, Excerpts from the Minutes of the Protestant Board of School Commissioners of the City of Montreal, Education – History and Chronology, folder 1870, 26 November 1874.

21 Shuchat, *supra* note 8; Rome, *supra* note 12 at 45; CJC, *supra* note 20 at 10 and 17 October 1870.

22 CJC, Shearith Israel, box 1, folder 1871, Extracts for the Minute Book of the Corporation of Portuguese Jews, Montreal, 24 September 1865–10 November 1910, 3 April 1871.

23 Report of the Joint Committee, October 1874, CJC Archives, Collection Shearith Israel, box 1, folder 1874.

24 Arthur Daniel Hart, "The Late DA Ansell" in *The Jew in Canada*, *supra* note 17 at 200.

25 CJC Archives, Ansell, David A, varia.

26 *Ibid.*

27 CJC, *supra* note 22.

28 *Ibid.* 17 November 1874 and 22 November 1874 and CJC, Education – History and Chronology, folder 1874.

29 CJC, Shaar Hashomayim, folder 1882.

30 *Ibid. Report of the Board of School Commissioners.*

31 Julie Châteauvert & Francis Dupuis-Déri, *Identités Mosaïques: Entretiens sur l'identité culturelle des Québécois juifs* (Montreal: Boréal, 2004); Ira Robinson & Mervin Butovsky, *Renewing Our Days: Montreal Jews in the Twentieth Century* (Montreal: Véhicule, 1995).

32 In 1882, the first Reform Congregation, Temple Emmanuel, was established and was incorporated the following year. An Act to incorporate the religious congregation called "Temple Emmanu-el," 46 Vict, c 67 (1883). In 1890, a new congregation, Benai Jacob, was created by statute. An Act to incorporate the religious congregation called Benai Jacob congregation, 53 Vict, c 84. For a contemporary account of the growing complexity of Mon-

treal Jewry at the time of the first school crisis, see YE Bernstein, *The Jews in Canada (North America)*, translated by Ira Robinson (Montreal: Hungry I Books, 2004).

33 Daniel J Elazar, Michael Brown, & Ira Robinson, eds, *Not Written in Stone: Jews, Constitutions and Constitutionalism in Canada* (Ottawa: University of Ottawa Press, 2003) at 8.

34 YMHBS Revised By-Laws, 1871, s 2.

35 The Young Men's Hebrew Benevolent Society, CJC, The David Ansell Collection.

36 For the history of the YMHBS/Baron de Hirsch Institute and its role in the development of Montreal Jewry, see *Baron de Hirsch Institute 1863–1963*, Centenary Book (Montreal: Baron de Hirsch Institute, 1963); Arthur Daniel Hart, "Baron de Hirsch Institute, Montreal" in *The Jew in Canada*, *supra* note 17 at 201–5.

37 *Ibid*.

38 "Baron de Hirsch Donates: Twenty Thousand Dollars to the Young Men's Hebrew Benevolent Society," *American Israelite* (28 August 1890).

39 An Act to change the name of the Young Men's Hebrew Benevolent Society of Montreal to "Baron de Hirsch Institute and Hebrew Benevolent Society of Montreal" and to extend its powers, 63 Vict, c 106, (1900).

40 Rome, *supra* note 12 at 81ff; Arlette Corcos, *Montréal, les Juifs et l'École* (Sillery, QC: Septentrion, 1997) at 153ff.

41 *Baron de Hirsch Institute 1863–1963*, *supra* note 36 at 23.

42 For an introduction to the history of these issues, see generally Jean-Philippe Croteau, "La question de la taxe scolaire à Montréal au XIXe siècle (1870–1903); un nouveau regard sur l'intégration des Juifs" (2009) 41 Canadian Ethnic Studies/Études Ethniques au Canada 1; Jean-Philippe Croteau and Robert Gagnon, "Les débats sur le partage de la taxe scolaire à Montréal (1869–1899): enjeux et rivalités" (2008) 20 Historical Studies in Education/Revue d'histoire de l'éducation 32.

43 Léo Pelland, *Défense et illustration de nos collèges classiques* (Joliette, QC: Carnets viatoriens, 1941).

44 Croteau, *supra* note 41; Croteau and Gagnon, *supra* note 42 at 46–8.

45 S 28 (3), An Act to amend the law respecting education in this Province, 32 Vict, c 16.

46 An Act to amend and extend the law respecting Education in this Province, 34 Vict, c 12.

47 CJC, PSBGM January 1871–November 1919, Education – History and Chronology, 1846–1989, 10 January 1871.

48 *Ibid*, 22 February 1877.

49 *Ibid*, 8 March 1877.
50 *Ibid.*
51 Roderick MacLeod and Mary Anne Poutanen, *A Meeting of the People: School Boards and Protestant Communities in Quebec, 1801–1998* (Montreal & Kingston: McGill-Queen's University Press, 2004).
52 CJC, *supra* note 47, 1 June 1877.
53 *Ibid*, letter, 7 June 1877.
54 Robert H Pfeiffer, "The Teaching of Hebrew in Colonial America" (1955) 45 Jewish Quarterly Review 363; Joe W Kraus, "The Development of a Curriculum in the Early American Colleges" (1961) 1 History of Education Quarterly 64; Shalom Goldman, "Biblical Hebrew in Colonial America: The Case of Dartmouth" (1989) 79 American Jewish History 173. De Sola was professor of Hebrew at McGill for many years.
55 An Act to amend the school law of Lower Canada, 12 Vict, c 50, 1849, ss 1 & 2.
56 An Act respecting provincial aid for superior education and normal and common schools, Consolidated Statutes of Lower Canada, 24 Vict, c 15 & 16, 1861, ss 66–67.
57 CJC, *supra* note 47, Minutes 13 September 1877 and 10 January 1878.
58 *Ibid*, Minutes 10 January 1878.
59 *Ibid*, Minutes 12 September 1878.
60 *Ibid*, Protestant Board Minutes, 14 November 1878.
61 *Ibid*, 15 November 1878.
62 *Ibid*, and 15 April 1880.
63 *Pinsler v The Protestant Board of School Commissioners* 23 CS 365 (1903).
64 CJC, *supra* note 47, 10 January and 20 May 1881.
65 CJC, Education – History and Chronology, folder 1883, Jewish Schools, Protestant School Board, 13 April 1883. Excerpts from the Minutes of the Protestant Board of School Commissioners of the City of Montreal, 19 February and 11 March 1880.
66 *Ibid.*
67 CJC, *supra* note 22.
68 Arthur Daniel Hart, "The Late Rev Meldola De Sola" in *The Jew in Canada, supra* note 17 at 87.
69 CJC, Education – History and Chronology, folder 1883, Jewish Schools, Protestant School Board, letter to the Jewish congregations 19 June; Protestant School Board Minutes, 29 June 1882.
70 This was, in fact, less problematic in Protestant schools, where the fear of "denominationalism" meant that exemption from religious instruction would be incorporated as a formal part of the regulations applicable to

all students established by the Protestant Committee of Public Instruction. Thus, "Religious Instruction shall be given in all public schools, but no person shall require any pupil in any public school to read or study in or from any religious book, or join in any exercise of devotion or religion, objected to in writing by his or her parents or guardians" and "the Holy Scriptures shall for such purposes be used as a text-book, but no denominational teaching shall be given in such schools." Sections 158 and 160, Regulations of the Protestant Committee of the Council of Public Instruction, in Paul De Cazes, ed, John Ahern, trans, *Code of Public Instruction of the Province of Quebec* (Montreal: Wm Drysdale, 1889).

71 CJC, *supra* note 69, Protestant School Board, letter and minutes, 28 July 1882.

72 *Ibid*, letter, 14 September 1882.

73 *Ibid*, minutes, 12 October 1882.

74 CJC, *supra* note 22 at 15 April 1883.

75 CJC, *supra* note 69, Protestant School Board Minutes, 12 December 1882.

76 *Ibid*, 14 October 1884.

77 *Ibid*, 2 July 1884.

78 *Ibid*, 13 June 1885.

79 *Ibid*, 13 March 1886.

80 *Ibid*, 18 April 1886.

81 *Ibid*, 8 May 1886.

82 *Ibid*, 30 June 1886.

83 CJC, *supra* note 22 at 20 June 1886.

84 Harold Ross, *The Jew in the Educational System of the Province of Quebec* (MA Thesis, McGill University, 1947) [unpublished] at 14.

85 Rome, *supra* note 12 at 59.

86 CJC, *supra* note 22 at 19 January 1897, 15 April 1888.

87 *Rapport du Surintendant de la Province du Québec pour l'Année 1888–89, Rapport Financier des Commissaires d'Écoles Catholiques Romains de la Cité de Montréal pour l'Année Scolaire 1888–89*, tableau 1 at 315.

88 *Ibid*, tableau J at 302.

89 *Rapport du Surintendant de la Province du Québec pour l'Année 1891–92, Rapport Financier des Commissaires d'Écoles Catholiques Romains de la Cité de Montréal pour l'Année Scolaire 1891–92*, tableau M at 211.

90 *Ibid*, tableau N at 236.

91 Born in 1820 in Pictou, Nova Scotia, Sir (John) William Dawson was the son of Scottish immigrants. He carried his family's Presbyterian faith throughout his life. Trained in the sciences, he returned to Canada from the University of Edinburgh and worked as an exploration geologist. He pursued a career in that field before also turning to higher education. He

died in Montreal in 1899. "Dawson, Sir John William" in Dictionary of Canadian Biography Online, <www.biographi.ca/en/bio/dawson_john_william_12E.html>.

92 William Dawson, *On Some Points in the History & Prospects of Protestant Education in Lower Canada* (Montreal: Becket, 1864).

93 See Jean-Philippe Croteau, "La communauté juive et l'éducation à Montréal: l'aménagement d'un nouvel espace scolaire (1874–1973)" in Pierre Anctil & Ira Robinson, eds, *Les Communautés Juives de Montréal: Histoire et enjeux contemporains* (Sillery, QC: Septentrion, 2004) at 65–91, 70–3.

94 *Report of the Protestant Board of School Commissioners*, 1889.

95 Harris Vineberg, president of the Baron de Hirsch Institute, letter to the editor, *Montreal Gazette* (1 June 1892).

96 See *Report of the Protestant Board of School Commissioners, 1886–87, 1887–88, 1888–89*, published in a single volume, 1889 at 8.

97 CJC, *supra* note 69, Protestant School Board Minutes, op. cit., 8 January 1887.

98 *Ibid*, 17 November 1888.

99 *Report, supra* note 96 at 11; CJC, Education – History and Chronology, 1846–1989, folder 1870, Excerpts from the Minutes of the Protestant Board of School Commissioners of the City of Montreal, 10 February 1881.

100 Procès-verbal de la réunion du Conseil de l'Instruction Publique, 15 May 1889.

101 Robert Gagnon, *Histoire de la Commission des Écoles Catholiques de Montréal* (Montreal: Boréal, 1996) at 85ff; Louis-Philippe Audet, *Histoire du Conseil de l'Instruction Publique de la Province du Québec 1856–1964* (Montreal: Éditions Leméac, 1964) at 108ff.

102 Montarville Boucher de LaBruère, *Le Conseil de l'Instruction Publique et le Comité Catholique* (Montreal: Le Devoir, 1918), 87.

103 *Ibid* at 91. "Dans ces circonstances, avec le respect dû aux membres de votre comité et à vous-même, je dois considérer comme exact le compte rendu écrit." See also *The Educational Record*, 1889, Department of Public Instruction, Minutes of the Protestant Committee of the Council of Public Instruction," 6 February 1889, 54ff.

104 Audet, *supra* note 101 at 114.

105 Boucher de LaBruère, *supra* note 101 at 88.

106 Croteau and Gagnon, *supra* note 42 at 60.

107 CJC, Education – History and Chronology, 1846–1989, folder 1870, Excerpts from the Minutes of the Protestant Board of School Commissioners of the City of Montreal, 14 March 1890.

108 Arlette Corcos, "École Baron de Hirsch, 1890–1907" in *Montréal, supra* note 40 at 153–6.
109 Rome, *supra* note 12 at 84.
110 CJC, MB1-A, box 4/1, *Baron de Hirsch Institute Annual Report*, 1891, 12.
111 *Annual Report*, Protestant Board of School Commissioners, 1890.
112 CJC, *supra* note 69, Protestant School Board Minutes, op. cit., 14 March 1890.

Chapter 4

1 CJC, MB1-A, 4/16, Minutes 1885–1891, Education.
2 *Ibid*, 29 March 1891.
3 Harris Vineberg came to Canada from Poland in the 1870s. He was a very successful clothing manufacturer and businessman. He was the first president of the Baron de Hirsch Institute, secretary of Shaar Hashomayim synagogue, and a leading advocate of Jewish educational rights. "Harris Vineberg" Canadian Jewish Heritage Network, online: <www.cjhn.ca/en/explore.aspx?q=harris+vineberg>.
4 Sam Jacobs was a leading lawyer of his generation. A graduate of McGill and Laval universities, he was fluent in French and English. He was made king's counsel in 1896. In addition to his work at the bar and his charitable contributions to the Jewish community, he was a long-serving member of Parliament for the Montreal riding of Cartier, the first Jewish MP from Quebec. First elected in 1917, he was sent back to Ottawa by the voters of his electorate in 1921, 1925, 1926, 1938, and 1935. He continued throughout his career at the Bar and in Parliament to use the public tribune to attack instances of anti-Semitism, and he would be among the leading advocates of Jewish educational equality. Bernard Figler, *Sam Jacobs: Member of Parliament* (Gardenvale, QC: Harpell's, 1959); Pierre Beullac & E Fabre Surveyer, "Samuel W (Sam) Jacobs" in *Le Centenaire du Barreau de Montréal, 1849–1949* (Montreal: Librairie Ducharme, 1949) at 168–71.
5 CJC, Education – History and Chronology, folder 1891.
6 *Ibid.*
7 *Ibid.*
8 CJC, CJC, MB1-A, 4/16, Minutes 1885–1891, Education, Meeting of 4 May 1891.
9 *Ibid.*
10 CJC, Shearith Israel, box 1, folder 1871, Minutes.
11 *Ibid*, Meeting of 17 May 1891.

12 Letter to the editor, *Montreal Witness* (25 January 1892).
13 Roger Magnuson, *The Two Worlds of Quebec Education during the Traditional Era, 1760–1940* (London, ON: Althouse, 2005) at 125–6.
14 CJC, Education – History and Chronology, 1846–1969, Minutes, School Committee, Spanish & Portuguese Jews, Montreal, 1874–1893, 22 April 1892.
15 CJC, Baron de Hirsch, MB1-A, box 4-11, Minutes 1891–94, Meeting of 29 May 1892.
16 *Ibid*, 22 May 1892; Provincial Secretary's Department to Meldola de Sola, 17 May, 1892; CJC, Education – History and Chronology, folder 1892; Spanish and Portuguese Synagogue to the provincial secretary, *ibid*, folder 1874.
17 CJC, MB1-A, box 4/1, Minutes 4 May 1892; "Memorial, Re Jewish School Tax, City of Montreal, Young Men's Hebrew Benevolent Society of Montreal, A Body Corporate" *29th Annual Report, Baron de Hirsch Institute*, 1 October 1892, 25–8.
18 *Ibid* at 27.
19 CJC, Education – History and Chronology, 1846–1969, folder 1891, Minutes of the Baron de Hirsch Institute School Committee, 23 May 1892.
20 "Hebrew School Taxes: The Deputation of Property Holders at Quebec to Interview the Government," *Montreal Star* (19 May 1891).
21 Editorial, *Montreal Star* (23 May 1892).
22 "Must Go Back Again," *Montreal Gazette* (17 May 1892).
23 As pointed out by "Interested," letter to the editor, *Montreal Gazette* (8 June 1892).
24 CJC, "Memorial," *supra* note 17 at 28.
25 Minutes, Protestant Committee, 20 May 1882.
26 Maxwell Goldstein was considered the leader among the few Jewish members of the Montreal Bar. He was called to the Bar upon reaching the age of majority in 1884 and became a KC in 1903. At around the time of the Baron de Hirsch struggle over school taxes, there were only three Jewish members of the Bar: Sam Jacobs, FT Judah, and Goldstein. He was a partner of the firm Carter and Goldstein, which later became Carter, Goldstein and Beullac. He was elected to the Bar Council. He was a leader of the Reform movement within Montreal Jewry and a founder of Temple Emmanuel. Throughout his career he was at the forefront of the struggle for the rights of Jewish children to attend the common schools of the city. Arthur Daniel Hart, "Maxwell Goldstein, KC, Montreal" in *The Jew in Canada* (Montreal: Jewish Publication, 1926) at 378; Pierre Beullac & E Fabre Surveyer, *Le Centenaire du Barreau de Montréal*, 166–8.
27 CJC, Baron de Hirsch, MB1-A, box 4-11, Minutes 1891–94, Meeting of 29 May 1892.

28 CJC, Education – History and Chronology, 1846–1969, folder 1872, letter 30 May 1892.
29 CJC, Education – History and Chronology, 1846–1969, folder 1872; and CJC, *29th Annual Report, supra* note 19 at 29.
30 CJC, Education – History and Chronology, 1846–1969, folder 1872.
31 CJC, Education – History and Chronology, 1846–1969, folder 1891, Minutes 11 July 1892; folder 1872, 12 July 1892.
32 CJC, Education – History and Chronology, 1846–1969, folder 1872; *ibid,* 2 August 1892.
33 19 August 1892, in CJC, *29th Annual Report, supra* note 19 at 29–30. Throughout the period involving the Spanish and Portuguese congregation and its agreement with the Roman Catholic Board and the first Jewish School Question, Gershom De Sola served as secretary of the School Committee.
34 CJC, Education – History and Chronology, 1846–1969, folder 1891, Minutes 9 August 1892.
35 In addition to being provincial treasurer, Hall was the member in the legislature for the West Ward or Fifth Division of Montreal. He was the son of a wealthy lumber merchant and pursued a successful career at the Bar, receiving silk after only eleven years in practice. He appeared before the Privy Council on several occasions. He was very active in McGill University affairs. J Douglas Borthwick, *History and Gazetteer of Montreal to the Year 1892* (Montreal: John Lovell & Son, 1892).
36 CJC, *29th Annual Report, supra* note 19 at 32.
37 CJC, Education – History and Chronology, 1846–1969, folder 1872. "Le Gouvernement considère qu'il a épuisé tous les moyens possibles de conciliation et que les délais accordés ont été suffisants pour vous permettre d'en venir à une entente." 14 October 1892.
38 *Ibid.*
39 *Ibid,* 27 November 1892.
40 CJC, Education – History and Chronology, 1846–1969, folder 1872, 29 November 1892.
41 *Ibid,* letter, 12 December 1892.
42 *Ibid.*
43 *Ibid,* letter, 16 December 1892.
44 *Ibid,* letter, 15 December 1892.
45 CJC, Education – History and Chronology, 1846–1969, folder 1892, letter, 20 December 1892.
46 CJC, Education – History and Chronology, 1846–1969, folder 1872, letter, 30 December 1892.
47 CJC, *29th Annual Report, supra* note 17.

48 An Act to incorporate the Congregation of Roumanian Jews, Beth David, of Montreal, 63 Vict, c 107, 1900.
49 Sara Ferdman Tauben, *Traces of the Past: Montreal's Early Synagogues* (Montreal: Véhicule, 2011).
50 CJC, Baron de Hirsch, box MB1-A, 4/11, Minutes 5 February 1893.
51 CJC, Education – History and Chronology, 1846–1969, folder 1874, letters, 20, 25, and 30 September, 4 October 1893.
52 CJC, *supra* note 50.
53 CJC, Excerpts from the Minutes of the Protestant Board of School Commissioners of the City of Montreal, Education – History and Chronology, folder 1870, Minutes 12 October, 14 December 1893.
54 "The City Schools: Many Subjects Discussed by the Protestant Board," *Montreal Gazette* (9 November 1893).
55 "The Hebrew Tax Question," *Montreal Gazette* (15 December 1893).
56 CJC, Education – History and Chronology, folder 1893, Extrait du registre des délibérations des Commissions d'Écoles catholiques romains de la Cité de Montréal, Séance du 19 décembre 1893. An English translation can be found at CJC, Education and History, Minutes, School Committee, Spanish and Portuguese Jews, Montreal, 1874–1893.
57 CJC, YMBHS, MB1-A, 4/15, School Committee – Day School, Year Ending 30 June 1893 and School Account to 30 September 1893, Night School at 10.
58 CJC, Education – History and Chronology 1846–1980, folder 1872, letter, 10 April.
59 CJC, Education and History, Minutes, School Committee, Spanish and Portuguese Jews, Montreal, 1874–1893, 18 April 1894; CJC, Education – History and Chronology 1846–1989, folder 1872, 24 April 1894.
60 CJC, Education – History and Chronology 1846–1989, folder 1872, letter, 12 May 1894.
61 CJC, Education – History and Chronology, folder 1874; folder 1872, letters, 28 and 30 May 1894.
62 CJC, MB1-A, 4/15, *Baron de Hirsch Institute Annual Report*, 1894, 3.
63 CJC, Baron de Hirsch, Minutes 1891–1895, MB1-A, 4/11, 12 September 1894.
64 CJC, Education – History and Chronology 1846–1989, folder 1872, 7 September 1894.
65 *Ibid*, 12, 17, and 18 September 1894.
66 *Ibid*, letters, 17 and 18 September 1894; CJC, Education – History and Chronology, 1846–1989, PSBGM January 1871–November 1919, Minutes of the Protestant Board of School Commissioners, 18 September 1894.

67 CJC, Education – History and Chronology, 1846–1989, PSBGM January 1871–November 1919, Minutes of the Protestant Board of School Commissioners, 20 September 1894.
68 *Ibid*, 21 September 1894.
69 *Ibid.*
70 CJC, Education – History and Chronology, 1846–1989, letter 20 September 1894, file 1894.
71 CJC, Education – History and Chronology, 1846–1989, PSBGM January 1871–November 1919, Minutes of the Protestant Board of School Commissioners, 29 September 1894.
72 CJC, Baron de Hirsch, Minutes 1891–1895, MB1-A, 4/11, 4 October 1894.
73 *Ibid.*
74 CJC, Education – History and Chronology, 1846–1989, PSBGM January 1871–November 1919, Minutes of the Protestant Board of School Commissioners, 31 October 1894.
75 *Ibid*, 24 November 1894.
76 Although the closing of its school had resulted in a breach of contract claim from one of its teachers, Miss Henrietta Featherstone, whose father was a member of the School Committee. CJC, Education – History and Chronology, folder 1874, letters, 15, 19, 25 November, 19, 21, 27 December. In the end it fell to the synagogue to pay the remainder of her annual salary, since the School Committee no longer received any money from the tax payments. CJC, Education – History and Chronology, Minutes, School Committee, Spanish & Portuguese Jews, Montreal, 1874–1893, 17 December 1894; CJC, Education – History and Chronology, 1846–1989, file 1872, G De Sola to the president and Board of Trustees, 18 December 1894.
77 In another context, see Jonathan Krasner, "The Limits of Cultural Zionism in America: The Case of Hebrew in the New York City Public Schools, 1930–1960" (2009) 95 American Jewish History 349.
78 CJC, Baron de Hirsch, Minutes 1891–1895, MB1-A, 4/11, 25 November 1894.
79 CJC, Education – History and Chronology, 1846–1989, file 1872.

Chapter 5

1 Gerald Tulchinsky, *Taking Root: The Origins of the Canadian Jewish Community* (Hanover, NH: Brandeis University Press/University Press of New England, 1993) at 143.
2 32 Vict, c 16, s 26; and School Laws relating to the City of Montreal, s 18.
3 CJC, Education – History and Chronology, folder 1874, letter, 21 February 1895.

4 CJC, Education – History and Chronology 1846–1989, PSBGM Minutes, Meeting of 27 May 1895. At the same meeting the board agreed to raise its subsidy of the Baron de Hirsch School.
5 Born in England and educated at Oxford and the University of Toronto, Edward Westhead Arthy became headmaster of the Preparatory High School in Montreal, and in 1883 he was named secretary-superintendent of the Protestant School Board. He stayed in the post until ill health forced him to resign in 1908. Therefore, he was at the heart of Montreal Protestant education during the key years of the Jewish School Question. "Arthy, Edward Westhead" in Dictionary of Canadian Biography Online, <www.biographi.ca/en/bio/arthy_edward_westhead_14E.html>.
6 CJC, Education – History and Chronology 1846–1989, folder 1872, letter, 28 May 1895.
7 *Ibid*, 31 May 1895.
8 CJC, Education – History and Chronology 1846–1989, folder 1872, letter, 10 June 1895.
9 *Ibid*, 21 June 1895.
10 *Ibid.*
11 CJC, Education – History and Chronology 1846–1989, PSBGM Minutes, 10 October 1895.
12 CJC, Education – History and Chronology 1846–1989, folder 1872, letter, 14 October 11, November 1895.
13 CJC, Education – History and Chronology 1846–1989, PSBGM Minutes, 11 November 1895.
14 CJC, Education – History and Chronology 1846–1989, folder 1872, letter, 28 May 1895, indicating that even the proposed $500 salary made De Sola the highest-paid employee; letter, 15 November 1895.
15 *Financial Statements and Statistics of Attendance of the Protestant Board of School Commissioners for Montreal for the Scholastic Year 1895–6* (Montreal: WH Eaton & Son, 1896) at 4.
16 CJC, MB1-A, 4/15, *Annual Report*, 1895, School Committee, 3.
17 *Financial Statements, supra* note 15.
18 "Montreal School Question" *Quebec Daily Mercury* (1 February 1896).
19 CJC, Education – History and Chronology 1846–1989, PSBGM Minutes, 15 February 1896.
20 "Montreal School Question" *supra* note 18.
21 CJC, Education – History and Chronology 1846–1989, PSBGM Minutes, 10 February, 10 March 1898.
22 CJC, Education – History and Chronology, 1846–1989, folder 1870, Excerpts from the Minutes of the Protestant Board of School Commissioners of the City of Montreal, 28 May, 12 July 1898.

23 *Financial Statements of the Protestant Board of School Commissioners for Montreal, from July 1st, 1897 to June 30th, 1898* at 4.
24 *Financial Statements of the Protestant Board of School Commissioners for Montreal, from July 1st, 1894 to June 30th, 1895*, 1894 at 3.
25 *Financial Statements of the Protestant Board of School Commissioners for Montreal, from July 1st, 1895 to June 30th, 1896*, 1895 at 2.
26 *Financial Statements of the Protestant Board of School Commissioners for Montreal, from July 1st, 1899 to June 30th, 1900*, 1899 at 5.
27 *Ibid* at 3.
28 CJC, Education – History and Chronology 1846–1989, folder 1872, 26 October 1898.
29 Jason A Gilliland, "Modelling Residential Mobility in Montreal, 1860–1900" (1998) 31 Historical Methods 27; Sherry Olson, "Occupations and Residential Spaces in Nineteenth-Century Montreal" (1989) 22 Historical Methods 81; Gregory J Levine, "Class, Ethnicity, and Property Transfers in Montreal, 1907–1909" (1988) 14 Journal of Historical Geography 360.
30 CJC, Education – History and Chronology, folder 1874, Baron de Hirsch Day School, Report for the Month of January 1899.
31 CJC, ZA 1895, *Report of the Montreal Board of Protestant School Commissioners for the Year Ending September 1899.*
32 "The School Taxes," *Montreal Gazette* (7 February 1899)
33 CJC, Education – History and Chronology, 1846–1989, folder 1870, "Excerpts from the Minutes of the Protestant Board of School Commissioners of the City of Montreal" 11 April 1899.
34 "Current Events," *Canadian Educational Monthly* (April 1889) at 188.
35 Jean-Philippe Croteau, "La question de la taxe scolaire à Montréal au XIXe siècle: un nouveau regard sur l'intégration sociale des Juifs" (2009) 41 *Canadian Ethnic Studies/Études Ethniques au Canada* at 6.
36 *Ibid.*
37 David Rome, *The Drama of Our Early Education* (Montreal: Canadian Jewish Congress National Archives, 1991), 90.
38 CJC, Baron de Hirsch Day School, Report of the Month of January 1899.
39 *Ibid*; "The School Question," *Canadian Jewish Times* (17 February 1899); "Jews and Public Schools" and "Hebrew Teaching in Public Schools," *Canadian Jewish Times* (19 April 1899).
40 CJC, YMBHS, MB1-A, 4/15, Baron de Hirsch Institute, *School Committee Annual Report*, 1893 at 7.
41 *Ibid*, 1901 at 8.
42 *Ibid.*
43 In 1891, the 6,501 Jews (by religion) in Montreal constituted 0.13 per cent of the total population. The 1901 census counted 16,131 Jews (by race) as

0.30 per cent, and 16,401 Jews (by religion) as 0.31 per cent of the city's populace. Louis Rosenberg, *Canada's Jews: A Social and Economic Study of the Jews of Canada* (Montreal: Bureau of Social and Economic Research, Canadian Jewish Congress, 1939), table 5 at 10.

44 Editorial, *Canadian Jewish Times* (6 July 1900).

45 "Discrimination against Jewish Pupils in the Protestant Schools," *Canadian Jewish Times* (5 July 1901).

46 *Ibid.*

47 EW Arthy, *Daily Witness* (20 July 1901); "The School Question," *Canadian Jewish Times* (2 and 16 August 1901).

48 For the persistence of these stereotypes at the time, among both Roman Catholic and Protestant Montrealers, despite clear structural evidence to the contrary, see Sylvie Taschereau, "Échapper à Shylock: la Hebrew Free Loan Association of Montreal entre antisémitisme et intégration, 1911–1913" (2006) 59 Revue d'histoire de l'Amérique française 451; Frank Myron Guttman, "The Hebrew Free Loan Association of Montreal" (2004) 12 Canadian Jewish Studies 45; Benjamin G Sack, *Canadian Jews: Early in the Century*, (Montreal: Canadian Jewish Congress National Archives, 1975) at 80; An Act to incorporate the Hebrew Free Loan Association, 3 Geo V, c 96, (1912).

49 "The School Question," *Canadian Jewish Times* (2 August 1901).

50 *Ibid.*

51 "His Rights at Stake: Court Asked to Decide Status of Hebrew Scholar: Suit Is a Friendly One," *Montreal Gazette* (27 November 1901).

52 "The Question of Scholarships in the Public Schools," *Canadian Jewish Times* (6 December 1901); "Jewish Pupils in Protestant Schools," *Canadian Jewish Times* (20 December 1901).

53 The family was apparently recorded under the surname "Prinsler" in the 1901 census. The father Paul and mother Rosa were born in Romania, but Jacob and his sisters Regina, Alice, and Etty were all Canadian-born, as were his brothers Harry, Mike, and Eddy. Glen Eker, *Index of Jews Resident in the Province of Quebec According to the 1861 to 1901 Censuses of Canada* (Toronto: Ontario Genealogical Society, 2004) at 172.

54 "Jews and the Schools" (18 December 1901); "The School Question," *Canadian Jewish Times* (20 December 1901). See also "The Public School Question in Montreal," *American Israelite* (26 December 1901).

55 "Rights Talk in Canada in the Late Nineteenth Century: 'The Good Sense and Right Feeling of the People'" (1996) 14 LHR 1.

56 They did so in other contexts. They attempted to use the courts to stop virulent anti-Semitic attacks in the French-Canadian press, first in Mon-

treal in 1902. See Sack, *supra* 13–14; and "Canadian Jews and Judaism," *American Israelite* (3 February 1902); and with greater success in the famous Plamondon case in Quebec in 1912. See *Ortenberg v Plamondon* 24 BR 69, (1914); David Fraser, "The Blood Libel in North America: Jews, Law, and Citizenship in the Early 20th Century," Law & Literature [forthcoming in 2015].

57 CJC, Education – History and Chronology, 1846–1989, folder Education 1870, Excerpts from the Minutes of the Protestant Board of School Commissioners of the City of Montreal, 9 January 1902; "The School Question," *Canadian Jewish Times* (17 January 1902).

58 CJC, YMBHS, MB1-A, 4/15, Baron de Hirsch Institute, *School Committee Annual Report*, 1902 at 39, 32; CJC, Education – History and Chronology, 1846–1989, folder Education 1870, Excerpts from the Minutes of the Protestant Board of School Commissioners of the City of Montreal, 13 March 1901.

59 CJC, Education – History and Chronology, 1846–1989, folder Education 1870, 13 March 1902.

60 *Rapport du Surintendant de l'Instruction Publique de la Province du Québec pour l'année 1902–03* (Quebec: Charles Pageau, 1904) at 383.

61 David Ansell, "Jews and the Protestant Schools," CJC, Education – History and Chronology, 1846–1989, folder Education 1870, 20 June 1902.

62 CJC, Education – History and Chronology, 1846–1989, folder 1872, letter, 6 October 1902.

63 CJC, Education – History and Chronology, 1846–1989, folder Education 1870, 9 October 1902.

64 "Attendu qu'il a été prouvé devant ce comité que ceux qui réclament l'enseignement de l'hébreu dans les écoles protestantes de cette province ne constitutent qu'une petite minorité des Juifs de Montréal, que la grande majorité s'oppose clairement à cet enseignement proposé; en conséquence, cette demande ne peut être agrée." *Rapport, supra* note 60 at 386, 28 November.

65 "The Pinsler Case," *Canadian Jewish Times* (24 October 1902).

66 23 CS 365, (1903).

67 *Ibid* at 366–7.

68 A fuller account of the situation of Protestant schools and the board's regulations can be found in the extensive documentation provided to British educational authorities in 1900. E Arthy, "Protestant Schools," in *Special Reports on Educational Subjects:* vol 4: *Educational Systems of the Chief Colonies of the British Empire* (London: HMSO, 1901) at 232–48.

69 *Pinsler*, 23 CS 365, (1903), 368.

70 *Ibid.*
71 *Ibid* at 370–4.
72 *Ibid* at 376.
73 *Ibid.*
74 The most likely figure is that thirty-six to forty Jewish students attended Roman Catholic schools at the time. Croteau, "La question de la taxe scolaire," *supra* note 35 at 22.
75 *Pinsler*, *supra* note 69 at 378.
76 *Ibid.*
77 *Ibid.*
78 *Pinsler*, 23 CS 365, (1903), 378.
79 "The Civil Courts," *Montreal Gazette* (16 February 1903).
80 "Pinsler Case Will Go before Privy Council," *Montreal Gazette* (21 February 1903).
81 CJC, Education – History and Chronology – 1903, Maxwell Goldstein to president of the institute and Notice of Meeting, 16 February 1903; "Jews Now Eager for Their Right," *Montreal Gazette* (19 February 1903).
82 Clarence de Sola was the third son of Abraham de Sola. He was a successful businessman and active in Jewish community affairs. He was a leading Canadian Zionist and a noted authority on Jewish history. From 1906 until his death he was parnass of the Spanish and Portuguese synagogue. From 1904 he was the consul for Belgium in Canada and played an important role in organizing aid to that country during the First World War, for which he was decorated by King Albert. Arthur Daniel Hart, "The Late Chevalier Clarence I De Sola" in *The Jew in Canada* (Montreal: Jewish Publication, 1926) at 314.
83 CJC, Jewish Education Council, 1 March 1903.
84 CJC, Jewish Education Council, Meeting of the Jewish Educational Rights Movement; "Will Appeal to Cabinet," *Montreal Gazette* (2 March 1903).
85 CJC, Education – History and Chronology 1846–1989, folder 1870, Excerpts from the Minutes of the Protestant Board of School Commissioners of the City of Montreal, 2 March 1903.
86 Croteau, *supra* note 35 at 21–2.
87 CJC, Education – History and Chronology 1846–1989, folder 1870, Excerpts from the Minutes of the Protestant Board of School Commissioners of the City of Montreal, 2 March 1903.
88 *Ibid.*
89 *Ibid.*
90 *Ibid.*
91 "Agreement of Jews and Protestants," *Montreal Gazette* (3 March 1903).

92 "School Question Is About to Be Settled: Montreal Deputation Interviews Quebec Ministers in Regard to Jewish Children," *Montreal Star* (5 March 1903).

93 CJC, Education – History and Chronology 1846–1989, folder 1870, Excerpts from the Minutes of the Protestant Board of School Commissioners of the City of Montreal, 9 April 1903.

94 *Ibid.*

95 3 Edw VII, c 16, 1903.

96 Michael Brown, *Jew or Juif?: Jews, French Canadians, and Anglo-Canadians, 1759–1914* (Philadelphia: Jewish Publication Society, 1986) at 241.

97 CJC, Education – History and Chronology, 1903, WH Baker to Arthy, 11 November 1903.

98 CJC, Education – History and Chronology, 1846–1989, PSBGM January 1871–1919, Meeting of 8 October 1903.

99 Rosenberg, *supra* note 43, table 19, "Comparative Number and Percentage of Jewish Population of Greater Montreal" and accompanying text at 31–3.

100 "System Works Ill: Absence of Jews on Holidays Hurts Schools," *Montreal Gazette* (8 October 1903); "Jews and the Schools," *Canadian Jewish Times* (18 December 1903).

101 A concise history of the school tax issue in Montreal and Quebec can be found in Walter Pilling Percival, *Across the Years: A Century of Protestant Education in the Province of Quebec* (Montreal: Gazette, 1946) at 35–8. Percival was for many years deputy minister and director of Protestant education for the province. See also George J Trueman, *School Funds in the Province of Quebec* (New York: Teachers College, Columbia University, 1920).

102 Sack, *supra* note 48 at 15–17; "Rabbi De Sola Objects to Any Distinction Being Made between Jews and Protestants," *Daily Witness* (11 December 1903); "Education of Jewish Children: Rabbi De Sola Complains about Amount of Talk Done; Views of Rev. Dr Barclay," *Montreal Star* (10 December 1903); "Protestant School Commissioners Meet: Rabbi De Sola Protests against Reference to Jews in Commissioners' Circular," *Montreal Gazette* (11 December 1903).

103 "Jews and the Schools," *Jewish Times* (18 December 1903).

104 An Act to amend the school law of Lower Canada, 12 Vict, c 50, 1849, ss 1 & 2; An Act respecting provincial aid for superior education and normal and common schools, Consolidated Statutes of Lower Canada, 24 Vict, c 15 & 16, 1861, ss 66–67.

105 See e.g. MS Katz, *A History of Compulsory Education Laws* (Bloomington, IN: Phi Delta Kappa Educational Foundation, 1976).

106 Allan D Talbot, *P.A.P.T: A History of the Provincial Association of Protestant Teachers of Quebec* (Gardenvale, QC: Harpell's Press, 1964) at 63–4; IO Vincent, *The Right Track: Compulsory Education in the Province of Quebec* (Toronto: J Dent & Sons, 1920).

107 Louis-Philippe Audet, "La Querelle de l'Instruction Obligatoire: 1875–1943" in Marcel Lajeunesse, ed, *L'Éducation au Québec: 19e–20e siècles* (Montreal: Boréal Express, 1971) at 115–29.

108 Yvan Lamonde, *The Social History of Ideas in Quebec, 1760–1896* (Montreal & Kingston: McGill-Queen's University Press, 2013) at 380ff.

109 Robert Gagnon, *Histoire de la Commission des Écoles Catholiques de Montréal: Le développement d'un réseau d'écoles catholiques en milieu urbain* (Montreal: Boréal, 1996) at 123–8; Charles-Édouard Dorion, *L'Enseignement Obligatoire* (Quebec: L'Action Sociale Catholique, 1919). Dorion was a judge of the Superior Court and professor of civil law at l'Université Laval.

110 C-J Magnan, *A propos de l'Instruction Obligatoire: La Situation Scolaire de la Province de Québec* (Quebec: L'Action Sociale, 1919). Magnan was inspector general for Catholic Schools and president of the St Vincent de Paul Society.

111 Antonin Dupont, *Les relations entre l'Église et l'État sous Louis-Alexandre Taschereau, 1920–1936* (Montreal: Guérin, 1972); *L'Instruction obligatoire: Ce qu'en pensent: Sir Lomer Gouin, MJ-M Tellier, MJ-A Langlois* (Montreal: L'Oeuvre des Tracts, 1919).

112 Dominique Marshall, Nicole Doone Danby, trans, *The Social Origins of the Welfare State: Quebec Families, Compulsory Education, and Family Allowances, 1940–1955* (Waterloo, ON: Wilfrid Laurier University Press, 2006) at 2ff.

113 Tamara Myers & Mary Anne Poutanen, "Cadets, Curfews, and Compulsory Schooling: Mobilizing Anglophone Children in WW II Montreal" (2005) 38 Social History 367.

114 Wendy Johnston, "Keeping Children in School: The Response of the Montreal Catholic School Commission to the Depression of the 1930s" (1985) 20 Historical Papers 193.

115 SQ, 7 Geo VI, c 13, (1943), Loi concernant la fréquentation scolaire obligatoire/An Act respecting Compulsory School Attendance.

116 James Tully, *Strange Multiplicity: Constitutionalism in an Age of Diversity* (Cambridge: Cambridge University Press, 1995), 209.

Chapter 6

1 Regulations for City Schools Under Control of the Protestant Board of School Commissioners for Montreal, 1908, s 39 (2).

2 "Protestant Commission Discusses Accommodation for Jews and Announces Dates for Holidays," *Montreal Star* (6 November 1904); editorial, *Daily Witness* (15 November 1904).
3 In 1905, for example, David Ansell submitted a list of fourteen Jewish holidays, nine of which fell on schooldays. CJC, Education – History and Chronology, PSBGM January 1871–November 1919, Minutes 15 September 1905.
4 David Rome, *On the Jewish School Question in Montreal, 1903–1931* (Montreal: Canadian Jewish Congress National Archives, 1975) at 43.
5 "Jewish Children and the Public Schools," *Canadian Jewish Times* (3 May 1907).
6 David Rome, "Those 'Good Old Nostalgic Days' at Baron Byng High Were Actually a Planned Affront to Jews of Montreal," *Canadian Jewish News* (3 April 1980); Arlette Corcos, *Montréal, les Juifs et l'École* (Sillery, QC: Septentrion, 1997) at 84.
7 J Ralph Watson, *Protestants in Montreal 1760–1992* (Hantsport, NS: Lancelot, 1992).
8 Roderick MacLeod & Mary Anne Poutanen, *A Meeting of the People: School Boards and Protestant Communities in Quebec, 1801–1998* (Montreal & Kingston: McGill-Queen's University Press, 2004) at 203.
9 Michael Brown, *Jew or Juif?: Jews, French-Canadians, and Anglo-Canadians, 1759–1914* (Philadelphia: Jewish Publication Society, 1987) at 242; Corcos, *supra* note 6 at 82–3.
10 CJC, Education – History and Chronology, PSBGM January 1871–November 1919, Minutes 12 June 1913.
11 Robert Tsai, *America's Forgotten Constitutions: Defiant Visions of Power and Community* (Cambridge, MA: Harvard University Press, 2014); Robert Cover, "*Nomos* and Narrative" (1983–84) 97 Harv Law Rev 4.
12 John Ferguson Snell, *Macdonald College of McGill University: A History from 1904–1955* (Montreal: McGill University Press, 1963), for an official history that makes no mention of Jewish students. See Shulamis Yelin, "I Become a Teacher" in *Shulamis: Stories from a Montreal Childhood* (Montreal: Véhicule, 1983) 147ff.
13 CJC, Education – History and Chronology, PSBGM January 1871–November 1919, Minutes 6 October 1905.
14 *Ibid.*
15 Bram de Sola, "The Jewish School Question," *University Magazine* 8 (1909) at 549. Abraham Charles Meldola de Sola was the son of Rabbi Meldola de Sola. He graduated from McGill and Oxford universities and turned to journalism before practising law in Montreal. He served as an officer in the Canadian Army during the First World War. Arthur Daniel Hart, "ACM

de Sola, MA, BCL, Montreal" in *The Jew in Canada* (Montreal: Jewish Publication, 1926) at 385.

16 "The Juvenile Strike," *Canadian Jewish Times* (7 March 1913).

17 Roderick MacLeod & Mary Anne Poutanen, "Little Fists for Social Justice: Anti-Semitism, Community, and Montréal's Aberdeen School Strike, 1913" (2012) 70 Labour 61; Reuben Brainin, "Strike of Yiddish Children in Aberdeen School, 2 March 1913" in Pierre Anctil, ed, *Through the Eyes of the Eagle: The Early Montreal Yiddish Press (1907–1916)*, translated by David Rome (Montreal: Véhicule, 2001) at 78–9.

18 "Jewish Women to Teach in School: Protestant School Board Will Employ Them under Certain Defined Conditions," *Montreal Gazette* (12 June 1913).

19 Protestant Board of School Commissioners, Minutes 12 June 1913.

20 *Ibid*; "Historical Week for Canadian Jewry," *Canadian Jewish Chronicle* (20 June 1913).

21 Protestant Board of School Commissioners, Minutes 13 November 1913.

22 A Wohliner, "The Jewish School Issue in Quebec," *Keneder Adler*, 1912, in Anctil, *supra* note 17 at 66; "The Institute and the People," 17 March 1909, *ibid* at 62; Simon Belkin, *Le Mouvement Ouvrier Yiddish au Canada, (1904–1920)*, translated by Pierre Anctil (Sillery, QC: Septentrion, 1999) at 348–50.

23 For contemporary debates elsewhere, see Alexander M Dushkin, *Jewish Education in New York City* (New York: Bureau of Jewish Education, 1918).

24 "A Vexed Question," *Canadian Jewish Times* (16 April 1909).

25 "Equal Rights in the Public Schools," *Canadian Jewish Times* (28 June 1907).

26 "The Baron de Hirsch School," *Canadian Jewish Times* (17 June 1904).

27 Department of Trade and Commerce, Census and Statistics Office, *Special Report on the Foreign-Born Population* (Ottawa: Government Printing Bureau, 1915), table 17 at 34.

28 "The Baron de Hirsch School," *Canadian Jewish Times* (17 June 1904).

29 CJC, ZA 1900–1905, 1904 1/5, Memorandum of Agreement and related correspondence.

30 *Ibid*, 11 October 1904.

31 CJC, Education – History and Chronology, 1846–1989, folder Education 1870, Excerpts from the Minutes of the Protestant Board of School Commissioners of the City of Montreal, Board of Protestant School Commissioners, Minutes 5 September 1905.

32 "School Accommodation," *Canadian Jewish Times* (29 November 1907).

33 CJC, MB1-A, box 1, Baron de Hirsch, Supplementary Chronological Material, Minutes 13 January 1907.

34 CJC, Education – History and Chronology, 1846–1989, folder Education 1870, Excerpts from the Minutes of the Protestant Board of School Com-

missioners of the City of Montreal, Board of Protestant School Commissioners, Minutes 18 April 1907.

35 *Ibid.*

36 *Ibid*, Minutes 14 November 1907.

37 *Ibid*, and 17 November 1907.

38 "Jewish Children and the Public Schools," *Canadian Jewish Times* (3 May 1907).

39 Protestant Board, letter to the editor, *Canadian Jewish Times* (20 October 1907).

40 CJC, Education – History and Chronology, 1846–1989, folder Education 1870, Excerpts from the Minutes of the Protestant Board of School Commissioners of the City of Montreal, Board of Protestant School Commissioners, Minutes 27 October 1907; "The School Question and the Baron de Hirsch Institute," *Canadian Jewish Times* (30 October 1930).

41 CJC, MR1, box 4, MB1-A, 4/6, Early Materials, YMHBA, B1, Report 12 March 1909.

42 CJC, Education – History and Chronology, PSBGM January 1871–November 1919, Minutes 22 September 1908; CJC, MB1-A, box 1, Baron de Hirsch, Supplementary Chronological Material, Minutes 8 October 1908; "Dufferin School Besieged: Police Had to Be Called to Stop Stampede of Pupils," *Montreal Gazette* (9 September 1908); "Record Enrolment," *Montreal Gazette* (10 September 1908).

43 "Les juifs veulent des écoles séparées," *Le Devoir* (9 October 1912).

44 32 Vict, c 16, s 17, (1869).

45 George J Trueman, *School Funds in the Province of Quebec* (New York: Teachers College Columbia University, 1920).

46 Jean-Philippe Croteau, "Le Mode de Nomination des Commissaires à la PBSCCM et la Communauté Juive: Confessionalité et Démocratisation (1906–1931)" (2008–09) 16–17 Canadian Jewish Studies/Études Juives Canadiennes 53; Ruby Heap, *L'Église, l'État et l'enseignement primaire public catholique au Québec, 1897–1920* (PhD Thesis, Université de Montréal, 1987) [unpublished].

47 Croteau, *supra* note 46 at 59–61.

48 Archives de la Ville de Montréal, Memo re: Jewish Schools, Montreal City Council, Trésorier Municipal, Memento Historique, 1897–1910, 13.

49 Christopher Benfield Carter (1844–1906) was named queen's counsel by both the federal and provincial governments. He was a prominent Montreal lawyer and served as *bâtonnier* of the Bar of Montreal and of the Bar of the province of Quebec. He also served as treasurer of the Canadian Bar Association. He was elected as a city councillor in Montreal and as mem-

ber of the Legislative Assembly. National Assembly, "Biographie" online: <www.assnat.qc.ca/fr/deputes/carter-christopher-benfield-2439/biographie.html>; "Christopher Benfield Carter 1844–1906" in Pierre Beullac & E Fabre Surveyer, *Le Centenaire du Barreau de Montréal 1849–1959* (Montreal: Librairie Ducharme, 1949) at 144–6.

50 There are no official accounts of Legislative Assembly proceedings for sessions before 1963. The Assembly is currently trying to reconstitute debates from contemporaneous newspaper reports, which did offer extensive and often verbatim accounts. No reports of the Carter Bill debates exist. See <www.assnat.qc.ca/archives/Debats-reconstitues/index.htm> for an account of the reconstitution process.

51 Gerald Tulchinsky, *Taking Root: The Origins of the Canadian Jewish Community* (Hanover, NH: Brandeis University Press/University Press of New England, 1993) at 246.

52 John Thomas Finnie (1847–1925) was a graduate of McGill and the Royal College of Surgeons, Edinburgh. He was elected to the Assembly from the 4th District of Montreal in 1908 and then from St Laurent in 1912 and again 1916. He was also elected whip by his party in the Assembly. "Biographie" online: <www.assnat.qc.ca/fr/deputes/finnie-john-thomas-3153/biographie.html>.

53 Rome, *supra* note 4 at 15.

54 "Loi de l'instruction publique, Art. 513," proposed amendment, Les débats de l'Assemblée legislative, 12e législature 1re session, 11 mars 1909. Godfroy Langlois (1866–1928) was a prominent Quebec journalist and liberal. He founded and edited *Le Canada* and *Le Pays*. "Biographie" online: <www.assnat.qc.ca/fr/deputes/langlois-godfroy-3955/biographie.html>.

55 Patrice A Dutil, "The Politics of Muzzling 'Lucifer's Representative': Godfroy Langlois's Test of Wilfrid Laurier's Liberalism, 1892–1910" (1993) 28 Journal of Canadian Studies 113.

56 Croteau, *supra* note 46 at 62.

57 Rome, *supra* note 4 at 13; see e.g. Henri Bernard, *La Ligue de l'Enseignement: Histoire d'une Conspiration Maçonnique à Montréal* (Montreal: np, 1904).

58 Circular, reproduced in EI Rexford, *Our Educational Problem: The Jewish Population and the Protestant Schools* (Montreal: Renouf, 1923 or 1924) at 23–4.

59 *Ibid* at 24.

60 Sir Lomer Gouin (1861–1929) had a long and illustrious career in politics. Admitted as a lawyer, he had a close personal and political friendship with Langlois and was associated with radical elements in the Liberal Party early in his career, although he became more moderate as the years passed.

He was first elected to the provincial Assembly in 1897 and was appointed to the Roman Catholic Committee of the Council of Public Instruction. In 1910–11, he was *bâtonnier* of the Montreal Bar. He would serve as Liberal premier until 1920. He would later chair the Commission into Education during another manifestation of the Jewish School Question. He became lieutenant governor of Quebec and died in office in 1929. "Gouin, Sir Lomer" in Dictionary of Canadian Biography Online, <www.biographi.ca/en/bio/gouin_lomer_15E.html>; G-Édouard Rinfret, *Histoire du Barreau de Montréal* (Cowansville, QC: Éditions Yvon Blais, 1989) at 278.

61 Robert Rumilly, *Histoire de Montréal*, vol 3 (Montreal: Fides, 1972) at 357, 381. Rumilly wrote extremely well-sourced histories of Quebec and Montreal politics. His political bias was, however, never far from the surface, nor particularly well disguised. Jean-François Nadeau, *Robert Rumilly, L'Homme de Duplessis* (Montreal: Lux, 2009).

62 CJC, Minutes Baron de Hirsch Institute, 8 October 1908; "School Board Representation," *Canadian Jewish Times* (20 March 1908).

63 "School Commissions," *Montreal Gazette* (30 March 1909).

64 *Ibid.*

65 Peter Samuel George Mackenzie (1862–1914) was member for Richmond, king's counsel, and *bâtonnier* for the Bar of the District of St François. In 1906 he was named to the Protestant Committee of the Council of Public Instruction. "Peter Samuel George Mackenzie," Assemblée Nationale, online: <www.assnat.qc.ca/fr/deputes/mackenzie-peter-samuel-george-4279/biographie.html>.

66 "School Commissions," *Montreal Gazette* (30 March 1909).

67 *Ibid*; "Protestant School Commissioners Opposed to Justice: Finnie Bill Killed," *Canadian Jewish Times* (2 April 1909).

68 Robert Campbell, "A Presbyterian View of the Proposals of Dr Finnie's Bill," *Montreal Gazette* (31 March 1909).

69 "Protestant School Commissioners Opposed to Justice," *Canadian Jewish Times* (2 April 1909).

70 *Ibid*; "Vexed Question," *supra* note 24; "Statements of Protestant Board Refuted," *Canadian Jewish Times* (30 April 1909).

71 Rexford, *supra* note 58 at 22.

72 Croteau, *supra* note 46 at 63.

73 "The School Question Redivivus," *Canadian Jewish Chronicle* (7 May 1909); "End of the School Question in Sight," *Canadian Jewish Times* (30 July 1909).

74 "Educational Difficulties in Canada," *Jewish Exponent* (27 August 1909); "Mr Hart Discusses the Position of the Jewish Pupil," *Montreal Gazette* (18 May 1909); see "Mr Hart and the School Issue," *Montreal Gazette* (21 May 1909).

75 "What World Owes to Jewish People: Rabbi de Sola in Sermon Replies to Dr Barclay's Remarks," *Montreal Star* (24 April 1909).

76 Bill 157, 5 April 1910; Bill 156, 3 February 1911; Bill 74, 27 November 1912.

77 David Rome, *The Drama of Our Early Education* (Montreal: Canadian Jewish Congress National Archives, 1991) at 130–4.

78 "The Education Problem in Montreal from a Jewish Standpoint," *Canadian Jewish Times* (24 February 1911).

79 35 CLT 262 (1915).

80 Sylvio Normand, "L'*affaire* Plamondon: un cas d'antisémitisme à Québec au début du XXe siècle" (2007), 48 C de D 477; and Constance Backhouse, "Anti-Semitism and the Law in Québec City: The *Plamondon* Case, 1910–15" in Daniel W Hamilton and Alfred Brophy, eds, *Transformations in American Legal History: Law, Ideology, and Methods, Essays in Honor of Morton J Horwitz*, vol 2 (Cambridge, MA: Harvard Law School & Harvard University Press, 2010) at 303–25.

81 *The Quebec Jewish Libel Case: Address Delivered by SW Jacobs KC* (Montreal: Jewish Times, 1913) at 26.

82 *Ibid* at 28.

83 CJC, letter, 26 February 1912, David Rome, Education Files, 1912.

84 *Report of the Superintendent of Public Instruction of the Province of Quebec for the Year 1915–1916* (Quebec: E-E Cinq-Mars, 1916), Meetings of the Roman Catholic Committee, 22 and 23 September 1915; Meeting of the Protestant Committee, 1 October 1915.

85 Baym Onhayb, *La Première École Yiddish de Montréal, 1911–1914*, edited and translated by Pierre Anctil (Sillery, QC: Septentrion, 2009).

86 "Jews Want Member in House," *American Israelite* (31 August 1911).

87 "School Troubles in Montreal," *American Israelite* (6 July 1911).

88 Arthur Daniel Hart, "Abraham Blumenthal, Montreal" in *The Jew in Canada, supra* note 15 at 363.

89 Rumilly, *supra* note 61 at 460; "Juifs et Protestants à la Commission Scolaire Dissidente," *Le Devoir* (15 April 1914); "To Complete Term on School Board," *Montreal Gazette* (8 June 1914); "Mayor Held Post for Five Minutes," *Montreal Gazette* (9 June 1914).

90 Arthur Daniel Hart, "Alderman Louis Rubenstein, Montreal" in *The Jew in Canada, supra* note 15 at 373.

91 Lyon Jacobs (1887–1971) graduated in law from McGill University after undergraduate degrees at Laval University. He was called to the Bar in 1913 and appointed king's counsel in 1923. He served as city councillor and as a federal prosecutor. "Obituary Lyon W Jacobs" *Jewish Advocate* (1 July 1971).

92 "Lyon W. Jacobs Elected Alderman in Montreal" *American Hebrew and Jewish Messenger* (19 April 1918); "Jew Acting Mayor of Montreal Que." *Jewish Advocate* (12 December 1918).
93 "The Public Schools," "Montreal School Problem," "Jewish Commissioner This Time," and "'No Jew on the Board,'" *Canadian Jewish Chronicle* (9 June 1916).
94 Letter to mayor, reproduced in Rexford, *supra* note 58 at 29.
95 For the details of the Protestant reaction, see *ibid* at 30ff.
96 Archives de la Ville de Montréal [AVM], Minutes, Montreal City Council, 7 May 1917.
97 AVM, Minutes, Montreal City Council, 29 May 1917.
98 Croteau, *supra* note 46 at 65.
99 Bram de Sola, *supra* note 15.
100 Rexford, *supra* note 58 at 31–5.
101 *Ibid* at 34.
102 "Synod's Strong Stand on Local School Question: Protestant Schools Must Remain Christian in Character: Let Jews Have Separate Board," *Montreal Star* (6 February 1918).
103 For a view of the "Jewish" holiday issue from the other side, see Joshua Eli Plaut, *A Kosher Christmas: 'Tis the Season to Be Jewish* (New Brunswick, NJ: Rutgers University Press, 2012).
104 Rexford, *supra* note 58 at 35.
105 Minutes, Board of Protestant School Commissioners, 14 November 1912; confirmed 29 May 1919.
106 "Separate Panel Only Solution: Synod's View on Jewish Demand for Place on School Board," *Montreal Gazette* (8 February 1918); "Synod's Strong Stand," *supra* note 104.
107 "Trouble in Montreal," *Jewish Advocate* (10 September 1909); Gerald Tulchinsky, *supra* note 51 at 248ff.
108 Bernard, *supra* note 57.

Chapter 7

1 Bettina Bradbury & Tamara Myers, *Negotiating Identities in 19th- and 20th-Century Montreal* (Vancouver: University of British Columbia Press, 2005).
2 Louis Rosenberg, *Canada's Jews: A Social and Economic Study of Jews in Canada in the 1930s* (Montreal: Bureau of Social and Economic Research, Canadian Jewish Congress, 1939), 3; Alexandra Szacka, "Immigration et Démographie" in *Juifs et réalités juives au Québec* (Montreal: Institut Québécois de Recherche sur la Culture, 1984), 95–121.

3 *Ibid.*

4 Robert Choinère, "Intégration Géographique et Sociale de la Population Juive à la Société Québécoise" (1982) 10 Cahiers québécois de démographie 381; and Jacques Légaré, "La population juive de Montréal est-elle victime d'une ségrégation qu'elle se serait elle-même imposée?" (1965) 6 Recherches sociographiques 311.

5 Sherry Olson & Patricia Thornton, *Peopling the North American City: Montreal 1840–1900* (Montreal & Kingston: McGill-Queen's University Press, 2011); Jason A Gilliland, *Residential Mobility in Montreal, 1861–1901* (MA Thesis, McGill University, 1993) [unpublished].

6 Joe King, *From the Ghetto to the Main* (Montreal: Montreal Jewish Publication Society, 2000); Edward Hillel, *The Main: Portrait of a Neighbourhood* (Toronto: Key Porter, 1987).

7 Ignace Olazabal, *Khaverim: Les Juifs Askénazes de Montréal au Début du XXe Siècle entre le Shtetl et l'Identité Citoyenne* (Montreal: Nota Bene, 2006); and Keinosuke Oiwa's excellent study, *Tradition and Social Change: An Ideological Analysis of the Montreal Jewish Immigrant Ghetto in the Early Twentieth Century* (PhD Thesis, Cornell University, 1988) [unpublished].

8 See e.g. Steven Lapidus, "'Magid of Montreal': Rabbi Hirsch Cohen on the Dilemmas of the Canadian Rabbi" (2009) 23 Jewish History 179; Lapidus, *Rabbis and Their Community: Studies in the Eastern European Orthodox Rabbinate in Montreal, 1896–1930* (Calgary: University of Calgary Press, 2007).

9 Geoffrey Ewen, *The International Unions and the Workers' Revolt in Quebec, 1914–1925* (PhD Thesis, York University, 1998) [unpublished]; Alan Gottheil, *Les Juifs Progressistes au Québec* (Montreal: Éditions Par Ailleurs, 1988).

10 Tamara Myers, "On Probation: The Rise and Fall of Jewish Women's Antideliquency Work in Interwar Montreal" in Bettina Bradbury & Tamara Myers, eds, *Negotiating Identities in 19th-and 20th-Century Montreal* (Vancouver: UBC Press, 2005), 175–201.

11 Rebecca E Margolis, "A Tempest in Three Teapots: Yom Kippur Balls in London, New York, and Montreal" (2001) 9 Canadian Jewish Studies 38; Irving Howe, *World of Our Fathers* (New York: Harcourt Brace Jovanovich 1976) at 106.

12 Yuu Nishimura, "On the Cultural Front: The Bund and the Yiddish Secular School Movement in Interwar Poland" (2013) 43 East European Jewish Affairs 265.

13 For an overview of the history of these debates and movements in Montreal's Jewish communities, see Arlette Corcos, *Montréal, Les Juifs et L'École* (Sillery, QC: Septentrion, 1997) at 151–250; S Wiseman, "The History of the

Jewish People's Schools of Montreal" in Arthur Daniel Hart, ed, *The Jew in Canada* (Montreal: Jewish Publication, 1926), 189–91; AJ Livinson, "The History of the United Talmud Torah" in *ibid* at 187–8; in North America, see Fradle Pomerantz Freidenreich, *Passionate Pioneers: The Story of Yiddish Secular Education in North America, 1910–1960* (Teaneck, NJ: Holmes & Meier, 2010).

14 Robert D Lewis, "A City Transformed: Manufacturing Districts and Suburban Growth in Montreal, 1850–1929" (2001) 27 Journal of Historical Geography 20.

15 John Adams, *The Protestant School System in the Province of Quebec* (Aberdeen: Aberdeen University Press/Longmans, 1902); WAF Hepburn et al, *Protestant Education in the Province of Quebec: Report of the Quebec Protestant Education Survey* (Montreal: Montreal Protestant Central School Board, 1938); Mary Anne Poutanen, "'Unless she gives better satisfaction': Teachers, Protestant Education, and Community in Rural Quebec, Lochaber and Gore District, 1863–1945" (2003) 15 Historical Studies in Education 237.

16 Wendy Johnston, "Contestation et continuité: les comités confessionnels et la gestion des écoles publiques au Québec" (1995) 48 Revue d'histoire de l'Amérique française 403.

17 Pierre Anctil, "Finding a Balance in a Dual Society: The Jews of Quebec" in Ezra Mendelsohn, ed, *Jews and the State: Dangerous Alliances and the Perils of Privilege*, Studies in Contemporary Jewry, An Annual, 19 (Oxford: Oxford University Press, 2003), 70–87.

18 Pierre Anctil, *Le Rendez-vous Manqué: Les Juifs de Montréal face au Québec de l'entre-deux-guerres* (Montreal: IQRC, 1988).

19 Pierre Anctil, *Le Devoir, Les Juifs et L'Immigration* (Montreal: IQRC, 1988); Anctil, *supra* note 18; Marc Hébert, "*Le Soleil*, Le *Quebec Chronicle Telegraph* et L'Immigration Juive 1925–1939" (1991) 3 Canadian Jewish Studies/Études Juives Canadiennes 55.

20 Max Nemni & Monique Nemni, William Johnson, trans, *Young Trudeau: Son of Quebec, Father of Canada* (Toronto: McClelland & Stewart, 2006) at 58–9.

21 John English, *Citizen of the World: The Life of Pierre Elliott Trudeau*, vol 1: *1919–1968* (Toronto: Knopf Canada, 2006) at 48–50.

22 Pierre Elliott Trudeau, *Memoirs* (Toronto: McClelland & Stewart, 1993).

23 "Interlude of Hostility: Judeo-Christian Relations in Quebec in the Interwar Period, 1919–1939" in Alan Davies, ed, *Antisemitism in Canada: History and Interpretation* (Waterloo, ON: Wilfrid Laurier University Press, 1992) at 135. While the focus in this chapter is the interwar period, the history of English Canadian Protestant anti-Semitism is not limited to that time-

frame. Michael Brown, *Jew or Juif?: Jews, French Canadians, and Anglo-Canadians, 1759–1914* (Philadelphia: Jewish Publication Society, 1987) at 224ff.

24 "Interlude," *supra* note 23; Mario Nigro & Clare Mauro, "The Jewish Immigrant Experience and the Practice of Law in Montreal, 1830 to 1990" (1998–99) 44 McGill LJ 999.

25 Michael Behiels, "Neo-Canadians and Schools in Montreal, 1900–1970" (1988) 8 Journal of Cultural Geography 5.

26 Mordecai Richler, *The Apprenticeship of Duddy Kravitz* (Don Mills, ON: Andre Deutsch, 1959) at 2–3.

27 Jiwu Wang, *"His Dominion" and the "Yellow Peril": Protestant Missions to the Chinese Immigrants in Canada, 1859–1967* (PhD Thesis, University of Ottawa, 2000) [unpublished]; Jeffrey P Plante, *Answering the Call for Reform: The Toronto and Montreal Chinese Missions 1894–1925* (MA Thesis, Wilfrid Laurier University, 1997) [unpublished].

28 In British Columbia, however, Chinese student and community activism was required to prevent the local school board in Victoria from establishing segregated classes for Chinese Canadian students. Timothy J Stanley, *Contesting White Supremacy: School Segregation, Anti-Racism, and the Making of Chinese Canadians* (Vancouver: UBC Press, 2011).

29 Lisa Rose Mar, *Brokering Belonging: Chinese in Canada's Exclusion Era, 1885–1945* (Oxford: Oxford University Press, 2010); Chan Kwok Bun, *Smoke and Fire: The Chinese in Montreal* (Hong Kong: Chinese University Press, 1991); Denise Helly, *Les Chinois à Montréal, 1877–1951* (Montreal: IQRC, 1987).

30 Iryna Melnyk, *Ukrainian Bilingual Education in the Montreal Public School System, 1911–1945* (MA Thesis, McGill University, 1987) [unpublished]; CM Bayley, *The Social Structure of the Italian and Ukrainian Immigrant Communities* (MA Thesis, McGill University, 1939) [unpublished].

31 Sherry Olson, "Silver and Hotcakes and Beer: Irish Montreal in the 1840s" (2013) 45 Canadian Ethnic Studies 179; Simon Jolivet, *Les deux questions irlandaises du Québec, 1898–1921: des considérations canadiennes-françaises et irlando-catholiques* (PhD Thesis, Concordia University, 2008) [unpublished]; Sherry Olson & Patricia Thornton, "The Challenge of the Irish Catholic Community in Nineteenth-Century Montreal" (2002) 35 Social History 331; Jean Huntley-Maynard, "English Catholic Education in Quebec: An Annotated Bibliography" (1993) 28 McGill Journal of Education 133.

32 Robert Gagnon, *Histoire de la Commission des Écoles Catholiques de Montréal* (Montreal: Boréal, 1996) at 128–31.

33 Bruno Ramirez & Michael Del Balso, *The Italians of Montreal: From Sojourning to Settlement, 1900–1921* (Montreal: Éditions du Courant, 1980).

34 Jeremy Boissevain, *The Italians of Montreal: Social Adjustment in a Plural So-*

ciety, Studies of the Royal Commission on Bilingualism and Biculturalism (Ottawa: Information Canada, 1970).

35 Anne MacLennan, "Charity and Change: Montreal's English Protestant Charity Faces the Crisis of Depression" (1987) 16 Urban History Review 1. These tensions between the Italian community and the French-speaking majority would continue for many years in Montreal, until they erupted in the St Leonard school controversy. Paul-André Linteau, "The Italians of Quebec: Key Participants in Contemporary Linguistic and Political Debates" in Roberto Perin & Franc Sturino, eds, *Arrangiarsi: The Italian Immigrant Experience in Canada* (Montreal: Guernica, 1989) 179; Claude Painchaud & Richard Poulin, "Italianité, conflit linguistique et structure du pouvoir dans la communauté italo-québécoise" (1983) 15 Sociologie et Sociétés 89; Henry Ergretaud, *L'Affaire Saint-Leonard* (Quebec: Société d'Éducation du Québec, 1970).

36 Tina Ioannou, *La Communauté Grecque du Québec* (Montreal: IQRC, 1983).

37 Leonidas C Bombas, *The Greek Day School Socrates in Montreal: Its Development and Impact on Student Identity, Adjustment and Achievement* (PhD Thesis, McGill University, 1988) [unpublished].

38 Nadia Brédimas-Assimopoulos, "Dynamique ethnique et évolution sociopolitique du Québec: Le Cas de la Population Grecque de Montréal" (1983) 15 Sociologie et Sociétés 105; Michel Paillé, "Quelques caractéristiques démolinguistiques des Québécois de langue maternelle grecque" (1981) 10 Cahiers québécois de démographie 307; Nadia Brédimas-Assimopoulos, "Intégration civique sans acculturation: Les Grecs à Montréal" (1975) 7 Sociologie et Sociétés 129.

39 Brian Aboud, "Power, Immigration and the 'Prescribed Amount' Rule: The Canadian Government and the Syrians in the Early Twentieth Century" (2014) 46 Canadian Ethnic Studies 67; Norman Marino, *The Antiochian Orthodox Syrians of Montreal: An Historical Study of Cultural and Social Change over Three Generations* (MA Thesis, Concordia University, 1994) [un published]; Diane Moser, *Hometown and Family Ties: The Marriage Registers of the Lebanese-Syrian Orthodox Churches of Montreal, 1905–1950* (MA Thesis, McGill University, 1990) [unpublished].

40 Archives nationales du Québec (ANQ), E13, Département de l'Instruction Publique, 1921–23, Non-Catholic, Non-Protestant.

41 Letter, 27 May 1921, *ibid*, "… de voir à faciliter à leurs enfants l'éducation qui doit en faire des citoyens pour le le [*sic*] grand bien du pays."

42 *Report of the Protestant Board of School Commissioners of the City of Montreal, October 1st, 1914–September 30th, 1915*. Under the regulations of the Protestant School Board, they would have been considered as children of parents

"not professing the Protestant or Jewish faith" and been permitted to attend Protestant-controlled schools only after places had been given to all Protestant and Jewish children. *Regulations for City Schools under Control of The Protestant Board of School Commissioners, Adopted June 17th, 1908* (Montreal: WH Eaton & Son, 1908), s XVI (2); *Regulations for City Schools under Control of The Protestant Board of School Commissioners, Adopted May 31st, 1914, Revised June, 1919* (Montreal: WH Eaton & Son, 1908).

43 *Report of the Protestant Board of School Commissioners of the City of Montreal, October 1st, 1915–September 30th,* 1916.

44 *Report of the Protestant Board of School Commissioners of the City of Montreal, October 1st, 1922–September 30th,* 1923; 23 March 1922 redrawing Protestant school districts.

45 *Report of the Superintendent of Public Instruction,* 1915–16 (Quebec: E-E Cinq-Mars, King's Printer, 1916), 23 September 1915.

46 David Rome, *On the Jewish School Question in Montreal* (Montreal: Canadian Jewish Congress National Archives, 1975), 45.

47 Miriam Lapp, *Ethnic Political Participation in Montreal: The Role of Community Leaders* (PhD Thesis, Université de Montréal, 1997) [unpublished]; M Michael Rosenberg & Jack Jewab, "Institutional Completeness, Ethnic Organizational Style and the Role of the State: The Jewish, Italian and Greek Communities of Montreal" (1991–92) 29 Canadian Review of Sociology and Anthropology 266; Huguette Ruimy & Léon Van Dromme, "Caractéristiques des associations ethniques de Montréal: bilan d'une enquête" (1985) 11 Revue des sciences de l'éducation 361.

48 *Report of the Protestant Board of School Commissioners of the City of Montreal, from October 1st, 1911 to September 30th, 1912.*

49 *Ibid.* See generally, Michael R Olneck & Marvin Lazerson, "The School Achievement of Immigrant Children, 1900–1930" (1974) 14 History of Education Quarterly 453.

50 *Report of the Protestant Board of School Commissioners of the City of Montreal, October 1st, 1914–September 30th, 1915.*

51 *Report of the Protestant Board of School Commissioners of the City of Montreal, October 1st, 1915–September 30th, 1916.*

52 *Report of the Protestant Board of School Commissioners of the City of Montreal, October 1st, 1922–September 30th, 1923.*

53 Louis Rosenberg, *Jewish Children in the Protestant Schools of Greater Montreal in the Period from 1878 to 1962: A Statistical Study,* CJC Research Papers, series E, no. 2, 1962, 3.

54 ANQ, E13, 775-30, Re. Jewish School Question, October 1930, Jewish Education, Protestant Board of School Commissioners of the City of Montreal, 14 December 1921.

55 David Rome, "Jews in Anglophone Quebec" in Gary Caldwell & Eric Waddell, *The English of Quebec: From Majority to Minority Status* (Montreal: ICRC, 1982) at 170–1.
56 Minutes of the Meeting of the Protestant Committee of the Council of Public Instruction, 26 May 1922.
57 Minutes of the Meeting of the Protestant Committee of the Council of Public Instruction, Montreal, 24 November 1922; Minutes of the Protestant Board of School Commissioners, 11 January 1923, 6 February 1923.
58 Minutes of the Protestant Board of School Commissioners, 11 January 1923, 6 February 1923.
59 CJC, ZA 1924, 16/10, Correspondence between the Jewish Community Council of Montreal and the Protestant Board, 26 June 1924 and 30 June 1924; Minutes of the Special Meeting of the Va'ad Hair, 30 July 1924.
60 Minutes of the Meeting of the Protestant Committee of the Council of Public Instruction, 23 February 1923.
61 According to Rexford, there were 13,954 Jewish students in Protestant schools in 1923–24 and this cost the board $837,240, far short of the amount received in Jewish taxes. At least the title of Rexford's book reveals the real issue in the minds of the Protestant educational establishment. *Our Educational Problem: The Jewish Population and the Protestant Schools* (Montreal: Renouf, 1924) at 35–6.
62 Rome, *supra* note 46 at 52–3.
63 Minutes of the Meeting of the Protestant Committee of the Council of Public Instruction, 23 February 1923.
64 1922, 13 Geo V, c 44.
65 "Temporary Settlement of the School Question," *Canadian Jewish Chronicle* (29 December 1922).
66 Rome, *supra* note 46 at 58–9.
67 Arthur Daniel Hart, "Peter Bercovitch" in *supra* note 13 at 381; Geneviève Richer, *Intervenir en faveur de la justice sociale et des droits de la minorité juive: La carrière politique de Peter Bercovitch à l'assemblée législative du Québec, 1916–1938* (MA Thesis, Université d'Ottawa, 2007) [unpublished]; Jean-Jacques Lefebvre & Louis-Philippe Gagnon, "Nos Disparus – Peter Bercovitch" (1943) 3 R du B 101.
68 Bercovitch also turned down the chance to run federally, and instead recommended Sam Jacobs to Sir Wilfrid Laurier as the best candidate. Jacobs became the first Quebec Jewish MP. "Sir Wilfrid Laurier and Our First M.P.'s" (1940–41) 2 Canadian Jewish Year Book 102.
69 Bill 169, introduced into the Legislative Assembly by Bercovitch on 21 February 1924 <www.assnat.qc.ca/fr/travaux-parlementaires/assemblee-nationale/16-1/journal-debats/19240221/91947.html>; 14 Geo V, c 68,

SQ (1923–24); An Act respecting the celebration of marriages, 15 Geo V, c 73, 3 April 1925, An Act to extend certain Privileges therein mentioned to persons professing the Jewish Religion and for obviating certain inconveniences to which others of His Majesty's Subjects might otherwise be exposed, 9 Geo IV, c 75, 1829.

70 Bernard Figler, *Sam Jacobs: Member of Parliament* (Gardenvale, QC: Harpell's Press Cooperative, 1959).

71 Joseph Cohen (1891–1973) was born in Russia but moved to Montreal as a young child. A graduate of Dufferin School and McGill and Laval universities in law, he clerked with SW (Sam) Jacobs and was admitted to the Bar in 1913 and named king's counsel in 1926. He was defeated as a Liberal candidate for St Laurent in 1923, but won the seat in that riding in 1927 and was re-elected in 1931 and 1935. He was therefore the second Jewish member in 1930 and 1931 when this part of the Jewish School Question reached its climax. He was a noted criminal lawyer and taught criminal law at McGill from 1952 to 1961. He was president of the Quebec Criminology Society from 1965 to 1969. "Joseph Cohen," Assemblée Nationale, online: <www.assnat.qc.ca/fr/deputes/cohen-joseph-2617/biographie.html>.

72 Howard Palmer, *Ethnicity and Politics in Canada since Confederation* (Ottawa: Canadian Historical Association, 1991).

73 Ira Robinson, "The Foundation Documents of the Jewish Community Council of Montreal" (1996) 8 Jewish Political Studies Review 69; Steven Lapidus, *Orthodoxy in Transition: The Vaad Ha'ir of Montreal in the Twentieth Century* (PhD Thesis, Concordia University, 2011) [unpublished]; Lapidus, "The Jewish Community Council of Montreal: A National *Kehillah* or a Local Sectarian Organization?" (1975) 16–17 Canadian Jewish Studies 267.

74 As early as 1915, Rabbi Herman Abramowitz of the Shaar Hashomayim synagogue and community leader Lyon Cohen had attempted to unite Montreal Jewry on issues of kashrut and on proper organization of the religious and secular needs of the Jewish communities of Montreal. Bernard Figler, *Rabbi Dr Herman Abramowitz, Lazarus Cohen, Lyon Cohen* (Ottawa: Author, 1968) at 13–14.

75 Frédéric Mole, *L'école laïque pour une République sociale: Controverses pédagogiques et politique, 1900–1914* (Rennes: Presses Universitaires de Rennes, 2010); see Jean-Claude Milner, *De l'école* (Paris: Verdier, 2009).

76 Ira Robinson, "'The Other Side of the Coin': The Anatomy of a Public Controversy in the Montreal Jewish Community, 1931" (2011) 40 Studies in Religion 271.

77 Ira Robinson, "The Kosher Meat Wars of the 1920s and Their Aftermath"

in *Rabbis and Their Community: Studies in the Eastern European Orthodox Rabbinate in Montreal, 1896–1930* (Calgary: University of Calgary Press, 2007) at 103ff; Robinson, "Toward a History of Kashrut in Montreal: The Fight over Municipal By-law 828 (1922–24)" in Ira Robinson & Mervin Butovsky, *Renewing Our Days: Montreal Jews in the Twentieth Century* (Montreal: Véhicule, 1995) at 30; Robinson, "The Kosher Meat War and the Jewish Community Council of Montreal, 1922–1925" (1990) 22 Canadian Ethnic Studies 41.

78 Nathan Gordon (1882–1938) came to Montreal in 1906 as rabbi of the Reform Congregation, Temple Emanu-El. In 1916 he left his position to take up the practice of law. He was originally associated with the firm of Peter Bercovitch but left to become a prosecutor for the City of Montreal. He succeeded Maxwell Goldstein as president of Temple Emanu-el, a post he held until his death. He was active in charities and became involved in the school question. Arthur Daniel Hart, "Nathan Gordon, MA, BCL, Montreal" in *supra* note 13 at 125; "Nathan Gordon Is Dead: Prominent Lawyer," *Montreal Gazette* (7 February 1938).

79 Michael Hirsch was a prominent Montreal businessman who worked extensively in Jewish charities and community work, and in the early 1920s he became involved in the school question. Arthur Daniel Hart, "Michael Hirsch, Montreal" in *supra* note 13 at 194.

80 Rome, *supra* note 46 at 61; Corcos, *supra* note 13 at 85ff.

81 CJC, Education – History and Chronology 1846–1989, file 1923 Education.

82 *Ibid.*

83 *Ibid*; Bernard Figler, *Louis Fitch, QC* (Ottawa: Author, 1968). When Sam Jacobs died in 1938, Peter Bercovitch took his federal seat by acclamation and Fitch presented himself as a candidate to fill Bercovitch's vacated provincial seat in St Louis ward. In the traditional Liberal and working-class seat, Fitch ran as a Duplessis Conservative, although he did distance himself from the anti-labour stance of the Conservatives and from legislation infringing civil liberties. He was elected.

84 Born in Lithuania, Garber came to Montreal as a child. He qualified as a lawyer and was active in Jewish community affairs. A founder of the Canadian Jewish Congress, he was its president from 1962 to 1968. "Garber, Michael," Canadian Jewish Heritage Network, online: <www.cjhn.ca/en/explore.aspx?q=Michael+Garber-05/05/15>.

85 Rabbi Hirsch Cohen was a monumental figure in the Montreal Jewish community. Born in Poland, he arrived in Montreal in 1892. He was chair of the Montreal Council of Orthodox Rabbis and of the Board of Education of the United Talmud Torahs and Yeshivas. He was a fervent advocate of

separate Jewish Schools. Arthur Daniel Hart "Rabbi Hirsch Cohen, Montreal" in *supra* note 13 at 186.

86 CJC, Education – History and Chronology 1846–1989, file 1923 Education, Minutes 16 November 1923.

87 "Jews of Montreal Oppose New Panel: Rally of Synagogues," *Montreal Gazette* (3 November 1923).

88 Library and Archives Canada [LAC], MG30 c 141, vol 1, Lyon Cohen Diary 1923, 16 May 1923.

89 Rome, *supra* note 46 at 59.

90 Harold Ross, *The Jew in the Educational System of the Province of Quebec* (MA Thesis, McGill University, 1947) [unpublished] at 29.

91 "Jewish Pupils May Exceed Protestant: New Panel Agitation," *Montreal Gazette* (23 November 1923); CJC, Education – History and Chronology 1846–1989, file 1923 Education, Minutes 16 November 1923.

92 *Report of the Protestant Board of School Commissioners of the City of Montreal from October 1st, 1922 to September 30th, 1923.*

93 *Report of the Protestant Board of School Commissioners of the City of Montreal from October 1st, 1923 to September 30th, 1924.*

94 Rexford, *supra* note 61 at 41; see "There Are No Jewish Teachers in the High Schools," *Canadian Jewish Chronicle* (12 October 1923).

95 CJC, ZA-S, 11/9, Resolution of 18 January 1924.

96 "'Fencing-In' the Jewish Soul," *Canadian Jewish Chronicle* (26 January 1923); Corcos, *supra* note 13 at 87–8.

97 Bill 150 concerning the education of non–Roman Catholic, non-Protestant children, 21 December 1923, 10 January 1924, 6 February 1924; <www.assnat.qc.ca/fr/travaux-parlementaires/assemblee-nationale/16-1/journal-debats/19231221/91881.html>, <www.assnat.qc.ca/fr/travaux-parlementaires/assemblee-nationale/16-1/journal-debats/19240110/91887.html>, <www.assnat.qc.ca/fr/travaux-parlementaires/assemblee-nationale/16-1/journal-debats/19240206/91925.html>.

98 LAC, Lyon Cohen Diary, *supra* note 88 at 3 February 1924.

99 *Ibid*, 5 February 1924.

100 *Ibid*, 6 February 1924; CJC, ZA 1924, 15/5, Nathan Gordon to Michael Hirsch, 18 January.

101 Rapport No. 1398, Comité de l'Honorable Conseil Exécutif, en date du 30 juillet 1924, approuvé par le Lieutenant-Gouverneur, le 31 juillet 1924, Sur la constitution d'une Commission concernant le système scolaire de l'Ile de Montréal; "Committee Named to Study Jewish School Question," *Montreal Gazette* (29 September 1923).

102 CJC, David Rome file, DA 11.1, box 6, Montreal School System, 1924–1931, Jewish Community Council to Taschereau 19 February 1923, Taschereau reply 20 February; Jewish Community Council to provincial treasurer 21 February, and to Taschereau 13 May 1924, reply from Taschereau 14 May 1924.

103 Victor Doré (1880–1954) was trained as an accountant but taught in the Roman Catholic schools of Montreal. He began to work for the Roman Catholic School Board as an accountant and then became a professor at the École des Hautes Études Commerciales. In 1918 he became financial comptroller of the Roman Catholic Board and from 1928 he was president of the Roman Catholic School Commission of Montreal. Raphaël Ouimet, ed, *Biographies canadiennes françaises*, 13th ed (Montreal: Éditions biographiques canadiennes-françaises, 1937) at 350.

104 Aimé Geoffrion (1872–1946), was a Montreal lawyer and graduate of McGill University who was named king's counsel in 1903. He taught civil law at McGill from 1905 to 1920 and was *bâtonnier* of the Montreal Bar in 1918–19. From 1917 to 1921 he was a member of the Roman Catholic Board of School Commissioners in Montreal. Ouimet, *supra* note 103 at 283; "Aime Geoffrion Dies: Legal Leader Dies; Acted in Many Famous Cases," *Montreal Gazette* (16 October 1946).

105 Sir Arthur Currie (1875–1933) led the Canadian Army in the First World War. From 1920 to 1933, he was principal and vice-chancellor of McGill University. He was a member of the Protestant Committee of the Council of Public Instruction. Hugh M. Urquhart, *Arthur Currie: The Autobiography of a Great Canadian* (Toronto: Dent, 1950).

106 Edward Wentworth Beatty (1877–1943), a lawyer, was named general counsel of the Canadian Pacific Railway in 1913 and became the first Canadian-born president of the company in 1918. He was chancellor of McGill University from 1920 until his death in 1943. He was knighted in 1935. Donald H. Miller-Barstow, *Beatty of the CPR* (Toronto: McClelland and Stewart, 1951).

107 Walter George Mitchell (1877–1935) was a graduate of McGill University who was called to the Bar in 1901 and was named king's counsel in 1912. He entered the Quebec Legislative Assembly as a Liberal in 1914 and was treasurer in the Cabinets of Lomer Gouin and Louis-Alexandre Taschereau. He was a member of the Protestant Committee of the Council of Public Instruction from 1914 to 1925. "Walter George Mitchell," Assemblée Nationale, online: <www.assnat.qc.ca/fr/deputes/mitchell-walter-george-4509/biographie.html>.

108 Samuel Cohen was born in Minnesota and became the first Jew to gradu-

ate from the School of Mines of the University of Minnesota. He spent his career in the mining industry. Arthur Daniel Hart, "Samuel W. Cohen, EM, Montreal" in *supra* note 13 at 429.

109 Joseph Schubert (1889–1952) was a Romanian-born socialist and member of the CCF. He was elected as Labour candidate to the City Council in 1924, where he served as acting mayor in 1927. Jewish Public Library, Montreal, Victor and Schubert Joseph L, file 2, Bibliographic information etc.

110 Livinson was an advertising agent who held several degrees from McGill and the Université de Montréal, including qualifications in law and teaching. He was active in the Dufferin School Association and in the Federation of Jewish Philanthropies. He taught English language and literature at the Jewish People's University. *Who's Who in American Jews, 1938–39* (New York: International News Association, 1939).

111 Robert Gagnon, *Histoire de la Commission des écoles catholiques de Montréal* (Montreal: Boréal, 1996).

112 CJC, ZA 1924/16/10; CJC, Protestant-Jewish School Question, Mtl 1925, letter to Taschereau 1 August; CJC, ZA 1924, 15/6 press release from Jewish Community Council, signed by Michael Garber, 19 August 1924.

113 CJC, David Rome file, *supra* note 102, "Opening Remarks by Michael Hirsch" 28 August 1924; CJC, ZA 1924/16/10, Minutes of the Meetings of the Jewish Commissioners. In order to ensure the full airing of views and the accuracy of the record, the meetings were stenographically recorded, in both English and Yiddish. The historical record of the debates within the Montreal Jewish communities on the "School Question" is a rich source of contemporary material.

114 CJC, David Rome file, *supra* note 102, memorandum to School Committee, Israel Figler, 28 August 1923.

115 CJC, ZA 1924/16/10, Minutes of the Meetings of the Jewish Commissioners.

116 *Ibid*, conferences of 2 and 4 September 1924.

117 CJC, ZA 1924,15/7, Livinson to various organizations and government officials, September 1924, and responses, CJC, Protestant-Jewish School Question, Mtl 1925.

118 CJC, David Rome file, *supra* note 102, Montreal School Question, Jewish Commissioners to the Commission Secretary, 6 November 1924; CJC, Protestant-Jewish School Question, Mtl 1925, Report Prepared for the Jewish Commissioners by AJ Livinson on 17 September 1924.

119 CJC, ZA 1924/15/4, letter, 24 November 1924.

120 CJC, ZA 1924/16/10, Minutes of the Meetings of the Jewish Commissioners, 11 and 12 September.

121 Minutes of Proceedings of Commission Appointed to Study and Report on the School System of the Island of Montreal, reproduced in Record of Proceedings, Supreme Court of Canada, *Michael Hirsch and Samuel W. Cohen*, Appellants and *The Protestant Board of School Commissioners of the City of Montreal et al*, 3ff.

122 John Jennings Creelman (1882–1949) was called to the Bar in Montreal in 1907 and was named king's counsel in 1919. He was active in business, holding many executive positions. He reached the rank of colonel in the Canadian Field Artillery, in which he served overseas in the First World War. He was a Montreal alderman from 1918 to 1926. Archives Canada, John Jennings Creelman Fonds, CAIN No 258596, Biographical Note.

123 Minutes, *supra* note 21.

124 *Ibid* at 11.

125 *Ibid* at 14.

126 *Ibid* at 15.

127 *Ibid* at 16–17.

128 *Ibid*; (Sir) Herbert Meredith Marler (1876–1940) was a member of a prominent anglophone family. A notary by profession, he served as a Liberal member of Parliament and minister without portfolio. He became Canada's first ambassador to Japan. "Marler, The Hon. Sir Herbert Meredith, PC" Parliament of Canada, online: <www.parl.gc.ca/parlinfo/Files/Parliamentarian.aspx?Item=d532de86-ad09-46e3-a8c4-9e590cdd3f60&Language=E&Section=ALL>.

129 Minutes of Proceedings, *supra* note 121 at 43.

130 *Ibid* at 43.

131 *Ibid* at 48–51.

132 Minutes of Proceedings, *supra* note 121, second and third sessions at 92ff.

133 *Ibid* at 93.

134 *Ibid* at 96.

135 Creelman returned to the commission and offered extensive evidence of what he claimed was the chaos caused by Jewish students being absent from certain schools on these days (*ibid* at 103).

136 *Ibid*; Minutes of a Private Conference held on Thursday afternoon, October 16th, 1924, at 4 o'clock, in the Montefiore Club, 399 Guy Street; CJC, David Rome file, *supra* note 102, Montreal School System. List of the persons invited to attend the private conference, Montefiore Club, 399 Guy Street, on Thursday, Oct. 16, 1924, at 4 p.m.

Chapter 8

1 CJC, David Rome file, DA 11.1, box 6, Montreal School System 1924–1931, Brief Report of the First Private Meeting of the Special School Commission, 22 October 1924.

2 *Ibid*, 29 October 1924.

3 *Ibid*, letter, 13 November 1924; CJC, David Rome, DA 11.1, box 6, Montreal School System 1924–1925, DA 11.1, box 6, translation of an article printed in Yiddish in the *Jewish Daily Eagle* (9 November 1924), "Jewish Interests in the School Question Will Be Betrayed."

4 CJC, David Rome file, *supra* note 1, Private Meeting, Commission of Nine, Wed. Dec. 3, 1924, Minutes.

5 *Ibid.*

6 Eugène Lafleur (1856–1930) was considered by many to be the outstanding lawyer in Canada during his lifetime. Former head boy at the High School of Montreal, he was of Swiss Protestant heritage. He received his law degree from McGill University in 1880 and was called to the Bar the following year. He was made a QC in 1899 and was *bâtonnier* of the Montreal and Quebec Bars in 1905–06. He served as a professor of law at McGill and became the leading advocate of his day, limiting his practice to appearances before the Supreme Court and the Privy Council. "Lafleur, Eugene" in Dictionary of Canadian Biography Online, <www.biographi.ca/en/bio/lafleur_eugene_15E.html>; Pierre Beullac & E Fabre Surveyer, "Eugene Lafleur" in *Le Centenaire du Barreau de Montréal, 1849–1949* (Montreal: Librairie Ducharme, 1949) at 177–9; "Eugene Lafleur: Canada's Late Outstanding Jurist Subject of Brilliant Address by Roger Brossard," *Montreal Gazette* (24 April 1933); Eugène Lafleur: *L'homme et l'avocat* (Montreal: Le Devoir, 1933); Elson I Rexford, I Gammell, & AR McBain, *The History of the High School of Montreal* (Montreal: The High School of Montreal, ca 1950), Appendix D, Head Boys since 1848 at 300–1.

7 Wallace Nesbitt (1858–1930) was called to the Bar in Ontario in 1881. By 1898 he had become one of the top litigators in the country. He was named to the Supreme Court of Canada in 1903 but resigned two years later and returned to private practice. He was elected as a bencher of the Law Society of Upper Canada in 1906 and became treasurer in 1927 and president of the Canadian Bar Association in 1928–29. "Nesbitt, Wallace" in Dictionary of Canadian Biography Online, <www.biographi.ca/en/bio/nesbitt_wallace_15E.html>.

8 CJC, David Rome file, *supra* note 1, Legal Opinion, 11 November 1924 and in ZCe 1924, 45.

9 *Ibid.*

10 *Ibid.*

11 *Ibid.*

12 CJC, David Rome file, *supra* note 1, Second Legal Opinion, 8 December 1924.

13 *Ibid*, Legal Opinion, 9 December 1924.

14 "Montreal Called City of Confusion," *Montreal Gazette* (3 October 1924); "Montreal behind Many Other Cities," *Montreal Star* (3 October 1924).

15 *Ibid.*

16 *Rapport des Représentants Catholiques de la Commission Spéciale d'Éducation*, 27 December 1924; An Act respecting the Montreal Catholic School Commission, 15 Geo V, c 43, (1925); An Act to amend the act respecting the Catholic schools of Montreal, *ibid* c 44; Robert Rumilly, *Histoire de la Province du Québec, tome XXX, Camilien Houde* (Montreal: Fides, 1958) at 43–5.

17 *Report of the Protestant Members, concerning the financial position of the School Commission of the Municipality of Verdun*, 22 December 1924; CJC, Protestant-Jewish School Question, Mtl 1925, Victor Doré, *Report to the Special Commission on the financial situation of the various school Municipalities of the Island of Montreal which are not under the jurisdiction of the Protestant School Commissioners of Montreal*; Minutes of the Commission re: Extension des pouvoirs de la Commission des Écoles Catholiques, 6 octobre and Financial Situation Protestant schools of Verdun; An Act respecting Protestant schools in and around the city of Montreal, 15 Geo V, c 45, (1925); "School Bill Is Settled after Strenuous Fight," *Montreal Star* (28 March 1923).

18 CJC, David Rome file, *supra* note 1, Memorandum to Commission Appointed to Study and Report on the School System of the Island of Montreal, 22 December 1924.

19 *Rapport de la Commission Spéciale d'Éducation*, 27 December 1924.

20 CJC, ZA 1924, 15/1, December, Schubert to Taschereau, 26 December 1924, with attached plan.

21 CJC, David Rome file, *supra* note 1, Memorandum of Majority of Jewish Commissioners.

22 *Ibid.*

23 No 129, Concerning the Reference to the Court of King's Bench, Appeal Side, of Questions relative to the Educational System in the island of Montreal.

24 *Ibid.*

25 Factum submitted in behalf of Messrs Michael Hirsch and Samuel Cohen, *In the Matter of a Reference by His Honour the Lieutenant Governor in Council of Certain Questions Relative to the Educational System in the Island of Montreal*, Court of King's Bench, Appeal Side, No 1228, 16 February 1925.

26 Charles Laurendeau KC was called to the Bar in 1892 and was *bâtonnier* in 1916–17. The Bar of Montreal, online: <www.barreaudemontreal.qc.ca/en/barreau/former_batonniers/1910-1919>; G-Édouard Rinfret, *Histoire du Barreau de Montréal* (Cowansville, QC: Éditions Yvon Blais, 1989) at 174.

27 George Archibald Campbell was a graduate of McGill University. Called to the Bar in 1901, he was named KC in 1912 and served as *bâtonnier* in 1930–31. Barreau du Québec, online: <www.barreau.qc.ca/fr/barreau/historique/administration/batonniers-1930-1959.html>. Rinfret, *supra* note 26 at 176. Campbell was a founder of the University Club. University Club of Montreal, online: <www.ucmontreal.ca/en/the-university-club-of-montreal>.

28 *Ibid*, Factum of the Protestant Board of School Commissioners of the City of Montreal.

29 *Ibid*, Factum of Joseph Schubert, Late Member of the Special Commission on Education in the Island of Montreal.

30 Antonio Perrault (1880–1955) was called to the Bar in 1906 and practised in the law firm of Lomer Gouin. He was made KC in 1916 and was a professor of law at the Université de Montréal. In 1944, he was elected *bâtonnier* of the Montreal Bar. Victor Morin, *Antonio Perrault 1880–1955* (Ottawa: Société Royale du Canada, 1955); Joseph-Papin Archambault, *Une Noble Carrière: Me Antonio Perrault* (Montreal: L'Oeuvre des Tracts, 1955); "Antonio Perrault, KC, Elected Bâtonnier of the Montreal Bar," *Montreal Gazette* (2 May 1944). He was intimately associated with French-Canadian Roman Catholic nationalism as a director of Lionel Groulx's Ligue de l'Action française. Antonio Perrault, "La Ligue de l'Action Française, Avant-propos" in *Consignes de demain: Doctrine et origines de l'Action française* (Montreal: L'action française, 1921) at 1–5.

31 Aymé Lafontaine, KC, had served as secretary to the Roman Catholic members of the Commission of Nine and was for many years general secretary and treasurer of the Roman Catholic School Board of Montreal.

32 31 R de J 440, (1925) [*Hirsch*].

33 Factum, *supra* note 25 at 5ff.

34 Gerald John Wheeler, *Confederation Law of Canada: Privy Council Cases on the British North-America Act, 1867* (London: Eyre & Spottiswoode, 1896) at 338.

35 Factum, *supra* note 28 at 10.

36 *Ibid* at 18.

37 Factum, *supra* note 29 at 3.

38 Mémoire de la Commission des Écoles Catholiques de Montréal.

39 The idea of Canada as a Christian nation had and would continue to have intellectual and ideological purchase outside Quebec as well. George Egerton, "Writing the Canadian Bill of Rights: Religion, Politics, and the Challenge of Pluralism, 1957–1960" (2004) 19 CJLS 1.

40 Henry Montor, "Is the Jew a Catholic or a Protestant? An Interview with Mr Louis Fitch, Leader of the Jewish Separate School Movement," *Jewish Exponent* (27 March 1925).

41 This was the long-standing position of the Roman Catholic Church, one that had stymied reform efforts from the time of the British conquest until Confederation and that continued in the province's schools into the twentieth century. See Louis Moreau, Aimé Chassé, & Bernard Boutet, *L'Éducation: Rôle de la Famille, de l'Église et de l'État* (Nicolet, QC: Séminaire de Nicolet, 1907).

42 *Hirsch, supra* note 32 at 456.

43 *Pinsler v The Protestant Board of School Commissioners* 23 CS 365 (1903).

44 *Ibid* at 461.

45 *Ibid* at 462.

46 *Ibid* at 470, "[I]l préjudicie aux droits et privilèges des protestants."

47 *Ibid* at 475.

48 *Ibid* at 472.

49 *Ibid* at 474.

50 *Ibid* at 495–6.

51 *Ibid* at 496–7. "Une loi qui donnerait aux non-chrétiens les droits aux écoles distinctes, ni catholiques, ni protestantes, serait contraire à l'esprit comme à la lettre de toute notre législation scolaire, créerait un état de choses contre lequel proteste le caractère essential imprimé à notre instruction publique, et porterait préjudice au droit qu'ont les chrétiens, en vertu de la Constitution, d'enseigner les enfants dans la province de Québec."

52 *Hirsch, supra* note 32 at 498.

53 *Ibid* at 500, "[Q]uant aux enfants des juifs qui, par l'un ou l'autre des modes pourvu par la loi, ont opté ou sont censés avoir opté pour les écoles protestantes (sauf que les règlements edictés par l'autorité compétente pour la régie de ces écoles et pour la sauvegarde du caractère confessionnel chrétien de l'éducation doivent être observés)."

54 *Ibid* at 503–4.

55 *Ibid* at 518.

56 The bi-confessional Quebec educational system continued to be met with approval by many. See e.g. EC Woodley, "The School System of the Province of Quebec, with Special Reference to Religious Differences" (1953) 4 History of Education Journal 97.

57 "Notre Législation Scolaire et Les Juifs" (1924–25) 3 R du D at 338; on the *Revue de Droit* and traditional Quebec legal thinking, Sylvio Normand, "Un thème dominant de la pensée traditionnelle au Québec: La sauvegarde du droit civil" (1987) 32 McGill LJ 559.

58 It is also important to note that an earlier generation of French-Canadian legal scholars, even those of an ultramontanist persuasion, had presented a subtler attitude towards the history of religious liberty and the presence of non–Roman Catholic minorities in the province. See Siméon Pagnuelo, *Études Historiques et Légales sur la Liberté Religieuse en Canada* (Montreal: CO Beauchemin & Valois, 1872).

59 Léo Pelland (1891–1970) was a Quebec lawyer, law professor, and journalist. He graduated at the top of his class in law from l'Université Laval in 1914 and taught there between 1925 and 1953. Earlier in his career he worked for the official Roman Catholic publication *L'Action Sociale Catholique* and published throughout his life in conservative nationalist, Roman Catholic publications, such as *La Semaine Religieuse de Québec, L'Action Catholique,* and *L'Action Nationale.* Bibilothèque et Archives Nationales du Québec, Fonds Léo Pelland, P626, Notice biographique.

60 "Notre Législation Scolaire et Les Juifs II" (1924–25) 3 R du D at 389–90 and 402, "une formule équivoque et dangereuse."

61 "Notre Législation Scolaire" (1924–25) 3 R du D at 435, 437–8.

62 Appelant's Factum, 24 August 1925; Factum of Respondent (The Protestant Board of School Commissioners of the City of Montreal); Mémoire de la Commission des Écoles Catholiques de Montréal, 1 September 1925,

63 CJC, ZA 1925, 18/1, Correspondence between Samuel W Cohen and Wallace Nesbitt, April and May 1925.

64 *Hirsch and another v Protestant Board of School Commissioners of Montreal et al,* [1925] SCR 246.

65 *Ibid* at 254.

66 Jean-Pierre Proulx (with Christian Dessureault & Paul Aubin), *La genèse de l'école publique et de la démocratie scolaire au Québec: les écoles de syndics (1814–1838),* (Ste Foy, QC: Les Presses de l'Université Laval, 2014); Yvan Lamonde, *The Social History of Ideas in Quebec, 1760–1896* (Montreal & Kingston: McGill-Queen's University Press, 2013) at 122–9, 248–9, 320–1, 380–3; Bruce Curtis, *Ruling by Schooling Quebec: Conquest to Liberal Governmentality – A Historical Sociology* (Toronto: University of Toronto Press, 2012).

67 *Hirsch, supra* note 64 at 257.

68 *Ibid* at 258.

69 *Ibid* at 259–60.

70 *Ibid* at 261.

71 *Ibid* at 264–8.
72 *Ibid* at 269.
73 *Ibid* at 271.
74 At the time, there were 19,341 Protestant students in the schools run by the Protestant Board. Jews numbered 10,918. *Annual Report, Protestant Board of School Commissioners of the City of Montreal, 1926–27.*
75 Abbé Antonio Huot, "Question des Écoles à Montréal" (1926) 15 L'Action Française 379.
76 15 Geo V, c 19, (1925), An act respecting the appeal to the Supreme Court of Canada and to His Majesty in His Privy Council from the opinion of the Court of King's Bench, (Appeal side), on questions relating to education in the Island of Montreal.
77 The Canadian Jewish Congress Archives has copies of the transcribed shorthand notes compiled at the request of Michael Hirsch and Samuel W Cohen, for all four days of oral argument before the Privy Council. They make fascinating reading, especially insofar as the interventions and questions of the Privy Council members are concerned, but the arguments at the technical level were the familiar ones.
78 Appellant's Case, *Hirsch v Protestant School Board*, In the Privy Council, Case 10, Volume 1928, No 67 of 1926.
79 Case for the Respondent, Protestant Board of School Commissioners, s 42 at 19.
80 *Ibid*, s 56 at 23–4.
81 Case for Respondent-Catholic Board of School Commissioners, s 44 at 15.
82 *Ibid*, s 80 at 27. Léo Pelland had put forward this view in his critique of the Supreme Court decision. "Notre Législation Scolaire et les Juifs" (1926) 4 R du D at 331.
83 Case of the Respondent Joseph Schubert, s 29 at 8.
84 *Hirsch and Another v Protestant Board of School Commissioners of Montreal and others*, [1928] AC 200.
85 *Ibid* at 209–10.
86 *Ibid* at 213–14.
87 *Ibid* at 215.
88 Leon D Crestohl, *The Jewish School Problem in the Province of Quebec* (Montreal: Eagle Publishing, 1926); Nathan Reich, "Letters from Abroad: The Quebec School Question" (1929) 16:6 Menorah Journal 539.
89 "Jewish School Issue Fails in Quebec Elections," *Jewish Advocate* (19 May 1927); Israel Medres, *Between the Wars: Canadian Jews in Transition*, translated by Vivian Felsen (Montreal: Véhicule, 2003) at 56–7.

90 Léo Pelland, "Notre Législation Scolaire et les Juifs" (1927–28) 6 R du D 321.
91 Antonio Perrault, "Problème scolaire juif" (1927–28) 6 R du D 381.
92 *Ibid*; for an earlier iteration, see Adélard Dugré, *L'École canadienne-française* (Montreal: L'Oeuvre des Tracts, 1919).
93 Abbé Antonio Huot, "Question des Écoles à Montréal" (1926) 15 L'Action Française 379. David Rome writes, "For Father Huot was one of the leading antisemites of his community." *On the Jewish School Question in Montreal 1903–1931* (Montreal: Canadian Jewish Congress National Archives, 1975) at 100. For evidence supporting Rome's claim, see Huot, *La Question Juive: Quelques Observations sur la Question du Meurtre Rituel* (Quebec: L'Action Sociale Catholique, 1914).
94 David Rome, "The Political Consequences of the Jewish School Question, Montreal, 1925–1933" (1977) 1 Jewish Historical Society of Canada Journal 3.

Chapter 9

1 David Rome, "The Political Consequences of the Jewish School Question, Montreal, 1925–1933" (1977) 1 Jewish Historical Society of Canada Journal at 6.
2 CJC, ZA 1928, 24/6B, Montreal Separate Jewish School Committee to Montreal Jewish School Committee, 17 February 1928; reply from Jewish Educational Committee, 5 March 1928. Hanniah Meyer Caiserman (1884–1950) was the Romanian-born general secretary of the Canadian Jewish Congress from its founding in 1919 until his death. He was an active Zionist and supporter of Jewish and Yiddish culture in Montreal. CJC, Caiserman, Fonds, History/Biographical.
3 Anathase David (1882–1953) was a lawyer and politician who served as provincial secretary in the governments of Lomer Gouin and Louis-Alexandre Taschereau. He resigned his seat in the provincial legislature to become a senator in 1940. Because education fell largely under his remit as provincial secretary, he would be a key player for the Liberal government in the unfolding drama of the Jewish School Question from 1928 to 1931. "Anathase David," Assemblée Nationale, online: <www.assnat.qc.ca/fr/deputes/david-athanase-2771/biographie.html>.
4 CJC, ZA 1928, 24/6B, Correspondence September and October 1928.
5 *Ibid*, letter to Michael Hirsch, 26 October 1928: Memorandum of Suggestions, Protestant School Board.
6 *Ibid*, s 1.

7 *Ibid*, s 3.
8 *Ibid*, s 4.
9 *Ibid*, s 2; Minutes, Protestant Board of School Commissioners; CJC, ZA 1928, 24/6B, letter to Michael Hirsch, 21 November 1928; letter with memorandum, Michael Hirsch to Peter Bercovitch, 7 December 1928,
10 CJC, ZA 1928, 24/6B, letter to Michael Hirsch, 21 November 1928. More broadly, see Claris Edwin Silcox & Galen M Fisher, *Catholics, Jews and Protestants: A Study of Relationships in the United States and Canada* (New York: Harper and Brothers, 1934).
11 CJC, ZA 1928, 24/6B, 1st meeting called by Mr Michael Hirsch for December 6th 1928.
12 *Ibid*, 2nd meeting called by Mr Hirsch by wire of Dec. 15th for Dec. 16th.
13 *Ibid*, letter to Michael Hirsch with attachments, 13 December 1928.
14 *Ibid*, 20th December meeting.
15 *Ibid*, 23 December 1928.
16 CJC, ZA 1929, 25/5, letter to Maxwell Goldstein reporting on the meeting, 16 January 1929, with attached agreement.
17 Daniel J Elazar, Michael Brown, & Ira Robinson, eds, *Not Written in Stone: Jews, Constitutions, and Constitutionalism in Canada* (Ottawa: University of Ottawa Press, 2003) at 6.
18 CJC, ZA 1929, 25/5, Resolution.
19 CJC, ZA 1929, letter from Taschereau, 16 March 1929.
20 ANQ, E13, 25, Département de l'Instruction Publique, Comité Protestant, Janvier 1930, Jewish Question, letter, 21 December 1929.
21 Pierre Anctil, *Le Rendez-vous manqué: Les Juifs de Montréal face au Québec de l'entre-deux-guerres* (Montreal: IQRC, 1988) at 204.
22 *Report of the Superintendent of Education of the Province of Quebec for the Year 1929–30* (Quebec: Rédempti Paradis, King's Printer, 1930), Meeting of the Protestant Committee, 3 January 1930, 512; ANQ, E13, 25, Département de l'Instruction Publique, Comité Protestant, Janvier 1930, Jewish Question.
23 ANQ, E13, 25, Département de l'Instruction Publique, Comité Protestant, Janvier 1930, Jewish Question, letter, 8 January 1930; "Protestant Body Oppose Change," *Montreal Star* (3 January 1930).
24 ANQ, E13, 25, Département de l'Instruction Publique, Comité Protestant, Janvier 1930, Jewish Question, letter, 10 January 1930; "Non-Protestants Refused Representation on Council of Education," *Canadian Jewish Chronicle* (10 January 1930); "The Protestants Protest," *Jewish Standard* (31 January 1930).
25 ANQ, E13, 25, Département de l'Instruction Publique, Comité Protestant,

Janvier 1930, Jewish Question, Copy of Resolution Passed by the Montreal Protestant Central Board at a Meeting Held on January 14th, 1930.

26 This is the point in history in which the English rendition changed from "Public Instruction" – a literal translation from the French "Instruction Publique" – to a more accurate "Public Education."

27 ANQ, E13, 25, Département de l'Instruction Publique, Comité Protestant, Janvier 1930, Jewish Question, letter of advice, 24 January 1930.

28 *Ibid*, 15 January 1924.

29 "Protestant Educational Rights," *Montreal Gazette* (7 January 1930); Elton I Rexford, "Jews and Protestant Schools," *Montreal Gazette* (7 January 1930); Peter Bercovitch, letter to the editior, *Montreal Gazette* (11 January 1930); see "Cohen Says Jews Would Pay Costs," *Montreal Star* (8 January 1930); "The Real Issues in the School Question," *Canadian Jewish Chronicle* (10 January 1930).

30 "Claim Jews Want Separate Schools," *Montreal Gazette* (11 January 1930); "Jewish School System Asked for Montreal," *Canadian Jewish Review* (31 January 1930).

31 CJC, ZA 1930, 37/13, letter, 13 January 1930; CJC, ZA 1930, 27/10B.

32 Antonin Dupont, *Les Relations entre l'Église et l'État sous Louis-Alexandre Taschereau, 1920–1936* (Montreal: Guérin, 1973).

33 David Rome, *On the Jewish School Question in Montreal 1903–1931* (Montreal: Canadian Jewish Congress National Archives, 1975) at 105.

34 Louis-Philippe Audet, "La question des écoles juives: 1870–1931" (1970) 8 Mémoires de la Société Royale du Canada, Série 4 at 115ff.

35 "Catholic Archbishop Denounces Montreal Jewish School Bills as Infringements," *Jewish Telegraphic Agency* (*JTA*) (21 March 1930).

36 "Discours de Mgr L'Archevêque à l'Oratoire Saint-Joseph" (1930) 89 La Semaine Religieuse at 181: "entouré les Juifs d'une sympathie absolument injustifié"; Audet, *supra* note 34 at 116.

37 "Jewish Schools in Quebec Protested," *Montreal Gazette* (19 March 1930); "Les Écoles Juives: Réponse de M Taschereau à la Lettre de S Eminence le cardinal Rouleau," *Le Devoir* (20 March 1930).

38 Louis-Philippe Audet, "L'épiscopat québécois et les écoles juives," in *Histoire de l'Enseignement au Québec, 1840–1971,* tome 2 (Montreal: Holt, Rinehart et Winston, 1971) at 261–2.

39 Léo Pelland, "Écoles juives" (1929–30) 8 R du D 451; Arlette Corcos, *Montréal, les Juifs et L'École* (Sillery, QC: Septentrion, 1997) at 102–6.

40 Robert Rumilly, *Histoire de la Province du Québec*, tome 32 (Montreal: Fides, 1959) at 75–84.

41 Hugues Théorêt, *Les Chemises Bleues: Adrien Arcand, journaliste antisémite canadien-français* (Sillery, QC: Septentrion, 2012).

42 "Bill for Separate Schools in Quebec Introduced by Bercovitch and Cohen," *Canadian Jewish Chronicle* (24 January 1930).

43 "The School Bill – May or Shall," *Canadian Jewish Chronicle* (7 February 1930); "Are We to Have Jewish Schools?," *Canadian Jewish Chronicle* (28 February 1930); "The Jewish School Bill," *Canadian Jewish Chronicle* (28 March 1930).

44 For an analysis of the legislative debates reflecting the views of the different parties, see Jocelyn Saint-Pierre, "Les écoles juives et les débats parlementaires de l'Assemblée Législative du Québec" (2001) 9 Canadian Jewish Studies/Études Juives Canadiennes 210.

45 "Matter of Jewish Schools Discussed," *Montreal Gazette* (29 March 1930).

46 Abel Vineberg, "Jewish School Bill Advances in Assembly," *Montreal Gazette* (2 April 1930); "Jewish School Bill Causes Hot Debate," *Montreal Star* (2 April 1930).

47 20 Geo V, c 61, 1930.

48 "Montreal Jews to Have Own School System: Long Standing Issue Has Been Finally Settled," *Jewish Advocate* (25 March 1930).

49 CJC, ZA 1930, 26/9, and Taschereau's response, 19 April 1930; "The Jewish School Board," *Canadian Jewish Chronicle* (2 May 1930).

50 ANQ, E13, Re. Jewish School Question, October 1930, 775–30, *Rapport d'un Comité de l'Honorable Conseil Exécutif en date du 23 Avril 1930 approuvé par le Lieutenant-Gouverneur le 24 Avril 1924, Concernant la nomination des members de la Commission des écoles juives de Montréal.*

51 Samuel Cohen of the Commission of Nine had apparently adopted his wife's maiden name, variously Livingston and Livingstone, and was appointed as head of the Jewish School Commission under this name. "Quebec Government Names 7 as Jewish School Committee," *JTA* (27 April 1930). "Mr Livingstone, a mining engineer, was born in St Paul, Minn., and came to Canada in 1906. He was a pioneer in the silver fields of the Cobalt District. In 1924, the Quebec government delegated him to study the question of Jewish education."

52 Berliner was a wealthy Canadian-American businessman who served as the Canadian representative of his family company Berliner Gram-o-phone, holding a virtual monopoly on the new technology. The company would later become part of RCA Victor. "The Virtual Gram-o-phone Company of Canada," LAC, online: <www.collectionscanada.gc.ca/gramophone/028011-3005-e.html>.

53 Wiseman was a leading Montreal physician and a moving force behind the fund-raising campaign that led to the establishment of the Jewish General Hospital. "Montreal Launches Drive for Jewish Hospital," *Jewish Telegraphic Agency* (10 May 1929); "New Montreal Hospital Opens Its Doors to Public," *Jewish Telegraphic Agency* (9 October 1934).
54 Abraham Zebulun Cohen was a Montreal businessman and philanthropist. He was the brother of the long-time leader of Montreal Jewry, Lyon Cohen, and, like his brother, had sought the creation of a separate Jewish school system.
55 Henry Broker, "The Montreal Jewish School Commission," *Canadian Jewish Chronicle* (2 May 1930).
56 Abramowitz was born in Russia and arrived in the United States as a ten-year-old in 1890. He attended public school in New York and graduated from City College. He became the first graduate of the Jewish Theological Seminary to receive the degree of Doctor of Hebrew Literature. In the First World War, he had been appointed as Jewish chaplain to the Canadian Army and rose to the rank of captain. He was a powerful force in the Jewish community. Arthur Daniel Hart, ed, "Reverend Dr H Abramowitz, Montreal," in *The Jew in Canada* (Toronto: Jewish Publication, 1926) at 92.
57 Broker, *supra* note 55.
58 *Report of the Superintendent of Education of the Province of Quebec for the Year 1930–31* (Quebec: Rédempti Paradis, King's Printer, 1931) at 228–9; letters, 4 and 6 September to the two boards. Reply from the Protestant Board 8 September.
59 *Report, supra* note 58, meeting of 24 September, 230; "Cardinal Wants to Supervise Montreal Jewish School Board," *JTA* (6 June 1930).
60 CJC, ZA 1930, 26/4.
61 "Jewish School Question Solved," *Montreal Gazette* (6 December 1930).
62 *Report, supra* note 58; *Report of the Superintendent of Education Respecting Jewish Schools of Montreal* at 236.
63 The recommendations of the Commission of Nine had been accepted and had led to a greater degree of administrative centralization in both the Roman Catholic and Protestant school systems (15 Geo V, c 45, 1925). On the Protestant side, the Montreal Protestant Central School Board was created but the local boards retained some degree of autonomy and a separate legal existence, as required in most cases by s 93 and its protections of pre-Confederation denominational boards.

64 Corcos, *supra* note 39 at 111.

65 Louis Rosenberg, *Canada's Jews* (Montreal: Bureau of Social and Economic Research, Canadian Jewish Congress, 1939) at 31.

66 CJC, ZA 1932, 29/11, City of Outremont, Apportionment between Catholic and Protestant School Authorities of neutral School taxes for year 1931/32.

67 *Report of the Superintendent of Education, supra* note 62, Annex H, 240.

68 "Reveals 3 of Jewish School Board Asked Jewish Subjects in Protestant School Course," *JTA* (15 December 1930).

69 "The Montreal School Question," *Jewish Exponent* (12 December 1930).

70 Anctil, *supra* note 21 at 202–5.

71 "The Protestant-Jewish School Agreement," *Montreal Daily Star* (5 December 1930).

72 "Secretary of Montreal Jewish School Commission Defends It from Attack by Advocates of Separate Jewish School System," *JTA* (10 December 1930).

73 Jules Dorion, "Une Page d'Histoire," *L'Action Catholique* (5 April 1930).

74 Protestant anti-Semites also voiced a strong opposition to the creation of a non-Christian school board. "Protestant Paper Terms Montreal Jewish School Bill 'Unchristian and Bolshevik,'" *JTA* (1 April 1930).

75 Corcos, *supra* note 39 at 106–12; Rome, *supra* note 33 at 100ff.

76 "Les Juifs et M Houde," *Le Devoir* (20 August 1931); Hector Grenon, *Camillien Houde* (Montreal: Stanké, 1979); Hertel LaRoque, *Camillien Houde: Le p'tit gars de Ste-Marie* (Montreal: Les Éditions de l'Homme, 1961) for different biographies.

77 "Montreal Mayor Would Repeal Bill Giving Jews Right to Have Own School System," *JTA* (10 October 1930); "Montreal Mayor Openly Anti-Semitic at Discussion of Jewish School Question," *JTA* (18 November 1930).

78 Rosenberg, *supra* note 65, chapter 3, "The Growth of Canada's Jewish Population," 9ff.

79 Cardinal Bézin, *Les conditions religieuses de la Société canadienne: Nos vertus traditionnels – Maux qui nous menacent – Résolutions à prendre* (Montreal: L'Oeuvre des Tracts, 1920); Euclide Lefebvre, *Le Cinéma corrupteur* (Montreal: L'Oeuvre des Tracts, 1919 or 1920).

80 "Les Juifs au Canada" (1933) 2 L'Action Nationale 5.

81 "Abbe Lavergne Makes Virulent Attack on Jews Via Radio Address on Communism," *Canadian Jewish Chronicle* (3 April 1931); "A Public Abuse," *Canadian Jewish Chronicle* (10 April 1931); RP Archambault SJ, *Sous la men-*

ace rouge: L'accroissement de la population cosmopolite de Montréal (Quebec: L'Oeuvre des Tracts, 1936).

82 Susan Mann Trofimenkoff, *Action Française: French Canadian Nationalism in the Twenties* (Toronto: University of Toronto Press, 1975). For the rest of Canada, see Janine Stingel, *Social Discredit: Anti-Semitism, Social Credit, and the Jewish Response* (Montreal & Kingston: McGill-Queen's University Press, 2000); Martin Robin, *Shades of Right: Nativist and Fascist Politics in Canada* (Toronto: University of Toronto Press, 1992); Lita-Rose Betcherman, *The Swastika and the Maple Leaf: Fascist Movements in Canada in the Thirties* (Toronto: Fitzhenry & Whiteside, 1975).

83 "Les Juifs au Canada," *supra* note 80.

84 I am aware of the point that anti-Semitism was not limited to Roman Catholic francophones and that other groups, including the Protestant elite, shared many anti-Semitic beliefs and stereotypes. One need refer only to some of the testimony by Protestant School Board members before the Commission of Nine for evidence. However, as a matter of population percentage, popular discourse, and political agitation in the late 1920s and early 1930s, there can be little doubt that French-Canadian ultramontane nationalism was the most significant form of anti-Semitism in the province. Pierre Anctil, "Interlude of Hostility: Judeo-Christian Relations in Quebec in the Interwar Period, 1919–1939" in Alan Davies, ed, *Antisemitism in Canada: History and Interpretation* (Waterloo, ON: Wilfrid Laurier University Press, 1992) at 135–66.

85 See David Rome, *Clouds in the Thirties*, 13 vols (Montreal: Canadian Jewish Congress National Archives, 1977–81), *passim*; Rome, *The Jewish Biography of Henri Bourassa: Part 1* (Montreal: Canadian Jewish Congress National Archives, 1988).

86 "L'assemblée des Jeune-Canada à la salle du Gesù hier soir: Protestation contre la reunion pro-juive de l'Arena," *Le Devoir* (21 April 1933); "'Nefarious Power' of Jewry Attacked: Mass Meeting under Auspices of Jeune Canada Is Largely Attended," *Montreal Gazette* (21 April 1933); Marie Catherine Agen, "Politics of the Société Saint-Jean-Baptiste de Montreal" (1999) 29 American Review of Canadian Studies 495; Alexandre Dugré SJ, *Saint Jean-Baptiste: Le Saint-La Fête-La Société* (Montreal: L'Oeuvre des Tracts, 1923).

87 "'Boycott Jews': Signs on Municipal-Owned Kiosks in Montreal: Jewish Paper Demand Test Case against City for Allowing Its Property to Be Used for Antisemitic Purposes," *JTA* (1 September 1931).

88 CJC, Personalia, Re: Sam Rabinovitch case 1934 copied from Notre Dame

Hospital and McGill Archives by Researcher Harold Toulch, May 1937; "Montreal Hospital Strike," *Jewish Standard* (22 June 1934); "Hospital Strike in Montreal Ends as Dr Rabinovitch Resigns Post," *Jewish Standard* (22 June 1934); Peter Wilson, "Days of Shame, Montreal, 1934" (2003) 9 Canadian Medical Association Journal at 1329.

89 An Act respecting the observance of Sunday, 1907, 7 Ed VII, c 42, s 6; Sheldon Indig, "Canadian Jewry and Their Struggle for an Exemption in the Federal Lord's Day Act 1906," parts 1 and 2, (1979) 3 Canadian Jewish Historical Society Journal at 27–56, 61–114; Paul Laverdure, *Sunday in Canada: The Rise and Fall of the Lord's Day* (Yorkton, SK: Gravelbooks. 2004); "Sunday in Quebec, 1907–1937" (1996) 62 CCHA Historical Studies 47. For a comparative example, see Batya Miller, "Enforcement of the Sunday Closing Laws on the Lower East Side, 1882–1903" (2003) 91 American Jewish History 269.

90 "La Semaine du dimanche" (1930) 197 École Sociale Populaire 2. See more generally, Richard Jones, *L'Idéologie de l'Action Catholique (1917–1939)* (Ste Foy, QC: Les Presses de l'Université Laval, 1974).

91 RP Archambault, SJ, *Contre le travail du dimanche* (Montreal: L'Oeuvre des Tracts, 1924); Archambault, *Pour un Dimanche chrétien: Vingt-cinq ans de bon combat* (Montreal: L'Oeuvre des Tracts, 1948).

92 "Le dimanche" (1930–31) 9 R du D 449; Léo Pelland, "Observance du dimanche" (1931–32) 10 R du D 129; "Le dimanche" (1931–32) 10 R du D, 513.

93 Antonin Dupont, *Les Relations entre l'Église et l'État sous Louis-Alexandre Taschereau, 1920–1936* (Montreal: Guérin, 1972) at 145–74.

94 *Réfèré Concernant la Loi du Dimanche*, 59 BR 491, (1935).

95 ANQ, E13, Jewish Question 783-21, and 775-30. Correspondence between the deputy minister of public education and the Protestant and Roman Catholic Committees and the superintendent of public education, February and March 1931; Audet, *supra* note 34 at 120.

96 L'assemblé legislative de la province du Québec, Session 1930, 24 February 1931; "Montreal School Bills Introduced," *Montreal Gazette* (7 March 1931).

97 "The Jewish School Question at Quebec," *Canadian Jewish Chronicle* (10 April 1931).

98 21 Geo V, c 63; "Jewish School Contract Will Be Confirmed," *Canadian Jewish Chronicle* (6 February 1931).

99 See also An Act to amend the Act 13 George V, c 44, 4 April 1931.

100 Gouvernement du Québec, *La Question des Écoles Juives: Comment le prob-*

lème a été réglé, Attitude du Cardinal et des Evêques (Quebec: Le Soleil, 1931).

101 Dominion Bureau of Statistics, Seventh Census of Canada, 1931, bulletin no 38, *Population of the Municipal Wards of Montreal City* at 30.

102 "Mr Hirsch Writes to the Premier on the School Issue," *Canadian Jewish Chronicle* (8 May 1931); "Mr Hirsch: It Should Never Have Been Written!!," *Canadian Jewish Chronicle* (8 May 1931).

103 "The Jewish School Commission Has Resigned!," *Canadian Jewish Chronicle* (17 April 1931); "To Be or Not To Be?" *Canadian Jewish Chronicle* (17 April 1931); Corcos, *supra* note 39 at 112.

104 "Jewish Commission Resignation Claims Superiority [*sic*] Forced upon Them through Repeal of 1930 Act," *Canadian Jewish Chronicle* (24 April 1931); "And Yet Another Chapter," *Canadian Jewish Chronicle* (24 April 1931).

105 "Jews Must Decide about Commission, Declares Premier," *Montreal Gazette* (21 April 1931).

106 An Act respecting the education of certain children in Montreal and Outremont, 21 Geo V, c 63, s 2.

107 Robert Rumilly, "L'affaire des écoles juives (1928–1931)" (1956) 10 Revue d'Histoire de l'Amérique française at 244.

108 Anctil, *supra* note 21 at 205. "En fait, près de cinquante ans de négociations et de compromis avec les instances scolaires en place n'avaient abouti à rien de plus que le droit pour les élèves de prendre place sur les bancs d'école, dans les classes où le personnel enseignant était pour la très grande majorité étranger à leurs traditions, et dans un contexte administratif où leurs parents étaient privés de droits de représentation."

109 Rome, *supra* note 33 at 133.

110 *Ibid.*

111 "Schubert Recalls Acadia to Critics: Statement on Auger-Quintal Motion Reminds French-Canadians of History," *Montreal Gazette* (23 September 1931); "Charge Schubert with Indelicacy," *Montreal Gazette* (26 September 1931); "Racial Trouble in Council Is Feared," *Montreal Gazette* (30 September 1931).

112 "Les Juifs et M Houde," *Le Devoir* (20 August 1931).

113 TRP Ceslas Forest, *La Question Juive au Canada* (Montreal: L'Oeuvre de Presse Dominicaine, 1935) at 5. Forest was dean of the Faculty of Philosophy at the Université de Montréal.

114 *Ibid* at 6.

115 *Ibid* at 28.

116 *Ibid* at 21–8.
117 ANQ, ANQ, E13, Jewish Question 783-21, letters, 5, 6, 7, and 11 October 1932.
118 *Ibid*, 11 September 1936.
119 *Ibid*, Resolution of 27 January 1936, Protestant School Board and Resolution of 27 March 1936; letter from Montreal director of finance, 6 April 1936.
120 *Ibid*, letter to WP Percival, 14 September 1936.
121 *Ibid*.

Chapter 10

1 Robert Cover, "*Nomos* and Narrative" (1983–84) 97 Harv L Rev 4.
2 The Education Act of the Province of Quebec, 62 Vict, c 26 (1899), as amended.
3 *Les Syndics d'écoles de la municipalité d'Outremont v Ainslie* 25 CS 348, (1904).
4 *The School Commissioners of the Village of Lake Megantic v Turgeon* (1897) 3 R de J 355.
5 *Syndics d'Écoles Dissidentes de St Romuald v Shannon*, [1930] SCR 599, (1930).
6 Jean-Pierre Proulx, "L'évolution de la législation relative au système électoral scolaire québécois" (1998) 10 Revue d'histoire de l'éducation 20.
7 *The School Commissioners of St Bernard de Lacolle v Bowman* (1865) 10 LCJ 103.
8 *Ibid* at 108. ("Mais une fois ce corps constitué, la loi ne distingue plus, elle déclare que le conseil de ces dissidents aura seul le pouvoir d'asseoir et de prélever l'impôt scolaire sur les habitants dissidents. C'est la croyance seule qui limite et désigne qui appartiennent à chaque corporation.")
9 *The School Commissioners of the Municipality of the Township of Roxton v Boston* (1879) 24 LCJ 122; see also *Les Commissaires d'écoles de St Ignace du Coteau du Lac v French* (1899) 16 CS 70.
10 *JA Cushing v Les Syndics d'Écoles pour la Municipalité d'Acton Vale* (1872) 18 LCJ 21.
11 Education, Revised Statutes of Quebec, 1925, c 133, s 576.
12 *Hirsch and Another v Protestant Board of School Commissioners of Montreal et al*, [1928] AC 200.
13 *Ibid* at 209.

14 Howard Gontovnick, "East European Jewish Migration and Its Impact: Farming Colonies across Canada" in Ira Robinson, ed, *Canada's Jews in Time, Space and Spirit* (Brighton, MA: Academic Studies, 2013) at 39–51; Vladimir Grossman, *The Soil's Calling* (Montreal: Edition Year Book Publishing, 1938).
15 Kennee Switzer-Rakos, "Baron de Hirsch, the Jewish Colonization Association and Canada" (1987) 32 Leo Baeck Institute Yearbook at 389.
16 Theodore Norman, *An Outstretched Arm: A History of the Jewish Colonization Association* (London: Routledge & Kegan Paul, 1985).
17 Simon Belkin, "Jewish Colonization in Canada" in Arthur Daniel Hart, ed, *The Jew in Canada* (Toronto: Jewish Publication, 1926) at 483–8.
18 Dominique Frischer, *Le Moïse des Amériques: Vies et Oeuvres du Munificent Baron de Hirsch* (Paris: Bernard Grasset, 2002); Samuel J Lee, *Moses of the New World: The Work of Baron de Hirsch* (New York: Thomas Yoseloff, 1970).
19 Simon Belkin, *Through Narrow Gates: A Review of Jewish Immigration, Colonization and Immigrant Aid Work in Canada (1840–1940)* (Montreal: Canadian Jewish Congress & the Jewish Colonization Association, 1966) at 40ff; Joseph Kage, *With Faith and Thanksgiving: The Story of Two Hundred Years of Jewish Immigration and Immigrant Aid Effort in Canada (1760–1960)* (Montreal: Eagle Publishing, 1962) at 41–59; Bernard Figler, *Sam Jacobs: Member of Parliament* (Ottawa: Author, 1959) at 29–31.
20 Belkin, *supra* note 17 at 487; Louis Rosenberg, *Canada's Jews* (Montreal: Bureau of Social and Economic Research, Canadian Jewish Congress, 1939) at 223–34.
21 Normand Champagne, *Le temps que je m'en souviens: Sainte-Sophie des origines à aujourd'hui* (Sainte-Sophie, QC: Municipalité de Sainte-Sophie, 2005) at 42.
22 *Ibid* at 52.
23 *Ibid* at 56.
24 Howard Gontovnick, "From Colony to Community: Ste-Sophie Quebec" (2001) 9 Canadian Jewish Studies 190.
25 Katherine Wilton, "Sainte-Sophie's Jewish Heritage to Be Celebrated," *Montreal Gazette* (14 September 2012); Janice Rosen, "A Tale of Two Willies in Ste-Sophie" (2003) 3 Montreal Forum 10.
26 Champagne, *supra* note 21 at 95.
27 *Ibid* at 95–100.
28 Roderick MacLeod & Mary Anne Poutanen, *A Meeting of the People: School Boards and Protestant Communities in Quebec, 1801–1998* (Montreal & Kingston: McGill-Queen's University Press, 2004) at 83.
29 Champagne, *supra* note 21 at 103; MacLeod & Poutanen, *supra* note 28 at 83.

30 Champagne, *supra* note 21 at 105.
31 CJC, ZD La Macaza, Jean-Paul Bélanger, "Aperçu Historique de la Colonie Juive de La Macaza," typescript, nd at 25.
32 *Ibid.*
33 CJC, Jewish Colonization Association, AA 162-436, 16 January 1911–15 December 1914, letters, 8 September, 12 December 1911, and 3 January 1913.
34 ANQ, E-13, 2065; MacLeod & Poutanen, *supra* note 28 at 210ff; Roderick MacLeod & Mary Anne Poutanen "Upstairs for Hebrew, Downstairs for English: The Jewish Community of Ste-Sophie, Quebec and Strategies for Public Education, 1914–1952" (2002) 10 Canadian Jewish Studies 29.
35 CJC, ZD, Ste Sophie Community Files, letter, to M J-E Parent, notary, 28 April 1916.
36 ANQ, E-13, 2065, letter, 16 July 1913.
37 *Ibid*, letter, 11 December 1913.
38 MacLeod & Poutanen, *supra* note 28 at 210.
39 ANQ, E-13, 2065, letter, 31 December 1913.
40 MacLeod & Poutanen, *supra* note 28 at 214; "Upstairs for Hebrew, Downstairs for English," *supra* note 34 at 35.
41 CJC, Jewish Colonization Association, AA3, 14 January 1915–16 December 1920, letter no 462, 12 July 1915.
42 Ste Sophie Protestant School, Scotland, Quebec, 1914–1937, McGill University Archives, microfilm, MG 4024, Minute Book, 11 July 1914.
43 *Ibid*, 10 August 1914.
44 *Ibid*, 7 December 1914; Education Act, ss 76–83.
45 Ste Sophie Protestant School, *supra* note 42, 7, 18 October 1915, 5 September, 16 November 1922, 22 October 1927, 13 May, 18 October 1916, 16 April 1917.
46 *Ibid*, 10 March 1917.
47 MacLeod & Poutanen, *supra* note 29, chapter 7, "The Rural School Problem," 95ff; WAF Hepburn et al, *Protestant Education in the Province of Quebec. Report of the Quebec Protestant Education Survey* (Montreal: Montreal Protestant Central School Board, 1938).
48 Minute Book, 6 March 1921.
49 Ste Sophie Protestant School, *supra* note 42, 26 August 1922, 17 August 1924, 6 April 1928, 8 July 1933, 5 February 1934, 30 March 1936.
50 Cover, *supra* note 1.
51 See also Minute Book, 14 May 1925.
52 *Ibid*, 10 October 1931.
53 *Ibid*, 23 April 1932.
54 *Ibid*, 4 December 1932.
55 *Ibid*, 7 January 1933.

56 *Ibid*, 4 March 1933.
57 *Ibid*, 17 April 1933.
58 *Ibid*, 5 October 1936, 1 March 1937; MacLeod & Poutanen, *supra* note 34 at 42.
59 Cover, *supra* note 1.
60 MacLeod & Poutanen, *supra* note 28 at 197.
61 Cover, *supra* note 1 at 39.
62 CJC, Jewish Colonization Association, AA2, *supra* note 33, letter no. 203.
63 The documents surrounding the transfer of land from Jacob Wrublewsky to Mark Isbisky in 1908, for example, demonstrate that school taxes were paid to the Roman Catholic Commissioners. CJC, La Macaza, P03/20, 1908.
64 CJC, La Macaza, P03/20, letter no. 196, 3 August 1911.
65 CJC, Jewish Colonization Association, AA2, *supra* note 33, letter no. 196.
66 *Ibid*.
67 Bélanger, *supra* note 31 at 29.
68 CJC, La Macaza file, Reuben Belansman, letter to the editor of *Der Veg*, 24 December 1915. Copy in CJC National Archives, La Macaza file. Translated from the Yiddish by Naomi Pascal Freeman. Freeman's website, La Macaza, Quebec, and the Colonization Association <jmarshallfreeman.com/macaza/>, offers a good introduction to the history of the La Macaza Jewish settlement.
69 CJC, Jewish Colonization Association, E 34 118, Hebrew School, La Macaza, Qué. 1918–1924, letter from superintendent of public instruction, 15 March 1918.
70 *Ibid*, letter, 1 April 1918 with enclosed list.
71 *Ibid*, 5 April 1918.
72 *Ibid*, R. Belansman, chairman of the School Board, to the JCA, 16 March 1920.
73 Bélanger, *supra* note 31.
74 CJC, Jewish Colonization Association, E 34 118, Hebrew School, La Macaza, Qué. 1918–1924, letter, JCA general manager to members of the committee, 19 March 1920.
75 ANQ, E13 1B01893, La Macaza, letters, 6 and 9 July.
76 CJC, Jewish Colonization Association E 42 170, La Macaza Colony Qué., List of Jewish Farmers in La Macaza, 6 May 1921.
77 *Ibid*, letters, 13 and 15 November 1922.
78 *Ibid*, letters, 11 and 13 June 1923.
79 *Ibid*, letter, 14 and 17 July 1924.
80 *Ibid*, letter, 2 August 1924.

81 *Ibid*, letter, 16 August 1924.
82 *Ibid*, letter, 19 August 1924.
83 *Ibid*, letter, 22 August, 1924.
84 *Ibid*.
85 *Ibid*, letter, 22 October 1924.
86 Davina Cooper, *Everyday Utopias: The Conceptual Life of Promising Spaces* (Durham, NC: Duke University Press, 2014).

Chapter 11

1 Robert Rumilly, *Histoire d'Outremont 1875–1975* (Montreal: Leméac, 1975) at 242. "La progression juive, à la manière d'une tache d'huile, n'arrête pas."
2 Louis Rosenberg, *Canada's Jews* (Montreal: Bureau of Social and Economic Research, Canadian Jewish Congress, 1939) at 31.
3 Rumilly, *supra* note 1 at 247.
4 Roderick MacLeod & Mary Anne Poutanen, *A Meeting of the People: School Boards and Protestant Communities in Quebec, 1801–1998* (Montreal & Kingston: McGill-Queen's University Press, 2004) at 216–18.
5 Rumilly, *supra* note 1 at 296. "Le fait saillant est le remplacement de 2.000 'Anglais,' partis pour Westmount, Hampstead ou Mont-Royal, par 2.000 Juifs."
6 Hyman Neamtan, "The Rise and Fall of Jewish Attendance in the Protestant Schools of Greater Montreal" (1940–1941) 2 Canadian Jewish Year Book at 185.
7 *Ibid* at 187.
8 Quebec *Official Gazette*, (No. 26), June 26/43. Vol 75, 1169.
9 Harold Ross, *The Jew in the Educational System of the Province of Quebec* (MA Thesis, McGill University, 1947) [unpublished] at 92. Ross was a member of the Outremont Committee for the Education of Jewish Children and participant in many of the events described here.
10 Omer Côté (1906–1999) was educated in Outremont and Montreal. He was called to the Bar in 1929, served as an alderman on the Montreal City Council, and was elected to the Quebec Legislature in 1944 as a Union Nationale member. He served as Maurice Duplessis's provincial secretary from 1944 when 1956 when he left the Legislative Assembly to take up a judicial appointment. "Omer Côté" Assemblée Nationale Québec <www.assnat.qc.ca/fr/deputes/cote-omer-2673/biographic.html>.
11 CJC, ZA 1945, 14/220, letter, 12 September 1944.
12 *Ibid*.

13 Rumilly, *supra* note 1 at 299.
14 CJC, ZA 1945 14/220.
15 Loi sur la fréquentation scolaire obligatoire/Compulsory School Attendance Act, 7 Geo VI, c 13, (1943).
16 MacLeod & Poutanen, *supra* note 4 at 219–20.
17 Eric M Adams, "'Guardians of Liberty': RMW Chitty and the Wartime Ideas of Constitutional Rights" in Constance Backhouse & W Wesley Pue, eds, *The Promise and Peril of Law: Lawyers in Canadian History* (Toronto: Irwin, 2009) at 173–90.
18 "Honor What He's Fighting For?," *Montreal Star* (12 December 1944). Dominant French-Canadian opinion, which had struggled against the Canadian presence in the war, would not have been moved by this argument. Ultramontanist elements continued to support the "conservatism" of Hitler's allies in Vichy France, even after the war ended. See Yves Lavertu, *The Bernonville Affair: A French War Criminal in Québec after World War II* (Montreal: Robert Davies, 1994).
19 CJC, ZA 1945, 14/220, letter to Protestant Central School Board, 12 October 1944; letter, Protestant Central Board to Phillips, 11 December 1944. Lazarus Phillips (1895–1986) was born in Montreal and served in the Canadian Expeditionary Force in Siberia at the end of the First World War. He graduated from McGill University, clerked with Sam Jacobs, and was called to the Bar in 1920. He practised in partnership with Jacobs until the latter's death. In addition to his law practice, he served on many corporate boards. He was a valued adviser to the Bronfman family and was active in Jewish communal organizations, including the Jewish Colonization Association and the United Talmud Torahs, and was founder of the Canadian Tax Foundation. He was appointed to the Senate in 1968. National Archives Canada, Fonds Lazarus Phillips, Biography, MAINS22093; "Obituary, Retired Senator, Lazarus Phillips," *Montreal Gazette* (31 December 1986).
20 Montreal Jewry played a significant role in the founding of the CJC and in its leadership for many years. The first four presidents of the congress were Montrealers: Lyon Cohen (1919–34); Sam Jacobs (1934–38); Samuel Bronfman (1939–62); and Michael Garber (1962–68). In 2011, the CJC amalgamated with other Jewish advocacy groups under the banner of the Centre for Israel and Jewish Affairs (CIJA).
21 Rebecca Margolis, *Jewish Roots, Canadian Soil: Yiddish Culture in Montreal, 1905–1945* (Montreal & Kingston: McGill-Queen's University Press, 2011).
22 Walter Pilling Percival (1885–1966) was for many years director of Protestant education, and then deputy minister of education in Quebec. He was the author, among other works, of *Across the Years: A Century of Education*

in the Province of Quebec (Montreal: Gazette Printing, 1946), and *Life in School: An Explanation of the Protestant School System of the Province of Quebec* (Montreal: Herald, 1940–41).

23 CJC, ZA 1945, 14/220, letter, 7 December 1944,

24 *Ibid*, memorandum, 7 December 1944; "School Agreement with Jews May End," *Montreal Gazette* (6 December 1944).

25 "Protests against School Board's Act," *Montreal Star* (11 December 1944).

26 Gerald Tulchinsky, *Taking Root: The Origins of the Canadian Jewish Community* (Hanover, NH: Brandeis University Press/University Press of New England, 1993) at 255–75.

27 CJC, ZA 1945, 14/220, letter to Percival, 19 December 1944.

28 *Ibid*, 22 December 1944.

29 *Ibid*, memorandum, 19 February 1945.

30 *Ibid*, Tentative Agenda, 27 February 1945.

31 CJC, DB01 3/19, Outremont School Question 48/9, Minutes of Special Meeting Quebec Federation of Home and School Associations Committee on Central School Board, 19 January 1945. Although there is an underlying trace of the fear of miscegenation here, the documentary record does not contain further or more specific evidence of this sexual fear. As a matter of historical fact, it is worth noting perhaps that at this time and for some time to come, the Montreal Jewish community had an extremely low rate of exogamous marriage. Jean-Claude Lasry & Evelyn Bloomfield-Schachter, "Jewish Intermarriage in Montreal, 1962–1972" (1975) 37 Jewish Social Studies 267.

32 CJC, ZA 1945, 14/220. On the rise of Jewish day schools, see Arlette Corcos, *Montréal, les Juifs et l'École* (Sillery, QC: Septentrion, 1997). In Outremont, in 1946, there were 245 students attending the Adath Israel Day School. In all likelihood, some Jewish students from that city also figured among the 1,169 Jewish students enrolled in the five Jewish day schools in Montreal. Ross, *supra* note 9 at 87, table V; An Act to incorporate Adath Israel Congregation and Community Centre of Outremont, 2 Geo VI, c 133, (1938). These developments in Montreal mirrored those elsewhere in Canada, especially in the post-war period, Michael Brown, "Good Fences Do Not Necessarily Make Good Neighbors: Jews and Judaism in Canada's Schools and Universities" (1999) 11 Jewish Political Studies Review 97.

33 CJC, ZA 1945, 14/220, Meeting of the Committee to deal with the Outremont School Question, 1 March 1945.

34 Stéphane Valiquette, SJ, "La Minorité Juive au Québec," *Relations*, March 1945, 72–4.

35 CJC, ZA 1945, 14/220 B, letter, 2 March 1945.
36 CJC, ZA 1945, 14/220 A, letters, 11 and 22 May 1945.
37 *Ibid*, 15 May 1945.
38 *Ibid*, letter, 26 May 1945.
39 *Ibid*.
40 *Ibid*, letter, 6 June 1945.
41 *Ibid*, letter, 12 June 1945.
42 *Ibid*, memorandum, 20 June 1945.
43 *Ibid*, Synopsis of Address by Michael Garber, KC.
44 CJC, DB01, 3/10 481 Q, Outremont Schools, Minutes of Public Meeting of Jewish Parents.
45 Ross, *supra* note 9 at 98.
46 *Ibid*. "Outremont Community Voices Deep Resentment of Making 'Jewish Children a Political Football,'" *Canadian Jewish Chronicle* (22 June 1945).
47 "School Crisis Relieved," *Montreal Gazette* (19 June 1945); "Jewish Children Assured Continued Education," *Montreal Herald* (19 June 1945).
48 CJC, ZA 1945, 14/220 A, Minutes of the Meeting of the Committee on Education of Jewish Children in Outremont, 25 June 1945; "Outremont Jewish Pupils Get One Year Extension," *Canadian Jewish Chronicle* (22 June 1945).
49 [1957] SCR 285; Abraham Feiner was an award-winning graduate of McGill Law School. Along with Joseph Cohen KC, Feiner represented Communist member of Parliament Fred Rose when he was prosecuted for violating the Official Secrets Act in the post-war Soviet spy scandals. *Rose v R*, [1947] 3 DLR 618; Dominique Clément, "The Royal Commission on Espionage and the Spy Trials of 1946–9: A Case Study in Parliamentary Supremacy" (2000) 11 Journal of the Canadian Historical Association 151.
50 *Boucher v R* [1951] SCR 265. Albert Louis Stein, QC, was active throughout his career in progressive causes in the legal protection of civil rights and liberties. He received the Montreal Bar Medal in 1997–98 for his role as an advocate for civil liberties, freedom of religion, and the rule of law. "1997–1998 Me Albert Louis Stein, QC," Bar of Montreal, online: <www.barreaudemontreal.qc.ca/en/barreau/1997-1998-me-albert-louis-stein-qc>.
51 *Roncarelli v Duplessis* [1959] SCR 121; Eric A Adams, "Building a Law of Human Rights: *Roncarelli v Duplessis* in Canadian Constitutional Culture" (2010) 55 McGill LJ 437.
52 Adams, *supra* note 51 at 444; Matthew Lewans, "*Roncarelli's* Green Card: The Role of Citizenship in Randian Constitutionalism" (2010) 55 McGill LJ 637.
53 Christopher MacLennan, *Toward the Charter: Canadians and the Demand for*

a National Bill of Rights, 1920–1960 (Montreal & Kingston: McGill-Queen's University Press, 2003).

54 OJA, JPRC correspondence, box 8, file 9A, Myerson to Laskin, 6 October 1958. Thanks to Philip Girard for the reference.

55 An Act to ensure the progress of education, 10 Geo VI, c 21, 17 April 1946. S 30 ensured the continuation of the 1931 contract until 1 July 1947. CJC to Duplessis, 26 June 1945.

56 CJC, ZA 1945, 14/220 A, Minutes of the Meeting of the Committee on Education of Jewish Children in Outremont, 27 March 1946; Michael Garber to Maurice Duplessis, 4 April 1946; Garber to Omer Côté and reply, 8 and 9 April 1946; "Quebec Government Asked to Secure Admission of Jewish Children to Montreal Schools," *JTA* (11 April 1946).

57 "Jamais Québec Ne Créera Une Commission Scolaire Juive, déclare M Maurice Duplesis premier-ministre du Québec," *La Presse* (31 May 1946).

58 The whole system of government spending and expanding state involvement in social welfare programs was on the political agenda at the time and throughout the Duplessis period. Dominique Marshall, *The Social Origins of the Welfare State: Quebec Families, Compulsory Education, and Family Allowances, 1940–1955*, translated by Nicola Doone Danby (Waterloo, ON: Wilfrid Laurier University Press, 2006).

59 CJC, ZA 1945, 14/220 A, Garber to Omer Côté, 12 April 1946.

60 CJC, ZA 1946, 11/191, *Submission to the Province of Quebec in the Matter of the Education of Jewish Children in the Protestant School System of Outremont.* Hyam Neamtan, *The Jews Bear the Main Burden of the Maintenance of the Protestant Schools in Outremont*, CJC, Neamtan, Hyam, file, 1946.

61 Ross, *supra* note 9 at 103–4.

62 "Quebec Legislature Adopts Law Compelling School Boards to Admit Jewish Students," *JTA* (21 April 1946).

63 CJC, ZA 1945, 14/220 A, letter from Garber, 21 November 1946.

64 CJC, BB, box 14/12, Minutes of Meeting of Committee of Education of Jewish Children in Outremont, 21 November 1946.

65 "Canadian Jewish Casualties in the Armed Forces," Canadian Jewish Congress Charities Committee National Archives, online: <www.cjccc.ca/en/cjccc-national-archives/canadian-jewish-military-casualties/>.

66 Ironically perhaps, an emerging literature argues that at the same time, anti-Semitism among the majority population was becoming more marginalized, although it remained problematically situated as part of the emerging national identity discourse. Sherry Simon, "Le Discours du Juif au Québec en 1948: Jean le Moyne, Gabrielle Roy," (1993) 15 Québec Studies 77.

67 CJC, ZA 1945, 14/220 A, Garber to Côté, 3 December 1946; reply 4 December 1946.
68 *Ibid*, Garber telegram to Duplessis, 14 April 1947.
69 *Ibid*, Outremont Delegation Meets Today with the Minister of Education, IOI, 18 April 1947; Outremont School Question, IOI, 21 April 1947.
70 CJC, ZA 1945, 14/220 A, Côté to Garber, 16 April 1947. "Nous essaierons toujours de donner justice à la minorité, quelle qu'elle soit."
71 *Ibid*, Garber to Côté, 17 April 1947.
72 *Ibid*, memorandum, Outremont School Problem, 25 April 1947; Garber reply to memorandum, 26 April 1947.
73 CJC, ZA 1947, 10/123, Minutes of Meeting of Committee on Education of Jewish children; CJC, ZA 1945, 14/220, Report by Michael Garber.
74 CJC, ZA 1947, 10/123, letter, 2 May 1947, and letter to Duplessis of the same date.
75 An Act respecting Protestant Schools in the city of Outremont, 11 Geo VI, c 86, 10 May 1947; CJC, ZA 1947, 10/123, Outremont School Problem Nearing Satisfactory Solution, IOI, 6 June 1947.
76 Arrêté en Conseil, numéro 1528, 18 September 1947.
77 CJC, ZA 1945, 14/220, letter, 22 July 1947.
78 Abstract from the Minutes of a Meeting of the Protestant Board of School Trustees for the City of Outremont, 8 September 1947.
79 CJC, ZA 1945, 14/220, letter to Côté, 10 September 1947, and enclosed Draft Agreement re Admission of Jewish Children to Protestant Schools in Outremont.
80 *Ibid*, letter, 12 September 1947.
81 *Ibid*, memorandum, 5 Years Agreement between the Protestant Board of Outremont and the Provincial Government Regarding Education of Jewish Children, 12 September 1947.
82 *Ibid*, letter, 17 September 1947.
83 CJC, ZA 1947, 10/123, Agreement; "Outremont's Protestant Schools Reopened to Jewish Children," *Montreal Gazette* (25 September 1947).
84 "Three-Way Pact Announced by Provincial Secretary: Long-Fought Issue Over as Pact Signed between Protestant School Syndicate, Suburb's Jewish leaders and Provincial Government," *Montreal Gazette* (25 September 1945).
85 CJC, ZA 1945, 14/220 A, New Agreement re Admission of Jewish Children to Protestant Schools in Outremont, 25 September 1947.
86 CJC, DB 101, Outremont School Question 1948–1951, Minutes of Meeting of the Committee on Education of Jewish Children in Outremont, 7 October.

87 CJC, ZA 1945, 14/220, Michael Garber, letter to the editor, *Montreal Star*, 6 November.
88 CJC, DB 101, Outremont School Question 1948–1951.
89 *Ibid*, Garber letter, 13 November 1947.
90 Canadian Jewish Congress, *Report of the National Executive Director to Delegates* at 20, CJC, DB 101, Outremont School Question 1948–1951.
91 Corcos, *supra* note 32 at 119–20.
92 CJC, ZA 1945, 14/220, Garber letter, 4 April 1946.
93 *Ibid*, letter, 15 June 1946.
94 CJC, ZA 1945, 14/220A, letter, 29 June 1945.
95 Minute Book of Outremont School Trustees, 6 May 1947; MacLeod & Poutanen, *supra* note 4 at 220–1.
96 Quoted in Ross, *supra* note 9 at 102.
97 *Ibid* at 100; *Report of the Committee Appointed to Study the Outremont School Situation*, Quebec Federation of Home and School Federations, Montreal, May 1947.
98 E.g., ANQ, E13, Jewish Questions, 783–21, Correspondence January–September 1936.
99 Rumilly, *supra* note 1 at 301.
100 Romuald Bourque (mayor of Outremont), "The Jews of Outremont," *Canadian Jewish Chronicle* (22 February 1952).
101 Rumilly, *supra* note 1 at 309–10.

Chapter 12

1 SQ, 1925, c 45; Andrew Sancton, *Governing the Island of Montreal: Language Differences and Metropolitan Politics* (Berkeley: University of California Press, 1985) at 48–50.
2 *Report, The Montreal Protestant Central School Board, 1930–1931.*
3 An Act Respecting the Department of Education (Education Act), RSQ, 1941, s 583.
4 ANQ, E13, Jewish Questions, 782/21, letter to Protestant Committee, 16 June 1941.
5 ANQ, E13, Jewish Questions, 782/21, letter from Percival, 27 June 1941.
6 *Hirsch v Commissioners of the Montreal Protestant School Board* [1928] AC 200.
7 *Ibid.*
8 *Ibid.*
9 *Report, The Montreal Protestant Central School Board, 1930–1931.*
10 Louis Rosenberg, *Canada's Jews* (Montreal: Bureau of Social and Economic Research, Canadian Jewish Congress, 1939) at 31.

11 Louis Rosenberg, *Jewish Children in the Protestant Schools of Greater Montreal in the Period from 1878 to 1962: A Statistical Study*, Canadian Jewish Congress, Research Papers, series E, no 2, 1962, table 4; *Changes in the Geographical Distribution of the Jewish Population of Metropolitan Montreal in the Decennial Periods from 1901 to 1961*, Canadian Jewish Congress, Research Papers, series A, no 7, 1966.
12 CJC, CA, box 47/439, Hampstead School, letter, 14 November 1949; memorandum, 8 December 1949.
13 *Ibid*, memorandum, 14 December 1949.
14 *Ibid*, Louis Rosenberg, memorandum, 14 December 1949.
15 *Ibid.*
16 CJC, PR, IOI no 97, memorandum, 22 January 1951.
17 CJC, CA, box 47/439, Hampstead School, Louis Rosenberg, memorandum, 19 July 1951.
18 *Ibid*, memoranda, 28 June and 1 August 1950.
19 *Ibid*, Louis Freedman, KC, to AHJ Zaitlin, chair, Anti-Diffamation [*sic*] Committee, 13 February 1951.
20 *Stephens v Les Commissaires d'Écoles pour la Municipalité de la Paroisse de Longeuil*, 9 CS 408, (1896), at 412–13.
21 CJC, CA, box 47/439, Hampstead School, letter to Harold Newman, 22 March 1951.
22 *Ibid*, letters, 25 and 30 April 1951.
23 *Official Gazette*, 1565.
24 CJC, CA, box 47/439, Hampstead School, Opinion of Harold Newman.
25 *Stephens v Les Commissaires, supra* note 20.
26 CJC, CA, box 47/439, Hampstead School, letter, 8 June 1951; CJC, IOI, no 1, 144, 8 June 1951; no 1, 145, 12 June 1951; no 1, 149, 18 June 1951.
27 *Ibid*, memorandum, 22 November 1951.
28 CJC, ZA 1951, 7/75, 11 December 1951.
29 CJC, IOI, no 1, 241, Congress Statement on Admission of Jewish Children to Protestant School in Hampstead, 20 November 1951; "Report Claims Anti-Jew Bias in Hampstead," *Montreal Gazette* (19 November 1951); "Correction Is in Order," *Montreal Herald* (21 November 1951); "Protestant Schools in Montreal Suburb Bar Jewish Pupils," *JTA* (27 November 1951).
30 CJC, CA, box 47/439, Hampstead School, letter, 7 December 1951.
31 *Ibid*, memorandum, Board of Protestant School of Hampstead Adopting Resolution Interpreted as Reversal of Policy of Exclusion of Children of Jewish Residents, 10 December 1951; "Hampstead School Won't Exclude Jews: New Board Policy Stated at Meeting with Jewish Parents," *Montreal Gazette*, 7 December 1951; "Hampstead School Said Open to All," *Montreal Gazette*, 7 December 1951.

32 CJC, IOI, no 1430, 2 September 1951.
33 "Jewish Parents to Bring Court Action against School Authorities," *JTA* (3 December 1951); "School Rejects Jewish Pupils," *Jewish Exponent* (14 December 1951); "Montreal Parents to Take Court Action," *Jewish Exponent* (21 December 1951).
34 CJC, IOI, no 1441, 17 September 1952.
35 Gérard Filion, *Les confidences d'un Commissaire d'Écoles* (Montreal: Les Éditions de l'Homme, 1960). See *L'Éducation, problème social: Semaines sociales du Canada 38e Session* (Montreal: Les Éditions Bellarmin, 1963).
36 Michael D Behiels, *Prelude to Quebec's Quiet Revolution: Liberalism versus Nationalism, 1945–1960* (Montreal & Kingston: McGill-Queen's University Press, 2011); Michael Gauvreau, *The Catholic Origins of Quebec's Quiet Revolution* (Montreal & Kingston: McGill-Queen's University Press, 2008); Gauvreau, *Une Certaine Révolution Tranquille 22 juin 1960–75* (Montreal: La Presse, 1975); Samuel H Barnes, "Quebec Catholicism and Social Change" (1961) 23 Review of Politics 52.
37 CJC, BB, box 14/12, Minutes, 27 November 1961.
38 "Canadian Jews Seek to Win Representation in Protestant School Board," *JTA*, (18 July 1961).
39 For a detailed view from a key participant in the St Martin case, see Yedidia "Eddy" Kaplansky, "The Landmark Case of Harvey Grotsky, et al., versus The Protestant School Board of St. Martin, et al. (A Memoir)" (1998) 6 Canadian Jewish Studies 65.
40 *Ibid*, 72–4; CJC, CD, box 4, file 809c, Protestant School Commission St Martin, 1961–1962.
41 CJC, ZA 1961, 3/38, legal opinion of 14 November 1961.
42 *Harvey Grotsky et al v The Protestant School Commissioners for the School Municipality of Greater St. Martin in the County of Laval et al.*, Province of Quebec, District of Montreal, No. 1162.
43 Law creating a Royal Commission of Inquiry into Education, 9–10 Eliz II, c 25, 1961.
44 Order in Council No. 1031, 21 April 1961.
45 See e.g., Benoît Laplante, "The Rise of Cohabitation in Quebec: Power of Religion and Power over Religion" (2006) 31 Canadian Journal of Sociology 1.
46 Robert Élie, ed, *L'École Laïque* (Montreal: Les Éditions du Jour, 1961); see René Hurtubise, "La confessionalité de notre système scolaire et les garanties constitutionnelles" (1962) 65 R du N 167.
47 Harold Troper, *The Defining Decade: Identity, Politics, and the Canadian Jewish Community in the 1960s* (Toronto: University of Toronto Press, 2010) at 52–68.

48 CJC, ZA 1958, box 4/35, Brief of Jewish Day Schools; Jack Jacob Hirschberg, *Secular and Parochial Education of Ashkenazi and Sephardi Jewish Children in Montreal: A Study in Ethnicity* (PhD Thesis, McGill University, 1988) [unpublished].
49 CJC, CA, box 81/809, Parent Commission, letter, 3 August 1961.
50 Brief Submitted by the Canadian Jewish Congress to the Royal Commission of Inquiry on Education, March 1962 at 6.
51 *Ibid* at 5.
52 "Jews in Canada Dissatisfied with Protestant Proposal on Schools," *JTA* (16 April 1962)
53 Roderick MacLeod & Mary Anne Poutanen, *A Meeting of the People: School Boards and Protestant Communities in Quebec, 1801–1998* (Montreal & Kingston: McGill-Queen's University Press, 2004) at 350–2.
54 Louis-Philippe Audet, *Histoire du Conseil de l'instruction publique de la province du Québec 1856–1964* (Montreal: Éditions Leméac, 1964) at 203–6.
55 *Ibid* at 207–13.
56 *Ibid* at 213.
57 Rosenberg, *supra* note 11 at 11, table 4.
58 CJC, DB 01 29, Hampstead-Protestant Schools, 1965–1967, CJC to Protestant School Board of Greater Montreal, 4 April 1966.
59 "'School Crisis' Emphasized in Congress Conference," *Canadian Jewish Chronicle* (24 February 1961).
60 CJC, DB 01 29, Hampstead-Protestant Schools, 1965–1967, memorandum, 25 February 1965.
61 CJC, DB 01 29, Hampstead-Protestant Schools, 1965–1967, CJC to Samuel Godinsky, QC, 5 May 1965.
62 *Ibid*, Minutes of Meeting of Committee on Position of Jews in Educational System of Quebec, 21 October 1965.
63 *Ibid*, CJC to Protestant School Board of Greater Montreal, 4 April 1966.
64 *Commissaires d'Écoles de St Ignace du Lac v French*, 16 CS 70, (1899); *Casgrain v The School Commissioners of St Grégoire le Thaumaturge*, 9 CS 225, (1895).
65 *Hirsch and Another v Protestant Board of School Commissioners of Montreal et al* [1928] AC 200, 213.
66 *Perron v Les Syndics d'Écoles de la Municipalité de Rouyn*, [1955] BR 841; John Ciaccia, "Perron v School Trustees of the School Municipality of Rouyn" (1955–56) 2 McGill LJ 42; *Chabot v Les Commissaires d'Écoles de Lamorandière*, [1957] BR 707; FR Scott, "Case and Comment – Quebec Education Act – Right of Parent over Religious Education of Child in Public School" (1958) 36 Can Bar Rev 248; James Hugessen, "Chabot vs Les Commissaires d'Écoles de la Morandière," *Chronique de Jurisprudence* (1957–58) 8 RJT ns

108; "Case and Comment – Chabot v Les Commissaires d'Ecoles de la Morandière" (1957–58) 4 McGill LJ 268.

67 CJC, DB 01 29, Hampstead-Protestant Schools, 1965–1967, CJC to T Palmer Howard, 3 May 1967.

68 *Ibid*, list of persons who have made written application to have their name added to the Electoral List for the School Municipality of the Town of Hampstead, April 1967.

69 *Ibid*, letter, 3 May 1967 to Julian Kotler.

70 *Ibid*, Minutes of Meeting of Committee on Position of Jews in the Educational System of Quebec, 12 July 1966; CJC, IOI, 3057, Eligibility of Jewish Residents in Hampstead to Vote and Be Elected to Local Protestant School Board, 14 July 1966; CJC, DB 01 29, Hampstead-Protestant Schools, 1965–1967, Correspondence July 1966.

71 CJC, DB 01 29, Hampstead-Protestant Schools, 1965–1967, letter to PSBGM, 13 July 1966.

72 *Ibid.*

73 Provincial Court, District of Montreal, *Lawrence Bessner et al v Protestant Board of School Commissioners of the Town of Hampstead*. Statement of Claim and attached affidavits in the appeal from the decision of the School Commissioners pertaining to the Electoral List, May 1967; Susan Altschul, "School List Problem: Jewish Test Cases," *Montreal Gazette* (1 May 1967).

74 CJC, DB 01 29, Hampstead-Protestant Schools, 1965–1967, letter, 26 February 1968.

Chapter 13

1 CJC, Louis Rosenberg, *Jewish Children in the Protestant Schools of Greater Montreal in the Period from 1878 to 1962*, Canadian Jewish Congress Research Papers, series E, no 2, 1962, table 8a, at 16.

2 Nathan H Mair, *Protestant Education in Quebec: Notes on the History of Education in the Protestant Public Schools of Quebec* (Quebec: Conseil Supérieur de l'Éducation, 1981).

3 CJC, ZA 1961, 3/38, Opinion of 14 November 1961.

4 CJC, ZA, 1965, 1/1, Minutes of Meeting of Committee on Position of Jews in the Educational System of Quebec, 11 June 1964.

5 Gordon Pape, "School Boards to Compromise on Tax System," *Montreal Gazette* (17 July 1964).

6 Bill 139, Legislative Assembly of Quebec, 13 Elizabeth II, 1964.

7 An Act respecting the Protestant School Board of Greater Montreal, 11–12 Eliz II, c 74, 1963.

8 CJC, ZA 1964, 6/39B, letter, 14 July 1964.

9 David H Kaplan, "Nationalism at a Micro-Scale: Educational Segregation in Montreal" (1992) 11 Political Geography 259.

10 CJC, ZA 1964, 6/39B, letter, 27 October 1964.

11 CJC, ZA 1964, 6/39B, letter, 29 October 1964; CJC, ZB Personalia, Godinsky Samuel, CJC to Godinsky, 27 October 1964.

12 CJC, ZA 1956, 1/1, memorandum to PSBGM, *The Right of the Jews to Obtain Representation on Certain School Boards in the Montreal Area*, 28 January 1965; "Jews and School Taxes in Quebec," *Canadian Jewish Chronicle* (2 April 1965).

13 9 CS 408, (1896).

14 CJC, ZA 1964, 6/39B, Memorandum of Discussions, 3 and 15 February 1965.

15 Andrew Sancton, *Governing the Island of Montreal: Language Differences and Metropolitan Politics* (Berkeley: University of California Press, 1985) at 149–52; "New Era for Quebec Education," *Home and School News* (1 May 1963).

16 3 March 1965; "Bill to Put Jews on Protestant School Board Ready in Quebec," *JTA* (18 February 1965); "Jews and School Taxes in Quebec," *Canadian Jewish Chronicle* (2 April 1965); Harold Troper, *The Defining Decade: Identity, Politics, and the Canadian Jewish Community in the 1960s* (Toronto: University of Toronto Press, 2010), for the position of Quebec Jewry in the 1960s, especially chapter 2, "A Third Solitude," 39–79.

17 An Act concerning education in the territory of the Protestant School Board of Greater Montreal, 13–14 Eliz II, c 87, 1965.

18 Arrêté en Conseil, no 1422, 3 August 1965; "Five Jews Named to School Board," *Canadian Jewish Chronicle* (6 August 1965).

19 The Labor Zionist Movement of Canada, for example, briefly challenged the CJC's claim of speaking for the Jewish community, but nothing came of it. CJC, ZA 1967, 3/26.

20 "Second Jew Elected to St Martin Board," *Canadian Jewish Chronicle Review* (23 June 1967).

21 Joan Marshall, *A Solitary Pillar: Montreal's Anglican Church and the Quiet Revolution* (Montreal & Kingston: McGill-Queen's University Press, 1995) at 46–8.

22 *Attorney General of Quebec v Quebec Association of Protestant School Boards et al* [1984] 2 SCR 66; *Attorney General of Quebec v Greater Hull School Board et al*, [1984] 2 SCR 575; *Reference re Bill 30, An Act to Amend the Education Act (Ont.)*, [1987] 1 SCR 1148; *Greater Montreal Protestant School Board v Quebec (Attorney General)*, [1989] 1 SCR 377; *Greater Montreal Protestant School Board*

v Quebec (Attorney General), [1989] 2 SCR 167; *In the matter of the reference re the Education Act, S.Q. 1988, c. 84*, [1993] 2 SCR 511.

23 *Miller et al v The Protestant Board of School Commissioners of the Town of Mount Royal*, Provincial Court, Province of Quebec, District of Montreal, no 7347, 10 May 1967.

24 Arlette Corcos, *Montréal, l'École et les Juifs* (Sillery, QC: Septentrion, 1997); CJC, ZA 1967, 1968.

25 Corcos, *supra* note 24 at 136.

26 CJC, K1/2 1968, 3 April 1968.

27 *Report of the Royal Commission of Inquiry on Education in the Province of Quebec* (Quebec: Government of Quebec, 1966).

28 *Ibid*, part 3, "Educational Administration, Religious and Cultural Diversity within a Unified Administration."

29 David Seljak, *The Catholic Church's Reaction to the Secularization of Nationalism in Quebec, 1960–1980* (PhD Thesis, McGill University, 1995) [unpublished].

30 Conseil de Restructuration Scolaire de l'Ile de Montréal, 30 September 1967; Rapport au Ministre de l'Éducation, October 1968; Corcos, *supra* note 24 at 137.

31 Corcos, *supra* note 24 at 138.

32 Conseil de Restructuration Scolaire de l'Ile de Montréal, 30 September 1967; Rapport au Ministre de l'Éducation, October 1968.

33 CJC, Louis Rosenberg, *Jewish Children in the Protestant Schools of Greater Montreal in the Period from 1878 to 1962*, Canadian Jewish Congress Research Papers, series E, no 2, 1962, table 8a at 16.

34 See *The Montreal Catholic School System v The Town of Montreal East*, [1970] SCR 393.

35 CJC, CA, box 96/2102, Ville St Laurent.

36 *Ibid*, Extract of the Minutes of a Meeting of the Protestant School Board of Greater Montreal Held in the City of Montreal on the Twenty-First Day of June, One Thousand Nine Hundred and Sixty-Six.

37 *Ibid*, letter, 18 December 1967.

38 *Ibid*, letter, 5 December 1967.

39 The Protestant School Commission of St Laurent, Notice, *St Laurent News* (31 October 1968); "Protestant Commission: Representation Tuesday topic," *St Laurent News* (31 October 1968).

40 CJC, DB/01 8012, no 25, St Laurent Protestant Schools 1969–1970, letter from Howard, 22 January 1969.

41 *Ibid*, letter 31 March 1969.

42 9 CS 408, (1896).

43 An Act to establish the Department of Education and the Superior Council of Education, 12–13 Eliz II, c 15, 1964; Chapter 58B, Superior Council of Education Act, s 2, "The Council shall consist of twenty-four members. At least sixteen shall be Catholics, at least four shall be Protestants, and at least one shall be neither Catholic nor Protestant"; An Act respecting the Conseil supérieur de l'éducation, SQ 1964, c 234, RSQ, c C-60. See generally Norman Henchey & Donald Burgess, *Between Past and Future: Quebec Education in Transition* (Calgary: Detselig, 1987).

44 CJC, ZA 1963, 2/27, Minutes of Meeting of Committee on Position of Jews in the Educational System of the Province of Quebec, 4 July 1963; "Quebec Government Appoints First Jew to Council of Education," *JTA* (9 February 1964).

45 CJC, ZA 1963, 2/27, opinion letter, 28 April 1969; CJC, DB 01 8012, no 25, St Laurent Protestant Schools 1969–1970, letter from T Palmer Howard, 11 April 1969.

46 *Ibid*, Howard to St Laurent Board, 7 May 1969.

47 *Ibid*, letter, 7 May 1969; letters, 15 May and 9 June re: *Sherker v The School Commissioners for the Saint Laurent Protestant School Municipality*; Statement of Claim, Provincial Court, District of Montreal, no 3187, 1 May 1969.

48 CJC, ZA 1963, 2/27, letter, 23 July 1969.

49 *Sherker v The School Commissioners for the Saint Laurent Protestant School Municipality*, Cour Supérieure, District de Montréal, no 773 402.

50 *The School Commissioners for the Saint Laurent Protestant School Municipality v Sherker*, Court of Appeal, District of Montreal, no 12, 601; CJC, DB 01 8012, no 25, St Laurent Protestant Schools 1969–1970, letter, 19 February 1970.

51 CJC, DB 01 8012, no 25, St Laurent Protestant Schools 1969–1970, letter, 22 May 1970.

52 *Ibid*, letters, 8 October, 11 December 1970.

53 CJC, DB 01, no 26, 80/3, Côte-St Luc Protestant Schools, 1968–1971.

54 *Ibid*, Resolution Submitted by Alderman Nathan Shuster at a Meeting of the Council of the City of Cote Saint Luc held March 18, 1968.

55 *Ibid*, IOI 3248, Voting Rights for Jews in Election of Protestant School Boards in Montreal, 21 March 1968.

56 *Ibid*, city clerk to minister of education, 21 March 1968.

57 "40,000 Montreal Jews Win Right to Vote in Protestant School Board Elections," *JTA* (1 April 1970).

58 CJC, DB/01, Committee on Position of Jews in Education System, 1969–1971, Minutes, 5 and 27 May, 12 June, 8 August, 6 October, 4 November 1969, 21 April 1971.

59 Education Act, RS Quebec 1964, c 235.
60 "Legislation Planned to Give Jews Right to Vote in Protestant School Board Elections," *JTA* (25 March 1971); An Act to amend the Education Act with respect to persons professing the Jewish religion in the Montreal region, 19–20 Eliz II, c 66, 1971.
61 CJC, DB/01, Committee on Position of Jews in Education System, 1969–1971, Minutes, 10 and 26 March 1969; *Brief submitted by the Canadian Jewish Congress Quebec Region to the Standing Parliamentary Committee on Education*, February 1970.
62 CJC, DB 01, no 26, 80/3, Côte-St Luc Protestant Schools, 1968–1971, CJC to Shuster, 23 April 1971.
63 CJC, DB/01 Committee on Position of Jews in Education System 1969–1971, Minutes, 21 April 1971.
64 CJC, DB 01, no 26, 80/3, Côte-St Luc Protestant Schools, 1968–1971, Resolution, 3 May 1971.
65 CJC, ZA 1971, 6/56, letter 3 May 1971.
66 CJC, ZB Personalia, Godinsky Samuel, letter of resignation, 25 January 1972, and other correspondence relating to the resignation; CJC, ZA 1971, 6/56, IOI, 17, 26 January, 4 February 1972.
67 An Act respecting the preparation of permanent electoral lists and amending legislative provisions, SQ, c 6, (1972); An Act to promote school development on the island of Montreal, SQ, c 60, (1972); Henry Milner, *The Long Road to Reform: Restructuring Public Education in Quebec* (Montreal & Kingston: McGill-Queen's University Press, 1986) at 30–1.
68 "Full Vote in School Elections Urged on Quebec Government," *Montreal Gazette* (13 May 1967).
69 CJC, ZA 1973 4/68, T Palmer Howard to CJC, 21 June 1973.
70 CJC, ZA 1973, 4/66, letter 27 February 1973; Richard G Townsend & Allan J Craig, "Running for School Board: A Survey of Campaigns on the Island of Montreal" (1978) 13 McGill Journal of Education 319
71 Murray Magor, "Constitutional Guarantees and Education in Quebec" (1980) 5 McGill Journal of Education 55.
72 Robert Gagnon, *Histoire de la Commission des Écoles Catholiques de Montréal* (Montreal: Boréal, 1996) at 239ff.

Chapter 14

1 "'J'-Designating Jewish-Removed from Montreal Tax Forms," *JTA* (14 March 1974).
2 CJC, DB/01/28, Committee on Position of Jews in Education System,

1965–1971, Minutes of Meeting of Committee on Position of Jews in Educational System of Quebec, 12 June 1969.

3 Jacques Gutwirth, "Hassidm et judaïcité à Montréal" (1973) 14 Recherches Sociographiques 291; William Shaffir, *Life in a Religious Community: The Lubavitcher Chassidim in Montreal* (Toronto: Holt, Rinehart & Winston, 1974).

4 Jan Feldman, *Lubavitchers as Citizens: A Paradox of Liberal Democracy* (Ithaca: Cornell University Press, 2003); William Shaffir, "Hassidim and the 'Accommodation' Debate in Quebec" (2008) 50 Jewish Journal of Sociology 33; Shaffir, "Hassidic Jews and Quebec Politics" (1983) 25 Jewish Journal of Sociology 105.

5 *Rosenberg v City of Outremont*, (2001) RJQ 1556; Myer Siemiatycki, "Contesting Sacred Urban Space: The Case of the *Eruv*" (2005), 6 Journal of International Migration and Integration 255; Valerie Stoker, "Drawing the Line: Hasidic Jews, Eruvim, and the Public Space of Outremont" (2003) 43 History of Religions 18.

6 "Purim Has Become a Flashpoint for Simmering Tensions in Outremont," *Montreal Gazette* (23 February 2013); "Outremont Councillor Says No Exemptions for Purim Buses," CBC (20 February 2013); Jeanne Corriveau, "Outremont: une séance du conseil sous haute tension," *Le Devoir* (7 April 2012); "Un Outremontais se plaint des hassidiques," *Le Devoir* (7 April 2012); Julie Elizabeth Gagnon, "Cohabitation interculturelle, pratique religieuse et espace urbain: quelques réflexions à partir du cas des communautés hassidiques d'Outremont/Mile End" (2002) 3 Les Cahiers du Gres 39. The position of Hasidim sits uncomfortably with many francophone understandings of Quebec identity; see e.g. Pierre Joncas, *Les accommodements raisonables: entre Hérouxville et Outremont: La Liberté de Religion dans un État de Droit* (Ste Foy, QC: Les Presses de l'Université Laval, 2009).

7 Louise Leduc, "Six Écoles Illégales Connues de Québec," *La Presse* (11 June 2014); Rima Elkouri, "Ces prisons appelés écoles," *La Presse* (26 May 2014); Lise-Marie Gervais, "Communauté juive orthodoxe: Virage à 180° à l'École Belz," *Le Devoir* (22 October 2012); Marie-Andrée Chouinard, "Financement des écoles juives- pas trop tôt," *Le Devoir* (22 October 2012); "Quebec Cuts Funding to Chasidic Schools," *JTA* (9 December 2009); "Chassidic Schools Pressured to Abide by Quebec Law," *Canadian Jewish News* (7 May 2009).

8 Yolande Cohen & Yann Scioldo-Zürcher, "Maghrebi Jewish Migrations and Religious Marriage in Paris and Montréal, 1954–1980" in Solange Lefebvre & Lori G Beaman, eds, *Religion in the Public Sphere: Canadian Case Studies* (Toronto: University of Toronto Press, 2014), 121–48; Yolande Co-

hen, "The Migrations of Moroccan Jews to Montreal: Memory, (Oral) History and Historical Narrative" (2011) 10 Journal of Modern Jewish Studies 245; Jean-Claude Lasry, "A Francophone Diaspora in Quebec" in M Weinfeld, W Shaffir, & I Cotler, eds, *The Canadian Jewish Mosaic* (Toronto: John Wiley & Son, 1981), 221–40.

9 Esther Benaim, "Francophone Jews and the French Fact" (1979) 10 Viewpoints: Canadian Jewish Quarterly 11.

10 "French-Speaking Jewish Day School Opens for Sephardim in Montreal Catholic Institution," *JTA* (24 September 1969); "Des Juifs réclament des écoles françaises," *Le Petit Journal* (18 May 1969); "French-Language Jewish Day Schools Demanded in Montreal by Rabbi," *JTA* (29 December 1966).

11 CJC, DB/01 28, Committee on Position of Jews in Educational System of Quebec, 1969–1971, Minutes, 6 October, 4 November 1969, 4 June 1970; Ignace (Ignaki) Olazabal, "Ethnicité et société nationale au Québec: Les relations entre Juifs ashkénazes et Québécois francophones à Montréal" (1998), 4 Cahiers du d'URMIS 21.

12 "Montreal Community Takes Steps to Integrate French-Speaking North African Immigrants," *JTA* (26 June 1969).

13 Régine Robin, "Francophone Jewish Intellectuals in Present-day Quebec," in Sander L Gilman & Milton Shain, eds, *Jewries at the Frontier: Accommodation Identity Conflict* (Urbana: University of Illinois Press, 1999), 380–92; Naïm Kattan, *Portraits d'un pays: récits* (Montreal: Hexagone, 1994).

14 Julian Bauer, "Jewish Communities, Jewish Education and Quebec Nationalism" (1984) 31 Social Compass 391.

15 Patrice Garant, "La déconfessionnalisation des structures scolaires au regard de l'article 93 de la Constitution et de la Charte québécoise des droits et libertés" (1984–1985) Canadian Human Rights Year Book 169.

16 Jean-Pierre Proulx, *La Restructuration Scolaire de l'Île de Montréal: Problématique et Hypothèses de Solution* (Montreal: Conseil Scolaire de l'Île de Montréal, 1976).

17 *Report of the Legal Committee on Constitutional Rights in the Field of Education in Quebec to the Protestant School Board of Greater Montreal* (Montreal: Protestant School Board of Greater Montreal, 1975); Sandra Djwa, "'Nothing by Halves': FR Scott" (2000) 34 Journal of Canadian Studies at 64ff.

18 *Attorney General of Quebec v Greater Hull School Board et al*, [1984] 2 SCR 575.

19 *In the matter of the reference re the Education Act*, SQ 1988, c 84, [1993] 2 SCR 511; see generally François Chevrette, Herbert Marx, & André Tremblay, *Les problèmes constitutionnels posés par la restructuration scolaire de l'île de Montréal* (Quebec: Ministère de l'Éducation, 1972).

20 Lomomba Emongo & Bob White, *L'interculturel au Québec: Rencontres historiques et enjeux politiques* (Montreal: Les Presses de l'Université de Montréal, 2014).

21 See the controversial Frédéric Bastien, *La Bataille de Londres: Dessous, Secrets et Coulisses du Repatriement Constitutionnel* (Montreal: Boréal, 2013), for an example for the continuing depth of feeling among some in Quebec on this question; see Philip Girard, "A Tempest in a Transatlantic Teapot: A Legal Historian's Critical Analysis of Frédéric Bastien's La Bataille de Londres" (2014) 51 Osgoode Hall LJ 673; Peter H Russell, *Constitutional Odyssey: Can Canadians Become a Sovereign People?* (Toronto: University of Toronto Press, 2004); Samuel V LaSelva, *The Moral Foundations of Canadian Federalism: Paradoxes, Achievements, and Tragedies* (Montreal & Kingston: McGill-Queen's University Press, 1996).

22 Barry L Strayer, *Canada's Constitutional Revolution* (Edmonton: University of Alberta Press, 2013).

23 *Re: Resolution to amend the Constitution*, [1981] 1 SCR 753.

24 Canada Act 1982 (UK), 1982, c 11; Constitution Act, 1982, being Schedule B to the Canada Act 1982 (UK), 1982, c 11; Canadian Charter of Rights and Freedoms, Part 1 of the Constitution Act, 1982, being Schedule B to the Canada Act 1982 UK, 1982, c 11.

25 *In the Matter of a Reference to the Court of Appeal of Quebec concerning the Constitution of Canada*, [1982] 2 SCR 793.

26 Patrick J. Monahan, *Meech Lake: The Inside Story* (Toronto: University of Toronto Press, 1991); Michael D. Behiels, ed, *The Meech Lake Primer: Conflicting Views of the 1987 Constitutional Accord* (Ottawa: University of Ottawa Press, 1989).

27 Kenneth McRoberts & Patrick J. Monahan, eds, *The Charlottetown Accord, the Referendum, and the Future of Canada* (Toronto: University of Toronto Press, 1993).

28 Michael B Stein, "Improving the Process of Constitutional Reform in Canada: Lessons from the Meech Lake and Charlottetown Constitutional Rounds" (1997) 30 Canadian Journal of Political Science 307.

29 Alan C Cairns, *Disruptions: Constitutional Struggles, from the Charter to Meech Lake*, edited by Douglas E Williams (Toronto: McClelland & Stewart, 1991); "Citizens (Outsiders) and Governments (Insiders) in Constitution-Making: The Case of Meech Lake" (1988) 14 Canadian Public Policy 121.

30 "The End of Mega Constitutional Politics in Canada?" in Kenneth McRoberts & Patrick J. Monahan, eds, *The Charlottetown Accord, the Referendum, and the Future of Canada*, op. cit., 211–21; see more generally, Peter H Russell, *Constitutional Odyssey: Can Canadians Become a Sovereign People?* (Toronto: University of Toronto Press, 2004).

31 "The End of Mega Constitutional Politics in Canada?," 220.

32 Robert A Young, *The Struggle for Quebec: From Referendum to Referendum?* (Montreal & Kingston: McGill-Queen's University Press, 1999); Louis Balthazar, "Quebec and the Ideal of Federalism" (1995) 538 Annals of the American Academy of Political and Social Science 40.

33 Robert Wright, *The Night Canada Stood Still* (Toronto: HarperCollins Canada, 2014).

34 Neil Nevitte, André Blais, Elisabeth Gidengil, & Richard Nadeau, *Unsteady State: The 1997 Canadian Federal Election* (Toronto: Oxford University Press, 2000); Alan Frizell & Jon H Pammett, eds, *The Canadian General Election of 1997* (Toronto: Dundurn, 1997).

35 *In the matter of the reference re the Education Act*, SQ 1988, c 84, [1993] 2 SCR 511.

36 *Toward the Establishment of Linguistic School Boards* (Quebec: Gouvernement du Québec, Ministère de l' Éducation, 1994).

37 *Ibid*, 19.

38 *Ibid*, 25.

39 *Les États Généraux de l'Éducation, 1995–1996, Rapport Final* (Quebec: États Généraux de l'Éducation, 1996); RSQ, c C-12.

40 *Ibid*, s 2.9.

41 Jean-Pierre Proulx, Émille Olivier, & Claude Lessard, "Le Rapport de la Commission des États généraux sur l'éducation" (1997) 38 Recherches sociographiques 335.

42 Edward W McWhinney, *Chrétien and Canadian Federalism: Politics and the Constitution, 1993–2003* (Vancouver: Ronsdale, 2003) at 159.

43 *Ibid.*

44 See generally, Peter Oliver, "Quebec and the Amending Formula: Protection, Promotion and Federalism" in Stephen Tierney, *Accommodating Cultural Diversity* (Farnham: Ashgate, 2007), 167; An Act respecting constitutional amendments, SC, 1996, c 1.

45 David R Cameron & Jacqueline D Krikorian, "Recognizing Quebec in the Constitution of Canada: Using the Bilateral Constitutional Amendment Process" (2008) 58 UTLJ 389.

46 Jean-Pierre Proulx & José Woehrling, "La restructuration du système scolaire québécois et la modification de l'article 93 de la Loi constitutionnelle de 1867" (1997) 31 RJT 399.

47 Constitutional Amendment 1997, (Québec), SI/97-141, 15 April 1997.

48 Letter September 1997, Pierre Morissette, bishop of Baie Comeau, head of the Assembly of Quebec Bishops; letter 3 November 1997 Rt Rev Andrew S. Hutchison, bishop of Montreal, Parliamentary Joint Committees, SJQS (36-1); Roderick MacLeod & Mary Anne Poutanen, *A Meeting of the People:*

School Boards and Protestant Communities in Quebec, 1801–1998 (Montreal & Kingston: McGill-Queen's University Press, 2004) at 400–16.

49 William J Smith, William F Foster, & Helen M Donahue, "The Transformation of Educational Governance in Québec: A Reform Whose Time Has Finally Come" (1999) 34 McGill Journal of Education 207.

50 Quebec, National Assembly, Committee on Education, "Consultations particulières sur le projet de loi modifiant la loi sur l'instruction publique, la Loi sur les élections scolaires et d'autres dispositions législatives" in *Hansard* (27 May 1997).

51 *Ibid*, Testimony of the English Speaking Catholic Council, Quebec Federation of Home and School Associations; *ibid*, Voice of English Quebec (28 May).

52 *Ibid*, Testimony of the Mouvement pour une école moderne et ouverte, Coalition pour la déconfessionnalisation du système scolaire; *ibid*, Mouvement National des Québécois et des Québécoises et Société Saint-Jean-Baptiste de Montréal (28 May).

53 *House of Commons Debates*, 36th Parl, 2nd Sess, No 161 (22 April 1997) at 10029–32 (Hon Stéphane Dion).

54 Pierre Blache, "La Charte canadienne: obstacle postmoderne à l'émergence d'un Québec moderne et rassembleur?" (1994) 28 RJT (ns) 333.

55 *Ibid*.

56 *House of Commons, Order Paper*, 36th Parl, 1st Sess, No 8 (1 October 1997).

57 Special Joint Committee to Amend Section 93 of the Constitution Act, 1867, concerning the Quebec School System, Evidence, SJQS 36-1, 29 October 1997.

58 *Ibid*.

59 *Ibid*.

60 *Ibid*.

61 *Ibid*.

62 Committee Report, SJQS 36-1.

63 Resolution, Constitutional Amendment, 1997, (Québec).

64 Constitutional Amendment 1997 (Quebec).

65 An Act to amend the Education Act, the Act respecting school elections and other legislative provisions, SQ, c 47, 1997; An Act to amend the Education Act and Various Legislative Provisions, SQ, c 96, 1997; David Young & Lawrence Bezeau, "Moving from Denominational to Linguistic Education in Quebec" (2003) 24 Canadian Journal of Educational Administration and Policy; Michael Fox, "The Geographic Implications of School Board Reform in Quebec" (1996) 40 Canadian Geographer 54; William J Smith, "Linguistic School Boards in Quebec – A Reform Whose Time Has Come: *Reference Re Education Act of Quebec* (Bill 107)" (1993–4) 39 McGill LJ 200.

66 *A School for the Future: Policy Statement on Educational Integration and Intercultural Education* (Quebec: Ministère de l'Éducation, 1998).

67 Joan Marshall, *A Solitary Pillar: Montreal's Anglican Church and the Quiet Revolution* (Montreal & Kingston: McGill-Queen's University Press, 1995) at 21–41; Richard Y Bourhis, ed, *The Vitality of the English-Speaking Communities of Quebec: From Community Decline to Revival* (Montreal: CEETUM & CIRLM, 2008); Garth Stevenson, *Community Besieged: The Anglophone Minority and the Politics of Quebec* (Montreal & Kingston: McGill-Queen's University Press, 1999); Ronald Rudin, *The Forgotten Quebeckers: A History of English-Speaking Quebec 1759–1980* (Quebec: IQRC, 1985); Gary Caldwell & Eric Waddell, *The English of Québec: From Majority to Minority Status* (Quebec: IQRC, 1982).

68 Robert T Brym & Rhonda L Lenton, "The Distribution of Anti-Semitism in Canada in 1984" (1991) 16 Canadian Journal of Sociology 411; Simon Langlois, "The Distribution of Anti-Semitism in Canada: A Hasty and Erroneous Generalization by Brym and Lenton" (1992) 17 Canadian Journal of Sociology 175; Brym & Lenton, "Anti-Semitism in Quebec; A Reply to Langlois" (1992) 17 Canadian Journal of Sociology 179.

69 Étienne Gérard, *La Question Raciale et Raciste dans le Roman Québécois* (Montreal: Les Éditions Balzac, 1995); Victor Teboul, *Mythes et Images du Juif au Québec* (Montréal: Éditions de Lagrave, 1977).

70 Paul M Sniderman et al, "Psychological and Cultural Foundations of Prejudice: The Case of Anti-Semitism in Quebec" (1993) 30 Canadian Review of Sociology and Anthropology 242.

71 Morton Weinfeld, "The Jews of Quebec: Perceived Antisemitism, Segregation, and Emigration" (1980) 22 Jewish Journal of Sociology 5; David Weiss, "Is There a Future for the Montreal Jewish Community?" (1979) 56 Journal of Jewish Communal Service 28; Jack Kantrovitz, "Jews in the New Quebec" (1979) 10 Viewpoints 5.

72 Mordecai Richler, *Oh Canada! Oh Quebec!: Requiem for a Divided Country* (Toronto: Penguin, 1992); Nadia Khouri, *Qui a peur de Mordecai Richler?* (Montreal: Les Éditions Balzac, 1994).

73 Jean-François Gaudreault-DesBiens, *Le Droit, La Religion et Le "Raisonnable": le fait religieux entre monisme étatique et pluralisme juridique* (Montreal: Les Éditions Thémis, 2009).

74 Gérard Bouchard & Charles Taylor, *Building the Future: A Time for Reconciliation*, abridged report, Commission de consultation sur les pratiques d'accommodement reliées aux différences culturelles (Quebec: Gouvernement du Québec, 2008).

75 Charte affirmant les valeurs de laïcité et la neutralité religieuse de l'État ainsi que d'égalité entre les femmes et les hommes et encadrant les de-

mandes d'accommodement, Projet de Loi no 60, 2013; Charter affirming the values of state secularism and religious neutrality, and of equality between women and men, and providing a framework for accommodation requests.

76 Un membre du personnel d'un organisme public ne doit pas porter, dans l'exercice de ses fonctions, un objet, tel un couvre-chef, un vêtement, un bijou ou une autre parure, marquant ostensiblement, par son caractère démonstratif, une appartenance religieuse.

77 Mélanie Marquis, "Agressions antisémites à Montréal: du 'jamais vu' selon un représentant," *La Presse* (24 July 2014).

78 Howard Adelman & Pierre Anctil, eds, *Religion, Culture, and the State: Reflections on the Bouchard-Taylor Report* (Toronto: University of Toronto Press, 2011).

79 *Commission scolaire régionale de Chambly v Bergevin*, [1994] 2 SCR 525.

80 Michel Laferrière, "L'éducation des enfants des groupes minoritaires au Québec: De la définition des problèmes par les groupes eux-mêmes à l'intervention de l'État" (1983) 15 Sociologie et sociétés 117.

81 *Multani v Commission scolaire Marguerite-Bourgeoys* [2006] 1 SCR 256; Valerie Stoker, "Zero Tolerance? Sikh Swords, School Safety and Secularism in Québec" (2007) 75:4 Journal of the American Academy of Religion 814; Shauna Van Praagh, *Hijab et Kirpan: Une histoire de cape et d'épée* (Ste Foy, QC: Les Presses de l'Université Laval, 2006).

82 Bruce Curtis, *Ruling by Schooling Quebec: Conquest to Liberal Governmentality – A Historical Sociology* (Toronto: University of Toronto Press, 2012); Jean-Pierre Proulx, with Christian Dessureault & Paul Aubin, *La genèse de l'école publique et de la démocratie scolaire au Québec: les écoles de syndics (1814–1838)* (Ste Foy, QC: Les Presses de l'Université Laval, 2014).

83 Officially, Canadian Charter of Rights and Freedoms, Part 1 of the Constitution Act 1982, being Schedule B to the Canada Act 1982 (UK, 1982), c 11. See also, Charter of Human Rights and Freedoms, RSQ, c C-12, under the provisions of which many current Quebec cases are fought.

84 Daniel J Elazar, Michael Brown, & Ira Robinson, *Not Written in Stone: Jews, Constitutions and Constitutionalism in Canada* (Ottawa: University of Ottawa Press, 2003) at 3–12.

Index

2015 Barry Wright, Eric Tucker, and Susan Binnie, eds., *Canadian State Trials, Volume IV: Security, Dissent, and the Limits of Toleration in War and Peace, 1914–1939*
David Fraser, *"Honorary Protestants": The Jewish School Question in Montreal, 1867–1997*
C. Ian Kyer, *A Thirty Years War: The Failed Public/Private Partnership that Spurred the Creation of the Toronto Transit Commission, 1891–1921*
Dale Gibson, *Law, Life, and Government at Red River: Settlement and Governance, 1812–1872*

2014 Christopher Moore, *The Court of Appeal for Ontario: Defining the Right of Appeal, 1792–2013*
Paul Craven, *Petty Justice: Low Law and the Sessions System in Charlotte County, New Brunswick, 1785–1867*
Thomas GW Telfer, *Ruin and Redemption: The Struggle for a Canadian Bankruptcy Law, 1867–1919*
Dominique Clément, *Equality Deferred: Sex Discrimination and British Columbia's Human Rights State, 1953–1984*

2013 Roy McMurtry, *Memoirs and Reflections*
Charlotte Gray, *The Massey Murder: A Maid, Her Master, and the Trial that Shocked a Nation*
C. Ian Kyer, *Lawyers, Families, and Businesses: The Shaping of a Bay Street Law Firm, Faskens 1863–1963*
G. Blaine Baker and Donald Fyson, eds., *Essays in the History of Canadian Law, Volume XI: Quebec and the Canadas*

2012 R. Blake Brown, *Arming and Disarming: A History of Gun Control in Canada*
Eric Tucker, James Muir, and Bruce Ziff, eds., *Property on Trial: Canadian Cases in Context*
Shelley Gavigan, *Hunger, Horses, and Government Men: Criminal Law on the Aboriginal Plains, 1870–1905*
Barrington Walker, ed., *The African Canadian Legal Odyssey: Historical Essays*

2011 Robert J. Sharpe, *The Lazier Murder: Prince Edward County, 1884*
Philip Girard, *Lawyers and Legal Culture in British North America: Beamish Murdoch of Halifax*
John McLaren, *Dewigged, Bothered, and Bewildered: British Colonial Judges on Trial, 1800–1900*
Lesley Erickson, *Westward Bound: Sex, Violence, the Law, and the Making of a Settler Society*

2010 Judy Fudge and Eric Tucker, eds., *Work on Trial: Canadian Labour Law Struggles*
Christopher Moore, *The British Columbia Court of Appeal: The First Hundred Years*
Frederick Vaughan, *Viscount Haldane: 'The Wicked Step-father of the Canadian Constitution'*
Barrington Walker, *Race on Trial: Black Defendants in Ontario's Criminal Courts, 1858–1958*

2009 William Kaplan, *Canadian Maverick: The Life and Times of Ivan C. Rand*
R. Blake Brown, *A Trying Question: The Jury in Nineteenth-Century Canada*
Barry Wright and Susan Binnie, eds., *Canadian State Trials, Volume III: Political Trials and Security Measures, 1840–1914*
Robert J. Sharpe, *The Last Day, the Last Hour: The Currie Libel Trial* (paperback edition with a new preface)

2008 Constance Backhouse, *Carnal Crimes: Sexual Assault Law in Canada, 1900–1975*
Jim Phillips, R. Roy McMurtry, and John T. Saywell, eds., *Essays in the History of Canadian Law, Volume X: A Tribute to Peter N. Oliver*
Greg Taylor, *The Law of the Land: The Advent of the Torrens System in Canada*
Hamar Foster, Benjamin Berger, and A.R. Buck, eds., *The Grand Experiment: Law and Legal Culture in British Settler Societies*

2007 Robert Sharpe and Patricia McMahon, *The Persons Case: The Origins and Legacy of the Fight for Legal Personhood*
Lori Chambers, *Misconceptions: Unmarried Motherhood and the Ontario Children of Unmarried Parents Act, 1921–1969*
Jonathan Swainger, ed., *A History of the Supreme Court of Alberta*
Martin Friedland, *My Life in Crime and Other Academic Adventures*

2006 Donald Fyson, *Magistrates, Police, and People: Everyday Criminal Justice in Quebec and Lower Canada, 1764–1837*
Dale Brawn, *The Court of Queen's Bench of Manitoba, 1870–1950: A Biographical History*
R.C.B. Risk, *A History of Canadian Legal Thought: Collected Essays*, edited and introduced by G. Blaine Baker and Jim Phillips

2005 Philip Girard, *Bora Laskin: Bringing Law to Life*
Christopher English, ed., *Essays in the History of Canadian Law: Volume IX – Two Islands: Newfoundland and Prince Edward Island*
Fred Kaufman, *Searching for Justice: An Autobiography*

2004 Philip Girard, Jim Phillips, and Barry Cahill, eds., *The Supreme Court of Nova Scotia, 1754–2004: From Imperial Bastion to Provincial Oracle*

Frederick Vaughan, *Aggressive in Pursuit: The Life of Justice Emmett Hall*
John D. Honsberger, *Osgoode Hall: An Illustrated History*
Constance Backhouse and Nancy Backhouse, *The Heiress versus the Establishment: Mrs Campbell's Campaign for Legal Justice*

2003 Robert Sharpe and Kent Roach, *Brian Dickson: A Judge's Journey*
Jerry Bannister, *The Rule of the Admirals: Law, Custom, and Naval Government in Newfoundland, 1699–1832*
George Finlayson, *John J. Robinette, Peerless Mentor: An Appreciation*
Peter Oliver, *The Conventional Man: The Diaries of Ontario Chief Justice Robert A. Harrison, 1856–1878*

2002 John T. Saywell, *The Lawmakers: Judicial Power and the Shaping of Canadian Federalism*
Patrick Brode, *Courted and Abandoned: Seduction in Canadian Law*
David Murray, *Colonial Justice: Justice, Morality, and Crime in the Niagara District, 1791–1849*
F. Murray Greenwood and Barry Wright, eds., *Canadian State Trials, Volume II: Rebellion and Invasion in the Canadas, 1837–1839*

2001 Ellen Anderson, *Judging Bertha Wilson: Law as Large as Life*
Judy Fudge and Eric Tucker, *Labour before the Law: The Regulation of Workers' Collective Action in Canada, 1900–1948*
Laurel Sefton MacDowell, *Renegade Lawyer: The Life of J.L. Cohen*

2000 Barry Cahill, *'The Thousandth Man': A Biography of James McGregor Stewart*
A.B. McKillop, *The Spinster and the Prophet: Florence Deeks, H.G. Wells, and the Mystery of the Purloined Past*
Beverley Boissery and F. Murray Greenwood, *Uncertain Justice: Canadian Women and Capital Punishment*
Bruce Ziff, *Unforeseen Legacies: Reuben Wells Leonard and the Leonard Foundation Trust*

1999 Constance Backhouse, *Colour-Coded: A Legal History of Racism in Canada, 1900–1950*
G. Blaine Baker and Jim Phillips, eds., *Essays in the History of Canadian Law: Volume VIII – In Honour of R.C.B. Risk*
Richard W. Pound, *Chief Justice W.R. Jackett: By the Law of the Land*
David Vanek, *Fulfilment: Memoirs of a Criminal Court Judge*

1998 Sidney Harring, *White Man's Law: Native People in Nineteenth-Century Canadian Jurisprudence*
Peter Oliver, *'Terror to Evil-Doers': Prisons and Punishments in Nineteenth-Century Ontario*

1997 James W.St.G. Walker, *'Race,' Rights and the Law in the Supreme Court of Canada: Historical Case Studies*

Lori Chambers, *Married Women and Property Law in Victorian Ontario*
Patrick Brode, *Casual Slaughters and Accidental Judgments: Canadian War Crimes and Prosecutions, 1944–1948*
Ian Bushnell, *The Federal Court of Canada: A History, 1875–1992*

1996 Carol Wilton, ed., *Essays in the History of Canadian Law: Volume VII – Inside the Law: Canadian Law Firms in Historical Perspective*
William Kaplan, *Bad Judgment: The Case of Mr Justice Leo A. Landreville*
Murray Greenwood and Barry Wright, eds., *Canadian State Trials: Volume I – Law, Politics, and Security Measures, 1608–1837*

1995 David Williams, *Just Lawyers: Seven Portraits*
Hamar Foster and John McLaren, eds., *Essays in the History of Canadian Law: Volume VI – British Columbia and the Yukon*
W.H. Morrow, ed., *Northern Justice: The Memoirs of Mr Justice William G. Morrow*
Beverley Boissery, *A Deep Sense of Wrong: The Treason, Trials, and Transportation to New South Wales of Lower Canadian Rebels after the 1838 Rebellion*

1994 Patrick Boyer, *A Passion for Justice: The Legacy of James Chalmers McRuer*
Charles Pullen, *The Life and Times of Arthur Maloney: The Last of the Tribunes*
Jim Phillips, Tina Loo, and Susan Lewthwaite, eds., *Essays in the History of Canadian Law: Volume V – Crime and Criminal Justice*
Brian Young, *The Politics of Codification: The Lower Canadian Civil Code of 1866*

1993 Greg Marquis, *Policing Canada's Century: A History of the Canadian Association of Chiefs of Police*
Murray Greenwood, *Legacies of Fear: Law and Politics in Quebec in the Era of the French Revolution*

1992 Brendan O'Brien, *Speedy Justice: The Tragic Last Voyage of His Majesty's Vessel Speedy*
Robert Fraser, ed., *Provincial Justice: Upper Canadian Legal Portraits from the Dictionary of Canadian Biography*

1991 Constance Backhouse, *Petticoats and Prejudice: Women and Law in Nineteenth-Century Canada*

1990 Philip Girard and Jim Phillips, eds., *Essays in the History of Canadian Law: Volume III – Nova Scotia*
Carol Wilton, ed., *Essays in the History of Canadian Law: Volume IV – Beyond the Law: Lawyers and Business in Canada, 1830–1930*

1989 Desmond Brown, *The Genesis of the Canadian Criminal Code of 1892*
Patrick Brode, *The Odyssey of John Anderson*

1988 Robert Sharpe, *The Last Day, the Last Hour: The Currie Libel Trial*
John D. Arnup, *Middleton: The Beloved Judge*

1987 C. Ian Kyer and Jerome Bickenbach, *The Fiercest Debate: Cecil A. Wright, the Benchers, and Legal Education in Ontario, 1923–1957*

1986 Paul Romney, *Mr Attorney: The Attorney General for Ontario in Court, Cabinet, and Legislature, 1791–1899*
Martin Friedland, *The Case of Valentine Shortis: A True Story of Crime and Politics in Canada*

1985 James Snell and Frederick Vaughan, *The Supreme Court of Canada: History of the Institution*

1984 Patrick Brode, *Sir John Beverley Robinson: Bone and Sinew of the Compact*
David Williams, *Duff: A Life in the Law*

1983 David H. Flaherty, ed., *Essays in the History of Canadian Law: Volume II*

1982 Marion MacRae and Anthony Adamson, *Cornerstones of Order: Courthouses and Town Halls of Ontario, 1784–1914*

1981 David H. Flaherty, ed., *Essays in the History of Canadian Law: Volume I*